Hong Kong

"All you've got to do is decide to go
and the hardest part is over.

So go!"

TONY WHEELER, COFOUNDER – LONELY PLANET

THIS EDITION WRITTEN AND RESEARCHED BY
Piera Chen, Emily Matchar

Contents

Plan Your Trip　　4

Explore Hong Kong　　66

Understand Hong Kong　　279

Survival Guide　　311

Hong Kong Maps　　360

(left) Fishing junk, Victoria Harbour

(above) Dragon dancers, Birthday of Tin Hau (p30)

(right) Stall, Temple Street Night Market (p142)

Welcome to Hong Kong

This enigmatic city of skyscrapers, ancient traditions and heavenly food will fascinate, whether it's your first visit or your fiftieth.

Neighbourhoods & Islands

The tantalising neighbourhoods and curious islands that make up Hong Kong are a sensory delight awaiting exploration. You may find yourself swaying along on a double-decker tramcar, cheering with the hordes at the city-centre horse races, or simply gazing out at the magnificent harbour. Over 70% of Hong Kong is mountains and sprawling country parks, some also home to geological gems. Escape the city limits on one of the world's best transport systems and spend your day wandering in a Song-dynasty village, hiking surf-beaten beaches or scouring for sea shards on a deserted island.

Cuisine

Asia's top culinary capital, the city that lives to eat is home to many a demon in the kitchen, whether the deliciousness in the pot is Cantonese, Shanghainese, Vietnamese, Japanese or European. Whatever your gastronomic desires, they're likely to be sated in Hong Kong – over a bowl of wonton noodles, freshly steamed dim sum, a pair of the sweetest prawns, your first-ever stinky tofu, or the culinary creations of the latest celebrity chef.

Shopping

From ready-to-wear Chinese jackets to bespoke kitchen knives, the sheer range and variety of products on Hong Kong's shelves is mind-bending. Every whim, need and pocket is catered for in true enterprising spirit by an equally dazzling number of venues – swanky malls where the moneyed shop, chic side-street boutiques, antique stores, gadget bazaars, and a colourful mix of markets where you can haggle to your heart's content. The city has no sales tax so prices are generally attractive to visitors.

Culture

Beyond the glass and steel of Hong Kong's commercial persona, the city also boasts a vibrant cultural scene that features the eclectic influences of its Chinese roots, colonial connections and a wondrous pool of homegrown talent. Here, you're just as likely to find yourself applauding at Asia's top film festival as joining in dawn taichi or reading the couplets of a local poet to the drumbeat of a dragon boat. Culture could also mean indie music under the stars, a classy art walk, your first Cantonese opera – not to mention the exhibitions and events staged year-round at the many museums and concert halls.

Why I Love Hong Kong

By Piera Chen, Author

I love Hong Kong because it has a complexity that eludes definition, sometimes even by its own people. I can be soul-searching near the Chinese border, lunching with Sikhs at a Sikh temple, splurging on a set of kitchen knives, arguing with bohos about the merits of a dress – all within five hours – followed by a night of Cantonese opera, tango or karaoke, anywhere I choose. Hong Kong is so intense and so full of possibilities that I'm glad there's the Rule of Law (and an awesome transport system) to stop it from whirling into chaos. For me, that's pretty darn perfect.

For more about our authors, see p384.

Top: Cantonese opera performers

Hong Kong's
Top 16

Star Ferry (p73)

1 A floating piece of Hong Kong heritage and a sightseeing bargain, the legendary Star Ferry was founded in 1880 and plies the calm waters of Victoria Harbour in the service of commuters craving a break from the sights and rhythms of the city. At only HK$2.50, the 15-minute ride with views of skyscrapers marching up jungle-clad hills must be one of the world's best-value cruises. While the vista is more dramatic when you're Island-bound, the art-deco Kowloon pier, resembling a finger pointing at the Island, is arguably more charming.

⦿ *Hong Kong Island: Central*

The Peak (p87)

2 Rising above the financial heart of Hong Kong Island, Victoria Peak offers superlative views of the city and the mountainous countryside beyond. Ride the hair-raising Peak Tram, Asia's first cable funicular (in operation since 1888) to the cooler climes at the top as skyscrapers and apartment blocks recede into the distance. At dusk Victoria Harbour glitters like the Milky Way on a sci-fi movie poster, mysterious and full of promise, as the lights come on. A view to die for!

BELOW: PEAK TRAM (P318)

⦿ *Hong Kong Island: The Peak & the Northwest*

PETER SCHOLEY / GETTY IMAGES ©

KIMBERLEY COOLE / GETTY IMAGES ©

Temple Street Night Market (p142)

3 Beneath the glare of naked bulbs, hundreds of stalls sell a vast array of booty, from sex toys to luggage. You can browse for handy gadgets or quirky souvenirs, and test your bargaining skills. Nearby, fortune-tellers beckon in English from dimly lit tents, and Cantonese opera singers strike a pose *en plein air*. If you're hungry, the many open-air stalls offer snacks or a seafood feast. Sure, it's touristy, but its mesmerising and impenetrable aura makes everyone – including locals – feel like a welcome visitor.

⊙ *Kowloon*

Wan Chai Dining (p117)

4 If you were to hurl yourself, eyes closed, into a random neighbourhood eatery and expect to emerge smacking your lips, you'd stand the best chance if you were in Wan Chai. The district is home to a great many restaurants suiting a range of pocket sizes. Regional Chinese cooking, European cuisines, Asian kitchens, East–West fusion, classy, midrange, hole in the wall... Just name your craving and head on down to the Wanch; you're certain to find it there.

Hong Kong Island: Wan Chai & the Northeast

Man Mo Temple (p88)

5 Ditch the Soho watering holes and experience Chinese folk religiosity in this atmospheric 19th-century institution. Forever wreathed in sandalwood smoke from the hanging incense coils, the popular temple is dedicated to Man and Mo, the gods of literature and of war. Formerly a cultural and political focal point for the Chinese, the dimly lit space now commands a following beyond conscientious students and the martially inclined, as locals and tourists come to perform age-old rites and have their fortunes told.

Hong Kong Island: The Peak & the Northwest

8

Shopping in Tsim Sha Tsui *(p161)*

6 An afternoon's visit to Tsim Sha Tsui's shopping quarters should yield a few gems. If you're seeking Chinese-style gifts, comb the streets near the southern end of the area for that silk gown, teapot or trinket. If glamour is what floats your boat, join the über-wealthy mainland tourists for a card-swiping marathon in the mile-long block of luxury malls along Canton Rd. Want something unique? Head over to Granville Rd for that super-sized orange blazer or a micromall nearby for those asymmetrical earrings and thigh-high boots. TOP LEFT: HARBOUR CITY MALL (P162)

 Kowloon

Hong Kong Wetland Park *(p174)*

7 Surreally nestled under an imposing arc of apartment towers, this 61-hectare ecological park in crowded Tin Shui Wai is a swampy haven of biodiversity. This is urban/nature juxtaposition at its best, and curiously, most harmonious. Precious ecosystems in this far-flung yet easily accessible part of the New Territories provide tranquil habitats for a range of waterfowl and other wildlife. Forget the man-made world for a moment and delve into a landscape of mangroves, rivers and fish-filled ponds.

⊙ *New Territories*

Mong Kok Markets *(p162)*

8 Mong Kok with its eclectic speciality markets is your best bet for a rewarding crawl. The Tung Choi St Market/Ladies' Market has a mile-long wardrobe covering everything from 'I Love HK' Ts and football jerseys, to granny swimwear and sexy lingerie. Exotic seeds and gardening tools sit next to buckets of fragrant florals in the flower market. Stalls displaying colourful aquatic life in softly humming, UV-lit tanks line the streets of the goldfish market. There are vertical markets too – a buzzing computer mall, and a multistorey gadget-lovers' heaven. ABOVE: TUNG CHOI ST MARKET (P164)

Kowloon

Tian Tan Buddha (p195)

9 A favourite with local day trippers and foreign visitors alike, the world's biggest outdoor seated Buddha lords over the western hills of Lantau. Visit this serene giant from the Ngong Ping 360 cable-car. Tuck into some monk food at the popular vegetarian restaurant in Po Lin Monastery below. Buddha's birthday in May is a lively time to visit this important pilgrimage site.

⊙ *Outlying Islands*

Happy Valley Races (p114)

10 Every Wednesday night the city horse-racing track in Happy Valley comes alive, with electrifying races and a carnival of food and beer. You can bet or simply enjoy the collective exhilaration and the thunder of ironed hooves. Races were first held here in the 19th century by European merchants who imported horses from Mongolia, which they rode themselves. Now there are races every week except in the heat of July and August, when beasts and jockeys retreat into air-conditioned comfort.

⊙ *Hong Kong Island: Wan Chai & the Northeast*

10

IMAGE SOURCE / GETTY IMAGES ©

Riding on the Trams (p318)

11 Nicknamed 'ding dings' by locals, trams have been sedately chugging back and forth, east to west, since 1904. A century later the world's largest fleet of still-operating double-decker tramcars continues to negotiate pathways through the city's heavy traffic. Board a ding ding and watch the city unfold like a carousel of images as you relax and ponder tomorrow's itinerary. It's the fun option, too: high fives between passengers on passing trams are not unheard of.

🏃 *Hong Kong Transport*

Tsim Sha Tsui East Promenade (p141)

12 Gleaming skyscrapers lined up between emerald hills and a deep-blue harbour with crisscrossing boats – Hong Kong's best-known imagery is of the Island but, like a hologram, its beauty only shimmers into view when you're looking from the Tsim Sha Tsui East Promenade in Kowloon, especially after sundown. Home to windswept museums and a world-class concert venue, the promenade offers pockets of culture as you stroll its length.

⊙ *Kowloon*

Hiking the Hong Kong Trail (p64)

13 Once you've made it past the formidable Dragon's Back ridge, the Hong Kong Trail sweeps you into emerald hills, secluded woodland and lofty paths that afford sumptuous views of the rugged south and its wavy shore. Starting from the Peak, the 50km route snakes across the entire length of Hong Kong Island, past picturesque reservoirs, WWII battlefields and cobalt bays. Spread over five country parks, this delightful trail invites both easy perambulations and harder hikes.

🏃 *Sports & Activities*

EURASIA/ROBERT HARDING ©

Exploring Lamma *(p196)*

14 If there were a soundtrack for the island of Lamma, it would be reggae. The island's naturally laid-back vibe attracts herb-growers, musicians and New Age therapists from a rainbow of cultures. Soak up the atmosphere in the village, and hike to the nearest beach; your unlikely compass will be three coal-fired plants against the skyline. Spend the afternoon chilling by the beach, and then, in the glow of the day's final rays, head back for steamed prawns, fried calamari and beer by the pier. RIGHT: YUNG SHUE WAN

🏃 *Outlying Islands*

Walled Villages of
Yuen Long *(p173)*

15 Let Yuen Long's walled villages take you back over half a millennium to a wild time when piracy was rife along the South China coast. Isolated from China's administrative heart, Hong Kong, with its treacherous shores and mountainous terrain, was an excellent hideout for pirates. Its earliest inhabitants built villages with high walls, some guarded by cannons, to protect themselves. Inside these walls today you'll see ancestral halls, courtyards, pagodas, temples, and ancient farming implements – vestiges of Hong Kong's precolonial history, all carefully restored. RIGHT: TEMPLE, PING SHAN HERITAGE TRAIL (P168)

⊙ New Territories

Ruins of the Church of St Paul, Macau *(p219)*

16 Macau's Eiffel Tower and Statue of Liberty is a dramatic gate perched on a hill 26m above sea level, smack in the middle of the city. A sweep of stairs with landings and balustrades take you to it, and then to nowhere. Once part of a 17th-century Jesuit church destroyed in a fire, the facade, with fine carvings and detailed engravings featuring Christian, Chinese and Japanese influences, is a captivating historical fragment and a document in granite of Macau's unique Mediterrasian culture.

⊙ Macau

What's New

Hong Kong Maritime Museum
The expanded Hong Kong Maritime Museum has reopened in a new harbourside location to show visitors the maritime history of Hong Kong and China. (p77)

Lui Seng Chun
In Mong Kok, a graceful 'shophouse' from the 1920s has been restored and turned into a school of Chinese medicine. Sip some herbal tea on the ground floor even if you don't take the tour to see the upper levels. (p152)

Liangyi Museum
This exquisite private space is one of the world's best museums of classical Chinese furniture from the Ming and Qing dynasties. Book a tour soon. (p89)

June 4th Museum
The world's first permanent museum dedicated to the student movement in Tiān'ānmén Square, Běijīng, on 4th June 1989. (p148)

Eslite
The mammoth Hong Kong branch of the famous Taiwanese bookstore specialises in arts, humanities and lifestyle titles. It's open until late on Friday and Saturday. (p127)

Art Basel
The world's leading modern and contemporary art fair launched its Hong Kong edition in May 2014, making the city one of three in the world to host the mega art show.

PMQ
The territory's first living quarters for married policemen (c 19th century) has reincarnated into an art village and creativity hub, after years of disuse. (p89)

Antique Shops
With China now the world's most dynamic antiques market, reputable and resourceful local dealers like Lam Gallery (p103), Andy Hei (p104), and Chan Shing Kee (p105) have upped their act.

Contemporary Bespoke Tailoring
Modern clothiers, Armoury and Browns-Tailor are rekindling Hong Kong's dying tradition of bespoke men's tailoring with their high-end, custom-made garments for the 21st-century gentleman. (p83; p161)

Latin American & Spanish Eateries
Fuelling Hong Kong's infatuation with Hispanic cuisines are Mexican restaurants Socialito (p94) and the Brickhouse (p94), and Spanish tapas bar 22 Ships (p117).

LMA & Senses 99
Macau's premier indie music venue Live Music Association (LMA) has reopened in a new location; Hong Kong's jammers' heaven Senses 99 welcomes visitors again after a refurbishment. (p239; p82)

Craft Beers, Cocktails & Whisky
Hong Kong's new favourite drinks are Japanese whisky and cocktails, and craft beers; they're available at Barsmith (p100), Butler (p158) and Roundhouse Taproom (p100).

Youth Hostels
New pocket-friendly hostels YesInn (p269), Urban Pack (p274) and Mei Ho House (p274) offer comfort and character.

For more recommendations and reviews, see **lonelyplanet. com/hong-kong**

Need to Know

For more information, see Survival Guide (p325)

Currency

Hong Kong dollar (HK$) for Hong Kong and pataca (MOP$) for Macau.

Language

Cantonese is spoken in Hong Kong and Macau. English is also widely used.

Visas

Not required for visitors from the US, Australia, New Zealand, Canada, the EU, Israel and South Africa for stays of up to 30 days.

Money

ATMs widely available. Credit cards accepted in most hotels and restaurants; some budget places only take cash.

Mobile Phones

Set your phone to roaming or buy a local SIM card.

Time

Hong Kong Time (GMT/UTC plus eight hours)

Tourist Information

Hong Kong Tourism Board (Star Ferry Concourse, Tsim Sha Tsui; ☺8am-8pm; Ⓜ East Tsim Sha Tsui, exit J) and Macau Government Tourist Office (Largo do Senado; ☺9am-6pm).

Daily Costs

Budget less than HK$700

➡ Guesthouse HK$150–400

➡ Meal at *cha chaan tang* (tea cafes) and *dai pai dong* (food stalls): HK$60–150

➡ Museum Wednesdays (free); night markets (free); horse races (HK$10)

➡ Bus, tram, Star Ferry ticket: HK$2.50–15

Midrange HK$700– HK$1700

➡ Double room in a hostel or budget hotel: HK$550–1000

➡ Chinese dinner with three dishes: HK$300

➡ Drinks and live music: HK$350

Top end over HK$1700

➡ Boutique or four-star hotel double room: HK$2000

➡ Dinner at top Chinese restaurant: from HK$800

➡ Cantonese opera ticket: HK$400

Advance Planning

Two months before Check dates of Chinese festivals; book accommodation and tickets for major performances and concerts; book a table at a top restaurant.

One month before Check listings and book tickets for fringe festivals and live entertainment; research dining options and book a table at a popular restaurant.

Two weeks before Book harbour cruises, nature tours; sign up for email alerts from entertainment and events organisers.

One week before Check the weather forecast.

Useful Websites

Lonely Planet (www.lonely planet.com/hong-kong, www.lonelyplanet.com/china/macau)

Discover Hong Kong (www.discoverhongkong.com)

Urbtix (www.urbtix.hk)

Time Out Hong Kong (www.timeout.com.hk)

Hong Kong Observatory (www.hko.gov.hk)

WHEN TO GO

October to early December is the best time to visit. June to August is hot and rainy. Beware of typhoons in September.

°C/°F Temp
40/104 —
30/86 —
20/68 —
10/50 —
0/32 —

Rainfall inches/mm
12/300
10/250
8/200
6/150
4/100
2/50
0

J F M A M J J A S O N D

Arriving in Hong Kong

Hong Kong International Airport Airport Express MTR train to city centre from 6am to 1.15am, HK$90 to HK$100; buses to various parts of Hong Kong from 6am to 12.30am, HK$22 to HK$48; taxi to city centre HK$220 to HK$360.

Lo Wu and Lok Ma Chau MTR train to city centre from 5.55am to 1.30am (Lo Wu), from 6.38am to 10.55pm (Lok Ma Chau), HK$36 to HK$48.

Macau Ferry Terminal MTR train to city centre from 6.05am to midnight, HK$4.50 to HK$13; taxi HK$20 to HK$80.

China Ferry Terminal MTR train to city centre from 6.04am to 12.40pm, HK$4.50 to HK$14; taxi HK$20 to HK$70.

For much more on **arrival** see p312

SMOKING

All indoor areas of eateries are now technically smoke-free. Smokers are seeking out restaurants with unsheltered outdoor spaces where the ban doesn't apply. In districts such as Soho, where restaurants tend to have open fronts, customers often step outside to smoke.

Useful Tours

➡ **Gray Line Tours** (☑2368 7111; www.grayline.com.hk) Over 20 different tours.

➡ **Little Adventures in Hong Kong** (www.littleadventuresinhongkong.com) Everything from food crawls to history walks.

➡ **Handmade in Hong Kong Tour** (www.hstvl.com; 8hr tour HK$850 per person; ⏰9.15am Tue-Thu) HS Travel International offers a tour showing Hong Kong's age-old handicrafts.

➡ **Land Between Tour** (www.grayline.com; full-/half-day tour HK$620/460) Grayline Tours guide hikes to walled villages, monasteries, fish farms and the like in the New Territories.

➡ **Hong Kong Foodie Tour** (www.hongkongfoodietours.com; adult/child HK$690/490; ⏰2.15pm Mon-Sat) A mouth-watering food crawl in Central and Sheung Wan.

For much more on **getting around** see p22

Sleeping

Hong Kong offers a full range of accommodation, from closet-sized rooms to palatial suites. Rooms are relatively expensive by Asian standards, though generally still cheaper than in the US and Europe.

Most hotels are on Hong Kong Island between Central and Causeway Bay, and on either side of Nathan Rd in Kowloon, where you'll also find more budget places. During low seasons prices fall sharply, particularly the midrange and top-end options, when you can get discounts of up to 60% if you book online. Check out the following websites:

➡ **Lonely Planet** (lonelyplanet.com/china/hong-kong/hotels) Book Lonely Planet's top accommodation picks online. Find Macau here too.

➡ **Hotel.com** (www.hotels.com/Hong-Kong) Specialises in cheap lodging.

➡ **Discover Hong Kong** (www.discoverhongkong.com) Provides a hotel search based on location and facilities.

➡ **Asia Travel** (www.hongkonghotels.com) Has better deals than others.

For much more on **sleeping** see p263

First Time Hong Kong

For more information, see Survival Guide (p311)

Checklist

➡ Make sure your passport is valid for at least one month past your intended stay

➡ Inform your debit-/credit-card company

➡ Arrange for appropriate travel insurance

➡ Check if your mobile phone service provider has roaming agreement with a Hong Kong operator

What to Pack

➡ Good walking shoes for the city and the countryside

➡ Light rain gear – Hong Kong has a subtropical climate with monsoons in summer

➡ Mosquito repellent, sunscreen and sunglasses in summer

➡ A small day pack

➡ Electric adaptor for Hong Kong

Top Tips for Your Trip

➡ Hong Kong's über-efficient Mass Transit Railway (MTR) system and buses can take you to most of the sights and allow you to pack a lot into a day. Most rural areas are no more than 1½ hours away from the city centre by public transport.

➡ If you have more than two days, visit the countryside or outlying islands. It will give you a completely different impression of the territory. Hong Kong is much more than just skyscrapers.

➡ Some of the world's best Chinese food is to be had in Hong Kong. Indulge in at least one excellent Chinese meal during your visit.

➡ To get a feel for local culture, explore the main areas of the city by foot. For our suggested itineraries, see p24.

➡ Take the Star Ferry and the trams at least once. They are living heritage and are well connected to some of the main sights.

What to Wear

Hong Kong has its share of fashion-obsessed people, but in general, Hong Kongers are casual. Many would go to dinner at a fancy restaurant in jeans (though not flip-flops). Central and Causeway Bay have the best dressers.

Summer is hot and humid. Dress lightly but bring a jacket for air-conditioned facilities. The aircon can be strong on empty buses and certain indoor areas.

When hiking in summer, pack your swimsuit and goggles for an impromptu dip.

Be Forewarned

Hong Kong is a very safe city, but you should always exercise common sense. See p330 for more information.

➡ Always be careful of your valuables when in crowded areas.

➡ When using a taxi, always make sure the driver starts the meter.

➡ Some shops and restaurants are closed on the first and second days of the Lunar New Year, some for a longer period of time.

Money

➡ ATMs are everywhere and operate 24/7. Many allow cash withdrawals with foreign cards, usually with a transaction surcharge.

➡ International credit cards are accepted at many hotels, shops and restaurants. Many premises display stickers at entrances showing the credit cards accepted. Visa or MasterCard are much more common than American Express and Diners Club.

➡ You can change money in most banks and any authorised moneychanger. The latter usually open well into the evening.

Taxes

There is no value-added tax (VAT) or sales tax in Hong Kong.

Tipping

➡ **Hotels** A HK$10 or HK$20 note for the porter; gratuity for cleaning staff at your discretion.

➡ **Restaurants** Most eateries, except very cheap places, impose a 10% to 15% service charge, but it is normal to still tip a little (under 5%) if you're happy with the experience. At budget joints, just rounding it off to the nearest HK$10 is fine.

➡ **Pubs and cafes** Not expected unless table service is provided, then something under 5% of your bill.

➡ **Taxis** Tips are never expected.

ANDREW WATSON / GETTY IMAGES ©

Street food stall, Kowloon

Etiquette

Though informal in their day-to-day dealings, Hong Kong people do observe certain rules of etiquette.

➡ **Greetings** Just wave and say 'hi' and 'bye' when meeting for the first time and when saying goodbye.

➡ **Dining** At budget places, people think nothing of sticking their chopsticks into a communal dish. Better restaurants provide separate serving spoons with each dish; if they're provided use them. Don't be afraid to ask for a fork if you can't manage chopsticks.

➡ **Queues** Hong Kongers line up for everything. Attempts to 'jump the queue' are frowned upon.

➡ **Bargaining** Haggling over the price of goods is not expected in shops. Do bargain when buying from street vendors (but not in food markets).

Language

Most people in Hong Kong speak some level of English. Don't be afraid to ask for directions in English. Ninety percent of restaurants have English menus.

If you know Mandarin, you can try using it in Hong Kong. Most people understand the dialect; some speak it reasonably well.

Getting Around

For more information, see Transport (p312)

Metro

Hong Kong's Mass Transit Railway (MTR) system covers most of the city and is the easiest way to get around. Most lines run from 6am to after midnight.

Bus

Relatively fast, buses are an indispensable form of transport to places not reachable by the MTR or after midnight.

Taxi

Cheap compared to Europe and North America. Most taxis are red; green ones operate in certain parts of the New Territories; blue ones on Lantau Island. All run on meter.

Ferry

The Star Ferry connects Hong Kong Island and Kowloon Peninsula via Victoria Harbour. Modern ferry fleets run between Central and the outlying islands.

Tram

Slow but the upper deck offers great views. Runs along the northern strip of Hong Kong Island, from 6am to midnight.

Public Light Buses (Minibuses)

Vans with a green or red roof that cover areas not reachable by bus.

Key Phrases

MTR The Mass Transit Railway runs nine lines serving Hong Kong Island, Kowloon, and the New Territories; the Airport Express to and from the airport; a Light Rail network in Northwestern New Territories; and trains to Běijīng, and Shànghǎi.

Octopus Card A rechargeable 'smart card' that can be used on most forms of public transport, and allows you to make purchases at convenience stores and supermarkets.

Cross-Harbour Taxi A taxi going from Hong Kong Island to Kowloon Peninsula or vice versa that requires passengers to pay the cross-harbour toll for a single trip.

Central-Mid-Levels Escalator A long, covered escalator that links up areas built on slopes in Central, Sheung Wan and Western District.

Key Routes

Star Ferry The scenic option.

MTR Island Line Covers Central, Admiralty, Wan Chai and Causeway Bay.

MTR Tsuen Wan Line Connects Central and Tsim Sha Tsui.

Peak Tram A funicular railway that takes you to the highest point on the island.

Tram 'Heritage' vehicles that run along the northern coast of the island.

How to Hail a Taxi

➡ Look for a stationary or approaching cab with a lit 'For Hire' sign.

➡ When the car is approaching, stand in a prominent place on the side of the road and stick out your arm. The driver should pull over when he sees you.

➡ Taxis do not stop if there are double yellow lines on the side of the road, or at bus stops.

➡ See p317 for advice on hailing a cross-harbour taxi.

TOP TIPS

➡ Opt to use the tram or walk if your end destination is only one Mass Transit Railway (MTR) station away.

➡ Download the app for the MTR system before you leave home.

➡ If you're short of time, combine the MTR with taxis for destinations that are located some walking distance from the MTR station.

➡ Carry the business card from your hotel with its name printed in Chinese characters so you can show your taxi driver on the way back.

When to Travel

➡ During rush hours (8am to 9.30am and 5.30pm to 7pm) the MTR's interchange stations (Central, Admiralty, Tsim Sha Tsui, Kowloon Tong) are jam packed.

➡ Vehicular traffic on major roads and the cross-harbour tunnels can also be painfully slow during peak hours.

Etiquette

➡ Have your ticket or Octopus Card ready before you go through the barrier in the MTR station. You'll feel the impatience at your back if you slow down the human traffic by three seconds.

➡ Stand on the right side of the escalator or you risk being asked to move aside by those in a hurry – and there are plenty of them in Hong Kong.

➡ Drinking and eating in MTR and buses is not allowed.

➡ People waiting to get on the MTR train usually let passengers disembark first before making their way inside. There's no need to push your way in. The train won't leave the station until all doors are properly closed. Wait for the next train rather than hold up the train.

➡ Hong Kongers are not very good at giving up their seats to pregnant women and elders.

Tickets & Passes

➡ A prepaid **Octopus Card** (www.octopus.com.hk) can be used on most forms of public transport. They can be bought at any MTR station, and topped up at MTR stations and convenience stores.

➡ If visiting for over two days, buy an Octopus Card; it will save you up to 5% per trip and you won't have to buy tickets and pay exact fares on buses.

➡ For shorter stays, buy a one-day or three-day pass for unlimited rides on the MTR (www.mtr.com.hk). Available at any MTR station.

For much more on **getting around** see p315

Top Itineraries

Day One

The Peak & the Northwest (p85)

 Catch the legendary Peak Tram up to **Victoria Peak** for stunning views of the city. Then descend and walk to **Sheung Wan**, checking out the shopping options along the way. Stop at **Man Mo Temple** for a taste of history and explore the burgeoning community on **Tai Ping Shan Street**.

> **Lunch** Elegant Luk Yu Tea House (p93) serves great dim sum.

Kowloon (p138)

Take the **Star Ferry** to Kowloon. Enjoy the views along **Tsim Sha Tsui East Promenade** and savour your stroll to the **Museum of History** where you'll get some context to your day's impressions.

> **Dinner** Dunk and dip Hong Kong–style at Great Beef Hot Pot (p154).

The Peak & the Northwest (p85)

After dinner in **Tsim Sha Tsui**, take the metro to **Soho** for drinks and dancing.

Day Two

Wan Chai & the Northeast (p107)

 Embrace (man-made) nature at the lovely **Hong Kong Park**, then head over to Queen's Rd East to explore the sights and streets of **old Wan Chai**. Tram it to **Causeway Bay** for some serious shopping.

> **Lunch** Irori (p119) is fabulously Japanese.

Kowloon (p138)

Take a peek inside **Chungking Mansions**. Then relax and people-watch at **Middle Road Children's Playground**, before taking afternoon tea in style at the **Peninsula**. Bus it north to **Yau Ma Tei**, where you can check out **Tin Hau Temple**, **Jade Market** and traditional shops along **Shanghai Street**.

> **Dinner** Temple Street Night Market (p142) for cheap food under the stars.

Kowloon (p138)

 Have your fortune told and catch some Cantonese opera at **Temple Street Night Market**. Then it's on to **Butler** for a crafted Japanese cocktail or two.

Day Three

Aberdeen & the South (p130)

 Bus it to **Aberdeen** for a cruise on the charming **Aberdeen Harbour**, then head over to **Ap Lei Chau** to check out the indoor **wet market** in the old town. Follow with shopping (for bargain designer furniture and clothing) at **Horizon Plaza** and a late lunch inside a spacious and attractive furniture shop.

> **Lunch** Tree Cafe (p134) for salads, sandwiches and coffee.

Kowloon (p138)

Spend the rest of the afternoon and early evening admiring temples in New Kowloon: the Taoist **Sik Sik Yuen Wong Tai Sin Temple** and the Buddhist **Chi Lin Nunnery**.

> **Dinner** Chi Lin Vegetarian (p157) for tasty Chinese vegetarian.

Kowloon (p138)

Still in New Kowloon, head to the Ritz Carlton for stellar drinks at Ozone, the world's highest bar, then, beset with the munchies, indulge in late-night dim sum at One Dim Sum.

Day Four

Kowloon (p138)

 Start your fourth day with a **taichi class** by the Tsim Sha Tsui waterfront. Boats to **Macau** are just around the corner at the **China Ferry Terminal** – why not hop aboard?

> **Lunch** Clube Militar de Macau (p237) for old-school Portuguese dining.

Macau (p218)

Explore the sights around the **Largo do Senado**. Walk along Rua Central through much of the Unesco-listed **Historic Centre of Macau**, including the **ruins of the Church of St Paul**. Then take a taxi to **Northern Macau Peninsula** to stroll among the designer shops and historic sites in the atmospheric **St Lazarus District**.

> **Dinner** António (p245) dishes up sumptuous Portuguese classics.

Macau (p218)

Make your way back to the Macau Peninsula to play the tables or sip cocktails at **MGM Grand Macau** before catching the ferry back to Hong Kong.

If You Like...

Views

Victoria Peak Pilgrims the world over come here for unbeatable views of the city. (p87)

Sevva A million-dollar view in every sense. (p82)

Tsim Sha Tsui Harbourfront Lap up Hong Kong's iconic skyline from the water's edge. (p141)

High Island Reservoir Climb the dramatic East Dam to survey this engineering feat and the polygonal rock formations below it. (p190)

Tung Ping Chau Mother Nature's flight of fancy brought stunning sedimentary rocks resembling layered sponge cakes to this remote island. (p192)

Lion Rock Visit the city's all-seeing guardian in Sha Tin for its cross-harbour study of population density. (p185)

Pak Nai Drink in the sunset at this westernmost edge of Hong Kong. (p174)

Ozone Overlooking West Kowloon from up in the clouds. (p158)

Modern Architecture

HSBC Building The Norman Foster masterpiece commands a special place in the city's hearts and minds. (p72)

Bank of China Some scoff at IM Pei's ingenious design as a futuristic meat cleaver. (p74)

Old Bank of China Six decades on, this art-deco gem still exudes terrific modernity. (p74)

Cable car, Ocean Park (p132)

Asia Society Hong Kong Centre A beautiful roof garden grows out of an overgrown former military site. (p110)

Two International Finance Centre A wannabe Angkor Wat? Or the ultimate phallic temple to Mammon? What do you think? (p76)

Hong Kong Convention & Exhibition Centre A stingray washed up on an artificial island. (p112)

Parks & Gardens

Victoria Peak Garden The peak above the Peak. This landscaped haven of calm commands untrammelled views of the city. (p87)

Kowloon Walled City Park The former sin city par excellence reincarnated as a traditional Jiāngnán (southern Yangzi) garden. (p153)

Nan Lian Garden A splendid Tang-style garden adorned with a pagoda, tea pavilion, koi pond, Buddhist pines and sedimentary cloud-like boulders. (p144)

Hong Kong Zoological & Botanical Gardens Enveloped by skyscrapers, this stronghold of nature has graced the city since 1871. (p76)

Hong Kong Park A rainforest-like aviary and the city's oldest colonial building lie in this heavily man-made leisure space. (p109)

Ocean Park The marine life is the best draw of this highly popular amusement park. (p132)

Astropark This park appeals to the stargazer in you with Chinese and Western astronomical instruments. (p190)

Kowloon Park The overworked urban lung throbs over the peninsula's artery that is Nathan Rd. (p146)

Unusual Eats

French toast, Hong Kong–style Probably the best-loved indigenous comfort food. Heart attack on a plate! Liberally served in any *cha chaan tang*, such as Sei Yik. (p136)

Snake soup A winter favourite trusted for its warming properties served at Ser Wong Fun. (p93)

Chiu Chow pig's blood with chives A timeless delicacy which comes in the form of jiggly russet cubes.

Cow innards Cheap and nutritious, they simmer away in vats of glorious stock behind steamy noodle-shop windows, like City Hall Maxim's Palace. (p77)

Turtle jelly A mildly bitter concoction of turtle shell and Chinese herbs available at Kung Lee. Ladies eat it for good skin. (p100)

Yin Yeung The quintessential Hong Kong drink of tea mixed with coffee; try it at Mido Café. (p156)

Stinky Tofu Fermented, bacterium-rich goodness, fried or steamed. They smell more pungent than they taste – really. Try them at Chuen Cheong Foods. (p117)

Hiking

Tai Long Wan Hiking Trail Emerge from the luxuriant mountains to find the idyllic Tai Long Wan beach. (p191)

Dragon's Back A popular see-the-sea ramble that undulates to the somnolent village of Shek O. (p64)

Lamma Island Take a gentle 4km hike across the leafy island to the embrace of waterside seafood restaurants. (p196)

For more top Hong Kong spots, see the following:

➡ Eating (p39)

➡ Drinking & Nightlife (p48)

➡ Entertainment (p53)

➡ Shopping (p56)

➡ Sports & Activities (p62)

Hong Kong Cemetery Wander through this hilly, overgrown, deeply atmospheric resting place of Hong Kong's good and naughty. (p111)

Pok Fu Lam Reservoir to the Peak A picturesque ascent past dense forests, waterfalls and military ruins. (p87)

Ng Tung Chai Waterfall Pack a picnic and aim for the waterfall amid the lush greenery. (p180)

Tai Mo Shan Several hiking trails thread up and around Hong Kong's tallest mountain. (p171)

Colonial & East-Meets-West Architecture

Former Legislative Council Building The most imposing colonial edifice left in town. (p74)

Government House Residence of Hong Kong's British governors between 1855 and 1997. An elegant, indubitably rare Georgian-Japanese hybrid. (p74)

Former Marine Police Headquarters Even blatant commercialism cannot detract from the poise and beauty of this neoclassical monument. (p145)

Hong Kong City Hall Classic Bauhaus. An ode to modernism. The place to get married in Hong Kong. (p77)

Tai Fu Tai Mansion A valuable fusion of East-meets-West interior designs for the old scholar-gentry class. (p176)

Central Police Station & Central Magistracy The stern cousins trace the history of law enforcement in Hong Kong. (p89)

Lui Seng Chun A surprisingly harmonious marriage between a Chinese 'shophouse' and an Italian villa. Chinese-medicine clinics occupy the premises. (p152)

St John's Cathedral Criticised for blighting the colony's landscape when it was first built, today it's an oft-forgotten reminder of dear old Blighty. (p74)

Béthanie Two octagonal cow sheds plus a neo-Gothic chapel equal a new performing-art space. (p132)

Shek Lo This Eurasian mansion with a classy rounded balcony resembles a minifort. (p177)

Festivals

Tin Hau's Birthday Don't miss the colourful procession of fishing boats to 'Big Temple' in Joss House Bay. (p30)

Dragon Boat Festival See dragon boats roaring down water courses to the pounding of drums in races across the city. (p30)

Hungry Ghost Festival Traditional Chinese theatre is performed in public playgrounds to entertain underworld visitors during their month-long holiday. (p30)

Mid-Autumn Festival An exhilarating fire dragon slithers through Tai Hang for three nights under the poetic full moon. (p30)

Cheung Chau Bun Festival Get up close and personal with the quirky islanders. (p30)

Chinese New Year This is the most significant occasion on the Chinese cultural calendar. Victoria Park in Causeway Bay erupts in a sea of colour, fireworks and fragrance during the annual Chinese New Year flower market. (p29)

Hong Kong International Film Festival It's action time for film buffs and casual viewers alike. (p29)

Traditional Culture

Tai O Visit the stilt-houses in Hong Kong's southwestern corner for a glimpse of the city's fishing past. (p208)

Walled villages Dotted around the New Territories, these preserve traces of an old, agricultural way of life. (p173)

Folk voodoo In full swing every March after the first (mythological) thunder of the year rouses the animal world.

Morning taichi Get out of bed and join other travellers for some meditative 'shadow boxing'. (p165)

Cantonese opera The endangered art is conserved at Sunbeam Theatre and the restored Yau Ma Tei Theatre. (p126)

Month by Month

February

The marquee of clammy clouds may seal up the city in perfect hibernation mode, but nothing can dampen the spirits around the most important festival on the Chinese cultural calendar.

✨ Chinese New Year

Vast flower markets herald the beginning of this best-loved Chinese festival. Wear red and be blessed at Sik Sik Yuen Wong Tai Sin Temple (p143). Then find a spot by Victoria Harbour (or failing that, a TV) and be awed by fireworks.

✨ Spring Lantern Festival

Lovers are the focus as colourful lanterns glow under the first full moon of the lunar year to mark the end of New Year celebrations, and a day known as Chinese Valentine's Day.

☆ Hong Kong Arts Festival

Over five to eight weeks, Hong Kong's premier cultural event (www.hk.artsfestival.org) is a feast of music and performing arts, ranging from classical to contemporary, by hundreds of local and international talents.

🏃 Hong Kong Marathon

In 2014, 64,000 athletes competed in this top Asian marathon (www.hkmarathon.com). The annual event also includes a half-marathon, a 10km race and a wheelchair race.

March

Rain and warm weather return, triggering the whirr of dehumidifiers in every home and office – as flowers and umbrellas bloom across the city.

◉ 'Villain Exorcism'

Witness folk sorcery performed by rent-a-curse grannies (p114) under the Canal Rd Flyover in Wan Chai or at Yau Ma Tei's Tin Hau Temple. Rapping curses, they hit cut-outs of clients' enemies with a shoe.

☆ Hong Kong Artwalk

Dozens of art galleries in Central, Sheung Wan, Wan Chai, Happy Valley and Aberdeen throw open their doors for a one-night experience (www.hongkongartwalk.com). There's much chin-stroking and wine-sipping as participants raise money for charity.

☆ Hong Kong International Film Festival

For two weeks from mid-to-late March, one of Asia's top film festivals, the four-decade-old HKIFF (www.hkiff.org.hk) screens the latest art-house and award-winning movies from Asia and around the world.

☆ Script Road – Macau Literary Festival

Writers, artists and filmmakers from Macau, Asia and Portuguese-speaking regions come together in March for 10 brilliant days of poetry reading, literary discussion, film screening, and cross-cultural performance (www.thescriptroad.org).

◉ Hong Kong Flower Show

For approximately 10 days, Victoria Park turns into a colourful sea of fragrant floral displays as horticulturalists from over 20 countries experiment with their green fingers.

🏃 Hong Kong Sevens

Hong Kong's most famous sporting event and probably its most original – the Rugby Sevens was invented here in 1975), this eternally popular tournament promises fierce competition and carnivalesque partying from the fans (www.hksevens.com.hk).

May

The city steams up, especially in urban areas, as the long summer months begin. The year's first heavy showers fall as religious celebrations heat up the mood.

🎆 Birthday of Tin Hau

A festival dedicated to the patroness of fisherfolk and one of the harbour city's most popular deities. Key celebrations include a colourful float parade in Yuen Long and traditional rites at the 'Big Temple' in Joss House Bay (p174).

🎆 Cheung Chau Bun Festival

This unique, week-long festival on Cheung Chau (p216) climaxes on Buddha's birthday when children 'float' through the island's narrow lanes

dressed up as mythological characters and modern-day politicians while the more daring townsfolk scramble up bun-studded towers at midnight.

🎆 Buddha's Birthday

Devotees head to Buddhist monasteries and temples on the eighth day of the fourth lunar month to pray to the founder of Buddhism and bathe his likenesses with scented water.

☆ Le French May

Misleadingly named, this celebration of all things Gallic often starts in April and ends in June – so much the better, as it returns with a rich arts program of consistently high quality, plus the obligatory fine food and wine (www.frenchmay.com).

June

The heavens are truly open, the mercury spikes, and strong air-conditioning switches on citywide to soothe the nerves of locals and visitors alike.

🎆 Hong Kong International Dragon Boat Races

Thousands of the world's strongest dragonboaters meet in Hong Kong over three days of intense racing and partying at Victoria Harbour (www.discoverhongkong.com), while smaller but equally heart-stopping races happen in waterways all over the city.

August

Seven million souls palpitate and perspire in the sweltering heat.

Torrential downpours are common but there is always a sun-toasted beach near you in this sprawling archipelago of 260-plus islands.

🎆 Hungry Ghost Festival

Restless spirits take leave from hell during the seventh moon to roam the earth. Hell money, food and earthly luxuries made of papier mâché are burned to propitiate the visitors. Fascinating folk traditions come alive across the city.

September

Summer lingers but the humidity factor starts to recede. Continue to hug the ocean coastlines for free respite as school kids swap their buckets and spades for mighty dunes of homework.

🎆 Mid-Autumn Festival

Pick up a lantern and participate in a moonlit picnic on the 15th night of the eighth lunar month. This family occasion commemorates a 14th-century, anti-Mongol uprising with much cheerful munching of the once-subversive 'mooncakes'.

November

At long last Hong Kong mellows. Temperatures sensibly cool down to around 22°C (72°F) and rainfall ceases significantly, much to the delight of ramblers and other countryside merrymakers.

(Top) 'Floating' child, Cheung Chau Bun Festival
(Bottom) Dragon dance, Birthday of Tin Hau

CARSTEN SCHAEL / GETTY IMAGES ©

HARALD SUND / GETTY IMAGES ©

☆ Hong Kong International Literary Festival

Held over 10 days, the festival (www.festival.org.hk) features established and emerging writers from around the world. Past authors have included luminaries Seamus Heaney and Louis de Bernières.

🏃 Oxfam Trailwalker

What began as a fundraising drill by local Ghurkha soldiers in 1981 is today a celebrated endurance test that challenges hikers in teams of four to complete the 100km MacLehose Trail (p187) in 48 hours (www.oxfamtrailwalker.org.hk).

December

Arguably the best time of the year to visit the city. The delightful weather is perfect for all outdoor activities, though brace for the Christmas shopping crowds.

🎇 Hong Kong Winterfest

Rejoice as neon Yuletide murals appear on the Tsim Sha Tsui harbourfront. Ferry across to Statue Sq to see illuminated Christmas trees and fake snow. Join teenage revellers around Times Sq to ring in the birth of the holy sprog.

🏃 Hong Kong International Races

Billed as the Turf World Championships, master horsemen and equine stars from across the planet descend on the beautifully set Sha Tin Racecourse (p187) to do battle. Expect fanatical betting from the 60,000-plus who pack the stands.

With Kids

Hong Kong is a great destination for kids, though the crowds, traffic and pollution might take a little getting used to. Food and sanitation are of a high standard. The city is jam-packed with things to entertain the young ones, often just a hop, skip and jump away from attractions for you.

Hong Kong Disneyland (p203)

COURTESY OF HONG KONG DISNEYLAND © DISNEY

Child-Friendly Museums

Hong Kong Science Museum

The three storeys of action-packed displays at Hong Kong's liveliest museum are a huge attraction for youngsters from toddlers to teens. There's a theatre where staff in lab coats perform wacky experiments. (p149)

Hong Kong Museum of History

This excellent museum brings the city's history to life in visually and aurally colourful ways. Kids will enjoy the 'Hong Kong Story' exhibition with its splendid replicas of local traditions, and a life-sized fishing junk. (p140)

Hong Kong Space Museum & Theatre

Kids eager to test their motor skills will go berserk – there are buttons to push, telescopes to peer through, simulation rides and computer quizzes. Older kids will enjoy the Omnimax films shown on the convex ceiling of the theatre. (p145)

Hong Kong Maritime Museum

Even if the exquisite ship models at this museum don't do the trick, there's plenty to fire junior's imagination – gun-toting pirate mannequins, real treasures salvaged from shipwrecks, a metal diving suit, fog-horn music, a digitised ancient map... (p77)

Hong Kong Railway Museum

Thomas and his friends jolt to life at this open-air museum converted from a historic railway station; it comes complete with old coaches and a train compartment. (p178)

Hong Kong Heritage Museum

Though some youngsters may appreciate the displays, the real gem is the hands-on children's discovery gallery where they can dress up, play puzzle games and enjoy an exhibition of vintage toys. (p184)

Parks Children Like

Ocean Park

Hong Kong's premier amusement park offers white-knuckle rides, a top-notch aquarium, real pandas and a cable-car ride overlooking the sea. (p132)

NEED TO KNOW

➡ **La Leche League Hong Kong** (☑Caroline 6492 7607, Cher 9314 9463, Jenny 2987 7792, Pauline 6331 5078; www.lllhk.org) English-speaking breastfeeding support group.

➡ **Nursing rooms** Available in large malls and most museums.

➡ **Rent-a-Mum** (☑2523 4868; www.rent-a-mum.com; per hr from HK$180) Babysitting for a minimum of four hours.

➡ **In Safe Hands** (☑9820 3363, 2323 2676; www.insafehands.com.hk; per hr from HK$200, plus transport costs) Childcare agency that provides full-time and part-time nanny services, and evening babysits (minimum four hours).

Hong Kong Park

Ducks, swans and turtles inhabit the ponds here, and the massive forest-like aviary has an elevated walkway that lets visitors move through the tree canopy to spy on the birds. (p109)

Hong Kong Zoological & Botanical Gardens

After a visit to this park, your offspring will have seen the American flamingo, the Burmese python, the two-toed sloth a buff-cheeked gibbon. (p76)

Middle Road Children's Playground

This breezy playground, with swings and slides for all ages, is a utopia of sorts, where you'll see kids of different ethnicities and social classes united in the language of play. (p146)

Hong Kong Wetland Park

Patience may be required for appreciation of the wetland habitats, but not for the themed exhibition galleries, the theatre and 'Swamp Adventure' play facility. (p174)

Kowloon Park

This large verdant venue has plenty of room, lakes with waterfowl, two playgrounds, swimming pools and an aviary. (p146)

Hong Kong Disneyland

The latest attraction at this famous theme park is Toy Story Land. (p203)

Tips for Visiting Theme Parks

Here are some tips if you're visiting Ocean Park (p132) and Disneyland (p203) with young ones in tow.

Practicalities

➡ Both parks are extremely popular with mainland Chinese tourists. For a quieter visit, avoid Chinese public holidays, in particular, Labour Day (1st May) and the ensuing two days, National Day holidays (1 to 7 October), Ching Ming Festival in April, and Chinese New Year in January or February. July and August are also very busy.

➡ If you have to go at the weekend, Sunday is slightly less busy than Saturday.

➡ Some of the rides have height restrictions.

➡ There's plenty of decent Chinese and Western food at both parks.

Ocean Park Tips

➡ Most teens and grown-ups will prefer Ocean Park to Disneyland; it's much bigger, has a lot more to offer, and the rides are more intense. Younger children may like Whisker's Harbour, the age-appropriate play area, and Pacific Pier where they can look at and feed seals and sea lions.

➡ Ocean Park consists of two parts – Waterfront near the entrance, and Summit on the headland. You can't walk between the two, but you can take the scenic Cable Car or the subterranean Ocean Express train. The former is busiest in the morning and just before closing. To avoid long lines, take the Ocean Express up and the Cable Car down.

Disneyland Tips

➡ Fantasyland is by far the best for the very young set. Here you'll find Dumbo, Mad Hatter's Teacups, It's a Small World, and the Many Adventures of Winnie the Pooh.

➡ The highly popular Toy Story Land and Grizzly Gulch usually have the longest lines.

➡ Though Hong Kong Disneyland is comparatively small, do bring a stroller if you have one. They're great for moving tired kids around and stowing your bags. Sidewalks are stroller-friendly and there's parking near the rides. The park also has a limited number of strollers for rent.

➡ There are lockers on Main Street, USA, where many of the shops are.

➡ Taking the train on Disneyland Railroad is nice if you're tired, but remember that seats are few. Also it does not take you all the way around the park. There are two stops – at the entrance and in Fantasyland.

➡ There's no need to stake out a position to watch the fireworks that come on at 8pm, unless you're looking to take awesome photos. However, watching near the entrance will allow a quick exit.

➡ Going to Disneyland in the afternoon may let you make flexible use of your time and avoid long lines. The park also takes on a special magic in the twilight hours (6pm to 9pm) – the Jungle Cruise ride becomes a 'night safari', the Orbitron flying saucers at Tomorrowland are lit up and the constellation globe and the planets will be twinkling with fibre-optic stars.

Boats & Trams

Peak Tram

Children will be fascinated by the ride on the gravity-defying Peak Tram (p87).

Star Ferry

Cruise liner, barge, hydrofoil, fishing junk... Your mini-mariner will have a blast naming passing vessels, as their own tugboat (p73) nimbly dodges the swipes of a gigantic dragon in tempestuous Victoria Harbour.

Trams

Looking out the window on the top deck of a narrow tram that rattles, clanks and sways amid the heavy traffic can be exhilarating.

MTR

The metro is interestingly colour-coded and full of myths and features of interest. See p315 for more information.

Symphony of the Stars Lightshow

Children will be awestruck by the dance of laser beams projected from skyscrapers on both sides of the harbour, to accompanying music. Bring the Darth Vader costume.

Shopping with Kids

Horizon Plaza (p137) has megastores selling kids' books and clothing. Tai Yuen St is known for traditional toy shops catering to youngsters of all ages.

For dozens of outlets dedicated to children, head to the ground floor of Ocean Terminal (p145) at Harbour City; level 2 of Festival Walk (p165); level 9 of Times Square (p128); or level 2 of Elements mall (p164).

Ice Skating

Elements (p164), Festival Walk (p165) and Cityplaza (p129) malls have indoor ice rinks. Check the websites for the latest rates and opening hours.

Dolphin Watching

See the second-smartest animal on earth in the wild – and it's in bubble-gum pink! Hong Kong Dolphinwatch (p320) runs three four-hour tours a week to waters where Chinese white dolphins may be sighted.

Play Pilot

If your children are over five, let them dress like a pilot and try flying a virtual Boeing 737 at **Flight Experience** (✆2359 0000; www.flightexperience.com.hk; 38 Wang Chiu Rd, Shop G20, Megabox; ⊕). Sweaty palms guaranteed. Advance booking essential.

Like a Local

Certain values and habits permeate everyday life in Hong Kong, but while they're prevalent, your experience of the city's cultural mores depends on the locals who cross your path – not everyone is the same. Here are some tips to help you navigate the social seas of this metropolis.

m sum restaurant

CULTURA TRAVEL/NANCY HONEY / GETTY IMAGES ©

Cultural Etiquette

Greetings

Some locals find hugging and cheek kissing too intimate; others secretly wish for more. Generally speaking, a simple 'Hello, how are you?' and a light handshake will do. Remove your shoes before entering someone's home.

Face

The cornerstone of human relations in this part of the world. Think status and respect: be courteous and never lose your temper in public.

Gifts

If you present someone with a gift, they may appear reluctant for fear of seeming greedy, but insist and they'll give in. Don't be surprised if they don't open a gift-wrapped present in front of you, though; to do so is traditionally considered impolite.

Dining Out

Most Hong Kongers like to 'go Dutch' when dining out with friends. The usual practice is to split the bill evenly, rather than for each person to pay for what they ordered, or asking for separate checks.

Colours

Red symbolises good luck, happiness and wealth (though writing in red can convey anger and unfriendliness). White is the colour of death in Chinese culture, so think twice before giving white flowers or attending an elderly person's birthday celebration in white.

Table Manners

Sanitary Consumption

Dishes are meant to be shared at Chinese meals. Expensive eateries provide serving chopsticks or spoons with each dish; most budget places don't, but you can ask for them.

Mind Your Chopsticks

Don't stand your chopsticks upright in the middle of a bowl (it resembles two incense sticks at a graveside offering). If you can't manage chopsticks, don't be afraid to ask for a fork. Nearly all restaurants have them.

Spirit of Sharing

Take a few pieces of food from a communal dish at a time, preferably those nearest to you. It is not necessary to shove half the dish into your bowl in one go. For shared staples, it is fine to fill your whole bowl up.

Tea Language

When someone refills your dainty teacup, you can tap two fingers (index and middle) gently on the table twice instead of saying thank you with a greasy mouth full of food. Mastering this (allegedly) centuries-old gesture will endear you to your hosts.

Bones & Tissues

Your plate is the preferred spot for bones, but at budget places diners put them on the table beside their plates or bowls. If you find that disconcerting, place a tissue under or over your rejects.

Food Obsessions

Swallow & Scribe

Legions of food critics, amateur or otherwise, post reports and photos on the user-driven, bilingual restaurant-review website www.openrice.com. Some bloggers have local celebrity status, such as Diary of a Growing Boy (www.diarygrowingboy.com).

Dim Sum – a Fact of Life

Morning dim sum is a daily ritual for many retirees and a tasty excuse for a weekend family reunion (though many pay more attention to their newspapers or smart phones than what's on the table).

Tea Break

When mid-afternoon comes, *cha chaan tang* (tea cafes) are full of elderly folks debating the morning's meat prices and stock-market fluctuations. These holes-in-the-wall function as community focal points for people to swap gossip. They're also bolt-holes for many a stressed office worker.

Late-Night Sweets

After dinner, locals like to head to a dessert shop for sweet soups and other Chinese-style or fusion desserts, such as black sesame soup, steamed egg pudding, mango pomelo sago, and durian crêpes.

Steamy Winter

In winter hotpot at a *dai pai dong* (food stall) or even a restaurant is a soul-warming, convivial experience. Dip slivers of meat, seafood and vegetables in a vat of steaming broth. Consume and repeat. Your night will be transformed.

Money Matters

Jockey Club

Step into any Jockey Club off-course betting centre (often found near public housing estates, markets or transport terminals) on any race day or night, and witness a maelstrom of emotions as punters struggle to defy the odds. Occasionally you'll hear a squeal of joy but, more often, invectives pepper deep sighs of desperation as numerals streak across the TV screens every 30 minutes. Outside, high rollers squat on the pavement, heads buried in race cards, in search of the ever elusive winning formula.

Stocks & Shares

Look out for the hole-in-the-wall brokerage firms on any weekday and you'll find crowds of (not all small-time) investors deeply engrossed in the live stock-market updates on the wall-mounted panels.

Local Hoods

Full-scale gentrification has yet to arrive in these areas but the dictates of urban development are already changing their character. Go and soak up their gritty, earthy, neighbourly vibes before it's too late.

Yau Ma Tei

Stroll Shanghai St for traditional barbers, Chinese wedding costume-makers and artisans of other time-honoured crafts.

Sham Shui Po

Find flea markets, 1930s shophouses, post-war housing estates and even an ancient tomb in this resilient working-class district.

Queen's Road West

The pungent smells of dried seafood and Chinese herbal medicine lead you into this meandering parade of small traders.

For Free

Iong Kong is not a cheap place to visit and prices creep up at every pportunity, as any veritable ocal can testify. But with a bit of planning, you can still indulge yourself for very little money.

chi, Victoria Park (p114)

Cheap & Cheerful

Not quite free but near enough to warrant inclusion, for a couple of dollars you can rattle your way through the urban canyon of high-rises on a tram; or give up pocket change for the voyage of a lifetime on the Star Ferry (p73).

Be seated by 11am and brunch on hearty dim sum – many Chinese restaurants offer discounted prices on either side of the noon–2pm lunch hours. For a taste of austerity, don't miss the mid-afternoon tea sets (HK$20 to HK$30) at the city's *cha chaan tang* (tea cafes) and fast-food chains.

At sundown and most of Sunday, generous happy hours are a feature of many bars. On Tuesdays, a movie ticket generally costs HK$10 to HK$25 less than usual. For only HK$10, you can experience a night at the races – pick the right horse(s) and you could recoup all of your travel expenses.

Museum Hopping

Wednesday is 'free admission' day at seven Hong Kong museums: Museum of Art (p145), Museum of History (p140), Heritage Museum (p184), Science Museum (p149), Space Museum (p145), excluding Space Theatre, Museum of Coastal Defence (p115) and Dr Sun Yat-sen Museum (p92). The Museum of Tea Ware (p110) and the Railway Museum (p178) are free of charge on all days of the week. And depending on your interest, there's also the Hong Kong International Hobby & Toy Museum (p152) and the even smaller Bruce Lee Club (p152).

Street Concerts

Don't miss the excellent concerts held every third Saturday of the month outside the Arts Centre (p126), and every second Thursday outside the Blue House (p111) in Wan Chai. Gigs by some of the best local musicians from classical through jazz to indie.

Liberal Views

Enjoy panoramic island views from the 43rd-floor viewing platform in the Bank of China building (p74); or bring your own booze to the public terrace at International Finance Centre (p76) and watch sunset over Victoria Harbour. Suffer from vertigo? Head up to Signal Hill Garden (p146) or Middle Road Children's Playground in Tsim Sha Tsui (p146), and gaze at the harbour.

Thrill Rides

White-knuckle bus rides can make a good poor man's alternative for the cable-car and thrill rides at Ocean Park. The following routes are scenic, if not hair-raising: 314 (Sunday only) from Siu Sai Wan via Tai Tam reservoir to Stanley; 14 (weekdays only) from Sai Wan Ho along the tram tracks to Stanley; 6 around the southern bays, and the open-top buses H1 and H2 that can pick you up in Central.

Taichi by the Harbour

Start the day on the right foot with a taichi lesson (p165) taught by experienced masters next to Victoria Harbour. Learn a martial art, enjoy stunning views, and shape up – not bad for HK$50.

Browse the Markets

Trawling through Hong Kong's vibrant markets will make you richer, as you will have pocketed the real gems – the unique atmosphere, brushing shoulders with locals, witnessing the bargaining culture.

Nature Escape

Over 60% of Hong Kong is officially countryside – rolling hills, sprawling country parks, surf-beaten coastlines, all gratis and within an hour from the nearest urban centre. Enjoy the luxuriant vistas by hiking, cycling, picnicking or taking long walks along dappled paths.

Hit the Beach

Whether it's a dip in the waves, engaging in long overdue sun worship, or dotting footprints along the shore, Hong Kong's beaches offer a free and enjoyable escape from the city. Admission is free and there are lifeguards. Just bring shades, sunblock, drinks and music, and you're ready to party.

Art & Antique Trail

The charming streets of Soho and Sheung Wan are lined with art galleries and shops selling Chinese antiques. You can take your time admiring the art and artefacts, or chat with the owners.

Spiritual Spaces

Hong Kong has hundreds of temples, a fair number of churches, and a handful of mosques and synagogues – a testimony to its religious freedom. Many of these are historically important; almost all are free of charge. Even if you're not a history buff, the architecture, artefacts and atmosphere will likely beguile. Admire the facades or enter for a few moments of quiet contemplation. For deeper introspection, saunter among the headstones of the famous dead at Happy Valley Cemetery (p111).

Peninsula Walkthrough

Wander through the gilded halls of one of Asia's most legendary hotels – the Peninsula (p145). Listen to the subtle clink of silverware as well-dressed patrons take afternoon tea in the opulent lobby, then climb the red-carpeted stairs to the 2nd floor to the colonnaded verandah.

Chungking Express

Chungking Mansions (p146), or CKM, has cleaned up its act since its heyday as a slum. Now it's an interesting maze of guesthouses, phone shops, and cheap South Asian eateries. The eclecticism earned it the title of the 'best example of globalistion in Asia' and inspired a movie by Wong Kar-wai.

Stock Exchange

Feel the throbbing in the air as dedicated punters of a different kind make money (or lose it) in Hong Kong's nerve centre.

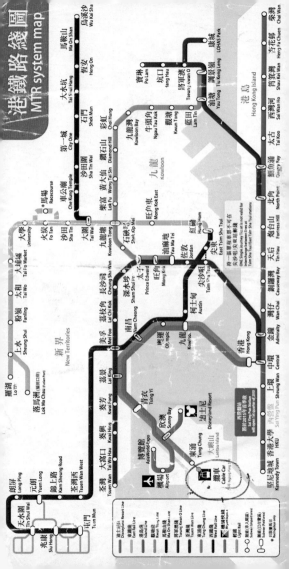

Steamed dumplings

 Eating

One of the world's most delicious cities, Hong Kong offers culinary excitement whether you're spending HK$20 on a bowl of noodles or HK$2000 on a seafood feast. The best of China is well represented, be it Cantonese, Shanghainese, Northern or Sichuanese. Similarly, the smorgasbord of non-Chinese – French, Italian, Spanish, Japanese, Thai, Indian – is the most diverse in all of Asia.

NEED TO KNOW

Price Ranges

The price indicators below are based on a two-course meal with a drink.

$	less than HK$200
$$	HK$200 to HK$500
$$$	more than HK$500

Opening Hours

➡ Lunch 11am–3pm

➡ Dinner 6–11pm

Some restaurants are open through the afternoon, while others are also open for breakfast. Most restaurants open on Sunday and close for at least two days during the Lunar New Year.

Reservations

Most restaurants (midrange or above) take reservations. At very popular addresses booking is crucial, especially for weekend dinners. Popular restaurants may serve two or even three seatings a night.

How Much?

Forty dollars will buy you noodles and some greens, or a set meal at fast-food chains such as **Cafe de Coral** (www.cafe decoralfastfood.com) or **Fairwood** (www. fairwood.com.hk). A proper sit-down lunch in a midrange restaurant costs at least HK$80 and dinner HK$120 per head. Dinner at upscale restaurants will set you back at least HK$600 per person.

Tipping

Tipping is not a must as every bill includes a 10% service charge, but this almost always goes into the owner's coffers, so if you're happy with the service, tip as you see fit. Most people leave behind the small change.

For help with ordering, see our Menu Decoder, p343.

Cantonese Cuisine

The dominant cuisine in Hong Kong is Cantonese and it's easily the best in the world. Many of China's top chefs had fled to the territory around 1949; it was therefore here

Egg tart

and not in its original home, Guǎngzhōu, that Cantonese cuisine flourished.

This style of cooking is characterised by an obsession with freshness. Seafood restaurants display tanks full of finned and shelled creatures enjoying their final moments on terra infirma. Flavours are delicate and balanced, obtained through restrained use of seasoning and light-handed cooking techniques such as steaming and quick stir-frying.

REGIONAL VARIETIES

Cantonese cuisine refers to the culinary styles of Guǎngdōng province, as well as Chiu Chow (Cháozhōu) and Hakka cuisines. Chiu Chow dishes reflect a penchant for seafood and condiments. Deep-fried soft-boned fish comes with tangerine oil; braised goose, a vinegar and garlic dip. Hakka cuisine is known for its saltiness and use of preserved meat. Salt-baked chicken and pork stewed with preserved vegetables fed many hungry families and famished workers back in leaner times.

MODERNISATION

Hong Kong's chefs are also an innovative bunch who'll seize upon new ingredients and find wondrous ways of using them. For example, dim sum has expanded to include mango pudding, and shortbread tarts stuffed with abalone and chicken. Black truffles – the kind you see on French or Italian menus – are sometimes sprinkled on rolled rice sheets and steamed. And it works.

Above: Po Lin Vegetarian Restaurant
(p195)
Right: Dim sum

YIU YU HOI / GETTY IMAGES ©

Dining Local
DIM SUM

Dim sum are Cantonese tidbits consumed with tea for breakfast or lunch. The term literally means 'to touch the heart' and the act of eating dim sum is referred to as yum cha, meaning 'to drink tea'.

In the postwar period, yum cha was largely an activity of single males, who met over their breakfast tea to socialise or exchange tips about job-seeking. Soon yum cha became a family activity.

Each dish, often containing two to four morsels steamed in a bamboo basket, is meant to be shared. In old-style dim sum places, just stop the waiter and choose something from the cart. Modern venues give you an order slip, but it's almost always in Chinese only. However, as dim sum dishes are often ready-made, the waiters should be able to show you samples to choose from.

SOY SAUCE WESTERN

'Soy sauce Western' (si yau sai chaan) features Western-style dishes prepared with a large dollop of wisdom from the Chinese kitchen. It's said to have emerged in the 1940s when the ingenious chef of Tai Ping Koon decided to 'improve' on Western cooking by tweaking recipes, such as replacing dairy products with local seasoning – lactose intolerance is common among East Asians – and putting rice on the menu.

His invention met its soul mate when White Russians, who had fled to Shànghǎi after the Bolshevik Revolution, sought refuge in Hong Kong in 1949; they soon cooked up what's known as Shanghainese–Russian food.

The two schools of Western-inspired cuisine offered affordable and 'exotic' dining to locals at a time when authentic Western eateries catered almost exclusively to expatriates. Eventually the two styles mingled, spawning soy sauce Western as we know it today. Popular dishes include Russian borscht, baked pork chop over fried rice and beef stroganoff with rice.

CHA CHAAN TANG

Tea cafes (茶餐廳, cha chaan tang) are cheap and cheery neighbourhood eateries that appeared in the 1940s serving Western-style snacks and drinks to those who couldn't afford Earl Grey and cucumber sandwiches. Their menus have since grown to include more substantial Chinese and soy sauce Western dishes.

Some tea cafes have bakeries creating European pastries with Chinese characteristics, such as pineapple buns (菠蘿包, bo law bao), which don't contain a trace of the said fruit; and cocktail buns, which have coconut stuffing (雞尾包, gai may bao).

Dai Pai Dong

A dai pai dong (大牌檔) is a food stall, hawker-style or built into a rickety hut crammed with tables and stools that sometimes spill out onto the pavement. After WWII the colonial government issued food-stall licences to the families of injured or deceased civil servants. The licences were big so the stalls came to be known as dai pai dong (meaning 'big licence stalls').

HOW HONG KONGERS EAT

Many busy Hong Kongers take their breakfast and lunch at tea cafes. A full breakfast at these places consists of buttered toast, fried eggs and spam, instant noodles and a drink. The more health-conscious might opt for congee, with dim sum of rolled rice sheets (chéung fán) and steamed dumplings with pork and shrimp (sìu máai).

Lunch for office workers can mean a bowl of wonton noodles, a plate of rice with Chinese barbecue or something more elaborate.

Afternoon tea is popular at the weekends. On weekdays it is the privilege of labourers and ladies of leisure (tai-tais). Workers are said to vanish, Cinderella fashion, at 3.15pm sharp for their daily fix of egg tarts and milk tea. For tai-tais, tea could mean scones with rose-petal jam with friends or a bowl of noodles at the hairdresser's.

Dinner is the biggest meal of the day. If prepared at home, what's on the table depends on the traditions of the family, but usually there's soup, rice, vegies and a meat or fish dish. Everyone has their own bowl of rice and/or soup, with the rest of the dishes placed in the middle of the table for sharing. Dining out is also extremely common, with many families eating out three to five times a week.

PLAN YOUR TRIP EATING

VEGIES BEWARE

There are 101 ways to accidentally eat meat in Hong Kong. A plate of greens is probably cooked in meat stock and served with oyster sauce. Broth made with chicken is a prevalent ingredient, even in dishes where no meat is visible. In budget restaurants, chicken powder is used liberally. The safe bet for vegies wanting to go Chinese is to patronise vegetarian eateries or upscale establishments. Vegie-friendly restaurants listed in this guide are marked with this icon: ✍.

Dai pai dong can spring up anywhere: by the side of a slope, in an alley or under a tree. That said, these vintage places for trillion-star dining are fast vanishing; most have now been relocated to government-run, cooked-food centres.

The culinary repertoire of *dai pai dong* varies from stall to stall. One may specialise in congee while its neighbour whips up seafood dishes that give restaurants a run for their money. In places where there's a cluster of *dai pai dong*, you can order dishes from different operators.

Walled Village Cuisine

The modern history of Hong Kong begins with the First Opium War, but the roots of its cuisine go much further back. The local inhabitants who dwelt here ate what they could herd, grow or catch from the sea. Certain ancient food traditions from these peoples remain, most notably walled village cuisine, best known for the 'basin feast' (盆菜, *poon choy*). The story has it that the last emperor of the southern Song dynasty (AD 1127–1279), fleeing from the Mongols, retreated to a walled village in Hong Kong with his entourage. The villagers, lacking decent crockery, piled all kinds of food into a large basin to serve the royal guests. *Poon choy* has become a dish for festive occasions in the New Territories ever since.

International Cuisine

From monkfish-liver sushi to French molecular cuisine, Hong Kong has no shortage of great restaurants specialising in the food of other cultures. The variety and quality of Asian cuisines is outstanding,

surpassing even that of Tokyo. Then there's the exceptional array of Western options. Hong Kong's affluent and cosmopolitan population loves Western food, especially European. This is evidenced by the number of international celebrity chefs with restaurants here, such as Joël Robuchon and Pierre Gagnaire. Prices at these and other top addresses can be steep, but there's also a burgeoning number of excellent eateries specialising in rustic French or Italian that cater to food lovers with medium-sized pockets.

Self-Catering

The two major supermarket chains, **Park'N'Shop** (www.parknshop.com) and **Wellcome** (www.wellcome.com.hk), have megastores that offer groceries as well as takeaway cooked food.

Great Food Hall (☎2918 9986; www.greatfoodhall.com; Basement, Two Pacific Place, Admiralty; meals from HK$100; ⊘10am-10pm; MAdmiralty, exit F) In the basement of the swish Pacific Place shopping mall, Great is one of the nicest gourmet supermarkets in Hong Kong. It has its own sit-down sushi bar and Spanish tapas

Tea urn and cups

BEST FOOD BLOGS

A few of our favourite English-language food blogs for getting the up-to-date dirt on restaurants new and old:

That Food Cray (www.thatfoodcray. com)

Sassy Hong Kong (www.sassyhong kong.com)

e-Ting (www.e-tingfood.com)

Food Craver (www.foodcraver.hk)

Hungry Hong Kong (http://hungryhk. blogspot.hk)

restaurant (always crowded; just stand politely behind the bar until someone finishes), as well as takeaway sushi and hearty create-your-own salads.

Citysuper (☑2506 2888; www.citysuper. hk; Basement 1, Times Square, Causeway Bay; ☉10.30am-10pm; ⓂCauseway Bay) There are also numerous other branches, including one in IFC.

Oliver's, the Delicatessen (☑2810 7710; www.oliversthedeli.com.hk; 10 Chater Rd, 201-205, Prince's Bldg, Central; ☉8.30am-8pm; ⓂCentral)

Taste (Festival Walk, Kowloon Tong; ☉7am-midnight; ⓂKowloon Tong) A classy version of Park'N'Shop. Other locations include Hopewell Centre in Wan Chai.

WET MARKETS

Wet markets for fresh produce (open 6am to 7pm) can be found all over town.

Graham St Market (Graham St, Central; ☐5B)

Bowrington Rd (Bowrington Rd, Causeway Bay; ⓂCauseway Bay, exit A)

Chun Yeung St (Chun Yeung St, North Point; ⓂNorth Point, exit A2)

Canton Rd (Canton Rd, Mong Kok; ⓂMong Kok, exit C3)

Cooking Courses

Hong Kong is a good place to hone your skills in the art of Chinese cookery.

Martha Sherpa (☑2381 0132; www.martha sherpa.com; North Point; courses HK$1600) Expert Cantonese home cook Martha Sherpa (her last name comes from her Nepali husband) has taught the likes of former Australian PM Julia Gillard how to make sweet-and-sour pork, fried noodles, glutinous rice dumplings and other

Hong Kong favourites. Small group classes cover topics like wok cookery, dim sum and vegetarian Chinese. Half-day, full-day and evening classes are available, all HK$1600.

Home's Cooking (www.homescookingstudio. com; classes HK$600) This highly rated cooking class, run out of the owner's home, offers three-hour morning or afternoon sessions. Students cook a three-course Chinese meal: think spring rolls, lotus-leaf chicken, ginger pudding. Classes include a trip to a local wet market and lunch or dinner.

Peninsula Academy (☑2696 6693; www. peninsula.com; Salisbury Rd, the Peninsula, Tsim Sha Tsui; per class HK$2000; Ⓜ Tsim Sha Tsui) One-and-half-hour dim-sum-making classes include lunch.

Publications

The popular website **Open Rice** (www.open-rice.com) has restaurant reviews penned by the city's armchair gourmands.

Time Out Hong Kong (www.timeout.com.hk/restaurants-bars/)

Good Eating (www.scmp.com)

HK Magazine Restaurant Guide (http://hk.asia-city.com/restaurants)

WOM Guide (www.womguide.com)

Eating by Neighbourhood

➡ **Hong Kong Island: Central** (p77) Power lunch spots for business wheelers and dealers, plus international food of all stripes.

➡ **Hong Kong Island: The Peak & the Northwest** (p92) Tourist traps around the Peak give way to low-key local spots further west.

➡ **Hong Kong Island: Wan Chai & the Northeast** (p116) Everything from the world's best *char siu* (roast pork) to ultra-authentic sushi in Hong Kong's foodie heart.

➡ **Hong Kong Island: Aberdeen & the South** (p134) Laid-back beach cafes and British-style pubs dot the island's sunny south side.

➡ **Kowloon** (p153) Cheap Indian dives sit next to glittering Cantonese banquet halls along Kowloon's screaming neon boulevards.

Top: Temple Street Night Market (p142)
Middle: Sweet and sour chicken
Bottom: Wonton noodles

Lonely Planet's Top Choices

Yat Lok Barbecue Restaurant (p180) The crispiest, juiciest roast goose in the territory.

Tim's Kitchen (p98) Healthy and refined Cantonese cooking with two Michelin stars.

NUR (p95) Extravagant tasting menus using local ingredients.

Lung King Heen (p78) Exquisite dim sum, pristine service and sweeping harbour views.

22 Ships (p117) The hippest of hip modern tapas joints.

Best by Budget

$

One Dim Sum (p156) Cheap, tasty dim sum.

Kau Kee (p98) Classic noodles worth waiting in line for.

Delicious Kitchen (p118) The best honey pork chop, fried tofu and wontons in town.

Wang Fu (p93) Heaping plates of meaty, Northern-style dumplings.

$$

Bistronomique (p98) Homey-French cooking at moderate prices.

Gaylord (p155) Venerable Indian establishment with a killer buffet.

Yardbird (p98) Trendy Japanese-style takes on all things chicken.

AMMO (p116) Elegant modern European in a cool all-glass setting.

Megan's Kitchen (p117) A fun twist on the classic hot-pot experience.

Sha Tin 18 (p187) To-die-for Peking duck in a swish hotel setting.

$$$

Bo Innovation (p118) Molecular gastronomy does Chinese cuisine.

Otto e Mezzo Bombana (p79) Top-notch Italian in a see-and-be-seen setting.

Caprice (p79) Luxurious Modern French in the Four Seasons.

Chairman (p99) Perfectly executed Cantonese classics.

Yè Shanghai (p154) Sophisticated Shànghǎi cuisine in a sultry retro setting.

Best for Dim Sum

City Hall Maxim's Palace (p77) The most famous of Hong Kong's dim sum palaces.

Luk Yu Tea House (p93) This venerable teahouse was once an artist's haunt.

Lin Heung Tea House (p78) Old-school cart dim sum in no-frills setting.

Tim Ho Wan, the Dim Sum Specialists (p77) The first-ever budget dim sum place to earn a Michelin star.

Fook Lam Moon (p156) Celeb haunt with swank menu but reasonably priced dim sum.

Best for Seafood

Tung Po Seafood Restaurant (p121) Modern *dai pai dong* in a wet market.

Lei Yue Mun (p157) Seafood village drawing crowds.

Loaf On (p191) Low-key but high-end seafood in seaside village of Sai Kung.

Chuen Kee Seafood Restaurant (p191) Classic seafood palace on Sai Kung waterfront.

Sam Shing Hui Seafood Market (p173) Bustling working seafood market in New Territories.

Best for Noodles

Ho To Tai Noodle Shop (p175) Shrimp-filled wonton noodles earn a devoted following.

Tasty Congee & Noodle Wonton Shop (p77) Shrimp wontons, prawn congee and more in luxe IFC mall.

Mak's Noodle (p93) Beloved shrimp wonton shop with multiple locations.

Ho Hung Kee (p119) Making noodles, wontons and congee for 68 years.

Best Dai Pai Dong

Sing Kee (p78) One of few surviving *dai pai dong* in Central.

Gi Kee Seafood Restaurant (p121) Gourmet seafood above a wet market.

Sei Yik (p136) Queues form for breakfast toast at this half-hidden Stanley mainstay.

Best Cha Chaan Tang

Lan Fong Yuen (p93) *The* place to sample Hong Kong's famous milk tea.

Cheong Kee (p121) Above a wet market, some say it has the best thick toast in town.

Capital Cafe (p117) Fluffy eggs and spam noodles draw crowds.

Mido Café (p156) A charmingly retro spot overlooking the Tin Hau temple.

Best for Vegetarian

Pure Veggie House (p116) Standout vegie dim sum and Cantonese classics.

Chi Lin Vegetarian (p157) Delightful Buddhist cuisine in a gorgeous nunnery.

Life Cafe (p92) Trendy quinoa salads and wrap sandwiches in SoHo.

Bookworm Cafe (p199) Beloved hippie haunt on laid-back Lamma.

Best for European

Otto e Mezzo Bombana (p79) Considered by many the finest Italian in Hong Kong.

Motorino (p93) Crowds dine on killer Neopolitan-style pizza at this hip New York import.

Bistronomique (p98) Yummy down-home Gallic specialties.

Amber (p79) Award-winning cuisine in dramatic setting.

Chef Studio (p135) Charming private kitchen on Hong Kong's south side.

Best for Japanese

Go Ya Yakitori (p121) Tasty skewers in trendy Tai Hang.

Irori (p119) Sushi and nibbles in Japanese-loving Causeway Bay.

Iroha (p119) Japanese-style grilled meat and vegies.

Inagiku (p79) Sumptuous sushi, grilled meat and tempura in the Four Seasons.

Best for Southeast Asian

Sabah (p117) Enormous roti and other Malaysian delights at this casual spot.

Chom Chom (p94) Trendy Vietnamese and cocktails in SoHo.

Good Satay (p154) Good satay indeed in a dumpy office building.

Best for Spicy Food

San Xi Lou (p116) Well-regarded Sichuān Mid-Levels tower building.

Yu (p119) Spicy and cheap Sichuān noodles.

Cheong Fat (p157) Spicy Thai in Little Bangkok neighbourhood.

Woodlands (p153) Sweat-producing vegie Indian.

Best for Sweets

Yuen Kee Dessert (p95) Glutinous Cantonese confections.

Tai Cheong Bakery (p93) The ultimate in Hong Kong egg tarts.

Lab Made Ice Cream (p119) Liquid-nitrogen-frozen ice cream in wild Asian-inspired flavours.

Pierre Hermé (p154) Heaven for Parisian-style macarons.

Honeymoon Dessert (p190) HK-based chain serving up sweet soups and icy treats.

Best for Ambience

Island Tang (p78) Cantonese cuisine with gorgeous art-deco decor.

Lock Cha Tea Shop (p116) Traditional tea shop resembling ancient scholar's study.

AMMO (p116) All-glass restaurant was once a weapon storage area.

Madam Sixty Ate (p118) Quirky art and funky European food.

Best Dining Away from the Crowds

Black Sheep (p136) Eclectic hippie cafe down a quiet back alley in beachside Shek O.

Chi Lin Vegetarian (Long Men Lou) (p157) Vegie cuisine on the grounds of a stunningly landscaped nunnery.

Yue Kee Roasted Goose (p173) Primo roast goose in a far-flung village.

Mavericks (p209) A chill beachfront cafe on the Lantau coast.

Central

Drinking & Nightlife

Energetic Hong Kong knows how to party and does so visibly and noisily. Drinking venues run the gamut from British-style pubs through hotel bars and hipster hang-outs, to karaoke bolt-holes aimed at a young Chinese clientele. The last few years have seen a heartening surge in the number of wine bars and live-music venues, catering to a diverse, discerning and fun-loving population.

How Much?

It's not especially cheap to drink in Hong Kong. An all-night boozy tour of the city's drinking landscape can set you back at least HK$800. That said, it's possible to cut corners while still soaking up the atmosphere – lots of youngsters do that. Buy your drinks from a convenience store and hang out with the revellers standing outside the bars. The alley near a convenience store in Soho is called 'Cougar Alley' for a reason.

Wine & Whisky Bars

A growing number of bars are dedicated to connoisseurship of whisky, gin or other spirits. Expect hand-carved ice, obscure bottles and nerdily expert bartenders.

Another recent trend is whisky-drinking, and a growing number of bars are devoted to savouring the amber liquid, including a couple of stylish Japanese whisky bars.

Cafes

Though still dominated by Starbucks and Pacific Coffee (essentially Hong Kong's homegrown Starbucks), Hong Kong has lately sprouted a very decent independent coffeehouse scene, complete with organic beans, micro-roasters and cupping events.

Cha Chaan Tang

Tea cafes (茶餐廳; *cha chaan tang*) are perhaps best known for their Hong Kong–style 'pantyhose' milk tea (奶茶; *nai cha*) – a strong brew made from a blend of several types of black tea with crushed egg shells thrown in for silkiness. It's filtered through a fabric that hangs like a stocking, hence the name, and drunk with evaporated milk. 'Pantyhose' milk tea is sometimes mixed with three parts coffee to create the quintessential Hong Kong drink, tea-coffee or *yin yeung* (鴛鴦), meaning 'mandarin duck', a symbol of matrimonial harmony. See also p42.

Dance

TANGO

Hong Kong has a small but zealous community of tango dancers, usually white-collar workers, professionals and expats. **Tango Tang** (www.tangotang.com), the most prominent of all the schools, has all tango events, including those by other organisers, posted on its website. You can join any of the many *milongas* (dance parties) held every week at restaurants and dance studios all over town.

SALSA

Hong Kong's vibrant salsa community holds weekly club nights that are open to anyone in need of a good time. Check out www.dancetrinity.com or www.hongkong-salsa.com. The annual **Hong Kong Salsa Festival** (http://hksalsafestival.com), held around February, features participants from the world over. The website has details of events including the after-parties.

SWING

If you like swing, there are socials with live jazz bands (and sometimes free beginners' class) at least six times a month. The calendar on www.hongkongswings.com has more.

Karaoke

Karaoke clubs are as popular as ever with the city's young citizens, with a sprinkling of clubs in Causeway Bay and Wan Chai,

NEED TO KNOW

Opening Hours

➡ Bars open noon or 6pm and stay open until 2am to 6am; Wan Chai bars stay open the latest.

➡ Cafes usually open between 8am and 11am and close between 5pm and 11pm.

Happy Hour

➡ During certain hours of the day, most pubs, bars and even certain clubs give discounts on drinks (usually from a third to half off) or offer two-for-one deals.

➡ Happy hour is usually in the late afternoon or early evening – 4pm to 8pm, say – but times vary widely from place to place. Depending on the season, the day of the week and the location, some happy hours run from noon until as late as 10pm, and some start up again after midnight.

Prices

➡ Beer from HK$45 per pint

➡ Wine from HK$50 per glass

➡ Whisky from HK$50 per shot

➡ Cocktail HK$80–200

➡ Cover charge for dance clubs HK$200–700 (including one drink)

Latest Information

➡ *Time Out* (www.timeout.com.hk)

➡ *HK Magazine* (http://hk.asia-city.com)

Dress Code

Usually smart casual is good enough for most clubs, but patrons wearing shorts and flip-flops will not be admitted. Jeans are popular in Hong Kong and these are sometimes worn with heels or a blazer for a more put-together look. Hong Kong's clubbers can be style-conscious, so dress to impress!

PLAN YOUR TRIP DRINKING & NIGHTLIFE

and local dives in Mong Kok. The aural wallpaper at these clubs is most often Canto-pop covers, compositions that often blend Western rock or pop with Chinese melodies and lyrics, but there is usually a limited selection of 'golden oldies' and pop in English.

GAY & LESBIAN HONG KONG

While Hong Kong's gay scene may not have the vibrancy or visibility of cities like Sydney, it has made huge strides in recent years and now counts more than two dozen gay bars and clubs.

Bars & Clubs

New Wally Matt Lounge (☑2721 2568; 152 Austin Rd, Tsim Sha Tsui; ☉5pm-4am, happy hour 5-10pm; ⓜJordan, exit D) The name comes from the old Waltzing Matilda pub, which was one of the daggiest gay watering holes in creation. But New Wally Matt is an upbeat and busy place and actually more a pub than a lounge.

DYMK (☑2868 0626; 16 Arbuthnot Rd, Central; ☉6pm-4am; ⓜCentral, exit D2) 'Does your mother know?' is an upmarket, gay-friendly bar catering to a discerning crowd of professionals who lounge in the dimly but stylishly lit booths.

Propaganda (☑2868 1316; 1 Hollywood Rd, lower ground fl, Central; ☉9pm-4am Tue-Thu, to 6am Fri & Sat, happy hour 9pm-1.30am Tue-Thu; ⓜCentral, exit D2) Hong Kong's default gay dance club and meat market; cover charge (HK$120 to HK$160) applies on Friday and Saturday. Enter from Ezra's Lane.

T:ME (☑2332 6565; www.time-bar.com; 65 Hollywood Rd; ☉6pm-2am Mon-Sat; ⓜCentral, exit D1) A small and chic gay bar located in a back alley off Hollywood Rd, close to Club 71; drinks are a bit on the pricey side but it has happy hour throughout the week.

Volume (☑2857 7683; 83-85 Hollywood Rd, Central; ☉6pm-4am, happy hour 7.30-9.30pm; ☐26) A swanky, kitsch, mirror-lined, late-night cocktail bar that pumps out a range of sounds, from '80s hits to the latest dance genres, to a mixed crowd of gay and expat locals.

Boo (☑2736 6168; www.boobar.com.hk; 225 Nathan Rd, 5th fl, Pearl Oriental Tower, Jordan; ☉7pm-2am Sun-Thu, to 4am Fri, 9pm-4am Sat, happy hour 7-9pm; ⓜJordan, exit C1) This low-key gay bar on Nathan Rd with a karaoke jukebox seems to attract huggable 'bear' types in the local gay community; there's a DJ every Saturday from 9pm.

Other Resources

Dim Sum (http://dimsum-hk.com) A free, monthly gay magazine with listings.

Les Peches (☑9101 8001; lespechesinfo@yahoo.com) Hong Kong's premier lesbian organisation has monthly events for lesbians, bisexual women and their friends.

Utopia Asia (www.utopia-asia.com/hkbars.htm) A website with listings of gay-friendly venues and events in town.

Drinking & Nightlife by Neighbourhood

➤ **Lan Kwai Fong** (p99) Synonymous with partying in Hong Kong, Lan Kwai Fong (LKF) is a raucous bar-lined alley packed with noisy bars and nightclubs. It's a popular after-work drink spot for Central's white collar workers, and becomes wilder as the night wears on. Holidays like New Year's and Halloween are slammed.

➤ **Soho** (p99) Soho, along the Central-Mid-levels Escalator, is a popular drinking and dining area for expats and tourists. Its bars aren't as wild as LKF's, but it gets hopping on weekends.

➤ **Sheung Wan** (p102) West of Soho, Sheung Wan is an increasingly hip hood with some lower-key cocktail bars and trendy speakeasies.

➤ **Wan Chai** (p124) While Wan Chai remains a byword for sleaze (and a long-standing port of call for American sailors and GIs since the Vietnam War), it has cleaned its act up of late. Much of the western part of the district offers lively, respectable bars, although hostess bars still line Lockhart Rd.

➤ **Old Wan Chai** (p124) Inland from Wan Chai around Queen's Rd East behind the tram tracks, Old Wan Chai is becoming another little epicentre of fine dining and sophisticated drinking.

➤ **Tsim Sha Tsui** (p158) If you head back from the bustle of Nathan Rd there are some nifty little bar areas, such as the karaoke bar scene around Minden Rd and the food-and-drink ghetto along Knutsford Tce in the north of Tsim Sha Tsui.

Lonely Planet's Top Choices

Globe (p100) Spacious but cosy with fine imported beers and the first cask-conditioned ale brewed in Hong Kong.

Executive Bar (p125) Exclusive whisky and cocktail bar where you can catch some serious Japanese mixology in action.

Club 71 (p99) Where all the activists, artists, musicians and the socially conscious go to rant and revel.

Pawn (p124) A gastropub housed in a historic pawn shop and three tenement houses overlooking the tram tracks.

Best for Views

Sevva (p82) See (both beautiful people and a beautiful harbour) and be seen atop the Prince's Building.

Ozone (p158) The highest bar in Asia.

Back Beach Bar (p136) Overlooking a deserted Shek O beach.

Sugar (p126) Dizzying views from atop an Island East hotel.

Intercontinental Lobby Lounge (p158) Floor-to-ceiling glass overlooks Victoria Harbour.

Best for a Cuppa

Peninsula Hong Kong (p276) The fanciest high tea in the territory.

Amical (p124) Pocket-sized indy coffee shop in trendy Star St hood.

Teakha (p99) Wake up and smell the jasmine at this elegant tea lounge.

Barista Jam (p99) Funky independent coffee house.

Lan Fong Yuen (p93) The classic spot to try Hong Kong's famous milk tea.

Best for Cocktails

Butler (p158) Japanese cocktail bar in quiet part of TST.

Executive Bar (p125) It's appointment-only at this swank whiskey lounge.

Sevva (p82) The pricey drinks are worth it, and the view...oh!

Best for Whisky

Butler (p158) The Japanese mixologist knows his whisky.

Angel's Share Whisky Bar (p99) It's all about this whisky here.

Best for Wine

Les Copains D'Abord (p211) Far-flung French cafe on an outer island.

Central Wine Club (p102) Baroque bar with fine European wines.

Best Pubs

Pawn (p124) Colonial charm in a renovated pawn shop.

Smugglers Inn (p136) Cosy pub in British-influenced Stanley.

Delaney's (p125) Spacious Irish pub perfect for a pint.

Best for Clubbing

Dragon-I (p102) Swank and celeb-filled hotspot.

Dusk Till Dawn (p124) The place to be rocking out to live music when the other bars close.

Tazmania Ballroom (p100) Grind with models on their night off.

Best for People-Watching

Peak Cafe Bar (p100) Watch the Mid-Levels elevator roll by from this Soho spot.

Quay West (p102) Sunset views from Kennedy Town.

China Bear (p210) Watch the ferry crowds come and go in sleepy Mui Wo village.

Bit Point (p102) German beers and international crowds.

Club 71 (p99) A mainstay of artists and writers.

Best for Unpretentious Drinking

Pier 7 (p82) Post-dinner drinks atop Star Ferry Pier.

Quay West (p102) Ungentrified Kennedy Town is the way Sheung Wan used to be.

Agave (p125) Enough tequila will make anyone lose their pretension.

Buddy Bar (p125) A low-key neighbourhood pub in hip but friendly Tai Hang.

Best for Watching Sports

Amici (p125) Football fans' fave thanks to big screens and beer on tap.

Liberty Exchange (p82) This American-style spot is big with the bankers.

Inn Side Out (p126) Throw peanuts on the floor and watch the big screen.

Dickens Bar (p125) This British-style pub plays any rugby and football to be found.

Delaney's (p125) An Irish pub with TVs and friendly crowds.

Best for Quirky Vibes

Ned Kelly's Last Stand (p158) Dixieland jazz, Aussie decor and expat crowds.

Snake King Yan (p159) Shot of snake bile? This is the place.

Wanch (p126) Rock out with tourists, locals, sailors, junkies and other assorted weirdos at this live-music spot.

Best for Local Vibes

Utopia (p159) Play darts with local office workers.

Buddy Bar (p125) Hang in Tai Hang with locals and their dogs.

Club 71 (p99) Talk politics with local radicals or chat up the artist on the next bar stool.

Fullcup Café (p159) Quirky decor and arty young crowds.

Back Beach Bar (p136) When the beach crowds leave, this waterfront spot is locals only.

Best for Bar Food

Dickens Bar (p125) Stuff yourself on Indian curry then watch the rugby.

Delaney's (p125) Solid Irish pub grub.

Classified (p124) Scrummy cheese plates go perfectly with a glass of red.

The Lawn (p124) Elegant bar snacks come from the hotel's own restaurant.

Cantonese opera, Sunbeam Theatre (p126)

☆ Entertainment

Hong Kong's arts and entertainment scene is healthier than ever. The increasingly busy cultural calendar includes music, drama and dance hailing from a plethora of traditions. The schedule of imported performances is nothing short of stellar. And every week, local arts companies and artists perform anything from Bach to stand-up to Cantonese opera and English versions of Chekhov plays.

The Arts

Local Western music ensembles and theatre troupes give weekly shows, while famous foreign groups are invited to perform often, particularly at the **Hong Kong Arts Festival** (www.hk.artsfestival.org) in March. The annual event attracts world-class names in all genres of music, theatre and dance, including the likes of the Bolshoi Ballet, Anne-Sophie Mutter and playwright Robert Wilson.

Cinema

Hong Kong is well served with cinema, screening both mainstream and art-house films. Cinemas usually show local productions and Hollywood blockbusters. The vast majority of films have both English and Chinese subtitles. Book tickets and seats online or in person well before the showing.

Cinema buffs from all over Asia make the pilgrimage to the **Hong Kong International Film Festival** (www.hkiff.org.hk) held each year in March and April.

NEED TO KNOW

Tickets & Reservations

These main ticket providers have tickets to every major event in Hong Kong. You can book through the website, by phone or purchase tickets at the performance venues.

Urbtix (☎2734 9009; www.urbtix.hk; ⏰10am-8pm)

Cityline (☎2317 6666; www.cityline.com.hk)

Hong Kong Ticketing (☎3128 8288; www. hkticketing.com; ⏰10am-8pm)

Prices

Expect to pay around HK$80 for a seat up the back for the Hong Kong Philharmonic and from about HK$600 for a performance by big-name international acts or an international musical such as *Chicago*.

Movie tickets cost between HK$65 and HK$100, but can be cheaper at matinees, at the last screening of the day, on weekends and holidays, or on certain days of the week. Most non-English-language films have both Chinese and English subtitles.

What's On

➡ **Artmap** (www.artmap.com.hk)

➡ **Artslink** (www.hkac.org.hk)

➡ **HK Magazine** (http://hk-magazine.com)

➡ **Time Out** (www.timeout.com.hk)

Concerts

Hong Kong is a stop on the big-name concert circuit, and a growing number of internationally celebrated bands and solo artists perform here. These include mainstream acts and those on the edge of the mainstream – from U2 and Red Hot Chilli Peppers, to Kings of Convenience and Mogwai.

Live Music

Hong Kong's live-music scene has been undergoing a renaissance of late with a growing number of venues hosting independent musicians (imported and local) at least several nights a week. The options range from jazz to goth metal, not to mention dub step, post-rock drum 'n' bass and electronica.

The Fringe Club (p102), Backstage Live (p102) and Grappa's Cellar (p82) are popular venues. And don't miss the clandestine live Hidden Agenda (p159).

The **Hong Kong International Jazz Festival** (http://hkja.org/blog) caters to jazz lovers.

Clockenflap

The highlight in Hong Kong's live-music calendar is the excellent multi-act outdoor music festival known as Clockenflap (p160). The two-day event has featured dozens of local, regional and international acts.

Flamenco

A couple of flamenco bands perform regularly in Hong Kong – Sol Y Flamenco (at Backstage Live or the Fringe Club) and Reorientate (a fusion world-music band). Flamenco dancer and teacher **Ingrid Sera-Gillet** (http://hkflamenco.com) performs with both. For more on performances and classes, check out **Felah Mengus** (www.felah-mengus.com), **Flamenco Hong Kong** (www. flamenco.hk) or **Hong Kong Flamenco Arts Centre** (find it on Facebook).

Cantonese Opera

The best time to watch Cantonese opera is during the Hong Kong Arts Festival (p53) in February/March and the Mid-Autumn Festival, when outdoor performances are staged in Victoria Park. You can also catch a performance at the Temple Street Night Market (p142) or during Chinese festivals.

There are daily performances at the Sunbeam Theatre (p126) and at the new Yau Ma Tei Theatre (p152). If you don't speak Cantonese, the best way to book tickets for the Sunbeam Theatre is through Urbtix or CityLine.

Entertainment by Neighbourhood

➡ **Hong Kong Island: Central** (p82) Lan Kwai Fong (LKF) is one of Asia's legendary party streets.

➡ **Hong Kong Island: The Peak & the Northwest** (p102) The hip Sheung Wan neighbourhood is the place for laid-back bars and speakeasies.

➡ **Hong Kong Island: Wan Chai & the Northeast** (p126) A former red light district, Wan Chai is still synonymous with all-night indulgence.

➡ **Hong Kong Island: Aberdeen & the South** Though it has a few great pubs, quiet Southside is more about beaches than bars.

➡ **Kowloon** (p160) Sing karaoke til the sun comes up in the peninsula that never sleeps.

Lonely Planet's Top Choices

Hong Kong International Film Festival (p53) Asia's top film festival features both esoteric titles and crowd pleasers.

Clockenflap Outdoor Music Festival (p160) Everyone in town attends this massive rock festival.

Hong Kong Arts Festival (p53) This is Hong Kong's most exciting outdoor music festival.

Hidden Agenda (p159)The city's most visible clandestine live-music venue.

Street Music Concert (p126) Free under-the-stars live music, from Bach to original jazz.

Best for Live Music

Peel Fresco (p102) Groovy jazz and arty crowds in a tiny club.

Backstage Live (p102) A restaurant created for the purpose of having live music of all sorts.

Hidden Agenda (p159) Hong Kong's most famous music dive offers a line-up of solid indie acts.

The Wanch (p126) Wan Chai's venerable live-music spot is tops for rock, jazz and lots of beer.

Grappa's Cellar (p82) This Italian restaurant turns to rock, jazz and comedy.

Fringe Club (p102) Jazz, world music and more are played inside this Victorian building.

Best Underground Vibe

XXX (p103) A dive bar with indie bands.

Cattle Depot Artist Village (p153) A Kowloon slaughter-house turned artists' village and music venue.

Hidden Agenda (p159) *The* underground music spot in Hong Kong – so cool the government wants to shut it down.

Best for Theatre

Hong Kong Arts Centre (p121) Theatre, dance and more.

Hong Kong Academy for the Performing Arts (p127) All manner of performances grace this school's stage.

Hong Kong Cultural Centre (p160) If it's culture, it's here.

Fringe Club (p102) Think of it as Hong Kong's off-Broadway.

Cattle Depot Artist Village (p153) See esoteric performance art in a former slaughterhouse.

Best Movie Theatres

Broadway Cinematheque (p160) Hong Kong's best art-house theatre shows indie films that don't play elsewhere.

AMC Pacific Place (p127) In the plush Pacific Place mall, here you can watch Hollywood and Hong Kong releases in comfort.

agnès b. Cinema (p112) In the Hong Kong Arts Centre, this small space plays festival releases on a limited basis.

Times Square (p128)

Shopping

Everyone knows Hong Kong as a place of neon-lit retail pilgrimage. This city is positively stuffed with swanky shopping malls and brand-name boutiques. All international brands worth their logo have outlets here. These are supplemented by the city's own retail trailblazers and a few creative local designers. Together they are Hong Kong's shrines and temples to style and consumption.

Antiques

Hong Kong has a rich and colourful array of Asian (especially Chinese) antiques on offer, but serious buyers will restrict themselves to reputable antique shops and auction houses only. Forgeries and expert reproductions abound. Remember that most of the quality pieces are sold through auction houses such as Christie's, especially at its auctions in spring and autumn.

Most of Hong Kong's antique shops are bunched along Wyndham St and Hollywood Rd in Central and Sheung Wan. The shops at the western end of Hollywood Rd tend to carry cheaper paraphernalia, including magazines, Chinese propaganda posters and badges from the Cultural Revolution.

For old-style Chinese handicrafts, the main places to go are the large emporiums.

Clothing

DESIGNER BRANDS & BOUTIQUES
The best places to find global designer brands and luxury stores are in malls such as

IFC and the Landmark in Central, Pacific Place in Admiralty and Festival Walk in Kowloon Tong. Some of these shops such as Prada have outlets at Horizon Plaza in Ap Lei Chau selling off-season items at discounted prices.

There's also an embarrassment of midrange malls showcasing second- or third-tier brands, fast fashion outlets like Mango and Zara and local retailers such as Giordano.

For something a little more unique, there are cool independents opened by local designers and retailers in Sheung Wan, Wan Chai and Tsim Sha Tsui. You'll see some brilliant pieces but the range of styles is limited, simply because these places are few and far between.

STREET MARKETS & MINIMALLS

The best hunting grounds for low-cost garments are in Tsim Sha Tsui at the eastern end of Granville Rd, and Cheung Sha Wan Rd in Sham Shui Po. The street markets on Temple St in Yau Ma Tei and Tung Choi St in Mong Kok have the cheapest clothes. You may also try Li Yuen St East and Li Yuen St West, two narrow alleyways linking Des Voeux Rd Central with Queen's Rd Central. They are a jumble of inexpensive clothing, handbags, backpacks and costume jewellery.

For a truly local shopping experience, the minimalls in Tsim Sha Tsui are teeming with all things young and trendy, both locally designed or imported from the mainland or Korea. Usually you can negotiate a lower price when you purchase more than one item. And if you have a good eye, you can end up looking chic for very little.

Handicrafts & Souvenirs

For old-school Chinese handicrafts and other goods such as hand-carved wooden pieces, ceramics, cloisonné, silk garments and place mats, head to the large Chinese emporiums, such as Chinese Arts & Crafts.

You'll also find a small range of similar items (but of a lesser quality) in the alleyways of Tsim Sha Tsui, but remember to check prices at different vendors and bargain.

If you prefer something in a modern Chinese style, Shanghai Tang (the fashion boutique with branches all over town) has a range of cushions, tableware, photo frames and other home accessories.

NEED TO KNOW

Opening Hours

➡ Central: generally 10am to 8pm

➡ Causeway Bay: 11am to 9.30pm or 10pm

➡ Tsim Sha Tsui: 11am to 8pm

➡ Most shops are open on Sunday

➡ Winter sales are in January; summer sales, late June and early July

Service

Service is attentive and credit cards are widely accepted.

Duty-Free

There's no sales tax in Hong Kong so ignore the 'Tax Free' signs in some stores. However, you will pay duty on tobacco, perfume, cosmetics and cars. In general, almost everything is cheaper when you buy it outside duty-free shops.

Warranties & Guarantees

Some imported goods have a Hong Kong–only guarantee. If it's a well-known brand, you can return the warranty card to the Hong Kong importer to get one for your country. Grey-market items imported by somebody other than the official agent may have a guarantee that's valid only in the country of manufacture, or none at all.

Refunds & Exchanges

Most shops won't give refunds, but they can be persuaded to exchange purchases if they haven't been tampered with and you have a detailed receipt.

Shipping Goods

Many shops will package and post large items for you, but check whether you'll have to clear the goods at the country of destination. Smaller items can be shipped from the post office or try DHL (p330).

Trouble?

HKTB's Quality Tourism Services (QTS; ☑2806 2823; www.qtshk.com)

Hong Kong Consumer Council (☑2929 2222; www.consumer.org.hk; ◷9am-5.45pm Mon-Fri)

The furniture store G.O.D. has a wide range of homewares and contemporary office products but with a cheeky Hong Kong twist.

Art

An increasing number of art galleries in Hong Kong sell paintings, sculptures, ceramic works and installations – some very good – by local artists. Like antique and curio shops, most of the city's commercial art galleries are found along Wyndham St and Hollywood Rd in Central and Sheung Wan.

The annual Hong Kong Art Fair, Hong Kong Artwalk in March, Le French May and Fotanian in October offer great opportunities to acquire art or simply acquaint yourself with the city's interesting visual-arts scene.

Gems & Jewellery

The Chinese attribute various magical qualities to jade, including the power to prevent ageing and accidents. The Jade Market in Yau Ma Tei is diverting, but unless you're knowledgeable about jade, limit yourself to modest purchases.

Hong Kong also offers a great range of pearls – cultured and freshwater. Retail prices for other precious stones are only marginally lower than elsewhere. The more reputable jewellery-shop chains – and there are many in Tsim Sha Tsui and Mong Kok catering to tourists from the mainland – will issue a certificate that states exactly what you are buying and guarantees that the shop will buy it back at a fair market price.

Leather Goods & Luggage

All the brand names such as Louis Vuitton, Samsonite and Rimowa are sold at Hong Kong department stores, and you'll also find some local vendors in the luggage business. The popularity of hiking and travel has triggered a proliferation of outdoor-

products shops that carry high-quality backpacks. If you're looking for a casual bag or daypack, check out Li Yuen St East and Li Yuen St West in Central or Stanley Market.

Cameras

One of the best spots in Hong Kong to buy photographic equipment is Stanley St in Central. Everything carries a price tag, though some low-level bargaining may be possible. Never buy a camera without a price tag. This will probably preclude many of the shops in Tsim Sha Tsui. That said, Tsim Sha Tsui has a couple of places on Kimberley Rd dealing in used cameras, and there are plenty of photo shops on Sai Yeung Choi St in Mong Kok.

Watches

Shops selling watches are ubiquitous in Hong Kong and you can find everything from a Rolex to Russian army timepieces and diving watches. Avoid the shops without price tags. The big department stores and City Chain are fine, but compare prices.

Local Brands & Designers

Hong Kong doesn't have a profusion of quirky, creative one-offs or unique vintage items as in London, New York or Copenhagen (have you seen the rent landlords charge here?). But the city has a small, passionate band of local designer boutiques offering value, character and style across a range of goods, especially in fashion and furniture.

Soho, Wan Chai, Causeway Bay and Tsim Sha Tsui are the best places to find them. Some stores like Homeless carry a smattering of chic, design-oriented goods (local and imported) while others, such as furniture store G.O.D. and fashion boutiques Shanghai Tang and Initial, have in-house design teams.

THE LOWDOWN ON HIGH-TECH SHOPPING

Hong Kong has a plethora of shops specialising in electronic and digital gadgets, but the product mix and prices may vary. Similarly, vendors' command of English can range from 'enough to close a deal' (Mong Kok, Sham Shui Po) to 'reasonable' (the rest). Shopkeepers are generally honest but some have been known to sell display or secondhand items as new ones. All things considered, Wan Chai is your safest bet, but if you're a bit of a geek, the malls and flea market in Sham Shui Po are worth exploring.

Defensive Shopping

Hong Kong is not a nest of thieves just waiting to rip you off, but pitfalls can strike the uninitiated.

Whatever you're in the market for, always check prices in a few shops before buying. The most common way for shopkeepers to cheat tourists is to simply overcharge. In some of the electronic stores in the tourist shopping district of Tsim Sha Tsui, many goods do not have price tags. Checking prices in several shops therefore becomes essential. Sometimes stores will quote a reasonable or even low price on a big-ticket item, only to get the money back by overcharging on accessories.

Spotting overcharging is the easy part, though. Sneakier (but rarer) tricks involve merchants removing vital components that should have been included for free (and demanding more money when you return to the shop to get them). Another tactic is to replace some of the good components with cheaper ones.

Bargaining

Sales assistants in department or chain stores rarely have any leeway to give discounts, but you can try bargaining in owner-operated stores and certainly in markets.

Some visitors believe that you can always get the goods for half of the price originally quoted. But if you can bargain something down that low, perhaps you shouldn't be buying it from that shop anyway. Remember you may be getting that DSLR cheap but paying high mark-ups for the memory card, or worse, it may have missing components or no international warranty.

Don't be too intent on getting the best deals. Really, what's HK$2 off a souvenir that's being sold for HK$20? Probably not much to you, but it may mean a lot to the old lady selling it.

Shopping by Neighbourhood

→ **Hong Kong Island: Central** (p83) Posh malls and designer brands abound in Hong Kong's business district.

→ **Hong Kong Island: The Peak & the Northwest** (p103) Trendy Sheung Wan is fast becoming the go-to spot for quirky boutiques and homewares shops.

→ **Hong Kong Island: Wan Chai & the Northeast** (p127) From street markets to fancy malls to funky hipster enclaves, Wan Chai has it all.

→ **Hong Kong Island: Aberdeen & the South** (p137) Ap Lei Chau is the place for outlet hauls; Stanley has a fun outdoor souvenir market.

→ **Kowloon** (p161) Shop for designer goodies and knock-offs galore along with half of China.

Lonely Planet's Top Choices

G.O.D (p137). Awesome lifestyle accessories, homewares and gifts – Hong Kong to the bone with a whiff of mischief.

Wattis Fine Art (p103) Antique maps and nostalgic photographs of Hong Kong and Macau.

Shanghai Tang (p83) Classy homewares and clothing in a modern chinoiserie style.

Gallery of the Pottery Workshop (p106) Excellent ceramic works by Hong Kong's home-grown artists.

Lane Crawford (p83) Luxury department store specialising in stylish clothing, homewares and accessories.

Daydream Nation (p127) Locally designed streetwear – edgy, wearable and with a touch of theatricality.

Best for Fashion

Joyce (p84) Hong Kong–born multi-designer department store.

Initial (p162) Hip urbanwear from multiple designers.

Vivienne Tam (p165) High-fashion dresses and more from a Hong Kong–bred designer.

Kapok (p127) Hipster fashions from local and international designers.

Horizon Plaza (p137) Cut-rates on luxury goods and clothing in a 27-floor warehouse.

Lu Lu Cheung (p105) Locally designed sophisticated casualwear.

Best for Gifts

Temple Street Night Market (p142) Has everything from chopsticks to jewellery – bargain hard.

Chinese Arts & Crafts (p128) Expensive but authentic handicrafts.

Stanley Market (p137) Carved name chops, satin baby shoes and more in a touristy but fun street market.

Picture This (p83) Cool vintage posters and antique books.

Lam Kie Yuen Tea Co (p106) Venerable tea shop with huge selection.

Best for Antiques

Arch Angel Antiques (p105) Costly but well-provinced Chinese antiques.

David Chan Photo Shop (p161) Amazing vintage camera selection.

Honeychurch Antiques (p104) Longstanding Asian antiques seller.

Indosiam (p106) Antiquarian bookshop specialising in Asia.

Picture This (p83) Vintage maps, books and posters.

Best for Art

Karin Weber Gallery (p105) Antiques and contemporary Asian art.

C&G Artpartment (p152) Edgy local art.

Pearl Lam Galleries (p103) Contemporary Hong Kong and Asian art.

Art in Chai Wan (p112) Multiple artists' studios in a warren of old factory buildings in this industrial neighbourhood.

Jockey Club Creative Arts Centre (p153) Artists studios in an old factory.

Best for Books

Flow (p104) Used books hidden inside a Soho building.

Eslite (p127) Massive Taiwanese bookstore/cafe/gallery/toy store.

Hong Kong Reader (p164) Bilingual bookstore with an intellectual edge.

Kubrick Bookshop Café (p159) Excellent selection of highbrow fiction, art books and literary journals.

Kelly & Walsh (p128) Well-rounded shop with good travel selection.

Best for Gadgets

Wan Chai Computer Centre (p127) A warren of all things electronic.

Golden Computer Arcade (p164) Computers and components for extra low prices.

Star Computer City (p162) The most expensive of the lot; strong in Mac products; no custom-made, white-box computers.

Ap Liu Street Flea Market (p164) A huge digital products flea market.

Sin Tat Plaza (p164) Everything mobile phone.

Mong Kok Computer Centre (p164) Cheap computer mall.

Best Malls

IFC Mall (p83) Swank and always crowded Central mall.

Pacific Place (p128) Ultra-luxe international clothing and accessories.

Elements (p164) One of Kowloon's fanciest shopping centres.

Festival Walk (p165) Over 200 shops plus an ice rink.

Rise Shopping Arcade (p162) Cheap, fun shopping mall.

Hysan Place (p128) The finest in Japanese and Korean fashions.

Best for Food & Beverages

Tak Hing Dried Seafood (p164) Trustworthy dried seafood shop.

Shanghai Street (p149) Woks, mooncake molds and other cooking implements galore.

Citysuper (p84) Huge variety of international gourmet groceries.

Sogo (p119) Basement food hall with every type of Japanese snack food imaginable.

Papabubble (p127) Hard candies in a variety of quirky local flavors.

Best Markets

Stanley Market (p137) Touristy street market, good for souvenirs.

Ap Liu Street Flea Market (p164) Massive electronics flea market.

Temple Street Night Market (p142) Iconic night market of kitsch and souvenirs.

Ladies Market (p164) Clothing, cell phone covers, knock-off purses and more.

Best for Quirky Items

Sino Centre (p164) Geek out at this anime mall.

Chan Wah Kee Cutlery Store (p162) One of Asia's few remaining master knife sharpeners.

Picture This (p83) Antique books, posters and maps.

Cat Street (p90) Junk shops hawk communist kitsch at this touristy street market.

Island Beverley Mall (p128) Eye-popping Japanese youth fashions.

Best for Beauty Products

Two Girls (p128) Hong Kong's cheap-and-cheerful local beauty brand, with fun vintage packaging.

Joyce (p84) High-end beauty products and scents from across the world.

Muji (p127) Elegantly packaged Japanese toiletries.

Hysan Place (p128) The 6th floor Garden of Eden is a paradise if you're looking for hard-to-find, youth-oriented Asian cosmetics.

Sea kayaking, Sai Kung Peninsula (p187)

🏃 Sports & Activities

Hong Kong offers countless ways to have fun and keep fit. From golf and frisbee to cycling and windsurfing, you won't be stumped for something active to do. There are also gyms, yoga studios and spas offering everything from aromatherapy to foot massage. If you prefer watching people play, the world's most exciting dragon boat racing takes place right here!

Climbing

Hong Kong is peppered with excellent granite faces and volcanic rocks in some striking wilderness areas. The best place to climb is on Tung Lung Chau, which has a technical wall, a big wall and a sea gully. Shek O beach has some excellent bouldering as well.

The **Hong Kong Climbing** (www.hongkong climbing.com) website is a handy resource for climbers.

Cycling

Hong Kong's natural terrain makes for some fabulous cycling. The ambitious New Territories Cycle Track Network construction project is currently under construction.

The longest bicycle track runs from Sha Tin through Tai Po to Tai Mei Tuk, taking you through parks, and past temples and the waterfront. The **Hong Kong Cycling Alliance** (http://hkcyclingalliance.org) website has information on road rules and safety for cyclists.

You need a (free) permit for mountain biking. Check with the **Mountain Biking Association** (www.hkmba.org) for permit details.

Dragon Boat Racing

Hong Kong is possibly the best place in the world to watch dragon boat racing because the traditions underlying the practice are still alive. The city has over 20 races a year with most taking place from May to July. The **Hong Kong Tourism Board website** (www.discoverhongkong.com) has information on the main events.

Football (Soccer)

Hong Kong has a fairly lively amateur soccer league. Games are played at the **Happy Valley Sports Ground**, a group of pitches inside the Happy Valley Racecourse (p114), and at **Mong Kok Stadium** (旺角大球場; 37 Flower Market Rd, Mong Kok; Ⓜ Prince Edward, exit B1). For match schedules and venues, check the sports sections of the English-language papers or contact the **Hong Kong Football Association** (www.hkfa.com). For casual football matches, visit http://casualfootball.net.

Golf

Hong Kong has only one public golf course but some private clubs open their doors on weekdays for a green fee (HK$700 to HK$2000 for 18 holes).

The **Hong Kong Golf Association** (☑2504 8659; www.hkga.com) has a list of driving ranges and tournaments held in the territory, including the **Hong Kong Open Championships**, one of Asia's leading professional golf tournaments (it's usually played in November or December).

Gyms & Yoga Studios

Yoga and fitness are big business here, with the largest slices of the pie shared out among a few big names. Pure Fitness (p84) has comprehensive gym facilities.

Hiking

Many visitors are surprised to learn that Hong Kong is an excellent place for hiking. Lengthy wilderness trails criss-cross the territory and its islands through striking mountain, coast and jungle trails. The four main ones are: **MacLehose Trail** (100km); **Wilson Trail** (78km), on both sides of Victoria Harbour; **Lantau Trail** (70km); and the **Hong Kong Trail** (50km). Hong Kong's excellent public transport network makes it feasible to tackle them a section at a time.

PLAN YOUR TRIP SPORTS & ACTIVITIES

NEED TO KNOW

Maps
The Map Publications Centre sells excellent maps of hiking and cycling trails; buy online (www.landsd.gov.hk/mapping/en/pro&ser/products.htm) or at major post offices.

Information & Facilities
Also check the sports sections of English-language newspapers.

➡ **Environmental Protection Department** (p111) Lists of country and marine parks.

➡ **Hong Kong Tourism Board** Website has a full list of what's on.

➡ **Leisure and Cultural Services Department** (www.lcsd.gov.hk) Lists of fields, stadiums, beaches, swimming pools, water-sports centres etc.

➡ **South China Athletic Association** (p129) Has sports facilities for hire.

For full details and advice on routes and itineraries, invest in one of the excellent hiking guides that are widely available in Hong Kong bookshops. Before heading out it's also a good idea to consult the official Hong Kong **hiking website** (www.hkwalkers.net) for updates on weather and the condition of the trails (landslides can sometimes mean route closures or diversions). Hikers can camp on remote beaches. For more information check out **Country & Marine Parks Authority** (www.afcd.gov.hk/english/country/cou_vis/cou_vis.html) and **Hong Kong Youth Hostels Association** (HKYHA; www.yha.org.hk)

Take care when bushwalking in the New Territories, particularly on Lamma and Lantau Islands. Poisonous snakes, the most common being the bamboo pit viper, are a hazard, although they will not attack unless surprised or provoked. Go straight to a public hospital if bitten; private doctors do not stock antivenene.

Horse Racing

Horse racing is Hong Kong's biggest spectator sport. There are two racecourses: one in Happy Valley (p114) and one at Sha Tin (p187). Attending one of the Wednesday race meetings (7pm, HK$10 entrance fee) at Happy Valley during the racing season (September to June) is a great way to experience horse racing in Hong Kong.

THE HONG KONG TRAIL

If you want to hike without exerting yourself too much, the **Hong Kong Trail** (港島徑) on Hong Kong Island is a great choice. The 50km route comprises eight sections of varying difficulty, beginning on the Peak (take the Peak tram up to the Peak and follow the signage) and ending near Shek O, on Island South.

One of the easiest and most scenic sections runs for about two hours along a mountain ridge called **Dragon's Back**. Voted by *Time* (Asia) as the best urban hike in Asia, it leads past woods, then up to the windy spine of the dragon where there are views of sundrenched beaches and billowing hills streaked with cloud shadow. Then head down to Shek O Rd, where you can walk or bus to Shek O's beach for a rewarding meal, swim or game of frisbee.

Martial Arts

Hong Kong has a glut of martial-arts programs, but only a few have special arrangements for English-speaking visitors. Check out **Hong Kong Tourism Board** (p325), which runs free taichi lessons outside the Cultural Centre; **Hong Kong Shaolin Wushu Culture Centre** (p212), which offers overnight stays; and **Wan Kei Ho International Martial Arts Association** (p106), which has a local and foreign following.

Rugby

The **Rugby World Cup Sevens** (www.hk sevens.com.hk) sees teams from all over the world come to Hong Kong in late March for three days of 15-minute matches at the 40,000-seat **Hong Kong Stadium** (www.lcsd. gov.hk/stadium; ⬛Happy Valley) in So Kon Po. Even nonrugby fans scramble for tickets, because the Sevens is also a giant three-day party, with costumes and Mardi Gras levels of drunkenness.

Running

The best places to run on Hong Kong Island include Harlech and Lugard Rds on the Peak, Bowen Rd above Wan Chai, the track in Victoria Park and the Happy Valley racecourse (as long as there aren't any horse races!). In Kowloon a popular place to run is the Tsim Sha Tsui East Promenade. Lamma makes an ideal place for trail runners, with plenty of paths and dirt trails, great views and, best of all, no cars.

Scuba Diving

Hong Kong has some surprisingly worthwhile diving spots, particularly in the far northeast, and there is certainly no shortage of courses. A good source of information for courses and excursions is Sai Kung–based **Splash Hong Kong** (www.splashhk.com).

Spa Treatments & Therapies

Whether you want a thousand-dollar caviar facial or a simple foot rub, Hong Kong's extensive pampering sector can assist. Most top hotels operate their own spas. For less elaborate routines, you'll find plenty of places in Central and Kowloon offering spa treatments, massages and reflexology. Be aware that some massage venues, especially in Wan Chai, may be 'happy ending' establishments.

Wakeboarding

Most operators of this popular sport are based in Sai Kung (New Territories) and Tai Tam (Hong Kong Island). Rates are about HK$700 per hour. Try **Tai Tam Wakeboarding Centre** (☑3120 4102; www.wakeboard.com. hk) or **Hong Kong Wakeboard** (☑9021 4221).

Windsurfing, Kayaking & Canoeing

The best time for windsurfing is October to December. Check the Leisure and Cultural Services Department website (www.lcsd.gov. hk) for government-run water-sports centres providing canoes, windsurfing boards, kayaks and other equipment for hire, some only to holders of the relevant certificates.

Activities by Neighbourhood

➡ **Hong Kong Island: Central** (p84) *The* place for relaxation, with some of the world's top spas.

➡ **Hong Kong Island: The Peak & the Northwest** (p106) Climbing the Peak is a don't-miss.

➡ **Hong Kong Island: Aberdeen & the South** (p137) Southside is all about beaches and family fun, with the city's biggest amusement park.

➡ **Kowloon** (p165) City parks are perfect for people-watching on this crowded peninsula.

➡ **New Territories** (p166) The mountains here contain some of the world's finest hiking.

➡ **Outlying Islands** (p194) These golden sands are neither Fiji nor Hawaii, but pure Hong Kong.

Lonely Planet's Top Choices

Dragon boat racing (p63) Feel the heart-pounding excitement of these atmospheric races that evolved from an ancient ritual.

Horse racing in Happy Valley (p114) The thunderous action at this urban racecourse makes for an unforgettable experience.

Rugby Sevens (p30) Join rugby fans for three days of lightning matches and wild partying.

Kayaking in Sai Kung (p187) Paddle in clear waters surrounded by hills and geological wonders.

Hiking Hong Kong's trails (p63) A palette of hills, history, grottoes and good food.

Morning taichi (p165) Learn the Chinese art of shadow boxing from a master.

Best Day Hikes

Lion Rock Country Park (p185) A steep climb past forests of monkeys to a craggy, lion-shaped peak.

Dragon's Back (p64) Hong Kong Island's best scenery.

The Morning Trail (p87) A shady paved path around The Peak, with stunning city views.

Sunset Peak (p210) On Lantau, Hong Kong's third-highest peak.

Lamma Island Family Trail (p196) A two-hour stroll

between this outer island's two main villages.

Best Beaches for Swimming

Lamma Island (p197) Small and laid-back.

Lantau Island (p201) Large, remote and good for watersports.

Cheung Chau Island (p213) Tops for windsurfing.

Sai Kung (p191) Scuba, kayaking and blue water galore.

Island South Sometimes crowded but gorgeous waters around Stanley and Shek O.

Best Scenery Experiences

Tai Long Wan Hiking Trail (p191) A glorious hike to an even more glorious beach.

Plover Cove Reservoir (p181) Cycling around the shimmering blue waters.

Eastern Nature Trail (p129) An easy day hike.

Tai Tam Waterworks Heritage Trail (p129) Nature and history come together.

Tung Ping Chau (p192) Hiking off the beaten path out-island.

Best for Martial Arts

Hong Kong Shaolin Wushu Culture Centre (p212) Teaches ancient Shaolin style of martial arts.

Wan Kei Ho International Martial Arts Association (p106) Kung fu for locals and foreigners.

Wing Chun Yip Man Martial Arts Athletic Association (p165) Runs six-week intensive courses.

Best for Toning Up

Spa at the Four Seasons (p84) Luxury, luxury and more luxury.

Ten Feet Tall (p84) Foot massages, pressure points and aromatherapy.

Happy Foot Reflexology Centre (p106) Hong Kong's go-to foot rub spot.

Best One-Stop Sports Facilities

South China Athletic Association (p129) A gym and other sports facilities.

Victoria Park (p129) Tennis, swimming, jogging track and more.

Kowloon Park (p165) Taichi, running, swimming, martial arts and beyond.

Best for Socialising

Rugby Sevens (p30) Epic annual spring debauchery.

Playing football (p63) Get to know the Anglo expat crowd.

Dragon boat races (p63) Down post-row beers with your team.

Explore Hong Kong

HONG KONG'S
TOP SIGHTS

Neighbourhoods
at a Glance

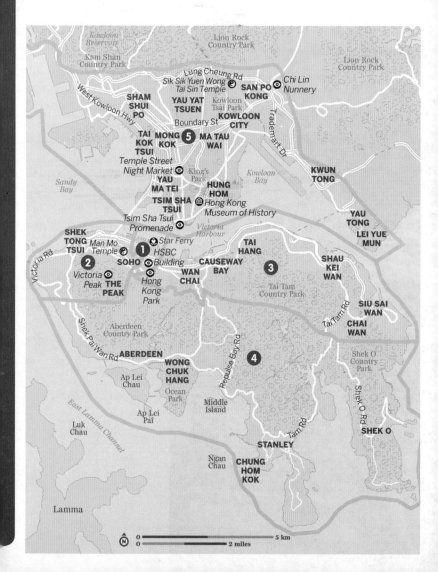

❶ Hong Kong Island: Central (p70)

The minted heart of Asia's financial hub comes replete with corporate citadels, colonial relics and massive monuments to consumerism. It's where you'll find the stock exchange, the Four Seasons, Prada and award-winning restaurants, all housed in a compelling mix of modern architecture, alongside graceful remnants of the city's colonial history. Dynamic during the day, it retires soon after sundown.

❷ Hong Kong Island: The Peak & the Northwest (p85)

Victoria Peak, soaring above the luxury residences in the Mid-Levels, offers a great vantage point from which to gaze back on Hong Kong. Down below, the charming old neighbourhoods of Sheung Wan, Sai Ying Pun and Western District have, between them, something for everyone, whether it's history, antiques and fine art, stylish hedonism, or a generous slice of local life as it has been in these hoods for decades.

❸ Hong Kong Island: Wan Chai & the Northeast (p107)

Quiet Admiralty offers class and quality over quantity for your shopping, dining and lodging needs. To its immediate east, versatile Wan Chai is a seat of culture, a showcase of dying age-old traditions and a nightlife guru. Wan Chai is also the area with the widest culinary repertoire in Hong Kong. In the crowded shopping hub of Causeway Bay, restaurants, traffic and department stores jockey for space with a racecourse and a cemetery.

❹ Hong Kong Island: Aberdeen & the South (p130)

The southern district is the island's backyard playground – from the beaches of Repulse Bay and Deep Water Bay to Stanley Market, the waterfront bazaar and Ocean Park, the amusement park. Aberdeen Harbour offers boat rides down memory lane to a bygone era when thousands lived on junks moored in the harbour, while sleepy Ap Lei Chau surprises with a shopping hot spot and top-notch seafood.

❺ Kowloon (p138)

Tsim Sha Tsui is endowed with four museums, an unbeatable harbour setting and all the superlatives Central has to offer on a more human scale. Other assets include leafy parks, colonial gems and the most diverse ethnic mix in all of Hong Kong. Indigenous Yau Ma Tei is a mosaic of night markets, guesthouses and martial-arts dens, while Mong Kok's distinguishing feature is its sardine-packed commercialism. In New Kowloon a Buddhist nunnery and a Taoist temple beckon the spiritually inclined.

Hong Kong Island: Central

Neighbourhood Top Five

1 Taking a cruise on the legendary **Star Ferry** (p73).

2 Getting personal with skyscrapers you saw in *Batman* by venturing inside buildings like the **Bank of China Tower** (p74).

3 Enjoying top-notch dim sum at **Lung King Heen** (p78).

4 Shopping with the wealthy (or watching the wealthy shop) at the **IFC Mall** (p83).

5 Taking your morning constitutional and paying the animals a visit at the **Zoological & Botanical Gardens** (p76).

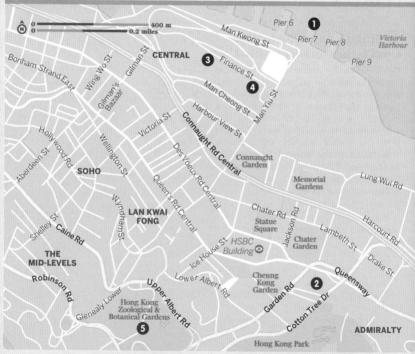

For more detail of this area, see Map p362 ➡

Explore: Central

Whatever time of the day you plan on visiting Hong Kong's central business district (CBD), it's worth remembering that shops here close relatively early (6pm or 7pm), and by mid-evening the dust has settled. It's also advisable to have lunch outside the noon-to-2pm insanity when hordes of hungry suits descend on every table in sight.

Travelling on the MTR, take the Statue Sq exit and spend an hour looking around the Former Legislative Council Building and other memorials to Hong Kong's past. In the next couple of hours, check out the architecture in the vicinity – glass-and-steel modernity like the HSBC Building and colonial-era survivors like Gothic St John's Cathedral.

Head over to the Zoological & Botanical Gardens for some hobnobbing with the rhesus monkeys. Recharged after an hour, make a beeline for the harbour for some retail therapy at the IFC Mall. Take as long as you like, then hop on the Star Ferry to Kowloon.

Local Life

➡ **Lil' Manila** Every Sunday, Filipina domestic helpers take over Statue Square (p74) and the nearby pavements to eat, sing, chat and read the Bible.

➡ **Hang-outs** On weekdays at 3pm, well-coiffed ladies of leisure congregate at Sevva (p82) for Marie Antoinette's Crave (it's a cake).

➡ **Shopping** If on a tight budget, World-Wide Plaza (p77) is handy for stocking up on affordable toiletries and snacks.

Getting There & Away

➡ **MTR** Central station on the Island and Tsuen Wan lines.

➡ **Airport Express** Hong Kong station below the IFC Mall connects (by underground walkway) with Central MTR station on one side and Central Piers on the other.

➡ **Star Ferry** Ferries from Tsim Sha Tsui in Kowloon arrive at Central Pier 7.

➡ **Bus** Buses start and end their journeys at Central Bus Terminus below Exchange Sq.

➡ **Tram** Runs east and west along Des Voeux Rd Central.

➡ **Outlying Islands Ferry** Ferries to Discovery Bay, Lamma, Cheung Chau, Lantau and Peng Chau (Central Piers 3 to 6).

➡ **Central Escalator** Runs from the former Central Market to the Mid-Levels.

➡ **Peak Tram** Runs from the lower terminus (33 Garden Rd) to the Peak.

Lonely Planet's Top Tip

To enjoy Central's top-notch French and Italian restaurants without breaking the bank, go for the midday specials. Most restaurants offer these for the convenience of business lunch eaters and frugal foodies. Some may even serve breakfast and/or afternoon tea, weekend lunch buffets or sell gourmet sandwiches at a takeaway station. Remember to book in advance if you're dining in for lunch.

HONG KONG ISLAND: CENTRAL

✕ Best Places to Eat

➡ Lung King Heen (p78)
➡ Otto e Mezzo Bombana (p79)
➡ Caprice (p79)
➡ Tasty Congee & Noodle Wonton Shop (p77)

For reviews, see p77 ➡

🍷 Best Places to Drink

➡ Sevva (p82)
➡ Liberty Exchange (p82)
➡ Pier 7 (p82)

For reviews, see p82 ➡

🛍 Best Places to Shop

➡ Shanghai Tang (p83)
➡ Blanc de Chine (p83)
➡ Lane Crawford (p83)
➡ Picture This (p83)

For reviews, see p83 ➡

TOP SIGHT
HSBC BUILDING

The stunning HSBC headquarters, designed by British architect Sir Norman Foster, is a masterpiece of precision, sophistication and innovation. And so it should be. On completion in 1985 it was the world's most expensive building (costing over US$1 billion). The HSBC Building reflects the architect's wish to create areas of public and private space, and to break the mould of previous bank architecture. A lighting scheme fitted later enabled the building to stand out at night.

The two bronze lions guarding the main entrance were designed for the bank's previous headquarters in 1935; the lions are known as Stephen – the one roaring – and Stitt, after two bank employees of the time. The Japanese used the lions as target practice during the occupation; you can still see bullet holes on Stitt. Rub their mighty paws for luck.

The 52-storey glass and aluminium building is full of examples of good feng shui (Chinese geomancy). There's no structure blocking its view of Victoria Harbour because water is associated with prosperity. The escalators are believed to symbolise the whiskers of a dragon sucking wealth into its belly. They're built at an angle to the entrance, supposedly to disorient evil spirits which can only travel in a straight line.

The ground floor is public space, which people can traverse without entering the bank. From there, take the escalator to the 3rd floor to gaze at the cathedral-like atrium and the natural light filtering through its windows.

DON'T MISS...

➡ Lighting scheme at night
➡ Stephen and Stitt
➡ Feng shui features
➡ The atrium

PRACTICALITIES

➡ 滙豐銀行總行大廈
➡ Map p362
➡ www.hsbc.com. hk/1/2/about/home/ unique-headquarters
➡ 1 Queen's Rd Central, Central
➡ admission free
➡ ⏱escalator 9am-4.30pm Mon-Fri, 9am-12.30pm Sat
➡ Ⓜ Central, exit K

You can't say you've 'done' Hong Kong until you've taken a ride on a Star Ferry, that legendary fleet of electric-diesel vessels with names like *Morning Star* and *Twinkling Star*. At any time of the day the ride, with its riveting views of skyscrapers and soaring mountains, must be one of the world's best-value cruises. At the end of the 10-minute journey, watch as a crew member casts a hemp rope to his colleague who catches it with a billhook, the way it was done in 1888 when the first boat docked.

The Star Ferry was a witness to major events in Hong Kong history, including on Christmas Day 1941, when the colonial governor, Sir Mark Aitchison Young, took the ferry to Tsim Sha Tsui, where he surrendered to the Japanese at the Peninsula Hotel.

Take your first trip on a clear night from Tsim Sha Tsui to Central. It's less dramatic in the opposite direction. That said, you can turn to face the rear and bid adieu to the glorious view as it slips away from you. If you don't mind the noise and diesel fumes, the lower deck (only open on the Tsim Sha Tsui–Central route) is better for pictures.

The pier you see on Hong Kong Island is an uninspiring Edwardian replica that replaced the old pier (Streamline Moderne style and with a clock tower) at Edinburgh Pl that was demolished despite vehement opposition from Hong Kong people. The Kowloon pier remains untouched.

The Star Ferry operates on two routes – Tsim Sha Tsui–Central and Tsim Sha Tsui–Wan Chai. The first is more popular. The coin-operated turnstiles do not give change but you can get it from the ticket window.

DON'T MISS...

➡ The views
➡ Kowloon pier
➡ The hemp rope and billhook routine

PRACTICALITIES

➡ 天星小輪
➡ Map p362
➡ ☎ 2367 7065
➡ www.starferry.com.hk
➡ adult HK$2.50-3.40, child HK$1.50-2.10
➡ ⊙ every 6-12min, 6.30am-11.30pm
➡ Ⓜ Hong Kong, exit A2

◉ SIGHTS

STATUE SQUARE
SQUARE

Map p362 (皇后像廣場; Edinburgh Pl, Central; MCentral, exit K) This leisurely square used to house effigies of British royalty. Now it pays tribute to a single sovereign – the founder of HSBC. In the northern area (reached via an underpass) is the **Cenotaph** (和平紀念碑; Chater Rd), built in 1923 as a memorial to Hong Kong residents killed during the two world wars. On the south side of Chater Rd, Statue Sq has a pleasant collection of fountains and seating areas, with tiling that's strangely reminiscent of a 1980s municipal washroom.

HSBC BUILDING
BUILDING

See p72.

OLD BANK OF CHINA BUILDING
BUILDING

Map p362 (1 Bank St, Central; MCentral, exit K) Constructed in 1950, the old Bank of China building now houses the bank's Central branch and, on its top floors, the exclusive **China Club**, which evokes the atmosphere of old Shanghai. The BOC is now headquartered in the awesome Bank of China Tower to the southeast.

FORMER LEGISLATIVE
COUNCIL BUILDING
HISTORIC BUILDING

Map p362 (前立法會大樓; 8 Jackson Rd, Central; MCentral, exit G) This colonnaded and domed building (c 1912) was built of granite quarried on Stonecutters Island, and served as the seat of the Legislative Council from 1985 to 2012. During WWII it was a headquarters of the Gendarmerie, the Japanese version of the Gestapo, and many people were executed here. Standing atop the pediment is a blindfolded statue of Themis, the Greek goddess of justice and natural law.

BANK OF CHINA TOWER
BUILDING

Map p362 (中銀大廈; BOC Tower; 1 Garden Rd, Central; MCentral, exit K) The awesome 70-storey Bank of China Tower designed by IM Pei rises from the ground like a cube, and is then successively reduced, quarter by quarter, until the south-facing side is left to rise on its own. The **public viewing gallery** (◷8am-6pm Mon-Fri) on the 43rd floor offers panoramic views of Hong Kong. Some geomancers believe the four prisms are negative symbols; being the opposite of circles, these triangles contradict what circles suggest – money, union and perfection.

The lobby of the BOC Tower features the **Prehistoric Story Room** (◷9am-6pm, Wed-Mon), a small exhibition depicting Earth's life history through fossil displays.

FORMER FRENCH
MISSION BUILDING
HISTORIC BUILDING

Map p362 (前法國外方傳道會大樓; 1 Battery Path, Central; MCentral, exit K) The **Court of Final Appeal**, the highest judicial body in Hong Kong, is housed in the neoclassical former French Mission building, a charming structure built in 1868. It served as the Russian consulate until 1915 when the French Overseas Mission bought it and added a chapel and a dome. The building was the headquarters of the provisional colonial government after WWII. Just before the mission building is the pretty **Cheung Kong Garden**.

ST JOHN'S CATHEDRAL
CHURCH

Map p362 (聖約翰座堂; ☎2523 4157; www.stjohnscathedral.org.hk; 4-8 Garden Rd, Central; ◷7am-6pm; ☐12A, 40, 40M, MCentral, exit K) **FREE** Services have been held at this Anglican cathedral since it opened in 1849, with the exception of 1944, when the Japanese army used it as a social club. It suffered heavy damage during WWII, and the front doors were subsequently remade using timber salvaged from HMS *Tamar*, a British warship that guarded Victoria Harbour. You walk on sacred ground in more ways than one here: it is the only piece of freehold land in Hong Kong. Enter from Battery Path.

HELENA MAY
HISTORIC BUILDING

Map p362 (梅夫人婦女會主樓; ☎2522 6766; www.helenamay.com; 35 Garden Rd, Central; ☐23) The Helena May was opened in 1916 by the wife of a governor as a social club for working, single European women, for whom the colony had little to offer by way of 'respectable' entertainment like ballet lessons and tea parties. The colonial building with features of the Palladian and beaux-arts styles was used to stable horses during the Japanese Occupation.

Currently a private club and hostel (p267), it runs 20-minute tours in English and Chinese once every two months on a Saturday (10am to noon; see the website for dates). Reservations are compulsory.

GOVERNMENT HOUSE
HISTORIC BUILDING

Map p362 (香港禮賓府; ☎2530 2003; www.ceo.gov.hk/gh; Upper Albert Rd, Central; MCentral,

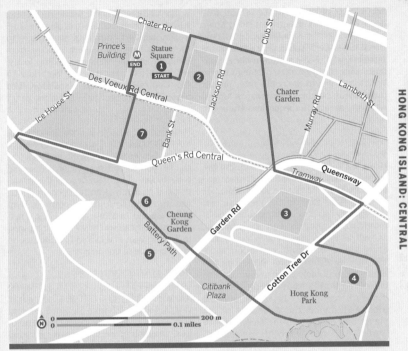

🏃 Neighbourhood Walk
Exploring Hong Kong's Heart

START STATUE SQ, CENTRAL
END CENTRAL MTR STATION
LENGTH 1.5KM, 45 MINUTES

Begin the walk at **❶ Statue Square** (p74) and take in the handsome outline of the neoclassical **❷ Former Legislative Council Building** (p74), one of the few colonial-era survivors in the area and the former seat of Hong Kong's modern legislature.

Walk southwest through Chater Garden and cross over Garden Rd to the angular, modern lines of the **❸ Bank of China Tower** (p74), which has amazing views from the 43rd floor.

Duck into Hong Kong Park for the free **❹ Flagstaff House Museum of Tea Ware** (p110), displaying valuable pots, cups and other elegant tea ware. Sample some of China's finest teas in the serene cafe.

From here take elevated walkways west over Cotton Tree Dr, through Citibank Plaza, over Garden Rd and through Cheung Kong Garden to **❺ St John's Cathedral** (p74), dating from 1849. It is a modest building to earn the title of cathedral, especially with the towering corporate cathedrals now surrounding it, but it is an important historic Hong Kong monument all the same.

Follow Battery Path past the **❻ Former French Mission Building** (p74) to Ice House St. Cross over and walk right (east) along Queen's Rd Central to the **❼ HSBC building** (p72) and up the escalator (if it's open) to the large airy atrium. Walk through the ground-floor plaza to pat Stephen and Stitt, the two lions guarding the exit to Des Voeux Rd Central. The closest Central MTR station entrance is a short distance to the north along the pedestrian walkway between Statue Sq and Prince's Building.

exit G) Parts of this erstwhile official residence of the chief executive of Hong Kong, and previously the colonial governors, date from 1855. Other features were added by the Japanese, who used it as military headquarters during the occupation of Hong Kong in WWII. It's open to the public three or four times a year, notably one Sunday in March, when the azaleas in the gardens are in full bloom.

HONG KONG ZOOLOGICAL & BOTANICAL GARDENS
PARK

Map p362 (香港動植物公園; www.lcsd.gov.hk/parks; Albany Rd, Central; ☺terrace gardens 5am-10pm, greenhouse 9am-4.30pm; ♿; ☐3B, 12) FREE Built in the Victorian era, this garden has a welcoming collection of fountains, sculptures and greenhouses, as well as a zoo and some fabulous aviaries. Along with exotic vegetation, some 160 species of bird reside here. The zoo is surprisingly comprehensive, and is also one of the world's leading centres for the captive breeding of endangered species. Albany Rd divides the gardens, with the plants and aviaries to the east, close to Garden Rd, and most of the animals to the west.

CENTRAL MARKET
HISTORIC BUILDING

Map p362 (中環街市; btwn Jubilee St, Queen Victoria St, Queen's Rd Central & Des Voeux Rd, Central; Ⓜ Central, exit C) Central Market (c 1938), built in the Bauhaus style, used to be one of Asia's premier food markets. Housewives and cooks would come as far as Happy Valley to shop. After the war, there were lines here whenever horsemeat was on sale. In 1967 the then governor crowned it the 'biggest meat market in Southeast Asia' after a visit. Pending further development, it's now a Sunday picnicking spot for over-

worked Filipina maids, a role in keeping with the utopian-socialism of Bauhaus.

The market is linked by footbridges to the Hang Seng Bank New Headquarters Building and the walkway leading to the IFC Mall (p83), and another footbridge to the **Central–Mid-Levels Escalator** (Map p366; ☺down 6-10am, up 10.30am-midnight).

EXCHANGE SQUARE
BUILDING

Map p362 (交易廣場; 8 Connaught Pl, Central; Ⓜ Central, exit A) This complex of office towers houses the Hong Kong Stock Exchange and the offices of global financial corporations. The main draw is the attractive and relatively peaceful open-air space, featuring fountains, and sculptures by Henry Moore and Ju Ming. Access is via a network of overhead walkways stretching west to Sheung Wan and linked to buildings on the other side of Connaught Rd.

ONE & TWO INTERNATIONAL FINANCE CENTRE
BUILDING

Map p362 (國際金融中心; One IFC: 1 Harbour View St, Two IFC: 8 Finance St, Central; Ⓜ Hong Kong, exit A or F) These pearl-coloured colossi resembling electric shavers sit atop the International Finance Centre (IFC) Mall (p83). Two IFC is the tallest building on Hong Kong Island. You can't get to the top, but you can get pretty high up by visiting the Hong Kong **Monetary Authority Information Centre** (金管局資訊中心; ☎2878 1111; www.info.gov.hk/hkma; 55th fl; ☺10am-6pm Mon-Fri, to 1pm Sat; Ⓜ Hong Kong, exit A2 or F) FREE, which has a library and an exhibition on Hong Kong's fiscal policy and banking history. There are half-hour guided tours daily from Monday to Saturday.

STAR FERRY
FERRY

See p73.

STAR FERRY'S STARS

The Star Ferry was founded in 1888 by Dorabjee Nowrojee, a Parsi from Bombay. At the time, most locals were crossing the harbour on sampans. Nowrojee bought a steamboat for his private use, and this eventually became the first Star Ferry. Parsis believe in the Persian religion of Zoroastrianism, and the five-pointed star on the Star Ferry logo is in fact an ancient Zoroastrian symbol. The Star Ferry features prominently in Hong Kong's history. In 1966 thousands gathered at the Tsim Sha Tsui pier to protest against a proposed 5¢ fare increase. It evolved into a riot as the protesters threw stones at buses and set vehicles on fire on Nathan Rd. The 1966 riot is seen as the trailblazer of local social protests leading to colonial reforms. No surprise then that, on an overcast day, the only stars you'll see over Victoria Harbour are those of the Star Ferry.

⭐ **HONG KONG MARITIME MUSEUM** MUSEUM

Map p362 (香港海事博物館; ☑3713 2500; www. hkmaritimemuseum.org; Central Ferry Pier 8, Central; adult/senior & child HK$30/15; ⏰9.30am-5.30pm Mon-Fri, 10am-7pm Sat & Sun; 🚹; Ⓜ Hong Kong, exit A2) Relocation and expansion have turned this into one of the city's strongest museums, with 15 well-curated galleries detailing over 2000 years of Chinese maritime history and the development of the Port of Hong Kong. Exhibits include ceramics from China's ancient sea trade, shipwreck treasures and old nautical instruments. A painted scroll depicting piracy in China in the early 19th century is one of Hong Kong's most important historical artefacts, and, like the rest of the museum, a real eye-opener.

The museum is located right next to Victoria Harbour. After leaving the MTR, walk towards the pier along Man Yiu St.

JARDINE HOUSE BUILDING

Map p362 (怡和大廈; 1 Connaught Pl, Central; Ⓜ Hong Kong, exit B2) This 52-storey silver monolith punctured with 1750 porthole-like windows was Hong Kong's first true 'skyscraper' when it opened in 1973. Inevitably the building has earned its own irreverent nickname: the 'House of 1000 Arseholes'. In the basement is the live-music venue and Italian restaurant Grappa's Cellar (p82).

WORLD-WIDE PLAZA BUILDING

Map p362 (環球商場; 19 Des Voeux Rd, Central; Ⓜ Central, exit G) A slice of Manila in Hong Kong's financial heart, the rabbit warren of tiny shops in this '80s-style shopping arcade cater to the needs of the Filipina domestic helpers working in Hong Kong, who, on Sundays, like to congregate in the streets around this area. Products for sale include food, toiletries and phonecards.

HONG KONG CITY HALL BUILDING

Map p362 (香港大會堂; www.cityhall.gov.hk; 5 Edinburgh Pl, Central; ⏰9am-11pm; Ⓜ Central, exit K) The City Hall, built in classic Bauhaus style in 1962, was Hong Kong's first large-scale civic centre. It remains a major cultural venue today, with concert and recital halls, a theatre and exhibition galleries. Within the Lower Block, entered to the east of City Hall's main entrance, the **City Gallery** (⏰10am-6pm) may awaken the Meccano builder in more than a few visitors.

🍴 **EATING**

⭐ **TIM HO WAN, THE DIM SUM SPECIALISTS** DIM SUM $

Map p362 (添好運點心專門店; ☑2332 3078; 8 Finance St, Shop 12a, Hong Kong Station, Podium Level 1, IFC Mall, Central; dishes HK$50; ⏰9am-8.30pm; Ⓜ Hong Kong, exit E1) Opened by a former Four Seasons chef, Tim Ho Wan was the first ever budget dim sum place to receive a Michelin star. Many relocations and branches later, the star is still tucked snugly inside its tasty tidbits, including the top-selling baked barbecue pork bun. Expect to wait 15 to 40 minutes for a table.

⭐ **TASTY CONGEE & NOODLE WONTON SHOP** NOODLES $

Map p362 (正斗粥麵專家; ☑2295 0101; www. tasty.com.hk; 1 Harbour View St, Central, Shop 3016, Podium Level 3, IFC Mall; dishes HK$90-200; ⏰11am-10.45pm; Ⓜ Hong Kong, exit E1) This clean and affordable eatery in the ultraposh IFC Mall has a long line at lunchtime. So learn from the ladies of leisure – shop first, eat later. Delayed gratification also means you'll be able to sample more of the Michelin-crowned deliciousness: shrimp wontons, prawn congee, stir-fried flat noodles with beef...

PETITE AMANDA BAKERY $

Map p362 (☑2234 7222; www.petiteamanda. com; 8 Finance St, Shop 2096, Podium Level 2, IFC Mall, Central; bread/pastries from HK$25/45; ⏰9am-8pm Mon-Fri, from 10am Sat & Sun; Ⓜ Hong Kong, exit E1) The creations at this petite patisserie opened by model turned pastry chef Amanda Strang are beautiful, delicious and fattening. The Charlotte aux Poires and the Amarina are very popular.

CITY HALL MAXIM'S PALACE DIM SUM $

Map p362 (美心皇宮; ☑2521 1303; 1 Edinburgh Pl, 3rd fl, Lower Block, Hong Kong City Hall, Central; meals from HK$150; ⏰11am-3pm Mon-Sat, 9am-3pm Sun; 🚹; Ⓜ Central, exit K) This 'palace' offers the quintessential Hong Kong dim sum experience. It's cheerful, it's noisy, and it takes place in a huge kitschy hall with dragon decorations and hundreds of locals. A dizzying assortment of dim sum is paraded on trolleys the old-fashioned way. There's breakfast on Sunday from 9am but people start queuing for a table at 8.30am.

SING KEE
DAI PAI DONG $

Map p362 (盛記; ☎2541 5678; 9-10 Stanley St, Soho; meals HK$200; ⏱11am-3pm & 6-11pm daily; 🖾; Ⓜ Central, exit D2) In the fine-dining enclave of Soho, finding a good and cheap meal can be tricky. Sing Kee, one of the few surviving *dai pai dong* (food stalls) in the area, has withstood the tide of gentrification, and still retains a working-class, laugh-out-loud character. There's no signage. Look for the crammed tables at the end of Stanley St.

YUE HING
DAI PAI DONG $

Map p362 (裕興; 76-78 Stanley St, Soho; meals HK$25-40; ⏱8.15am-2pm; Ⓜ Central, exit D2) One of a gang of *dai pai dong* earmarked for preservation, easygoing Yue Hing reinvents the Hong Kong sandwich by topping the usual suspects (ham, spam and egg) with peanut butter and cooked cabbage. And it works! Allow 15 minutes for preparation as these wacky wedges are made to order.

LIN HEUNG TEAHOUSE
DIM SUM, CANTONESE $

Map p362 (蓮香樓; ☎2544 4556; 160-164 Wellington St, Sheung Wan; lunch/dinner from HK$60/120; ⏱6am-11pm daily; 🚃26, Ⓜ Sheung Wan, exit E1) This 80-year-old restaurant, packed with older men reading newspapers and extended families, has decent dim sum (until 5pm) and old-school Cantonese dishes. The grandfather-like waiters still wear traditional white tunics over black trousers, and pour tea from huge brass kettles. Tables are shared at this no-frills place, giving a feel of community even for first-timers.

ISLAND TANG
CANTONESE, DIM SUM $$

Map p362 (港島廳; ☎2526 8798; www.islandtang. com; 9 Queen's Rd Central, Shop 222, Galleria, Central; set lunch from HK$308, dinner from HK$400; ⏱noon-2.30pm & 6-10.30pm; 🖥; Ⓜ Central, exit D1) Island Tang can easily be a place where, as the Chinese say, one goes to 'devour the decor' – the 1930s art-deco interior is sheer elegance. But admirably, the restaurant has kept its culinary standards extremely high. The exquisite selections range from Cantonese home-cooking to banquet-style seafood dishes, which means a meal can set you back HK$300 or HK$3000.

LEI GARDEN
CANTONESE, DIM SUM $$

Map p362 (利苑酒家; ☎2295 0238; 1 Harbour View St, Shop 3008-3011, Level 3, IFC Mall, Central; meals HK$180-900; ⏱11.30am-2.30pm & 5.30-10.30pm; 🖥🖾; Ⓜ Hong Kong, exit E1) Military-like control of food quality has earned seven of the 10 Lei Garden outlets, including this one, a Michelin star, but this IFC branch has the most contemporary environment and the most professional staff. Signature dishes include roast meats, dim sum and the award-winning dessert – sweet sago soup with mango and pomelo. Booking essential.

WATERMARK
EUROPEAN $$

Map p362 (☎2167 7251; www.cafedecogroup.com; Central Pier 7/Star Ferry Pier, Shop L, Level P, Central; lunch & brunch from HK$400, dinner HK$600; ⏱noon-2.30pm & 6pm-late Mon-Fri, 11.30am-3pm & 6pm-late Sat & Sun; 🖥🖾; Ⓜ Hong Kong, exit A2) With its location on the Star Ferry Pier, Watermark commands panoramic views of Victoria Harbour. It's airy during the day and romantic at night, and you can feel the sway of the waves at some of the tables. Dry-aged rib-eye and seafood are the highlights of its solid European menu.

GREYHOUND CAFÉ
THAI, FUSION $$

Map p362 (☎2383 1133; www.greyhoundcafe. com.hk; 3 Harbour View St, Central, Shop 1082, Podium Level 1, IFC Mall, Central; meals from HK$200; ⏱11am-10.30pm; 🖥🖾; Ⓜ Hong Kong, exit E1) This popular Bangkok cafe brings its hip Asian fusion to Hong Kong. The long menu features both modernised Asian favourites like pad Thai and Vietnamese curry, as well as burgers and pizzas with an Asian twist – all deftly executed and presented in a crisp and airy setting. Save room for the tropical-fruit-infused Thai desserts.

HEICHINROU
CANTONESE $$

Map p362 (聘珍樓; ☎2868 9229; www.heichinrou.com; 41 Connaught Rd, G05 & 107-108, Nexxus Bldg, Central; lunch/dinner from HK$200/350; ⏱10.30am-midnight; 🖥🖾; Ⓜ Central, exit C) It's everything you'd expect from a modern Cantonese restaurant of this calibre in Hong Kong – polished service, a somewhat formal ambience, refined cooking, and good tea. This makes its self-touting as the 'oldest Chinese restaurant in Japan' a little baffling. The afternoon tea set with four kinds of dim sum, snack, staple and dessert for HK$128 is a steal.

★ LUNG KING HEEN
CANTONESE, DIM SUM $$$

Map p362 (龍景軒; ☎3196 8888; www.fourseasons.com/hongkong; 8 Finance St, Four Seasons Hotel, Central; set lunch/dinner HK$500/1560; ⏱noon-2.30pm & 6-10.30pm; 🖥; Ⓜ Hong Kong, exit E1) The world's first Chinese restaurant to receive three stars from the Michelin people, still retains them. The Cantonese food, though by no means peerless in Hong Kong, is excellent in both taste and presentation, and when combined with the harbour views and the impeccable service, provides a truly stellar dining experience. The signature steamed lobster and scallop dumplings sell out early.

OTTO E MEZZO
BOMBANA
MODERN ITALIAN $$$

Map p362 (☑2537 8859; www.ottoemezzobombana.com; Shop 202, Landmark Alexandra, 18 Chater Rd, Central; lunch from HK$700, dinner from HK$1380; ⊙noon-2.30pm & 6.30-10.30pm Mon-Sat; ☎; ⓂCentral, exit H) Asia's only Italian restaurant with three Michelin stars lives up to its name, and Chef Bombana is here, sleeves rolled, to see that it does. 'Eight and a Half' is the place for white truffles, being the host of the local bid for these pungent diamonds. To eat here though you'll need the tenacity of a truffle hound – book two months ahead.

★CAPRICE
FRENCH $$$

Map p362 (☑3196 8888; www.fourseasons.com/hongkong; 8 Finance St, Four Seasons Hotel; set lunch/dinner from HK$540/1740; ⊙noon-2.30pm & 6-10.30pm; ☎; ⓂHong Kong, exit E1) In contrast to its opulent decor, Caprice, with two Michelin stars, has a straightforward menu. The meals are masterfully crafted from ingredients flown in daily from France. The selections change, but experience says anything with duck, langoustine or pork belly is out of this world. Their artisanal cheeses, imported weekly, are the best you can get in Hong Kong.

DUDDELL'S
CANTONESE $$$

Map p362 (都爹利會館; ☑2525 9191; www.duddells.co; 1 Duddell St, Level 3 & 4 Shanghai Tang Mansion, Central; lunch HK$500-800, dinner HK$800-1600; ⊙noon-2.30pm & 6-10.30pm Mon-Sat; ☎; ⓂCentral, exit G) Light Cantonese fare served in riveting spaces enhanced by artwork – a graceful dining-room awash in diffused light; a marble-tiled salon in modernided '50s chic; a leafy terrace. Saturday brunch (HK$588; served noon to 3.30pm) with free-flowing champagne and all-you-can-eat dim sum is a welcome treat, especially given the usually petite serving portions. Duddell's is also an art gallery holding regular exhibitions and talks.

L'ATELIER DE JOËL ROBUCHON
FRENCH $$$

Map p362 (☑2166 9000; www.robuchon.com; 15 Queen's Rd Central, Shop 401, Landmark, Central; lunch HK$450-1900, dinner HK$800-2000, tapas from HK$350; ⊙noon-2.30pm & 6.30-10.30pm; ☎; ⓂCentral, exit G) One-third of celebrity chef Joël Robuchon's Michelin-crowned wonder in Hong Kong, this red-and-black workshop has a tantalising list of tapas and a 70-page wine list. If you prefer something more formal, visit Le Jardin in the next room. Le Salon de The, one floor down, has the best sandwiches and pastries in town for dine-in or takeaway.

PIERRE
FRENCH $$$

Map p362 (☑2825 4001; www.mandarinoriental.com/hongkong; 5 Connaught Rd, 25th fl Mandarin Oriental, Central; set lunch HK$470-1500, set dinner HK$900-1500; ⊙noon-2.30pm & 7-10.30pm; ☎; ⓂCentral, exit F) The godfather of fusion, Pierre Gagnaire, has created a provocative menu in the city that embodies the concept. Amuse bouche might be a marshmallow sprinkled with shrimp powder; dessert a caramelised rocket salad. The decor, with portholes and chandeliers, reminds one of a cruise liner, especially when adding the harbour view. Pierre has three Michelin stars.

INAGIKU
JAPANESE $$$

Map p362 (稻菊日本餐廳; ☑2805 0600; www.fourseasons.com/hongkong; 8 Finance St, Level 4, Four Seasons Hotel, Central; lunch/dinner from HK$600/900; ⊙11.30am-3pm & 6-11pm; ⓂCentral, exit A) Inagiku, meaning 'rice chrysanthemum', is perfection. It's a formal place with subtle interiors and stunning views of the harbour, where attention is lavished on every dish. You can choose to sit at one of the sushi, teppanyaki or tempura bars and watch the chefs work their magic, or bask in the romantic privacy of a table.

AMBER
MODERN EUROPEAN $$$

Map p362 (☑2132 0066; www.mandarinoriental.com/landmark; 15 Queen's Rd Central, 7th fl, Landmark Mandarin Oriental, Central; set lunch HK$560-760, set dinner HK$1800-2100; ⊙noon-2.30pm & 6.30-10.30pm; ⓂCentral, exit G) This elegant restaurant with dusk-like lighting and 3000 hanging 'organ pipes' may feel a tad formal, but once you've sampled Chef Ekkebus' masterful takes on traditional French dishes, such as the Mieral Bresse pigeon, you will warm to Amber. It's food intelligently cooked with a lot of heart. Amber has two Michelin stars.

1. New Central Government Offices
Located in the harbourfront Tamar Park (p110), this is the headquarters of the Hong Kong government.

2. Star Ferry (p73)
Hong Kong's iconic Star Ferry fleet cruises Victoria Harbour.

3. Statue Square (p74)
Statue Square offers views of Hong Kong's landmarks, including the Bank of China Tower.

4. Former Legislative Council Building (p74)
Constructed in 1912, this is one of few colonial-era buildings remaining in the area.

🍷 DRINKING & NIGHTLIFE

SEVVA
COCKTAIL BAR

Map p362 (📞2537 1388; www.sevva.hk; 10 Chater Rd, 25th fl, Prince's Bldg, Central; ⊙noon-midnight Mon-Thu, to 2am Fri & Sat; 🛜; Ⓜ Central, exit H) If there was a million-dollar view in Hong Kong, it'd be the one from the balcony of ultra-stylish Sevva – skyscrapers so close you can see their arteries of steel, with the harbour and Kowloon in the distance. At night it takes your breath away. To get there though, you have to overcome expensive drinks and patchy service. Book ahead if you want a table on the balcony.

PIER 7
BAR

Map p362 (📞2167 8377; www.cafedecogroup.com; Central Pier 7/Star Ferry Pier, Shop M, Roof Viewing Deck, Central; ⊙9am-midnight, happy hour 6-9pm; 🛜; Ⓜ Hong Kong, exit A1) Sitting atop the Star Ferry terminal, Pier 7 has a large outdoor terrace with views of neighbouring skyscrapers, the hills of Kowloon and a sliver of the harbour. It's an unpretentious spot for a quiet pre-movie (or postdinner) drink and some light refreshments. On random weekends there are reggae DJs in the house and the vibe turns shaggy.

LIBERTY EXCHANGE
SPORTS BAR

Map p362 (📞2810 8400; www.lex.hk; 8 Connaught Pl, Two Exchange Sq, Central; ⊙noon-11.30pm Mon-Sat, to 5.30pm Sun, happy hour 3-8pm, to 5.30pm Sun; 🛜; Ⓜ Hong Kong, exit A1) This American bar and bistro beckons with open frontage, generous pourings and a casual atmosphere. No surprise then that it's hugely popular with the bankers and hedgies who work in the vicinity. On any given Friday evening, it's packed with people exchanging industry gossip over cocktails, wine or beer, or watching sports on one of the big TV screens.

RED BAR
BAR

Map p362 (📞8129 8882; www.pure-red.com; 8 Finance St, L4, Two IFC; ⊙noon-midnight Mon-Wed, to 1am Thu, to 3am Fri & Sat, to 10pm Sun, happy hour 6-9pm; 🛜; Ⓜ Hong Kong, exit E1) Red Bar's combination of alfresco drinking and harbour views is hard to beat. Expect to meet lots of smartly dressed finance types from the corporate offices nearby. DJs playing funk and jazz turn up the volume as the weekend approaches.

MO BAR
BAR

Map p362 (📞2132 0077; 15 Queen's Rd Central, Landmark, Central; ⊙7am-1.30am; 🛜; Ⓜ Central, exit D1) If you want to imbibe in quiet or to catch up with a chat, the swish MO Bar, attached to the Mandarin's swanky outpost at the Landmark, offers peace, soft lighting and a first-rate drinks list of wines and cocktails.

CAPTAIN'S BAR
BAR

Map p362 (船長吧; 📞2825 4006; www.mandarinoriental.com.hk; 5 Connaught Rd Central, ground fl, Mandarin Oriental, Central; ⊙11am-2am Mon-Sat, to 1am Sun; 🛜; Ⓜ Central, exit F) Captain's Bar has been attracting drinkers with its clubby atmosphere and polished service for half a century. Though looking slightly old-fashioned now, it still makes some of the best martinis in town and serves ice-cold draught beer in chilled silver mugs. It's a good place to talk business, at least until the cover band strikes up at 9pm.

GOOD SPRING CO
HERBAL TEA

Map p362 (春回堂藥行; 📞2544 3518; 8 Cochrane St, Soho; tea HK$7-30; ⊙8.45am-8pm daily; Ⓜ Central, exit D2) This Chinese medicine shop has a counter selling herbal teas – for detoxing, getting rid of water, cooling the body or treating colds. The most popular is the bitter 24-herb tea. There's also the fragrant chrysanthemum infusion. If you like, the English-speaking herbalist will take your pulse and prescribe a (black and bitter) medicinal soup.

☆ ENTERTAINMENT

GRAPPA'S CELLAR
LIVE MUSIC

Map p362 (📞2521 2322; www.elgrande.com.hk/outlets/HongKong/GrappasCellar; 1 Connaught Pl, Central; ⊙9pm-late; Ⓜ Hong Kong, exit B2) For at least two weekends a month, this subterranean Italian restaurant morphs into a jazz or rock music venue – chequered tablecloths and all. Call or visit the website for event and ticketing details.

SENSES 99
LIVE MUSIC

Map p362 (📞9466 2675; www.sense99.com; 2nd & 3rd fl, 99 Wellington St, Soho; ⊙9pm-late Fri & Sat; Ⓜ Sheung Wan, exit E2) This two-floor speakeasy inside a pre-WWII building has all the features of a tasteful mid-century residence – high ceilings, balconies overlooking a quiet street, folding screen door and distressed couches. Music sessions begin after 10pm but before that you can take charge of the drum set and electric guitar on the 3rd floor to start a jam session or join one.

PALACE IFC CINEMA

Map p362 (☎2388 6268; 8 Finance St, Podium L1, IFC Mall, Central; M Hong Kong, exit F) This eight-screen cinema complex in the IFC Mall is arguably the most advanced and comfortable in the territory.

🛍 SHOPPING

⭐**SHANGHAI TANG** CLOTHING, HOMEWARE

Map p362 (上海灘; ☎2525 7333; www.shanghai-tang.com; 1 Duddell St, Shanghai Tang Mansion, Central; ⊙10.30am-8pm; M Central, exit D1) This elegant four-level store is the place to go if you fancy a body-hugging *qipao* (cheong-sam) with a modern twist, a Chinese-style clutch or a lime-green mandarin jacket. Custom tailoring is available; it takes two weeks to a month and requires a fitting. Shanghai Tang also stocks cushions, picture frames, teapots, even mah-jong tile sets, designed in a modern chinoiserie style.

⭐**ARMOURY** MEN'S CLOTHING

Map p362 (☎2804 6991; www.thearmoury.com; 12 Pedder St, 307, 3rd fl, Pedder Bldg, Central; ⊙11am-8pm Mon-Sat) The Armoury can help any man look like a dapper gentleman, whatever your build – the elegant shop is a specialist in refined menswear sourced from around the world. You can choose from British, Italian and Asian-tailored suits, and a high-quality selection of shoes and ties to match. Still not good enough? Ask about the bespoke suits and custom footwear.

PRINCE'S BUILDING MALL

Map p362 (太子大廈; ☎2504 0704; www.cen-tralhk.com; 10 Chater Rd, Central; M Central, exit K) You may find the layout of Prince's Building disorienting, but it's worth a look for its speciality fashion, toy and kitchenware shops, and the latest art galleries. The selection is rather eclectic but invitingly so.

⭐**PICTURE THIS** GIFTS

Map p362 (☎2525 2803; www.picturethiscollec-tion.com; 10 Chater Rd, Shop 212, Prince's Bldg, Central; ⊙10am-7pm Mon-Sat, noon-5pm Sun; M Central, exit H) The vintage posters, photographs, prints and antique maps of Hong Kong and Asia on sale here will appeal to collectors or anyone seeking an unusual gift. There's also an assortment of antiquarian books related to Hong Kong. Prices are not cheap but they guarantee all maps and prints to be originals.

⭐**BLANC DE CHINE** CLOTHING, ACCESSORIES

Map p362 (源; ☎2104 7934; www.blancdechine. com; 10 Chater Rd, Shop 123, Prince's Bldg, Central; ⊙10.30am-7.30pm Mon-Sat, noon-6pm Sun; M Central, exit H) This sumptuous store specialises in Chinese men's jackets and silk dresses for women, both off-the-rack and made-to-measure. A gorgeous sequined gown takes about four weeks to make, including one fitting. If you will have left Hong Kong by then, the shop will ship it to you.

IFC MALL MALL

Map p362 (☎2295 3308; www.ifc.com.hk; 8 Finance St, Central; M Hong Kong, exit F) Hong Kong's most luxurious shopping mall boasts 200 high-fashion boutiques linking the One and Two IFC towers and the Four Seasons Hotel. Outlets include Patrick Cox, Geiger, Longchamp, Kenzo, Vivienne Tam, Zegna... we could go on. The Hong Kong Airport Express Station is downstairs.

⭐**LANE CRAWFORD** DEPARTMENT STORE

Map p362 (連卡佛; ☎2118 3388; www.lanecraw-ford.com; 8 Finance St, Level 3, Podium 3, IFC Mall, Central; ⊙10am-9pm; M Central, exit A) The territory's answer to Harrods in London, Lane Crawford (c 1850) was Hong Kong's original Western-style department store, and one which, admirably, has succeeded in rejuvenating itself while remaining classy over the decades. This flagship store sells everything from fashion to crockery. There are four other branches in town.

FOOK MING TONG TEA SHOP FOOD, DRINK

Map p362 (福茗堂; ☎2295 0368; www.fook-mingtong.com; 8 Finance St, Shop 3006, Podium Level 3, IFC Mall, Central; ⊙10.30am-8pm Mon-Sat, 11am-8pm Sun; M Central, exit A) Tea-making accoutrements and carefully chosen teas of various ages and grades are available here, from gunpowder to Nanyan Ti Guan Yin Crown Grade – costing anything from HK$10 to HK$9000 per 100g.

DYMOCKS BOOKS

Map p362 (☎2489 8868; www.dymocks.com. hk; 1 Harbour View St, Shop 3002-3005, 3rd fl, IFC Mall, Central; ⊙10am-9pm; M Hong Kong, exit F)

Has a mainstream selection of books and magazines, mostly English-language, in several branches.

CITYSUPER
FOOD, DRINK

Map p362 (www.citysuper.com.hk; 8 Finance St, Shop 1041-1049, IFC Mall, Central; ⊗10.30am-9.30pm; MHong Kong, exit F) Citysuper sells a range of top-notch hard-to-find ingredients from all over the world, as well as natural and organic foods. The prices are high.

LANDMARK
MALL

Map p362 (置地廣場; ☑2525 4142; www.centralhk.com; 1 Pedder St, Central; MCentral, exit G) The most central of all shopping centres, the Landmark has high fashion and good eating in a pleasant, open space. It has become a home almost exclusively to the very high-end fashion brands and boutiques (Gucci, Louis Vuitton, TODs etc).

HARVEY NICHOLS
DEPARTMENT STORE

Map p362 (☑3695 3389; www.harveynichols.com; 1 Pedder St, Landmark Bldg, Central; ⊗10am-9pm Mon-Sat, to 7pm Sun; MCentral, exit G) Britain's Harvey Nichols has brought its diverse, profuse and on-the-pulse range of couture and smart street fashions to Hong Kong, occupying four floors at the Landmark.

HONG KONG BOOK CENTRE
BOOKS

Map p362 (☑2522 7064; www.hongkongbookcentre.com; 25 Des Voeux Rd, Basement, On Lok Yuen Bldg, Central; ⊗9am-6.30pm Mon-Fri, to 5.30pm Sat; MCentral, exit B) This basement shop has a vast selection of English-language books and magazines, particularly business titles.

JOYCE
CLOTHING, ACCESSORIES

Map p362 (☑2810 1120; www.joyce.com; 16 Queen's Rd Central, ground fl, New World Tower, Central; ⊗10.30am-7.30pm; MCentral, exit D1) This multi-designer store is a good choice if you're short of time rather than money: Marc Jacobs, Comme des Garçons, Chloé, and several of the hottest Hong Kong fashion designers are just some of the brands you'll find here. For the same duds at half the price, visit **Joyce Warehouse** (Map p376; ☑2814 8313; 2 Lee Wing St, 21st fl, Horizon Plaza Arcade, Ap Lei Chau; ⊗closed Mon) in Horizon Plaza in Ap Lei Chau.

OH MY GLASSES
GLASSES

Map p362 (☑2581 1986; www.ohmyglasseshk.com; 3rd fl, 154 Des Voeux Rd, Central; ⊗noon-8pm Mon-Sat; MSheung Wan, E1) If you ever had the misfortune to scream this shop's name while in Hong Kong (or even if you don't), you'll find spectacles to your liking here. OMG is a local label of shades and opticals that are 30–50% cheaper than imported brands. Styles are middle-of-the-road trendy, with the odd neon yellow frame thrown in.

🏃 SPORTS & ACTIVITIES

TEN FEET TALL
FOOT MASSAGE

Map p362 (☑2971 1010; www.tenfeettall.com.hk; 139 Queen's Rd Central, 20th & 21st fl, L Place, Central; ⊗11am-midnight Mon-Thu, 10.30am-1.30am Fri & Sat, 10.30am-12.30am Sun; MCentral, exit D2) Opened by the owner of Dragon-I (p102), this sprawling comfort den (745 sq metres) offers a range of treatments from foot reflexology and shoulder massage to hardcore pressure-point massage and aromatic oil treatments. The interiors are created by French restaurant designers.

SPA AT THE FOUR SEASONS
SPA

Map p362 (☑3196 8900; www.fourseasons.com/hongkong/spa.html; 8 Finance St, Central; ⊗8am-10pm; MHong Kong, exit F) A 1860-sq-metre, ultra-high-end spa with a comprehensive range of beauty, massage and health treatments, plus ice fountain, hot cups, moxibustion and even a 'herbal cocoon room'.

PURE FITNESS
GYM

Map p362 (☑8129 8000; www.pure-fitness.com; 8 Finance St, 3rd fl, IFC Mall, Central; ⊗6am-midnight Mon-Sat, 8am-10pm Sun; MHong Kong, exit F) A pleasant gym offering comprehensive facilities and/or classes for cardio-strength training, cycling, kickboxing, yoga, Pilates and dance fitness. It's a favourite among those working in the area.

IMPAKT MARTIAL ARTS & FITNESS CENTRE
MARTIAL ARTS

Map p362 (☑2167 7218; www.impakt.hk; 110-116 Queen's Rd Central, 2nd fl, Wing's Bldg, Central; ⊗7am-10pm Mon-Fri, 8am-7pm Sat, 10am-5pm Sun; MCentral, exit D2) One of few martial arts centres with female trainers. They teach Muay Thai, kickboxing, jiu jitsu, karate etc to GI Jane wannabes and experienced fighters alike. You can walk in for a one-off class or use the gym facilities for HK$250 or book personal private training for upwards of HK$300 per person per hour.

Hong Kong Island: The Peak & the Northwest

LAN KWAI FONG | SOHO | SHEUNG WAN | WESTERN DISTRICT | MID-LEVELS

Neighbourhood Top Five

❶ Making the white-knuckle ascent to Victoria Peak on the **Peak Tram** (p87) and taking in the night views from the summit.

❷ Strolling the streets of **Sheung Wan** (p89) to uncover the fascinating history of 19th-century Hong Kong.

❸ Bar-hopping your way over the inviting slopes of **Lan Kwai Fong** (p101).

❹ Enjoying delicious food under ceiling fans and stained-glass windows at **Luk Yu Tea House** (p93).

❺ Trawling through the **galleries and boutiques in Soho** (p103).

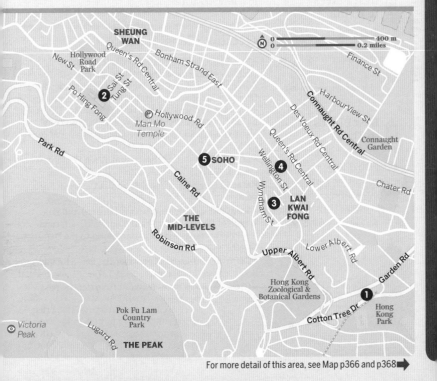

For more detail of this area, see Map p366 and p368 ➡

Lonely Planet's Top Tip

Besides partying in Lan Kwai Fong and Soho, don't miss the neighbourhood around Tai Ping Shan St in Sheung Wan. The area is a burgeoning boho haven, with cafes, galleries and boutiques – all quite low-key and tasteful – mushrooming alongside weather-beaten shrines.

 Best Places to Eat

→ Luk Yu Tea House (p93)

→ Chairman (p99)

→ Ser Wong Fun (p93)

→ Boss (p95)

For reviews, see p92 ➡

Best Places to Drink

→ Club 71 (p99)

→ Stockton (p99)

→ Angel's Share Whisky Bar (p99)

For reviews, see p99 ➡

Best Places to Shop

→ Grotto Fine Art (p103)

→ Hulu 10 (p103)

→ Gallery of the Pottery Workshop (p106)

→ Lam Gallery (p103)

For reviews, see p103 ➡

Explore: The Peak & the Northwest

Begin by exploring Sheung Wan's old neighbourhoods in the morning when the temples and the dried seafood stores get into full swing. Sample some local fare in the area before heading to Hollywood Rd to browse the antique shops and art galleries. If time allows, trek up to the Mid-Levels to check out the museums and religious monuments. Take the Peak Tram in Central to Victoria Peak; wait to see the lights come on in the city. Descend and return to Sheung Wan for dinner, followed by pub crawling in Lan Kwai Fong and Soho.

Local Life

→**Hang-outs** For intellectual banter and a bohemian vibe, head to Club 71 (p99), the haunt of activist-artist types.

→**Shopping** Li Yuen St East and West, two alleys that link Des Voeux Rd Central with Queen's Rd Central, have a jumble of inexpensive clothing, handbags and jewellery.

→**Old Chinese Quarter** The area around Tai Ping Shan St is where the old Chinese quarter used to be in the 19th century; you'll see temples and shops specialising in funeral-related services.

Getting There & Away

→**Bus** Lan Kwai Fong and Soho: bus 26 along Hollywood Rd links Sheung Wan with Central, Admiralty and Wan Chai. Western District: bus 3B from Jardine House in Central, and buses 23, 40 and 40M from Admiralty stop along Bonham Rd. The Peak: bus 15 from the terminus below Exchange Sq runs along Queen's Rd East and terminates below the Peak Galleria.

→**MTR** Central station (Island and Tsuen Wan lines); Sheung Wan station (Island line).

→**Macau Ferry** Terminal at Shun Tak Centre in Sheung Wan.

→**Tram** Runs along Des Voeux Rd Central and Des Voeux Rd West (Sheung Wan). The Peak Tram runs from the lower terminus on Garden Rd to the Peak Tower.

→**Central–Mid-Levels Escalator** For Caine Rd and Robinson Rd (Mid-Levels).

→**Green Minibus** Buses 8 and 22 from Central pass Caine Rd (Mid-Levels).

TOP SIGHT
VICTORIA PEAK

Standing at 552m, Victoria Peak is the highest point on Hong Kong Island. The Peak is also one of the most visited spots by tourists in Hong Kong, and it's not hard to see why. Sweeping views of the vibrant metropolis, verdant woods, easy but spectacular walks – all reachable in just eight minutes from Central by Hong Kong's earliest form of transport.

The best way to reach the Peak is by the 125-year-old gravity-defying **Peak Tram** (Map p362; ☎2522 0922; www.thepeak.com.hk; Lower Terminus, 33 Garden Rd, Central; one-way/return adult HK$28/40, seniors over 65yr & child 3-11yr HK$11/18; ⊙7am-midnight). Rising almost vertically above the high-rises nearby, Asia's oldest funicular clanks its way up the hillside to finish at the **Peak Tower** (凌霄閣; ☎2849 0668; 128 Peak Rd; ⊙10am-11pm Mon-Fri, 8am-11pm Sat, Sun & public holidays; 🚋Peak Tram). The lower terminus in Central has an interesting gallery that houses a replica of the earliest carriage. The **Peak Galleria** (山頂廣場; 118 Peak Rd; 🚌15, alight at the stop btwn Stubbs Rd & Peak Rd), adjoining the anvil-shaped Peak Tower, has an admission-free viewing deck.

Some 500m to the northwest of the upper terminus, up steep Mt Austin Rd, is the site of the old governor's summer lodge, which was burned to the ground by Japanese soldiers during WWII. The beautiful **gardens** remain, however, and have been refurbished with faux-Victorian gazebos and stone pillars. They are open to the public.

The dappled **Morning Trail**, a 3.5km circuit formed by Harlech Rd on the south, just outside the Peak Lookout (p94), and Lugard Rd on the northern slope which it runs into, takes about 45 minutes to cover. A further 2km along Peak Rd will lead you to Pok Fu Lam Reservoir Rd. Hatton Rd, reachable by Lugard or Harlech Rds, on the western slope goes all the way down to the University of Hong Kong. The 50km Hong Kong Trail also starts on the Peak.

DON'T MISS

➡ Peak Tram
➡ Peak Trails
➡ Victoria Peak Garden

PRACTICALITIES

➡ 太平山頂
➡ ☎2522 0922
➡ www.thepeak.com.hk
➡ admission free
➡ ⊙24hr
➡ 🚌15 from Central, below Exchange Sq, 🚋Peak Tram Lower Terminus

TOP SIGHT
MAN MO TEMPLE

One of Hong Kong's oldest temples, atmospheric Man Mo Temple is dedicated to the god of literature ('Man'), who's always holding a writing brush, and the god of war ('Mo'), who wields a sword. Built in 1847 during the Qing dynasty by wealthy Chinese merchants, it was, besides a place of worship, a court of arbitration for local disputes when trust was thin between the Chinese and the colonialists. Oaths taken at this Taoist temple (often accompanied by the ritual beheading of a rooster) were accepted by the colonial government.

Outside the main entrance are four **gilt plaques** on poles that used to be carried around at processions. Two describe the gods being worshipped inside, one requests silence and a show of respect within the temple's grounds, and the last warns menstruating women to keep out of the main hall. Inside the temple are two 19th-century sedan chairs with elaborate carvings, which used to carry the two gods during festivals.

Lending the temple its beguiling and smoky air are rows of large earth-coloured spirals suspended from the roof, like strange fungi in an upside-down garden. These are incense coils burned as offerings by worshippers.

Off to the side is **Lit Shing Kung**, the 'saints' palace', a place of worship for other Buddhist and Taoist deities. Another hall, **Kung Sor** ('Public Meeting Place'), used to serve as a court of justice to settle disputes among the Chinese community before the modern judicial system was introduced. A couplet at the entrance urges those entering to leave their selfish interests and prejudices outside. **Fortune-tellers** beckon from inside.

DON'T MISS

➡ The main temple
➡ Lit Shing Kung
➡ Fortune-tellers

PRACTICALITIES

➡ 文武廟
➡ Map p366
➡ ☎2540 0350
➡ 124-126 Hollywood Rd, Sheung Wan
➡ admission free
➡ ⊘8am-6pm
➡ 🚌26

WIBOWO RUSLI / GETTY IMAGES ©

SIGHTS

⊙ Lan Kwai Fong & Soho

VICTORIA PEAK
PEAK
See p87.

★ LIANGYI MUSEUM
MUSEUM
Map p366 (兩依藏博物館; ☑2806 8280; www.liangyimuseum.com; 181-199 Hollywood Rd, Soho; admission HK$200; ⊙10am-6pm Tue-Sat; Ⓜ Central, exit D2) This private three-floor museum houses two exquisite collections – antique Chinese furniture from the Ming and Qing dynasties, and Chinese-inspired European vanities from the 19th and 20th centuries. The former is one of the world's best. The 400 pieces of precious *huanghuali* and *zitan* (wood) furniture are shown in rotating exhibitions that change every six months. The only way to visit is by contacting the museum at least a day in advance to join a small tour. Visitors can touch or sit on the pieces which are not separated by rope or glass. The vanities collection shows gem-studded clutches and toiletry cases in intricate Chinoiserie motifs popular in art nouveau and art deco.

★ PMQ
ARTS HUB
Map p366 (元創方; ☑2811 9098; www.pmq.org.hk; 35 Aberdeen St, S614, Block A, PMQ, Soho; ⊙9am-1pm & 2-5pm; 🚌26, Ⓜ Central, exit D2) This new arts hub occupies the modernist buildings and breezy courtyard of the old Police Married Quarters (c 1951). You'll see the usual suspects – design studios, cafes, galleries and a bookstore. The site's earliest incarnation was a temple built in 1843, which was subsequently replaced by Central School, where Nationalist leader Dr Sun Yatsen once studied. Remnants of the school remain. PMQ is bounded by Hollywood Rd (north), Staunton St (south), Aberdeen St (east) and Shing Wong St (west).

CENTRAL POLICE STATION
HISTORIC BUILDING
Map p366 (10 Hollywood Rd, Lan Kwai Fong; 🚌26, Ⓜ Central, exit D2) Built between 1841 and 1919, Hong Kong's oldest symbol of law and order is this now-disused police-magistracy-prison complex modeled after London's Old Bailey. The large compound is being redeveloped into an arts hub with cinema, museum and boutique shopping mall, due to open in 2015.

⊙ Sheung Wan

MAN MO TEMPLE
TEMPLE
See p88.

★ PAK SING ANCESTRAL HALL
TEMPLE
Map p368 (廣福祠, Kwong Fuk Ancestral Hall; 42 Tai Ping Shan St, Sheung Wan; ⊙8am-6pm; 🚌26) In the 19th century, many Chinese who left home in search of better horizons died overseas. As it was the wish of traditional Chinese to be buried in their hometowns, this temple was built in 1856 to store corpses awaiting burial in China, and to serve as a public ancestral hall for those who could not afford the financial costs of bone repatriation. Families of the latter have erected 3000 memorial tablets for their ancestors in a room behind the altar.

KWUN YUM TEMPLE
TEMPLE
Map p368 (觀音廟; 34 Tai Ping Shan St, Sheung Wan; ⊙9am-6pm; 🚌26) Built in 1840, Sheung Wan's oldest temple honours Kwun Yum, the goddess of mercy. It's a quaint-looking structure, with a magnificent and intricate brass carving just above the doorway. The temple has been renovated with funky structural additions – orange iron railings and a yellow awning printed with Buddhist swastika symbols.

PALACE OF MOON AND WATER KWUN YUM TEMPLE
TEMPLE
Map p368 (水月觀音堂; 7 Tai Ping Shan St, Sheung Wan; ⊙9am-6pm; 🚌26) Not to be confused with Kwun Yum Temple nearby, this dimly lit temple honours Kwun Yum of a Thousand Arms. Kwun Yum aka Guanyin is the goddess of compassion. According to legend, Buddha gave her a thousand arms so she could help everyone who needed it. For a small donation, you can give the small wooden windmill at the entrance a spin; it will presumably change your luck.

TAI SUI TEMPLE
TEMPLE
Map p368 (太歲廟; 9 Tai Ping Shan St, Sheung Wan; ⊙9am-6pm; 🚌26) A quirky temple featuring statuettes of deities governing the different Chinese zodiac animals (there are 12 altogether). For under HK$100 and four red packets (of any amount), they will help you burn incense and offer prayer to bless your animal, which will translate into blessings for you.

LEUNG CHUN WOON KEE   BURIAL GARMENTS

Map p366 (梁津焕記; 17 Square St, Sheung Wan; ⊙9am-5.30pm Mon-Sat; 🚌26) Leung Chun Woon Kee (1904) is one of the last remaining burial garment producers in Hong Kong. White, black, brown or blue are preferred colours for the clothing, never red. The Chinese believe only those who want revenge on the living depart in red. Sleeves cover the hands completely – exposed hands make beggars of one's descendants. The outfits also come without pockets to prevent the dead from taking money or luck from his family. Photos are not allowed in the shop.

CAT STREET   STREET

Map p366 (摩羅上街; Upper Lascar Row, Sheung Wan; ⊙9am-6pm; 🚌26) Just north of (and parallel to) Hollywood Rd is Upper Lascar Row, aka 'Cat Street', a pedestrian-only lane lined with antique and curio shops and stalls selling found objects, cheap jewellery and newly minted ancient coins. It's a fun place to trawl through for a trinket or two, but expect most of the memorabilia to be mass-produced fakes.

POSSESSION STREET   STREET

Map p368 (Possession St, Sheung Wan; 🚌26) Just before Hollywood Rd meets Queen's Rd West is Possession St, where Commodore Gordon Bremmer and a contingent of British marines planted the Union Jack flag on 26 January 1841 and claimed Hong Kong Island for the Crown (though no plaque marks this birthplace of colonial Hong Kong).

QUEEN'S ROAD WEST
INCENSE SHOPS   PAPER OFFERINGS

Map p368 (Queen's Rd W, Sheung Wan; ⊙8am-7pm; 🚌26) At 136–150 Queen's Rd West, there are shops selling incense and paper offerings for the dead. The latter is burned to propitiate departed souls and the choice of combustibles is mindblowing: dim sum, iPads, Rolexes, Viagra tablets, and – the latest – solar-powered water heaters. You may buy them as souvenirs, but remember that keeping these offerings meant for the dead (rather than burning them) is supposed to bring bad luck.

WESTERN MARKET   HISTORIC BUILDING, MALL

Map p368 (西港城; ☎6029 2675; www.western-market.com.hk; 323 Des Voeux Rd Central & New Market St, Sheung Wan; ⊙9am-7pm; 🚇Sheung Wan, exit B) Textile vendors driven off nearby streets in the 1990s moved into this renovated market building (1906) with its red-and-white facade, four-corner towers and other Edwardian features. Now bolts of cloth flank the corridors of the 1st floor. Souvenir shops and restaurant Grand Stage (p95) occupy the ground and top floors.

MAN WA LANE   STREET

Map p368 (文華里; Man Wa Lane, Sheung Wan; ⊙10am-6pm; 🚇Sheung Wan, exit A1) Kiosks in this alley just east of the Sheung Wan MTR station specialise in name *chops* – a stone (or wood or jade) seal with the owner's name carved in Chinese on its base. It's combined with Chinese red ink or cinnabar paste to make a seal imprint that can be used in lieu of a handwritten signature. Tell the shop owner your name and he will create an auspicious Chinese version for you.

⊙ Western District

SAI YING PUN
COMMUNITY COMPLEX   HISTORIC BUILDING

(西營盤社區綜合大樓; ☎2540 2812; 2 High St, Western District; ⊙9am-5.30pm; 🚌12M, 13, 14M) A high-rise imposed on Victorian remains constitute this complex that's fondly nicknamed the High Street Haunted House. The grey stone facade and arched verandah, both heritage structures (c 1892), were part of a nurses' dormitory, then a mental asylum and an execution hall during the Japanese Occupation. Rumours of men bursting into flames, women wailing and decapitated spirits spread in the 20 years the building was abandoned. Fires subsequently swallowed everything, except what you see today.

WESTERN DISTRICT
COMMUNITY CENTRE   HISTORIC BUILDING

(西區社區中心; ☎2119 5001; 36A Western St, Western District; ⊙9am-10.30pm; 🚌37A, 90B) NGO offices and amenity rooms occupy this red-brick Georgian house at the junction of Western and Third Sts. The listed building was opened in 1922 as the Tsan Yuk Maternity Hospital to offer obstetrics and gynaecological services and to train midwives for the British colony.

UNIVERSITY OF HONG KONG   UNIVERSITY

(香港大學; ☎2859 2111; www.hku.hk; Pok Fu Lam Rd, Pok Fu Lam; 🚌23, 40 from Admiralty) Established in 1911, HKU is the oldest university in Hong Kong. The **Main Building**,

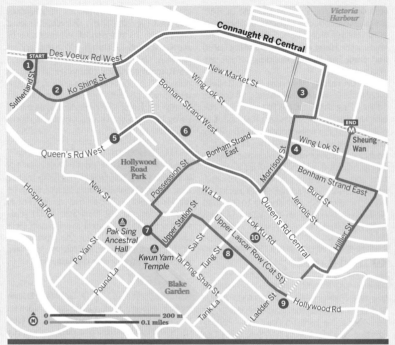

Neighbourhood Walk
Hong Kong's Wholesale District

START SUTHERLAND ST STOP OF
KENNEDY TOWN TRAM
END SHEUNG WAN MTR STATION, EXIT B
LENGTH 1.9KM, ONE HOUR

Set off from the Sutherland St stop of the
Kennedy Town tram. Have a look at (and a
sniff of) Des Voeux Rd West's many
① dried seafood shops piled with all
manner of desiccated sea life. Walk south
on Sutherland St to Ko Shing St, to browse
the medieval-sounding goods on offer from
the **② herbal-medicine traders**.

At the end of Ko Shing St, re-enter Des
Voeux Rd West and head northeast. Continue along Connaught Rd West, where you'll
find the attractive colonial building that
houses the **③ Western Market** (p90).

At the corner of Morrison St, walk south
past Wing Lok St and Bonham Strand, which
are both lined with **④ shops selling
ginseng root and edible birds' nests**.
Then turn right onto Queen's Rd Central
and progress to Queen's Rd West to the

⑤ incense shops (p90) selling paper
funeral offerings for the dead.

Retrace your steps, and if you're hungry,
stop for a quick Chiu Chow meal at **⑥ Chan
Kan Kee** (p98). Climb up Possession St,
then take a left into Hollywood Rd, before
turning right to ascend Pound Lane to
where it meets Tai Ping Shan St. Here you'll
see four charming **⑦ temples** (p89).

Head southeast down Tai Ping Shan St,
then left to descend Upper Station St to the
start of Hollywood Rd's **⑧ antique shops**.
There's a vast choice of curios and rare,
mostly Chinese, treasures.

Continue east on Hollywood Rd to
⑨ Man Mo Temple (p88), one of the oldest
and most significant temples in the territory.

Take a short hop to the left down Ladder St to Upper Lascar Row, home of the
⑩ Cat Street Market (p90), which is well
stocked with inexpensive Chinese memorabilia. Ladder St brings you back to Queen's
Rd Central. Cross the road and follow Hillier
St to Bonham Strand. Sheung Wan MTR
station is due north.

completed in the Edwardian style in 1912, is a declared monument. Several other early 20th-century buildings on the campus, including the **Hung Hing Ying Building** (1919) and **Tang Chi Ngong Building** (1929), are also protected.

The **University Museum & Art Gallery** (☑2241 5500; www.hku.hk/hkumag; 94 Bonham Rd, Fung Ping Shan Bldg, Pok Fu Lam; ⊙9.30am-6pm Mon-Sat, 1-6pm Sun; ☑23, 40M) **FREE** is to the left of the university's Main Building and opposite the start of Hing Hon Rd. It houses collections of ceramics and bronzes spanning 5000 years, including exquisite blue and white Ming porcelain; decorative mirrors from the Warring States period to the Qing dynasty; and almost 1000 small Nestorian crosses from the Yuan dynasty, the largest such collection in the world.

◉ Mid-Levels

DR SUN YAT-SEN MUSEUM   MUSEUM
Map p366 (孫中山紀念館; ☑2367 6373; http://hk.drsunyatsen.museum; 7 Castle Rd, Mid-Levels; adult/concession HK$10/5, Wed free; ⊙10am-6pm Mon-Wed & Fri, to 7pm Sat & Sun; ☑3B) The museum, dedicated to the father of modern China, is housed in an Edwardian-style building, which is arguably more interesting than the solemn displays of archival materials. Built in 1914, the mansion belonged to Ho Kom-tong, a tycoon from a Eurasian family. It was converted into a Mormon church in 1960, and became a museum in 2006. If you're taking the bus, alight at the Hong Kong Baptist Church on Caine Rd.

HONG KONG MUSEUM OF
MEDICAL SCIENCES   MUSEUM
Map p368 (香港醫學博物館; ☑2549 5123; www.hkmms.org.hk; 2 Caine Lane, Mid-Levels; adult/concession HK$20/10; ⊙10am-5pm Tue-Sat, 1-5pm Sun; ☑3B) This small museum features medical accoutrements, including an old autopsy table and herbal medicine chests; a rundown of how Hong Kong coped with the 1894 bubonic plague; and exhibits comparing Chinese and Western medical approaches. Equally interesting is the building, a breezy Edwardian-style brick-and-tile structure (1905) fronted by bauhinia trees. From the Central–Mid-Levels Escalator exit on Caine Rd, walk west to Ladder St. Descend one flight of steps and turn left. If you take the bus, alight at the Ladder St bus stop on Caine Rd.

OHEL LEAH SYNAGOGUE   SYNAGOGUE
Map p368 (猶太教莉亞堂; ☑2589 2621; www.ohelleah.org; 70 Robinson Rd, Mid-Levels; ⊙ by appointment only 10.30am-7pm Mon-Thu, services 7am Mon-Fri, 6pm Mon-Thu; ☑3B, 23) This Moorish Romantic temple, completed in 1902, is named after Leah Gubbay Sassoon, the matriarch of a philanthropic Sephardic Jewish family. It's Hong Kong's earliest synagogue. Bring ID if you plan on visiting the sumptuous interior.

ROMAN CATHOLIC CATHEDRAL OF
THE IMMACULATE CONCEPTION   CHURCH
Map p368 (香港聖母無原罪主教座堂; ☑2522 8212; www.cathedral.catholic.org.hk; 16 Caine Rd, Mid-Levels; ⊙9.30am-5.30pm Mon-Fri, to 12.30pm Sat, mass 9.30am Sun; ☑23) This Gothic Revival cathedral was built in 1888 and financed largely by the Portuguese faithful from Macau. If taking the bus, alight at Caritas Centre on Caine Rd.

JAMIA MOSQUE   MOSQUE
Map p366 (些利街清真寺; ☑2523 7743; 30 Shelley St, Mid-Levels) Also called Lascar Mosque, Hong Kong's oldest mosque was erected in 1849. Non-Muslims can only admire the facade from the terrace out front. Jamia Mosque is accessible by the Central–Mid-Levels Escalator.

✕ EATING

Restaurants in Soho have a pre-clubbing vibe; the majority are midrange or above. Sheung Wan has more local flavour, and is known for Chinese places that keep their quality high but profiles low. Further west, a hip new dining scene is taking shape. Quality choices on the Peak are sparse, though eateries make smart use of the gorgeous views.

✕ Lan Kwai Fong & Soho

LIFE CAFE   VEGETARIAN, INTERNATIONAL $
Map p366 (☑2810 9777; www.lifecafe.com.hk; 10 Shelley St, Soho; meals HK$100; ⊙noon-10pm; ⊙☑☑; Ⓜ Central, exit D1) Next to the Central–Mid-Levels Escalator, Life is a vegetarian's dream, serving organic vegan salads, guilt-free desserts, and tasty dishes free of gluten, wheat, onion, garlic – you name it – over three floors stylishly decked out in reclaimed teak and recycled copper-domed lamps.

⭐**SER WONG FUN** CANTONESE $

Map p366 (蛇王芬飯店; ☎2543 1032; 30 Cochrane St, Soho; meals HK$70; ⏱11am-10.30pm; Ⓜ Central, exit D1) This snake-soup specialist whips up old Cantonese dishes that are as tantalising as its celebrated broth, and the packed tables attest to it. Many regulars come just for the homemade pork-liver sausage infused with rose wine – perfect over a bowl of immaculate white rice, on a red tablecloth. Booking advised.

MANA! FAST SLOW FOOD VEGAN $

Map p366 (☎2851 1611; www.mana.hk; 92 Wellington St, Soho; meals HK$100-200; ⏱10am-10pm; 🛜🍴; Ⓜ Central, exit D2) 🍃 A vegan and raw food haven that whips up smoothies, salads and desserts for the professional crowd. Flatbreads (available gluten-free) are baked in-shop by the cheerful staff then smothered with organic vegies and Mediterranean dips. Besides tasty, guilt-free food, Mana offers a hippy vibe that makes one forget its physical smallness and not-so-bohemian prices.

MOTORINO PIZZA $

Map p366 (☎2801 6881; www.motorinopizza. com; 14 Shelley St, Soho; meals HK$150-380; ⏱noon-midnight; 🛜🍴; Ⓜ Central, exit D2) The buzzing debut outpost of the famed NYC pizzeria puts out charcoal-kissed Neapolitan pies with a bubbly and flavourful crust that will give your jaws a delectable workout. Reservations accepted for lunch.

YAT LOK NOODLES $

Map p366 (一樂燒鵝; ☎2524 3882; 34-38 Stanley St, Soho; meals HK$45-90; ⏱7.30am-9pm Mon-Fri, 9am-5.30pm Sat & Sun; Ⓜ Central, exit D2) Be prepared to bump elbows with locals at this tiny joint known for its roast goose. Anthony Bourdain gushed over the bird. Foodies prefer it to fowls from pricey 'goose specialists'. Our favourite cut is the leg, over rice or slippery rice noodles. Order it unchopped and rip it – crispy skin, tender flesh and all!

VBEST TEA HOUSE CANTONESE $

Map p366 (緻好茶館; ☎3104 0890; www.vbest. com.hk; 17 Elgin St, Soho; lunch/dinner from HK$120/200; ⏱noon-3pm & 6-11pm Mon-Sat; 🍴; Ⓜ Central, exit D1) Tucked away on a steep street off Soho, this understated family-run restaurant serves MSG-free comfort food. The owners' children grew up on this, so you can't go too wrong. We recommend the homemade wontons and prawns with rice vermicelli. Vbest offers set lunch and set dinner for HK$80 and HK$100 respectively.

MAK'S NOODLE NOODLES, CANTONESE $

Map p366 (麥奀雲吞麵世家; ☎2854 3810; 77 Wellington St, Soho; noodles HK$32-48; ⏱11am-8pm; 🚇40M) At this legendary shop, noodles are made the traditional way with a bamboo pole and served perched on a spoon placed over the bowl so they won't go soggy. The beef brisket noodles are equally remarkable.

LAN FONG YUEN CAFE $

Map p366 (蘭芳園; ☎2854 0731, 2544 3895; 2 & 4A Gage St, Soho; meals from HK$60; cover charge HK$20; ⏱7am-6pm Mon-Sat; 🚇5B) The rickety facade hides an entire *cha chaan tang* (tea cafe). Lan Fong Yuen (1952) is believed to be the inventor of the 'panty-hose' milk tea. Over a thousand cups of the strong and silky brew are sold daily alongside pork-chop buns, tossed noodles and other hasty tasties. Watch staff work their magic while you wait for a table.

TAI CHEONG BAKERY BAKERY $

Map p366 (泰昌餅家; ☎8300 8301; 35 Lyndhurst Tce, Central; pastries from HK$8; ⏱7.30am-9pm Mon-Sat, 8.30am-9pm Sun; 🚇40M) Tai Cheong was best known for its lighter-than-air beignets (deep-fried dough rolled in sugar; *sa yung* in Cantonese) until former governor Chris Patten was photographed wolfing down its egg-custard tarts. Since then 'Fat Patten' egg tarts have hogged the limelight.

FLYING PAN AMERICAN $

Map p366 (☎2140 6333; www.the-flying-pan.com; 9 Old Bailey St, Soho; breakfast combos HK$86-120; ⏱24hr; 🍴; 🚇26) Fancy eggs Benedict, chocolate waffles, even a full English breakfast for dinner? No problem. Breakfast is served 24/7 in a 1950s-American-diner setting at the Flying Pan.

WANG FU NORTHERN CHINESE $

Map p366 (王府; ☎2121 8089; 65 Wellington St, Soho; meals HK$40; ⏱11am-3pm & 6-10pm Mon-Sat; 🚇40M) At this cosy eatery, you'll see visitors from the mainland demolishing plate after plate of dumplings. There are nine delicious varieties, as well as hearty noodles and Northern-style appetizers.

⭐**LUK YU TEA HOUSE** CANTONESE, DIM SUM $$

Map p366 (陸羽茶室; ☎2523 5464; 24-26 Stanley St, Lan Kwai Fong; meals HK$300; ⏱7am-10pm, dim sum to 5.30pm; ♿; Ⓜ Central, exit D2) This gorgeous teahouse (c 1933), known for its masterful cooking and Eastern art-deco decor, was the haunt of opera artists, writers and painters, who came to give recitals and discuss the national fate. Today some of the waiters who served the tousled glamourati will pour your tea in the same pleasantly irreverent manner.

Tea connoisseurs can order special teas served in a *guk dzung* (焗盅), a bowl with lid and saucer that better preserves the flavour of the infusion.

SOCIALITO
LATIN AMERICAN $$

Map p366 (⌨3167 7380; www.socialito.com.hk; 60 Wyndham St, Shop 2, ground fl, The Centrium, Lan Kwai Fong; taquería HK$150-300, restaurante HK$300-600; ☺taquería noon-midnight Mon & Tue, to 2am Wed-Thu, to 3am Fri & Sat, restaurant 6-11.30pm Mon-Sat; ☎; Ⓜ Central, exit D2) Beckoning with 1950s lights, Socialito's laidback *taquería* pays tribute to the taco stand with a tin roof and tasty tidbits. Behind a silver door is the *restaurante*, an opulent dining room worthy of old Mexico. Here in the half-light of chandeliers, gold surfaces flicker and carved wood stands guard as fashionable patrons tackle sumptuous lamb tamales and lobster tacos.

SUSHI KUU
JAPANESE $$

Map p366 (⌨2971 0180; 2-8 Wellington St, 1st fl, Wellington Pl, Lan Kwai Fong; lunch/dinner from HK$200/800; ☺noon-11pm Mon-Thu & Sun, noon-12.30am Fri & Sat; Ⓜ Central, exit D2) If you order the *omakase* ('I'll leave it to you') at this elegant sushi bar, the chef will lavish you with a multicourse meal prepared with the sweetest fruits of the sea available. Though not cheap at HK$1500 per person, it's excellent value for jet-fresh seafood of this quality. The lunch sets are also much raved about. Bookings essential.

PEAK LOOKOUT
INTERNATIONAL, ASIAN $$

(太平山餐廳; ⌨2849 1000; www.thepeaklookout.com.hk; 121 Peak Rd, the Peak; lunch/dinner from HK$250/350; ☺10.30am-11.30pm Mon-Thu, to 1am Fri, 8.30am-1am Sat, 8.30am-11.30pm Sun; ☐15, ☐Peak Tram) This 60-year-old colonial establishment, with seating in a glassed-in verandah and on an outside terrace, has more character than all the other Peak eateries combined. The food is excellent – especially the Indian and Western selections – as are the views.

BRICKHOUSE
MEXICAN $$

Map p366 (⌨2810 0560; www.brickhouse.com.hk; 20A D'Aguilar St, Lan Kwai Fong; meals HK$350; ☺6pm-midnight Mon-Wed, to 2am Thu-Sat; ☎; Ⓜ Central, exit D2) Glowing in an alley off D'Aguilar, Brickhouse draws hipsters and young expats with its funky atmosphere. Graffiti art is splattered over walls distressed to look raw, and the food, thoughtfully homemade from scratch, is served by friendly, tattooed waiters. It's no-reservations so take a few tequila shots at the bar while you wait for a table.

YUNG KEE RESTAURANT
CANTONESE $$

Map p366 (鏞記; ⌨2522 1624; 32-40 Wellington St, Lan Kwai Fong; lunch HK$150-400, dinner from HK$450; ☺11am-10.30pm; ♿; Ⓜ Central, exit D2) The roast goose here, made from fowls raised in the restaurant's own farm and roasted in coal-fired ovens, has been the talk of the town since 1942. Celebrities and well-to-dos are regulars at this well-illuminated and welcoming place, and its lunch dim sum is popular with the Central workforce.

CHOM CHOM
VIETNAMESE $$

Map p366 (⌨2810 0850; www.chomchom.hk; 58-60 Peel St, Soho; meals HK$250-500; ☺4pm-late Wed-Sun, from 6pm Mon & Tue; ☎; Ⓜ Central, exit D1) Lively Chom Chom re-creates Vietnamese street food with bold flavours and charcoal grill, which are best washed down with the craft beers on tap. The corner location makes for great people-watching – alfresco by a slope or indoors from a marble-topped bistro table. *Pho* fans take note: noodles are only served in a (refreshing) roll with beef and peppermint.

LUPA
ITALIAN $$

Map p366 (⌨2796 6500; www.diningconcepts.com.hk/lupa; 31 Queen's Rd Central, 3rd fl, LHT Tower, Central; lunch/dinner from HK$300/500; ☺noon-3pm & 6-11pm, La Terrazza 3-11.30pm Sun-Thu, to 1.30am Fri & Sat; Ⓜ Central, exit D2) A trattoria opened by celebrity chef Mario Batali, Lupa specialises in rustic New York–style Italian food that includes fried whitebait, pasta with rabbit ragu, and chewy pizzas. Despite word that Lupa doesn't measure up to Batali's outlets in New York, our only complaint was his orange Crocs. The pasta tasting menu includes four kinds of noodles and dessert for HK$568.

★ NUR
WESTERN $$$

Map p366 ([☎]2871 9993; www.nur.hk/restaurant; 1 Lyndhurst Tce, 3rd fl, Soho; set menu from HK$788; ⏰6pm-1am Mon-Sat; [M]Central, exit D2) NUR is known for delicious and healthy food that's presented like poetry. Headed by Chef Nurdin Topham, who spent time at Copenhagen's Noma, NUR forages local farms for organic produce and grows herbs on its terrace for two highly creative tasting menus. Ingredients are often slow-cooked then painstakingly paired with sauces to preserve and highlight their flavours.

★ BOSS
MODERN CANTONESE $$$

Map p366 (波士廳; [☎]2155 0552; www.theboss1.com; Basement, 58-62 Queen's Rd Central, Central; meals from HK$500; ⏰11.30am-midnight Mon-Sat, from 11am Sun; [☎]; [M]Central, exit D2) Awarded one Michelin star, the Boss is a perfectionist. Flawless service, austere modern decor and a meticulous kitchen point to high expectations being imposed. The old-school Cantonese dishes are impressive, notably the deep-fried chicken pieces with home-fermented shrimp paste, and the baked-crab casserole. Dim sum, made with first-rate ingredients, is available at lunch.

HARLAN GOLDSTEIN'S COMFORT
INTERNATIONAL $$$

Map p366 ([☎]2521 8638; 15-16 Lan Kwai Fong, 5th fl, Grand Progress Bldg; meals HK$500; ⏰noon-2pm & 6-11pm; [☎]; [M]Central, exit D2) This affordable addition to the empire of the Michelin-crowned chef has relaxing decor to match – brick wall panels, wooden tables, lots of windows. The menu is full of nods and namastes to Goldstein's roots in Lower East Side New York and culinary adventures worldwide. Curry and truffle mash are both comfort food, and why not, when they're this delicious?

✖ Sheung Wan, Western District & Mid-Levels

GRAND STAGE
CANTONESE $

Map p368 (大舞臺飯店; [☎]2815 2311; 323 Des Voeux Rd Central, 2nd fl, Western Market, Sheung Wan; lunch/dinner from HK$120/200; ⏰11.30am-3pm & 7pm-midnight; [♿]; [M]Sheung Wan, exit E2) This restaurant serves great-value dim sum at lunch in a grand-ish setting that hasn't quite forgotten its previous incarnation as a ballroom. Sitting atop the historical West-

DRUNK FOOD

On your left as you make your way down short Wo On Lane from D'Aguilar St, **Sharkie's** (鯊仔記; Map p366; [☎]2530 3232; 8-12 Wo On Lane, Lan Kwai Fong; snacks HK$5-25; ⏰11.30am-6am daily; [M]Central, exit D2) is a brightly lit stall selling Hong Kong–style snacks, such as curry fish balls and egg waffles, that are a cut above convenience store grub. Like the convenience stores in the neighbourhood, it's earned the reputation of being a 'cougar hot spot' because of its – presumably – young, hungry and male following.

ern Market (p90), the Grand Stage is also one of the few dining venues that occupies a heritage site yet manages not to be wallet-shatteringly expensive.

CAFE HUNAN
HUNAN $

(書湘門第; [☎]2803 7177; 420-424 Queen's Rd W, Koon Wah Bldg, Sheung Wan; lunch/dinner HK$50/180; ⏰11am-11pm; [M]Sheung Wan, exit A1) Honest prices, a neat environment and the culinary genius of 21-year-old Chef Huang have won Cafe Hunan a well-deserved mention in the Michelin guide. But even before this, discerning foodies had been raving about the earthy dishes prepared with spices from Hunan, a province known for its chillies and Chairman Mao.

SUN HING RESTAURANT
DIM SUM $

(新興食家; [☎]2816 0616; 8C Smithfield Rd, Kennedy Town, Western District; meals HK$50; ⏰3am-4pm; [🚌]101) Many a drunken Soho reveler have trudged westward after a long night seeking cheap dim sum, but to no avail. Then just before they pass out, there appears, vision-like – Sun Hing in all its scrumptious glory! They weep. True story, though some say tears are shed over the runny custard bun. Ask the HKU students sharing your table.

YUEN KEE DESSERT
DESSERTS, CANTONESE $

(源記甜品專家; [☎]2548 8687; 32 Centre St, Sai Ying Pun, Western District; meals from HK$25; ⏰noon-11.30pm; [🚌]101, 104) This old-timers' favourite has been whipping out its famous sweet mulberry mistletoe tea with lotus seeds and egg (桑寄蓮子雞蛋茶) since 1855. It pairs well with the eggy sponge cake.

. Man Mo Temple (p88)
Hanging incense coils wreath Man Mo Temple, dedicated to the gods of literature and war, in sandalwood smoke.

2. Ceramic figurines, Cat Street (p90)
Upper Lascar Row, aka Cat Street, is lined with antique shops and stalls..

3. Victoria Peak (p87)
Viewing decks on the Peak, the island's highest point, offer sweeping views over Hong Kong.

4. D'Aguilar St, Lan Kwai Fong (p99)
Lan Kwai Fong is synonymous with partying in Hong Kong, with all-night street parties and plenty of bars and pubs to crawl between.

CHAN KAN KEE
CHIU CHOW $

Map p368 (陳勤記鹵鵝飯店; ☑2858 0033; 11 Queen's Rd W, Sheung Wan; meals HK$50; ☺11am-10pm; 🚇5) For an authentic Chiu Chow treat, this family-run eatery does hearty marinated goose, baby oyster omelette and duck soup. It's jam-packed during lunch hours. Chiu Chow is a city in the northeastern part of Guǎngdōng province, but its cooking is so refined and distinctive that it's often mentioned separately from Cantonese cuisine.

KAU KEE RESTAURANT
NOODLES $

Map p366 (九記牛腩; ☑2850 5967; 21 Gough St, Sheung Wan; meals from HK$40; ☺12.30-7.15pm & 8.30-11.30pm Mon-Sat; Ⓜ Sheung Wan, exit E2) You can argue till the noodles go soggy about whether Kau Kee has the best beef brisket in town. Whatever the verdict, the meat – served with noodles in a beefy broth – is hard to beat. During the 90 years of the shop's existence, film stars and politicians have joined the queue for a table.

KWUN KEE RESTAURANT
CANTONESE $

(坤記煲仔小菜; ☑2803 7209; Wo Yick Mansion, 263 Queen's Rd W, Sai Ying Pun, Western District; meals from HK$80; ☺11am-2.30pm & 6-11pm Mon-Sat, 6-11pm Sun; 🚇101) Hong Kong's top brass make pilgrimages to this local place for its claypot rice (HK$40 to HK$60, available only at dinner) – a meal-in-one in which rice and toppings such as chicken are cooked in claypots over charcoal stoves until the grains are infused with the juices of the meat and a layer of crackle is formed at the bottom of the pot.

★ TIM'S KITCHEN
CANTONESE $$

Map p368 (桃花源; ☑2543 5919; 84-90 Bonham Strand, Sheung Wan; lunch HK$130-500, dinner HK$300-1300; ☺11.30am-3pm & 6-11pm; 🚹; Ⓜ Sheung Wan, exit A2) This restaurant is considered one of Hong Kong's best – as evidenced by the Michelin honour and the praises lavished by local gourmands. It serves masterfully executed Cantonese fare over two clean, modern and well-illuminated floors. Signature dishes such as the crab claw poached with wintermelon (HK$250) require preordering. Reservations essential.

ON LOT 10
FRENCH $$

Map p366 (☑2155 9210; 34 Gough St, Sheung Wan; lunch/dinner from HK$140/500; ☺noon-2.30pm & 6.30-10pm Mon-Sat, 6.30-10pm Sun; 🚇26, Ⓜ Sheung Wan, exit E2) At On Lot 10, rustic French dishes are prepared with passion

by chef-owner David Lai, who helmed Alain Ducasse restaurants in Monaco and Hong Kong. The menu changes regularly.

MAN MO CAFÉ
FUSION DIM SUM $$

Map p366 (☑2644 5644; 40 Upper Lascar Row, Sheung Wan; meals HK$300-500; ☺noon-2.30pm & 6-10.30pm Tue-Sun; 🛜🚹; Ⓜ Central, exit D2) At this welcoming place, chefs from culinary giants in Taiwan (Din Tai Fung) and France (Robuchon) team up to create high-end fusion dim sum. Forget sweet-and-sour sauce. Silky wontons swim in a rich bouillabaisse, Nutella oozes seductively from sesame-speckled balls, and ratatouille is a decent dumpling. Portions are dainty, but well, this is hardly Panda Express.

YARDBIRD
JAPANESE $$

Map p366 (☑2547 9273; www.yardbirdrestaurant.com; 33-35 Bridges St, Sheung Wan; meals HK$300; ☺6pm-11.45pm Mon-Sat; 🚇26) Yardbird is a hipster's ode to the chicken. Every part of the cluck-cluck, from thigh to gizzard, is seasoned, impaled with a stick, then grilled, *yakitori* style. The resulting skewers are flavourful with just the right consistency. The highly popular eatery doesn't take reservations, so sample the sakes at the convivial bar area while you wait for a table.

LITTLE BAO
ASIAN FUSION $$

Map p366 (☑2194 0202; www.little-bao.com; 66 Staunton St, Sheung Wan; meals HK$200-500; ☺6-11pm Mon-Sat; Ⓜ Central, exit D2) A trendy diner that wows with its *bao* (Chinese buns; snow-white orbs crammed with juicy meat and slathered with a palette of Asian condiments). The signature pork-belly *bao* comes with hoisin ketchup, sesame dressing, and a leek and shiso salad. If spot-on flavours and full-on sauces appeal, go early – it doesn't take reservations.

BISTRONOMIQUE
FRENCH $$

(☑2818 8266; 1B Davis St, ground fl, Kennedy Town, Western District; lunch/dinner from HK$150/400; ☺noon-2.30pm & 6-10pm Tue-Sun, 6-10pm Mon; 🚇5B, 5X from Central) Owned by David Lai of On Lot 10, high-ceilinged Bistronomique fulfils the market's need for affordable yet expertly made French food. The menu is decidedly rustic and features bone marrow, frog legs and pig's ears alongside more commonplace ingredients – all cooked in a homey Gallic kind of way. The set lunches are incredibly good value.

★**CHAIRMAN** CANTONESE **$$$**

Map p366 (大班樓; ☑2555 2202; www.the-chairmangroup.com; 18 Kau U Fong, Sheung Wan; lunch/dinner from HK$200/560; ⊘noon-3pm & 6-11pm; 🕾; Ⓜ Sheung Wan, exit E2) Understated faux-retro decor and warm service impart a homely feel at this upmarket place serving Cantonese classics with a healthy twist. Ingredients are sourced locally; cured meat and pickles are made at Chairman's own farm. The website even has a manifesto! No surprise, almost all the dishes hit all the right notes, from flavour to presentation. Reservation absolutely essential.

UPPER MODERN BISTRO MODERN FRENCH **$$$**

Map p368 (☑2517 0977; www.upper-bistro.com; 6-14 Upper Station St, Sheung Wan; lunch HK$180-450, dinner from HK$850; ⊘noon-10.30pm Mon-Sat; Ⓜ Central, exit D2) Bland menu descriptions belie the complexity of flavours and clever Asian touches of the cooking here. Likewise, the 'bistro' label falls short of the chic interiors that include a ceiling overlaid with petal-like 'eggs'. Michelin-starred Philippe Orrico's latest take on French cuisine is full of surprises.

🍷 DRINKING & 🍸 NIGHTLIFE

Expect all-night street parties in Lan Kwai Fong, and occasionally in Soho. Hong Kong Pub Crawl (www.hongkongpubcrawl.com) organises an event every Thursday night (ticket HK$100) that lets you experience Hong Kong's nightlife and meet new friends.

🍷 Lan Kwai Fong & Soho

★**STOCKTON** COCKTAIL BAR

Map p366 (☑2565 5268; www.stockton.com.hk; 32 Wyndham St, Lan Kwai Fong; ⊘6pm-late Mon-Sat; Ⓜ Central, exit D2) Stockton evokes the ambience of a private club in Victorian London with Chesterfield sofas, dark-wood panelling and the odd candelabra. These are cleverly arranged to form intimate corners that are best for sipping rum- and whisky-based cocktails with a date. Make a reservation if you're coming after 9pm on a weekend.

From the big iron gate diagonally across the road from the Fringe Club, walk three steps west and turn left into an alley. Go to the back and up the stairs to Stockton.

★**ANGEL'S SHARE WHISKY BAR** BAR

Map p366 (☑2805 8388; www.angelsshare.hk; 23 Hollywood Rd, 2nd fl, Amber Lodge, Lan Kwai Fong; ⊘3pm-2am Mon-Thu, to 3am Fri & Sat; Ⓜ Central, exit D1) One of Hong Kong's best whisky bars, this clubby place has over 100 whiskies from the world over – predominantly Irish, but also French, Japanese and English. One of these, a 23-year-old Macallan, comes straight out of a large 180L oak barrel placed in the centre of the room. If you're hungry, there's a selection of whisky-inspired dishes.

★**CLUB 71** BAR

Map p366 (67 Hollywood Rd, Basement, Soho; ⊘3pm-2am Mon-Sat, 6pm-1am Sun, happy hour 3-9pm; 🚌26, Ⓜ Central, exit D1) This friendly bar with a bohemian vibe is named after a

---

THE PERFECT BREW

Atmospheric cafes have been sprouting in Sheung Wan, thanks to Central's soaring rentals which have driven small businesses westward.

Teakha (茶・家; Map p368; ☑2858 9185; www.teakha.com; 18 Tai Ping Shan St, Shop B, Sheung Wan; ⊘11am-7pm Tue-Sun; 🕾; 🚌26) Fancy organic tea concoctions are best enjoyed with the homemade scones in this oasis just off the main street. The cute teaware also makes good souvenirs.

Cafe Loisl (Map p368; ☑9179 0209; www.cafeloisl.com; Tai On Tce, Sheung Wan; ⊘8am-7pm Tue-Sun; 🕾; 🚌26) A tribute to a Viennese coffee house, this attractive little spot has a laid-back vibe and a serene terrace where you can relax over a foamy Weiner Melange.

Barista Jam (Map p368; ☑2854 2211; www.baristajam.com.hk; 126-128 Jervois St, Shop D, ground fl, Sheung Wan; ⊘8am-6pm Tue-Fri, from 10am Mon & Sat; 🕾; Ⓜ Sheung Wan, exit A2) Connoisseurs should make the pilgrimage to this grey-walled institution that also sells coffee beans and professional coffee-making equipment.

LOCAL KNOWLEDGE

'SECRET' PUBLIC GARDEN

If you want a change of air during your pub crawl, come to the amphitheatre at the end of Wo On Lane in Lan Kwai Fong. An open secret of sorts, it's the hang out of young expats who buy smokes and drinks from convenience stores nearby and come to play charades or shoot the breeze. The official name is **Lok Hing Lane Park** (Map p366; Wo On Lane, Lan Kwai Fong; MCentral, exit D2).

protest march on 1 July 2003. It's a favourite haunt of local artists and activists who come for the beer and music jamming sessions. In the garden out front, revolutionaries plotted to overthrow the Qing dynasty a hundred years ago. Enter from the alley next to 69 Hollywood.

BARSMITH COCKTAIL BAR
Map p366 (☑2613 2680; www.barsmith.com. hk; 60 Wellington St, 4th fl, Lan Kwai Fong; cover HK$200; ☺6pm-midnight Mon-Thu, to 2am Fri & Sat; MCentral, exit D2) A cosy Japanese bar run by the impeccably mannered Ayako, who kneels to speak to customers at eye level when taking orders. Her cocktails are fresh-tasting and inventive – 'Italian Bloody Mary' features real tomatoes and a drop of truffle oil. Ayako also does custom cocktails.

The entrance to the building's lift lobby is in an alley just off Wellington. Turn right when you see the large Evisu sign.

ROUNDHOUSE TAPROOM BAR
Map p366 (☑2366 4880; www.roundhouse.com. hk; 62 Peel St, Soho; ☺noon-11pm, happy hour noon-8pm; MCentral, exit D1) One of the best places in town for microbrews on tap – there are 24 from all over the world! Roundhouse is small and brightly lit. If you want more atmosphere, pick your brew from the iPad menu and savour it on the steps just outside the bar.

GLOBE PUB
Map p366 (☑2543 1941; www.theglobe.com.hk; 45-53 Graham St, Soho; ☺10am-2am, happy hour 9am-8pm; MCentral, exit D1) Besides an impressive list of 150 imported beers, including 13 on tap, the Globe serves T8, the first cask-conditioned ale brewed in Hong Kong.

Occupying an enviable 370 sq metres, the bar has a huge dining area with long wooden tables and comfortable banquettes.

FEATHER BOA COCKTAIL BAR
Map p366 (☑2857 2586; 38 Staunton St, Soho; ☺9pm-midnight Mon-Sat; ☐26) At the end of Staunton St in Soho, you'll see a shop with velvet drapes drawn over the door, and no signage. Feather Boa is a dimly lit, bordello-like chamber, with candles, gold-plated mirrors and faux-antique furniture. Its strawberry-chocolate daiquiris are popular with the predominantly European clientele. Bring ID.

PEAK CAFE BAR BAR
Map p366 (☑2140 6877; www.cafedecogroup. com; 9-13 Shelley St, Soho; ☺11am-2am Mon-Fri, 9am-2am Sat, 9am-midnight Sun, happy hour 5-8pm; ☐13, 26, 40M) This welcoming bar with great cocktails is decorated with charming fixtures and fittings of the old Peak Cafe, from 1947, which was replaced by the Peak Lookout. The cafe comprises two parts, both next to the Central–Mid-Levels Escalator, linked by a courtyard.

TAZMANIA BALLROOM CLUB
Map p366 (☑2801 5009; www.tazmaniaballroom. com; 33 Wyndham St, 1st fl, LKF Tower, Lan Kwai Fong; ☺5pm-late, happy hour 5-8pm; MCentral, exit D2) Skipped the gym? This sophisticated cavern whips out ping-pong tables every Tuesday, Thursday and Sunday night. The dress code, however, is casual glam, not Chinese national team. You can also shoot pool with bankers at a gold-plated table, join model types for verbal back-and-forth on the balcony, or groove to jazzy house music on the sleek dance floor.

TASTINGS WINE BAR
Map p366 (☑2523 6282; www.tastings.hk; 27 & 29 Wellington St, Basement, Yuen Yick Bldg, Lan Kwai Fong; ☺5pm-2am Mon-Sat; MCentral exit D2) This bar on a side street off Wellington offers 40 wines from 'enomatic' wine dispensers that pour by a few millilitres, a half-glass or a full glass. This allows you to taste rare varietals without bankrupting yourself. You create a tab by handing over your credit card in exchange for a smart card that you use to operate the machines.

KUNG LEE JUICE
Map p366 (公利真料竹蔗水; ☑2544 3571; 60 Hollywood Rd, Soho; juice from HK$11; ☺11am-

🏃 Neighbourhood Walk
Pub Crawl

START BIT POINT, LAN KWAI FONG
END CLUB 71, SOHO
LENGTH 800M, TAKING AS LONG AS YOU
CAN LAST!

Order a round of schnapps at ❶ **Bit Point** (p102) to kick things off. Then climb uphill to ❷ **Stockton** (p99) to explore the nooks of the clubby Victorian-style bar. Finish your cocktail and cross over to the ❸ **Tazmania Ballroom** (p100) for the most glamorous (and inebriated) game of ping pong in your life. Slam and spin as model types gape. Head back to the other side of the road to ❹ **Dragon-I** (p102) where Cantopop stars and more models await if you can get past the door police.

Stop for a glass of Prosecco at ❺ **Tivo** (p102), where you'll be mixing with a well-dressed crowd under red lampshades.

Ready for a change of air? Head east to the ❻ **Fringe Club** (p102) to check out the night's gig and hang out with artsy hipsters. If you're hungry, go down D'Aguilar St and make a left into Wo On Lane. Grab some snacks from ❼ **Sharkie's** (p95) then plant yourself at the relaxing ❽ **amphitheatre** (p100) for as long as you want.

Once recharged, walk up to ❾ **Peel Fresco** (p102) on Peel St for great jazz. Wrap up the night at ❿ **Senses 99** (p82) where a jamming session may still be on, or in friendly ⓫ **Club 71** (p99).

11pm; 26) This institution in the heart of Soho has been quietly selling herbal teas and fresh sugarcane juice since 1948. Their quality is unchanged, as are the charming vintage tiles, posters and signage.

BIT POINT
BAR

Map p366 (2523 7436; 31 D'Aguilar St, Lan Kwai Fong; 1pm-late Mon-Fri, 5pm-late Sat & Sun, happy hour 3-9pm; Central, exit D2) Smack in the thick of the LKF action, German-style Bit Point has a good selection of German beers on tap, including exclusive-to-Hong-Kong Bitburger, and a sausage platter to pleasantly stoke your thirst. The amicable Eurasian owner, Cindy, is happy to give you sightseeing recommendations.

DRAGON-I
BAR, CLUB

Map p366 (3110 1222; www.dragon-i.com.hk; 60 Wyndham St, upper ground fl, the Centrium, Lan Kwai Fong; noon-late, terrace happy hour 3-9pm Mon-Sat; 26, Central, exit D2) This fashionable venue has both an indoor bar and a terrace over Wyndham St filled with caged songbirds. Go after midnight and watch Ukrainian models and Cantopop stars sipping Krug and air kissing, as DJs fill the dance floor with hip hop, R&B and jazz. Go early or dress to kill if you want to be let in.

TIVO BAR
BAR

Map p366 (2116 8055; www.aqua.com.hk; 43-55 Wyndham St, Lan Kwai Fong; 6pm-midnight Sun-Thu, to late Fri & Sat; Central, exit D2) Sophisticated Tivo delights with open frontage, an exuberant crowd and *aperitivo*-type snacks. On the first and third Sunday of the month, lovely drag hostesses take over from 7pm and whip up the action for the Tivo Tea Dance.

CENTRAL WINE CLUB
WINE BAR

Map p366 (2147 3448; www.thecentralwineclub.com; 22-28 Wyndham St, 3rd fl, Sea Bird House, Lan Kwai Fong; 2pm-2am Mon-Fri, 4pm-2am Sat, happy hour 3-9pm; Central, exit D1) If you're serious about your tipple and don't mind over-the-top modern-baroque decor, CWC is a great place to sample fine old-world wines. The bar's iPad wine list features over 500 bottles, in addition to Cognac and whisky. Blues and jazz provide the soundtrack to your evening. Nonmembers are subject to a 15% service charge.

🍷 Sheung Wan & Western District

QUAY WEST
BAR

(2817 0198; www.quaywest.hk; 25 New Praya, Shop 5, ground fl, Ka Fu Bldg, Kennedy Town, Western District; 3pm-midnight, happy hour 3-9pm; 5, 5B, 10, 43X) Tucked away towards the end of Kennedy Town, this neighbourhood bar by the Praya commands views of the sunset and the harbour. The decor is simple and the vibe unpretentious.

DHARMA DEN
BAR

(5400 3327; 38-40 Davis St, Kennedy Town, Western District; 5pm-late, happy hour 5-9pm; 101) A cosy Tibetan-themed bar on a quiet street with a post-industrial feel, Dharma Den is decorated with multicoloured ribbons, sorcerer's masks and Buddhist sutras. Besides standard alcoholic beverages, it offers shisha and a Nepalese snack *du jour*.

☆ ENTERTAINMENT

★ PEEL FRESCO
JAZZ

Map p366 (2540 2046; www.peelfresco.com; 49 Peel St, Soho; 5pm-late Mon-Sat; 26, 13, 40M) Charming Peel Fresco has live jazz six nights a week, with local and overseas acts performing on a small but spectacular stage next to teetering faux-Renaissance paintings. The action starts around 9.30pm, but go at 9pm to secure a seat.

FRINGE CLUB
LIVE MUSIC, THEATRE

Map p366 (藝穗會; 2521 7251, theatre bookings 2521 9126; www.hkfringe.com.hk; 2 Lower Albert Rd, Lan Kwai Fong; noon-midnight Mon-Thu, to 3am Fri & Sat; Central, exits D1, D2 & G) The Fringe, housed in a Victorian building (c 1892) once part of a dairy farm, offers original music in the Dairy several nights a week – mostly jazz, rock and world music. The intimate theatres host eclectic local and international performances. The Fringe sits on the border of Lan Kwai Fong.

BACKSTAGE LIVE
LIVE MUSIC

Map p366 (2167 8985; www.backstagelive.hk; 52-54 Wellington St, 1st fl, Somptueux Central, Lan Kwai Fong; noon-late Mon-Fri, 7pm-late Sat; Central, exit D1) New indie, alternative and post-punk gigs from Hong Kong and overseas are played here four or more nights a week. Check out the program online.

TAKEOUT COMEDY CLUB   COMEDY

Map p366 ([☎]6220 4436; www.takeoutcomedy. com; 34 Elgin St, Basement, Soho; [🚇]26) In need of some LOL? Hong Kong's first full-time comedy club, founded by Chinese-American Jameson Gong, has stand-up and improv acts in English, Cantonese and Mandarin. It also hosts visiting comedians from overseas. See website for program.

CULTURE CLUB   LIVE MUSIC

Map p366 ([☎]2127 7936; www.cultureclub.com. hk; 15 Elgin St, Soho; [🕐]2.30-11.30pm; [🚇]26) Besides the tango *milongas* that take place here some Saturdays, this multipurpose venue is where amateur musicians hold their debut performances. It also features photography exhibition, and the occasional Chinese music performance such as the blindman *nányīn* (a vanishing genre of Cantonese music).

XXX   LIVE MUSIC

Map p368 ([☎]9156 2330; www.xxxgallery.hk; 212 Wing Lok St, Basement, Fui Nam Bldg, Sheung Wan; [Ⓜ]Sheung Wan, exit A2) Accessible from the door next to the main entrance of the building, this basement dive features bare concrete and indie music performances, and art exhibitions. Opening hours are irregular. Check the website for upcoming events.

LES BOULES CAFE PETANQUE   LIVE MUSIC

([☎]2872 0102; www.lesboules.hk; 18 Woo Sung St, Shek Tong Tsui, Western District; [🕐]4-11pm Tue-Sat; [🚇]1, 5B, 18, stop Hill Rd, Des Voeux Rd West, [Ⓜ]Sheung Wan, exit A1) This hidden bar and live-music venue has five lanes of sand for playing petanque in its spacious basement. Petanque is a metal-ball-throwing game that men play in the south of France. Non-players are entertained by live French gigs and performances by Hong Kong's veteran expatriate bands. If you're taking the bus get off at the stop on Hill Rd and Des Voeux Rd West.

🛍 SHOPPING

Gentrifying Hollywood Rd, which stretches from Central to Sheung Wan, is home to some of Hong Kong's best art galleries and antique shops, with a couple of fashion boutiques thrown in. Western Market (p90) is good for buying fabrics.

🏯 Lan Kwai Fong & Soho

⭐GROTTO FINE ART   GALLERY

Map p366 (嘉圖; [☎]2121 2270; www.grottofine-art.com; 2nd fl, 31C-D Wyndham St, Lan Kwai Fong; [🕐]11am-7pm Mon-Sat; [Ⓜ]Central, exit D2) This exquisite gallery, founded by a scholar in Hong Kong art, is one of very few that represents predominantly local artists. The small but excellent selection of works on display ranges from painting and sculpture to ceramics and mixed media. Prices are reasonable too.

⭐HULU 10   CLOTHING

Map p366 ([☎]2179 5500; www.hulu10.com; 10 Glenealy, Lan Kwai Fong; [🕐]10am-7pm Mon-Sat; [Ⓜ]Central, exit D1) This pleasant shop sells Chinese-style tunics, jackets, dresses and fashionably loose *qipao* as worn by educated women of the 1910s. Materials have a raw feel whether it's tie-dyed cotton, patterned wool or mud-treated silk. Going uphill from the five-way intersection on Wyndham St, the shop is on your right just before the public toilets.

⭐WATTIS FINE ART   ANTIQUES

Map p366 (www.wattis.com.hk; 20 Hollywood Rd, 2nd fl, Lan Kwai Fong; [🕐]10.30am-6pm Mon-Sat; [🚇]26) This upstairs gallery has an excellent collection of antique maps for sale. The selection of old photographs of Hong Kong and Macau is also impressive. Enter from Old Bailey St.

PEARL LAM GALLERIES   GALLERY

Map p366 ([☎]2522 1428; www.pearllam.com; 12 Pedder St, 601-605 Pedder Bldg, Central; [🕐]10am-7pm Mon-Sat; [Ⓜ]Central, exit H) This elegant space showcases mainland Chinese, Hong Kong and Asian contemporary art – mostly paintings and sculptures. The owner Pearl Lam has a good eye for talent. Lam has been a fervent promoter of Chinese contemporary art and design since the 1990s. She also has galleries in Shanghai and Singapore.

LAM GALLERY   ANTIQUES

Map p366 (松心閣; [☎]2554 4666; 44 Hollywood Rd, Lan Kwai Fong; [🕐]10.30am-6.30pm Mon-Fri, 11am-6pm Sat; [🚇]26, [Ⓜ]Central, exit D2) Arguably the best shop in the area for sculptures, this is the largest of several owned by the Lam family on Hollywood Rd. Sculpted pieces from the Neolithic period to the Qing dynasty predominate. Other products

DESIGNERS TO WATCH

The following are designers we love who do not have their own shops. If you like what you see on the websites, contact them about stockists or a visit to their showrooms.

Yi Ming (☑3111 2268; www.yi-ming.asia) Stunning modern cheongsam (aka *qipao*); wear them to cocktail parties or weddings (including your own).

Injury (www.theinjury.com.au) Moody, futuristic with a hint of Goth, Injury's men's and women's wear is well tailored or fashionably loose in monochrome with metallic accents.

Mischa (www.mischadesigns.com) Beautiful bags of all shapes and sizes, including clutches created from vintage Japanese kimonos.

include ceramics, bronze, paintings, gold and silverware. Lam is known by collectors and auction dealers worldwide, and offers restoration services.

MY GALLERY ANTIQUES
Map p366 (有明堂; ☑2850 4882; 61 Hollywood Rd, Lan Kwai Fong; ◷10am-6pm Mon-Sat; 🚇26, Ⓜ️Central, exit D2) My Gallery focuses on ceramics, paintings, jade and bronze from the Qing dynasty, the last dynasty before the establishment of the Republic era. Porcelain and paintings from this period are characterised by a bold use of colour and more fanciful designs than those from earlier times.

KOWLOON SOY COMPANY FOOD
Map p362 (九龍醬園; ☑2544 3695; www.kowloonsoy.com; 9 Graham St, Soho; ◷8am-6.15pm Mon-Fri, to 6pm Sat; Ⓜ️Central exit D1) *The* shop (c 1917) for artisanal soy sauce, premier cru Chinese miso, and other high-quality condiments; also sells preserved eggs (*pei darn*, 皮蛋) and pickled ginger (*suen geung*, 酸姜) which are often served together at restaurants. Did you know that preserved eggs, being alkaline, can make young red wines taste fuller-bodied? Just try it.

ANDY HEI CLASSICAL FURNITURE
Map p366 (研木得益; ☑3105 2002; www.andyhei.com; 84 Hollywood Rd, Lan Kwai Fong; ◷10am-12.30pm & 1.30-6pm Mon-Sat; 🚇26, Ⓜ️Central, exit D2) This world-class furniture dealer specialises in classical Chinese furniture from the Ming and Qing dynasties, and scholar's objects. It also restores rare *huanghuali* and *zitan* wood pieces. Hei is the founding chairman of **Fine Art Asia** (www.fineartasia.com), which showcases art and antiquities of Asian heritage.

JOHANNA HO CLOTHING
Map p366 (☑2722 6776; www.johannaho.com; 13 Wyndham St, Lan Kwai Fong; ◷11am-8pm; Ⓜ️Cen-

tral, exit D1) A graduate of Central St Martin's College of Art and Design, Johanna Ho specialises in ecofriendly, feminine-with-a-twist streetwear for women. Her forte is knitwear and these feature soft ruffles, biased cuts and vivid colours. Ho recently launched a men's line.

FLOW BOOKS
Map p366 (☑9278 5664, 2964 9483; www.flowbooks.net; 38 Hollywood Rd, 7th fl, 1A Wing On Bldg, Lan Kwai Fong; ◷noon-7pm; 🚇26) A sprawling jumble of secondhand English titles covers almost every inch of Flow. You'll need some patience to find whatever you're seeking; alternatively, let the friendly owner Lam Sum guide you to the right shelf.

FANG FONG PROJECTS CLOTHING
Map p366 (69 Peel St, Lan Kwai Fong; ◷11am-8pm Sun-Thu, noon-9pm Fri & Sat; 🚇26) Wu Lai-fan's very wearable dresses are a clever mix of vintage fabric and modern 1980s silhouettes.

L'S FINE ARTS ANTIQUES
Map p368 (松心閣; ☑2540 5569, 6606 1818; 233 Hollywood Rd, Room G8, Hollywood Centre, Sheung Wan; ◷noon-6pm Mon-Sat; 🚇26, Ⓜ️Central, exit D2) L's is littered with curios, including early Chinese ceramics and Tang dynasty figurines. The reputable shop, located in the drab-looking Hollywood Centre, also sells consigned items for collectors worldwide.

HONEYCHURCH ANTIQUES ANTIQUES
Map p366 (☑2543 2433; www.honeychurch.com/hong_kong.html; 29 Hollywood Rd, Lan Kwai Fong; ◷9am-6.30pm Mon-Sat; 🚇26) This fine shop, run by an American couple for 30 years, specialises in antique Chinese furniture, jewellery and English silver. There's a wide range of stock, with items from the early Chinese dynasties right up to the 20th century.

LIANCA
LEATHER GOODS

Map p366 (☎2139 2989; www.liancacentral.com; 27 Staunton St, Basement, Soho; ⏰12.30-9pm; ☒26) An understated boutique offering good-quality shoes, solid handbags and small leather goods in classic, office-friendly designs. All items except a few imported accessories are crafted in Lianca's own workshop. Enter from Graham St.

9TH MUSE
JEWELLERY, ACCESSORIES

Map p366 (☎2537 7598; 1 Lyndhurst Tce, Unit 1204, One Lyndhurst Tower, Soho; ⏰10.30am-7.30pm; Ⓜ Central, exit D2) This secret treasure trove on the 12th floor attracts fashionistas with its electic selection of costume jewellery, handcrafted bags and vintage accessories. The good news is you don't have to break the bank to own them.

ARCH ANGEL ANTIQUES
ANTIQUES

Map p366 (☎2851 6848; 53-55 Hollywood Rd, Lan Kwai Fong; ⏰9.30am-6.30pm Mon-Sat, to 6pm Sun; ☒26) Though the specialities are ancient porcelain and tombware, Arch Angel packs a lot more into its three floors: it has everything from mah-jong sets and terracotta horses to palatial furniture.

10 CHANCERY LANE GALLERY
GALLERY

Map p366 (10 號贊善里畫廊; ☎2810 0065; www.10chancerylanegallery.com; 10 Chancery Lane, Soho; ⏰10am-6pm Tue-Sat; Ⓜ Central, exit D2) Located in Chancery Lane, this gallery focuses on thought-provoking works by promising Asian, mainland Chinese and Hong Kong artists. It also runs seminars and art walks.

L PLUS H
CLOTHING

Map p366 (☎2923 2288; www.lplush.com; 11 Stanley St, 17th fl, Soho; ⏰10am-7pm Mon-Sat; Ⓒ Central, exit D2) Founded by a group of socially driven entrepreneurs, L Plus H teams up with local designers to create a 100% 'Designed and Made in Hong Kong' label. Classic-looking, highly wearable knitwear is its forte.

LINVA TAILOR
CLOTHING, ACCESSORIES

Map p366 (年華時裝公司; ☎2544 2456; 38 Cochrane St, Soho; ⏰9.30am-6.30pm Mon-Sat; ☒26) Fancy a cheongsam (aka *qipao;* body-hugging Chinese dress)? Bring your own silk or choose from the selection here. If you're pushed for time, the bespoke tailors, Mr and Mrs Leung, are happy to mail the completed items to you.

KARIN WEBER GALLERY
ARTS & CRAFTS

Map p366 (☎2544 5004; www.karinwebergallery.com; 20 Aberdeen St, Soho; ⏰11am-7pm Tue-Sat, Sun by appointment only; ☒26) Karin Weber has an interesting mix of Chinese country antiques and contemporary Asian artwork. She is able to arrange antique-buying trips to Guǎngdōng for serious buyers.

PHOTO SCIENTIFIC
PHOTOGRAPHY

Map p366 (攝影科學; ☎2525 0550; 6 Stanley St, Lan Kwai Fong; ⏰10am-7pm Mon-Sat; Ⓜ Central, exit D2) This is the favourite shop of Hong Kong's professional photographers. You may find cheaper equipment elsewhere, but Photo Scientific has a rock-solid reputation with labelled prices, and zero leeway for bargaining.

LU LU CHEUNG
CLOTHING

Map p366 (☎2537 7515; www.lulucheung.com.hk; 50 Wellington St, Lan Kwai Fong; ⏰10.30am-8pm Sun-Thu, to 9pm Fri & Sat; Ⓜ Central, exit D2) Local designer Lu Lu Cheung makes sophisticated casual wear, work clothes and evening gowns for the urban woman. There's lots of cotton, silk and linen, in whites and earth tones.

CITY CHAIN
WATCHES

Map p366 (時間廊; ☎2537 6518; www.citychain.com; 44-46 Des Voeux Rd Central, ground fl, Yat Fat Bldg, Central; ⏰10am-8pm; Ⓜ Central, exit C1) With over 60 outlets in Hong Kong, City Chain has a wristwatch for almost every whim, look and occasion, ranging from the slightly dressy to the downright sporty. But look elsewhere if you're after diamond-studded timepieces.

GIORDANO LADIES
CLOTHING

Map p366 (☎2921 2955; www.giordanoladies.com; 43-45 Queen's Rd Central, ground fl & 1st fl, Lansing House, Central; ⏰11am-9pm Mon-Sat, to 8pm Sun; Ⓜ Central, exit D1) Giordano Ladies offers graceful clothing for women that feature lots of soft, flowing lines and a conservative palette. There is office attire, leisurewear and basic items, meant to mix and match well with most wardrobes.

🍴 Sheung Wan

⭐ **CHAN SHING KEE** CLASSICAL FURNITURE

Map p366 (陳勝記; ☎2543 1245; www.chanshingkee.com; 228-230 Queen's Rd Central, Sheung Wan; ⏰9am-6pm Mon-Sat; ☒101, 104) A shop with a three-storey showroom run by Daniel Chan, the third generation of a family that's been in the business for 70 years, Chan Shing Kee is known to collectors and museums worldwide for its fine classical Chinese furniture (16th to 18th century). Scholar's objects, such as ancient screens and wooden boxes, are also available.

★ GALLERY OF THE POTTERY WORKSHOP
ART, HOMEWARES

Map p368 (樂天陶社; ☑2525 7949, 9842 5889; www.potteryworkshop.com.cn; 24 Upper Station St, Sheung Wan; ◑1-6pm Tue-Sun; ☒26) This gallery showcases playful ceramic objects made by local ceramic artists and artisans from the mainland and overseas. The lovely pieces range from crockery to sculptures.

WING ON DEPARTMENT STORE
DEPARTMENT STORE

Map p368 (永安百貨; ☑2852 1888; www.wingonet.com; 211 Des Voeux Rd Central, Wing On Centre, Central; ◑10am-7.30pm; Ⓜ Sheung Wan, exit E3) The last truly one-stop-shop department store in Hong Kong. It's a little old-fashioned but you can find almost everything you need here, from garden hoses to iPhone covers, baby pacifiers and Italian leather jackets.

SIN SIN FINE ART
ART

Map p368 (☑2858 5072; www.sinsin.com.hk; 53-54 Sai St, Sheung Wan; ◑9.30am-6.30pm Mon-Sat; Ⓜ Sheung Wan, exit A2) This eclectic gallery owned by a fashion designer with a flair for ethnic designs shows good-quality Hong Kong, mainland Chinese and Southeast Asian art.

INDOSIAM
BOOKS, ANTIQUES

Map p366 (☑2854 2853; 89 Hollywood Rd, 1st fl; ◑1-7pm; ☒26) Hong Kong's first truly antiquarian bookshop deals in rare titles relating to Asian countries, with Thailand, China and the former French colonies being its areas of strength. Indosiam also sells vintage newspapers and old Chinese prints.

NGAI TILE WAVE
ANTIQUES

Map p368 (藝雅廊; ☑2517 2586; 172 Hollywood Rd, Sheung Wan; ◑11am-6pm Mon-Sat; ☒26, Ⓜ Central, exit D2) You can find Tang figurines, tricoloured ancient pottery, and porcelain from the Ming and Qing dynasties costing between HK$1000 and HK$100,000 in this shop. Older and more expensive artefacts are kept in a room upstairs. Tell the staff what you're looking for and they'll let you know if they have it.

LAM KIE YUEN TEA CO
TEA

Map p368 (林奇苑茶行; ☑2543 7154; www.lkytea.com; 105-107 Bonham Strand E, Sheung Wan; ◑9am-6.30pm Mon-Sat; Ⓜ Sheung Wan, exit A2) This shop, which has been around since 1955, is testament to just how much tea there is in China. From unfermented to fully fermented, and everything in between, there's simply too much to choose from.

CAPITAL GALLERY
ANTIQUES

Map p368 (長安美術; ☑2542 2271; 27E Tung St, Sheung Wan; ◑10am-6pm Mon-Sat, Sun by appointment; ☒26, Ⓜ Central, exit D2) Located on a slope between Upper Lascar Row and Hollywood Rd, this tiny shop is crammed with sculptures, ceramics and other curios dating from 4000 to 5000 years ago. Highlights include Silk Road pieces, such as minority textiles from northwest China, and jewellery.

🏃 SPORTS & ACTIVITIES

HAPPY FOOT REFLEXOLOGY CENTRE
SPA

Map p366 (知足樂; ☑2522 1151; www.happyfoot.hk; 1 D'Aguilar St, 19th & 20th fl, Century Sq, Lan Kwai Fong; ◑10am-midnight; Ⓜ Central, exit D2) Foot/body massage starts at HK$200/2500 for 50 minutes.

WAN KEI HO INTERNATIONAL MARTIAL ARTS ASSOCIATION
MARTIAL ARTS

Map p368 (尹圻灝國際武術總會; ☑2544 1368, 9506 0075; www.kungfuwan.com; 304 Des Voeux Rd Central, 3rd fl, Yue's House, Sheung Wan; ◑10am-8pm Mon-Fri, 9am-1pm Sat & Sun; Ⓜ Sheung Wan, exit A) English-speaking Master Wan teaches northern Shaolin Kung Fu to a wide following of locals and foreigners. Classes are offered in the evenings from Monday to Thursday. Depending on how many classes you take, the monthly fees may range from HK$300 to HK$1400.

FLAWLESS HONG KONG
SPA

Map p366 (☑2869 5868; www.flawless.hk.com; 22-28 Wyndham St, 4th fl, Sea Bird House, Lan Kwai Fong; ◑10am-10pm; Ⓜ Central, exit D1) This award-winning spa attracts a youngish clientele with its homey setting and vast array of no-nonsense treatments for the face (from HK$980) and nails (manicures from HK$140).

Hong Kong Island: Wan Chai & the Northeast

ADMIRALTY | WAN CHAI | CAUSEWAY BAY | HAPPY VALLEY | ISLAND EAST

Neighbourhood Top Five

1 Combing the rows of **narrow streets** (p113) sandwiched between Queen's Rd East and Johnston Rd for old houses, Taoist temples, traditional shops, open-air bazaars and screaming wet markets.

2 Feeling your adrenalin soar at the **Happy Valley Racecourse** (p114) on a Wednesday night, beer in hand.

3 Experiencing sublime taste in Admiralty: aesthetic at the **Asia Society Hong Kong Centre** (p110) and culinary at its resident restaurant, AMMO.

4 Shopping for Japanese and Korean fashions among the hordes of teeny-boppers in **Causeway Bay** (p127).

5 Having a night of debauchery on **Lockhart Road** (p124) in Wan Chai.

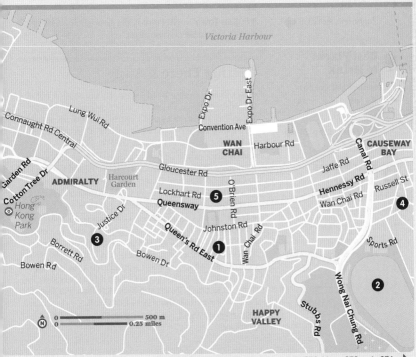

For more detail of this area, see Map p370, Map p372 and p374 ➡

Lonely Planet's Top Tip

Viewing the Island's east districts from a moving tram imparts a charming cinematic quality to your impressions, as these primarily residential areas can underwhelm on foot. Add speed to the uniformity of housing blocks and you get rhythm and pattern. The bonus is that you can hop off when something tickles your fancy. The district is served by some 30 stops on the eastbound tramline.

✖ Best Places to Eat

➜ Irori (p119)

➜ Tung Po Seafood Restaurant (p121)

➜ 22 Ships (p117)

➜ Megan's Kitchen (p117)

➜ AMMO (p116)

For reviews, see p116 ➡

🍷 Best Places to Drink

➜ Executive Bar (p125)

➜ Pawn (p124)

➜ Sugar (p126)

For reviews, see p124 ➡

🛍 Best Places to Shop

➜ Kapok (p127)

➜ Eslite (p127)

➜ Wan Chai Computer Centre (p127)

For reviews, see p127 ➡

Explore Wan Chai & the Northeast

Stroll through the Pacific Place mall connected to Admiralty MTR station and pay a leisurely 2½-hour visit to Hong Kong Park and the Asia Society Hong Kong Centre. Head downhill and over to Queen's Rd East nearby. Spend two hours exploring the 'old' Wan Chai area. Have some ethnic food; choices are plenty. Continue your journey to 'new' Wan Chai, closer to the harbour, to the Wan Chai Computer Centre or further north to the Hong Kong Convention & Exhibition Centre. Tram it to Causeway Bay, arriving after the lunch hour to avoid the crowds. Spend some time shopping or head east to Victoria Park to people-watch under a tree. Enjoy happy-hour drinks here or hop on an eastbound 'ding ding' and play it by ear.

Local Life

➜ **Lil' Jakarta** Indonesian maids gather at Victoria Park (p114) on Sundays to eat, sing and pray.

➜ **Toy shops** Gen-Xers bring their kids to the Tai Yuen St toy shops (p128) to relive childhood innocence, and buy lanterns during the Mid-Autumn Festival.

➜ **Hipsterville** The atmospheric area around Star, Moon and St Francis Sts is where hipsters and tastemakers hang out.

➜ **Fújiàn Town** North Point is the stronghold of Hong Kong's Fujianese community.

Getting There & Away

➜ **Bus** Buses operate from Admiralty bus station below Queensway Plaza. To get to Causeway Bay and Happy Valley from Admiralty and Central, buses 5, 5B and 26 stop along Yee Wo St. Green minibus 40 from Stanley calls along Tang Lung St and Yee Woo St.

➜ **MTR** Admiralty station is on the Island and Tsuen Wan lines. Wan Chai station is on the Island line. Get to Causeway Bay and Happy Valley from the Causeway Bay and Tin Hau stations on the Central line. Take the Island line from Causeway Bay to get to Island East.

➜ **Tram** Trams run east along Queensway, Johnston Rd and Hennessy Rd to Causeway Bay, and west to Central and Sheung Wan. To get to Causeway Bay and Happy Valley, trams run along Hennessy Rd and Yee Wo St to Central and Shau Kei Wan; along Percival St to Happy Valley; and along Wong Nai Chung Rd to Causeway Bay, Central, Kennedy Town and Shau Kei Wan. For Island East, trams run all the way to Chai Wan.

➜ **Star Ferry** Wan Chai ferry pier to Tsim Sha Tsui, Kowloon.

TOP SIGHT
HONG KONG PARK

Designed to look anything but natural, **Hong Kong Park** emphasises artificial creations such as its fountain plaza, conservatory, waterfall, playground, taichi garden and viewing tower. Yet the 8-hectare park is beautiful and, with a wall of skyscrapers on one side and mountains on the other, makes for dramatic photographs.

The best feature is the Edward Youde Aviary (p110). Home to more than 600 birds representing some 90 species, it's like a rainforest planted in the middle of the city. Visitors walk along a wooden bridge suspended some 10m above the ground and at eye level with tree branches. The **Forsgate Conservatory** (⊙9am-5pm) overlooking the park is the largest in Southeast Asia.

At the park's northernmost tip is Flagstaff House Museum of Tea Ware (p110). Built in 1846, it now houses a collection of antique Chinese tea ware. The ground-floor cafe is a great place to recharge over a pot of fine tea.

The **KS Lo Gallery** (羅桂祥茶藝館; ☑2869 0690; 10 Cotton Tree Dr; ⊙ 10am-5pm Wed-Mon) **FREE** contains rare Chinese ceramics and stone seals.

On the eastern edge of the park, the **Hong Kong Visual Arts Centre** (香港視覺藝術中心; ☑2521 3008; www.lcsd.gov. hk/ce/Museum/Apo/en/vac.html; 7A Kennedy Rd; ⊙10am-9pm Wed-Mon) **FREE**, housed in beautiful former Victoria Barracks, supports local artists and stages exhibitions.

DON'T MISS

➡ Edward Youde Aviary
➡ Flagstaff House Museum of Tea Ware
➡ KS Lo Gallery
➡ Hong Kong Visual Arts Centre

PRACTICALITIES

➡ 香港公園
➡ Map p370
➡ ☑2521 5041
➡ www.lcsd.gov.hk/parks/hkp/en/index.php
➡ 19 Cotton Tree Dr, Admiralty
➡ admission free
➡ ⊙park 6am-11pm
➡ 🚻
➡ Ⓜ Admiralty, exit C1

MANFRED GOTTSCHALK / GETTY IMAGES ©

SIGHTS

⊙ Admiralty

ASIA SOCIETY HONG KONG CENTRE
HISTORIC BUILDING, GALLERY

Map p370 (亞洲協會香港中心; Hong Kong Jockey Club Former Explosives Magazine; ☎2103 9511; www.asiasociety.org/hong-kong; 9 Justice Dr, Admiralty; ⊙gallery 11am-5pm Tue-Sun, to 8pm last Thu of month; MAdmiralty, exit F) An architectural feat, this magnificent site integrates 19th-century British military buildings, including a couple of explosives magazines, and transforms them into an exhibition gallery, a multipurpose theatre, an excellent restaurant and a bookstore, all open to the public. The architects Tod Williams and Billie Tsien eschewed bold statements for a subdued design that deferred to history and the natural shape of the land. The result is a horizontally oriented site that offers an uplifting contrast to the skyscrapers nearby. Experience it with a meal at AMMO (p 116).

HONG KONG PARK
PARK

See p 109.

EDWARD YOUDE AVIARY
AVIARY

Map p370 (尤德觀鳥園; Hong Kong Park; ⊙9am-5pm; MAdmiralty, exit C1) The best feature of Hong Kong Park is the delightful Edward Youde Aviary, named after a former Hong Kong governor (1982–86) and China scholar. Home to more than 600 birds representing some 90 different species, it's nothing like a conventional aviary and more like a bit of rainforest planted in the middle of the city. Visitors walk along a wooden bridge suspended some 10m above the ground and at eye level with tree branches, where most of the birds are to be found. The Forsgate Conservatory on the slope overlooking the park is the largest in Southeast Asia.

FLAGSTAFF HOUSE MUSEUM OF TEA WARE
MUSEUM

Map p370 (茶具文物館; ☎2869 0690; www.lcsd.gov.hk/ce/museum/arts/english/tea/intro/eintro.html; 10 Cotton Tree Dr; ⊙10am-6pm Wed-Mon; MAdmiralty, exit C1) FREE At Hong Kong park's northernmost tip is the Flagstaff House Museum of Tea Ware. Built in 1846 as the home of the commander of the British forces, it is the oldest colonial building in Hong Kong still standing in its original spot. The museum, a branch of the Hong Kong Museum of Art, houses a collection of antique Chinese tea ware.

Peruse bowls, teaspoons, brewing trays, sniffing cups (used particularly for enjoying the fragrance of the finest oolong from Taiwan) and, of course, teapots made of porcelain or purple clay from Yixing. The ground-floor cafe is a great place to recharge over a pot of fine tea.

LIPPO CENTRE
ARCHITECTURE

Map p370 (89 Queen's Way; MAdmiralty, exit B) Though the HSBC building (p72) and the Hong Kong International Airport in Chep Lap Kok (1998) – both by English architect Norman Foster, in late modern high-tech style – may be Hong Kong's best-known modern architecture, there are quite a number of fine modernist buildings in the territory designed by old masters. The Lippo Centre, which resembles koalas hugging a tree, is a pair of office towers built in 1987 by American Paul Rudolph.

TAMAR PARK
PARK

Map p370 (添馬公園; Tamar St, Admiralty; MAdmiralty, exit A) This harbour-front park on the site of the New Central Government Offices (新政府總部) is an inviting sprawl of verdant lawns where you can soak up the rays while watching the ships go by. It's part of a 4km promenade along the northern shoreline of Hong Kong Island, from Central Piers, outside the IFC Mall, past Wan Chai, all the way to North Point. Concerts and other cultural activities are sometimes held here.

The HMS *Tamar* was a British naval vessel moored in Victoria Harbour that served as the operational headquarters of the Royal Navy until 1946. The New Central Government Offices comprise the headquarters of the HKSAR government, the legislature and the Chief Executive's Office.

⊙ Wan Chai

PAK TAI TEMPLE
TEMPLE

Map p372 (北帝廟; 2 Lung On St; ⊙8am-5pm; MWan Chai, exit A3) A short stroll up Stone Nullah Lane takes you to a majestic Taoist temple built in 1863 to honour a god of the sea, Pak Tai. The temple – the largest on Hong Kong Island – is impressive. The main hall contains a 3m-tall copper likeness of Pak Tai cast in the Ming dynasty.

HONG KONG HOUSE OF STORIES MUSEUM

Map p372 (香港故事館; ☑2835 4372; http://houseofstories.sjs.org.hk; 74 Stone Nullah Lane; ⊙11am-5pm; ⮑6, 6A) Opened by local residents and fans of Wan Chai, this tiny museum is in the historic Blue House, a prewar building with cast-iron Spanish balconies reminiscent of New Orleans. The not-for-profit museum sells local handicrafts and runs private tours in English. Email a month in advance to arrange. A two-hour tour is HK$600, so the more of you, the cheaper.

OLD WAN CHAI POST OFFICE BUILDING

Map p372 (舊灣仔郵政局; 221 Queen's Rd E; ⊙10am-5pm Wed-Mon; ⮑6 or 6A) A short distance to the east of Wan Chai Market is this tiny colonial-style building erected in 1913 and now serving as a resource centre operated by the **Environmental Protection Department** (☑2893 2856; ⊙10am-5pm Mon-Tue & Thu-Sat, 10am-1pm Wed, 1-5pm Sun).

HUNG SHING TEMPLE TEMPLE

Map p372 (洪聖古廟; 129-131 Queen's Rd E; ⊙8am-5.30pm; ⮑6, 6A, Ⓜ Wan Chai, exit A3) Nestled in a nook on the southern side of Queen's Rd East, this narrow, dark and rather forbidding temple (c 1847) is built atop huge boulders. It was erected in honour of a deified Tang dynasty official who was known for his virtue (important) and ability to make predictions of great value to traders (ultra-important).

SOUTHORN PLAYGROUND PARK

Map p372 (修頓球場; ⊙6am-11.30pm; Ⓜ Wan Chai, exit A3) This unspectacular-looking sportsground is in fact the social hub of old Wan Chai, offering up a cross-section of life in the hood at any time of the day. Seniors come to play chess, students and amateur athletes to shoot hoops and kick ball. There are hip-hop dance-offs, housewives shaking a leg, outreach social workers, cruisers looking for a booty call, and a daily trickle of lunchers from the banks and construction sites. Southorn is bound by Hennessy, Luard and Johnston Rds, and the Wan Chai Computer Centre.

KHALSA DIWAN SIKH TEMPLE SIKH TEMPLE

Map p372 (☑2572 4459; www.khalsadiwan.com; 371 Queen's Rd E, Wan Chai; ⊙4am-9pm; ⮑10 from Central) Sitting quietly between a busy road and a cemetery is Hong Kong's largest Sikh temple, a descendant of a small original built in 1901 by Sikh members of the British army. The temple welcomes people of any faith, caste or colour to join in the services. Sunday prayer (9am to 1.30pm) sees some 1000 believers and nonbelievers in collective worship (fewer at the daily prayers, 6am to 8.30am and 6.30pm to 8pm).

More famous are its free vegetarian meals (11.30am to 8.30pm), a simple dhal or *sabzi* (vegetable stew) handed to anyone walking through the blue-and-white gates. You could return the favour by helping to wash the dishes.

HONG KONG CEMETERY CEMETERY

(香港墳場; www.fehd.gov.hk/english/cc/introduction.html; ⊙7am-6pm or 7pm; ⮑1, 8X, 117) Crowded and cosmopolitan, dead Hong Kong is no different from the breathing city. Tombstones jostle for space at this Christian cemetery (c 1845) located on Wong Nai Chung Rd alongside the Jewish, Hindu, Parsee and Muslim Cemeteries, and St Michael's Catholic Cemetery. Burial plots date to the mid-1800s and include colonialists, tycoons and silver-screen divas.

After exiting the MTR, follow Russell St, turn left into Wong Nai Chung Rd, and walk south for 15 minutes. The entrances of

---

CLOCK OF COLOURS

Central Plaza in Wan Chai, the lanky skyscraper sticking out from behind the Hong Kong Convention & Exhibition Centre when you're looking from Kowloon, is one of the world's biggest clocks. Between 6pm and midnight daily, there are four illuminated lines shining through the glass pyramid at the top of the building.

The bottom level indicates the hour: red is 6pm, white 7pm, purple 8pm, yellow 9pm, pink 10pm and green 11pm. When all four lights are the same colour, it's right on the hour. When the top light is different from the bottom ones, it's 15 minutes past the hour. If the top two and bottom two are different, it's half-past the hour. If the top three match, it's 45 minutes past the hour.

So what time is it now?

ART IN CHAI WAN

The old, industrial town of Chai Wan is fast gaining a reputation as a hipster-ville, with artists and nonprofits setting up shop in its dystopian-looking waterfront warehouses. Most of the boutiques and galleries here have no signs, which makes for fun (if sometimes frustrating) exploring. Try your luck in the Chai Wan Industrial City Phase 1 and Phase 2 warehouses, or the Asia One Tower. Warehouses are closed Sundays.

the cemeteries are scattered close to each other, opposite the public entrance of the Happy Valley Racecourse.

LOVER'S ROCK
LANDMARK

(姻緣石; off Bowen Rd; green minibus 24A) Lover's Rock or Destiny's Rock (Yan Yuen Sek) is a, well, phallus-shaped boulder on a bluff at the end of a track above Bowen Rd. It's a favourite pilgrimage site for women with relationship or fertility problems. It's busy during the Maidens' Festival , held on the seventh day of the seventh moon (mid-August). The easiest way to reach here is to take green minibus 24A from the Admiralty bus station. Get off at the terminus (Shiu Fai Tce) and walk up the path behind the housing complex.

POLICE MUSEUM
MUSEUM

(警隊博物館; 2849 7019; www.police.gov.hk/hkp-home/english/museum; 27 Coombe Rd, The Peak; 2-5pm Tue, 9am-5pm Wed-Sun; 15) FREE Fans of Hong Kong crime thrillers should make a trip to this museum in pretty Wan Chai Gap. The protagonist in this former police station is the Hong Kong police force, formed in 1844, but the real star is the Triads (ie Hong Kong Mafia). The eye-opening **Triad Societies Gallery** uncovers the rituals they follow. Equally intriguing is the well-supplied **Narcotics Gallery**. If taking the bus, alight at the stop between Stubbs Rd and Peak Rd.

HONG KONG CONVENTION & EXHIBITION CENTRE
BUILDING

Map p372 (香港會議展覽中心; 2582 8888; www.hkcec.com.hk; 1 Expo Dr; 18) Due north of the Wan Chai MTR station, the massive Convention & Exhibition Centre, which was built in 1988 and extended onto an artificial island in the harbour for the official ceremony of the return of sovereignty to China in 1997, has been compared with a bird's wing, a banana leaf and a lotus petal. It's a leading venue for large trade fairs, exhibitions and conventions.

GOLDEN BAUHINIA SQUARE
MONUMENT

Map p372 (金紫荊廣場; 1 Expo Dr, Golden Bauhinia Sq; 18, Wan Chai, exit A5) A 6m-tall statue of Hong Kong's symbol stands on the waterfront just in front of the Hong Kong Convention & Exhibition Centre to mark the establishment of the Hong Kong SAR in 1997. The flag-raising ceremony, held daily at 8am and conducted by the Hong Kong police, is a must-see for mainland tourist groups. There's a pipe band on the first day of each month at 7.45am.

CENTRAL PLAZA
BUILDING

Map p372 (中環廣場; 18 Harbour Rd; 18, Wan Chai, exit A5) Central Plaza, Hong Kong's third-tallest building, looks garish with its glass skin of three colours – gold, silver and terracotta. But it provides direct connection to the Hong Kong Convention & Exhibition Centre and Wan Chai MTR station through an elevated pedestrian footbridge.

HONG KONG ARTS CENTRE
BUILDING

Map p372 (香港藝術中心; www.hkac.org.hk; 2 Harbour Rd; Admiralty, exit E2) Along with theatres, including the **agnès b. Cinema** (2582 0200; Upper Basement; 18), the Hong Kong Arts Centre contains the two-floor **Pao Sui Loong & Pao Yue Kong Galleries** (包玉剛及包兆龍畫廊 (包氏畫廊); 10am-6pm, to 8pm during exhibitions) FREE, which hosts retrospectives and group shows in all visual media, several boutiques, an art bookstore and a cafe.

HONG KONG ACADEMY FOR THE PERFORMING ARTS
BUILDING

Map p372 (香港演藝學院; www.hkapa.edu; 1 Gloucester Rd; Admiralty, exit E2) With its striking triangular atrium and an exterior Meccano-like frame (a work of art in itself), the academy building (1985) is a Wan Chai landmark and an important venue (p127) for music, dance and scholarship. Check out the online event calendar for exhibits and performances.

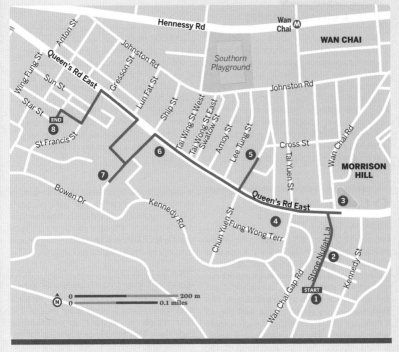

Neighbourhood Walk
Old Wan Chai's Forgotten Streets

START PAK TAI TEMPLE
END STAR ST
LENGTH 1.2KM; TWO HOURS

A short stroll from the main bus routes and Wan Chai metro (exit A3), you'll start to get a feel for the neighbourhood as it was in the 19th century at **1 Pak Tai Temple** (p110), a stunning temple built 150 years ago by local residents. Further down the slope, the **2 House of Stories** (p111) will show you what life was like in Wan Chai in the last century.

The Streamline Moderne exterior of the historic **3 Wan Chai Market** is all that remains of the place now fronting a shopping centre. Once the hub of the neighbourhood, the market was used as a mortuary by Japanese forces in WWII. Just to the west, the pocket-sized **4 Old Wan Chai Post Office** (p111) is Hong Kong's oldest post office.

Take a quick look at **5 Spring Garden Lane**, one of the first areas developed by the British, and imagine what it was like when prostitutes hawked their wares here in the 1900s. Then head along Queen's Rd East to peep inside the mysterious **6 Hung Shing Temple** (p111), once a seaside shrine.

Just west of the temple turn up the hill along Ship St and stand before the now derelict **7 Ghost House** at 55 Nam Koo Tce. Its history is a wretched one: it was used by Japanese soldiers as a brothel housing 'comfort women' in WWII.

The **8 Star Street neighbourhood** is a quiet little corner of town that manages to contain the old, including a family-run *dai pai dong* (food stall) on St Francis St, and the new, in the form of quaint boutiques and restaurants. On 31 Wing Fung St is a six-storey balconied building in art-deco style. Admiralty MTR can be reached by an escalator and underground travelator entered at the bottom of Wing Fung St.

LOCAL KNOWLEDGE

RENT-A-CURSE GRANNIES

Under the Canal Rd Flyover between Wan Chai and Causeway Bay, you can hire little old ladies to beat up your enemy. From their perch on plastic stools, these rent-a-curse grannies will pound paper cut-outs of your romantic rival, office bully or whiny celeb with a shoe (their orthopaedic flat or your stilettos – your call) while rapping rhythmic curses. All for only HK$50. Hung Shing Temple (p111) has a 'master' who performs the same with a symbolic 'precious' sword for the exorbitant sum of HK$100.

Villain hitting or villain exorcism (打小人; *da siu yan*) is a practice related to folk sorcery. It's performed throughout the year but the most popular date is the **Day of the Awakening of Insects** when the sun is at an exact celestial longitude of 345° (usually between 5 and 20 March on the Gregorian calendar). It's believed to bring reconciliation or resolution, though that too could be symbolic.

◉ Causeway Bay

NOONDAY GUN
HISTORIC SITE

Map p374 (怡和午炮; 221 Gloucester Rd; ⊘7am-midnight; ⓂCauseway Bay, exit D1) A colonial tradition dating back to the mid-1800s, the daily firing of this Hotchkiss 3-pounder naval gun was made famous by the Noël Coward song 'Mad Dogs and Englishmen' ('In Hong Kong, they strike a gong, and fire off a noonday gun/To reprimand each inmate who's in late'). The gun stands in a small garden opposite the Excelsior Hotel on the waterfront, where its noon-on-the-dot firing always draws a small crowd.

The Noonday Gun is tricky to find – it's accessible via a tunnel through the basement car park in the World Trade Centre, just west of the Excelsior Hotel. From the taxi rank in front of the hotel, look west for the door marked 'Car Park Shroff, Marina Club & Noon Gun'.

CAUSEWAY BAY TYPHOON SHELTER
TYPHOON SHELTER

Map p374 (銅鑼灣避風塘; off Hung Hing Rd, Causeway Bay; ⓂCauseway Bay, exit D1) Not so long ago the waterfront in Causeway Bay was a mass of junks and sampans huddling in the typhoon shelter for protection, but these days it's nearly all yachts. The land jutting out to the west is Kellett Island, home to the Royal Hong Kong Yacht Club (p129).

VICTORIA PARK
PARK

Map p374 (維多利亞公園; www.lcsd.gov.hk/en/ls_park.php; Causeway Rd; ⊘6am or 7am-11pm; ⓂTin Hau, exit B) **FREE** Victoria Park is the biggest patch of public greenery on Hong Kong Island. The best time to go is on a weekday morning, when it becomes a forest of people practising the slow-motion choreography of taichi. The park becomes a flower market a few days before the Chinese New Year. It's also worth a visit during the **Mid-Autumn Festival** , when people turn out en masse carrying lanterns.

TIN HAU TEMPLE
TEMPLE

Map p374 (天后廟; 10 Tin Hau Temple Rd; ⊘7am-5pm; ⓂTin Hau, exit B) Southeast of Victoria Park, Hong Kong Island's most famous Tin Hau temple is dwarfed by surrounding high-rises. This temple dedicated to the patroness of seafarers has been a place of worship for three centuries, though the current structure is only about 200 years old. The central shrine contains an effigy of Tin Hau with a blackened face.

LIN FA TEMPLE
BUDDHIST TEMPLE

Map p374 (蓮花宮; Lin Fa Kung St W, Tai Hang; ⊘8am-5pm; ⓂTin Hau, exit B) 'Lotus' is a pretty Buddhist temple with an octagonal front, a boulder jutting into its rear, and elaborate frescos.

◉ Happy Valley

★HAPPY VALLEY RACECOURSE
HORSE RACING

Map p374 (跑馬地馬場; www.hkjc.com; 2 Sports Rd, Happy Valley; admission HK$10; ⊘7pm-10.30pm Wed Sep-Jun; ⓶Happy Valley) An outing at the races is one of the quintessential Hong Kong things to do, especially if you happen to be around during one of the weekly Wednesday evening races here. The punters pack into the stands and trackside, cheering, drinking and eating, and the atmosphere is electric.

The first horse races were held here in 1846. Now meetings are held both here and at the newer and larger (but less atmospheric) Sha Tin Racecourse (p187) in the New Territories. Check the website for details on betting and tourist packages.

HONG KONG RACING MUSEUM   MUSEUM
(Wong Nai Chung Rd, 2nd fl, Happy Valley Stand; ☻noon-7pm, to 9pm race days; ☑Happy Valley) FREE Though probably one for racing buffs only, you can also visit the Hong Kong Racing Museum, which has eight galleries and a cinema showcasing celebrated trainers, jockeys and horseflesh, and key races over the past 150 years. The most important event in the history of the Happy Valley Racecourse – individual winnings notwithstanding – was the huge fire in 1918 that killed hundreds of people. Many of the victims were buried in the cemeteries surrounding the track.

⊙ Island East

CHUN YEUNG STREET MARKET   MARKET
(春秧街街市; Chun Yeung St, North Point; MNorth Point, exit A4) Hop on an eastbound tram, and past Fortress Hill you'll turn into an old narrow street teeming with market stalls and old tenement buildings. This is the famous Chun Yeung Street Market, and at 5pm it's so busy you wonder why no one ever got hit by the tram.

Flanking the tram tracks are vegetable stalls, meat vendors and stores selling foodstuff from Fújiàn, such as pig intestines stuffed with egg and all kinds of meat balls. North Point has a huge Fujianese community, and you'll hear their dialect spoken on Chun Yeung St.

As the tram turns the corner into King's Rd, you'll pass the nondescript **Wah Fung Chinese Department Store**. Once Hong Kong's largest Chinese department store, its rooftop served as a hideout for underground communists during the 1967 riots.

ISLAND EAST MARKET   MARKET
(www.hkmarkets.org; Tong Chong St, Quarry Bay; ☻11am-5.30pm Sun spring-autumn; MQuarry Bay, exit A) Hong Kong Island's largest farmers' market, inaugurated in 2012, has dozens of booths of organic produce, local snacks, craft makers and street musicians, all in a typically Hong Kong setting in a busy urban plaza.

HONG KONG FILM ARCHIVE   MUSEUM
(香港電影資料館; ☏2739 2139, bookings 2734 9009, bookings 2119 7383; www.filmarchive.gov.hk; 50 Lei King Rd, Sai Wan Ho; ☻10am-8pm, box office noon-8pm; MSai Wan Ho, exit A) FREE The archive is worth a visit, even if you know little about Hong Kong film. It has over 6300 reels and tapes, as well as magazines, posters and scripts. There's a small **exhibition hall** (opening hours vary) and a **cinema**. Check online for exhibitions and screenings. From the MTR station, walk north on Tai On St and west on Lei King Rd.

HONG KONG MUSEUM OF
COASTAL DEFENCE   MUSEUM
(香港海防博物館; ☏2569 1500; http://hk.coastaldefence.museum; 175 Tung Hei Rd, Shau Kei Wan; adult/concession HK$10/5; ☻10am-5pm Fri-Wed; MShau Kei Wan, exit B2) This museum occupies a knockout location in the Lei Yue Mun Fort (1887), which has sweeping views down to the Lei Yue Mun Channel and southeastern Kowloon. Exhibitions in the old redoubt cover Hong Kong's coastal defence over six centuries.

HONG KONG ISLAND: WAN CHAI & THE NORTHEAST SIGHTS

VICKIE'S ANGRY UNCLES

Victoria Park has always been associated with freedom of expression, a reputation owed mainly to the candlelight vigil which takes place here on 4 June, but also to the current affairs debate 'City Forum' which turns it into a mini Hyde Park every Sunday.

Spanning two MTR stations and with multiple entrances, the park provides a leafy detour and short cut for many locals. Among the regulars are a group of retired, pro-communist old men who during 'City Forum' on Sundays (noon to 1pm), would hang out near the venue and holler against speechifying pro-democracy politicians to drown them out.

These men came to be known as the 'Uncles of Victoria Park' (維園阿伯), but the term has since evolved to include any politically minded old man with a gripe. And Hong Kong certainly has no shortage of these.

There's a historical trail through the casemates, tunnels and observation posts almost down to the coast.

As you leave the MTR, follow the signs for the museum on Tung Hei Rd for about 15 minutes. Bus 85, which is accessible via exit A3 and runs along Shau Kei Wan Rd between North Point and Siu Sai Wan, stops on Tung Hei Rd outside the museum.

LAW UK FOLK MUSEUM   MUSEUM
(羅屋民俗館; ☑2896 7006; www.lcsd.gov.hk/CE/Museum/History/en_US/web/mh/about-us/law-uk-folk-museum.html; 14 Kut Shing St, Chai Wan; ⊙10am-6pm Fri-Wed; MChai Wan, exit B) FREE This teeny museum occupies two restored Hakka village houses that have stood in a district of office buildings, warehouses and workers' flats for over two centuries. The courtyard and bamboo groves are peaceful, and the displays – furniture, household items and farming implements – simple but charming.

✖ EATING

Admiralty has a few exceptional restaurants. Wan Chai, with its wealth of cuisines in all price ranges, is Hong Kong's food capital. Causeway Bay is an eclectic amalgam of eateries, many upscale. Down-at-heel North Point is home to a number of old Chinese restaurants and *dai pai dong* (food stalls).

✖ Admiralty

BEEF & LIBERTY   BURGERS $
Map p370 (☑2811 3009; www.beef-liberty.com/hk; 23 Wing Fung St, 2nd fl; burgers HK$78-108; ⊙noon-3pm & 6-10.30pm Mon-Fri, 11am-10.30pm Sat & Sun; MAdmiralty, exit F) For our money, this trendy new spot has the best burgers in town. Juicy Tasmanian beef is cooked any way you like, and topped with bacon jam, green chilli, pickled onions and other goodies. Sweet-potato fries are killer, and boozy spiked milkshakes add to the fun. Book ahead during peak times. Enter through the elevator in the pizza restaurant downstairs.

GREAT FOOD HALL   SUPERMARKET $
Map p370 (☑2918 9986; www.greatfoodhall.com; Basement, Two Pacific Place, Admiralty; meals from HK$100; ⊙10am-10pm; MAdmiralty, exit F)

In the basement of the swish Pacific Place shopping mall, Great is one of the nicest gourmet supermarkets in Hong Kong. It has its own sit-down sushi bar and Spanish tapas restaurant (always crowded; just stand politely behind the bar until someone finishes), as well as takeaway sushi and hearty create-your-own salads.

AMMO   EUROPEAN $$
Map p370 (☑2537 9888; www.ammo.com.hk; 9 Justice Dr, Asia Society Hong Kong Centre; meals HK$200-400; ⊙noon-midnight Sun-Thu, to 1am Fri & Sat; MAdmiralty, exit F) Awash in a coppery light the colour of bullets, this sleek glass-walled cafe at the Asia Society Hong Kong Centre (p110) features chandeliers and copper panels evoking the site's past as an explosives magazine. The excellent menu is well thought out and pricey, with a selection of mostly Italian mains, preceded by tapas available at cocktail hour. Bookings essential.

PURE VEGGIE HOUSE   VEGETARIAN, CHINESE $$
Map p370 (☑2525 0556; 51 Garden Rd, 3rd fl, Coda Plaza; meals HK$200-400; ⊙11am-10pm; ☑; MAdmiralty, then bus 12A) This Buddhist restaurant goes way beyond the usual tofu-n-broccoli to serve innovative, exquisitely presented vegetarian dishes – sautéed lily bulb, fried rice with black truffle and pine nuts, seaweed-wrapped tofu rolls. Excellent all-vegie dim sum will please even dedicated carnivores. The tranquil setting resembles a rustic inn.

SAN XI LOU   SICHUANESE $$
Map p370 (三希樓; ☑2838 8811; 51 Garden Rd, 7th fl, Coda Plaza; meals HK$150-300; ⊙11am-10.30pm; MAdmiralty, then bus 12A) One of Hong Kong's more popular Sichuan restaurants, San Xi Lou specialises in hotpot, but its à la carte menu will satisfy chilli heads too. Crowd-pleasers include chilli chicken with cashews, Mandarin fish, and *mapo tofu* (chilli tofu), while the adventurous might consider deer sinew or spicy frog legs. Decor is typical Chinese banquet hall, with peach tablecloths and high-backed chairs.

LOCK CHA TEA SHOP   VEGETARIAN, CHINESE $$
Map p370 (樂茶軒; ☑2801 7177; www.lockcha.com; ground fl, KS Lo Gallery, Hong Kong Park; dim sum HK$15-28, tea from HK$25; ⊙10am-10pm; ☑; MAdmiralty, exit C1) Set in the lush environs of Hong Kong Park, Lock Cha

offers a dozen teas and 20 varieties of tiny but tasty vegetarian dim sum in a replica of an ancient scholar's study. On most Sunday afternoons (4pm to 6pm), there are Chinese music performances or tea talks for HK$100 per person (see website for details). Do reserve a seat. The music is popular; the tea shop is dainty.

✕ Wan Chai

JOY HING ROASTED MEAT CANTONESE $
Map p372 (再興燒臘飯店; ☑2519 6639; 1C Stewart Rd; meals HK$25-60; ☺10am-10pm; ⓜWan Chai, exit A4) This basic stall is one of your best bets for Cantonese barbecue – succulent slivers of barbecued pork, goose, chicken and liver over freshly steamed rice. The menu is simply cards stuck on the wall. Just see what your neighbours are having and point.

LA CREPERIE CREPERIE $
Map p372 (☑2529 9280; 100 Queen's Rd E, 1st fl; meals HK$70-200; ☺11.30am-11pm Mon-Sun; ⓜWan Chai, exit A3) Decorated like a seaside town in Brittany, this quaint 20-seat creperie whips out sumptuous galettes and airy crêpes, which are best savoured with some imported cider served in bowls. If you fancy French andouille sausage, La Creperie is one of the only places in town where you'll find that pungent delicacy.

CHUEN CHEONG FOODS CHINESE $
Map p372 (泉昌美食; 150 Wan Chai Rd, Wan Chai; stinky tofu HK$18; ☺1-9pm Mon-Sat; ⓜWan Chai, exit A4) So you're walking through Wan Chai and you smell something...wait, is there a *horse stable* nearby? Nope, that's just the manure-like stench of stinky tofu, a paradigm case of 'tastes better than it smells'. This popular street stall (no English sign) serves the beloved snack Hong Kong–style, which means deep-fried with hot chilli sauce.

BAO WOW TAIWANESE, FAST FOOD $
Map p372 (☑2528 9505; www.baowowhk.com; 28 Tai Wong St E, Wan Chai; bao HK$38; ☺noon-9pm; ⓜ Wan Chai, exit A3) Hong Kong is in the midst of a love affair with Taiwanese *gua bao,* steamed bun 'sandwiches' wrapped, taco-style, around a variety of fillings. This ultra-casual new spot satisfies demand with a short menu of creative *bao* (we like the original pork and peanut, or the Thai

fish with cabbage) and funky sides like taro fries with Sriracha mayo.

SABAH MALAYSIAN $
Map p372 (☑2143 6626; Shops 4 & 5, 98-108 Jaffe Rd; meals HK$68-100; ☺7.30am-midnight; ⓜWan Chai, exit A1) Sabah in the heart of Wan Chai serves Malaysian food tempered for the Hong Kong palate, though that doesn't seem to keep the peeps from the Consulate General of Malaysia from coming. The pièce de résistance is the fluffy *roti canai* , which is tossed, twirled and kneaded before your eyes.

CAPITAL CAFE TEA CAFE $
Map p372 (華星冰室; ☑2666 7766; 6 Heard St, Shop B1, ground fl, Kwong Sang Hong Bldg; meals HK$35-50; ☺7am-11pm; ⓜWan Chai, exit A2) Designed to resemble a vintage *cha chaan tang* (tea cafe), but cleaner and more gimmicky than the real thing, this joint is the pet project of the owner of an eponymous Canto-pop record label that was famous in the '70s and '80s. It serves good old classics like toast with fluffy scrambled eggs and iced red-bean drink, as well as fancier laced-with-black-truffle versions.

MEGAN'S KITCHEN CANTONESE, HOTPOT $$
Map p372 (☑2866 8305; www.meganskitchen.com; 165-171 Wan Chai Rd, Wan Chai, 5th fl, Lucky Centre; hot pot per person HK$200-300; ☺noon-3pm & 6-11.30pm; ⓜWan Chai, exit A3) Broth choices like Thai-flavoured tom yum and 'lobster borsch' make for a modern twist on the classic hotpot experience at Megan's, though standbys like spicy Sichuan soup are just as good. The vast menu of items to dip runs the gamut from the standard (mushrooms, fish slices, tofu) to the avant garde (don't miss the fabulous rainbow cuttlefish balls). Like all hotpot restaurants, Megan's is best visited with a crowd of at least four. Subdivided hotpots mean you can sample up to three broths, so the more the merrier. Call ahead for reservations, especially on weekends.

★22 SHIPS TAPAS $$
Map p372 (☑2555 0722; www.22ships.hk; 22 Ship St, Wan Chai; tapas HK$68-178; ☺noon-3pm & 6-11pm; ⓜWan Chai, exit B2) The star of the recent crop of new tapas restaurants to open in Hong Kong, this tiny, trendy spot is packed from open to close. But the long wait (the restaurant doesn't take reservations) is worth it for exquisite, playful small

HONG KONG ISLAND: WAN CHAI & THE NORTHEAST EATING

plates by much-buzzed-about young British chef Jason Atherton. Molecular gastronomy techniques are on display in some dishes while others are pure luxe comfort food.

KIN'S KITCHEN
CANTONESE $$

Map p372 (留家廚房; ☑2571 0913; 314 Hennessy Rd, 5th fl, Wan Chai; meals HK$180-450; ⊙noon-3pm & 6-11pm; Ⓜ Wan Chai, exit A2) Opened by art critic turned restaurateur Lau Kin-wai, this understated restaurant touts its Cantonese classics with a modern spin. The owner, looking quite the *bon vivant* with silver hair and rosy cheeks, is sometimes seen discussing the delicious smoked chicken with customers.

CHE'S CANTONESE RESTAURANT
CANTONESE $$

Map p372 (車氏粵菜軒; ☑2528 1123; 54-62 Lockhart Rd, 4th fl, the Broadway; meals HK$180-800; ⊙11am-3pm & 6-11pm; Ⓜ Wan Chai, exit C) This Cantonese restaurant, favoured by suits, serves home-style dishes and a small but delectable selection of dim sum. The crispy barbecued pork bun is a clever take on the *char siu bao*. The decor is simple but tables are a tad too close for comfort.

LIU YUAN PAVILION
SHANGHAINESE $$

Map p372 (留園雅敘; ☑2804 2000; 54-62 Lockhart Rd, 3rd fl, the Broadway; meals HK$200-600; ⊙noon-3pm & 6-11pm; Ⓜ Wan Chai, exit C) This pretty restaurant in airy yellows makes superb Shanghainese classics, including tasty Shanghainese pastries. It has a loyal following among the local Shanghainese community, so do book ahead.

★ YIN YANG
CHINESE $$$

Map p372 (鴛鴦飯店; ☑2866 0868; www.yin-yang.hk; 18 Ship St; lunch from HK$180, chef's menu dinners HK$580-2000; ⊙noon-2.30pm Sun, dinner by reservation; Ⓜ Wan Chai, exit B2) Margaret Xu, the chef of Yin Yang, calls her cooking New Hong Kong. A former ad-agency owner who taught herself how to cook, Margaret grows her own organic vegetables and uses old-fashioned tools, such as stone-grinds and terracotta ovens, to create Hong Kong classics with a clean, contemporary twist.

Yin Yang is housed in a three-storey 1930s heritage building. Dinner is a tasting menu, but you'll have to book at least five days in advance. The website mentions a deposit, but that's negotiable. There are takeaway options as well.

BO INNOVATION
CHINESE $$$

Map p372 (廚魔; ☑2850 8371; www.boinnovation.com; 60 Johnston Rd, 2nd fl; lunch set/tasting menu HK$288/780, dinner tasting menu HK$1380-2180; ⊙noon-2pm Mon-Fri, 7-10pm Mon-Sat; Ⓜ Wan Chai, exit B2) This self-identified 'X-Treme' restaurant takes classic Chinese dishes apart and reassembles them in surprising ways using the sci-fi techniques of molecular gastronomy. The pork dumpling is a wobbly blob of ginger-infused pork soup encased in a transparent wrapper that explodes in the mouth. The 'Dead Garden' dish of various fungi with green onions and avocados is characteristically surreal. The lift entrance is at 18 Ship St.

GRISSINI
ITALIAN $$$

Map p372 (☑2588 1234; www.hongkong.grand.hyatt.com; 1 Harbour Rd, Grand Hyatt Hotel; set lunch HK$458, dinner mains from HK$260; ⊙noon-2.30pm Sun-Fri, 7-10.30pm daily; ☑; Ⓜ Wan Chai, exit A1) Fluffy, chewy and addictive, the foot-long grissini here are – appropriately – the best in town. But leave room for the Milanese specialities and pair them with a bottle from the 1000-strong cellar. This stylish restaurant has floor-to-ceiling windows commanding views of the harbour (and construction in progress).

MADAM SIXTY ATE
MODERN EUROPEAN $$$

Map p372 (☑2527 2558; www.madamsixtyate.com.hk; 60 Johnston Rd, Shop 8, 1st fl, the Podium, J Senses; set lunch/dinner from HK$188/498; ⊙noon-11pm; Ⓜ Wan Chai, exit B2) Hong Kong has chic eats aplenty, yet few are fun like Madam. The modern European dishes here may not be the best in town, but they're evocatively named and playfully plated, and when served against the restaurant's surrealist paintings, make dinner (or lunch) a very pleasant experience.

✕ Causeway Bay

★ DELICIOUS KITCHEN
SHANGHAINESE $

Map p374 (☑2577 7720; 9-11B Cleveland St; meals HK$40-100; ⊙11am-11pm; Ⓜ Causeway Bay, exit E) The Shanghainese rice cooked with shredded Chinese cabbage is so good at this *cha chaan tang* (tea cafe) that fashionistas are tripping over themselves to land a table here. It's best with the legendary honey-glazed pork chop. Fat, vegie-stuffed wontons and perfectly crispy fried tofu are also winners.

★LAB MADE ICE CREAM DESSERTS $

Map p374 (☑2670 0071; www.labmade.com.hk; 6 Brown St, Tai Hang; ice cream HK$42; ⊗3pm-midnight; Ⓜ Tin Hau, exit B) A very delicious science experiment, the ice cream at Lab Made is created with liquid nitrogen and a mixer, each scoop made to order and emerging with a poof of vapour. A rotating menu offers four flavours daily, a blend of the prosaic (chocolate, mango) and the only-in-Hong-Kong magical (condensed milk with crispy toast bits, purple yam, mooncake).

SOGO JAPANESE, SELF-CATERING $

Map p374 (☑2833 8338; www.sogo.com.hk; 555 Hennessy Rd, Causeway Bay, Basement; snacks from HK$20; ⊗10am-10pm; Ⓜ Causeway Bay, exit D3) In the basement of the landmark Sogo Japanese department store, this packed supermarket and foodhall is the place to come for all manner of Japanese snacks. Look for *onigiri* (fish-stuffed rice balls), fresh crêpes with fillings like green-tea ice cream, fried-octopus pancakes, and almost-too-pretty-to-eat *mochi* (sweet glutinous rice cakes).

HO HUNG KEE NOODLES $

Map p374 (何洪記; ☑2577 6558; 500 Hennessy Rd, Hysan Place, 12th fl; wonton soup HK$53; ⊗11.30am-11.30pm; Ⓜ Causeway Bay, exit F2) The tasty noodles, wontons and congee at this 68-year-old shop are cooked according to the ancient recipes of the Ho family, and clearly they still work. Though the new location, inside shiny Hysan Place mall, lacks character, Ho Hung Kee is always packed during lunch, even before it was awarded one Michelin star.

SCHOOL FOOD KOREAN $

Map p374 (☑2480 3666; 1 Matheson St, Times Square Mall, 13th fl, Causeway Bay; meals HK$60-120; ⊗noon-11pm; Ⓜ Causeway Bay, exit A) Hong Kong teeny-boppers are mad for all things Korean: K-Pop, K-Fashion and, yes, K-Food. On the 13th floor of Times Square, this nouveau Korean snack-food joint is always utterly thronged with 13-to-25 year olds. They come for the creative *gimbap* (Korean sushi) with stuffings like squid ink rice, the sugary smoothies and the cheese-smothered Korean rice cakes. Relive your own youth by grabbing a queue number and joining them.

YU SICHUANESE, NOODLES $

Map p374 (渝酸辣粉; ☑2838 8198; 4 Yiu Wa St; meals from HK$100; ⊗noon-5pm & 6-11pm; Ⓜ Causeway Bay, exit A) Addicts of the Sichua-nese peppercorn flock to this guileless little shop for that tingling and numbing feeling, which only happens when the Sichuanese fare is done right. From tame to full-blown, you can choose the level of spiciness for your noodles; there are some nonspicy offerings too. Yu doesn't take reservations for Friday and Saturday.

FIAT CAFFE ITALIAN $

Map p374 (www.fiat.com.hk; 77 Leighton Rd, Shop G5-G6, Leighton Centre; meals from HK$100; ⊗11am-10pm; Ⓜ Causeway Bay, exit A) This cafe belonging to the Italian automotive brand offers one of the best deals in town for a casual bite and a decent espresso. Perhaps after munching on grilled sardines, customers will be in the mood to hop over to the Fiat showroom and buy a Panda.

HONG KEE CONGEE SHOP CANTONESE $

Map p374 (康記粥店; ☑2808 4518; 11 King St, Tai Hang; congee from HK$13; ⊗6am-midnight; Ⓜ Tin Hau, exit B) Family-run Hong Kee has been sitting quietly in this corner of Tai Hang for 30 years. The food is fresh, home-made and inexpensive – a generous bowl of congee for as little as HK$13. Try the rice dumpling, fried bread stick and congee with liver, frog or tripe, fish or chicken, or maybe thousand-year-old egg.

IRORI JAPANESE $$

Map p374 (酒處; ☑2838 5939; Yiu Wa St, 2nd fl, Bartlock Centre; lunch/dinner from HK$150/300; ⊗noon-3pm & 6-11pm; Ⓜ Causeway Bay, exit A) Irori's versatile kitchen turns out raw and cooked delicacies of an equally impressive standard. Seasonal fish is flown in regularly from Japan and carefully crafted into sushi and sashimi. To warm the stomach between cold dishes, there's a creative selection of tasty tidbits, such as fried beef roll and *yakitori* (grilled skewers).

IROHA JAPANESE $$

Map p374 (伊呂波燒肉; ☑2882 9877; www.iroha.com.hk; 50 Jardine's Bazaar, 2nd fl; lunch sets from HK$110, dinner from HK$300; ⊗noon-3pm & 6-11pm; Ⓜ Causeway Bay, exit E) Bright and noisy, Iroha specialises in *yakiniku,* the Japanese style of grilling meat or vegetables over a burner. Among the dizzying range of Wagyu cuts on offer, the beef rib finger *(nakaochi karubi)* with its perfect fat-to-meat ratio and just-right chewiness comes highly recommended. If you love steak, be prepared to spend.

THE SOUND & SCENT OF TAI HANG

To get to Tai Hang, take bus 26 from Central. The single- or double-decker lets you off on a slope under a *bak lan* tree, a white orchid that stands about eight storeys high. Alight into scent, then descend the stairs, thousands of leaves overhanging, and more scent: incense from a neighbourhood temple. Just ahead is Tai Hang, a quiet, low-rise pocket of Hong Kong tucked in a valley.

Many of the residents have grown up in Tai Hang. Friendliness prevails. Children are doted on. Whole families take walks. Many elders like to sit in plastic chairs along the main road to watch the days continue, one after another, a thermos of tea at hand. Mornings are calmest.

At mealtimes and especially in the evenings, Tai Hang bursts with many happy people eating: homemade congee 19 hours a day, gourmet cheese, late-night sweets, Vietnamese and Japanese and Thai, pasta and pizzerias, wine bars, beer bars, coffee bars, an oyster bar and more.

The congee shop is a centre of the community open from 6am until 1.30am the following day. At least eight members of the family work here together. The youngest have slept in a crib alongside the shop, then used stools as desks, and now help serve a customer or two. The teenagers help after school. It's the grandparents and parents and an uncle or two who run the shop.

But there is more to Tai Hang than food. Small-scale walk-ups, an art-deco building from the 1930s, a clay-tile roofed home (one of the oldest remaining single-family homes of its kind on Hong Kong Island), sidewalk furniture, three picturesque temples, a public garden full of flowering trees, several rooftop gardens, and at least one skyscraper in the making, probably green-skirted with scaffolding nets.

And birdsong in Tai Hang is plentiful. The first round starts at about 3.30am. Raptors loop from time to time, cockatoos may perch on aerials, screeching, and the family who runs the fruit shop keeps a huge turtle on the rooftop. Plus there are the cats and dogs, many for the lap.

Lin Fa Temple (p114) was named for the lotus, for the purity and shape of the blossom. Step inside to find a huge and holy stone, a goddess who used to be male, and 60 divinities of time. A corner window stays open during the day for passersby to have direct access to the goddess of mercy, and many people bow, hands in prayer, from 50m away.

Flowers. *Bak lan. Lin fa.* One of the best places for flowers is a tiny alley off Tung Lo Wan Rd near the Metropark Hotel. A family has been selling flowers there for about 55 years, and a generous bunch goes for far less than HK\$55. If you arrive or leave Tai Hang by MTR (nearest station: Tin Hau), you will pass the alley with blooms and buckets.

Tai Hang is recognised by Unesco for its **Mid-Autumn Festival**, when residents lead a handmade dragon measuring 68m and stuck with thousands of incense sticks through their streets to cleanse the neighbourhood of all that may be unwell. For three nights, scent and smoke enter each street, lane, home, all to the sound of drum and dance and gong. The tradition has been happening annually since 1880, when it was conducted to control the plague. Nowadays a lion dance might also happen on Buddha's Birthday, closer to springtime.

Tai Hang: a community at any time of day and season.

Madeleine Slavick is a former Tai Hang resident and author of Fifty Stories Fifty Images.

TAI PING KOON   SOY SAUCE WESTERN, CHINESE **\$\$**
Map p374 (太平館餐廳; ☑2576 9161; www.taipingkoon.com; 6 Pak Sha Rd, Causeway Bay; meal sets from HK\$188; ⊙11am-11.20pm; ⓂCauseway Bay, exit F) Soy sauce Western is believed to have been invented by the first Tai Ping Koon in Guăngzhōu. Today tasty classics such as smoked pomfret and ox tongue with rice are still served in neat, if slightly worn, surrounds by the waiters who have been here for decades. There are branches in Central, Yau Ma Tei and Tsim Sha Tsui.

GO YA YAKITORI JAPANESE $$

Map p374 ([☎]2504 2000; 21 Brown St, Tai Hang; skewers from HK$30; ⊙6pm-midnight daily, noon-2.30pm Sat & Sun; [M]Tin Hau, exit B) This wood-panelled *yakitori* joint in the cozy Tai Hang neighbourhood makes you feel like you're in a quiet Japanese village. After your complimentary cup of sake, choose from dozens of skewers – popular picks include duck tongue, *kurobuta* pork, and savoury charred leeks. Don't panic when you see the prices – they're listed in Japanese yen!

FORUM CANTONESE, DIM SUM $$$

Map p374 (富臨飯店; [☎]2891 2555; Sino Plaza, Jaffe Rd, Causeway Bay; meals HK$500-1600; ⊙11am-11pm; [M]Causeway Bay, exit D4) The abalone dishes at this expensive eatery have fans from across the world. What restaurant owner Yeung Koon-yat does with these molluscs has earned him membership of Le Club des Chefs des Chefs and the moniker 'King of Abalone'. If on a budget, you can make a meal of dim sum for under HK$350.

FARM HOUSE CANTONESE $$$

Map p374 (農圃飯店; [☎]2881 1331; www.farm-house.com.hk; 8 Sunning Rd, 1st fl Taiping Tower, Causeway Bay; meals HK$300-1300; ⊙11am-3pm & 6-11pm; [M]Causeway Bay, exit F) Families from the expensive residences nearby come for dinner when their maids are on leave. And it's not hard to see why. The masterful takes on home cooking, such as the steamed pork patty with duck egg and squid, are so well executed it would be hard for any maid or housewife to beat. Ambience is relaxing and upscale.

WEST VILLA CANTONESE, DIM SUM $$$

Map p374 (西苑酒家; [☎]2882 2110; www.westvillahk.com; 33 Hysan Ave, 5th fl, Lee Gardens One, Causeway Bay; meals from HK$350; ⊙11am-11.30pm; [M]Causeway Bay, exit E) West Villa does the *char siu* (barbecued pork) job well – just slightly charred at the edges and with a golden lean-to-fat ratio. It also makes some of the best soy-sauce chicken in town, and a soup (pre-ordering required) comprising chicken, conch meat, honeydew melon and a dozen other ingredients its competitors would kill to know.

SUSHI FUKU-SUKE JAPANESE $$$

Map p374 (鮨福助; [☎]2955 0005; www.fuku-suke.com.hk; 525 Hennessy Rd, 11th fl, Macau Yat Yuen Centre; meals HK$260-1000; ⊙noon-11pm; [M]Causeway Bay, exit D4) An elegant sushi bar with clean lines and pine wood like you'd find in Tokyo, which is where the chef/owner used to work. If you're not too hungry, there's a fairly reasonable lunch set for under HK$200. The two chef's menus (from HK$800) at dinner comprise sushi or sashimi and some hot side dishes.

✗ Happy Valley

GI KEE SEAFOOD
RESTAURANT DAI PAI DONG, CANTONESE $

(銖記海鮮飯店; [☎]2574 9937; 2 Yuk Sau St, Shop 4, 2nd fl, Wong Nai Chung Municipal Services Bldg; meals from HK$100; ⊙5.30-10pm; [🚌]1 from Des Voeux Rd Central) Reserve a table or expect to queue for a plastic stool at this *dai pai dong* perched above a wet market. Chan Chung-fai, the man in the kitchen who turns out tantalising dishes such as chicken with fried garlic, is an award-winning cordon bleu chef with a huge fan following that includes the likes of Zhang Ziyi and Jackie Chan.

CHEONG KEE CHA CHAAN TANG $

(昌記; [☎]2573 5910; 2 Yuk Sau St, 2nd fl Wong Nai Chung Municipal Services Bldg, Happy Valley; meals from HK$30; [🚌]1 from Des Voeux Rd Central) One of Hong Kong's most venerable *cha chaan tang* (tea cafes), scrappy little Cheong Kee is beloved for its ultra-thick toast drenched in condensed milk and peanut butter. Milk tea is silky-sweet, while local comfort foods like pork chop noodles and *char siu* with egg are well above average. It's above the wet market.

✗ Island East

★TUNG PO SEAFOOD
RESTAURANT DAI PAI DONG, CANTONESE $

(東寶小館; [☎]2880 9399; 99 Java Rd, 2nd fl, Municipal Services Bldg, North Point; meals HK$80-200; ⊙5.30pm-midnight; [M]North Point, exit A1) Atop the Java Rd wet market, Tung Po has revolutionised *dai pai dong* cooking. Beer is served in chilled porcelain bowls, to be downed bandit style. The young staff strut around in rubber boots, serving Cantonese dishes with a twist. Book ahead (reservations 2.30pm to 5.30pm) or go before 7pm.

Must-tries here include the crispy, garlicky wind-sand chicken, the sinus-clearing wasabi cucumber salad, the lotus-leaf rice and the midnight-black squid-ink pasta.

PETE SEAWARD / LONELY PLANET ©

CASARSA / GETTY IMAGES ©

3

JOE CHEN / GETTY IMAGES ©

1. Double-decker tramcars (p14)
Known as 'ding dings', these trams have been swaying through Hong Kong's traffic since 1904.

2. Bowrington Rd wet market (p44)
Fresh produce, including seafood, can be found at this Causeway Bay market.

3. Happy Valley Racecourse (p114)
Weekly Wednesday evening races bring cheering punters and an electric atmosphere.

4. Hong Kong Park (p109)
Home to more than some 90 species of bird, Hong Kong Park is like a rainforest planted in the centre of the city..

GRAND CUISINE
SHANGHAI KITCHEN   SHANGHAINESE $
(君頤上海小廚; ☎2568 9989; 1 Tai Yue Ave, Tai Koo; meals HK$80-120; ⏰11am-11pm; Ⓜ Tai Koo, exit D1) In a blandly upscale residential neighbourhood, this warmly lit spot serves excellent Shanghainese specialities at excellent prices. You can't go wrong with the soup dumplings, sautéed bamboo shoots, or any of the noodle dishes (we especially like the thick, chewy Shànghǎi fried noodles with salty cabbage). English menu.

HUNG'S DELICACIES   CHIU CHOW, CANTONESE $
(阿鴻小吃; ☎2570 1108; 84-94 Wharf Rd, Shop 4, ground fl, Ngan Fai Bldg, North Point; meals HK$45-100; ⏰1-10pm Wed-Sun; Ⓜ North Point, exit A3) Ever since it plucked a Michelin star, there's always a line outside this humble shop. Go outside peak meal times and you'll land a seat (tables are shared), or buy takeout from the missus. The signature Chiu Chow dishes such as marinated goose lend themselves well to consumption anywhere.

LITTLE CHILLI   SICHUAN $
(小辣椒; ☎2571 9822; 33 North Point Rd, North Point; meals HK$50-100; ⏰11am-5am; Ⓜ North Point, exit A1) This Sichuan greasy spoon has been slinging hotpot beef and peanutty *dan dan* noodles to crowds of local teenagers and vacationing mainland families for years. It's especially tasty after a night at the bars, which is convenient, since it's open until 5am.

🍷🍸 DRINKING & NIGHTLIFE

🍴 Admiralty

CLASSIFIED   CAFE
Map p370 (☎2528 3454; 31 Wing Fung St; ⏰8am-midnight; Ⓜ Admiralty, exit F) We love the scrubbed wooden table, the designer lamp and the open frontage of this quiet and stylish cafe. Take a seat near the pavement and people-watch as you enjoy your pick from 100-plus bottles and some quality tapas.

THE LAWN   BAR
Map p370 (☎3968 1106; www.upperhouse.com/en/Inside-and-Out/Inside-the-Hotel/The-Lawn.aspx; 88 Queensway, 6th fl, the Upper House,

Admiralty; ⏰from 10am; Ⓜ Admiralty, exit F) Atop the Upper House boutique hotel, this secret garden of a roof bar is the place for cooling your heels with a Pimm's Cup beneath a lacquered parasol. Occasional Sunday DJ parties are see-and-be-seen events.

AMICAL   CAFE
Map p370 (☎5489 5330; 1 Sun St, 1st fl, Wan Chai; ⏰10am-7pm Fri-Wed; Ⓜ Admiralty, exit F) In a charming 1st-floor eyrie in Wan Chai's hip Star St district, this teeny cafe makes its exquisite drip coffees and espresso drinks from fairly traded organic Cameroonian beans. Ask about off-menu items like the cucumber cappuccino.

🍴 Wan Chai

★ PAWN   BAR
Map p372 (www.thepawn.com.hk; 62 Johnston Rd; ⏰11am-2am, to midnight Sun; Ⓜ Wan Chai, exit A3) This handsome three-storey establishment used to be a row of tenement houses and the century-old Woo Cheong pawn shop. Now it's occupied by a restaurant and a bar. The slouchy sofas with space to sprawl, shabby-chic interiors designed by a filmmaker, plus great little terrace spaces overlooking the tram tracks, make this an ideal location to sample a great selection of lagers, bitters and wine.

MES AMIS   BAR
Map p372 (☎2527 6680; www.mesamis.com.hk; 81-85 Lockhart Rd; ⏰noon-4am, happy hour 4-9pm; Ⓜ Wan Chai, exit C) A slightly more stylish place in the lap of girly club land, Mes Amis has a good range of wines and a Mediterranean-style snacks list. There's a DJ from 11pm on Friday and Saturday. Mes Amis stays open till 6am Friday and Saturday.

CHAMPAGNE BAR   BAR
Map p372 (1 Harbour Rd, ground fl, Grand Hyatt Hotel; ⏰5pm-2am; Ⓜ Wan Chai, exit A1) Take your fizz in the sumptuous surrounds of the Grand Hyatt's Champagne Room, kitted out in art-deco furnishings to evoke Paris of the 1920s. Live blues or jazz happens most evenings and the circular main bar is always busy.

DUSK TILL DAWN   LIVE MUSIC
Map p372 (☎2528 4689; ground fl, 76-84 Jaffe Rd; ⏰noon-5am Mon-Fri, 3pm-7am Sat & Sun, happy

hour 5-11pm; Ⓜ Wan Chai, exit C) True to its name, when the other bars begin to peter out, Dusk Till Dawn is just getting started. A noisy Filipino rock band keeps the eclectic crowd of locals, expats and backpackers dancing until the sun comes up.

COYOTE'S BAR AND GRILL BAR
Map p372 (www.coyotebarandgrill.com; 114-120 Lockhart Rd; ⊙noon-2am, happy hour 3-8pm; Ⓜ Wan Chai, exit C2) Coyote's has some 70 margaritas made from a choice of 35 tequilas. If that's not enough, go for the 'dentist chair' challenge. The said piece of furniture is usually hidden in the back of the bar and brought out only on request. For HK$50, you can lie back and have the bartender pour a deluge of spirits direct from the bottles into your throat.

DELANEY'S BAR, PUB
(www.delaneys.com.hk; 18 Luard Rd, ground & 1st fl, One Capital Place, Wan Chai; ⊙noon-3am, happy hour noon-9pm; Ⓜ Wan Chai, exit C) At this immensely popular Irish watering hole you can choose between the black-and-white-tiled pub on the ground floor and a sports bar and restaurant on the 1st floor. The food is good and plentiful; the kitchen allegedly goes through 400kg of potatoes a week.

AMICI SPORTS BAR
Map p372 (www.amicihongkong.com; Lockhart Rd, 1st fl, Empire Land Commercial Centre; ⊙noon-1am Sun-Thu, to 2am Fri & Sat; Ⓜ Wan Chai, exit C) The champion of Wan Chai sports bars features ample screens, five beers on tap, decent American-Italian food and a long happy hour. A few local football supporters' clubs have made Amici their base, and it's easy to see why. The atmosphere during live broadcasts of big sporting events is contagious.

AGAVE BAR
Map p372 (www.epicurean.com.hk; 93 Lockhart Rd, Shop C & D; ⊙noon-1am Sun-Thu, to 2am Fri & Sat, happy hour 3-9pm; Ⓜ Wan Chai, exit C) Fans of tequila will be ecstatic here – there are 170 brands of the spirit, and the bartenders are heavy-handed with it. Interiors are brightly coloured with cactus-themed adornments and jovial atmosphere.

CARNEGIE'S PUB
Map p372 (www.carnegies.net; 53-55 Lockhart Rd, ground fl; ⊙11am-late Mon-Thu, from noon Sat, from 5pm Sun, happy hour 11am-9pm Mon-

Sat; Ⓜ Wan Chai, exit C) The rock memorabilia festooning the walls makes it all seem a bit Hard Rock Café-ish, but this place is worth a look all the same. From 9pm on Friday and Saturday, Carnegie's fills up with young revellers, many of whom will end up dancing on the bar which has brass railings in case they fall.

📍 Causeway Bay

EXECUTIVE BAR LOUNGE
Map p374 (☑2893 2080; 3 Yiu Wa St, 7th fl, Bartlock Centre; ⊙5pm-1am Mon-Sat; Ⓜ Causeway Bay, exit A) You won't be served if you just turn up at this clubby, masculine bar high above Causeway Bay – it's by appointment only. Odd perhaps, but worth the trip if you are serious about whisky and bourbon. Several dozen varieties are served here, in large brandy balloons with large orbs of ice hand-chipped by the Japanese proprietor to maximise the tasting experience.

THE CHAPEL BAR
(☑2834 6565; 27 Yik Yam St, Happy Valley; ⊙noon-11pm, happy hour 4.30-8.30pm; ☑30) A low-key neighbourhood bar, the Chapel has beers on tap, the sports channel and British-Indian food. What more can one ask for? Thursday is quiz night (from 9.30pm), but book if you want to go because it's popular.

DICKENS BAR BAR
Map p374 (www.mandarinoriental.com/excelsior/dining/dickens_bar; 281 Gloucester Rd, Basement, Excelsior Hong Kong; ⊙noon-1am Mon-Fri, to 2am Fri & Sat, happy hour 4-8pm; Ⓜ Causeway Bay, exit D1) Dickens has been popular with expats and locals for decades. Designed to resemble a British pub, it has a longer beer list that includes rare selections like Black Sheep Ale, and improved modern UK pub grub. The big-screen sports coverage is still there, and so is the still-popular curry buffet at lunch.

BUDDY BAR BAR
Map p374 (☑2882 9780; 22 School St, Tai Hang; ⊙to 3am; Ⓜ Tin Hau, exit B) In the up-and-coming Tai Hang neighbourhood, this low-key neighbourhood bar is the kind of place where everybody knows your name (or they would, if you lived in Tai Hang) and your dog is welcome to snooze at your feet while you down a pint of Belgian ale.

HONG KONG ISLAND: WAN CHAI & THE NORTHEAST DRINKING & NIGHTLIFE

INN SIDE OUT PUB

Map p374 (☑2895 2900; 88 Caroline Hill Rd, Causeway Bay; ☺11.30am-1am; ☑23) A chill, American-style bar overlooking the South China Athletics Association's golf driving range, Inn Side Out has a good beer selection, plenty of classic bar snacks, and free peanuts to shell and toss on the floor. A 15-minute stroll south of Causeway Bay.

☕ Island East

★**SUGAR** LOUNGE

(29 Taikoo Sing Rd, 32nd fl, East Hotel, Quarry Bay; ☺5pm-2am Mon-Sat, noon-11.30pm Sun; ⓂTai Koo, exit D1) This new bar inside a new business hotel has a lounge with illuminated floors, and an open deck which maximises the impact of the superb East Island views – silvery high-rises on one side and the old Kai Tak airport runway on the other. On a clear night, it's a stunning backdrop to your rendezvous, so understandably, tables fill up fast. Go at 6pm.

☆ ENTERTAINMENT

★**STREET MUSIC CONCERTS** LIVE MUSIC

(☑2582 0280; www.kungmusic.hk; Wan Chai) **FREE** Don't miss one of the free outdoor gigs thrown by eclectic musician Kung Chi-sing. One Saturday a month, the musician holds a concert outside the Hong Kong Arts Centre (6.30pm to 9pm). The exciting line-ups have included anything from indie rock, punk and jazz to Cantonese opera and Mozart. It's excellent, professional-quality

music performed in an electrifying atmosphere. There's also performances at the Blue House (p111) on the second Thursday of the month (7.30pm to 9.30pm). Check the website for dates.

WANCH LIVE MUSIC

Map p372 (☑2861 1621; www.thewanch.hk; 54 Jaffe Rd, Wan Chai; ⓂWan Chai, exit C) This place, which derives its name from what everyone calls the district, has live music (mostly rock and folk with the occasional solo guitarist thrown in) seven nights a week from 9pm. Jam night is Monday from 8pm.

HONG KONG ARTS CENTRE DANCE, THEATRE

Map p372 (香港藝術中心; ☑2582 0200; www. hkac.org.hk; 2 Harbour Rd, Wan Chai; ⓂWan Chai, exit C) The Hong Kong Arts Centre is a popular venue for dance, theatre and music performances.

SUNBEAM THEATRE THEATRE

(新光戲院; ☑2563 2959, 2856 0161; www.sun beamtheatre.com/hk; 423 King's Rd, Kiu Fai Mansion, North Point; ⓂNorth Point, exit A4) Cantonese opera is performed at this vintage theatre throughout the year. Performances generally run for about a week, and are usually held five days a week at 7.30pm, with occasional matinees at 1pm or 1.30pm.

PUNCHLINE COMEDY CLUB COMEDY

Map p372 (☑2598 1222; www.punchlinecomedy.com/hongkong; 30 Harbour Rd, Tamarind, 2nd fl, Sun Hung Kai Centre, Wan Chai; ☑18, alight at Wan Chai Sports Ground) A veteran on the scene, the Punchline hosts local and imported acts approximately every third Thursday, Friday and Saturday from

---

WAN CHAI'S UPRIGHT ARTISTS' VILLAGE

Foo Tak Building (富德樓; 365 Hennessy Rd; Ⓜ Wan Chai, exit A2), overlooking the tram tracks, looks no different from any old tenement block in Wan Chai, but tucked away in its 14 storeys are the studios and/or living quarters of artists, activists, indie film groups, publishers and musicians.

Foo Tak was built in 1968 as a residential building, but in the 2000s, its landlady turned the property into an art village. Now young, 'starving' artists can rent the units within the premises for a small sum of money.

The best way to experience Foo Tak is to proceed to the 14th floor and check out each level from top down. The building itself is interesting to walk around in. Despite a major renovation in 2003, it still retains some of the features of late 1960s local architecture.

You can check out the websites of the following for the latest events: Ying e Chi, on the 4th floor, is an indie film group that hosts regular free screenings (look for their schedule on their Facebook page). **Visible Record** (www.visiblerecord.com), on the 3rd floor, promotes documentary films.

9pm to 11pm. Entry costs around HK$300. Book tickets online or call.

HONG KONG ACADEMY FOR THE PERFORMING ARTS
DANCE, THEATRE

Map p372 (香港演藝學院; ☑ 2584 8500; www.hkapa.edu; 1 Gloucester Rd, Wan Chai; Ⓜ Admiralty, exit E2) The APA (p112) is a major performance venue for dance, music and theatre.

AMC PACIFIC PLACE
CINEMA

Map p370 (☑ 2869 0322; www.amccinemas.com.hk; 1st fl, 1 Pacific Pl, Admiralty; Ⓜ Admiralty, exit F) This cinema inside the Pacific Place mall in Admiralty screens some of the more interesting current releases.

WINDSOR CINEMA
CINEMA

Map p374 (皇室戲院; ☑3516 8811; www.uacinemas.com.hk; Gloucester Rd, 4th fl, Windsor House, Causeway Bay; Ⓜ Causeway Bay, exit E) Part of the 12-strong UA circuit, this comfortable cineplex is just west of Victoria Park.

🛍 SHOPPING

Admiralty's sleek shopping mall, Pacific Place, can be accessed via Admiralty MTR station. Wan Chai is a good spot for medium- and low-priced clothing, sporting goods and footwear. Causeway Bay is a crush of shopping malls, department stores and smaller outlets selling designer and street fashion, electronics, sporting goods and household items.

★DAYDREAM NATION
CLOTHING

Map p372 (☑3741 0758; www.daydream-nation.com; 2 Harbour Rd, 2nd fl, Hong Kong Arts Centre, Wan Chai; ⊙11am-10pm; Ⓜ Wan Chai, exit C) Soaring rent has exiled this dreamy nation from its home near Star St to the Hong Kong Arts Centre. A 'Vogue Talent 2010' brand founded by two of the most creative local designers around (Kay Wong and her brother Jing, who's also a musician), DN is known for its highly wearable fashion and accessories that come with a touch of theatricality.

★KAPOK
CLOTHING, ACCESSORIES

Map p370 (☑2549 9254; www.ka-pok.com; 5 St Francis Yard, Wan Chai; ⊙11am-8pm, to 6pm Sun; Ⓜ Admiralty, exit F) In the hip Star St area, this boutique has a fastidiously edited selection of luxe-cool local and international clothing and accessory labels. Look for its

new line of Kapok-label made-in-HK men's shirts, and graphic Mischa handbags by local designer Michelle Lai. The sister boutique is around the corner at 3 Sun St.

★ESLITE
BOOKS

Map p374 (☑3419 6789; 500 Hennessy Rd, Causeway Bay, Hysan Place, 8th-10th fl; ⊙10am-11pm Sun-Thu, to 2am Fri & Sat; Ⓜ Causeway Bay, exit F2) You could spend an entire evening in this swank three-floor Taiwanese bookstore (really – it's open til 2am on weekends), which features a massive collection of English and Chinese books and magazines, a shop selling gorgeous stationery and leather-bound journals, a cafe, a bubble-tea counter, and a huge kids toy and book section.

★WAN CHAI COMPUTER CENTRE
ELECTRONICS

Map p372 (灣仔電腦城; 130-138 Hennessy Rd, 1st fl, Southorn Centre, Wan Chai; ⊙10am-8pm Mon-Sat; Ⓜ Wan Chai, exit B2) This gleaming, beeping warren of tiny shops is a safe bet for anything digital and electronic.

CHINA GOODS CENTRE
DEPARTMENT STORE

(☑2856 0333; 395-421 King's Rd, North Point; ⊙10am-6pm; Ⓜ North Point, A4) This very local Chinese department store has everything from ginseng to silk baby slippers to acupuncture models to calligraphy brushes. Crowded, dusty and entirely non-English, it's a fun place to poke around for gifts and souvenirs without the hassle of bargaining.

MUJI
CLOTHING, HOUSEWARES

Map p374 (☑3971 3120; 99 Percival St, Lee Theatre, Causeway Bay; ⊙11am-10.30pm; Ⓜ Causeway Bay, exit F1) The Hong Kong flagship of the cult-hit Japanese brand, this two-storey Muji is chock full of charmingly designed, neutral-toned clothing, housewares, beauty products and toys. The section of Japanese snacks like sour plum candy and animal-shaped seaweed crackers is irresistible.

PAPABUBBLE
FOOD

Map p374 (☑2367 4807; www.papabubble.com.hk; 34 Tung Lo Wan Rd, Tai Hang; ⊙11am-10pm; Ⓜ Tin Hau, exit B) This Spanish artisan candy company's Hong Kong outpost sells unique-to-here flavours like lemon tea and durian, featuring local designs such as Chinese zodiac animals and the character for 'double happiness'. Great gifts. Kids will love watching the hot sugar being pulled behind the counter.

HYSAN PLACE
MALL

Map p374 (☎2886 7222; www.hp.leegardens.com.
hk; 500 Hennessy Rd, Causeway Bay; MCauseway
Bay, exit F2) This shiny new 17-storey mall is
filled with hundreds of ever-trendy Japanese
and Korean clothing and beauty brands in a
more upscale environment than other local
teeny-bopper havens. The 6th-floor Garden
of Eden features youth-oriented Asian cosmetics and lingerie labels.

TWO GIRLS
BEAUTY

Map p374 (www.twogirls.hk; 2-10 Great George
St, Causeway Bay, Causeway Place, Shop 207;
☉noon-10pm; MCauseway Bay, exit E) Hong
Kong's first cosmetics brand has been selling fragrant, highly affordable creams and
potions since 1898. The pretty, retro packaging featuring two cheongsam-clad beau-
ties makes these excellent gifts. We like the
spicy Florida Water cologne.

PACIFIC PLACE
MALL

Map p370 (太古廣場; ☎2844 8988; www.pacific-
place.com.hk; 88 Queensway, Admiralty; MAdmiralty, exit F) Pacific Place mall has a couple
of hundred outlets, dominated by high-end
men's and women's fashion and accessories.
There's also a **Lane Crawford department
store** (連卡佛; ☎2118 3398; level 1, Pacific Place;
☉10am-9pm) and a **Joyce boutique** (☎2523
5944; Shop 334, 3rd fl, Pacific Place).

KELLY & WALSH
BOOKS

Map p370 (☎2522 5743; www.kellyandwalsh.com;
88 Queensway, Glass House, L2, Pacific Place, Admiralty; ☉10.30am-8pm; MAdmiralty, exit F) A
good selection of art, design and culinary
books plus a handy kids' reading lounge.

CHINESE ARTS & CRAFTS
DEPARTMENT STORE

Map p370 (88 Queensway, Shop 220, Pacific Place;
☉10am-9pm; MAdmiralty, exit F) Mainland-
owned CAC is probably the best place in
Hong Kong to buy quality jade, porcelain,

chopsticks and other pricey Chinese crafts;
it's positively an Aladdin's cave of souvenirs. On Hong Kong Island there are also
branches in Central (Map p370; ☎2901 0338;
59 Queen's Rd, ground fl, Asia Standard Tower;
MAdmiralty, exit F) and Wan Chai (Map p372; 28
Harbour Rd, 2nd Causeway Centre; MWan Chai,
exit A5).

COSMOS BOOKS
BOOKS

Map p372 (天地圖書; ☎2866 1677; www.cos-
mosbooks.com.hk; 30 Johnston Rd, ground &
1st fl, Wan Chai; ☉10am-8pm; ☐6, 6A, 6X) This
chain-store branch has a good selection of
China-related books in the basement. Upstairs are English-language books (nonfic-
tion is strong). Enter from Lun Fat St.

KUNG FU SUPPLIES
SPORTS

Map p372 (功夫用品公司; ☎2891 1912; www.
kungfu.com.hk; 188-192 Johnston Rd, Room
6a, 6th fl, Chuen Fung House, Wan Chai; ☉Mon-
Sat; ☐6, 6A, 6X) If you need to stock up on
martial-arts accessories, including uni-
forms, nunchakus and safety weapons for
practice, or just want to thumb through a
decent collection of books and DVDs, this
is the place to go. The staff here is very
helpful.

ISLAND BEVERLEY MALL
MALL

Map p374 (金百利商場; 1 Great George St, Causeway Bay; MCauseway Bay, exit E) Crammed
into buildings, up escalators and in back
lanes are Hong Kong's malls of microshops
selling local designer threads, garments
from other parts of Asia and a kaleidoscope
of kooky accessories.

TIMES SQUARE
MALL

Map p374 (時代廣場; www.timessquare.com.
hk; 1 Matheson St, Causeway Bay; MCauseway
Bay, exit A) The 10 floors of retail organised
by type are slightly less high-end than in
Central, but with selections of electronics,

WAN CHAI'S MARKETS

The area sandwiched by Queen's Rd East and Johnston Rd in Wan Chai is a lively
outdoor bazaar thronged with vendors, shoppers and parked cars. Cross St and the
northern section of Stone Nullah Lane feature **wet markets** (☉7.30am-7pm) in all their
screaming splendour. **Tai Yuen Street**, aka 'toy street' (玩具街; *woon gui kaai*) to locals, has hawkers selling goldfish, plastic flowers and granny underwear, but it's best
known for its traditional **toy shops** (Map p372; 14-19 Tai Yuen St; ☉10am-8.30pm) where
you'll find not only kiddies' playthings, but clockwork tin and other kidult collectibles.
Spring Garden Lane and Wan Chai Rd are a treasure trove of quirky shops selling
everything from Indian and Southeast Asian spices to funerary offerings and gadgets.

There are restaurants on the 10th to 13th floors, and snack bars, cafes and a supermarket in the basement.

CITYPLAZA
MALL

(太古城; ☑2568 8665; www.cityplaza.com.hk; 18 Tai Koo Shing Rd, Tai Koo Shing, Quarry Bay; Ⓜ Tai Koo, exit D2) The largest shopping centre in eastern Hong Kong Island, with 180 shops, Cityplaza is directly linked to the MTR.

MOUNTAIN SERVICES
OUTDOOR EQUIPMENT

Map p374 (名峰行; 52–56 King's Rd, Shop 1, Fortress Hill; ⊙11am-7pm Mon-Sat; Ⓜ Fortress Hill, exit A) This excellent shop sells climbing and hiking gear and pretty much everything you need for tackling Hong Kong's hills and country parks. Turn left when you exit the MTR station and walk for three minutes.

BUNN'S DIVERS
SPORTS

Map p372 (賓氏潛水學院; ☑3422 3322; www.bunnsdivers.com; 188-192 Johnston Rd, Mezzanine, Chuen Fung House, Wan Chai; Ⓜ Wan Chai, exit A3) Masks, snorkels, fins, regulators, tanks – Hong Kong's longest-established dive shop also runs dive tours and training courses.

🏃 SPORTS & ACTIVITIES

EASTERN NATURE TRAIL
HIKING

(東區自然步道) Belonging to Stage 5 of the Hong Kong Trail, this 9km, three-hour nature trail, so called because of the indigenous trees and birds you'll meet along it, starts on Mount Parker Rd in Quarry Bay and ends on Wong Nai Chung Gap Rd in Tai Tam. The trail features historic sites including WWII military relics and a house in red brick that belonged to a sugar refinery.

You'll pass beautiful Tai Tam Country Park as you descend to Tai Tam Reservoir. Following Tai Tam Reservoir Rd, you'll reach Wong Nai Chung Gap Rd.

To get to the start, take exit B from Tai Koo MTR station, head 600m west and turn into Quarry St. The start of the trail is near the Quarry Bay Municipal Services Building at 38 Quarry St.

TAI TAM WATERWORKS HERITAGE TRAIL
HIKING

(大潭水務文物徑) This 5km scenic trail will take you past reservoirs and a handsome collection of some 20 historic waterworks structures. These bridges, aqueducts, valve houses, pumping stations and dams, many still working, are feats of Victorian utilitarian engineering.

The trail, which ends at Tai Tam Tuk Raw Water Pumping Station, takes about two hours. Enter at Wong Nai Chung Gap near the luxury flats of Hong Kong Parkview, or at the junction of Tai Tam Rd and Tai Tam Reservoir Rd. On weekends you'll see residents taking a walk with their dogs, kids, maids, chauffeurs and nannies.

From Admiralty MTR station, bus 6 takes you to Wong Nai Chung Reservoir. Walk east along Tai Tam Reservoir Rd.

HONG KONG TENNIS CENTRE
TENNIS

(香港網球中心; ☑2574 9122; 133 Wong Nai Chung Gap Rd, Happy Valley; per hour day/evening HK$42/57; ⊙7am-11pm; 🚌6) The Hong Kong Tennis Centre, with 17 courts, is on a spectacular hill pass between Happy Valley and Deep Water Bay on Hong Kong Island. It's usually easy to get a court during working hours.

ROYAL HONG KONG YACHT CLUB
BOATING

Map p374 (香港遊艇會; ☑2832 2817; www.rhkyc.org.hk; Hung Hing Rd, Kellett Island, Causeway Bay; Ⓜ Causeway Bay, exit D1) It's private but you can try to get visiting membership if you belong to a reciprocal club. Subscription fees are waived for the first two weeks for visitors.

SOUTH CHINA ATHLETIC ASSOCIATION
GYM

Map p374 (南華體育會; ☑2577 6932; www.scaa.org.hk; 88 Caroline Hill Rd, 5th fl, South China Sports Complex, Causeway Bay; visitor membership per month HK$60; 🚌31) The SCAA has a 1000-sq-metre gym, with modern exercise machinery and an aerobics room, as well as a sauna, steam room and massage room.

VICTORIA PARK
TENNIS

Map p374 (Hing Fat St, Causeway Bay; ⊙6am or 7am-11pm; Ⓜ Causeway Bay, exit E) The park has 13 standard tennis courts, two lawn bowls greens and swimming pools, as well as football pitches, basketball courts and jogging trails.

Hong Kong Island: Aberdeen & the South

ABERDEEN | POK FU LAM | DEEP WATER BAY | REPULSE BAY | STANLEY | SHEK O

Aberdeen & the South Top Five

1 Lounging on the golden sands of the laid-back beach village of **Shek O** (p134).

2 Having hair-raising fun in **Ocean Park** (p132) and befriending the resident pandas.

3 Downing a pint or two at the British-style pubs in the seaside colonial town of **Stanley** (p136).

4 Catching a glimpse into the lives of seafarers by hopping on a **sampan** (p137) at Aberdeen.

5 Shopping till you drop at Hong Kong's **largest outlet mall** (p137) in Ap Lei Chau.

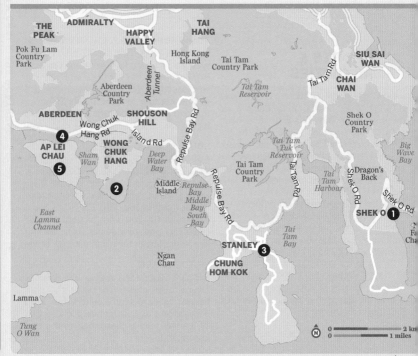

For more detail of this area see Map p376 and p377 ➡

Explore: Aberdeen & the South

The long coastline along the south of the island means you'll need a half to a full day to explore each of the areas listed below. Beach hopping is doable.

Aberdeen's theme park, Ocean Park, is a store of fun for kids and adults alike. Expect a full day there. More sedentary travellers can opt for a boozy brunch or a hearty seafood lunch in Aberdeen. Treasure hunters can find designer bargains in Ap Lei Chau in Aberdeen.

A posh beach suburb, Repulse Bay has Hong Kong's most famous beach and some of its richest residents. The hills around the beach are strewn with luxury apartment blocks, the iconic Repulse Bay being the most famous.

Stanley, with a lively market and friendly beaches, plus a fascinating mix of museums and heritage sites, certainly deserves another full day of exploration.

On Hong Kong Island's far southeast, Shek O is a laid-back village that still oozes an old-world charm and has one of the best (and quietest) beaches on the island. Shek O has enough activities to keep you amused plus several passable dining and drinking options.

Local Life

→ **Shopping** When shopping in the mammoth Horizon Plaza (p137), wear sensible shoes like the locals, and have a taxi call-centre number ready (☏2368 1318).

→ **Seafood** It's common for foodies to buy their own seafood in a wet market and have it cooked in a *dai pai dong* (food stall) of their choice. Ap Lei Chau Market and its associated Cooked Food Centre (p134) offer seafood lovers that winning formula.

Getting There & Away

For Shek O, take bus 9 from Shau Kei Wan MTR station (exit A3). For Stanley from Shau Kei Wan, take bus 14 from Shau Kei Wan Rd, a short walk from the MTR station (exit A3). Buses 6, 6A, 6X, 66 and 260 come here via Repulse Bay. These routes all begin in Central, below Exchange Sq. For Aberdeen, Buses 73 and 973 from Stanley call at Repulse Bay and Aberdeen Main St. Green minibus 40 runs from Tang Lung St in Causeway Bay to Stanley via Ocean Park. Buses 40 and 40M leave for Pok Fu Lam from Wan Chai Ferry Pier via Admiralty. Buses 7, 90B and 91 link Pok Fu Lam with Aberdeen Praya Rd in Aberdeen. To get to Repulse Bay from Central, below Exchange Sq, take bus 6, 6A, 6X, 66 or 260. To get here from Aberdeen take bus 73 or 973 – both stop on Aberdeen Main Rd. To get to Deep Water Bay from Central, below Exchange Sq, take bus 6A, 6X or 260. To get here from Aberdeen take bus 73 or 973.

Lonely Planet's Top Tip

The beaches on the south side of Hong Kong are best enjoyed on weekdays when you can have them to yourself. The discreet **St Stephen's Beach** (p134) boasts fine water quality and near-perfect sunset views.

✖ Best Places to Eat

→ Verandah (p136)
→ Happy Garden (p136)
→ Saffron Bakery Café (p135)

For reviews, see p134 ➡

◉ Best Beaches to Visit

→ Shek O (p134)
→ Repulse Bay (p133)
→ St Stephen's (p134)

For reviews, see p132 ➡

🛍 Best Places to Shop

→ Horizon Plaza (p137)
→ G.O.D. (p137)

For reviews, see p137 ➡

SIGHTS

◉ Aberdeen

OCEAN PARK   AMUSEMENT PARK

(☑3923 2323; www.oceanpark.com.hk; Ocean Park Rd; adult/child 3-11yr HK$320/160; ⏱10am-7.30pm; ⓦ; ▣629 from Admiralty, ▣973 from Tsim Sha Tsui, ▣6A, 6X, 70, 75 from Central, ▣72, 72A, 92 from Causeway Bay) It may have to compete with the natural crowd-pulling powers of Disneyland on Lantau, but for many Ocean Park remains the top theme park in Hong Kong. The park's constant expansion and addition of new rides and thrills, as well as the presence of four giant pandas plus two very cute, rare red pandas – all gifts from the mainland – have kept this a must-visit for families.

The park is divided into two main sections. The main entrance is on the Waterfront (lowland) side and is linked to the main section on the Summit (headland) via a scenic **cable car** ride and a marine-themed funicular train called the **Ocean Express**.

The major attractions at the Waterfront are **Amazing Asian Animals** and **Aqua City**, where animals and sea creatures come with some worthwhile educational content. The newest addition is the **Grand Aquarium** which boasts the world's largest aquarium dome with a 5.5m diameter and is home to 5000 fish (400 species). Another new zone, **Old Hong Kong**, is a replica of the old buildings and communities that once graced Wan Chai and older parts of Kowloon. To the north is **Whiskers Harbour**, which thrives on an assortment of kid-oriented rides.

On the Summit, the **Thrill Mountain** has plenty of white-knuckle rides, such as the celebrated roller coaster, Hair Raiser. In **Marine World** you'll find sea lions and seals plus daily dolphin and killer-whale shows. Meanwhile, the **Chinese Sturgeon Aquarium** showcases another living gift from the mainland.

TIN HAU TEMPLE   TEMPLE

Map p376 (天后廟; Aberdeen Main Rd; ▣70) If you have time to spare, a short walk through Aberdeen will bring you to a Tin Hau temple from 1851. Once you're in the vicinity, check out the series of quirky shrines that are dedicated to local deities; you'll see them on the slope behind the rest area on Old Main St.

◉ Pok Fu Lam

BÉTHANIE   HISTORIC BUILDING

(伯大尼修院; ☑2854 8918; www.hkapa.edu/asp/general/general_visitors.asp; 139 Pok Fu Lam Rd; admission HK$30; ⏱11am-5pm; ▣7, 40, 40M, 90B, 91) Perched on hilly Pok Fu Lam, a college and residential area northwest of Aberdeen, this beautiful restoration is a highlight in this part of town. The complex, which now houses a film school, was built by the French Mission in 1875 as a sanatorium for priests from all over Asia to rest and recover from tropical diseases before they returned to their missions.

The guided tour will include a visit to the neo-Gothic Béthanie Chapel, a new theatre in the two octagonal Dairy Farm cowsheds, and the wine-cellar-converted museum which displays the history of the mission. Tours are run hourly and it's wise to call ahead, as some venues may not be accessible when they've been hired. The nearest bus stop is at the junction of Pok Fu Lam Reservoir and Pok Fu Lam Rd.

POK FU LAM VILLAGE   VILLAGE

(薄扶林村; www.pokfulamvillage.org; ▣7, 40, 40M, 90B, 91) On a sloping hillside, Pok Fu Lam Village, a settlement full of shacks and makeshift huts, is quite a contrast to the condos behind. You can catch a glimpse of the Hong Kong of yesteryear when refugees from China built their temporary-turned-permanent homes here. There's a 200-year-old pagoda on the northern side of the village, and a spectacular fire dragon dance takes place here during the Mid-Autumn Festival.

◉ Deep Water Bay

DEEP WATER BAY   BEACH

(▣6, 6A, 6X, 260) A quiet little inlet with a beach flanked by shade trees, Deep Water Bay is a few kilometres northwest of Repulse Bay. There are a handful of places to eat and have a drink, and some barbecue pits at the southern end of the beach. If you want a dip in the water, this spot is usually less crowded than Repulse Bay. Deep Water Bay beach is a centre for wakeboarding.

◉ Repulse Bay

REPULSE BAY
BEACH

(淺水灣; 🚍6, 6A, 6X, 260) The long beach with tawny sand at Repulse Bay is visited by Chinese tourist groups year-round and, needless to say, packed on weekends in summer. It's a good place if you like people-watching. The beach has showers and changing rooms and shade trees at the roadside, but the water is pretty murky.

Middle Bay and **South Bay**, about 10 and 30 minutes to the south respectively, have beaches that are usually much less crowded.

KWUN YAM SHRINE
TEMPLE

(觀音廟; 🚍6, 6A, 6X, 260) Towards the southeast end of Repulse Bay beach is Kwun Yam Shrine, an unusual shrine to Kwun Yam, the goddess of mercy. The surrounding area has an amazing assembly of deities and figures – goldfish, rams, the money god and other southern Chinese icons, as well as statues of Tin Hau. Most of the statues were funded by local personalities and businesspeople during the 1970s.

In front of the shrine to the left as you face the sea is **Longevity Bridge** (長壽橋); crossing it is supposed to add three days to your life.

◉ Stanley

MURRAY HOUSE
HISTORIC BUILDING

Map p377 (美利樓; Stanley Bay; 🚍6, 6A, 6X, 260) Across the bay from Stanley Main St stands this three-storey colonnaded affair. Built in 1846 as officers' quarters, it took pride of place in Central, on the spot where the Bank of China Tower now stands, for almost 150 years until 1982. It was re-erected here stone-by-stone and opened in 2001. Today it's home to a number of restaurants, many with lovely sea views.

TIN HAU TEMPLE
TEMPLE

Map p377 (119 Stanley Main St; 🚍6, 6A, 6X, 260) At the western end of Stanley Main St, past a tiny **Tai Wong shrine** (大王廟; Map377) and through the Stanley Plaza shopping complex, is a Tin Hau temple, built in 1767. Its appearance has completely changed over the years, however, and it's now a concrete pile. The walk here is well worthwhile for the sea views.

THE BUILDING WITH THE HOLE

Anyone passing through Repulse Bay can't help but notice the enormous residential tower with the giant square hole in the middle, like an architectural doughnut. According to feng shui principles, it's unlucky to block the dragon who lives in the mountain from accessing the sea. If he can't get through, he might just knock the building down. The hole accommodates the dragon, and keeps the building, called The Repulse Bay, standing.

A sign in the temple explains that the tiger skin hanging on the wall came from an animal that 'weighed 240 pounds, was 73 inches long, and three feet high [and] shot by an Indian policeman, Mr Rur Singh, in front of Stanley Police Station in the year 1942'.

OLD STANLEY
POLICE STATION
HISTORIC BUILDING

Map p377 (舊赤柱警署; 88 Stanley Village Rd; 🚍6, 6A, 6X, 260) The most interesting building in the village itself is this two-storey structure from 1859. It now contains, less interestingly, a Wellcome supermarket.

STANLEY MILITARY CEMETERY
CEMETERY

(赤柱軍人墳場; ☎2557 3498; Wong Ma Kok Rd; ⊙8am-5pm; 🚍14, 6A) South of Stanley Market, this cemetery for armed forces personnel and their families is also a highlight in Stanley. The oldest graves date back to 1843 and are an intriguing document of the colonial era. The earlier graves show just how great a toll disease took on European settlers, while the number of graves from the early 1940s serves as a reminder of the many who died during the fight for Hong Kong and subsequent internment at the hands of occupying Japanese forces.

To reach the cemetery, walk south along Wong Ma Kok Rd for 15 minutes.

ST STEPHEN'S COLLEGE
HISTORIC SITE

Map p377 (聖士提反書院文物徑; ☎2813 0360; www.ssc.edu.hk/ssctrail/eng; 22 Tung Tau Wan Rd; 🚍6, 6A, 6X, 260) FREE WWII history buffs can visit the beautiful campus of St Stephen's College which sits right next to Stanley Military Cemetery. Founded in 1903, the school was turned into an emergency military hospital on the eve of the

Japanese invasion of Hong Kong in 1941 and became an internment camp after the city fell. The 1½-hour guided tour by students takes you to eight sites in the campus.

Poignant reminders of the war include the colonial-style School House, which witnessed what has become known as the St Stephen's College Massacre when Japanese soldiers stormed into the building and killed 56 British and Canadian soldiers who were still wounded in their beds, on Christmas Eve in 1941. The austere chapel was built in 1950 on the highest point of the campus in memory of the war victims. There's also a museum showing the school's interesting history as the Eton of the East. Admission to the trail is by guided tour only – reserve in advance via the website.

HONG KONG CORRECTIONAL SERVICES MUSEUM
MUSEUM

Map p377 (香港懲教博物館; ☎2147 3199; www.csd.gov.hk/emuseum; 45 Tung Tau Wan Rd; ⊘10am-5pm Tue-Sun; 🚌6, 6A, 6X, 260) FREE Mock cells, gallows and flogging stands are the gruesome draws at this museum, about 500m southeast of Stanley Village Rd, which traces the history of jails, prisons and other forms of incarceration in Hong Kong.

ST STEPHEN'S BEACH
BEACH

(🚌6A, 14) A short walk south of Stanley village is this great little bolthole which comes handily with a cafe, showers and changing rooms. In summer you can hire windsurfing boards and kayaks from the watersports centre.

◉ Shek O

SHEK O
BEACH

(🚌9 from Shau Kei Wan MTR station, exit A3) Shek O beach has a large expanse of sand, shady trees to the rear, showers, changing facilities and lockers for rent.

BIG WAVE BAY
BEACH

(🚌18M from Chai Wan MTR) The fine and often deserted Big Wave Bay beach, 2km north of Shek O, is popular with surfers for its (occasional) big waves. One of eight prehistoric rock carvings discovered in Hong Kong is on the headland above Big Wave – just follow the signs.

✗ EATING

Choices in Shek O and Repulse Bay are sparse, but you'll still manage to eat decently, and enjoy the views on the coast. Stanley boasts the largest number of midrange restaurants, with a few standing out. Aberdeen and Ap Lei Chau are home to a few hidden gems if you dig beneath the kitsch.

✗ Aberdeen

TREE CAFE
CAFE $

Map p376 (☎2870 1582; www.tree.com.hk/cafe; 2 Lee Wing St, 28/F, Horizon Plaza, Ap Lei Chau; meals from HK$60; ⊘10.30am-7pm; 🚼; 🚌90 from Central) The Horizon Plaza shopping mall is quite out of the way, so if you're feeling peckish after a shopping spree, why not rest your legs in this eco-chic cafe hidden in the eponymous furniture shop on the very top floor of the building? The coffee is arguably among the best on the island. Thoughtfully, there is also a play area for the little ones.

AP LEI CHAU MARKET COOKED FOOD CENTRE
DAI PAI DONG, SEAFOOD $

Map p376 (鴨脷洲市政大廈; 8 Hung Shing St, 1st fl, Ap Lei Chau Municipal Services Bldg; meals from HK$40; 🚌minibus 36X from Lee Garden Rd, Causeway Bay) Sharing a building with a market, six *dai pai dong* operators cook up a storm in sleepy Ap Lei Chau. **Pak Kee** (栢記; ☎2555 2984; ⊘dinner) and **Chu Kee** (珠記; ☎2555 2052; ⊘dinner) both offer simple but tasty seafood dishes in the HK$40 to HK$60 range. You can also buy seafood from the wet market downstairs and pay them to cook it for you the way you want.

Every evening fishermen and dragon boaters come here for the cheap beer and the food. You can also reach the market from Aberdeen Promenade by taking a sampan (p137).

JUMBO KINGDOM FLOATING RESTAURANT
CANTONESE $$

Map p376 (珍寶海鮮舫; ☎2553 9111; www.jumbo.com.hk; Shum Wan Pier Dr, Wong Chuk Hang; meals from HK$120; ⊘11am-11.30pm Mon-Sat, from 9am Sun; 🚌90 from Central) A three-storey floating extravaganza moored in Aberdeen Harbour, the Jumbo looks like Běijīng's Imperial Palace crossbred with

BEACH BBQ, HONG KONG–STYLE

Show up at any Hong Kong beach or country park on a weekend, and you'll see dozens, if not hundreds, of locals enthusiastically brandishing long sharp metal forks. Ancient Hong Kong ritual? Sort of. Here in the SAR, barbecue parties at public beaches and parks replace the kind of indoor or backyard entertaining done in countries where the average home size is larger.

Throwing your own BBQ is surprisingly easy and makes for a great day out. Here's a list of items to bring:

➡ Barbecue forks (sold at most supermarkets for around HK$3)

➡ Tin foil and paper plates

➡ Meat: pre-marinated chicken wings, fish balls, beef cubes and more are sold at most supermarkets

➡ Vegies (corn and mushrooms are good, easy picks)

➡ Salt, oil and condiments of your choice

➡ 'Barbecue honey': This thick syrup is sold at supermarkets, and is used to baste grilled bread, chicken wings, corn and much more

➡ Bread

➡ Charcoal and a lighter

➡ Beer

Best BBQ Spots

Just show up early enough to claim a pit in a public area, start your fire, and you're on your way to barbecuing like a local!

Some of our favorite free public BBQ spots:

➡ Shek O beach (p134)

➡ Stanley beach (p134)

➡ Silvermine Bay Beach at Mui Wo in Lantau (p204)

➡ Lo So Shing Beach in Lamma (p197)

➡ Lion Rock Country Park (p185)

Macau's Casino Lisboa – a spectacle so kitsch it's fun. Celebrity visitors have included everyone from Queen Elizabeth to Tom Cruise to Chow Yun Fat. Eschew the overpriced Dragon Court on the 2nd floor and head to the 3rd floor for dim sum.

There's free transport for diners from the pier on Aberdeen Promenade (p137).

CHEF STUDIO FRENCH $$$
Map p376 (☑3104 4664; chefstudiohk@gmail.com; 40 Wong Chuk Hang Rd, Kwai Bo Industrial Bldg; 7-course tasting menu per person from HK$780; ☺6-10pm Mon-Sat; ☒70 from Exchange Sq in Central) You may not be sure what you're walking into (the factory building housing the restaurant is yet to be revitalised), but once you enter the cavernous fine-dining private kitchen, you'll be in a far better world. This high-end speakeasy flaunts minimalist chic, and there's a mini organic farm on the balcony.

The open kitchen allows you to chit chat with the chef and see how the ingredients are carefully prepared. Eddy Leung, the mastermind here and a lauded practitioner of eco-foodism, wows diners with his French-inspired dishes. Reservation a must, at least a week in advance. No corkage fee. No website, but look for 'Chef Studio by Eddy' on Facebook.

✖ Stanley

SAFFRON BAKERY CAFÉ CAFE, BAKERY $
Map p377 (☑2813-0270; http://saffronbakery.com; ground fl, Stanley Plaza; breakfast from HK$50, meals from HK$80; ☺8am-8pm; ☎❖) Families love the truly organic bread and the kid-friendly atmosphere in this spacious and inviting cafe. Savoury roast vegie salads, face-sized chocolate-chip cookies, and free wi-fi complete the package.

SEI YIK
CANTONESE, DAI PAI DONG **$**

Map p377 (泗益; ☑2813 0503; 2 Stanley Market St; meals from HK$30; ☺6am-7pm Wed-Mon) Weekenders flock to this small tin-roofed *dai pai dong*, right opposite the Stanley Municipal Building, for its fluffy Hong Kong–style French toast with *kaya* (coconut jam) spread. No English signage; look for the long queue of pilgrims and the piles of fruits that hide the entrance.

LUCY'S
INTERNATIONAL **$$**

Map p377 (☑2813 9055; lucys@netvigator.com; 64 Stanley Main St; meals from HK$180; ☺noon-10pm) If the waterfront restaurants are too formulaic for you, seek out this cosy restaurant hidden away in Stanley Market. Lucy's has earned a loyal local following for its tasty French-inspired recipes, friendly service and relatively reasonable prices.

KING LUDWIG BEER HALL
GERMAN **$$**

Map p377 (☑2899 0122; www.kingparrot. com; Shop 202, Murray House, Stanley; meals from HK$180; ☺noon-midnight) This absurd medieval-themed German restaurant has five locations in Hong Kong, but this one has the advantage of being in historic Murray House, with its killer verandah views over the ocean. After a long hike, you just might be able to finish King Ludwig's famous enormous pork knuckle. All-you-can eat weekend brunch is massively popular.

✖ Repulse Bay

SPICES RESTAURANT
SOUTHEAST ASIAN **$$**

(香辣軒; ☑2292 2821; www.therepulsebay.com; 109 Repulse Bay Rd, the Repulse Bay; meals from HK$200; ☺noon-2.30pm & 6.30-10.30pm Mon-Fri, 11.30am-10.30pm Sat & Sat; ☐6, 6A, 6X, 260) The high ceilings, rattan chairs and sparkling wooden flooring evoke the romantic vibes that you'd expect from a beachfront hang-out in Bali. The interior is oriental minimalism, and the open terrace is the best spot for a sundowner. The menu runs the gamut of seafood, satay and curry.

★ VERANDAH
INTERNATIONAL **$$$**

(露台餐廳; ☑2292 2822; www.therepulsebay. com; 109 Repulse Bay Rd, 1st fl, the Repulse Bay; meals from HK$400; ☺noon-2.30pm, 3-5.30pm & 7-10.30pm, brunch 11am-2.30pm Sun; ☐6, 6A, 6X, 260) A meal in the grand Verandah, run by the prestigious Peninsula, is a special occasion indeed. The large restaurant features a recently restored and refurbished interior that is literally dripping with colonial nostalgia, what with the grand piano at the entrance, the wooden fans dangling from the ceiling, and the marble staircases with wooden banisters. The Sunday brunch is famous (book ahead), and the afternoon tea the best this side of Hong Kong Island.

✖ Shek O

HAPPY GARDEN
THAI **$**

(石澳樂園; ☑2809 4165; 786 Shek O Village; lunch/dinner from HK$50/80; ☺11.30am-11pm; ☐9 from Shau Kei Wan MTR station, exit A3) This humble mum-and-dad operation makes everyone happy with fresh seafood, authentic Thai fare and decent prices. Upstairs, the terrace offers some views of the ocean. The restaurant is in front of the car park by the beach.

BLACK SHEEP
INTERNATIONAL **$$**

(黑羊餐廳; ☑2809 2021; 330 Shek O Village; meals from HK$180; ☺6-9pm Mon-Fri, noon-9pm Sat & Sun; ☑; ☐9 from Shau Kei Wan MTR station, exit A3) With batik tablecloths, a plant-filled patio and a hand-written chalkboard menu, this back-alley bistro exudes hippie vibes. Pizzas and seafood are favourites, and there's always a vegie option.

☕ DRINKING & NIGHTLIFE

★ BACK BEACH BAR
BAR

(273 Shek O Village, Shek O Back Beach, Shek O; ☺7pm-1am Tue-Fri, 2pm-1am Sat & Sun; ☐9 from Shau Kei Wan MTR station, exit A3) Hidden on the quiet Shek O Back Beach, locals and expats munch burgers and sip cold brews beneath a rustic awning. A sea-facing shrine stands right next to this rugged ensemble. Enjoy reggae beats and the sound of the lapping waves while sipping beer. From Shek O bus terminal, turn right into the path that leads to an abandoned school and a health centre. The beach is at the end of the path.

SMUGGLERS INN
PUB

Map p377 (90A Stanley Main St, ground fl, Stanley; ☺10am-2am; ☐6, 6A, 6X or 260) This is arguably the most popular pub on the Stanley waterfront, offering perhaps the closest thing to an English pub in Hong Kong.

🛍 SHOPPING

★ G.O.D. — CLOTHING, HOUSEWARES

Map p377 (Goods of Desire; ☎2673 0071; www.god.co.hk; 22-23 Stanley Rd, Stanley, Shop 105, Stanley Plaza; ⏱10.30am-8pm; 🚌6, 6A, 6X, 260) One of the coolest born-in-Hong Kong shops around, G.O.D. does irreverent takes on classic Hong Kong iconography. Think cell phone covers printed with pictures of Hong Kong housing blocks, light fixtures resembling the ones in old-fashioned wet markets, pillows covered in lucky koi print. There are a handful of G.O.D. shops in town, but this is one of the biggest.

HORIZON PLAZA — OUTLETS

Map p376 (新海怡廣場; 2 Lee Wing St, Ap Lei Chau, Aberdeen; ⏱10am-7pm; 🚌90 from Exchange Sq in Central) Tucked away on the southern coast of Ap Lei Chau, this enormous outlet, in a converted factory building, boasts more than 150 shops over 28 storeys. Most locals come here to buy furniture, but you'll also find Alexander McQueens on offer and Jimmy Choos at knock-down prices.

Our favourites are **Tree**, a chic wooden furniture shop on the top floor; **Lane Crawford**, with up to 90% off luxe frocks and footwear; and **Bluebell Fashion Warehouse**, another multibrand outlet that carries a number of designer labels that won't bust a hole in your wallet. (A heads-up: waiting for the lifts is a frustrating exercise here; it's wise to start from the top floor and work your way down.)

To get there, take bus 90 and alight at Ap Lei Chau Estate Terminus. Then take the free shuttle minibus that operates (irregularly) between 7.45am and 7.30pm. There's no bus stop for the shuttles. Wait at the bus station's staff booth near the taxi stand, or it's a 20-minute walk to the outlet.

STANLEY MARKET — MARKET

Map p377 (赤柱市集; Stanley Village Rd; ⏱9am-6pm; 🚌6, 6A, 6X or 260) No big bargains or big stings, just reasonably priced casual clothes, bric-a-brac, souvenirs and formulaic art, all in a nicely confusing maze of alleys running down to Stanley Bay. It's best to go during the week; on the weekend the market is bursting at the seams with tourists and locals alike.

Good choices for gifts and souvenirs include stone 'chops' (stamps) carved with the owner's name, embroidered baby shoes, and pretty, though factory-produced, painted wooden boxes. Do bargain here, though not aggressively.

🏃 SPORTS & ACTIVITIES

SAMPAN TOURS — BOAT TRIPS

Map p376 (Aberdeen Promenade; 🚌70 to Aberdeen) Sampan tours are a fun way to see parts of the island's south coast, and you can easily find sampan operators milling around the eastern end of the Aberdeen Promenade. Usually they charge around HK$68 per person for a 30-minute ride (about HK$120 to Sok Kwu Wan and HK$150 to Yung Shue Wan on Lamma).

If you want just a glimpse of the harbour, you can take a small ferry across to Ap Lei Chau Island (adult/child under 12 HK$2/1.10), which is also a destination for bargain hunters drawn to its outlet stores. Alternatively, just hop on the free ferry to Jumbo Kingdom Floating Restaurant (p134) and come back.

The promenade can be easily accessed from Aberdeen bus terminus. To get to it just take the pedestrian subway under Aberdeen Praya Rd.

ABERDEEN BOAT CLUB — BOATING

Map p376 (香港仔遊艇會; ☎2552 8182; www.abclubhk.com; 20 Shum Wan Rd, Aberdeen; 🚌70, 73, 793) This boat club offers sailing and windsurfing courses to both members and nonmembers.

ABERDEEN MARINA CLUB — BOATING

Map p376 (深灣遊艇俱樂部; ☎2555 8321; www.aberdeenmarinaclub.com; 8 Shum Wan Rd, Aberdeen; 🚌70, 73, 793) Nonmembers must be accompanied by a member in this swish clubhouse.

SHEK O GOLF & COUNTRY CLUB — GOLF

(石澳高爾夫球會; ☎2809 4458; 5 Shek O Rd, Shek O; greens fees HK$300-500; 🚌9, 309) An 18-hole course located on the southeastern edge of Hong Kong Island. Nonmembers must be accompanied by a member.

Kowloon

TSIM SHA TSUI | YAU MA TEI | MONG KOK | NEW KOWLOON

Neighbourhood Top Five

1 Strolling the **Tsim Sha Tsui East Promenade** (p141) against the backdrop of Victoria Harbour.

2 Enjoying scones and Earl Grey at the **Peninsula lobby** (p145), as a string quartet saws away.

3 Taking in the sounds, smells and flavours of the **Temple Street Night Market** (p142).

4 Experiencing a Taoist ceremony or having your fortune told at **Sik Sik Yuen Wong Tai Sin Temple** (p143).

5 Browsing with gadget geeks and comb-over uncles at **Ap Liu Street Flea Market** (p164).

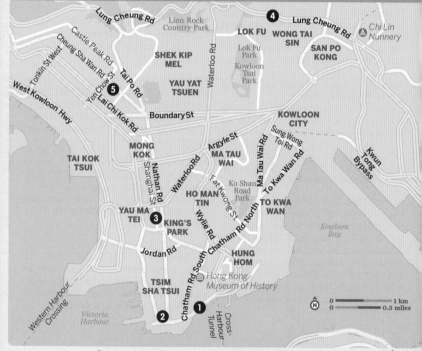

For more detail of this area see Map p378, Map p380, Map p382 and Map p383 ➡

Explore Kowloon

Start your day by spending an hour or two at the Museum of History, then take a leisurely half-hour stroll to the Star Ferry Concourse via the scenic Tsim Sha Tsui East Promenade. Check out the sights along the way, such as the Cultural Centre and the clock tower, and follow up with lunch at an Indian or Shanghainese restaurant.

Walk to Yau Ma Tei, stopping at St Andrew's Church and Kowloon British School along the way. Spend 90 minutes exploring: Tin Hau Temple, the Jade Market and Shanghai St. Then do any one or two of the following: take the MTR to Prince Edward for the Yuen Po St Flower and Bird Market followed by a visit to Mong Kok; visit Sham Shui Po and the Ap Liu Street Flea Market; or go to Diamond Hill to immerse yourself in the tranquillity of Chi Lin Nunnery.

Have dinner at one of the roadside stalls in Yau Ma Tei, then it's on to the Temple Street Night Market. Wrap up your day with drinks in Tsim Sha Tsui (TST).

Local Life

➡ **Hang-out** Film buffs and the artsy crowd like to chill on the upper floor of Mido Café (p156).

➡ **Shopping** Fashionistas seek affordable additions to their wardrobes at the Rise Shopping Arcade (p162) and street-level shops at Granville Circuit.

➡ **Singalong parlours** College kids like to celebrate birthdays in Yau Ma Tei's singalong parlours, like Canton Singing House (p161).

Getting There & Away

➡ **Bus** Buses 2, 6, 6A and 9 run up Nathan Rd to Yau Ma Tei. Buses 5 and 26 leave Tsim Sha Tsui for Ma Tau Chung Rd in New Kowloon.

➡ **MTR** For Tsim Sha Tsui: Tsim Sha Tsui, East Tsim Sha Tsui and Hung Hong stations. For Yau Ma Tei: Yau Ma Tei station. For Mong Kok: Mong Kok and Prince Edward stations. New Kowloon: Sham Shui Po and Cheung Sha Wan stations on the Tsuen Wan line; Kowloon Tong, Lok Fu, Wong Tai Sin, Diamond Hill and Kowloon Bay stations on the Kwun Tong line; Kowloon Tong station on the East Rail line; and Kowloon Station on the Tung Chung line and Airport Express line.

➡ **Macau Ferries** The China Ferry Terminal is on Canton Rd (Tsim Sha Tsui).

➡ **Star Ferry** The Tsim Sha Tsui concourse is at the western end of Salisbury Rd.

KOWLOON

Lonely Planet's Top Tip

Ethnic pockets abound in Kowloon, especially in Tsim Sha Tsui. Indians, Pakistanis and Africans reside in and around Chungking Mansions where you can find the best Indian grocery stores in town; Korean eateries and minimarts proliferate on Kimberley St and Austin Ave; Nepalese (former Gurkhas) congregate near the Temple Street Night Market in Yau Ma Tei; and Kowloon City lays claim to an elephant's share of Hong Kong's Thai eateries.

✕ Best Places to Eat

➡ Sun Tung Lok (p155)
➡ Great Beef Hot Pot (p154)
➡ Yoga Interactive Vegetarian (p153)
➡ Sun Sin (p156)
➡ Yè Shanghai (p154)

For reviews, see p153 ➡

🍷 Best Places to Drink

➡ InterContinental Lobby Lounge (p158)
➡ Butler (p158)
➡ Aqua Spirit (p158)

For reviews, see p158 ➡

☉ Best Places for Culture

➡ Museum of Art (p145)
➡ West Kowloon Cultural District (p160)
➡ Cattle Depot Artist Village (p153)
➡ Hidden Agenda (p159)

For reviews, see p145 ➡

TOP SIGHT
HONG KONG MUSEUM OF HISTORY

If you have time for only one museum, make it the Hong Kong Museum of History. Its whistle-stop overview of the city's natural history, ethnography and indigenous culture will give some lively context to your impressions of Hong Kong. **There are free guided tours in English at 10.30am and 2.30pm on weekends.**

The eight galleries of the **Hong Kong Story** exhibition take you on a fascinating walk through the territory's history, starting with the natural environment and prehistoric Hong Kong (about 6000 years ago), and ending with the territory's return to China in 1997. Interestingly, there's hardly anything on life post-1997.

You'll encounter colourful replicas of a Chinese marriage procession, and the dwellings of the Tanka boat people and the Puntay who built walled villages. You'll see traditional costumes and recreated shophouses from 1881, and board a tram from 1913. You'll watch WWII footage that features interviews with Chinese and foreigners taken prisoner by the Japanese.

The section devoted to Hong Kong urban culture contains replicas of a retro grocery store, a soda fountain and the interiors of a poor man's home. There's a cinema decorated in '60s style, with three screenings daily (11am, 2pm, 4pm) of old Cantonese films – an attraction for the older set who comes here for the movies and the free airconditioning.

The gallery for **special exhibitions** features topics of significance in Hong Kong and Chinese history, which change every few months.

DON'T MISS

➡ The Hong Kong Story
➡ Special exhibitions

PRACTICALITIES

➡ 香港歷史博物館
➡ Map p380
➡ ☎ 2724 9042
➡ http://hk.history. museum
➡ 100 Chatham Rd South, Tsim Sha Tsui
➡ adult/concession HK$10/5, Wed free
➡ ⏱10am-6pm Mon & Wed-Sat, to 7pm Sun
➡ ♿
➡ Ⓜ Tsim Sha Tsui, exit B2

TOP SIGHT
TSIM SHA TSUI EAST PROMENADE

The resplendent views of Victoria Harbour make this walkway one of the best strolls in Hong Kong. Go during the day to take pictures and visit the museums. Then after sundown, revisit the views, now magically transformed, with the skyscrapers of Central and Wan Chai decked out in neon robes.

A good place to begin your journey is at the Former KCR Clock Tower (p145), a landmark of the age of steam, near the Star Ferry Concourse. In 1966 thousands gathered here to protest against a fare increase. The protest erupted into the 1966 riot, the first in a series of social protests leading to colonial reform.

Passing the Cultural Centre and the Museum of Art, you'll arrive at the **Avenue of the Stars** (星光大道; Map p378; Tsim Sha Tsui East Promenade), Hong Kong's lacklustre tribute to its once-brilliant film industry. The highlight here is a 2.5m tall bronze statue of kung fu icon Bruce Lee.

From here, every evening, you can watch the **Symphony of Lights** (⏲ 8-8.20pm), the world's largest permanent laser light show projected from atop dozens of skyscrapers.

The walk takes you past the hotels of the reclaimed area known as Tsim Sha Tsui East, and past that to the **Hong Kong Coliseum** and the Hung Hom train station. The further north you go, the quieter it gets, and tourists and pleasure boats are replaced by container barges and men angling for fish.

The promenade is packed during the **Chinese New Year** fireworks displays in late January/early February and in June during the **Dragon Boat Festival** .

DON'T MISS

➡ The views
➡ Clock Tower
➡ Bruce Lee statue
➡ Symphony of Lights

PRACTICALITIES

➡ 尖沙嘴東部海濱花園
➡ Map p380
➡ Salisbury Rd, Tsim Sha Tsui
➡ Ⓜ Tsim Sha Tsui, exit E

TOP SIGHT
TEMPLE STREET NIGHT MARKET

Hong Kong's liveliest night market, Temple St extends from Man Ming Lane in the north to Nanking St in the south, and is cut in two by historic Tin Hau Temple (p149). It's a great place to go for the bustling atmosphere, the smells and tastes on offer from the *dai pai dong* (food stalls), the free Cantonese opera performances, and some fortune-telling. The market is at its best from about 7pm to 10pm, when it's clogged with stalls and people.

While you may find better bargains over the border in Shēnzhèn, people still shop here for cheap clothes, watches and everyday items. Any marked prices should be considered suggestions – this is definitely a place to bargain.

For alfresco dining, head for Woo Sung St, running parallel to the east, or to the section of Temple St north of the temple. You can get anything from a bowl of wonton noodles to oyster omelettes and Nepalese curries. There are also seafood and hotpot restaurants in the area. For an unusual experience, take a seat at a **singalong parlour** and order delivery.

Every evening a gaggle of **fortune-tellers** sets up tents in the middle of the market where they make predictions about your life (for HK$100 up) by reading your face and palm, or based on your date of birth. Some keep birds that have been trained to pick out 'fortune' cards. Most operators speak some English.

If you're in luck, you'll catch snippets of a Cantonese opera performed under the stars. Some of the most famous stars of the opera stage began their careers in this humble fashion – or so they say.

If you want to carry on, visit the charming Yau Ma Tei Wholesale Fruit Market (p149) which comes alive from 4am.

To get here from Yau Ma Tei MTR station, follow Man Ming Lane.

DON'T MISS

➡ Shopping
➡ Street food
➡ Fortune-tellers
➡ Temple St singalong parlours
➡ Wholesale Fruit Market

PRACTICALITIES

➡ 廟街夜市
➡ Map p382
➡ Yau Ma Tei
➡ ⏲6-11pm
➡ Ⓜ Yau Ma Tei, exit C

MIRSOV RUSU / GETTY IMAGES ©

TOP SIGHT
SIK SIK YUEN WONG TAI SIN TEMPLE

An explosion of pillars, roofs, and lattice work in bright colours, this busy Taoist temple is a destination for all walks of life, from pensioners to young professionals. Some come simply to pray, others to divine the future with chìm (bamboo 'fortune sticks') which are shaken out of a box onto the ground and interpreted by a fortune-teller.

The complex, built in 1973, is dedicated to a deified healer named Wong Tai Sin who, as a shepherd in Zhèjiāng province, was said to have transformed boulders into sheep. In fact, the whole district is named after him – ironic given he is said to have been a hermit. When he was 15 an immortal taught Wong how to make a herbal potion that could cure all illnesses. He is thus worshipped both by the sick and those trying to avoid illness. The term 'Wong Tai Sin' is sometimes used to describe people who are generous to a fault.

Taoist ceremonies take place at the **main altar** . The image of the deity was brought to Hong Kong from Guǎngdōng province in 1915. Behind the main altar and to the right are the **Good Wish Gardens**, replete with pavilions (the hexagonal **Unicorn Hall**, with carved doors and windows, is the most beautiful), zigzag bridges and carp ponds.

To the left as you enter the complex is an arcade of fortune-tellers (consultation from HK$100), some of whom speak English. The busiest times at the temple are around Chinese New Year, Wong Tai Sin's birthday (23rd day of the eighth month – usually in September) and on weekends.

DON'T MISS

➡ The architecture
➡ *chìm*
➡ The main altar
➡ Ceremonies
➡ Good Wish Gardens
➡ Unicorn Hall

PRACTICALITIES

➡ 嗇色園黃大仙祠
➡ ☑ 2351 5640, 2327 8141
➡ www.siksikyuen.org.hk
➡ 2, Chuk Yuen Village, Wong Tai Sin
➡ donation HK$2
➡ ⊙7am-5.30pm
➡ Ⓜ Wong Tai Sin, exit B2

TOP SIGHT
CHI LIN NUNNERY

One of the most beautiful and arrestingly built environments in Hong Kong, this large Buddhist complex, originally dating from the 1930s, was rebuilt completely of wood in the style of a Tang-dynasty monastery in 1998. It's a serene place with lotus ponds, bonsai tea plants, bougainvillea and silent nuns delivering offerings of fruit and rice to Buddha or chanting behind intricately carved screens.

Built to last a thousand years, Chi Lin Nunnery is the world's largest cluster of handcrafted timber buildings, one exhibiting a level of artistry rarely found in other faux-ancient architecture. The design, involving interlocking sections of wood joined without a single nail, is intended to demonstrate the harmony of humans with nature.

You enter through the **Sam Mun**, a series of 'three gates' representing the Buddhist precepts of compassion, wisdom and 'skilful means'. The first courtyard, which contains the delightful **Lotus Pond Garden**, gives way to the **Hall of Celestial Kings**, with a large statue of the seated Buddha surrounded by deities. Behind that is the **Main Hall**, containing a statue of the Sakyamuni Buddha.

Connected to the nunnery is **Nan Lian Garden** (南蓮園池; ☑3658 9311; www.nanliangarden.org; ◷10am-6pm; Ⓜ Diamond Hill, exit C2), a Tang-style garden featuring a golden pagoda, a koi pond and a collection of bizarre rocks.

Also here is the small but excellent Chi Lin Vegetarian (p157) and the elegant Song Cha Xie (p157).

To get here from Diamond Hill MTR, go through Hollywood Plaza and turn east on to Fung Tak Rd.

DON'T MISS

- ➡ Faux-Tang architecture
- ➡ Sam Mun
- ➡ Lotus Pond Garden
- ➡ Hall of Celestial Kings
- ➡ Main Hall
- ➡ Nan Lian Garden

PRACTICALITIES

- ➡ 志蓮淨苑
- ➡ ☑2354 1888
- ➡ www.chilin.org
- ➡ 5 Chi Lin Dr, Diamond Hill
- ➡ admission free
- ➡ ◷nunnery 9am-4.30pm, garden 6.30am-7pm
- ➡ Ⓜ Diamond Hill, exit C2

SIGHTS

⊙ Tsim Sha Tsui

FORMER KCR
CLOCK TOWER HISTORIC BUILDING
Map p378 (前九廣鐵路鐘樓; Southern tip of Salisbury Rd, Tsim Sha Tsui Star Ferry Concourse; ⛴Star Ferry, MEast Tsim Sha Tsui, exit J) This 44m-high clock tower (1915) in red-brick and granite was once part of the southern terminus of the Kowloon–Canton Railway (KCR). It was demolished in 1978 after operations moved to the modern train station at Hung Hom, but you can still see what it looked like at the Hong Kong Railway Museum in Tai Po. The clocks began ticking on the afternoon of 22 March 1921 and have not stopped since, except during the Japanese Occupation.

OCEAN TERMINAL BUILDING BUILDING
Map p378 (www.oceanterminal.com.hk; Salisbury Rd, Tsim Sha Tsui; ⊙10am-9pm; ⛴Star Ferry, MEast Tsim Sha Tsui, exit J) The building jutting 381m into the harbour is a cruise terminal and a shopping mall. Originally Kowloon Wharf Pier (c 1886), it was rebuilt and reopened in 1966 as the Ocean Terminal – then the largest shopping centre in all of Hong Kong. Today it's part of the Harbour City (p162) complex that stretches for half a kilometre along Canton Rd and offers priceless views of the waterfront. You enter it at the western end of the Former KCR Clock Tower.

HONG KONG CULTURAL CENTRE BUILDING
Map p378 (香港文化中心; www.lcsd.gov.hk; 10 Salisbury Rd, Tsim Sha Tsui; ⊙9am-11pm; ⛴Star Ferry, MEast Tsim Sha Tsui, exit J) Overlooking the most beautiful part of the harbour, the aesthetically challenged and windowless Cultural Centre is a world-class venue (p160) containing a 2085-seat concert hall, a Grand Theatre that seats 1750, a studio theatre for up to 535, and rehearsal studios. On the building's south side is the beginning of a viewing platform from where you can gain access to the Tsim Sha Tsui East Promenade.

TSIM SHA TSUI
EAST PROMENADE HARBOUR
See p141.

FORMER MARINE POLICE
HEADQUARTERS HISTORIC BUILDING
Map p378 (前水警總部; ☎2926 8000, tour reservation 2926 1881; www.1881heritage.com; 2A Canton Rd, Tsim Sha Tsui; ⊙10am-10pm; ⛴Star Ferry, MEast Tsim Sha Tsui, exit L6) **FREE** Built in 1884, this gorgeous Victorian complex, is one of Hong Kong's four oldest government buildings. It was used continuously by the Hong Kong Marine Police except during WWII when the Japanese navy took over. The complex is now a nakedly commercial property called 'Heritage 1881'. Some of the old structures are still here, including stables, pigeon houses and bomb shelter. Why 1881? Because '4' has a similar pronunciation to 'death' in Chinese, and the developer was superstitious. There are two 30-minute guided tours daily (2.30pm and 4pm) in English, Cantonese or Mandarin.

HONG KONG SPACE
MUSEUM & THEATRE MUSEUM
Map p378 (香港太空館; ☎2721 0226; www.lcsd.gov.hk; 10 Salisbury Rd, Tsim Sha Tsui; adult/concession HK$10/5, shows HK$24/12, Wed free; ⊙1-9pm Mon & Wed-Fri, 10am-9pm Sat & Sun; ♿; MEast Tsim Sha Tsui, exit J) This golf-ball-shaped building on the waterfront houses two exhibition halls and a planetarium with a large screen on the ceiling. The museum has a dated feel, but the Omnimax films, the virtual paraglider and the 'moonwalking' simulator hold a timeless fascination for kidults. The museum shop also sells dehydrated 'astronaut' ice cream in three flavours.

HONG KONG MUSEUM OF ART MUSEUM
Map p378 (香港藝術館; ☎2721 0116; http://hk.art.museum; 10 Salisbury Rd, Tsim Sha Tsui; adult/concession HK$10/5, Wed free; ⊙10am-6pm Mon-Fri, to 7pm Sat & Sun; ⛴Star Ferry, MEast Tsim Sha Tsui, exit J) This excellent museum has seven galleries spread over six floors, exhibiting Chinese antiquities, fine art, historical pictures and contemporary Hong Kong art. Highlights include the Xubaizhi collection of painting and calligraphy, contemporary works, and ceramics and other antiques from China. Audio guides are available for HK$10. Refer to the tour schedule in the lobby for free English-language tours.

PENINSULA HONG KONG HISTORIC BUILDING
Map p378 (香港半島酒店; www.peninsula.com; cnr Salisbury & Nathan Rds, Tsim Sha Tsui;

East Tsim Sha Tsui, exit L3) The Peninsula (c 1928), in a throne-like building, is one of the world's great hotels. Though it was once called 'the finest hotel east of Suez', the Pen was in fact one of several prestigious hotels across Asia, lining up with (but not behind) the likes of the Raffles in Singapore and the Cathay (now the Peace) in Shànghǎi. Taking afternoon tea here is a wonderful experience – dress neatly and be prepared to queue for a table.

MIDDLE ROAD CHILDREN'S PLAYGROUND
PARK

Map p380 (中間道兒童遊樂場; Middle Rd, Tsim Sha Tsui; ⏰7am-11pm; 🚇; MEast Tsim Sha Tsui, exit K) Accessible via a sweep of stairs from Chatham Rd South, this hidden gem atop the East Tsim Sha Tsui MTR station has play facilities, shaded seating and views of the waterfront. On weekdays it's the quiet backyard playground of the residents nearby, but on weekends it's filled with children and picnickers of as many ethnicities as there are ways to go down a slide (if you're eight).

The park's eastern exit is connected to the handsome **Tsim Sha Tsui East Waterfront Podium Garden** (尖沙咀東海濱平台花園; Map p380)with its sleek granite structures and white sail canopies. On weekends skateboarders and traceurs come to practise. The podium sits atop the Tsim Sha Tsui East (Mody Rd) Bus Terminus.

SIGNAL HILL GARDEN & BLACKHEAD POINT TOWER
PARK

Map p380 (訊號山公園和訊號塔; Minden Row, Tsim Sha Tsui; ⏰tower 9-11am & 4-6pm; MEast Tsim Sha Tsui, exit K) The views from the top of this knoll are quite spectacular, and if it were the 1900s the ships in the harbour might be returning your gaze – a copper ball in the handsome Edwardian-style tower was dropped at 1pm daily so seafarers could adjust their chronometers. The garden is perched above the Middle Road Children's Playground. Enter from Minden Row (Mody Rd).

NATHAN ROAD
STREET

Map p378 (彌敦道; Tsim Sha Tsui; MTsim Sha Tsui, Jordan) Kowloon's main drag is a bit of a traffic- and pedestrian-choked scrum of jewellery stores and fashion boutiques. It's nonetheless an iconic Hong Kong scene where guesthouses rub shoulders with luxury hotels. And it's completely safe – which is just as well since you won't be able to avoid using it if you spend any time in the area.

CHUNGKING MANSIONS
BUILDING

Map p378 (重慶大廈, CKM; 36-44 Nathan Rd, Tsim Sha Tsui; MTsim Sha Tsui, exit D1) FREE Say 'budget accommodation' and 'Hong Kong' in one breath and everyone thinks of Chungking Mansions. This huge, ramshackle high-rise caters to virtually all needs – from finding a bed (p273) and a curry lunch to changing your Burmese kyat and getting your hair cut. The building's infamy is fuelled by tales both tall and true of conflagrations and crimes. Everyone should come here once.

KOWLOON PARK
PARK

Map p378 (九龍公園; www.lcsd.gov.hk; Nathan & Austin Rds, Tsim Sha Tsui; ⏰6am-midnight; 🚇; MTsim Sha Tsui, exit C2) Built on the site of a barracks for Indian soldiers in the colonial army, Kowloon Park is an oasis of greenery and a refreshing escape from the hustle and bustle of Tsim Sha Tsui. Pathways and walls criss-cross the grass, birds hop around in cages, and ancient banyan trees dot the landscape. In the morning the older set practise taichi amid the serene surrounds, and on Sunday afternoon Kung Fu Corner stages martial arts displays.

FOOK TAK ANCIENT TEMPLE
TEMPLE

Map p378 (福德古廟; 30 Haiphong Rd, Tsim Sha Tsui; ⏰6am-8pm; MTsim Sha Tsui, exit C2) Tsim Sha Tsui's only temple is a smoke-filled hole in the wall with a hot tin roof. Little is known about its ancestry except that it was built as a shrine in the Qing dynasty and renovated in 1900. Before WWII, worshippers of its Earth God were the coolies from Kowloon Wharf nearby, where the Ocean Terminal (p145) now stands. Today most incense offerers are octogenarians – the temple specialises in longevity.

KOWLOON MOSQUE & ISLAMIC CENTRE
MOSQUE

Map p378 (九龍清真寺; ☎2724 0095; http://kowloonmosque.com; 105 Nathan Rd, Tsim Sha Tsui; ⏰5am-10pm; MTsim Sha Tsui, exit C2) This structure, with its dome and carved marble, is Hong Kong's largest mosque. It serves the territory's 70,000-odd Muslims, more than half of whom are Chinese, and accommodates up to 3000 worshippers. The mosque was originally established to serve the Indian Muslim troops of the

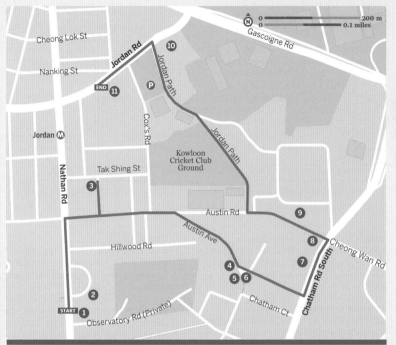

Neighbourhood Walks
Vestiges of Local & Colonial Life in TST

START KOWLOON BRITISH SCHOOL
END KOWLOON UNION CHURCH
LENGTH 2.5KM, TWO HOURS

Tsim Sha Tsui's lesser-known northern end is a treasure trove of postwar buildings and colonial relics. Start your journey at the **1 Former Kowloon British School** (p148) and **2 St Andrew's Church** (p148), respectively Kowloon's oldest 'international' school and Anglican church.

Further north on Nathan Rd, turn right into Austin Rd, a former stronghold of Shanghainese migrants. Explore **3 Pak On Building**, with its lobby full of shops, including, at the Tak Shing St end, a liquor store that stocks absinthe.

Return to Austin Rd. At the corner where it branches out into Austin Ave, you'll see a late-1960s building with rounded balconies. Further on, at 15 Austin Ave, stands **4 Carnival Mansion**. Here a vortex of rickety postwar homes hangs above the courtyard and buildings have terrazzo staircases with

green balustrades made by Shanghainese craftsmen 50 years ago.

Next door, chaotic **5 Success** (成功文具行) is the oldest surviving stationery shop in TST. From here, you'll see the curious **6 'triangular public toilet'** which doubles up as a power substation.

Continue down Austin Ave and make a left on Chatham Rd South. **7 Rosary Church** (p149), Kowloon's oldest Catholic church, stands next to **8 St Mary's Canossian College** (嘉諾撒聖瑪利書院), built in 1900. At the canon-guarded gate of **9 Gun Club Hill Barracks** now occupied by the People's Liberation Army, turn right into leafy Jordan Path.

As you walk, functional buildings belonging to the PLA loom up on your right, while the manicured lawns of the colonial recreation clubs unfurl on your left. Just before Jordan Rd, you'll see the **10 PLA hospital** (解放軍駐軍醫院) with its darkened windows. Crossing Cox's Rd takes you to the Victorian-style Anglican **11 Kowloon Union Church** (p149).

TST, BREEZE FOR THE FEET

The crowds and the traffic might have you thinking otherwise, but Tsim Sha Tsui is one of Hong Kong's most walkable urban areas. Its pavements are between 250m and 300m long. Metro stations have a catchment radius of 500m – the rough equivalent of an eight-minute stroll. At half the length, streets in TST take only four minutes to cover.

T-junctions link most of TST's meandering avenues. The very layout of the T-junction, where one road meets another at right angles but does not cross it, creates neighbourly enclosures while dangling the promise of fresh horizons at every corner. So reaching Canton Rd from Peking Rd, would it be right to the Macau Ferry Terminal or left to the Space Museum? Compare this to the sprawling, crisscrossing grid that is Yau Ma Tei – a fascinating area buzzing with life that could also alienate or disorient newcomers.

No matter where you're at in TST, good old Nathan Rd is never more than four blocks away. Born just shy of the harbour, Kowloon's earliest strip of asphalt runs past Yau Ma Tei to end in Mong Kok, offering the reassurance of a linear narrative in a labyrinthine plot, and a choice of many, many endings.

British army who were stationed at what is now Kowloon Park. Muslims are welcome to attend services, but non-Muslims should ask permission to enter. Remember to remove your footwear.

FORMER KOWLOON BRITISH SCHOOL
HISTORIC BUILDING

Map p378 (前九龍英童學校; www.amo.gov.hk; 136 Nathan Rd, Tsim Sha Tsui; MTsim Sha Tsui, exit B1) The oldest surviving school building for expat children is a listed Victorian-style structure that now houses the **Antiquities and Monuments Office** (古物古蹟辦事處). Established in 1902, it was subsequently modified to incorporate breezy verandahs and high ceilings, prompted possibly by the fainting spells suffered by its young occupants.

ST ANDREW'S ANGLICAN CHURCH CHURCH

Map p378 (聖安德烈堂; ☑2367 1478; www.standrews.org.hk; 138 Nathan Rd, Tsim Sha Tsui; ⊙7.30am-10.30pm, church 8.30am-5.30pm; MTsim Sha Tsui, exit B1) Sitting atop a knoll, next to the Former Kowloon British School, is a charming building in English Gothic style that houses Kowloon's oldest Protestant church. St Andrew's was built in 1905 in granite and red brick to serve Kowloon's Protestant population; it was turned into a Shinto shrine during the Japanese occupation. Nearby you'll see the handsome former vicarage with columned balconies (c 1909). Enter from the eastern side of Nathan Rd via steps or a slope.

INTERNATIONAL COMMERCE CENTRE
BUILDING

(環球貿易廣場, ICC; www.shkp-icc.com; 1 Austin Rd W, Tsim Sha Tsui; adult/concession HK$168/118; ⊙from 10am; MKowloon, exit C) At 118 stories, the sleek ICC is Hong Kong's tallest building and the world's seventh tallest. Besides the Ritz-Carlton (p278) and Elements (p164), it houses, on its 100th floor, a panoramic observation deck – **Sky100**. And 60 seconds are all it takes for the high-speed elevators to whisk you there for stunning views of Kowloon and part of the island. From Element's 2nd floor ('Metal Zone'), look for signage for Sky100. Last entry is at 8pm.

HONG KONG MUSEUM OF HISTORY
MUSEUM

See p 140.

JUNE 4TH MUSEUM
MUSEUM

Map p380 (六四紀念館; ☑ 2782 6111; www.64museum.org; 3 Austin Ave, 5th fl, Foo Hoo Centre, Tsim Sha Tsui; adult/concession HK$10/5; ⊙10am-6pm Mon, Wed-Fri, to 7pm Sat & Sun; MJordan, exit D) The world's first permanent museum dedicated to the 1989 prodemocracy protests in Běijīng's Tiān'ānmén Square. The 800 sq ft space has artefacts, photographs, books and microfilm related to the incident including casings of bullets supposedly fired by the People's Liberation Army and T-shirts signed by the Běijīng student leaders such as Wang Dan. A copy of the Goddess of Democracy statue built by the students stands at the heart of the museum.

ROSARY CHURCH
CHURCH

Map p380 (玫瑰堂; ☑2368 0980; http://rosarychurch.catholic.org.hk; 125 Chatham Rd South, TsimSha Tsui; ⏱7.30am-7.30pm; ⓜJordan, exit D) Kowloon's oldest Catholic church was built in 1905 with money donated by a Portuguese doctor in Hong Kong, initially for the benefit of the Catholics in an Indian battalion stationed in Kowloon, and later for the local Catholic community. Rosary Church features a classic Gothic style with a yellowish facade reminiscent of churches in Macau.

HONG KONG SCIENCE MUSEUM
MUSEUM

Map p380 (香港科學館; ☑2732 3232; http://hk.science.museum; 2 Science Museum Rd, Tsim Sha Tsui; adult/concession HK$25/12.50, Wed free; ⏱10am-7pm Mon-Wed & Fri, to 9pm Sat & Sun; ♿; ⓜTsim Sha Tsui, exit B2) Illustrating the fundamental workings of technology with practical demonstrations of the laws of energy, physics and chemistry, the Hong Kong Science Museum is a great hands-on experience capable of entertaining adults as well as children from toddlers to teens.

☉ Yau Ma Tei

TEMPLE STREET NIGHT MARKET
MARKET
See p 142.

SHANGHAI STREET
STREET

Map p382 (上海街; Yau Ma Tei; ⓜYau Ma Tei, exit C) Strolling down Shanghai St will take you back to a time long past. Once Kowloon's main drag, it's flanked by stores selling Chinese wedding gowns, sandalwood incense, hardcore kitchenware, and Buddha statues. There are also mah-jong parlours and an old pawn shop at the junction with Saigon St. It's rich in local flavour and filled with unusual souvenirs.

TIN HAU TEMPLE
TEMPLE

Map p382 (天后廟; ☑2385 0759; www.ctc.org.hk; cnr Temple St & Public Square St, Yau Ma Tei; ⏱8am-5pm; ⓜYau Ma Tei, exit C) This large, incense-filled sanctuary built in the 19th century is one of Hong Kong's most famous Tin Hau (Goddess of the Sea) temples. The public square out front is Yau Ma Tei's communal heart where fishermen once laid out their hemp ropes to sun next to Chinese banyans that today shade chess players and elderly men. Yau Ma Tei Police Station is a listed blue-and-white structure one block to the east along Public Square St.

YAU MA TEI POLICE STATION
HISTORIC BUILDING

Map p382 (油麻地警署; 627 Canton Rd, Yau Ma Tei; ⓜYau Ma Tei, exit C) A stone's throw from Tin Hau Temple is this handsome Edwardian police station (c 1922) with arcades and arches. You may have caught a glimpse of it in the film *Rush Hour 2* . Some of its architectural features have been adapted for feng shui reasons – crime-fighting is a high-risk profession. For instance, the portico at the main entrance is set in an indented corner to better protect the building's inhabitants.

JADE MARKET
MARKET

Map p382 (玉器市場; Battery St & Kansu St, Yau Ma Tei; ⏱10am-6pm; ⓜYau Ma Tei, exit C) The covered Jade Market, split into two parts by Battery St, has hundreds of stalls selling all varieties and grades of jade. But unless you really know your nephrite from your jadeite, it's not wise to buy expensive pieces here.

CHIN WOO ATHLETIC ASSOCIATION
MARTIAL ARTS SCHOOL

Map p382 (香港精武體育會; ☑2384 3238; 300 Nathan Rd, flat B & C, 13th fl, Wah Fung Bldg, Yau Ma Tei; ⏱2.30-9pm; ⓜJordan, exit B1) This is the 88-year-old branch of the Chin Woo Athletic Association, founded 100 years ago in Shanghai by the famed kung-fu master Huo Yuanjia (霍元甲). The Shanghai school was featured in Bruce Lee's *Fist of Fury* and Let Li's *Fearless*. You can visit the school during opening hours. Classes, however, are taught mainly in Cantonese.

KOWLOON UNION CHURCH
CHURCH

Map p382 (九龍佑寧堂; ☑2367 2585; www.kuc.hk; 4 Jordan Rd, Tsim Sha Tsui; ⏱9am-5pm Mon-Fri; ⓜJordan, exit B2) The red-bricked church with Protestant roots was constructed in 1930 with money from an English businessman of Armenian descent. It was built in a Neo-Gothic style – quite unusual for Kowloon – and features a Chinese-tiled pitched roof (which makes it typhoon-proof), a battlemented tower, and windows with Gothic tracery. Sunday service starts at 10.30am.

WHOLESALE FRUIT MARKET
MARKET

Map p382 (油麻地果欄; cnr Shek Lung St & Reclamation St, Yau Ma Tei; ⏱2-6am; ⓜYau Ma Tei, exit B2) This historic and still operating market, founded in 1913, is a cluster of one- or two-storey brick and stone buildings with pre-WWII signboards. It is a hive of activity from 4am to 6am when fresh fruit is loaded

1. Temple Street Night Market (p142)
Hong Kong's liveliest market is full of activity, from the food stalls to Cantonese opera and fortune-telling.

2. Statue, Sik Sik Yuen Wong Tai Sin Temple (p143)
This Taoist temple is dedicated to a deified healer who was said to have transformed boulders into sheep.

3. Amulets, Jade Market (p149)
Hundreds of stalls sell all varieties and grades of jade.

4. Avenue of the Stars (p141)
A tribute to the Hong Kong film industry forms part of the Tsim Sha Tsui East Promenade.

on and off trucks, and bare-backed workers manoeuvre piles of boxes under the moon. The market is bounded by Ferry St, Waterloo Rd and Reclamation St with Shek Lung St running through it. To get here from Yau Ma Tei MTR exit B2, turn right.

YAU MA TEI THEATRE   BUILDING
Map p382 (油麻地戲院; ☎2264 8108, tickets 2374 2598; www.lcsd.gov.hk/ymtt; 6 Waterloo Rd, cnr Waterloo Rd & Reclamation St, Yau Ma Tei; ⓂYau Ma Tei, exit B2) Yau Ma Tei Theatre (1920) with art-deco interiors, and adjacent to the Wholesale Fruit Market, had for decades kept coolies and rickshaw drivers entertained, but losing business to modern cinemas in the '80s, it began showing erotic films and selling porn videos to stay afloat. At 8 Waterloo Rd next door, the neoclassical **Red Brick House** (紅磚屋; Map p382) once belonged to a pumping station (1895). The buildings now house a Cantonese opera performance and training centre.

BRUCE LEE CLUB   MUSEUM
Map p382 (李小龍會; ☎2771 7093; www.bruceleeclub.com; 530 Nathan Rd, Shop 160-161, In's Point, Mong Kok; ⓧ 1-9pm; ⓂYau Ma Tei, exit A1) FREE Founded by Bruce Lee's fans, this mini-museum and souvenir shop has action figures, toys, movie products and other memorabilia related to the kung-fu icon.

HONG KONG INTERNATIONAL HOBBY & TOY MUSEUM   MUSEUM
Map p382 (香港國際玩具博物館; www.hktoymuseum.org; 1st fl, 330 Shanghai St, Yau Ma Tei; ⓧ2-7pm Mon & Wed-Fri, 1-7pm Sat & Sun; ⓂYau Ma Tei station, exit C) FREE The collection here is by no means overwhelming but there are action figures, anime, sci-fi characters, dolls and quite a number of Gundam robots.

LOCAL KNOWLEDGE

UPSTAIRS MONG KOK
Mong Kok can be intense. After all, it *is* the most densely populated spot on the face of the earth. But you don't have to shun it. Experience MK without the insanity by making a beeline for its upstairs spaces. Above-the-ground oases include C&G Artpartment (p152), Hong Kong Reader (p164), Fullcup Café (p159) and Bruce Lee Club (p152).

⊙ Mong Kok

★YUEN PO STREET BIRD GARDEN & FLOWER MARKET   PARK, MARKET
Map p383 (園圃街雀鳥花園, 花墟; Yuen Po St & Boundary St, Mong Kok; ⓧ7am-8pm; ⓂPrince Edward, exit B1) In this enchanting corner of Mong Kok, you will find a handful of old men out 'walking' their caged songbirds. Stick around long enough and you should see birds being fed squirming caterpillars with chopsticks. There are also feathered creatures for sale, along with elaborate cages carved from teak. Adjacent to the garden is the **flower market** (Map p383; Flower Market Rd), which theoretically keeps the same hours, but only gets busy after 10am.

★LUI SENG CHUN   HISTORIC BUILDING
Map p383 (雷春生堂; ☎3411 0628; http://scm.hkbu.edu.hk/lsctour; 119 Lai Chi Kok Rd, cnr Lai Chi Kok & Tong Mi Rds; ⓧguided tour 2.30pm & 4pm Mon-Fri, 9.30am & 11am Sat; consultation 9am-1pm & 2-8pm Mon-Sat, 9am-1pm Sun.; ⓂPrince Edward, exit C2) FREE Hugging a street corner is this beautiful four-storey Chinese 'shophouse' belonging to a school of Chinese medicine. A historic construction (c 1931), it features a mix of Chinese and European architectural styles – deep verandahs, urn-shaped balustrades and other fanciful takes on a Neoclassical Italian villa. The ground floor, which has a herbal tea shop, is open to public. Free guided tours to the upper-floor clinics is available by registration. The tours are in Cantonese, but exhibits have bilingual labels.

An English tour can be arranged for groups of more than four. Make an appointment if you want to have your pulse taken by a Chinese doctor.

C&G ARTPARTMENT   GALLERY
Map p383 (☎2390 9332; www.candg-artpartment.com; 222 Sai Yeung Choi St S, 3rd fl, Mong Kok; ⓧ2-7.30pm Thu, Fri, Sun & Mon, from 11am Sat; ⓂPrince Edward, exit B2) Clara and Gum, the founders of this edgy art space behind the Pioneer Centre (始創中心) are passionate about nurturing the local art scene and representing socially minded artists. They close late when there are events. See website for the latest.

⊙ New Kowloon

CATTLE DEPOT ARTIST VILLAGE VILLAGE

(牛棚藝術村; 63 Ma Tau Kok Rd, To Kwa Wan; ⊙10am-10pm; ⬚106, 12A, 5C, 101, 111) This century-old slaughterhouse deep in the entrails of Kowloon has reincarnated into an artists' village, its red-brick buildings housing studios and exhibition halls. There are some 20 art organisations inside, including On and On Theatre Workshop (p160). The nonprofit visual art organisation **1a Space** (☑2529 0087; www.oneaspace.org.hk; 63 Ma Tau Kok Rd, Unit 14, Cattle Depot Artist Village, To Kwa Wan; ⊙noon-7pm Tue-Sun; ⬚106, 12A, 5C, 101, 111) is one of the most active tenants in the village, holding regular exhibitions of high-quality local and international art, as well as concerts and theatrical performances. The village itself is an interesting place to visit even when nothing's happening. Its next to a Town Gas storage facility, in the northern part of To Kwa Wan, an area on Kowloon's east coast.

LEI CHENG UK HAN TOMB MUSEUM MUSEUM

(李鄭屋漢墓博物館; ☑2386 2863; www.lcsd. gov.hk; 41 Tonkin St; ⊙10am-6pm, closed Thu; Ⓜ️Cheung Sha Wan, exit A3) 🆓 Don't expect a terracotta army, but for those interested in the area's ancient history, this is a significant burial vault dating from the Eastern Han dynasty (AD 25–220). The tomb consists of four barrel-vaulted brick chambers set around a domed central chamber. It's encased in a concrete shell for protection and visitors can only peep through a plastic window.

JOCKEY CLUB CREATIVE ARTS CENTRE ARTS CENTRE

(賽馬會創意藝術中心, JCCAC; www.jccac.org. hk; 30 Pak Tin St, Shek Kip Mei; ⊙10am-10pm; Ⓜ️Shek Kip Mei, exit C) Over 150 artists have moved into these factory premises that used to churn out shoes and watches. Many studios are closed on weekdays, but you can visit the breezy communal areas, the cafes and the shops with regular opening hours.

KOWLOON WALLED CITY PARK PARK

(九龍寨城公園; ☑2716 9962; www.lcsd.gov.hk; Tung Tau Tsuen, Tung Tsing, Carpenter & Junction Rds, Kowloon City; ⊙park 6.30am-11pm; exhibition 10am-6pm, closed Wed; ⬚1 from Star Ferry pier) This attractive park was the site of the mysterious Kowloon Walled City, a Chinese garrison in the 19th century that technically remained part of China throughout British rule. Neither government wanted to have anything to do with the 3-acre enclave, so it became a lawless slum infamous for its gangs, prostitution and drug dens. The British eventually relocated the 30,000 residents and built a park in its place. There's a model of it on display at the park. If you're taking the bus, alight opposite the park at Tung Tau Tsuen Rd.

SIK SIK YUEN WONG TAI SIN TEMPLE TEMPLE

See p 143.

CHI LIN NUNNERY BUDDHIST NUNNERY

See p 144.

✗ EATING

Kowloon doesn't have quite as many upmarket restaurants as Hong Kong Island but there's a riveting assortment of Chinese and Asian eateries to fit all budgets in Tsim Sha Tsui. For hearty local fare, head for Yau Ma Tei or Mong Kok. Kowloon City is renowned for its many Thai eateries.

✗ Tsim Sha Tsui

★YOGA INTERACTIVE VEGETARIAN VEGETARIAN, ASIAN $

Map p380 (互動瑜伽素食; ☑9327 7275, 3422 1195; www.yogafitnesshk.com; 30 Hillwood Rd, 15B, Hillview Ct, Tsim Sha Tsui; meals HK$200; ⊙noon-3pm & 7-10pm; ☑; Ⓜ️Jordan, exit D) The Asian vegetarian here, cooked by a yoga teacher, is among the best in town. But you'll need to book at least a week in advance. That said, if there's only one or two of you, they might be able to fit you in sooner. This homey place is one flight of stairs above the 14th floor.

WOODLANDS INDIAN, VEGETARIAN $

Map p380 (活蘭印度素食; ☑2369 3718; 62 Mody Rd, upper ground fl, 16 & 17 Wing On Plaza, Tsim Sha Tsui; meals HK$70-180; ⊙noon-3.30pm & 6.30-10.30pm; ☑ ♿; Ⓜ️East Tsim Sha Tsui, exit P1) Located above a department store, good old Woodlands offers excellent-value Indian vegetarian food to compatriots and the odd local. Dithering gluttons should order the *thali* meal, which is served on a round metal plate with 10 tiny dishes, a dessert and bread.

GOOD SATAY
SOUTHEAST ASIAN $

Map p380 (好時沙嗲; ☑2739 9808; 63 Mody Rd, Shop 144-148, 1st fl, Houston Centre, Tsim Sha Tsui; meals from HK$80; ⊙noon-10pm; Ⓜ East Tsim Sha Tsui, exit P2) This place on the 1st floor of a dowdy shopping and office complex doesn't look promising but its Southeast Asian cooking is great value for money. We loved the stir-fried turnip cake, and satays. It's packed at lunch.

PEKING DUMPLING SHOP
NORTHERN CHINESE $

Map p380 (北京水餃店; ☑2368 3028; 15B Austin Ave, Shop A2, Tsim Sha Tsui; servings HK$10-40; ⊙11.30am-11.30pm; Ⓜ Jordan, exit D) This tiny shop whips up decent pastries and noodles of the chewy northern variety. Get your carb fix seated in booths or, if the smell of grease gets to you, on the go.

SWEET DYNASTY
CANTONESE, DESSERTS $

Map p378 (糖朝; ☑2199 7799; 28 Hankow Rd, Shop A, Basement, Hong Kong Pacific Centre, Tsim Sha Tsui; meals HK$70-$300; ⊙8am-midnight Mon-Thu, 8am-1am Fri, 7.30am-1am Sat, 7.30am-midnight Sun; ⓓ; Ⓜ Tsim Sha Tsui, exit A1) Sweet Dynasty's extensive menu encompasses a plethora of casual Cantonese dishes, but the desserts, noodles and congee, for which they became famous years ago, are still the best. The restaurant is clean and modern but gets crowded when busy.

PIERRE HERMÉ
MACARONS $

Map p378 (☑2155 3866; www.pierreherme.com/hk; 7-27 Canton Rd, Shop 2410, Level 2, Harbour City, Tsim Sha Tsui; macarons HK$30; ⊙10am-10pm; Ⓜ Tsim Sha Tsui, exit C3) Sweet, tender and transient like young love, the legendary macarons of the French confectioner feature dazzling flavour pairings, all beautifully named. Jardin Dans Les Nuages (Garden in the Clouds) is 'chocolate and smoked salt' which translates on the tongue to a hint of smokiness in velvety chocolate.

TAK FAT BEEF BALLS
NOODLES $

Map p378 (德發牛肉丸; Haiphong Rd, Haiphong Rd Temporary Market, Tsim Sha Tsui; beef ball noodles HK$26; ⊙9am-8pm; Ⓜ Tsim Sha Tsui, exit A1) This famous *dai pai dong* is one of a handful operating in this market. Pick a seat in the cacophonous sprawl and order the beef ball noodles, famed for their bounce and hint of dried mandarin peel. The market is next door to Fook Tak Ancient Temple (p146). Venture past the florists and halal meat stalls to reach the *dai pai dong* .

★ YÈ SHANGHAI
SHANGHAINESE, DIM SUM $$

Map p378 (夜上海; ☑2376 3322; www.elite-concepts.com; Canton Rd, 6th fl, Marco Polo Hotel, Harbour City, Tsim Sha Tsui; meals HK$400-800; ⊙11.30am-2.30pm & 6-10.30pm; ⓓ; Ⓜ Tsim Sha Tsui, exit C2) The name means 'Shànghǎi Nights'. Dark woods and subtle lighting inspired by 1920s Shànghǎi fill the air with romance. The modern Shanghainese dishes are also exquisite. The only exception to this Jiāngnán harmony is the Cantonese dim sum being served at lunch, though that too is wonderful. Sophisticated Yè Shanghai has one Michelin star.

★ GREAT BEEF HOT POT
HOTPOT $$

Map p380 (禾牛薈火焗館; ☑3997 3369; 48 Cameron Rd, 1st & 2nd fl, China Insurance Bldg, Tsim Sha Tsui; meals HK$350-600; ⊙5.30pm-2am; Ⓜ Tsim Sha Tsui, exit B3) Indecisive gluttons will scream at the mind-blowing hotpot choices here – 200 ingredients (the majority fresh or homemade; HK$25-270), 20 kinds of broth (from clam soup to fancy herbal concoctions; HK$68-468), and an embarrassment of condiments (all-you-can-dip)! There's no escaping the menu either, the lights are too bright! Now onto the sashimi options... Booking essential.

SEN HOTPOT RESTAURANT
CANTONESE $$

Map p382 (千鍋居; ☑2377 2022; 26E Jordan Rd, 1st fl, Liberty Mansion, Tsim Sha Tsui; meals HK$300; ⊙11.30am-3pm & 5.30pm-1am; Ⓜ Jordan, exit A) A wallet-friendly misnomer, Sen specialises in (rustic) dishes served in pots, rather than 'hotpot' aka steamboat, though that is available too. Rustic cuisine evokes dew-fresh ingredients in heart-warming combos – and this modern eatery fares well, notably with the braised goose. That said, it's noisy, unlike the portraits of old Hong Kong gracing its walls. Enter from Temple St.

DONG LAI SHUN
CHINESE $$

Map p380 (東來順; ☑2733 2020; www.rghk.com.hk; 69 Mody Rd, B2, the Royal Garden, Tsim Sha Tsui; meals HK$250-1500; ⊙11.30am-2.30pm & 6pm-10.30pm; ☎ ⓓ; Ⓜ East Tsim Sha Tsui, exit P2) Besides superbly executed Northern Chinese dishes, the phonebook of a menu here also features Shanghainese,

Sichuanese, and Cantonese favourites. But Dong Lai Shun is best known for its mutton hotpot which involves dunking paper-thin slices of mutton into boiling water and eating it with sesame sauce. The atmosphere is a little formal but the service is warm.

TYPHOON SHELTER HING KEE RESTAURANT
CANTONESE $$

Map p378 (避風塘興記; ☑2722 0022; 180 Nathan Rd, 1st fl Bowa House, Tsim Sha Tsui; meals HK$380-1200; ☺6pm-5am; ⓂJordan, exit D) This celebrity haunt is run by a feisty fisherman's daughter who's known for her brilliant dishes prepared the way they were on sampans. The signature crabs smothered in a mountain of fried garlic are a wonder to taste and behold. The service can be a little edgy. Be sure you know the price of every dish before you order.

GAYLORD
INDIAN $$

Map p378 (爵樂印度餐廳; ☑2376 1001; 23-25 Ashley Rd, 1st fl Ashley Centre, Tsim Sha Tsui; meals from HK$250; ☺noon-3pm & 6-11pm; ☑; ⓂTsim Sha Tsui, exit E) Dim lighting and live sitar music set the scene for enjoying the excellent rogan josh, dhal and other favourite dishes at Hong Kong's oldest – and Kowloon's classiest – Indian restaurant, which has been operating since 1972. There are lots of vegetarian choices as well. Though pricier than other Indian places in town, the cosy alcoves and attentive service more than compensate.

CHING YAN LEE CHIU CHOW RESTAURANT
CHIU CHOW $$

Map p380 (正仁利潮州菜館; ☑2366 6556; 10A Hau Fook St, Tsim Sha Tsui; meals from HK$300; ☺11.30am-midnight; ⓂTsim Sha Tsui, exit B1) Resist the hard sell at this family-run establishment. If staff can't sell you the shark's fin and the cold crab, they'll suggest adding conch meat to your vegies, which will inflate your bill by HK$500. Be firm. Stick with the menu or agree on the price beforehand. All said, the Chiu Chow food here is excellent.

DIN TAI FUNG
TAIWANESE, NOODLES $$

Map p378 (鼎泰豐; ☑2730 6928; www.dintaifung.com.hk; 30 Canton Rd, Shop 130, 3rd fl, Silvercord, Tsim Sha Tsui; meals HK$120-300; ☺11.30am-10.30pm; ☑; ⓂTsim Sha Tsui, exit C1) Whether it's comfort food or a carb fix you're craving, the juicy Shanghai dumplings and hearty Northern-style noodles at this Taiwanese chain will do the trick.

> ### ⓘ BEWARE: FAKE MONKS
>
> Real monks never solicit money. But during your stay, you may be approached by con artists in monk outfits who try to make you part with your money. Some may even offer Buddhist amulets for sale, or force 'blessings' on you then pester you for a donation. When accosted, just say 'no' firmly and ignore them.

Queues are the norm and it doesn't take reservations, but service is excellent. DTF has one Michelin star.

SPRING DEER
NORTHERN CHINESE $$

Map p380 (鹿鳴春飯店; ☑2366 4012; 42 Mody Rd, 1st fl, Tsim Sha Tsui; meals HK$80-500; ☺noon-3pm & 6-11pm; ⓂEast Tsim Sha Tsui, exit N2) Hong Kong's most authentic Northern-style roasted lamb is served here. Yet better known is the Peking duck which is very good. That said, the service can be about as welcoming as a Běijīng winter, c 1967. Booking is essential.

AL MOLO
ITALIAN $$

Map p378 (☑2730 7900; www.diningconcepts.com.hk; 7-23 Canton Rd, Shop G63, Ocean Terminal, Harbour City, Tsim Sha Tsui; meals HK$360-700; ☺noon-10.30pm; ☑; ☑Star Ferry, ⓂEast Tsim Sha Tsui, exit J) The Hong Kong venture of New York–based chef and restaurateur Michael White has brick walls, iron fittings and an alfresco area where you can savour homemade semolina pasta with seafood to the delicious views of the Tsim Sha Tsui harbourfront. Lunch sets start from HK$150.

★ SUN TUNG LOK
CANTONESE, DIM SUM $$$

Map p378 (新同樂; ☑2152 1417; www.suntunglok.com.hk; 132 Nathan Rd, 4th fl, Miramar Shopping Centre, Tsim Sha Tsui; lunch HK$250-3000, dinner HK$500-5000; ☺11.30am-3pm & 6-10.30pm; ⓂTsim Sha Tsui, exit B2) Crowned with two Michelin stars, elegant Sun Tung Lok (c 1969) proudly upholds the fine traditions of Cantonese cooking. It's evident in the dim sum (available at lunch) which food critics hail as the best in town, and dishes like braised abalone which are a litmus test of culinary skill. STL is pricey but sets are available and dim sum come in half-baskets.

GADDI'S
FRENCH $$$

Map p378 (☏2696 6763; www.peninsula.com/Hong_Kong; 19-21 Salisbury Rd, 1st fl, the Peninsula, Tsim Sha Tsui; set lunch/dinner HK$500/2000; ☺noon-2.30pm & 7-10.30pm; Ⓜ Tsim Sha Tsui, exit E) Gaddi's, which opened just after WWII, was the kind of place where wealthy families went to celebrate special occasions. Today the classical decor may be a tad stuffy, the live Filipino band gratuitous, but the food – traditional French with contemporary touches – is without a doubt still among the best in town.

STEAK HOUSE
INTERNATIONAL $$$

Map p380 (☏2313 2323; http://hongkong-ic.din ing.intercontinental.com; 18 Salisbury Rd, InterContinental Hong Kong, Tsim Sha Tsui; meals HK$700; ☺6-11pm Mon-Fri, noon-2.30pm & 6-11pm Sat & Sun; ⎙; Ⓜ East Tsim Sha Tsui, exit J) At this first-rate steakhouse, the imported beef exhilarates, and there are trimmings to enhance your experience – a flight of eight exotic salts, multiple mustards, fancy steak knives. The extravagant salad bar (HK$350 per person) is a meal in itself; and the desserts are awesome, but beware: they're huge even for American portions!

T'ANG COURT
CANTONESE, DIM SUM $$$

Map p378 (唐閣; ☏2375 1133; www.hongkong.langhamhotels.com; 8 Peking Rd, 1st, Langham Hotel, Tsim Sha Tsui; lunch HK$300-2000, dinner HK$500-2000; ☺noon-2.30pm & 6-10.30pm; ⎙; Ⓜ Tsim Sha Tsui, exit L4) As befitting its name T'ang Court, with two Michelin stars has mastered the art of fine Cantonese cooking. Deep-pile carpets, heavy silks and mindful staff contribute to a hushed atmosphere. If that seems too formal, rest assured, the polished service will make you feel right at home, like an emperor in his palace. The signature baked oysters with port require pre-ordering.

FOOK LAM MOON
CANTONESE, DIM SUM $$$

Map p380 (福臨門; ☏2366 0286; www.fooklammoon-grp.com; 53-59 Kimberley Rd, Shop 8, 1st fl, Tsim Sha Tsui; meals HK$400-2000; ☺11.30am-2.30pm & 6-10.30pm; Ⓜ Tsim Sha Tsui, exit B1) Locals call FLM 'celebrities' canteen'. But even if you're not rich and famous, FLM will treat you as if you were. The huge menu contains costly items such as abalone which would shoot your bill up to at least HK$1000 per head. But no one will snub you if you stick to the dim sum (from HK$60 a basket), which is divine and available only at lunch.

🍴 Yau Ma Tei & Mong Kok

★ SUN SIN
NOODLES $

Map p382 (新仙清湯腩; ☏2332 6872; 37 Portland St, Yau Ma Tei; meals HK$40-65; ☺11am-midnight; Ⓜ Yau Ma Tei, exit B2) A Michelin-praised brisket shop in a 'hood known for brothels, Sun Sin has kept quality up and prices down despite its laurel. The succulent cuts of meat are served in a broth with radish, in a chunky tomato soup, or as a curry. At peak times, makeshift tables are available upstairs for those who prize food over comfort.

NATHAN CONGEE AND NOODLE
CONGEE, NOODLES $

Map p382 (彌敦粥麵家; ☏2771 4285; 11 Saigon St, Yau Ma Tei; meals HK$60; ☺7.30am-11.30pm; Ⓜ Jordan, exit B2) This low-key eatery has been making great congee and noodles for the last half-century. Order a side of fritters (to be dunked into congee and eaten slightly soggy), tackle a pyramidal rice dumpling, or conquer the blanched fish skin tossed with parsley and peanuts.

GOOD HOPE NOODLE
NOODLES $

Map p382 (好旺角麵家; ☏2384 6898; 18 Fa Yuen St, Shop 5-6, Mong Kok; meals HK$30-90; ☺11am-12.45am; Ⓜ Mong Kok, exit D3) Despite a relocation and makeover, this 40-year-old shop has managed to retain its Michelin commendation and fan following. Now al dente egg noodles, bite-sized wontons, and silky congee that have won hearts for decades continue to be cooked the old way, but are served in neat, modern surrounds.

MIDO CAFÉ
CAFE $

Map p382 (美都餐室; ☏2384 6402; 63 Temple St; meals HK$40-90; ☺9am-10pm; Ⓜ Yau Ma Tei, exit B2) This retro *cha chaan tang* (1950) with mosaic tiles and metal latticework stands astride a street corner that comes to life at sundown. Ascend to the upper floor and take a seat next to a wall of iron-framed windows overlooking Tin Hau Temple (p149). Atmosphere is what makes it Kowloon's most famous tea cafe, despite passable food and service.

ONE DIM SUM
DIM SUM $

Map p383 (一點心; ☏2789 2280; 15 Playing Field Rd, Shop 1 & 2, Kenwood Mansion, Mong Kok; meals HK$35-60; ☺11am-1am; Ⓜ Prince Edward, exit A) This cheery place is known for all-day, bang-for-the-buck dim sum. Customers

LOCAL KNOWLEDGE

LEI YUE MUN VILLAGE

Popular seafood venue Lei Yue Mun has around two dozen restaurants lining a winding road that overlooks a typhoon shelter. Once you've settled down in a restaurant, go outside and pick your dinner from one of the stalls with live seafood tanks, making sure you know how much you're paying and for what, before committing. The restaurant will take care of the rest. Expect to pay upwards of HK$800 per person for a meal.

After leaving Yau Tong MTR station (exit A2), follow Cha Kwo Ling Rd and Shung Shun St south for 15 minutes or catch green minibus 24M from outside the station.

Lung Mun Seafood Restaurant (龍門海鮮酒家; ☑ 2717 9886; 20 Hoi Pong Rd W; meals HK$800-2000; ☺noon-10.30pm) Founded in 1967, this is one of the oldest restaurants here. Lobster baked with cheese and fried mantis shrimp with salt and pepper are the specialities.

Sea King Garden Restaurant (海皇園林酒家; ☑ 2348 1800, 2348 1408; 39 Hoi Pong Rd Central; meals HK$800-2000; ☺noon-10pm) Restaurant with a dated feel and an indoor garden and pool where turtles are kept. Throwing money into the shallow water is supposed to bring luck.

Lung Yue Restaurant (龍如海鮮酒樓; ☑ 2348 6332; 41 Hoi Pong Rd Central; meals HK$800-2000; ☺11.30am-11pm) Another veteran, Lung Yue is known for its skills in steaming fish and abalone.

place orders by ticking their selections of 45 items. There's always a line but the wait is usually under 30 minutes. Nonpeak hours are 3pm to 5pm, and 9pm to midnight.

BBQ LOBSTER — SKEWERS $$

Map p382 (龍蝦燒; ☑2374 9888; www.bbqlobster.com.hk; 7 Man Ying St, Ferry Point, Yau Ma Tei; skewers HK$12-35; ☺5pm-3am; Ⓜ Jordan, exit A) The most comfortable of three neighbouring branches, this buzzing eatery lures Kowloon gluttons with scrumptious grilled skewers that are 30% to 50% cheaper than the same in Soho. With fresh seven-inch prawns at only HK$17 each and vegetarian options aplenty, indulgence is the norm. In between sticks, cleanse your palate with a sip of Hoegaarden or a zesty white.

🍴 New Kowloon

KUNG WO TOFU FACTORY — DESSERT $

(公和荳品廠; ☑2386 6871; 118 Pei Ho St, Sham Shui Po; meals HK$8-30; ☺9am-9pm; Ⓜ Sham Shui Po, exit B2) A charming 50-year-old shop of a brand established in 1893, Kung Wo wears its name proudly in red clerical script. Regulars come for fresh soymilk, pan-fried tofu, and sweet tofu pudding, made the traditional way from beans ground using a hand-operated millstone. The silky tofu has nutty notes, and the hue is off-white – reassuringly imperfect, just like the service.

CHI LIN VEGETARIAN — VEGETARIAN, CHINESE $

(志蓮素齋, 龍門樓, Long Men Lou; ☑3658 9388; 60 Fung Tak Rd, Nan Lian Garden; meals from HK$200; ☺noon-9pm Mon-Fri, 11.30am-9pm Sat & Sun; ⌘; Ⓜ Diamond Hill, exit C2) Tasty vegetarian food and the location behind a waterfall make dining here a superb way to begin or end your visit to Chi Lin Nunnery and Nan Lian Garden (p144). The elegant **Song Cha Xie** (松茶榭, Pavilion of Pine & Tea; ☑3658 9390; 60 Fung Tak Rd, Nan Lian Garden; ☺noon-6.30pm; Ⓜ Diamond Hill, exit C2) nearby specialises in the art of Chinese tea drinking.

QUEEN'S CAFE — SOY SAUCE WESTERN $

(☑2265 8288; www.queenscafe.com; 80 Tat Chee Ave, Shop 18, L1/F, Festival Walk, Kowloon Tong; lunch from HK$100, dinner from HK$300; ☺11am-11pm; ⌘; Ⓜ Kowloon Tong, exit C) Queen's specialises in what's known as 'soy sauce Western' (the earliest fusion cuisine in Hong Kong featuring the influence of White Russian chefs who fled to Shanghai after the Bolshevik victory). The highlights at Queen's are baked dishes, cold cuts, and of course, the Hong Kong version of Russian borscht.

CHEONG FAT — THAI, NOODLES $

(昌發泰國粉麵屋; ☑2382 5998; 27 South Wall Rd, Kowloon City; noodles from HK$30; ☺noon-11.30pm) Blasting music videos in this hole-in-the-wall eatery set the rhythm as you slurp up the tasty Chiang Mai noodles. The open kitchen has appetising cooked dishes on display too, such as pork trotters with preserved vegetables. To get to Kowloon City, take minibus 25M from Kowloon Tong station (exit B2).

KOWLOON TANG
CHINESE, DIM SUM **$$**

(九龍廳; ☑2811 9398; www.kowloontang.com; 1 Austin Rd W, Shop R002-003, Civic Square, 3rd fl, roof deck, Elements Mall; meals HK$300-2000; ◷noon-10.30pm; ☷; ▥Kowloon, exit U3) Sophisticated Kowloon Tang serves impeccable Cantonese dishes, including a few Dong Guan classics, a laudable Peking duck, and an impressive selection of Western-style desserts in an art deco–inspired setting, reminiscent of its cousin across the harbour, Island Tang (p78).

TIN LUNG HEEN
CANTONESE **$$$**

(天龍軒; ☑2263 2270; www.ritzcarlton.com/hongkong; 1 Austin Rd W, 102nd fl, Ritz-Carlton Hong Kong, International Commerce Centre; meals HK$400-1700; ◷noon-2.30pm & 6-10.30pm; ▥Kowloon, exit U3) Though the decor is imposing – Xi Jinping could walk in any minute and feel at home – the service is personable and we were floored by the views. The signature *char siu* made with Spanish Iberico pork is the priciest plate of barbecue in town, but also the most succulent. Do not ask for a window seat if you suffer from vertigo.

🍷 DRINKING & NIGHTLIFE

🍷 Tsim Sha Tsui

★BUTLER
COCKTAIL BAR

Map p380 (☑2724 3828; 30 Mody Rd, 5th fl, Mody House, Tsim Sha Tsui; cover HK$200, snacks HK$30; ◷6.30pm-3am Mon-Fri, 6.30pm-2am Sat & Sun; ▥East Tsim Sha Tsui, exit N2) A cocktail and whisky heaven hidden in the residential part of TST. You can flip through its whisky magazines as you watch bartender Uchida create magical concoctions with the flair and precision of a master mixologist in Ginza. We loved the cocktails made from fresh citruses. A discreet and welcome addition to the TST drinking scene.

★INTERCONTINENTAL LOBBY LOUNGE
BAR

Map p380 (☑2721 1211; www.hongkong-ic.intercontinental.com; 18 Salisbury Rd, Hotel InterContinental Hong Kong, Tsim Sha Tsui; ◷24hr;

☎; ▥East Tsim Sha Tsui, exit J) Soaring plate glass and an unbeatable waterfront location make this one of the best spots to soak up that Hong Kong Island skyline and take in the busy harbour, although you pay for the privilege. It's also an ideal venue from which to watch the evening lightshow at 8pm.

★AQUA SPIRIT
BAR

Map p378 (☑3427 2288; www.aqua.com.hk; 1 Peking Rd, 29, 30th fl, Tsim Sha Tsui; ◷4pm-2am, happy hour 4-6pm; ☎; ▥Tsm Sha Tsui, exit L5) When night falls, you'll know why this über-fashionable bar has dim iilumination and black furniture – the two-storey, floor-to-ceiling windows command sweeping views of the Hong Kong Island skyline that come to life after sundown. The tables by the windows are awesome for bringing a date. On the weekends, a DJ spins hip hop and lounge jazz.

OZONE
BAR

(☑2263 2263; www.ritzcarlton.com; 1 Austin Rd, 118th fl, ICC, Tsim Sha Tsui; ◷5pm-1am Mon-Wed, to 2am Thu, to 3am Fri, 3pm-3am Sat, noon-midnight Sun; ☎; ▥Kowloon, exit U3) Ozone is the highest bar in Asia. The imaginative interiors, created to evoke a cyberesque Garden of Eden, have pillars resembling chocolate fountains in a hurricane and a myriad of refracted glass and colour-changing illumination. Equally dizzying is the wine list, with the most expensive bottle selling for over HK$150,000. Offers potential for a once-in-a-lifetime experience.

TAPAS BAR
BAR

Map p380 (☑2733 8756; www.shangri-la.com; 64 Mody Rd, Lobby, Kowloon Shangri-La, Tsim Sha Tsui; ◷3.30pm-1am Mon-Fri, from noon Sat & Sun; ☎; ▥East Tsim Sha Tsui, exit P1) An intimate vibe and bistro-style decor make this a good place to unwind over champagne, tapas and the sports channel after a day of sightseeing. A table in the alfresco area will let you smoke and take in harbour views, visible beyond a river of cars.

NED KELLY'S LAST STAND
PUB

Map p378 (☑2376 0562; 11A Ashley Rd, Tsim Sha Tsui; ◷11.30am-2am, happy hour 11.30am-9pm; ▥Tsim Sha Tsui, exit L5) Named after a gun-toting Australian bushranger, Ned's is one of Hong Kong's oldest pubs. Most of the expat regulars here (and there are many) are drawn to the laid-back atmosphere and the Dixieland jazz band that cracks jokes

LOCAL KNOWLEDGE

HONG KONG'S HIDDEN AGENDA

Located in the gritty industrial hub of Kwun Tong, **Hidden Agenda** (☑ 9170 6073; www.hiddenagendahk.com; 15-17 Tai Yip St, 2A, Wing Fu Industrial Bldg, Kwun Tong; Ⓜ Ngau Tau Kok, exit B6) is synonymous with underground music in Hong Kong. Hong Kong's best known music dive has the setting (former warehouse), line-up (solid indie acts), and elusiveness (it's off the way) all other dives wish they had.

As the city sheds its role as a manufacturing hub, artists and musicians have been setting up shop in abandoned factories where the rent is cheap and space is abundant. However, complications often arise with the lease of these premises, neighbours complaining about the noise and landlords hoping to develop their property into something lucrative.

No stranger to these problems, Hidden Agenda is now living it up at its third location – a warehouse-turned-venue accommodating 300 people. Its lineup features a plethora of genres including post-rock, reggae, jazz, techno and punk.

Strong bands from Greater China (Chochukmo, Hungry Ghosts, Carsick Cars) and overseas (Tahiti 80, The Chariot, Anti-Flag, Alcest, Pitchtuner) have performed here. See the website for the latest. Hidden Agenda is about a five-block walk from the MTR. The entrance has a small metal gate that's open after-hours.

between songs. The bar is filled with old posters, rugby shirts and Oz paraphernalia.

AMUSE
BAR

Map p380 (☑2317 1988; 4 Austin Ave, Tsim Sha Tsui; ⊙5pm-4am Mon-Fri, 6pm-4am Sat, 6pm-3am Sun; 🛜; Ⓜ Jordan, exit D) An airy bistro-like bar frequented by white-collar locals and university students who come for their draught beers, decent wines and funky cocktails. The best seats are the leather couches next to a row of large windows; the communal table is great if you want to meet people; and the banquettes make for intimate tête-à-têtes.

UTOPIA
BAR

Map p378 (☑3188 0816; 7 Hillwood Rd, 26th fl, Hon Kwok Jordon Centre, Tsim Sha Tsui; ⊙5pm-2am Mon-Thu, to 3am Fri & Sat, to 1am Sun; 🛜; Ⓜ Jordan, exit D) A favourite haunt of young local office workers, Utopia has good views but doesn't charge for them. The drinks list of 50 Old and New World bottles, and draught beer, is also reasonably priced. And there's a dart board if you're bored. Happy hour runs from 5pm to 9pm and midnight to late Monday to Thursday, plus all day Sunday.

VIBES
LOUNGE

Map p378 (☑2315 5999; www.themirahotel.com; 118 Nathan Rd, 5th fl, Mira Hong Kong, Tsim Sha Tsui; ⊙5pm-midnight Sun-Wed, 5pm-1am Thu-Sat; 🛜; Ⓜ Tsim Sha Tsui, exit B1) This open-air lounge bar comes with plush seating, exotic cabanas, and random greenery. You can take your pick among their 'molecular'

cocktails, which feature liquid nitrogen and foam, or smoke a fruit-flavoured shisha. From 8pm daily (except Sunday), a resident DJ spins groovy tunes from his station.

🍷 Yau Ma Tei & Mong Kok

KUBRICK BOOKSHOP CAFÉ
CAFE

Map p382 (☑2384 8929; www.kubrick.com.hk; 3 Public Square St, Shop H2, Prosperous Garden, Yau Ma Tei; ⊙11.30am-9.30pm; Ⓜ Yau Ma Tei, exit C) The airy bookstore-cafe attached to the Broadway Cinematheque (p160) serves decent coffee and simple eats. While waiting for your cuppa, you can browse the shop's strong collection of art, film and cultural studies titles.

SNAKE KING YAN
SNAKE BILE

Map p382 (蛇王恩; ☑2384 5608; 80A Woo Sung St, Yau Ma Tei; ⊙noon-10pm; Ⓜ Jordan, exit A) Challenge yourself to a shot of rice wine mixed with snake bile at this specialty shop near the Temple Street Night Market (p142). If that reviles you, there are jars of exotic infusions on display that you might prefer. Snake bile is believed to increase virility.

FULLCUP CAFÉ
CAFE

Map p382 (呼吸咖啡茶館; 36 Dundas St, 4-6th fl, Hanwai Commercial Centre, Mong Kok; ⊙noon-3am; 🛜; Ⓜ Yau Ma Tei, exit A1) 'Full cup' sounds similar to the Cantonese for 'breathe' and it's what this quirky three-storey cafe does: offer a breather in the midst of Mong Kok.

With retro furniture and an alfresco space, it attracts a young local artsy crowd. Full-cup serves decent coffee, smoothies, and beer. There are live gigs on some weekends.

KNOCKBOX COFFEE COMPANY — COFFEE
Map p383 (☑2781 0363; http://knockboxcoffee. hk; 21 Hak Po St, Mong Kok; ⊗11am-9pm; ☞; MMong Kok, exit E) This tiny cafe in hectic Mong Kok offers good espresso-based coffees, and the baristas are ready to share their encyclopaedic knowledge of beans. If you're hungry, there's fish and chips. The cafe closes at 10pm Monday to Thursday, and 11pm on Friday, Saturday and Sunday though last order is always 9pm.

☆ ENTERTAINMENT

WEST KOWLOON CULTURAL DISTRICT — CULTURAL VENUE
(西九文化區, WKCD; ☑2200 0000; www. westkowloon.hk; West Kowloon Waterfront Promenade; ⊗6am-11pm; MKowloon, exit D) Taking up a dramatic spot on the West Kowloon harbourfront, WKCD is developing into Hong Kong's premier cultural quarter. Construction of cultural spaces began in 2013. In the meantime, (quasi-)outdoor events take place at the picturesque venue, notably, music festivals **Freespace Fest** and **Clockenflap** (www.clockenflap.com), in November and December, and West Kowloon Bamboo Theatre, a Chinese opera extravaganza in January. Parts of the site are open to public even when there are no events on.

After exiting the metro station, head to Nga Cheung Rd, followed by a 10-minute walk to the WKCD entrance. The website has detailed instructions.

TONGTHREE — LIVE MUSIC
Map p383 (妖物唐三; https://www.facebook. com/tongthree; 716 Shanghai St, 2nd fl, Mong Kok; MPrince Edward, exit C2) This atmospheric studio and artists' hideout on the 3rd floor of a Chinese tenement building, or *tong lau*, stages cultural events several times a month, its charming turn-of-the-century setting providing the backdrop to live gigs, poetry readings, dance performances, and movie screenings. See their Facebook page for the latest.

ON AND ON THEATRE WORKSHOP — THEATRE
(前進進戲劇工作坊; ☑2503 1630; www.onan-don.org.hk; 63 Ma Tau Kok Rd, Unit 7, Cattle Depot Artist Village, To Kwa Wan; ☐106, 12A, 5C, 101, 111) This independent theatre group at the Cattle Depot Artist Village (p153) puts on thought-provoking works by local and international playwrights and runs workshops for professional actors. Their website has more.

BROADWAY CINEMATHEQUE — CINEMA
Map p382 (百老匯電影中心; ☑2388 3188; 3 Public Square St, ground fl, Prosperous Gardens, Yau Ma Tei; MYau Ma Tei, exit C) The place for new art-house releases and rerun screenings. The Kubrick Bookshop Café (p159) next door serves decent coffee and simple meals.

LEE SHAU KEI SCHOOL OF CREATIVITY ARTS CENTRE — LIVE PERFORMANCE
(香港兆基創意書院文化藝術中心; www. creativehk.edu.hk/artscentre; 135 Junction Rd, Kowloon City; ☐11D, 11K, 75K, 85, 891, MLok Fu, exit B) This off-the-way performance arts academy has a rich cultural program that covers music, film and a book fair. Though some events are meant for students, many are professional and interestingly experimental in nature, such as noise concerts by internationally renowned artists. See the calendar for what's on.

DADA — LIVE MUSIC
Map p380 (39 Kimberley Rd, 2nd fl, Luxe Manor, Tsim Sha Tsui; ⊗11am-2am Mon-Sat, to 1am Sun; ☞; MTsim Sha Tsui, exit B1) Upstairs in a quirky hotel, Dada is an intimate cocktail bar decked out with florid wallpaper, plush velvet seats, and a couple of Dalí-esque paintings. Jazz and blues bands play to a professional mid-30s crowd a few times a month.

HONG KONG CULTURAL CENTRE — THEATRE, MUSIC
Map p378 (香港文化中心; www.lcsd.gov.hk; 10 Salisbury Rd, Tsim Sha Tsui; ⊗9am-11pm; ☞; MEast Tsim Sha Tsui, exit L6) Hong Kong's premier arts performance venue, the world-class Cultural Centre (p145) contains a 2085-seat concert hall with an impressive Rieger pipe organ, two theatres and rehearsal studios.

GRAND OCEAN CINEMA — CINEMA
Map p378 (☑2377 2100; www.goldenharvest. com; 3 Canton Rd, Marco Polo Hong Kong Hotel Shopping Arcade, Zone D, Harbour City, Tsim Sha Tsui; MEast Tsim Sha Tsui, exit L6) Featuring local and international blockbusters.

TEMPLE STREET'S SINGALONG PARLOURS
....

A highlight of Yau Ma Tei is its old-fashioned singalong parlours (歌廳). These originated 20 years ago to offer shelter to street singers on rainy days.

Most parlours have basic setups – tables, a stage, and Christmas lights for an upbeat atmosphere. All have their own organist and troupe of freelance singers – ladies who'll keep you company and persuade you to make a dedication or sing along with them for a fee. Their repertoir spans from Chinese operatic extracts to English oldies. You'll see many regulars at these places – kooky types from the neighbourhood; old men who drink from whisky flasks and know all the dames...

It's more fun to go after 9pm. As parlours don't provide food, you're welcome to order delivery. Some sell beer but you can also get your own from convenience stores.

Canton Singing House (艷陽天歌座; Map p382; 49-51 Temple St, Yau Ma Tei; entrance HK$20; ⊘ 3-7pm & 8pm-5am; Ⓜ Yau Ma Tei, exit C) The oldest and most atmospheric of the singalong parlours, Canton resembles a film set with its mirror balls and glowing shrines. Each session features 20 singers, all with fan following. Patrons tip a minimum of HK$20 (per patron) if they like a song. But even if you don't, it's nice to tip every now and then for the experience – just slip your money into a box on stage. For HK$100, you can sing a song.

Jyut Wan Go Zo (粵韻歌座, Yuèyùn Gēzuò; Map p382; 53-57 Temple St, Yau Ma Tei; entrance HK$20; ⊘ 3.30-7.30pm & 8pm-4am; Ⓜ Yau Ma Tei, exit C) Larger but shabbier than Canton Singing House next door, this place has been around for 10 years. The ladies here are sweet and persuasive. For HK$50, you can make a dedication or sing with them.

🔒 SHOPPING

Tsim Sha Tsui has the greatest range of goods on offer, from HK$20 trinkets to HK$12,000 leather boots, but they are mainly upmarket. To the north of Tsim Sha Tsui, Yau Ma Tei and Mong Kok offer good prices on clothing, sporting goods, camping gear, computers and other daily necessities. The highlight of shopping in New Kowloon is the cut-price computer centres of Sham Shui Po.

🔒 Tsim Sha Tsui

BROWNSTAILOR — MEN'S CLOTHING
Map p378 (☏3996 8654; www.brownstailor.com; 88 Nathan Rd, Unit E, 2nd fl, Comfort Bldg, Tsim Sha Tsui; ⊘11am-7pm Mon-Fri, to 6.30pm Sat; ⓂTsim Sha Tsui, exit B1) Like Armoury (p83), BrownsTailor belongs to a new generation of bespoke tailoring shops for men. It's adept at making traditional gentlemen's attire and instilling modern elements into a classic look. Depending on the fabric used, a suit can cost you anywhere between HK$4200 and HK$18,000.

SWINDON BOOKS — BOOKS
Map p378 (☏2366 8001; 13-15 Lock Rd, Tsim Sha Tsui; ⊘9am-6pm Mon-Fri, to 1pm Sat; ⓂTsim Sha

Tsui, exit A1) One of the best 'real' (as opposed to 'supermarket') bookshops. An excellent range and knowledgeable staff. Strong on local books and history in particular.

BIZET — SHOES
Map p380 (☏3621 0878; www.bizetleather.com; 87-105 Chatham Rd S, Room 1610, 16th fl, Beverley Commercial Centre, Tsim Sha Tsui; ⊘1-8pm Tue-Fri, to 7pm Sat, to 5.30pm Sun; ⓂTsim Sha Tsui, exit B2) Bizet's owner orders quality shoes directly from Italian artisans for her small but exquisite women's collection. Everything from ballerinas and Oxfords to peek-a-boo sandals and combat boots, at prices modest for the '100% made in Italy' label.

DAVID CHAN PHOTO SHOP — PHOTOGRAPHY
Map p378 (陳烘相機; ☏2723 3886; 16 Kimberley Rd, Shop 15, ground fl, Champagne Court, Tsim Sha Tsui; ⊘10am-8pm Mon-Sat; ⓂTsim Sha Tsui, exit B1) If you've decided to give the digital age a miss altogether, or at least still use film cameras, this dealer is the most reputable used-camera shop in town. The owner David Chan has been working in the business since the 1960s and has some precious equipment in his collection.

HEAVEN PLEASE — CLOTHING
Map p380 (☏23119533; www.heaven-please.com; 77-79 Granville Rd, 7th fl, Kolling Centre, Tsim Sha

Tsui; 1-9pm Mon-Sat; MTsim Sha Tsui, exit B2) Lady Gaga meets punk Lolita for cocktails at this fun place. The designers are liberal with lace and '80s glam. Even if you don't want the whole look, the pieces will add whimsical touches to any classic wardrobe. Building entrance on Chatham Rd South.

K11
MALL

Map p380 (18 Hanoi Rd, Tsim Sha Tsui; MEast Tsim Sha Tsui, exit D2) A pleasant shopping mall catering to the young, middle-class market, K11 features exhibition spaces for local artists and Daydream Nation. It's right above the MTR station.

DAYDREAM NATION
CLOTHING

Map p378 (2177 7208; www.daydream-nation. com; 18 Hanoi Rd, Shop 101, Level 1, K11, Tsim Sha Tsui; 11am-10pm; MEast Tsim Sha Tsui, exit N3, N4) A 'Vogue Talent' brand founded by two creative designers, Kay Wong and her brother Jing, DN is known for its penchant for theatricality in its designs. Clothes and accessories often feature allusions to folklore and romantic literature, while remaining highly wearable.

INITIAL
CLOTHING

Map p380 (www.initialfashion.com; 48 Cameron Rd, Shop 2, Tsim Sha Tsui; 11.30am-11.30pm; MTsim Sha Tsui, exit B2) This attractive shop and cafe carries stylish, multifunctional urbanwear with European and Japanese influences. The clothes created by local designers are complemented by imported shoes, bags and costume jewellery.

PREMIER JEWELLERY
JEWELLERY

Map p378 (愛寶珠寶有限公司; 2368 0003; 50 Nathan Rd, Shop G14-15, ground fl, Holiday Inn Golden Mile Shopping Mall, Tsim Sha Tsui; 10am-7.30pm Mon-Sat, to 4pm Sun; MTsim Sha Tsui, exit G) This third-generation family firm is directed by a qualified gemmologist. The range isn't huge but if you're looking for something particular, give Premier Jewellery a day's notice and a selection will be ready in time for your arrival. Staff can also help you design your own piece.

RISE SHOPPING ARCADE
CLOTHING

Map p380 (利時商場; www.rise-hk.com; 5-11 Granville Circuit, Tsim Sha Tsui; 3-9pm; MTsim Sha Tsui, exit B2) Bursting the seams of this minimall is cheap streetwear from Hong Kong, Korea and Japan, with a few knockoffs chucked in for good measure. Patience

and a good eye could land you purchases fit for a Vogue photo shoot. It's best visited between 4pm and 8.30pm when most of the shops are open.

CURIO ALLEY
GIFTS, SOUVENIRS

Map p378 (10am-8pm; MTsim Sha Tsui, exit C1) This is a fun place to rummage for name chops, soapstone carvings, fans and other Chinese bric-a-brac. It's found in an alleyway between Lock and Hankow Rds, just south of Haiphong Rd.

I.T.
CLOTHING, ACCESSORIES

Map p378 (www.ithk.com; 30 Canton Rd, Shop LG01 & LG16-17, Basement, Silvercord, Tsim Sha Tsui; 11.30am-9pm; MTsim Sha Tsui, exit A1) I.T. carries a chic and edgy selection of first-to third-tier designer brands from Europe and Japan, with high but not outrageous price tags. The I.T. group has shops in almost all the major shopping areas in town.

STAR COMPUTER CITY
ELECTRONICS

Map p378 (星光電腦城; 2730 4382; 3 Salisbury Rd, 2nd fl, Star House, Tsim Sha Tsui; 10am-7.30pm; Star Ferry, MTsim Sha Tsui, exit L6) This handy and relatively uncrowded mall right next to Victoria Harbour has one floor devoted to computers. It's a good place to shop if you don't mind paying a bit more.

HARBOUR CITY
MALL

Map p378 (www.harbourcity.com.hk; 3-9 Canton Rd; MTsim Sha Tsui, exit C1) This is an enormous place, with 700 shops, 50 food and beverage outlets and five cinemas. Outlets are arrayed in four separate zones: for kids, sport, fashion, and cosmetics and beauty. Almost every major brand is represented.

Yau Ma Tei & Mong Kok

CHAN WAH KEE CUTLERY STORE
HOMEWARES

Map p382 (陳華記刀莊; 2730 4091; Temple St, 278D, Yau Ma Tei; 11am-6pm, closed Wed; MJordan, exit C2) At this humble shop, 80-year-old Mr Chan, one of Asia's few remaining master knife-sharpeners, uses nine different stones to grind each blade, and alternates between water and oil. If you bring him your blade, he charges between HK$100 and HK$600 with a three-month wait. But if you buy one from him, he'll do it there and then. Prices range from HK$200 for a small paring knife to around HK$2000 for a Shun knife.

🏃 City Walk
Kowloon's Teeming Market Streets

START PRINCE EDWARD MTR STATION, EXIT A
END JORDAN MTR STATION, EXIT A
LENGTH 4.5KM, TWO HOURS

A 10-minute walk away from Prince Edward station (exit A), ❶ **Yuen Po Street Bird Garden** (p152) is the gathering place for older men who air their caged birds here. A little further along, Flower Market Rd is lined with fragrant and exotic blooms.

At the end of the street, take a left turn onto Sai Yee St, then a right onto Prince Edward Rd West and then take a left turn onto Tung Choi St. Walk two blocks to the ❷ **Goldfish Market**, a dozen or so shops trading in these extravagantly hued fish. You'll see an amazing variety, with the real rarities commanding high prices.

Sharpen your elbows. ❸ **Tung Choi St market** (p164), also known as the Ladies' Market, is crammed with shoppers and stalls selling mostly inexpensive clothing.

Beneath the naked light bulbs, hundreds of stalls at the ❹ **Temple Street Night Market** (p142) sell a vast array of booty from sex toys to luggage. Coming from Tung Choi St, turn right on Dundas St and then left into Shanghai St, cut down Hi Lung Lane to Temple St and turn right. The market runs right down to Jordan Rd.

Fragrant smoke curls from incense spirals at ❺ **Tin Hau Temple** (p149). Fortune-tellers nearby use everything from tarot cards to palmistry and even tame sparrows to deliver their predictions.

A good place to pick up an inexpensive trinket, the large covered ❻ **Jade Market** (p149) contains dozens of stalls selling jade of all grades. At Jordan Rd turn east, then south into Nathan Rd to find Jordan MTR station.

HONG KONG READER
BOOKS

Map p383 (序言書室; ☑2395 0031; www.hkreaders.com; 68 Sai Yeung Choi St S, 7th fl, Mong Kok; ⏱2pm-midnight; Ⓜ Mong Kok, exit D3) Run by a handful of young people, this bilingual bookstore-cafe has an intellectual bent. If you're looking for the likes of Derrida or Milosz, this is the place to go. Check the website for the latest literary readings, though most are conducted in Cantonese. It is located above a 1010 telecommunications shop.

TUNG CHOI ST MARKET
MARKET

Map p383 (通菜街, 女人街, Ladies' Market; Tung Choi St; ⏱noon-11.30pm; Ⓜ Mong Kok, exit D3) The Tung Choi St market is a cheek-by-jowl affair offering cheap clothes and trinkets. Vendors start setting up their stalls as early as noon, but it's best to get here between 1pm and 6pm when there's much more on offer. Beware, the sizes stocked here tend to suit the lissom Asian frame.

TAK HING DRIED SEAFOOD
FOOD

Map p382 (德興海味; ☑2780 2129; 1 Woosung St, Yau Ma Tei; ⏱ 9am-7.30pm; Ⓜ Yau Ma Tei, exit C) One of very few honest dried-seafood stores in the area, this delightful old corner establishment has glass jars stuffed with dried scallops, crocodile meat and bird's nests, though you might prefer the figs, cashews, candied lotus seeds and ginseng.

SINO CENTRE
MALL

Map p382 (信和中心; 582-592 Nathan Rd, Mong Kok; ⏱10am-10pm; Ⓜ Yau Ma Tei, exit A2) This shabby go-to place for all things related to Asian animation and comics will give you a taste of local culture. Its tiny shops carry new and back issues of Japanese manga, action figures, old-fashioned video games and other kidult bait.

SIN TAT PLAZA
MALL

Map p383 (83 Argyle St, Mong Kok; ⏱11am-10pm; Ⓜ Mong Kok, exit D2) Popular with locals, Sin Tat Plaza on busy Argyle St is dedicated to mobile phones of all persuasions, including a Chinese-made phone that doubles up as a lighter! It's also where to go to get your phone fixed and unlocked.

MONG KOK COMPUTER CENTRE
MALL

Map p383 (旺角電腦中心; 8-8A Nelson St, Mong Kok; ⏱1-10pm; Ⓜ Mong Kok, exit D3) Prices at this computer mall are cheap but language can be a barrier, and you'll see more finished products than computer components.

PROTREK
OUTDOOR EQUIPMENT

Map p382 (保捷行; www.protrek.com.hk; 5 Tung Fong St, Yau Ma Tei; ⏱noon-8pm Mon-Sat, 11.30am-9.30pm Sun; Ⓜ Yau Ma Tei, exit C) This reliable shop with branches all over town is your best bet for outdoor gear that will see you through from sea to summit. It also runs training courses on outdoor activities The English-speaking staff are very helpful.

LANGHAM PLACE MALL
MALL

Map p383 (朗豪坊; ☑3520 2800; 8 Argyle St, Mong Kok; ⏱11am-7pm; Ⓜ Mong Kok, exit C3) This 15-storey supermall has some 300 shops that stay open till as late as 11pm. The focal point of the mall is the high-tech Digital Sky, where special events take place.

🅰 New Kowloon

★GOLDEN COMPUTER ARCADE & GOLDEN SHOPPING CENTER
ELECTRONICS

(黃金電腦商場, 高登電腦中心; www.goldenarcade.org; 146-152 Fuk Wa St, Sham Shui Po; ⏱11am-9pm; Ⓜ Sham Shui Po, exit D2) Occupying different floors of a building opposite Sham Shui Po MTR station, these are *the* places to go for low-cost computers and peripherals. Golden Computer Arcade comprises the basement and ground floor; Golden Shopping Centre, the 1st floor. The 3Cs are generally considered the best shops – Centralfield (Golden Shopping Centre), Capital (Golden Computer Arcade), and Comdex (both places).

AP LIU STREET FLEA MARKET
MARKET

(鴨寮街; Ap Liu St, btwn Nam Cheong & Yen Chow Sts, Sham Shui Po; ⏱noon-midnight; Ⓜ Sham Shui Po, exit A1) A geek's heaven, this flea market specialises in all things digital and electronic. The market spills over into Pei Ho St.

ELEMENTS
MALL

(圓方; www.elementshk.com; 1 Austin Rd W, West Kowloon; ⏱11am-9pm; Ⓜ Kowloon, exit U3) Located inside the ICC (p148), Kowloon's most upmarket shopping mall comprises five pleasant sections each decorated according to one of the five natural elements. Thoughtful touches include good nursing facilities and helpful staff. Austin Rd West is built on reclaimed land that's connected to Austin Rd in Tsim Sha Tsui at its eastern end.

FESTIVAL WALK — MALL

(又一城; www.festivalwalk.com.hk; 80-88 Tat Chee Ave, Kowloon Tong; ⊙11am-10pm; ⓂKowloon Tong, exit C) Festival Walk's design lends it an airiness that makes it nice to walk around in. As well as some 200 shops, it has a cinema and an ice-skating rink.

VIVIENNE TAM — CLOTHING, ACCESSORIES

(☑2265 8381; www.viviennetam.com; LG1 Shop 05, Festival Walk, Kowloon Tong; ⊙11am-8.30pm Sun-Thu, to 9pm Fri & Sat; ⓂKowloon Tong, exit C2) This enduring brand from New York–based designer Tam, who was trained in Hong Kong, sells eminently wearable, feminine but also streetwise women's foundation pieces, light gossamer dresses and slinky tops, plus a range of accessories.

CHEUNG SHA WAN ROAD — MARKET

(長沙灣道; ⊙10am-6.30pm Mon-Fri, to 4pm Sat; ⓂSham Shui Po, exit C1) A riot of shops selling fabrics, trimmings, buttons, ribbons, other raw materials, and prét-à-porter clothing. You'll bump into fashion designers here.

🏃 SPORTS & ACTIVITIES

★ TAICHI — TAICHI

Map p378 (☑Pandora 9415 5678, William 9554 6928; Tsim Sha Tsui East Promenade; taichi HK$50; ⊙7.30-9am Mon, Wed & Fri; ⓂTsim Sha Tsui, exit J) Let sprightly masters show you how to 'wave hands like clouds' against the stunning views of Victoria Harbour, just outside the Museum of Art. Taichi or shadow boxing is supposed to give you a sharper mind and a fitter heart. Just show up.

MEI WAH TATTOO — TATTOO PARLOUR

Map p383 (美華刺青; ☑2757 0027, 6333 5352; kowloonink@gmail.com; 703 Shanghai St, 4th fl, Mong Kok; per hr HK$1000; ⓂPrince Edward, exit C1) Tattoo artist Nic Tse is Chinese but speaks perfect English. His impressive repertoire includes abstract contemporary designs, lines of poetry, interpretations of childhood dreams and minimalist armscapes. Interested parties should email Nic as early as possible to discuss specifics and book. Payment is in cash or via PayPal.

WING CHUN YIP MAN MARTIAL ARTS ATHLETIC ASSOCIATION — MARTIAL ARTS

Map p378 (葉問國術總會; ☑2723 2306; 27-33 Nathan Rd, Unit A, 5th fl, Alpha House, Tsim Sha Tsui; ⓂTsim Sha Tsui, exit E) The cost for three lessons a week (two or three hours each) for a month is HK$500. A six-month intensive course (six hours a day, six days a week) is around HK$5000, depending on the student.

OCEAN SKY DIVERS — WATER SPORTS

Map p378 (海天潛水訓練中心; ☑2366 3738; www.oceanskydiver.com; 19 Lock Rd, 1st fl, Tsim Sha Tsui; ⊙noon-9pm; ⓂTsim Sha Tsui, exit C1) Along with a full range of diving and snorkelling gear, this place is also worth consulting about dive courses and ideal dive sites all around the Hong Kong's coastline and islands.

KOWLOON PARK SWIMMING COMPLEX — SWIMMING

Map p378 (九龍公園游泳池; ☑2724 3577; Nathan & Austin Rds, Tsim Sha Tsui; adult/concession HK$19/9; ⊙6.30am-noon, 1-5pm & 6-10pm; ⓂTsim Sha Tsui, exit C2) This complex comes complete with four pools and waterfalls. Visit on a weekday; on weekends there are so many bathers it's difficult to find the water.

KING'S PARK TENNIS COURTS — TENNIS

Map p382 (☑2385 8985; 23 King's Park Rise, Yau Ma Tei; ⊙7am-11pm; ⓂYau Ma Tei, exit D) There are six tennis courts here at the King's Park Recreation Ground – not to be confused with the King's Park, home of the Hong Kong Rugby Football Union.

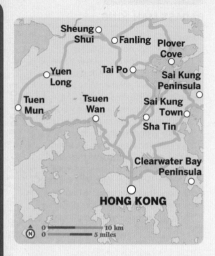

New Territories

Tsuen Wan p169
Has some of Hong Kong's most important Buddhist and Taoist monasteries.

Tuen Mun p171
Visit at leisure the temples and monasteries that dot the landscape.

Yuen Long p173
Hong Kong Wetland Park, laid-back Pak Nai and old walled villages.

Fanling & Sheung Shui p176
A heaven for history buffs, with fortified villages and historic ruins.

Tai Po p177
Lively markets and temples, plus an encyclopaedia of flora and fauna.

Plover Cove p181
Plover Cove is where you go to hike, hike, hike or bike, bike, bike!

Sha Tin p184
A New Town with a historical feel, temples and a heritage museum.

Sai Kung Peninsula p187
Pristine beaches and deserted coves grace this dramatic coastline.

Clearwater Bay Peninsula p192
The name says it all – beaches with crystal-clear water.

TOP SIGHT
MAI PO MARSHES

Witness the magic of migration in Mai Po Marshes, one of the world's most significant wetlands and a major pit stop for the tens of thousands of migratory waterfowl travelling from Siberia to Australasia every winter. These months are the best time to visit this Hong Kong treasure as you're likely to spot a number of rare birds; in other months, nature lovers and urbanites alike come here for the sheer beauty and biodiversity of Mother Nature.

Mai Po Marshes comprise some 1500 hectares of wetlands at the centre of which is a nature reserve. Here, the fragile ecosystem abutting Deep Bay simply teems with life. It is a protected network of mudflats, gei wai (shallow shrimp ponds), reed beds and dwarf mangroves, offering a rich habitat of up to 380 species of migratory and resident birds, more than a third of them rarely seen elsewhere in the territory. The area attracts birds in every season but especially winter, when an average of 54,000 migratory birds – including such endangered species as the Dalmatian pelican, black-faced spoonbill, spotted and imperial eagle and black vulture – pass through the marshes.

The **World Wide Fund for Nature Hong Kong** (世界自然基金會香港辦事處, WWFHK; ☑24hr hotline 2526 1011; www.wwf.org.hk; 1 Tramway Path, Central) does guided visits to the marsh. Three-hour tours leave the **Visitor Centre** (☑2471 8272) on Saturdays, Sundays and public holidays. The tours can be booked online, but reserve well in advance, especially during winter.

Bus 76K or red minibus 17 will drop you off at Mai Po Lo Wai, a village along the main road just east of the marsh. The WWFHK car park is about a 20-minute walk from there. Alternatively, a taxi from Sheung Shui will cost HK$70.

DON'T MISS

➡ Guided tours to the Reserve

➡ Floating boardwalks

PRACTICALITIES

➡ 米埔自然保護區

➡ ☑2471 3480

➡ www.wwf.org.hk

➡ Mai Po, Sin Tin, Yuen Long

➡ admission HK$120

➡ ⊘9am-5pm

➡ ▭76K from Sheung Shui East Rail or Yuen Long West Rail stations

This meandering 1km trail through three old but lively (partially walled) villages in northwestern New Territories will lead you down the memory lane of pre-colonial Hong Kong, including the spectacular Ping Shan Village. The trail boasts 12 well-restored historic buildings and a museum at Ping Shan dedicated to the powerful Tang clan, the founders of this 500-year-old village and considered the first immigrants to settle in Hong Kong.

Start with the **Ping Shan Tang Clan Gallery** (屏山鄧族文物館; ⓇPing Shan) at the eastern end of the trail. Housed in a beautifully restored former police station, the gallery showcases the history of the Tang clan and its relation to Ping Shan. The colourful collections include a traditional sedan chair, ritual wares and a giant wooden bed. The building itself, by the way, was built in 1899 and was a colonial outpost to monitor 'untoward' villagers.

Retrace your steps to Ping Ha Rd and turn right. The small **Hung Shing Temple** is on your right-hand side, followed by **Ching Shu Hin Chamber** and **Kun Ting Study Hall** where you turn right again. North of them are the **Tang Ancestral Hall** and **Yu Kiu Ancestral Hall**, two of the largest ancestral halls in Hong Kong. The Tangs justifiably brag about them, especially the hall that bears their name, since it follows a unique three-halls-two-courtyards structure which shows the clan's prestigious status inside the imperial court.

Further on are some more temples and an old well. At the end of the trail is the three-storey **Tsui Sing Lau** (聚星樓; ⓇTin Shui Wai), the only surviving ancient pagoda in Hong Kong.

DON'T MISS

➡ Ping Shan Tang Clan Gallery
➡ Tang Ancestral Hall
➡ Yu Kiu Ancestral Hall

PRACTIALITIES

➡ 屏山文物徑
➡ ☎2617 1959
➡ ⊙ancestral halls 9am-1pm & 2-5pm, Tsui Sing Lau 9am-1pm & 2-5pm, closed Tue
➡ Ⓜ West Rail Tin Shui Wai, exit E

Tsuen Wan

Explore

The industrial and residential New Town of Tsuen Wan is nothing special, but its outskirts can be rewarding, especially if you are an early bird.

Eating yum cha in the morning at one of the Chuen Lung Village teahouses is an experience. After breakfast hikers usually continue up to Tai Mo Shan Country Park. If you want to see vibrant temples, head back to the town centre and take a minibus bound for the serene Western Monastery and colourful Yuen Yuen Institute, the latter stuffed with all manner of deities, or make a pilgrimage to Chuk Lam Sim Monastery.

Do not miss the Hakka-themed Sam Tung Uk Museum before you head back to the MTR station.

The Best...

➡ **Sight** Western Monastery (p169)

➡ **Place to eat** Duen Kee Restaurant (p171)

➡ **Activity** Climbing Tai Mo Shan

Top Tip

Tak Wah Park in the centre of town, with ancient trees and footbridges over ponds, is an ideal spot to take a break from the hustle and bustle of Tsuen Wan.

Getting There & Away

➡ **Bus** Many buses from around the New Territories arrive at Tsuen Wan's central bus station, including bus 60M from Tuen Mun and 68M from Yuen Long. Bus 51 from Tai Mo Shan and Kam Tin stops along Tai Ho Rd. The main bus station is opposite the MTR on Castle Peak Rd (exit A2), but buses and green minibuses pick up and disgorge passengers throughout the New Town.

➡ **MTR** Tsuen Wan MTR station is on the Tsuen Wan line; it's on Sai Lau Kok Rd, with the Luk Yeung Galleria shopping centre above it. Tsuen Wan West station is on the West Rail line.

Need to Know

➡ **Area code** ☑852

➡ **Location** 11km northwest of Kowloon Peninsula

◉ SIGHTS

YUEN YUEN INSTITUTE   RELIGIOUS CENTRE
(圓玄學院; ☑2492 2220; Lo Wai Rd; ⊙8.30am-5pm; 🚌green minibus 81) Stuffed with vivid statuary of Taoist and Buddhist deities plus Confucian saints, the Yuen Yuen Institute, in the hills northeast of Tsuen Wan, gives a fascinating look into Hong Kong's tripartite religious system. The main building is a replica of the Temple of Heaven in Běijīng. On the upper ground floor are three Taoist immortals seated in a quiet hall; walk down to the lower level to watch as crowds of the faithful pray and burn offerings to the 60 incarnations of Taoist saints lining the walls.

To reach the institute, take minibus 81 from Shiu Wo St, two blocks due south of Tsuen Wan MTR station (exit B1). A taxi from the MTR station will cost around HK$40.

WESTERN MONASTERY   BUDDHIST MONASTERY
(西方寺; ☑2411 5111; Lo Wai Rd; ⊙8.30am-5.30pm; 🚌green minibus 81) This Buddhist monastery is a tranquil complex in which to pass the time, observing points of interest both architectural and spiritual. After being greeted by a Bodhisattva statue in the entrance, you'll see the main building lying behind, styled as a classical Chinese palace. Further behind is another two-storey building where, depending on what time of day you visit, you may witness scores of monks chanting mantras. This building is topped by a spectacular nine-storey pagoda.

To reach the monastery, take minibus 81 from Shiu Wo St. A taxi from the MTR station will cost around HK$40.

CHUK LAM SIM
MONASTERY   BUDDHIST MONASTERY, TEMPLE
(竹林禪院; ☑2490 3392; Fu Yung Shan Rd; ⊙9am-4.30pm; 🚌green minibus 85) In a lovely bucolic setting, Chuk Lam Sim (Bamboo Forest) Monastery is one of the larger temple complexes in Hong Kong. The temple was completed in 1932 when (legend has it) Tou Tei, the earth god, told an elderly monk to build it. The second temple contains three of the largest golden Buddhas in the

Tsuen Wan

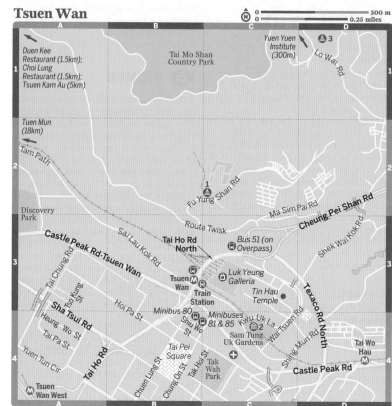

Tsuen Wan

◉ Sights	(p169)
1 Chuk Lam Sim Monastery	C2
2 Sam Tung Uk Museum	C4
3 Western Monastery	D1

territory, while the third contains another large image of Lord Gautama.

The monastery is northeast of Tsuen Wan MTR station. To reach it, take green minibus 85 from Shiu Wo St.

SAM TUNG UK MUSEUM   MUSEUM
(三棟屋博物館; ☎2411 2001; 2 Kwu Uk Lane; ⊙9am-5pm Wed-Mon; Ⓜ Tsuen Wan) FREE This well-tended museum aims to portray rural life as it was lived in this late-18th-century Hakka walled village, the former residents of which (the Chan clan) were resettled in 1980. Within the complex a dozen three-

beamed houses contain traditional Hakka furnishings, kitchenware, wedding items and agricultural implements, most of which came from two 17th-century Hakka villages in Guǎngdōng province. Behind the restored halls is the old village school, with interactive displays and videos on such topics as Hakka women, traditional crafts and food.

At the Tsuen Wan MTR station, take exit E and walk five minutes southeast along Sai Lau Kok Rd to Kwu Uk Lane and the museum.

✖ EATING

The two old-style Cantonese teahouses in the village of Chuen Lung, located to the west of Tai Mo Shan and 5km northeast of Tsuen Wan, are favourite breakfast joints for hikers bound for Tai Mo Shan Country Park. To get there, catch minibus 80 that leaves from Chuen Lung St in Tsuen Wan (MTR exit B1) and hop off when you reach the last stop.

CHOI LUNG RESTAURANT   CANTONESE $
(彩龍茶樓; ☑2415 5041; 2 Chuen Lung Village, Route Twisk; dim sum from HK$10; ◷5.30am-3pm; 🚌minibus 80 from Tsuen Wan) In a two-storey house near the village entrance, this 40-year-old establishment is renowned for using the mountain spring water from Tai Mo Shan to make sweet bean curds. The teahouse is self-service – you pick your dim sum from the kitchen and make your own tea. The best dim sum time is between 8am and 10am when the widest choices are served. There is no English signage but it's identifiable by the stools in its open area.

DUEN KEE RESTAURANT   CANTONESE $
(端記茶樓; ☑2490 5246; 57-58 Chuen Lung Village, Route Twisk; dim sum from HK$10; ◷6am-2pm; 🚌minibus 80 from Tsuen Wan) Not far from Choi Lung Restaurant and located closer to the fields is this popular – and no-frills – yum-cha joint. You can have dim sum under one of the parasols on the ground floor, but the true attraction lies upstairs where older villagers show off their caged birds while sipping tea. The home-grown watercress is the signature vegetable here.

Tuen Mun

Explore

Industrial-residential Tuen Mun is not a particularly attractive part of Hong Kong, but several historic temples make it worth the trek. If you want to stretch your legs, walk uphill to Tsing Shan Monastery and enjoy the sweeping views of Tuen Mun Valley; lazybones can head to Miu Fat Monastery and Ching Chung Temple, both of which are conveniently served by Light Rail.

Foodwise, try the local speciality, roast goose, in the neighbourhood of Shem Tseng, or seafood along the coast.

The Best...
➡**Sight** Miu Fat Monastery (p172)
➡**Place to eat** Yue Kee Roasted Goose Restaurant (p173)

Top Tip

If you're travelling to Tuen Mun from Tsuen Wan, Kowloon or Hong Kong Island by bus, sit on the upper deck on the left side for spectacular views of the Tsing Ma Bridge.

Getting There & Away
➡**Bus** Bus 60M from Tsuen Wan MTR station (exit A3) travels along the coast to Tuen Mun.

WORTH A DETOUR

TAI MO SHAN

Hong Kong's tallest mountain is Tai Mo Shan (957m). Several hiking trails thread up and around it, but you'll need to bring your own food and water. The Countryside Series *North-east & Central New Territories* map is the one you want for this area.

The **Tai Mo Shan Country Park Visitor Centre** (大帽山郊野公園遊客中心; ☑2498 9326; ◷9.30am-4.30pm Sat, Sun & holidays) is at the junction of Route Twisk (the name is derived from 'Tsuen Wan into Shek Kong') and Tai Mo Shan Rd, which is crossed by the MacLehose Trail.

The nearest MTR station is Tsuen Wan. From there, catch bus 51 on Tai Ho Rd North, alighting at the junction of Route Twisk and Tai Mo Shan Rd in Tsuen Kam Au. Follow Tai Mo Rd, which forms part of stage No 9 of the MacLehose Trail, east to the summit. On the right-hand side, about 45 minutes from the bus stop, a fork in the road leads south along a concrete path to the Sze Lok Yuen Hostel. Bus 64 also links Tai Mo Shan with Yuen Long and Tai Po Market, and bus 25K runs between Tai Po Market and Tai Mo Shan.

➡ **Ferry** Services to Tuen Mun ferry pier arrive from Tung Chung, Sha Lo Wan and Tai O (all on Lantau). Ferries to the airport, Tung Chung and Tai O on Lantau depart from the pier to the southwest of the town centre.

➡ **Light Rail** Tuen Mun is towards the southern end of the useful Light Rail network. Other major points include Tin Shui Wai, Yuen Long and Siu Hong. The station is linked to the MTR station.

➡ **MTR** Tuen Mun is on the West Rail line.

Need to Know

➡ **Area code** ☑852

➡ **Location** 30km northwest of Kowloon Peninsula

➡ **Last train to Kowloon** 12.15am from Tuen Mun West Rail station

◉ SIGHTS

MIU FAT MONASTERY   BUDDHIST MONASTERY

(妙法寺; ☑2461 8567; 18 Castle Peak Rd; ⊙9am-5pm; 🚊line 751) Miu Fat Monastery in Lam Tei, due north of Tuen Mun town centre, is one of the most eye-catching Buddhist complexes in the territory. Wander through the peaceful rock garden to find two stone lions and two stone elephants guarding the entrance. Inside you'll find a golden likeness of Buddha and three larger statues of Lord Gautama. You can't miss the soaring new extension, a 45m tower resembling a huge crystal lotus blossom. Unsurprisingly, the structure glows at night.

This is an active monastery; you'll see brown-robed nuns in droves. To get here take Light Rail line 751 from the Tuen Mun or Town Centre stops to Lam Tei station. The complex is on the opposite side of Castle Peak Rd; cross over the walkway and walk north 150m. Bus 63X, from the Mong Kok MTR station, also stops in front of the monastery.

TSING SHAN
MONASTERY   BUDDHIST MONASTERY

(青山禪院; ☑2461 8050; Tsing Shan Monastery Path; ⊙24hr; 🚊line 610, 615, 615P) Also known as Castle Peak Monastery, this temple complex perched on the hill of Castle Peak is the oldest in Hong Kong. Founded by Reverend Pui To (literally, 'travelling in a cup') 1500 years ago, the complex you see today was rebuilt in 1926. Check out shrines and temples for different saints and Bodhisattvas, including one to Pui To in a grotto, as you ascend the hill. Some of these have slid into dilapidation; nonetheless they're imbued with a spooky charm.

The temple was also one of the shooting locations for the Bruce Lee classic *Enter the Dragon*. To reach here, board Light Rail line 610, 615 or 615P and alight at Tsing Shan Tsuen. From there follow the sign to Tsing Shan Monastery Path, which is due

---

WORTH A DETOUR

TSING YI

Blemished by oil depots and extended by land reclamation, Tsing Yi is the large island to the east of Ma Wan on the MTR's Tung Chung and the Airport Express lines. The only reason to visit this island is to take in the gigantic **Tsing Ma Bridge**. Feel free to admire the 1377m suspension bridge but don't even think about visiting the beaches here.

The **Lantau Link Visitors Centre** (青嶼幹線訪客中心; ☑2495 7583, 2495 5825; ⊙10am-5pm; 🚌green minibus 308M, Ⓜ Tsing Yi) **FREE** and its viewing platform is where you can get a close-up of the enormity of Tsing Yi Bridge and the **Lantau Link**, the combined road and rail transport connection between the New Territories and Lantau. The centre contains models, photographs and videos of the construction process – very much a crowd-pleaser for trainspotters and the hard-hat brigade.

The Lantau Link has since been overshadowed somewhat by the **Stonecutter's Bridge**, a graceful 1.5km span bridging the gap between the massive international container terminal in the New Territories and Tsing Yi Island.

The visitors centre for the Lantau Link is in the northwest corner of Tsing Yi Island just to the south of Ting Kau Bridge. To reach it, take the MTR to Tsing Yi station on the Tung Chung line, use exit No A1 and board minibus 308M in Maritime Sq, which will drop you off at the centre's car park.

west of the station. The steep path to the entrance of the monastery is a 30-minute hike.

CHING CHUNG TEMPLE
TAOIST TEMPLE

(青松觀, Green Pine Temple; ☑2370 8870; Tsing Lun Rd; ⊘7am-6pm; ⎗line 505) Green Pine Temple is a peaceful Taoist temple complex northwest of Tuen Mun town centre. Walk through the rows of bonsai trees, bamboo and ponds and you'll reach the main temple which is dedicated to Lu Sun Young, one of the eight immortals of Taoism who lived in the 8th century. An annual **Bonsai Festival** is held here in April or May.

Ching Chung Temple is directly opposite Ching Chung Light Rail station. To reach it from the Tuen Mun or Town Centre stations, catch line 505.

EATING

You'll find plenty of Chinese restaurants and noodle shops in Tuen Mun town centre, but it's best to travel out a bit further for something unusual and delicious.

★YUE KEE ROASTED
GOOSE RESTAURANT
CANTONESE $$

(裕記大飯店; ☑2491 0105; www.yuekee.com.hk/en; 9 Sham Hong Rd, Sham Tseng; meals HK$100-200; ⊘11am-11pm; ⎕minibus 302 from Tai Wo Hau MTR) In an alley lined with roast-goose restaurants, 54-year-old Yue Kee is king. Order gorgeous plates of coppery-skinned charcoal-roasted goose (half is plenty for four people) and sample house specialties like soy-braised goose web (feet), garlic-fried goose kidneys, and spicy goose intestines. If that's not your speed, there are plenty of standard Cantonese dishes on offer. English menu.

SAM SHING HUI
SEAFOOD MARKET
SEAFOOD, CANTONESE $$

(三聖墟海鮮市場; Sam Shing St, Castle Peak Bay, Tuen Mun; meals HK$150-300; ⊘10am-midnight; ⎕minibus 140M from Tsing Yi) Along Castle Peak Beach, this busy working seafood market sits adjacent to rows of *dai pai dong* (food stalls), as well as fancier enclosed establishments, ready to cook up whatever you've picked. English is limited here, but pointing and smiling should get you going – just be sure to ask for prices first.

Yuen Long

Explore

Yuen Long is an important transport hub and a gateway to the Mai Po Marshes and the nearby walled villages.

Bring your binoculars and set off early for Mai Po. Morning hours are the best time to go birdwatching. If you didn't manage to book a guided tour, Hong Kong Wetland Park is a more than worthy substitute. Head back to town, enjoy lunch at Dai Wing Wah, after which you could visit one or two of those fortified hamlets in Kat Hing Wai and Shui Tau Tsuen.

An even better place to spend an hour or two in the afternoon is along the popular Ping Shan Heritage Trail. Watching the sunset in Pak Nai at the westernmost edge of Hong Kong is an unforgettable experience. Afterwards, a seafood dinner in Lau Fau Shan is the best way to end the day.

The Best...

➡**Sight** Mai Po Nature Reserve (p167)
➡**Sunset** Pak Nai (p174)
➡**Place to eat** Dai Wing Wah (p175)

Top Tip

There are several bird hides in Hong Kong Wetland Park. The mudflat hide at the end of the mangrove boardwalk is where you can see the greatest variety of birds.

Getting There & Away

➡**Bus** From Yuen Long West Bus Terminal on Kik Yeung Rd, bus 968 leaves for Tin Hau on Hong Kong Island; bus 76K calls at Mai Po, Pak Wo Rd in Fanling and Choi Yun Rd in Sheung Shui.

➡**Green minibus** Buses 35 and 33 from Tai Fung St travel respectively to Lau Fau Shan and Pak Nai via Ping Shan.

➡**MTR** Yuen Long, Long Ping and Tin Shui Wai stations are on the West Rail line; Ping Shan station is on the Light Rail line.

Need to Know

➡**Area code** ☑852
➡**Location** 30km northwest of Kowloon Peninsula
➡**Last train to Kowloon** 12.26am from Yuen Long West Rail station

◉ SIGHTS

MAI PO NATURE RESERVE   NATURE RESERVE
See p167.

PING SHAN HERITAGE TRAIL   OUTDOORS
See p168.

★**HONG KONG WETLAND PARK**   PARK
(香港濕地公園; ☎2708 8885; www.wetland-park.com/en/; Wetland Park Rd, Tin Shui Wai; adult/child HK$30/15; ☺10am-5pm Wed-Mon; ⊞; ⊠line 705 or 706) This 60-hectare eco-logical park is a window on the wetland ecosystems of northwest New Territories. The natural trails, bird hides and view-ing platforms make it a handy and excel-lent spot for bird-watching. The futuristic grass-covered headquarters houses inter-esting galleries (including one on tropical swamps), a film theatre, a cafe and a view-ing gallery. If you have binoculars then bring them; otherwise be prepared to wait to use the fixed points in the viewing gal-leries and hides.

To reach the Hong Kong Wetland Park, take the MTR West Rail to Tin Shui Wai and board Light Rail line 705 or 706, alighting at the Wetland Park stop. It can also be reached directly from Hong Kong Island: jump on a 967 bus at Admiralty MTR bus station.

LAU FAU SHAN   VILLAGE
(流浮山; ⊠33 minibus from Tin Shui Wai MTR) Towards the northwestern edge of Hong Kong waters is Lau Fau Shan, a rural fish-ing village that hosts the only **oyster farm** in the territory. Today most people come here for the seafood restaurants, but the small oyster market is interesting enough to merit a peep. You'll see oyster farmers shucking the shelled creatures on the wa-terfront. Sweeping Deep Bay and Shékŏu in Shēnzhèn lie just across the waters.

To get to the shore, walk through the paved path (next to the public toilet) that's lined with restaurants and fish tanks.

PAK NAI   BEACH
(白泥; ⊠33 minibus from Tin Shui Wai MTR) Lit-erally 'white mud', Pak Nai is one of the best places to see the sunset in Hong Kong. This 6km stretch of coastline is dotted with mangroves, fish ponds, farms, shacks and muddy beaches sprinkled with oyster shells. Sunset can be watched from most parts of Deep Bay Rd (it continues as Nim Wan Rd after Upper Pak Nai), the only road meandering along the coastline.

Green minibus 33 goes from Yuen Long via Lau Fau Shan. Check the website of **Hong Kong Observatory** (www.hko.gov. hk) for sunset times.

KAT HING WAI   VILLAGE
(吉慶圍; ⊠64K) This tiny village is 500 years old and was walled during the early years of the Ming dynasty (1368–1644). It contains just one main street, off which a host of dark and narrow alleyways lead. There are quite a few new buildings and retiled older ones in the village. A small temple stands at the

---

TIN HAU BIRTHDAY FESTIVAL

Like the Taoist god Pak Tai, Tin Hau, the queen of heaven, is the protector of seafarers and is widely worshipped along the South China coast. Her birthday, which will fall on 11 May in 2015 and 2 May 2016, is a key saintly festivity for the older generations and swaggering businessmen alike. There is a parade in Yuen Long featuring lion dances and Cantonese opera, and Tin Hau temples throughout the city swell with visitors. But Tai Miu Temple (p193) is *the* place to go as elaborate rites are performed starting four days before Tin Hau's birthday.

You can take a minibus to go there, but you are totally missing the point if you don't take the special ferry (round trip HK$60) from North Point Pier (北角碼頭), which only operates on Tin Hau's birthday and the day before. About 50 boats carry the faithful to and from the temple.

The 40-minute journey itself is quite a spectacle. Once the voyage begins, the ferry transforms into a floating temple, with grannies praying, preparing joss sticks and pa-per offerings, and burning them in the furnace on the deck. Hell money is thrown into the sea along the journey to appease the water deities. If you set off at around noon on the red-letter day, you'll see a flotilla of colourful fishing boats parading through Victoria Harbour. Finally the sea procession arrives in Joss House Bay to pay homage to their protector.

MA WAN

Ma Wan was once an important gateway to Kowloon, where foreign vessels would drop anchor before entering Chinese waters. If you want to get away from it all, Ma Wan, a flat, rapidly developing island between the northeastern tip of Lantau and the New Territories, is hardly the place to go. It has a couple of **temples** devoted to Tin Hau, a long beach on the east coast at **Tung Wan**, a few stilt houses, and a massive, high-end residential community called **Park Island**. You can't fail to notice **Noah's Ark**, a 'lifesize' version of the biblical craft with plastic versions of the world's animals strolling down the gangplank.

The real reason to come to Ma Wan is to see **Tsing Ma Bridge**, the world's seventh-longest span suspension bridge, to the east and, to a lesser extent, **Kap Shui Mun Bridge** on the west. Together they form the rail and road link connecting Lantau with the New Territories via Tsing Yi Island. While catapulting Ma Wan headlong into the next century, the bridge has guaranteed an end to the island's solitude. Neighbouring Tsing Yi has a special viewing platform (p172) for those particularly interested in seeing the bridge up close.

end of the street. Visitors are asked to make a donation when they enter the village; put the money in the coin slot by the entrance.

You can take photographs of the old Hakka women in their traditional black trousers, tunics and distinctive bamboo hats with black cloth fringes, but they'll expect you to pay (around HK$10).

To get here from Yuen Long, get off at the first bus stop on Kam Tin Rd, cross the road and walk east for 10 minutes. Alternatively, take a taxi from Kam Sheung Rd West Rail station for about HK$20.

SHUI TAU TSUEN   VILLAGE

(水頭村; ⊟64K) This 17th-century village, a 15-minute north of Kam Tin Rd, is famous for its prow-shaped roofs decorated with dragons and lucky fish.

The **Tang Kwong U Ancestral Hall** (⊘9am-1pm & 2-5pm Sat, Sun & public holidays) and the **Tang Ching Lok Ancestral Hall** (⊘9am-1pm & 2-5pm Wed, Sat & Sun) were built in the early 19th century. South of them is the village's most impressive sight, the 19th-century **Yi Tai Study Hall** (⊘9am-1pm & 2-5pm Wed, Sat & Sun), named after the gods of literature and martial arts. The **Tin Hau temple** just north of the village was built in 1722.

To reach Shui Tau Tsuen, which is signposted from Kam Tin Rd, walk north, go through the subway below the Kam Tin bypass, pass Kam Tai Rd and cross over the river to Chi Ho Rd. Go over the small bridge spanning a stream, turn right and then left to enter the village from the east. The first thing you'll pass is the Yi Tai Study Hall.

✖ EATING

DAI WING WAH   HAKKA $

(大榮華酒樓; 2nd fl, Koon Wong Mansion, 2-6 On Ning Rd; dim sum HK$16, dishes from HK$70; ⊘6am-midnight; ⊞Tai Tong Rd Light Rail station) The brainchild of celebrated chef Leung Man-to, Dai Wing Wah is most famous for its walled-village dishes. Leung sources local ingredients from small farms and food producers whenever possible, and complements them with his innovations in cooking. Must-eats include lemon-steamed grey mullet, smoked oysters and Malay sponge cake.

From Tai Tong Rd Light Rail station, walk north along Kuk Ting St then turn left on to Sai Tai St. The restaurant sits 30m away.

HO TO TAI NOODLE SHOP   CANTONESE $

(好到底麵家; ✆2476 2495; 67 Fau Tsoi St; won-ton noodles HK$23; ⊘8am-8pm; ⊞Tai Tong Rd Light Rail station) This 60-year-old Yuen Long institution is one of the world's cheapest Michelin restaurants. It is best known for its fresh Cantonese egg noodles and shrimp roe noodles. Foodies from all corners come to slurp the delightful wonton noodles. An English menu is available at the cashier. The haunt is a three-minute walk south of Tai Tong Rd Light Rail station.

HAPPY SEAFOOD RESTAURANT   SEAFOOD $$

(歡樂海鮮酒家; ✆2472 3450; 12 Shan Ting St, Lau Fau Shan; meals HK$250-800; ⊘11am-10.30pm; ⊟minibus 35 from Tai Fung St) The world's youngest cordon bleu chef, Lau Ka-lun, dishes out innovative seafood in this rural restaurant. Try the signature fried rice with crab roe, scallops and ostrich meat.

Fanling & Sheung Shui

Explore

Begin with a visit to the Fung Ying Sin Temple, which is just a stone's throw from Fanling East Rail station. After a vegetarian lunch in the temple, head to Lung Yeuk Tau Heritage Trail for some village immersion.

For the more adventurous, off-the-beaten-path options include the seldom-visited walled village of Ping Kong, or Sha Tau Kok, where Japanese pillboxes from WWII lie intact in the (still) unspoilt countryside.

The Best...

➡ **Sight** Fung Ying Sin Temple (p176)

➡ **Place to eat** IPC Foodlab (p176)

➡ **Activity** Lung Yeuk Tau Heritage Trail (p177)

Top Tip

Some walled villages along the Lung Yeuk Tau Heritage Trail are private properties; be discreet and show common sense when you visit.

Getting There & Away

➡ **Bus** Most onward travel connections depart from the East Rail stations. Bus 76K to Yuen Long and Mai Po Marshes departs from Pak Wo Rd in Fanling and Choi Yun Rd in Sheung Shui. Bus 77K to Ping Kong stops at Yuen Long Jockey Club Rd in Fanling and Po Shek Wu Rd in Sheung Shui.

➡ **Green minibus** Bus 58K heads to Ping Kong from San Wan Rd in Sheung Shui.

➡ **MTR** Take the MTR to Fanling and Sheung Shui East Rail stations.

Need to Know

➡ **Area code** ☑852

➡ **Location** Fanling and Sheung Shui are in north-central New Territories, much closer to the mainland (5km) than to Tsim Sha Tsui (20km).

➡ **Last train to Kowloon** leaves at 12.35am from Sheung Shui East Rail station; 12.37am from Fanling East Rail station

◉ SIGHTS

FUNG YING SIN TEMPLE   TEMPLE

(☑2669 9186; 66 Pak Wo Rd, Fanling; ☺8am-6pm, restaurant 10am-5pm; ⓂFanling) This huge Taoist temple complex opposite the Fanling East Rail station has wonderful exterior murals of Taoist immortals and the Chinese zodiac, an orchard terrace, a herbal clinic and a **vegetarian restaurant** (ground and 1st floors, Bldg A7). Most important are the dozen ancestral halls behind the main temple, where the ashes of the departed are deposited in niche urns.

TAI FU TAI MANSION   HISTORIC BUILDING

(大夫第; San Tin, Yuen Long; ☺9am-1pm & 2-5pm Wed-Mon; ☐76K) Located between Yuen Long and Sheung Shui, this splendid Mandarin-style building complex from 1865 is eclectically fused with Western design. Members of the Man clan, another powerful family in the New Territories, lived here for well over a century until they moved out in 1980. The courtyard is encircled by stone walls with a guarded checkpoint. Inside, auspicious Chinese symbols are found in the woodcarvings along with art-nouveau glass panels, and there is a European fountain.

Board bus 76K in Sheung Shui and get off at the San Tin stop.

PING KONG   VILLAGE

(丙崗; ☐77K) This sleepy walled village in the hills south of Sheung Shui is seldom visited by outsiders. Like other walled villages still inhabited in Hong Kong, it is a mix of old and new, and has a lovely little **Tin Hau temple** (天后廟) in the centre.

To get to Ping Kong from Sheung Shui East Rail station (exit A), catch green minibus 58K from the huge minibus station south of Landmark North shopping centre on San Wan Rd. A taxi from the Sheung Shui East Rail station to Ping Kong costs about HK$32.

✗ EATING

IPC FOODLAB   HEALTH FOOD $$

(☑2676 6900; www.ipcfoodlab.com; 26 On Lok Mun St, Fanling; meals from HK$150; ☺11.30am-10pm; ☑; ⓂFanling) Incongruously located on an industrial block in Fanling, IPC is one of Hong Kong's most hardcore farm-to-table restaurants. Most of the vegies

SHA TAU KOK

An off-limit frontier area for over 60 years, Sha Tau Kok (沙頭角), which lies 11km north-east of Fanling, was sealed off from the rest of Hong Kong in 1951 following the Communist takeover of China. While access to the border town itself is still restricted to local residents, the 400 hectares of land – and the patchwork of time-warped villages that it contains – to the west and southwest were partially reopened in February 2012.

Tam Shui Hang Village (担水坑村), the village right next to the frontier checkpoint, is worth a wee wander. It has a cluster of old and new village houses and several intact ancestral halls. To the northeast, WWII buffs may want to venture out to the rolling hills behind Shan Tsui Village to look for a group of **Japanese pillboxes** (日軍碉堡). From Tam Shui Hang Village, walk north (200m) to the antiquated **Kwan Ah School** (群雅學校), identifiable by a basketball court in front of it. Pass the **Pak Kung shrine** and descend to Shan Tsui Village. From here, take the path to your left and walk uphill for five minutes, and you'll see some trenches that will lead you to the pillboxes.

There are at least six pillboxes hidden in the mountains but the trails are not well marked. If you want to go further off the beaten path, the villagers may have some interesting pointers.

Bus 78K or green minibus 55K from Landmark North shopping centre in Sheung Shui take you to Sha Tau Kok. When you arrive at the frontier checkpoint, the friendly police will signal you to get off.

come from local organic farms, though some come from IPC's own vertical garden. The menu skews towards fancy salads and artfully presented dishes involving trendy health ingredients like quinoa. Decor is sleek and modern, service friendly.

⚡ SPORTS & ACTIVITIES

LUNG YEUK TAU
HERITAGE TRAIL   HERITAGE WALK
(龍躍頭文物徑; 🚐54K) This 4.5km-long trail northeast of Fanling meanders through five relatively well-preserved walled villages and, like the village of Ping Shan, they are home to the Tang clan. The most attractive of the lot is the oldest (800 years) but most intact **Lo Wai**, identifiable by its 1m-thick fortified wall. Unfortunately, it's not open to the public. Admire the exterior, before carrying on to the more welcoming villages of **Tung Kok Wai** to the northeast and **Sun Wai** towards the northern end of the trail.

Other attractions here include the **Tang Chung Ling Ancestral Hall** and the adjacent **Tin Hau temple**. The ancestral hall was built during the Ming dynasty and the dragon motif that you'll see on some of the spirit tablets inside the building was a symbol of the clan's royal status. The temple houses two bronze bells; one is from 1695,

the other, 1700. **Shek Lo**, literally 'stone cottage' and built in 1925, is an eclectic mix of colonial and traditional Chinese architectural styles. The cottage appears to be permanently locked, but it can be seen clearly from the east of **Tsung Kyam church**, the start of the trail.

To get there from Fanling East Rail station (Exit C), take the green minibus 54K and ask to be dropped at Tsung Kyam church (Shun Him Tong in Cantonese).

Tai Po

Explore

Tai Po is perhaps the most interesting New Town in the New Territories. Formed from two former market towns on either side of the Lam Tsuen River, today it has a lively waterfront downtown ringed by housing estate skyscrapers and, beyond, rolling rural hills.

Tai Po offers quirky temples, a cute railway museum, and several countryside nature areas, including a lush butterfly reserve. But the best thing about this ever-changing New Town is the street life. Barter for lychees in the crowded street markets, queue for tofu or noodles at hole-in-the-wall stalls, or watch proud parents photograph their babies toddling along the pedestrian bridge crossing the river. This is old-school Hong Kong living at its finest.

....

The Best...

➡**Sight** Tai Po Market (p178)

➡**Place to eat** Yat Lok Barbecue Restaurant (p180)

➡**Activity** Cycling from Tai Po to Plover Cove Reservoir

....

Top Tip

Tai Po has a number of markets and nature sanctuaries that are more than worth a visit, so wake up early!

....

Getting There & Away

➡**Bus** Bus 71K runs between the Tai Wo and Tai Po Market East Rail stations.

➡**Green minibus** For onward travel, start at Tai Po Market East Rail station or from Heung Sze Wui St, take bus 20K for San Mun Tsai; catch bus 25K at Tsing Yuen St to get to Ng Tung Chai for Tai Mo Shan.

➡**MTR** Take the MTR to Tai Po Market or Tai Wo East Rail stations.

....

Need to Know

➡**Area code** ☎852

➡**Location** 13km to the Hong Kong–China border at Lo Wu; 18km north of Kowloon Peninsula

➡**Last train to Kowloon** 12.42am from Tai Wo East Rail station; 12.45am from Tai Po Market East Rail station

◉ SIGHTS

TAI PO MARKET   MARKET

(大埔街市; Fu Shin St; ⊙6am-8pm; ⓂTai Wo) Not to be confused with the East Rail station of the same name, this street-long outdoor wet market is one of the most winning in the New Territories. Feast your eyes on a rainbow of fruits and vegetables, tables lined with dried seafood, old ladies hawking glutinous Hakka rice cakes, and stalls selling fresh aloe and sugarcane juices.

HONG KONG RAILWAY MUSEUM   MUSEUM

(香港鐵路博物館; ☎2653 3455; www.heritagemuseum.gov.hk/eng/museums/railway.aspx; 13 Shung Tak St; ⊙9am-6pm Wed-Mon; 👶; ⓂTai Wo) **FREE** Housed in the former Tai Po Market train station (built in 1913 in traditional Chinese style), this small museum is a fun stop for trainspotters and families with train-crazy kids. There are a few exhibits about the history of the Hong Kong railways, but the real draws are the historical train carriages open to visitors.

MAN MO TEMPLE   TEMPLE

(文武廟; Fu Shin St; ⊙8am-6pm; ⓂTai Wo) In the middle of the Tai Po Market street, the double-hall Man Mo Temple from the late 19th century is a centre of worship for the Tai Po area. Jointly dedicated to the gods of literature and of war, it's got an incense-scented, otherworldly charm.

FUNG YUEN BUTTERFLY RESERVE   WILDLIFE RESERVE

(鳳園蝴蝶保育區; ☎3111 7344; www.fungyuen.org; 150 Fung Yuen Rd; admission HK$20; ⊙9am-5pm; 🚐green minibus 20A) Just 2km northeast of Tai Po town lies this sprawling 42-hectare Special Site of Scientific Interest

LOCAL KNOWLEDGE

TWO-WHEELERS' TAI PO

One cycling route not to miss is the ride from Tai Po to Plover Cove Reservoir on the northeastern side of Tolo Harbour. Another is to the Chinese University of Hong Kong (p184) in Ma Liu Shui, on the southwestern side of the harbour. Allow half a day for either trip. There is also an inland route that goes to the university, but the coastal route linking the university with Tai Mei Tuk has the better views. Another option is to follow Ting Kok Rd east to the fishing village of San Mun Tsai.

Bicycles can be rented in season from several stalls around Tai Po Market East Rail station, but try to arrive early – they often run out during the busiest times. A number of bicycle shops line Kwong Fuk Rd northwest of the station.

Tai Po

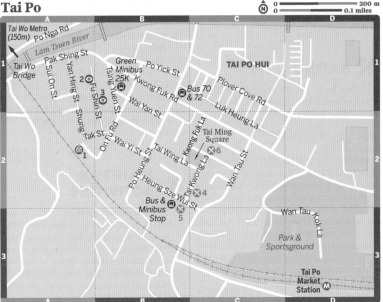

where more than 180 butterfly species will dazzle your eyeballs. A third of them are rare breeds, including the common birdwing and white dragontail. The best time to spot them is before 10am.

Green minibus 20A leaves every half hour from Tai Po Market East Rail station. Ask to be dropped off at Fung Yuen Chun Kung Sor (鳳園村公所).

LAM TSUEN WISHING TREE   TEMPLE

(林村許願樹; Lam Kam Rd, Fong Ma Po; 🚌64K)
This large banyan tree, laden with coloured streamers of paper tied to oranges, was long considered a good-luck spot. The idea was to write your wish on a piece of paper, tie it to the citrus fruit and then throw it as high as you could up into the tree. If your fruit lodged high in the branches, you were in luck. But damage to the tree has recently altered – though not erased – this tradition.

In 2005 a large branch of the tree came crashing to the ground, dashing most punters' wishes once and for all. Now the tree is being left alone to recover and, in the name of conservation, wish makers can only tie their wishing papers to Chinese-style wooden racks, or throw plastic fruits

Tai Po

◎ Sights   (p178)
1 Hong Kong Railway Museum A2
2 Man Mo Temple A1
3 Tai Po Market B1

✖ Eating   (p180)
4 Ah Po Tofu C2
5 Tai Po Hui Market B3
6 Yat Lok Barbecue Restaurant............C2

(available from the on-site vendors) onto a plastic tree. There's a small **Tin Hau temple** nearby, replete with fortune-tellers, to compensate for your curtailed wish making.

To reach the tree catch bus 64K from the Tai Po Market East Rail station and alight at Fong Ma Po.

KADOORIE FARM & BOTANIC GARDEN   WATERFALL, GARDEN

(梧桐寨瀑布、嘉道理農場暨植物園; 📞2483 7200; www.kfbg.org.hk; Lam Kam Rd; ◐9.30am-5pm; 🚌64K) FREE Kadoorie Farm & Botanic Garden, southwest of Ng Tung Chai, is primarily a conservation and teaching centre, but the gardens are especially lovely, with many indigenous birds, animals, insects and plants in residence. You can reach the farm most easily on bus 64K.

✕ EATING

Tai Ming Sq in Tai Po town centre has a wealth of restaurants, as well as shops serving old-style Hakka snacks.

★ YAT LOK BARBECUE
RESTAURANT   CANTONESE $
(一樂燒臘飯店; ☏2656 4732; 5 Tai Ming Lane; meals HK$40-100; ⊙11am-11pm; ⓂTai Po Market) Glossy roast goose with shatteringly crisp skin and a pillow of succulent fat is the order of the day at this family-run eatery, which counts celebrity chef Anthony Bourdain among its many fans. *Char siu* (roast pork) is a bit dry, so focus on the bird. Chinese menu only, but friendly servers will help you order.

AH PO TOFU   DESSERTS $
(亞婆豆腐花; Tai Kwong Ln, shop 2A; dau fu fa HK$7; ⊙10am-6pm; ⓂTai Po Market) You'll recognise this beloved *dau fu fa* (sweet silky tofu pudding) shop by the line snaking down the busy pedestrian street. Sprinkle on palm sugar to taste, then eat your pudding while standing before returning the bowl to the counter.

TAI PO HUI MARKET   DAI PAI DONG $
(大埔舊墟; 8 Heung Sze Wui St; meals HK$30-50; ⊙market 6am-8pm, cooked-food centre to 2am; ⓂTai Po Market) This modern silver building houses a large, clean and always-busy wet market, with a spacious cooked-food centre on top. Local favourites include stall 27 for pork chop noodles, and stall 8–9 for dim sum.

⚐ SPORTS & ACTIVITIES

NG TUNG CHAI WATERFALL   HIKE
(梧桐寨瀑布; ▣64 from Tai Po Market MTR) The scenic area around the Ng Tung Chai Waterfall is a retreat from the bustle of downtown Tai Po. Reach the series of streams and waterfalls by bus 64K from Tai Po Market East Rail station, and get off at Ng Tung Chai stop. Enter the eponymous village and hike through the bamboo groves towards the **Man Tak Monastery** (萬德苑), which can be reached in 30 minutes. From the monastery, hike uphill for 20 minutes and you'll see the waterfalls sliding down.

WORTH A DETOUR

TAI PO KAU NATURE RESERVE

The **Tai Po Kau Nature Reserve** (大埔滘自然護理區; Tai Po Rd; ▣70, 72) is a thickly forested 460-hectare 'special area' and is Hong Kong's most extensive woodlands. It is home to many species of butterflies, amphibians, birds, dragonflies and trees, and is a superb place in which to enjoy a quiet walk. The reserve is criss-crossed with four main tracks ranging in length from 3km (red trail) to 10km (yellow trail), plus a short nature trail of less than 1km. The reserve is supposed to emphasise conservation and education rather than recreation.

About 1km northwest of the reserve entrance and down steep Hung Lam Dr is the **Kerry Lake Egret Nature Park** (☏2657 6657; www.lakeegret.com; 2 Hung Lam Drive, Tai Po Kau; minibus 72) and the overpriced **Museum of Ethnology** (☏2657 6657; www.taipokau.org; 2 Hung Lam Dr; adult/concession HK$18/12; ⊙2-3pm & 5-6pm Sun & public holidays).

Tai Po Kau Nature Reserve lies south of Tai Po, less than 1km inland from Tolo Harbour. The main entrance and the information centre are at the village of **Tsung Tsai Yuen** in the northernmost part of the reserve along Tai Po Rd. The reserve is well served by buses. Bus 70 passes through Jordan and Mong Kok on its way here. Bus 72 can be used to get here from nearby the Sha Tin and Tai Po Market East Rail stations. A taxi from Tai Po Market East Rail station will cost around HK$27, and from the University East Rail station about HK$42.

Plover Cove

Explore

Plover Cove has only two themes: hiking and cycling. Large parts of it are designated Geopark areas, so you'll see rugged rocks and mineral marvels, especially around Plover Cove Reservoir. Plan to spend a full day here.

For an easy walk, the 4.4km Pat Sin Leng Nature Trail is a good alternative.

The Best...

➡**Place to eat** Cafe de Country Art (p181)

➡**Activity** Biking around Plover Cove Reservoir (p181)

Top Tip

The challenging (uphill) but also scenic route to cycle is to begin in Tai Mei Tuk and go all the way north to the border at Sha Tau Kok.

Getting There & Away

➡**Bus** Take bus 75K (and additionally either 74K or 275R on Sundays and holidays) from Tai Po Market East Rail station in Tai Po.

➡**Green minibus** Bus 20C passes Tai Po Market East Rail station and Heung Sze Wui St in Tai Po on its way to Plover Cove.

Need to Know

➡**Area code** ☑852

➡**Location** 12km northeast of Tai Po

➡**Last train to Kowloon** leaves at 12.45am from Tai Po Market East Rail station

EATING

CAFE DE COUNTRY ART   CAFE $

(藝程雅聚; ☑2824 1812; 64B Lung Mei Village; ⊙11am-10pm; minibus 20C) This funky European-style casual dining spot is located in a colourful town house

🏃 SPORTS & ACTIVITIES

★PLOVER COVE RESERVOIR   OUTDOORS

(☐75K) Part of the Hong Kong Geopark, this vast reservoir was completed in 1968, in a very unusual way. Rather than build a dam across a river, of which Hong Kong has very few, a barrier was erected across the mouth of a great bay. The sea water was siphoned out and fresh water – mostly piped in from the mainland – was pumped in.

The area around Plover Cove Reservoir is glorious hiking and cycling country, and well worth at least a full day's exploring.

The village of **Tai Mei Tuk**, the springboard for most of the activities in the Plover Cove area, is about 6km northeast of Tai Po Market East Rail station. Bicycles can be rented at several locations in Tai Mei Tuk, including **Lung Kee Bikes** (☑2662 5266; bicycle rental per day HK$30; ⊙9.30am-6pm). A bicycle track along the coast runs from Tai Mei Tuk to Chinese University (p184) at Ma Liu Shui. Ting Kok Rd in **Lung Mei Village** is also where you'll find a row of popular restaurants.

The **Plover Cove Country Park Visitor Centre** (船灣郊野公園遊客中心; ☑2665 3413; Tai Mei Tuk; ⊙9.30am-4pm Sat, Sun & public holidays), a short distance further east from the car park on Ting Kok Rd, is where the Pat Sin Leng Nature Trail to Bride's Pool starts.

PAT SIN LENG NATURE TRAIL   HIKING

(八仙嶺自然教育徑; ☐75K) This excellent 4.4km-long trail, which should take from two to 2½ hours, leads from the Plover Cove Country Park Visitor Centre at Tai Mei Tuk and heads northeast for 4km to **Bride's Pool**; there are signboards numbered 1 to 22, so there is little danger of getting lost. The scenery is excellent and the two waterfalls at Bride's Pool are delightful, but the place gets packed on the weekend.

You can either return to Tai Mei Tuk via Bride's Pool Rd on foot or catch green minibus 20C, which stops at Tai Mei Tuk before heading to Tai Po Market East Rail station.

Those looking for a more strenuous hike can join stage No 9 of the **Wilson Trail** at Tai Mei Tuk on the Plover Cove Reservoir and head west into the steep Pat Sin Leng range of hills to **Wong Leng Shan** (639m). The trail then carries on westward to **Hok Tau Reservoir** and **Hok Tau Wai** (12km, four hours).

Tai Long Wan (p191)
The Tai Long Wan Hiking Trail passes through Tai Long Wan, one of the most beautiful beaches on the Sai Kung Peninsula.

Western Monastery (p169)
The main building of this tranquil monastery is styled as a classical Chinese palace.

10,000 Buddhas Monastery (p185)
There are actually more than 10,000 Buddhas to be found in this temple – including 12,800 miniature statues lining the walls of the main temple alone.

IAN TROWER / GETTY IMAGES ©

MANFRED GOTTSCHALK / GETTY IMAGES ©

Sha Tin

Explore

You're likely to arrive in New Town Plaza, a claustrophobic shopping mall connected to Sha Tin station on the East Rail line, if you visit this busy part of the New Territories. There are a couple of noteworthy religious establishments in the ar ea – 10,000 Buddhas Monastery on Po Fook Shan Hill and Che Kung Temple by Shing Mun River.

The town's other key drawcard is the Hong Kong Heritage Museum, where you can relive Hong Kong's past in a range of thoughtfully constructed exhibitions.

If you'd rather have some raw outdoor action, then time your visit with one of the rip-roaring weekend race days at the beautifully set Sha Tin Racecourse.

The Best...

➡ **Sight** Hong Kong Heritage Museum (p184)

➡ **Place to win big** Sha Tin Racecourse (p187)

➡ **Place to eat** Lung Wah Hotel Restaurant (p187)

Top Tip

On race days, entry to the Sha Tin Racecourse is free from around 3pm (roughly halfway through the afternoon program).

Getting There & Away

➡ **Bus** Buses into and out of Sha Tin leave from/terminate at City One Plaza Sha Tin bus station. Bus 182 links Sha Tin with Wan Chai, Admiralty and Central. Bus 170 connects Sha Tin East Rail bus station with Causeway Bay and Aberdeen. Bus 299 shuttles between Sha Tin and Sai Kung.

➡ **MTR** Sha Tin, Tai Wai and Racecourse stations are on the East Rail line; Che Kung Temple station is on Ma On Shan line.

Need to Know

➡ **Area code** ☑852

➡ **Location** 12km north of Kowloon Peninsula

➡ **Last train to Kowloon** 12.57am from Sha Tin East Rail station

◉ SIGHTS

HONG KONG HERITAGE MUSEUM
MUSEUM

(香港文化博物館; ☑2180 8188; www.heritage-museum.gov.hk; 1 Man Lam Rd; adult/concession HK$10/5, Wed free; ⊙10am-6pm Mon & Wed-Sat, to 7pm Sun; ⊞; Ⓜ Che Kung Temple) Southwest of Sha Tin town centre, this spacious, high-quality museum gives a peek into local history and culture. Highlights include a **children's area** with interactive play zones, the **New Territories Heritage Hall** with mock-ups of traditional minority villages,

---

WORTH A DETOUR

UNIVERSITY SIGHTS

Chinese University of Hong Kong (香港中文大學; ☑2609 7000; www.cuhk.edu.hk; Ⓜ University) has its main campus in Sha Tin. If you are in this neck of the woods, it's worth making time to see the university's **art museum** (香港中文大學文物館; ☑3943 7416; www.cuhk.edu.hk/ics/amm; Institute of Chinese Studies, Central Campus; ⊙10am-5pm, closed public holidays) **FREE**. The four-floor **East Wing Galleries** house a permanent collection of Chinese paintings and calligraphy, but it is the ceramics and jade objets d'art that are especially worth inspecting, including 2000-year-old bronze seals and a large collection of jade flower carvings. The **West Wing Galleries** stage five to six special exhibitions each year.

Other than that, the **lotus pond** in Chung Chi Campus (you'll see it when you step out of the train station) is a photogenic spot, especially when the lotuses are blooming in spring; and the **Pavilion of Harmony** (合一亭) in hilly New Asia Campus offers panoramic views of Tolo Harbour.

A shuttle bus from University station travels through the campuses. The bus runs every 20 to 30 minutes daily and is free.

Sha Tin

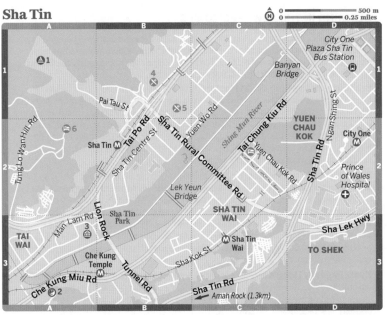

the **Cantonese Opera Heritage Hall**, where you can watch old operas with English subtitles, and an elegant **gallery** of Chinese art. Lately, the big draw is a semi-permanent **Bruce Lee exhibit**, with some 600 items of the Kung Fu star's memorabilia on display until 2018.

To reach the Hong Kong Heritage Museum from Che Kung Temple MTR station, walk east along Che Kung Miu Rd, go through the subway and cross the footbridge over the channel. The museum is 200m to the east.

10,000 BUDDHAS
MONASTERY
BUDDHIST MONASTERY

(萬佛寺; ☏2691 1067; ⊙10am-5pm; Ⓜ Sha Tin, exit B) **FREE** This quirky temple about 500m northwest of Sha Tin station is worth the uphill hike to visit. Built in the 1950s, the complex actually contains more than 10,000 Buddhas. Some 12,800 miniature statues line the walls of the main temple and dozens of life-sized golden statues of Buddha's followers flank the steep steps leading to the monastery complex. There are several temples and pavilions split over two levels, as well as a nine-storey pagoda.

To reach the monastery, take exit B at Sha Tin station and walk down the ramp, passing a series of traditional houses at Pai

Tau Village on the left. Take the left onto Pai Tau St, and turn right onto Sheung Wo Che St. At the end of this road, a series of signs in English will direct you to the left along a concrete path and through bamboo groves to the first of some 400 steps leading up to the monastery.

AMAH ROCK
LANDMARK

(望夫石; Ⓜ Tai Wai) This oddly shaped boulder southwest of Sha Tin, like many local landmarks in Hong Kong, carries a legend. For many years a fisherman's wife would stand on this spot in the hills above **Lion Rock Country Park**, watching for her

SLEEPING IN THE NEW TERRITORIES

Good-value accommodation is in short supply in the New Territories. There are four official HI-affiliated hostels, all in the remote parts of the region. Walkers and hikers can pitch a tent at any one of 40 New Territories campsites managed by the **Country & Marine Parks Authority** (☎1823; www.afcd.gov.hk).

Bradbury Jockey Club Youth Hostel (☎2662 5123; www.yha.org.hk; 66 Tai Mei Tuk Rd; dm members under/over 18yr HK$65/95, d/q members HK$290/420; ☒75K) This is the HKYHA's flagship hostel in the New Territories and is open daily year-round. Bradbury is next to the northern tip of the Plover Cove Reservoir dam wall, a few hundred metres south of Tai Mei Tuk. To get here take bus 75K (or 275R on Sundays and public holidays) from Tai Po Market KCR East station to the Tai Mei Tuk bus terminus. The hostel is on the road leading to the reservoir.

Bradbury Hall Youth Hostel (☎2328 2458; www.yha.org.hk; Chek Keng, Sai Kung; dm members under/over 18yr HK$45/65; ☒94, 96R, 698R) This hostel is in the beautiful cove of Chek Keng, where some unspoilt beaches are just a flip-flop's throw away. The dorms are slightly dated but clean. To get there, take bus 94 from Sai Kung bus terminal to Pak Tam Au. Walk along stage 2 of the MacLehose Trail towards Chek Keng Village. The walk takes about 40 minutes. A faster way to the hostel is to take bus 96R or 698R to Wong Shek Pier, and then take a scheduled ferry to Chek Keng Pier. The boat journey is about 10 minutes.

Hyatt Regency Hong Kong (☎3723 1234; www.hongkong.shatin.hyatt.com; 18 Chak Cheung St; r HK$2500-3000, ste HK$3500-12,500; ☒University) This is the plushest sleeping option as you head out towards the border with China. Views of Tolo Harbour or the rolling hills of Sha Tin can be seen in most rooms. It's a five-minute walk from University East Rail station.

Regal Riverside Hotel (Map p185; ☎2649 7878; www.regalriverside.com; 34-36 Tai Chung Kiu Rd; r HK$1300-1700, ste from HK$3800; ☒284, ☒Sha Tin Wai, exit A) Don't judge this hotel from the outside: a handsome and cavernous lobby will lead you to the well-decorated and spacious rooms. Those overlooking Shing Mun River have excellent views.

Pilgrim's Hall (Map p185; ☎2691 2739; www.tfssu.org/pilgrim.html; 33 Tao Fong Shan Rd; s/d with shared bathroom HK$260/400; ☒Sha Tin, exit B) This Lutheran Church–affiliated hostel provides a nice escape from the city as it's set on a peaceful hillside above the town. To get here, take the MTR East Rail to Sha Tin station, leave via exit B and walk down the ramp, passing a series of old village houses on the left. To the left of these houses is a set of steps signposted 'To Fung Shan'. Follow the path all the way to the top and you'll see Pilgrim's Hall. The walk should take around 20 minutes. A taxi from the nearest MTR station in Sha Tin will cost around HK$20. The canteen serves simple and healthy meals (advance booking required).

husband to return from the sea while carrying her baby on her back. One day he didn't come back – and she waited and waited. The gods apparently took pity on her and transported her to heaven on a lightning bolt, leaving her form in stone. Today it's a great day hike.

As you take the MTR south from Sha Tin to Kowloon, Amah Rock is visible to the east (ie on the left-hand side) up on the hillside after Tai Wai East Rail station, but before the train enters the tunnel.

CHE KUNG TEMPLE   TAOIST TEMPLE

(車公廟; ☎2691 1733; Che Kung Miu Rd; ⊗7am-6pm; ☒Che Kung Temple) **FREE** This large Taoist temple complex, rebuilt in 1993, is on the opposite bank of the Shing Mun River channel. It's dedicated to Che Kung, a Song-dynasty general credited with ridding Sha Tin of the plague. The best time to visit the temple is on the third day of Chinese New Year, when hordes of worshippers come here to rotate the sails of the copper windmill inside the temple for good luck.

SHA TIN RACECOURSE RACECOURSE

(沙田馬場; www.hkjc.com; Penfold Park; race day public stands HK$10, members enclosures HK$100-150; ⓜRacecourse) Northeast of Sha Tin town centre is Hong Kong's second racecourse, which can accommodate up to 80,000 punters. Races are usually held on Sunday afternoon (and sometimes on Saturday and public holidays) from September to early July; a list of race meetings is available from the Hong Kong Jockey Club website (www.hkjc.com).

The Racecourse East Rail station, just west of the track, opens on race days only.

 EATING

LUNG WAH HOTEL
RESTAURANT CANTONESE $

(龍華酒店; ☑2691 1828; www.lung wahhotel. hk; 22 Ha Wo Che; pigeon HK$79; ⊘11am-11pm; ⓜSha Tin, exit B) This is where Bruce Lee is said to have stayed during the filming of *The Big Boss*. It's now a restaurant, frequented by nostalgic adults. You'll find a small playground out front where peacocks are kept in cages, and an outdoor area where old men come to play mah jong. Foodwise, stick with the roast pigeon.

To reach the hotel, walk north for 10 minutes along the railway line after exiting the station.

SHING KEE DAI PAI DONG, CANTONESE $

(盛記; ☑2692 6611; Shop 5, Lek Yuen Estate Market; meal from HK$80; ⊘6am-4pm & 7-11pm; ⓠ83K from Sha Tin New Town Plaza, ⓜSha Tin) Tucked in the oldest public housing estate in Sha Tin, this 30-year-old establishment is no ordinary *dai pai dong* (food stall). It resembles a gallery, with black-and-white photos stuck on the wall, CDs, toys, and potted plants in other corners. All, including the chairs, were picked up from public wheelie bins and arty-craftily recycled by the owner.

Noodles are served in the daytime. In the evening, it turns into a popular hotpot joint, with several dozens of broths on offer. To get there, take bus 83K, or it's a 15-minute walk northeast from Sha Tin station.

SHA TIN 18 CANTONESE, NORTHERN CHINESE $$

(沙田18; ☑3723 1234; www.hongkong.shatin. hyatt.com; 18 Chak Cheung St, Hyatt Regency Hong Kong; meals HK$300-500; ⊘11.30am-3pm & 5.30-10.30pm; ⓜUniversity) The Peking duck (whole HK$538, half HK$328) here has put this hotel restaurant, adjacent to the campus of the Chinese University, in the gastronomic spotlight since its opening in 2009. Book your prized fowl 24 hours in advance. Tantalise your taste buds in two ways – pancakes with the crispy skin, and wok-fried mince duck with iceberg lettuce. The restaurant also boasts a tempting dessert counter.

Sai Kung Peninsula

Explore

The rugged and massive Sai Kung Peninsula is an outdoor-pursuits paradise. The hiking is excellent here – the MacLehose Trail runs right across it. Sai Kung Town is a good base for exploring the easily accessible countryside. This eclectic waterfront town has a cluster of restaurants and is also a stopping point and transport hub to and from the surrounding countryside. A *kaido* (small, open-sea ferry) trip to one or more of the little offshore islands and their secluded beaches is recommended.

Tai Long Wan is among the most beautiful (and popular) beaches to loll around. For a shoal of seafood possibilities, Sai Kung Town has a variety of fish menus to drool over.

The 100km **MacLehose Trail** traverses the New Territories from Tuen Mun in the west to Sai Kung in the east.

The Best...

➡**Sight** Tai Long Wan (p191)
➡**Place to eat** Loaf On (p191)
➡**Place to drink** Steamers (p191)

Top Tip

Near the Sai Kung Town pier, you'll find one of the liveliest fish markets in Hong Kong, where fishermen sell their catch directly from their boats.

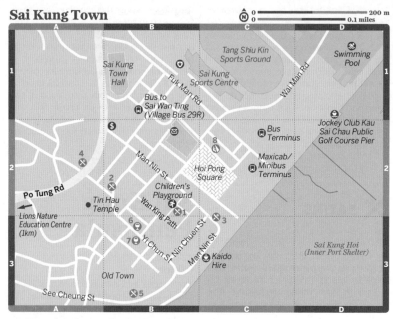

Sai Kung Town

NEW TERRITORIES SAI KUNG PENINSULA

Getting There & Away

➡ **Bus** To/from Sai Kung Town, bus 299 connects to Sha Tin East Rail station, bus 92 to Diamond Hill and Choi Hung, bus 96R (Sunday and public holidays) connects to Wong Shek, Hebe Haven, and Choi Hung and Diamond Hill MTR stations. Bus 792M calls at Tseung Kwan O and Tiu Keng Leng MTR stations. Bus 94 goes to Wong Shek.

➡ **Green minibus** To/from Sai Kung Town, buses 1A, 1M and 1S (12.30am to 6.10am) connect with Hebe Haven and Choi Hung MTR station.

Need to Know

➡ **Area code** ✆852

➡ **Location** 21km northeast of Kowloon

➡ **Last train to Kowloon** leaves at 12.20am from Tseung Kwan O station, 12.22am from Tiu Keng Leng MTR station

➡ **Tourist information** Sai Kung District Council (www.travelinsaikung.org.hk)

◎ SIGHTS

HEBE HAVEN YACHT CLUB   YACHT CLUB
(白沙灣遊艇會; ✆2719 9682; www.hhyc.org. hk) The very small bay of Hebe Haven (白沙灣), which Cantonese speakers call Pak Sha Wan (White Sand Bay), is home to the Hebe Haven Yacht Club, which has a large fleet of yachts and other pleasure craft all but choking Marina Cove.

To swim at **Trio beach**, opposite the marina, catch a sampan from Hebe Haven to the long, narrow peninsula called Ma Lam Wat; along the way you'll pass a small **Tin Hau temple** on a spit of land jutting out to the south. The beach is excellent and the sampan trip should only cost a few dollars.

You can also walk to the peninsula from Sai Kung Town; it's about 4km.

LIONS NATURE EDUCATION CENTRE
OUTDOORS

(獅子會自然教育中心; ☏2792 2234; www. lnec.gov.hk; Pak Kong; ◷9am-5pm Wed-Mon; ♿; 🚌92) **FREE** One of the best kid-pleasing destinations around, this 34-hectare attraction, 2km northwest of Hebe Haven, is Hong Kong's first nature education centre. It comprises everything from an arboretum, a medicinal plants garden and an insectarium to a mineral and rocks corner and a shell house. The **Dragonfly Pond**, which boasts up to a quarter of the more than 100 dragonfly species found in Hong Kong, is the star of the show.

You can reach the centre on bus 92 from Diamond Hill MTR and Choi Hung, bus 96R on Sunday and holidays from Diamond Hill, and green minibus 1A from Choi Hung.

SAI KUNG COUNTRY PARK VISITOR CENTRE
OUTDOORS

(西貢郊野公園遊客中心; ☏2792 7365; Tai Mong Tsai Rd; ◷9.30am-4.30pm Wed-Mon; 🚌94) Pak Tam Chung (北潭涌) is the start of the MacLehose Trail. While you're in Pak Tam Chung, visit the Sai Kung Country Park Visitor Centre, which is to the south of the village, just by the road from Sai Kung. It has excellent maps, photographs and displays of the area's geology, fauna and flora, as well as useful information on the traditional villages nearby and Hoi Ha Wan Marine Park.

SHEUNG YIU FOLK MUSEUM
MUSEUM

(☏2792 6365; ◷9am-4pm Wed-Mon; 🚌94) **FREE** The museum is part of a restored Hakka village typical of those found here in the 19th century. The village was founded about 150 years ago by the Wong clan, which built a kiln to make bricks. In the whitewashed dwellings, pigpens and cattle sheds – all surrounded by a high wall and watchtower to guard against pirate raids – there are farm implements, objects of daily use, furnishings and Hakka clothing.

The museum is a leisurely 20-minute walk south of Pak Tam Chung along the 1km-long **Pak Tam Chung Nature Trail**.

EATING

Food is the raison d'être for the flocks who descend on Sai Kung Town every weekend. It's reachable by minibus 1 or 1A from Choi Hung MTR.

WORTH A DETOUR

TAP MUN CHAU

The very isolated Tap Mun Chau, also known as 'Grass Island', is definitely worth the trip, and you will be rewarded with something that's hard to come by in Hong Kong: isolation and an otherworldly feel. The sailing is particularly scenic from **Wong Shek**, as the boat cruises through the fjord **Tai Tan Hoi Hap**.

Tap Mun Village is noted for its **Tin Hau temple**, which was built in the early 18th century and is northeast from where the boat docks. The **Birthday of Tin Hau festival**, celebrated in late April/early May, is big here. Part of the temple is devoted to the god of war Kwan Tai.

Other attractions include seafood drying on racks in the sun, dragon boats bobbing in the harbour and, strangely, a herd of cows. It's an easy (and signposted) walk northward to **Mau Ping Shan** (125m), the island's highest point; a windy pebble **beach** on the southeastern shore; and an odd stone formation called **Balanced Rock**, 200m south of the beach.

If you want to stay here, the only option is to pitch a tent. There are shops selling snacks and drinks, and **New Hon Kee** (新漢記; ☏2328 2428; 4 Tap Mun Hoi Pong St; meals from HK$100; ◷lunch Mon-Fri, 11am-4.30pm Sat & Sun), a seafood restaurant popular with islanders and visitors alike, is a short walk northeast of the ferry pier on the way to Tin Hau temple.

The island is off the northeast coast of the New Territories, where the Tolo Channel empties into Mirs Bay (Tai Pang Wan in Cantonese). Ferries depart from Wong Shek in Sai Kung and Ma Liu Shui near University East Rail station.

ISLAND-HOPPING IN SAI KUNG

Exploring the islands that encircle the peninsula is a delightful way to see Sai Kung. Most *kaido* (small, open-sea ferries) leave from the piers on the waterfront, just in front of Hoi Pong Sq.

The first island to the east of Sai Kung Town is **Yeung Chau** (Sheep Island). You'll be able to spot a horseshoe-shaped burial plot up on the slope; it's so designed for reasons dictated by feng shui. Southeast of Yeung Chau, **Pak Sha Chau** (White Sand Island) has a popular beach on its northern shore.

Just beyond Pak Sha Chau is the northern tip of the much larger **Kiu Tsui Chau** (Sharp Island), arguably the most popular island destination. Kiu Tsui Chau has several fine beaches: Kiu Tsui and, connected to it by a sand spit, Kiu Tau on the western shore; and **Hap Mun** on the island's southern tip. Both can be reached by *kaido* (HK$40) directly from Sai Kung Town.

The charming island of **Yim Tin Tsai** is accessible by 'scheduled' *kaido* (return HK$35, 15 minutes, departs hourly 10am to 3pm Saturday and Sunday). Literally 'Little Salt Field', the island is so-called because the original fisherfolk who lived here augmented their income by salt-panning. A few minutes' walk from the jetty up a small flight of steps to the left is **St Joseph's Chapel**, the focal point of the island. The villagers, who all belong to the same clan, converted to Catholicism 150 years ago after St Peter appeared on the island to chase away pirates who had been harassing them. There's also a modest **cafe** open daily.

Yim Tin Tsai is connected to the much larger island of **Kau Sai Chau** by a narrow spit of land that becomes submerged at high tide. Kau Sai Chau is the site of the 36-hole **Jockey Club Kau Sai Chau Public Golf Course** (☑2791 3388; www.kscgolf.org.hk/index-e.asp; Kau Sai Chau, Sai Kung), a public links course that can be reached by the course's direct ferry from Sai Kung (adult/concession HK$60/35 return, departs every 20 minutes daily from 6.40am to 7pm). Boats dock in Sai Kung Town at the long pier opposite the new Sai Kung Waterfront Park. The 19th-century Hung Shing Temple at the southern tip of Kau Sai Chau won a Unesco restoration award in 2000.

Beyond Kau Sai Chau is **Leung Shuen Wan** (糧船灣; High Island), a long trip from Sai Kung Town, and the **High Island Reservoir** (萬宜水庫), which is now part of the Hong Kong Geopark. This largest reservoir of Hong Kong was built in 1978 by damming what was once a large bay with dolooses (huge cement barriers shaped like jacks); sea water was then siphoned out and fresh water pumped in. To the west of the dam is the newly opened **Astropark** (天文公園; ☑2792 6810; http://astropark.hk.space.museum; ⏰24hr), located in a water-sports centre, where you can stargaze from the naked-eye observation area. The park also has a replica of a 17th-century Chinese celestial globe and a campground. Reservations a must.

If you want to be out on the water for a longer period or have greater flexibility as to where you go, you can hire your own boat. *Kaido* owners can usually be found trawling for fares. Explain where you want to go, how long you want to spend there and which way you wish to return. The usual price for this kind of trip is about HK$300 on weekdays, more on the weekend.

ALI OLI BAKERY CAFE   EUROPEAN, BAKERY **$**

(☑2792 2655; 11 Sha Tsui Path; pastries from HK$18; ⏰8am-7.30pm Mon-Fri, to 9pm Sat & Sun; ▣1) This much-loved bakery is a hiker's best friend, with simple sandwiches on European-style homemade bread, pies and preserves. Breakfast and set lunches are also offered here and best enjoyed at its outdoor tables.

HONEYMOON DESSERT   DESSERTS **$**

(滿記甜品; ☑2792 4991; 9, 10A, B&C Po Tung Rd; per person HK$30; ⏰1pm-2.45am; ▣1) This shop specialising in Chinese desserts such as sweet walnut soup and durian pudding is so successful that it has branches all over China and in Indonesia, not to mention some 20 locations in Hong Kong.

★ **LOAF ON** CANTONESE, SEAFOOD $$
(六福菜館; ☎2792 9966; 49 See Cheung; dishes from HK$100; ⏰11am-11pm; 🚇1) The motto here is: eat what they hunt. This three-storey Michelin-star restaurant is where fish freshly caught from the Sai Kung waters in the morning lands on customers' plates by midday. The signature fish soup and steamed fish sell out fast. There is no English signage, but it's identifiable by a lone dining table set outside and the shiny brass sign. Reservations recommended.

CHUEN KEE SEAFOOD RESTAURANT CANTONESE, SEAFOOD $$
(全記海鮮菜館; ☎2792 6938; 87-89 Man Nin St; meals from HK$180; ⏰7am-11pm; 🚇1) Chuen Kee has two locations in Sai Kung. This is the plush branch of the flagship on the promenade. The elaborate display of fish and crustaceans at the door may make you cringe, but cringe will turn to crave once you've had a bite of the cooked versions.

ANTHONY'S RANCH AMERICAN $$
(☎2791 6113; www.anthonys-ranch.com; 28 Yi Chun St, Sai Kung; meals HK$150; ⏰11.30am-midnight Mon-Thu, to 2am Fri & Sat, from 8.30am Sun; 🚇1) The Disney-fied cowboy decor is goofy, but the excellently executed American-style burgers, ribs, pulled pork and apple pie are no joke. Especially good after a long hike or kayak.

🍷 DRINKING & NIGHTLIFE

STEAMERS BAR
(66 Yi Chun St; ⏰happy hour 2-8pm Mon-Fri; 🚇1) Steamers is graced by a blissful alfresco bar area where you can chill out with some excellently blended cocktails and tasty bar grub.

POETS PUB
(55 Yi Chun St; ⏰happy hour noon-9pm Mon-Fri; 🚇1) This down-to-earth pub opposite Steamers is a pleasant place for a pint and serves typical pub meals, such as pies, chips and beans.

🏃 SPORTS & ACTIVITIES

WINDSURFING CENTRE WINDSURFING
(☎2792 5605; basic windsurfing lessons HK$450, board rentals weekday/weekend HK$50/150; ⏰9.30am-6pm Sat & Sun, call ahead on weekdays; 🚇94) Windsurfing equipment can be hired from the Windsurfing Centre at Sha Ha, just north of Sai Kung Town. Bus 94, heading for the pier at Wong Shek and the springboard for Tap Mun Chau, will drop you off, or you could walk there from town in about 15 minutes.

TAI LONG WAN HIKING TRAIL HIKING
(大浪灣遠足徑; 🚌village bus 29R) The northern end of Sai Kung Peninsula boasts several rewarding hikes that will take you through some of the most pristine scenery in Hong Kong. The breathtaking 12km Tai Long Wan Hiking Trail, which starts from the end of Sai Wan Rd and passes through beautiful coves like Sai Wan, Tai Long Wan and Chek Keng, is a perennially popular option. On weekdays you're likely to have the trail to yourself. The walk takes five to six hours.

Take the village bus 29R at Chan Man Rd (the stop is in front of McDonald's), get off at the last stop (Sai Wan Ting) and start the hike there. Departures are more frequent on Sundays and public holidays. A taxi ride will be under HK$100. The trail ends at Pak Tam Au, from where you can catch a minibus back to Sai Kung Town.

HOI HA WAN MARINE PARK OUTDOORS
(海下灣; ☎hotline 1823; Hoi Ha; 🚌green minibus 7) A rewarding 6km walk in the area starts from the village of Hoi Ha (literally 'Under the Sea'), now part of the Hoi Ha Wan Marine Park, a 260-hectare protected area blocked off by concrete booms from the Tolo Channel and closed to fishing vessels. It's one of the few places in Hong Kong waters where coral still grows in abundance and is a favourite with snorkellers and kayakers.

Snorkels, masks and kayaks can be rented from **Wan Hoi Store** on the beach. Green minibus 7 makes the run from Sai Kung Town daily, with the first departure at 8.25am and the last at 6.45pm. A taxi from there will cost around HK$120.

WORTH A DETOUR

TUNG PING CHAU

The easternmost point of Hong Kong, kidney-shaped Tung Ping Chau (東平洲) sits in splendid isolation in Mirs Bay in the far northeast of the New Territories. The distance from Ma Liu Shui to the southwest, from where the ferry serving the island departs, is around 25km.

The island is part of **Hong Kong Geopark**, which encompasses eight sites of special geologic significance that are protected from development. Together with the waters around it – which teem with sea life (especially corals) – it forms Hong Kong's fourth marine park.

Tung Ping Chau's highest point is only about 40m, but it has unusual rock layers in its cliffs, which glitter after the rain. The eastern coast hosts some of the best coral communities in Hong Kong and is good for **snorkelling**. There is a small **Tin Hau temple** on the southwestern coast of the island, and some small **caves** dotting the cliffs. A good 6km **walking trail** encircles the whole island.

At one time the island, which is called Tung Ping Chau (East Peace Island) to distinguish it from Peng Chau (same pronunciation in Cantonese) near Lantau, supported a population of 3000, but now it is virtually deserted. There are several food stalls in **Sha Tau**, a village east of the pier. All provide simple lodging (ie bunk beds) if you have a burning desire to stay here. One of them is **Ping Chau Store** (坪洲士多; ☑2661 6941; bed HK$30). Book ahead (a must); or pitch your tent in the campground at the eastern tip of the island.

Tsui Wah Ferry Services (☑2272 2022; www.traway.com.hk; round trip HK$90) runs ferries here on Saturdays, Sundays and public holidays. Boats depart from Ma Liu Shui near University East Rail station.

Clearwater Bay Peninsula

Explore

Tseung Kwan O, accessible via the MTR station of the same name, is the springboard to the Clearwater Bay Peninsula. There are several wonderful beaches for whiling away an afternoon. The most beautiful and popular are Clearwater Bay First Beach and Clearwater Bay Second Beach. They are often packed with local weekenders during the warmer months.

The Clearwater Bay Country Park offers some easy but exceptional walks with sweeping views of the bay. The secluded Tai Miu Temple, dedicated to the goddess of heaven, is best visited during Tin Hau's Birthday Festival in April or May. Seafood lovers will not want to miss Po Toi O Village: this is where you can enjoy sumptuous seafood and home-style cooking at its best.

The Best...

➡ **Sight** Silverstrand Beach (p193)

➡ **Beach** Clearwater Bay Second Beach (p193)

➡ **Place to eat** Seafood Island (p193)

Top Tip

Early birds shouldn't miss the breathtaking sunrise that can be watched from Clearwater Bay Second Beach. The first minibus starts at 6am.

Getting There & Away

➡ **Bus** Bus 91 runs between Diamond Hill and Choi Hung MTR stations to Tai Au Mun.

➡ **Green minibus** Bus 103M runs between Tseung Kwan O MTR station and Clearwater Bay. Bus 103 runs to Kwun Tong ferry pier, and bus 16 to Po Lam MTR station.

Need to Know

➡ **Area code** ☑852

➡ **Location** 15km east of Tsim Sha Tsui, Kowloon. Junk Bay (Tseung Kwan O) is to the west of the peninsula and Clearwater Bay (Tsing Sui Wan) sits to the east; Joss House Bay (Tai Miu Wan) lies to the south.

➡ **Last train to Kowloon** leaves at 12.16am from Po Lam MTR station.

SIGHTS

SILVERSTRAND BEACH
BEACH

(銀線灣; Ngan Sin Wan; 🚌91) Bus 91 passes Silverstrand beach north of Hang Hau before reaching Tai Au Mun; if you wish, you can get off at Silverstrand and go for a dip. If you're heading for Lung Ha Wan, get off the bus at Tai Au Mun Village and start walking. From Sai Kung, take bus 92 to where Hiram's Hwy and Clearwater Bay Rd meet and change there to bus 91.

CLEARWATER BAY BEACHES
BEACH

(🚌91) From Tai Au Mun, Tai Au Mun Rd leads south to two fine, sandy beaches: **Clearwater Bay First Beach** (清水灣一灘) and, a bit further southwest, **Clearwater Bay Second Beach** (清水灣二灘). In summer try to go during the week, as both beaches get very crowded on the weekend.

TAI MIU TEMPLE
TEMPLE

(大廟; 📞2519 9155; ⊙8am-5pm; minibus 16) This far-flung temple further south along Tai Au Mun Rd is one of the most important Tin Hau temples in the territory. Built in the 13th century by two Fujianese in gratitude to the goddess for saving them during a sea storm, the temple was restored in 2009 and is the prime celebration venue during the Tin Hau Birthday Festival (p174).

Just behind the temple is a Song-dynasty rock carving dating from 1274 and recording both the visit of a superintendent of the Salt Administration and the history of two temples in Joss House Bay. It is the oldest inscription extant in Hong Kong.

From Tai Miu, hikers can follow the 6.6km-long **High Junk Peak Country Trail** up to Tin Ha Shan (273m) and then continue on to High Junk Peak (Tiu Yu Yung; 344m) before heading eastward back to Tai Au Mun.

EATING

Po Toi O is a small fishing village southeast of Clearwater Bay. The two seafood restaurants there draw in gourmands from all over Hong Kong.

SEAFOOD ISLAND
CANTONESE, SEAFOOD $$

(海鮮島海鮮酒家; 📞2719 5730; Shop B, 7 Po Toi O Chuen Rd; meals from HK$180; ⊙10.30am-11.30pm) Crustaceans of every kind are on full display at this energetic restaurant hidden in discreet Po Toi O Village. A totally non-luxe setting but with no-nonsense fare, Seafood Island is famed for its cuttlefish sashimi and razor clams. It's more a group activity to dine here. Grab a couple of friends and enjoy all the treats on offer.

SPORTS & ACTIVITIES

CLEARWATER BAY COUNTRY PARK
OUTDOORS

(minibus 103) The heart of the country park is **Tai Au Mun**, from where trails go in various directions, through the **Clearwater Bay Country Park Visitor Centre** (📞2719 0032; ⊙9.30am-4.30pm, closed Tue) to the southeast in Tai Hang Tun. Take Lung Ha Wan Rd north from Tai Au Mun to the beach at **Lung Ha Wan** (Lobster Bay) and return via the 2.3km **Lung Ha Wan Country Trail**.

CLEARWATER BAY GOLF & COUNTRY CLUB
GOLF

(清水灣高爾夫球鄉村俱樂部; 📞2335 3700; www.cwbgolf.org; 139 Tau Au Mun Rd, Clearwater Bay; greens fees HK$1600-2000; 🚌91) A 27-hole course at the tip of Clearwater Bay in the New Territories.

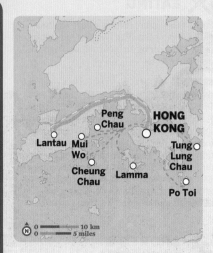

Outlying Islands

Lamma p196

The quickest island escape from downtown Hong Kong, laid-back Lamma exudes a bohemian charm and is home to many a commuter who prefers more space and greenery.

Lantau p201

The largest of the islands boasts bountiful sights and recreational possibilities: country parks, hiking trails, fishing villages, beaches, monasteries and the unmissable Big Buddha.

Cheung Chau p213

Think seafood and seafaring culture on this bustling isle of great windsurfing beaches and temples dedicated to water deities. The annual Bun Festival is a highlight.

Worth a Detour

At **Peng Chau** (p211), glimpse the last echoes of traditional village life in Hong Kong. **Po Toi** (p213) is the southernmost island of Hong Kong, and offers scenic walks and delicious seafood. Camping, rock climbing and stargazing are the drawcards of 'East Dragon Island', **Tung Lung Chau** (p217).

 TOP SIGHT
NGONG PING PLATEAU

No trip to Hong Kong is complete without visiting Ngong Ping Plateau for the seated Tian Tan Buddha statue, the biggest of its kind in the world. It can be seen aerially as you fly into Hong Kong, or on a clear day from Macau, but nothing beats coming up close and personal with this much-loved spiritual icon sitting at over 500m up in the western hills of Lantau.

Commonly known as the 'Big Buddha', the 202-tonne **Tian Tan Buddha** (天壇大佛; ⏰10am-6pm) **FREE** is a representation of Lord Gautama some 23m high (or just under 34m if you include the podium and lotus). Unveiled in 1993, it still holds the honour as the tallest seated bronze Buddha statue in the world. It's well worth climbing the 268 steps for a closer look at the statue and the surrounding views. The large bell within the Buddha is controlled by computer and rings 108 times during the day to symbolise escape from what Buddhism terms the '108 troubles of mankind'.

Po Lin Monastery (寶蓮禪寺; ☎2985 5248; Lantau; ⏰9am-6pm), a huge Buddhist complex built in 1924, is more of a tourist honeypot than a religious retreat today, attracting hundreds of thousands of visitors a year, and it's still being expanded. Most of the buildings you'll see on arrival are new, with the older, simpler ones tucked away behind them. **Po Lin Vegetarian Restaurant** (寶蓮禪寺齋堂; ☎2985 5248; Ngong Ping; set meals regular/deluxe HK$60/100; ⏰11.30am-4.30pm) in the monastery is famed for its inexpensive but filling vegetarian food.

The most spectacular way to get to the plateau is by the 5.7km **Ngong Ping 360** (昂坪360纜車; adult/child/concession one way HK$86/44/70, return HK$125/62/98; ⏰10am-6pm Mon-Fri, 9am-6.30pm Sat, Sun & public holidays), a cable car linking Ngong Ping with the centre of Tung Chung. The glassed-in gondola journey over the bay and the mountains takes 25 minutes. The upper station is at the skippable theme-park-like **Ngong Ping Village** just west of the monastery.

DON'T MISS

➜ Tian Tan Buddha
➜ Po Lin Monastery
➜ Ngong Ping 360

PRACTICALITIES

➜ Map p202
➜ ☎3666 0606
➜ 11 Tat Tung Rd
➜ admission free
➜ 🚌2 from Mui Wo, 21 from Tai O, 23 from Tung Chung or cable car

ⓘ CENTRAL TO OUTLYING ISLANDS FERRY SERVICES

There are two types of ferries: the large 'ordinary ferries' that, with the exception of those to Lamma, offer ordinary and deluxe classes; and the smaller 'fast ferries' that cut travel time by between 10 and 20 minutes, but cost between 50% and 100% more.

Prices are higher on Sunday and public holidays. Unless stated otherwise, children aged three to 11 years, seniors over 65 years and people with disabilities pay half-fare on both types of ferries and in both classes. Return is double the single fare.

Tickets are available from booths at the ferry piers, but avoid queuing at busy times by using an Octopus card or putting the exact change into the turnstile as you enter.

Ferry timetables are prominently displayed at all ferry piers, or you can read them on the ferry companies' websites.

Listed below are some of the more popular routes:

Central (Pier 6)–Mui Wo on Lantau Island Adult ordinary/deluxe class/fast ferry HK$15.20/25.40/29.90 (HK$22.50/37.20/42.90 on Sunday and public holidays); 50 to 55 minutes with large ferry and 31 minutes with fast ferry; departures around every half-hour from 6.10am (from 7am Sunday and public holidays). The last ferry from Mui Wo to Central departs at 11.30pm.

Central (Pier 4)–Yung Shue Wan on Lamma Island Adult HK$16.10 (HK$22.30 on Sunday and public holidays); 30 to 35 minutes; departures approximately every half-hour to an hour. The last boat to Central from Yung Shue Wan departs at 11.30pm.

Central (Pier 4)–Sok Kwu Wan on Lamma Island Adult HK$19.80 (HK$28 on Sunday and public holidays); 40 minutes; departures every 1½ hours or so from 7.20am to 11.30pm. The last ferry to Central from Sok Kwu Wan is at 10.40pm.

Central (Pier 5)–Cheung Chau (ordinary ferry) Adult ordinary/deluxe class/fast ferry HK$12.60/19.70/24.60 (HK$18.40/28.70/35.30 on Sunday and public holidays); 55 to 60 minutes with large ferry and 35 minutes with fast ferry; departures approximately every half-hour from 6.10am. The last boat to Central from Cheung Chau departs at 11.45pm.

Lamma

....

Explore

Lamma, Hong Kong's laid-back 'hippie is-land', is easily recognisable at a distance by the three coal chimneys crowning its hilly skyline. The chimneys stand out so much because Lamma, home to 6000 or so, is otherwise devoid of high-rise development. Here it's all about lush forests, hidden beaches and chilled-out villages connected by pedestrian paths. You won't see any cars here, but be prepared for spotting the odd snake.

Most visitors arrive in the main town of Yung Shue Wan, a counterculture haven popular with expats. From here, the most interesting way to see a good portion of the island is to amble along the 4km-long Fam-ily Trail that runs between Yung Shue Wan and Sok Kwu Wan, the island's second town (really little more than a strip of seafood restaurants). Those happy to be out in the hot sun should carry on to Tung O Wan, an idyllic bay some 30 minutes further south, and perhaps return to Sok Kwu Wan via Mo Tat Wan.

....

The Best...

➜**Sight** Lo So Shing Beach (p197)
➜**Place to eat** Bookworm Cafe (p199)
➜**Place to drink** Island Bar (p200)

....

Top Tip

Want huge swaths of the island all to your-self? Visit on a weekday to avoid the week-end crowds.

....

Getting There & Away

➜**Ferry** Ferries (☎2375 7883; www.ferry. com.hk) run from Yung Shue Wan pier to Pier 4 of Central's Outlying Islands ferry terminal, Pak Kok Tsuen (Lamma) and Aberdeen; they also go from Sok Kwu Wan pier to Pier 4 of Central's Outlying Islands ferry terminal, Mo Tat Wan (Lamma) and Aberdeen.

··

Need to Know

➡**Area code** ☑852

➡**Location** 3km across the East Lamma Channel from Aberdeen. There are two main settlements on the island: Yung Shue Wan to the northwest and Sok Kwu Wan on the east coast of the island.

➡**Last ferry to Central** 11.30pm from Yung Shue Wan; 10.40pm from Sok Kwu Wan

◉ SIGHTS

YUNG SHUE WAN   VILLAGE

(榕樹灣; ⬛Yung Shue Wan) Yung Shue Wan (Banyan Tree Bay) may be the largest settlement on the island but it remains a small village with little more than a car-free main street following the curve of the bay. Despite encroaching development, the village has somehow managed to retain more than a whiff of rustic charm. The main street is lined with cafes, bars, vegie stalls and New Age shops, all popular with locals and tourists alike.

At the southern end of the bay, look for a small **Tin Hau Temple** (天后廟) dating from the late 19th century, with a pair of eccentric Western lion statues guarding the entrance.

HUNG SHING YEH   BEACH

(⬛Yung Shue Wan) A 25-minute walk southeast from the Yung Shue Wan ferry pier, Hung Shing Yeh beach is the most popular beach on Lamma. Arrive early in the morning or on a weekday and you'll probably find it deserted, though you may find the view of the power station across the bay takes some getting used to. The beach is protected by a shark net and has toilets, showers and changing rooms. There are a few restaurants and drinks stands nearby, open in season.

LO SO SHING   BEACH

(⬛Yung Shue Wan) Lo So Shing beach is the most beautiful stretch of sand on Lamma, a small gold crescent fringed by thickly forested hills. Since getting here requires some walking, it's often practically deserted, even on weekends.

To get here, continue south from Hung Shing Yeh beach. The path climbs steeply until it reaches a Chinese-style pavilion. You'll pass a second pavilion that offers splendid sea views; from here a path leads from the Family Trail down to Lo So Shing.

SOK KWU WAN   VILLAGE

(索罟灣; ⬛Sok Kwu Wan) Though still a small settlement (population 500), Lamma's secondary village of Sok Kwu Wan supports at least a dozen waterfront seafood restaurants, which are popular with boaters. The small harbour is filled with rafts from which cages are suspended and fish are farmed. It's a lovely place to end your **Family Trail** walk with a seafood feast and a few cold beers. There's also a totally renovated **Tin Hau Temple** (天后廟) dating back to 1826.

Sok Kwu Wan's peaceful vibe may not last much longer, as there are plans for a new housing development in the village's abandoned quarry. The high-rise apartments would house some 5000 residents, nearly doubling Lamma's population.

LAMMA FISHERFOLK'S
VILLAGE   VILLAGE, MUSEUM

Map p198 (漁民文化村; ☑2982 8585; www.fisherfolks.com.hk/english; 2nd fl, 20 Sok Kwu Wan First St, Sok Kwu Wan; adult/child HK$80/60; ⊙10am-6pm; ⬛Sok Kwu Wan) This 2000-sq-metre floating museum and theme park on a raft showcases the fishing culture and history of the fishery industry in Hong Kong. Fishing tools and model vessels are on display, including a real 60-year-old junk. You can also try your hand at angling and rope weaving.

KAMIKAZE CAVES   CAVE

(神風洞; ⬛Sok Kwu Wan) The three so-called Kamikaze Caves (神風洞), grottoes measuring 10m wide and 30m deep, were built by the occupying Japanese forces to house motorboats wired with explosives to disrupt Allied shipping during WWII. They were never used. You'll pass the caves when entering Sok Kwu Wan from the south (ie from the Family Trail linking this village with Yung Shue Wan).

HERBOLAND   FARM

(☑9094 6206; off Hung Shing Yeh beach; ⊙10am-5pm; ⬛Yung Shue Wan) Nestled in the leafy fringes of Hung Shing Yeh beach is Herboland, the first organic herb farm in

Lamma

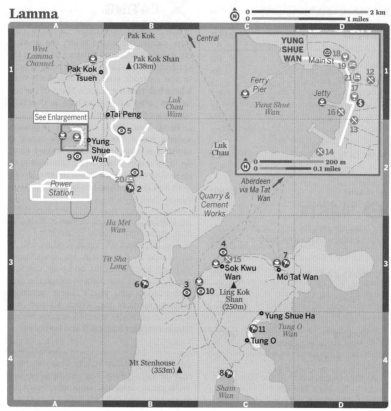

the territory. Stroll past fragrant bushes of rosemary and verbena, or choose from more than 40 types of herbal tea in the farm's blissful tea garden.

LAMMA WINDS
LANDMARK

(南丫風采發電站; ⏱7am-6pm; ⛴Yung Shue Wan) Standing in elegant contrast to that carbon-dioxide-belching, coal-fired power station, Lamma's giant wind turbine, dramatically positioned atop the ridge just southeast of Tai Peng old village, makes a stirring sight (although in reality it is something of a white elephant generating far less power than was hoped for). There's a small **exhibition centre** on wind power, but there's not much else to do here but admire its feathered blades scything the breeze.

To reach it, follow the paths from Yung Shue Wan up to Tai Peng old village and turn right once you hit the concrete roadway linking the power station with Pak Kok.

TUNG O WAN
BEACH

(⛴Sok Kwu Wan) Long coveted by developers as a prime location for new condos and marina facilities, unspoiled Tung O Wan is still holding out against the might of the property dollar thanks to the combined resistance of local residents and environmentalists from other shores. Ringed by a long sandy beach, this small and secluded bay makes a rewarding detour while walking to Sok Kwu Wan from Yung Shue Wan or from Sok Kwu Wan itself.

Just before the Tin Hau Temple at the entrance to Sok Kwu Wan, follow the signposted path to the right southward, up and over the hill to the tiny village of Tung O. The walk takes about 30 minutes over a

Lamma

rugged landscape, and the first half is a fairly strenuous climb up steps and along a path.

MO TAT WAN BEACH

(⛴Sok Kwu Wan) The clean and relatively uncrowded beach at Mo Tat Wan is a mere 20-minute coastal path walk east of Sok Kwu Wan village. Mo Tat Wan is OK for swimming, but has no lifeguards. You can also reach it by *kaido* (small open-sea ferry) from Aberdeen, which continues on to Sok Kwu Wan.

SHAM WAN BEACH

(Deep Bay; ◷closed Jun-Oct; ⛴Sok Kwu Wan) Sham Wan is a beautiful bay in the south of the island that can be reached from Tung O Wan by clambering over the hills. A trail on the left about 200m up the hill from Tung O Wan leads south to this small and sandy beach. Don't come here from June to October, when Hong Kong's endangered green turtles nest and the beach is closed to the public.

✖ EATING

While seafood dominates Lamma's culinary palate, the island offers the greatest choice of eateries and cuisines of any of the Outlying Islands. Most people head directly to the seafront stretch of Sok Kwu Wan, where fish rule the menus. Many of the restaurants offer a free ferry back to Central if you dine at their establishment.

Yung Shue Wan, the most populated village, has a vast and eclectic range of inviting restaurants, mostly spread along its main street. There are a couple of good spots for refreshment at the remote Mo Tat Wan and Hung Shing Yeh beaches.

BOOKWORM CAFE CAFE, VEGETARIAN $

(南島書蟲; ☎2982 4838; 79 Main St, Yung Shue Wan; meals from HK$80; ◷9am-9pm Fri-Wed; ⛴Yung Shue Wan) 🌱 Vegie foodies will be in heaven at Bookworm, the granddaddy of Hong Kong's healthy and eco-conscious dining scene. Tasty dishes include the dhal and salad combo, goat's cheese sandwich and shepherdess pie, which all pair well with the carefully selected organic wines. The cafe is also a secondhand bookshop.

WATERFRONT INTERNATIONAL $

(☎2982 1168; 58 Main St, Yung Shue Wan; meals from HK$90; ◷9am-2am; ⛴Yung Shue Wan) With great views and lapping waves a few steps from the terrace, this restaurant is both a popular breakfast joint and sundowner spot. It serves traditional British and Italian fare, as well as Indian grub.

BEER GARDEN INDIAN $

(☎2982 6168; http://lammahk.com/; Main St, Yung Shue Wan; meals about HK$80; ⛴Yung Shue Wan) Located just off Yung Shue Wan's main drag, locals and visitors kick back here with frosty beers and plates of cheap, tasty Indian food in a plant-filled covered patio. A large TV makes this the place to be when there's a football or rugby match on.

BEST KEBAB & PIZZA TURKISH $

(☎2982 0902; 4 Yung Shue Wan Back St, Yung Shue Wan; meals from HK$40; ◷2-10pm Mon-Fri, noon-10pm Sat; ⛴Yung Shue Wan) This small, unpretentious Turkish-run eatery serves exactly what it says on the tin. The pizza, lamb chops and sizzling shish kebab are what the local residents rave about. Wash them down with freshly brewed Turkish coffee and fruit teas.

LAMMA'S ENDANGERED TURTLES

Sham Wan has traditionally been the one beach in the whole of Hong Kong where endangered green turtles (Chelonia mydas), one of three species of sea turtle found in Hong Kong waters, still struggle onto the sand to lay their eggs from early June to the end of August.

Female green turtles, which can grow to a metre in length and weigh 140kg, take between 20 and 30 years to reach sexual maturity and always head back to the same beach they were born on to lay their eggs, which takes place every two to six years. Fearing that Sham Wan would catch the eye of housing-estate developers and that the turtles would swim away forever, the area was declared a Site of Special Scientific Interest in 1999 and closed for part of the year. It is patrolled by the Agriculture, Fisheries & Conservation Department (AFCD) from June to October, when the beach is closed to the public. Some eight turtles are known to have nested here since 1997 and some are now being tracked by satellite.

As well as developers, a major hurdle faced by the long-suffering turtles is the appetite of Lamma locals for their eggs. In 1994 three turtles laid about 200 eggs, which were promptly harvested and consumed by villagers. Several years later villagers sold eggs to Japanese tourists for HK$100 each. There is now a HK$50,000 fine levied on anyone caught on the beach during the nesting season. Anyone taking, possessing or attempting to sell one of the eggs faces a fine of HK$100,000 and one year in prison.

RAINBOW SEAFOOD RESTAURANT
CHINESE, SEAFOOD $$

(天虹海鮮酒家; ☑2982 8100; www.rainbow-rest.com.hk; Shops 1A-1B, Ground fl, 23-25 First St, Sok Kwu Wan; meals from HK$180; ⊙10am-10.30pm; ⊠Sok Kwu Wan) Gigantic Rainbow may boast 800 seats but you still need to book ahead for prime hours. Steamed grouper, lobster and abalone are the specialities at this waterfront restaurant. You have the option of being transported by its own ferries from Central Pier 9 or Tsim Sha Tsui Public Pier; call or check its website for sailings.

🍷 DRINKING & NIGHTLIFE

Lamma is no party island, but there are several cosy bars in Yung Shue Wan where you can converse and watch the sun set over a cold one. Most bars serve what is very much a local crowd, consisting mostly of expats, in the evenings. You may be asked to sign a members' book, as some places operate on club licences.

ISLAND BAR
BAR

(⊙5pm-late Mon-Fri, noon-late Sat & Sun, happy hour 5-8pm; ⊠Yung Shue Wan) The closest bar to Yung Shue Wan's ferry pier, this place is a favourite with older expats and hosts the best jam sessions on the island.

7TH AVENUE
BAR

(7 Main St, Yung Shue Wan; ⊙noon-late; ⊠Yung Shue Wan) Though the city-sounding name doesn't match Lamma's rural ambience, this new kid on the block has a welcoming atmosphere with hookahs and outdoor seating, thanks to the 20-year-old entrepreneur who runs it. All food and booze is reasonably priced.

FOUNTAIN HEAD
BAR

(17 Main St, Yung Shue Wan; ⊙4pm-late; ⊠Yung Shue Wan) Recognisable by the colourful graffiti-style mural out the front, cheerfully no-frills Fountain Head has a good mix of Chinese and expats in regular attendance, decent music and beer at affordable prices.

🛌 SLEEPING

There are holiday flats aplenty in Yung Shue Wan.

BALI HOLIDAY RESORT
HOTEL $

(☑2982 4580; www.lammabali.com; 8 Main St, Yung Shue Wan; r Sun-Fri HK$300-750, Sat & holidays HK$700-1400; ⊠Yung Shue Wan) Near the ferry in Yung Shue Wan, Bali has basic, pleasant, tile-floored rooms with TVs and fridges, as well as family apartments. Upper-floor rooms with balconies are the nicest. Wi-fi in the patio.

JACKSON PROPERTY AGENCY ACCOMMODATION SERVICES **$**
Map p198 (☑2982 0606; www.lammaresort.com; 15 Main St, Yung Shue Wan; d Sun-Fri from HK$480, Sat HK$780-1080; ☑Yung Shue Wan) This property agency has studios and apartments for rent on Lamma. All of them have a TV, private bathroom, microwave and fridge. Rooms start at HK$480 per night for two people from Sunday to Friday and increase in price substantially on Saturday.

CONCERTO INN HOTEL **$$**
Map p198 (☑2982 1668; www.concertoinn.com.hk; 28 Hung Shing Yeh beach, Hung Shing Yeh; r Sun-Fri HK$800-1188, r Sat & eve of public holidays HK$1068-1488; ☎; ☑Yung Shue Wan) This cheerful beachfront hotel, southeast of Yung Shue Wan, is quite some distance from the action, so you should stay here only if you really want to get away from it all. Rooms for three or four people are actually doubles with a sofa bed or pull-out bed.

Lantau

Explore
The sheer size of Lantau, Hong Kong's largest island, makes for days of exploration. The north tip of the island, home to the airport, Disneyland and the high-rise Tung Chung residential and shopping complex, is highly developed. But much of the rest of Lantau is still entirely rural. Here you'll find traditional fishing villages, empty beaches and a mountainous interior crisscrossed with quad-burning hiking trails.

Most visitors come to Lantau to visit Mickey or see the justly-famous 'Big Buddha' statue, but be sure you get beyond the north side for a taste of a laid-back island where cows graze in the middle of the road, schoolkids gather seaweed with their grandparents in the shallow bays, and the odd pangolin is said to still roam the forested hillsides.

The Best...
→**Sight** Tai O (p208)
→**Place to Eat** Mavericks (p209)
→**Place to Sleep** Espace Elastique (p212)

Top Tip
There are only 50 taxis serving the whole island. Have the call-service numbers ready, especially after hours.

Getting There & Away
→**Airport Express** This MTR line takes you to Airport station at Chek Lap Kok.
→**Bus** Bus S1 connects Lantau's Tung Chung and the airport. Bus N11 connects Tung Chung and Central, while bus N21 connects Tung Chung with Kowloon.
→**Ferry** Major services from Central (☑2131 8181; www.nwff.com.hk) leave from pier 6 at the Outlying Islands ferry terminal for Mui Wo. Ferries also depart from Chi Ma Wan (also on Lantau), Cheung Chau and Peng Chau for Mui Wo. Chi Ma Wan is served by the inter-island ferry from Mui Wo, Cheung Chau and Peng Chau.
→**MTR** The Tung Chung line runs between Central and Lantau, and is the main way (other than the Mui Wo ferry) tourists access Lantau from Hong Kong Island.

Getting Around
→**Taxi** Telephone the call service on ☑2984 1328 or ☑2984 1368. Sample fares to Ngong Ping/Tian Tan Buddha from Mui Wo and Tung Chung/Hong Kong International Airport are HK$140/160.

Need to Know
→**Area code** ☑852
→**Location** 8km west of Hong Kong Island. The most inhabited town Tung Chung is on the northern coast, while Mui Wo, the second-largest settlement, is on the eastern coast. The airport is directly north of Tung Chung.
→**Last ferry to Central** 11.30pm from Mui Wo

◉ SIGHTS

◉ North Lantau

NGONG PING PLATEAU TEMPLE, STATUE
See p195.

Lantau

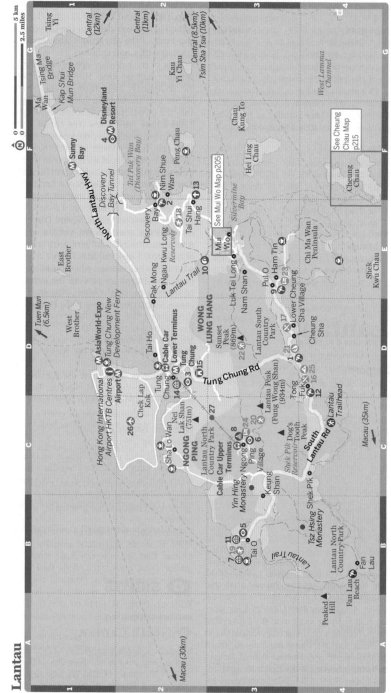

See Cheung Chau Map p215

See Mui Wo Map p205

Lantau

HONG KONG DISNEYLAND AMUSEMENT PARK
Map p202 (香港迪士尼樂園; ☑183 0830;
http://park.hongkongdisneyland.com; adult/child
HK$450/320; ⊙10am-8pm Mon-Fri, to 9pm Sat
& Sun; ⊛; Ⓜ Disney Resort Station) Ever since
it claimed Hong Kong in 2005, Disneyland
has served as a rite of passage for the flocks
of Asian tourists who come daily to steal a
glimpse of one of America's most famous
cultural exports. It's divided into seven areas – Main Street USA, Tomorrowland, Fantasyland, Adventureland, Toy Story Land,
Mystic Point, and Grizzly Gulch – but it's
still quite tiny compared to the US version,
and most of the attractions are geared to
families with small children.

Most of the rides are appropriate for all
but the smallest kids. Highlights include
the goofy-scary tour through the Mystic
Manor, and classics like 'It's a Small World'
and the Mad Hatter teacups. Adrenalin
junkies have only a few true thrills – the
whipping-through-utter-darkness Space
Mountain roller coaster in Tomorrowland,
the Big Grizzly Mountain coaster in Grizzly
Gulch, and the stomach-dropping RC Racer
half-pipe coaster in Toy Story Land. The
Iron Man Experience 3D motion simulator
is slated to open in 2016.

While most of Hong Kong Disney is
essentially a scaled-down version of the
American Disneyland, there are a number
of nods to Chinese culture. Disney consulted a feng shui master when building the
park, and ended up moving the entrance
12 degrees to avoid *chi* slipping into the
ocean. The lucky number eight is repeated
throughout the park (the Western min-
ing town of Grizzly Gulch was said to be
founded on 8 August 1888), and Canto-pop
singer Jacky Cheung is the park's official
spokesperson.

The hungry will never be far from a
snack or a sit-down meal, whether Eastern
(dried squid, fish balls on a stick, dim sum)
or Western (burgers, cotton candy, muf-
fins). And you'll certainly never be far from
a souvenir shop.

There's a parade daily through Main
Street at 3.30pm, and a music, light and
fireworks show centred on Sleeping Beauty's Castle nightly at 8pm. As in any Disney
theme park, costumed characters wander around ready to be greeted by excited
children.

Disneyland is linked by rail with the
MTR at Sunny Bay station on the Tung
Chung line; passengers just cross the
platform to board the dedicated train
for Disneyland Resort station and the
theme park. Journey times from Central/
Kowloon/Tsing Yi stations are 24/21/10
minutes respectively.

TRAPPIST MONASTERY CHRISTIAN MONASTERY
Map p202 (熙篤會聖母神樂院; ☑2987 6292;
Tai Shui Hang; ⛴ kaido from Peng Chau or Discov-
ery Bay) Northeast of Mui Wo and south of
Discovery Bay is the Roman Catholic Lady

KAIDO SERVICES

Kaido are small ferries that serve more remote islands or destinations, with less frequent services than regular ferries and schedules that change from time to time. Check the website of the **Transport Department** (www.td.gov. hk) for the most up-to-date timetables before you set off.

of Joy Abbey, better known as the Trappist Monastery. The Trappists gained a reputation as one of the most austere religious communities in the Roman Catholic Church and the Lantau congregation was established at Peking in the 19th century. All of the monks here now are local Hong Kongers. Their medieval-style stone chapel is a peaceful spot for quiet contemplation.

The monastery is known throughout Hong Kong for its cream-rich milk, sold in half-pint bottles everywhere, but the cows have been moved to the New Territories and Trappist Dairy Milk is now produced in Yuen Long.

One of the nicest ways to visit the monastery is by hiking the three hours from Mui Wo to Discovery Bay – just follow the well-marked coastal trail at the northern end of Tung Wan Tau Rd. The monastery makes a good halfway stopping place. You can then have dinner at Discovery Bay and catch a ferry back to Central.

TUNG CHUNG HISTORIC SITE

(🚌3M from Mui Wo, 11 from Tai O, 23 from Ngong Ping, Ⓜ Tung Chung) Before 1994 Tung Chung, on Lantau's northern coast, was still an inaccessible farming village. Less than four years later, it was transformed into a new town and a new airport was added to nearby Chek Lap Kok. Today Tung Chung has the largest population on the island with a 760-hectare residential estate served by the MTR. Most people come here to shop at the Citygate Outlets, but there are some interesting historical sights in the vicinity too.

Annals record a settlement at Tung Chung as early as the Ming dynasty. There are several Buddhist establishments in the upper reaches of the valley, but the main attraction here is **Tung Chung Fort** (Map p202; Tung Chung Rd; admission free; ⏱10am-5pm Wed-Mon), which dates back to 1832, when

Chinese troops were garrisoned on Lantau. The Japanese briefly occupied the fort during WWII. Measuring 70m by 80m and enclosed by granite-block walls, it retains six of its muzzle-loading cannons pointing out to sea.

About 1km to the north are the ruins of **Tung Chung Battery** (Map p202), which is a much smaller fort built in 1817. All that remains is an L-shaped wall facing the sea, with a gun emplacement in the corner. The ruins were only discovered in 1980, having been hidden for about a century by scrub.

Facing Tung Chung Bay to the southwest in the village of Sha Tsui Tau is double-roofed **Hau Wong Temple** (侯王廟; Map p202), founded at the end of the Song dynasty. The temple contains a bell dating from 1765 and inscribed by the Qing-dynasty emperor Qian Long.

DISCOVERY BAY BEACH, GOLF

Map p202 (🚢 Discovery Bay) With a fine stretch of sandy beach ringed by luxurious condominiums, 'DB' is a dormitory suburb on Lantau's northeastern coast for professionals who commute to Central. There is no pressing need to visit except to ogle at residents in their converted golf carts, which cost HK$200,000 a pop, or perhaps to eat dinner and watch the nightly Disneyland fireworks, visible across the water.

There is a handful of decent restaurants in **Discovery Bay Plaza** (愉景灣廣場), just up from the ferry pier and the central plaza. The 27-hole Discovery Bay Golf Club (p212) is perched in the hills to the southwest.

Buses make the run to and from Tung Chung and the airport at Chek Lap Kok via the Discovery Bay Tunnel and the North Lantau Hwy. A trail leading from the golf course will take you down to Silvermine Bay and the rest of Lantau in a couple of hours.

◉ Mui Wo

MUI WO VILLAGE

Map p205 (🚢 Mui Wo) Mui Wo (Plum Nest) was Lantau's largest settlement before Tung Chung was born. These days, this sleepy town functions as a shopping, eating and transport hub for the island's south side. The big draw for visitors is Silvermine Bay beach (銀礦灣), a decent

Mui Wo

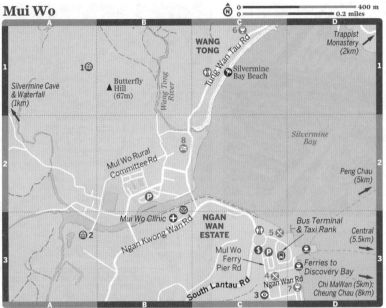

stretch of sand with toilets and changing facilities just east of town.

There are several decent places to stay and eat in Mui Wo. **Friendly Bicycle Shop** (老友記單車專門店; ☑2984 2278; 13 Mui Wo Ferry Pier Rd; ⊙10am-6pm Wed-Mon) near the Park 'n' Shop supermarket rents bikes.

SILVERMINE BAY BEACH   BEACH

(銀礦灣; 🚹; 🚇Mui Wo) Just east of Mui Wo town, Silvermine Bay beach is a popular spot for day trippers. The long, wide beach fringed by houses and a few small hotels is not the most pristine, but it's plenty nice for an afternoon of sun and surf. There are changing facilities and lifeguards, but only in season (April to October).

SILVERMINE WATERFALL   WATERFALL

Map p202 (🚇Mui Wo) If time allows, hike from Mui Wo town to Silvermine Waterfall (銀礦瀑布), near the old Silvermine Cave northwest of town (the cave was mined for silver in the 19th century but has now been sealed off). The waterfall is quite a spectacle when it gushes during the rainy season. The walk to the waterfall from Mui Wo is about 3km; head westward along Mui Wo Rural Committee Rd and then follow the marked path north.

WATCHTOWERS   HISTORIC BUILDING

(🚇Mui Wo) There are several old granite watchtowers in the viscinity of Mui Wo, including **Luk Tei Tong Watchtower** (鹿地塘更樓; Map p205) on the Silver River and **Butterfly Hill Watchtower** (蝴蝶山更樓; Map p205) further north. They were built in the late 19th century as safe houses and as coastal defences against pirates, and are now scenic ruins.

MARK SIMONS / GETTY IMAGES ©

藏行

1. Drying fish, Cheung Chau (p214)
Seafood restaurants and stalls serve fish along the Cheung Chau waterfront.

2. Po Lin Monastery (p195)
Through the moon gate is a huge Buddhist complex, built in 1924 and still expanding.

3. Tian Tan Buddha (p195)
Weighing 202 tonnes and reaching some 23m in height, the Tian Tan Buddha is the largest of its kind in the world.

4. Cheung Chau harbour (p213)
Waterfront restaurants offer seafood galore, as well as plenty of fishing-village atmosphere.

◉ South Lantau Road

PUI O
BEACH, VILLAGE

Map p202 (☐3M from Mui Wo) Along South Lantau Rd is a succession of beaches that attract surfers, beach-goers and retirees alike. Just 5km southwest of Mui Wo, Pui O has a decent beach, but as it's the closest one to Mui Wo it can get very crowded. The village has several restaurants, holiday flats galore and, in season, stalls renting bicycles.

CHEUNG SHA
BEACH

Map p202 (☐3M from Mui Wo) Cheung Sha (Long Sand), is Hong Kong's longest beach, stretching over 3km on the southern coast of Lantau. It's divided into 'upper' and 'lower' sections; a trail over a hillock links the two. Upper Cheung Sha, with occasional good surf, is the prettier and longer beach, and boasts changing facilities and a snack bar. Lower Cheung Sha has a beachfront restaurant and a water-sports centre. This is said to be the best windsurfing beach in Hong Kong, especially from November to March.

TONG FUK
BEACH

Map p202 (☐3M from Mui Wo) The beach at Tong Fuk is not Lantau's nicest, but the village has holiday flats, several shops and restaurants, and its distance from Mui Wo means it's usually quite peaceful. To the northwest is the not-so-scenic sprawl of Ma Po Ping Prison.

◉ Tai O

TAI O
VILLAGE

(☐1 from Mui Wo, 11 from Tung Chung, 21 from Ngong Ping) On weekends, droves of visitors trek to the far-flung west coast of Lantau to see a fascinating way of life. Here in Tai O, historical home to the Tanka boat people, life is all about the sea. Houses are built on stilts above the ocean, sampans ply the dark-green waterways, and elderly residents still dry seafood on traditional straw mats and make the village's celebrated shrimp paste.

Tai O is built partly on Lantau and partly on a tiny island about 15m from the shore. Until the mid-1990s the only way to cross was via a rope-tow ferry pulled by elderly Hakka women. That and the large number of sampans in the small harbour earned Tai O the nickname 'the Venice of Hong Kong'. Though the narrow iron Tai Chung footbridge now spans the canal, the rope-tow ferry is resurrected on some

---

THE PINK DOLPHINS OF THE PEARL RIVER

Between 100 and 200 misnamed Chinese white dolphins *(Sousa chinensis)* – they are actually bubble-gum pink – inhabit the coastal waters around Hong Kong, finding the brackish waters of the Pearl River estuary to be the perfect habitat. Unfortunately these glorious mammals, which are also called Indo-Pacific humpback dolphins, are being threatened by environmental pollution, and their numbers are dwindling.

The threat comes in many forms, but the most prevalent – and direct – dangers are sewage, chemicals, overfishing and boat traffic. Some 200,000 cu metres of untreated sewage is dumped into the western harbour every day, and high concentrations of chemicals such as DDT have been found in tissue samples taken from some of the dolphins. Several dolphins have been entangled in fishing nets and, despite the dolphins' skill at sensing and avoiding surface vessels, some have collided with boats. Pleasure boats buzzing around the Tai O area are a particular menace.

The dolphins' habitat has also been diminished by the destruction of the natural coastline of Lantau Island. The North Lantau Hwy consumed about 10km of the natural coastline. The Hong Kong Disneyland theme park required large amounts of reclamation in Penny's Bay.

Hong Kong Dolphinwatch (p320) was founded in 1995 to raise awareness of these wonderful creatures and promote responsible ecotourism. It offers 2½-hour cruises to see the pink dolphins in their natural habitat every Wednesday, Friday and Sunday year-round. Guides assemble in the lobby of the Kowloon Hotel Hong Kong in Tsim Sha Tsui at 9am for the bus to Tung Chung via the Tsing Ma Bridge, from where the boat departs; the tours return at 1pm.

weekends and holidays: drop HK$1 in the box as you disembark.

Some of the tiny, traditional-style village houses still stand in the centre, including some of Tai O's famed stilt houses on the waterfront. There are a few houses that escaped a fire in 2000, plus a number of shanties, their corrugated-iron walls held in place by rope, and houseboats that haven't set sail for years.

The main activity for visitors in Tai O is simply wandering the back alleys, photographing the stilt houses, strolling the long causeway, and buying seafood at the crowded street markets.

STILT HOUSES
HISTORIC BUILDING

Map p202 (🚌1 from Mui Wo, 11 from Tung Chung, 21 from Ngong Ping) Tai O's remaining stilt houses and the local **Kwan Tai Temple** (Map p202; 關帝廟), dedicated to the god of war, are on Kat Hing St. To reach them, cross the bridge from the mainland to the island, walk up Tai O Market St and go right at the Fook Moon Lam restaurant. There are a couple of other temples here too, including an 18th-century one erected in honour of Hung Shing, patron of fisherfolk; it's on Shek Tsai Po St, about 600m west of the Fook Moon Lam restaurant.

OLD TAI O POLICE STATION
HISTORIC BUILDING

Map p202 (舊大澳警署; Tai O Heritage Hotel; 📞2985 8383; www.taioheritagehotel.com; Shek Tsai Po St; ⊙tours 3pm & 4pm; 🚌1 from Mui Wo, 11 from Tung Chung, 21 from Ngong Ping) **FREE** At the end of Shek Tsai Po St stands the beautifully restored colonial-style Old Tai O Police Station. Built in 1902, the former marine police station was originally set up to protect the surrounding waters from pirate activity. In 2012, the restored building was reopened as the charming Tai O Heritage Hotel. Even if you aren't staying here, it's worth joining the free guided tour; online reservation is a must.

EATING

Lantau might not be able to compete with Lamma or Cheung Chau in the cuisine stakes, but there are enough decent eateries to soothe your belly. Tung Chung and Mui Wo have the island's largest concentration of restaurants, while Discovery Bay has its own line-up of dining venues around Discovery Bay Plaza. There are also some good choices further afield in Ngong Ping Plateau and Tai O, as well as the villages scattered along South Lantau Rd.

⭐MAVERICKS
BURGERS, INTERNATIONAL $

Map p202 (📞5402 4154; Pui O beach; meals from HK$100; ⊙5.30-11.30pm Fri, 11.30am-11.30pm Sat & Sun; 🚌1 from Mui Wo) 🍴 Sunburned beach-goers gather for house-made sausages and burgers on artisan buns at this hip new surf-themed weekend spot, right on the water in Pui O. Many of the vegies are grown on the restaurant's own farm, the meat and dairy used are hormone-free, and menus are printed on recycled bamboo paper. Wash your meal down with a locally brewed Young Master Ale.

SOLO
CAFE $

Map p202 (📞9153 7453; 86 Kat Hing St, Tai O; meals from HK$40; ⊙11am-6pm Mon-Sat; 🚌1 from Mui Wo) Framed by a backdrop of stilt houses and lush mountains, this sunny terrace right on the water invites lazy afternoons spent enjoying coffee. The tiramisu and the apple crumble with ice cream are as tempting as its fresh roasted coffee.

BAHÇE
TURKISH $

Map p205 (📞2984 0222; Shop 19, Ground fl, Mui Wo Centre, 3 Ngan Wan Rd, Mui Wo; mains from HK$95; ⊙11am-10.30pm Mon-Fri, 9.30am-10.30pm Sat & Sun; 🚢Mui Wo) Near the ferry pier is this small, busy place where many locals and expats alike opt for its outdoor tables in the warmer months. Chow down on heaping plates of savoury lamb, falafel, hummus, *fattoush* (a pitta bread and vegetable salad) and more before hitting the beaches or taking the ferry back to Central.

GALLERY
INTERNATIONAL, PIZZERIA $

Map p202 (📞2980 2582; 26 Tong Fuk Village; meals from HK$80; ⊙6pm-1am Mon-Sat, noon-1am Sun; 🚌3M from Mui Wo) This laid-back alfresco spot in the poky little village of Tong Fuk has some of Hong Kong's better steaks, at way-better-than-Central prices. Ideal for a post-hike feast. Pizzas get high marks as well.

MUI WO COOKED FOOD CENTRE
CANTONESE, SEAFOOD $

Map p205 (next to ferry pier, Mui Wo; meals from HK$50; ⊙6am-2am, individual restaurants may have different hours; 🚢Mui Wo) Next to the Mui Wo ferry pier, this smallish cooked-food centre has a handful of seafood restaurants with tables overlooking the water. **Wah Kee** is the pick for Cantonese-style seafood, while **K's British** does a shockingly authentic fish 'n' chips and steak pie.

TAI O LOOKOUT   FUSION $$
Map p202 (📞2985 8383; www.taioheritagehotel.com; Tai O Heritage Hotel, Shek Tsai Po St, Tai O; dishes from HK$100; ⏰7.30am-10pm; 🚌1 from Mui Wo, 11 from Tung Chung, 21 from Ngong Ping) The rotating ceiling fans, wooden booths and tiled floor of this rooftop glasshouse restaurant ooze old-world charm, and no one would blame you if you came to just sip coffee and chill. But the food – fried rice tossed with Tai O's famous shrimp paste, cheesecake with local mountain begonia – is well rated too.

STOEP RESTAURANT   MEDITERRANEAN $$
Map p202 (📞2980 2699; http://thestoep.com; 32 Lower Cheung Sha Village; meals from HK$85; ⏰11am-10pm Tue-Sun; 🚌1 from Mui Wo) This Mediterranean-style restaurant with a huge terrace on Lower Cheung Sha beach has decent meat and fish dishes and a South African *braai* (barbecue). Be sure to book on the weekend.

🍷 DRINKING & NIGHTLIFE

CHINA BEACH CLUB   BAR
Map p205 (📞2983 8931; 18 Tung Wan Tau Rd; ⏰noon-11pm Fri-Sun; 🚢Mui Wo) This cheerful restaurant has an airy rooftop and balcony overlooking Silvermine Bay beach for those who want to chill over their home-style Greek moussaka or just kick back with a cocktail or beer. The two-for-one cocktail 'hour' can go on well into the night.

CHINA BEAR   PUB
Map p205 (📞2984 9720; Ground fl, Mui Wo Centre, Ngan Wan Rd; ⏰10am-2am, happy hour 5-9pm Mon-Fri, 5-8pm Sat & Sun; 🚢Mui Wo) The most popular expat pub-restaurant in Mui Wo, China Bear boasts a wonderful open bar facing the water. It's right by the ferry terminal, making it the perfect spot for your first and last beer in Mui Wo, and perhaps also for those in-between.

🏃 SPORTS & ACTIVITIES

LANTAU PEAK   HIKING
Map p202 (Fung Wong Shan) Known as Fung Wong Shan (Phoenix Mountain) in Cantonese, this 934m-high peak is the second-highest in Hong Kong after Tai Mo Shan (957m) in the New Territories. The view from the summit is absolutely stunning, and on a clear day it's possible to see Macau 65km to the west. Watching the sun rise from the peak is a popular choice among hardy hikers. Some choose to stay at the Ngong Ping SG Davis Hostel (p212) and leave around 4am for the two-hour summit push.

If you're hiking Lantau Peak as a day trip, take the MTR to Tung Chung, then take bus 3M to Pak Kung Au (tell the driver where you're getting off beforehand). From here, you'll follow the markers for section 3 of the Lantau Trail, ascending the peak then descending the steps into Ngong Ping. This 4.5km route takes about three hours.

SUNSET PEAK   HIKING
Map p202 (Tai Tung Shan) Hong Kong's third highest peak (869m) is a good sweaty climb with lovely panoramic views of the surrounding mountains. Plan for three hours. The ambitious can combine it with Lantau Peak (this is popularly known as the 'two peak challenge'). Check out the creepy 'ghost houses' near the peak – ruins of British holiday bungalows from colonial days.

To get to the start, take the ferry to Mui Wo and bus 1 towards Pui O. Get off the bus just before the top of the hill where there's a fenced trailhead and noticeboard with the Lantau Trail map. This section ends at Pak Kung Au, where the Lantau Peak section begins. From here catch a bus back to Mui Wo, or on to Tung Chung and the MTR.

SHEK PIK RESERVOIR TO TAI O   HIKING
Sections 8 and 7 (in that order) of the Lantau Trail are a long but relatively flat walk along the Lantau's southwestern hillsides and down into Tai O fishing village. You'll pass a postcard-pretty beach and, with a quick 30-minute detour, the ruins of Fan Lau Fort and a Tin Hau temple. If you time it right, you can have a sunset seafood feast in Tai O before catching the bus back to Tung Chung. Plan for five hours.

To get to the trailhead, take the ferry to Mui Wo and then catch a Tai O–bound bus.

PENG CHAU

Backwater Peng Chau does not possess much wow factor but it is perhaps the most traditionally Chinese of the Outlying Islands, with narrow alleyways, crowded housing, a covered wet **market** (坪洲街市) near the ferry pier, a couple of small but important temples, and interesting shops selling everything from humble household goods to religious paraphernalia. Come any day and you can count on the clatter of mah-jong tiles and Cantonese opera tunes leaking from old transistors to act as a soundtrack to this sleepy getaway.

Ferry services from Central leave from Pier 6 of the Outlying Islands ferry terminal. Ferries also depart from Mui Wo and Chi Ma Wan on Lantau and from Cheung Chau. Additionally, regular *kaido* (small open-sea ferries) operate to Peng Chau from the Trappist Monastery and Discovery Bay on Lantau.

There are no cars on Peng Chau, and you can walk around it easily in an hour. Here are a few activities for a perfect day trip:

Finger Hill Climbing the steps to Finger Hill (95m), the island's highest point, offers some light exercise and excellent views. To get here from the ferry pier, walk up Lo Peng St, turn right at the Tin Hau temple (天后廟), containing a century-old 2.5m-long whale bone blackened by incense smoke, and walk south along Wing On St. This gives way to Shing Ka Rd, and Nam Shan Rd leads from here east up to Finger Hill. It's an easy half-hour walk.

Peng Chau Heritage Trail (www.greenpengchau.org.hk) Follow the signs around Peng Chau to see the ghostly remains of the island's past life as an industrial hub. Though it may seem hard to believe, this was once one of Hong Kong's major industrial centres, with a large match factory and a lime kiln. All that remains today is picturesque ruins. Don't miss the cool octagonal well just off the town square.

Tung Wan The water at otherwise-pleasant Tung Wan beach, a five-minute walk from the ferry pier, is too dirty for swimming and is not served by lifeguards, but it's a great place to watch the sun set.

Les Copains d'Abord (☑9432 5070; Lo Peng St; cheese & meat plates from HK$80; ☷11am-9pm) Don't dare leave Peng Chau without sipping a glass of *vin rouge* and nibbling a plate of charcuterie under parasols at Les Copains d'Abord, an incongruously located French-owned wine bar and cafe. Opening hours can be erratic. Don't be surprised if it's closed for a neighbourhood party; it's that kind of place. You'll find it on the island's main square straight up from the pier.

Get off the bus just after Shek Pik Reservoir on your right.

FAN LAU   HIKING

Only accessible on foot, Fan Lau (Divided Flow), a small peninsula on the southwestern tip of Lantau, has a couple of good beaches and the remains of **Fan Lau Fort**, built in 1729 to protect the channel between Lantau and the Pearl River estuary from pirates. It remained in operation until the end of the 19th century and was restored in 1985. The sea views from here are sterling.

To the southeast of the fort is an **ancient stone circle**. The origins and age of the circle are uncertain, but it probably dates from the neolithic or early Bronze Age and may have been used in rituals.

To get here from Tai O, walk south from the bus station for 250m and pick up section 7 of the coastal Lantau Trail, a distance of about 8km. The trail then carries on to the northeast and Shek Pik for another 12km, where you can catch bus 1 back to Mui Wo.

BOAT TOURS   BOAT TOUR

(Tai O; ☐1 from Mui Wo, 11 from Tung Chung, 21 from Ngong Ping) As soon as you step off the bus in Tai O you'll be greeted by elderly women offering 'dolphin tours'. While you're unlikely to spot one of the increasingly rare pink dolphins, this can be a nice chance to take a spin around the village waterways. Always agree on a price beforehand – expect to pay about HK$20 per person for a 20-minute trip.

LONG COAST SEASPORTS
WINDSURFING, KAYAKING

Map p202 (☏8104 6222; www.longcoast.hk; 29 Lower Cheung Sha Village; ☺10am-sunset Mon-Fri, 9am-sunset Sat & Sun) If sun, surf and sand are what you're after, then you need look no further. This water-sports centre has its own lodge and campground and offers windsurfing, sea kayaking and wakeboarding. Day-long windsurfing lessons are HK$1400, while a single kayak rents for HK$70/210 for an hour/half-day.

HONG KONG SHAOLIN WUSHU CULTURE CENTRE
MARTIAL ARTS

Map p202 (香港少林武術文化中心; ☏2985 8898; http://shaolincc.org.hk; Shek Tsai Po St, Tai O; courses from HK$650) Located outside the centre of Tai O is this low-key martial arts school, one of the few in Hong Kong that runs intensive short courses for curious first-timers. However, classes are offered on an irregular basis, so check the website. On-site accommodation is available. It's next to the Hung Shing Temple.

DISCOVERY BAY GOLF CLUB
GOLF

Map p202 (愉景灣高爾夫球會; ☏2987 7273; www.dbgc.hk; Valley Rd, Discovery Bay; green fees weekday/weekend HK$2000/3100; ☻Discovery Bay) Perched high on a hill, this 27-hole course has impressive views of the Outlying Islands. Nonmembers can only book two days in advance.

🛏 SLEEPING

You can rent holiday flats from kiosks set up at the Mui Wo ferry pier. Expect to pay HK$250 on weekdays and HK$350 on the weekend for a double room or studio. Not all the places are within walking distance of the pier. Needless to say, the airport has plenty of hotels geared towards tourists.

PALM BEACH
CAMPGROUND $

Map p202 (☏2980 4822; www.palmbeach.com. hk; Cheung Sha; 4-person tepee Mon-Thu/Fri-Sun HK$620/$950, 6-person safari bush camper HK$980/1350; ☐3M from Mui Wo) Never mind the incongruity of sleeping in a Native American–style tepee on a Hong Kong beach. These cosy, family-size tepees, complete with sleeping bags, are ideal for those who want to camp, but don't fancy roughing it too much. Go even more upscale with a canvas 'safari bush camper' permanent tent, which comes

with air beds and camping tables. If you've got a group, the largest teepee sleeps 20! Palm Beach also offers water sports and other activities.

NGONG PING SG DAVIS HOSTEL
HOSTEL $

Map p202 (☏2985 5610; www.yha.org.hk; Ngong Ping; dm members under/over 18yr HK$60/85, nonmembers HK$95/120; ☐2 from Mui Wo, 23 from Tung Chung) Near the Tian Tan Buddha statue, this is an ideal place to stay if you want to watch the sunrise at Lantau Peak. The hostel is only open to HKYHA/HI cardholders or the guests of a cardholder.

From the Ngong Ping bus terminus, take the paved path to your left as you face the Tian Tan Buddha, pass the public toilets on your right and follow the signs.

★ TAI O HERITAGE HOTEL
BOUTIQUE HOTEL $$

Map p202 (大澳文物酒店; www.taioheritageho-tel.com; Shek Tsai Po St, Tai O; r HK$1900-2500; @🛜🌀; ☐1 from Mui Wo, 11 from Tung Chung, 21 from Ngong Ping) Housed in a century-old former police station, this is Lantau's newest hotel. All nine rooms are handsomely furnished in a contemporary style, offering top-of-the-line comfort. Our favourite is the inspector-office-turned–Sea Tiger Room, the smallest digs (24 sq metres) but with picture windows ushering in the sea breeze.

ESPACE ELASTIQUE
B&B $$

Map p202 (歸田園居; ☏2985 7002; www.espace elastique.com.hk; 57 Kat Hing St, Tai O; r Sun-Thu HK$500-1400, Fri & Sat HK$540-1700; @🛜🌀; ☐1 from Mui Wo, 11 from Tung Chung, 21 from Ngong Ping) This cosy four-room B&B is one of the best-kept gems on Lantau. All rooms are tastefully decorated; the 2nd-floor double room with a balcony overlooking the main Tai O waterway gets booked up quickly. The friendly owner Veronica provides multilingual travel advice, plus a hearty breakfast in the cafe. The jacuzzi on the rooftop is a delight.

SILVERMINE BEACH RESORT
HOTEL $$

Map p205 (銀鑛灣渡假酒店; ☏6810 0111; www. silvermineresort.com; Silvermine Bay beach, Mui Wo; r HK$1480-1980; 🛜🌀; ☻Mui Wo) This 128-room hotel has rooms that look out to the hills, sideways to the bay and directly onto the bay. It's nothing special, but it's the most convenient spot for a quick Lantau beach getaway. Eschew the rooms in the south wing for those in the superior north wing. Rates are negotiable.

PO TOI

A solid favourite of weekend holidaymakers with their own seagoing transport, Po Toi is the largest of a group of five islands – one is little more than a huge rock. Hong Kong's territorial border lies just 2km to the south. Visitors frequent the seafood restaurants beyond the jetty at **Tai Wan**, the main settlement, in the island's southwest.

There's some decent walking on Po Toi, a tiny **Tin Hau temple** across the bay from the pier, and, on the southern coast, rock formations that (supposedly) look like a palm tree, a tortoise and a monk, and some mysterious **rock carvings** resembling stylised animals and fish. You can see everything here in an hour.

Kaido run to the ferry pier from Aberdeen and Stanley on Tuesdays, Thursdays, weekends and public holidays.

Ming Kee Seafood Restaurant (明記海鮮酒家; ☑2849 7038; ⊙11am-11pm) is one of a handful of restaurants in the main village of Po Toi, and is by far the most popular with day trippers. Make sure you book ahead on the weekend.

Cheung Chau

Explore

This small, dumb-bell-shaped island is a popular getaway thanks to its beaches and its cute downtown lined with snack shops and incense-smokey temples. Come here for an afternoon of temple touring, noshing on fish balls and exploring the rocky coastline. Or stay for a weekend at one of the many holiday rentals and treat yourself to a day of windsurfing lessons followed by an alfresco seafood dinner at one of several harbourside restaurants.

The Best...

➡**Place to eat** Kam Wing Tai Fish Ball Shop (p214)
➡**Place to drink** Hing Kee Beach Bar (p216)
➡**Activity** Cheung Chau Windsurfing Centre (p216)

Top Tip

During the Bun Festival, it's wise to take a ferry to Mui Wo, and then take the inter-island ferry to Cheung Chau to avoid the long wait on Central ferry pier.

Getting There & Away

➡**Ferry** Services from Central leave from Pier 5 of the Outlying Islands ferry terminal (regular/fast 45 minutes/one hour). Ferries can also be taken from Mui Wo and Chi Ma Wan on Lantau and from Peng Chau. Additionally, regular *kaido* operate between Cheung Chau village (sampan pier) and Sai Wan in the south of the island.

Need to Know

➡**Area code** ☑852
➡**Location** Cheung Chau is just off the southeast coast of Lantau Island.
➡**Last ferry to Central** 11.45pm Monday to Saturday, 11.30pm Sunday and public holidays

⊙ SIGHTS

There are temples galore on Cheung Chau, including four dedicated to Tin Hau, empress of heaven and patroness of seafarers. Strolling along the coastline paths will take you past numerous craggy vistas and the occasional hidden cave. But the main draws on Cheung Chau are the pleasant, though sometimes crowded, beaches. The island is also a popular spot for Hong Kong windsurfers.

PAK TAI TEMPLE TEMPLE
(北帝廟; ☑2981 0663; ⊙7am-5pm; ⊛Cheung Chau) This colourfully restored temple from 1783 is the epicentre of the annual Cheung Chau Bun Festival in late April or early May. The most important and oldest temple on the island, it is dedicated to the Taoist deity Pak Tai, the 'Supreme Emperor of the Dark Heaven', military protector of the state, guardian of peace and order, and protector of fisherfolk.

Legend tells that early settlers from Canton province brought an image of Pak Tai with them to Cheung Chau and, when the statue was carried through the village, Cheung Chau was spared the plague that had decimated the populations of nearby islands. A temple dedicated to the saviour was built six years later.

CHEUNG CHAU VILLAGE   VILLAGE

(🚢Cheung Chau) The island's main settlement lies along the narrow strip of land connecting the headlands to the north and the south. The waterfront is a bustling place and the maze of streets and alleyways that make up the village are filled with old Chinese-style houses and tumbledown shops selling everything from plastic buckets to hell money and other combustible grave offerings. The streets close to the waterfront are pungent with the smell of incense and fish hung out to dry in the sun.

CHEUNG PO TSAI CAVE   CAVE

(張保仔洞; 🚢Cheung Chau) This 'cave' – in truth not much more than a hole in some rocks – on the southwestern peninsula of the island is said to have been the favourite hideout of the notorious pirate Cheung Po Tsai, who once commanded a flotilla of 600 junks and had a private army of 4000 men. Cheung Po Tsai surrendered to the Qing government in 1810 and became an official himself, but his treasure is said to remain hidden here.

It's a 2km walk from Cheung Chau village along Sai Wan Rd, or take a *kaido* (adult/child from HK$3/2) from the cargo ferry pier to the pier at Sai Wan. From here the walk is less than 200m (uphill).

TUNG WAN   BEACH

Tung Wan beach, east of the ferry pier, is not Cheung Chau's prettiest beach but it's the longest and most popular. The far southern end of Tung Wan is a great area for windsurfing. There are plenty of facilities here, as well as lifeguard stations overlooking the roped-off swimming area.

KWUN YAM WAN   BEACH

East of the ferry pier and just south of Tung Wan beach is Kwun Yam Wan, a quieter spot popular with windsurfers. At the southeastern end of Kwun Yam Wan a footpath leads uphill past a **Kwun Yum Temple** (觀音廟), which is dedicated to the goddess of mercy.

Continue up the footpath and look for the sign to the Fa Peng Knoll. From the knoll you can walk down to signposted Don Bosco Rd; it leads due south to rocky **Nam Tam Wan** (aka 'Morning Beach'), where swimming is possible.

PAK TSO WAN   BEACH

(Italian Beach) Peak Rd is the main route to the island's **cemetery** in the southwestern part of the island; you'll pass several pavilions along the way built for coffin bearers making the hilly climb. Once at the cemetery it's worth dropping down to Pak Tso Wan (known by local Westerners as 'Italian Beach'), a sandy, isolated spot that is good for swimming.

✗ EATING

There are seafood restaurants galore on Pak She Praya Rd. Alternatively, around the south of the pier and at the start of Tai Hing Tai Rd, you can pick your fish or other seafood from the food stalls with fish tanks, and then pay the stallholders to cook them the way you like. To get off the well-trodden waterfront, we recommend the following places.

KAM WING TAI FISH BALL SHOP   CHINESE $

(甘永泰魚蛋; ☏2981 3050; 106 San Hing St; balls HK$10-15; ⊙10am-8pm; 🚢Chueng Chau) The long line snaking along the alley should tell you something about this celebrated pit stop. Hakka-style snack balls of minced fish and meat are served piping hot. A stick of chewy assorted balls is highly recommended.

HOMETOWN TEAHOUSE   JAPANESE $

(故鄉茶寮; ☏2981 5038; 12 Tung Wan Rd; sushi from HK$16; ⊙11.30am-9pm; 🚢Cheung Chau) Run by an amiable Japanese couple, this tiny backstreet eatery is positively flooded with both locals and tourists who come for its sushi and red-bean pastries, served through a walk-up window.

KWOK KAM KEE CAKE SHOP   BAKERY $

(郭錦記餅店; ☏2986 9717; 46 Pak She St; buns from HK$4; ⊙6am-7pm; 🚢Cheung Chau) Not far

Cheung Chau

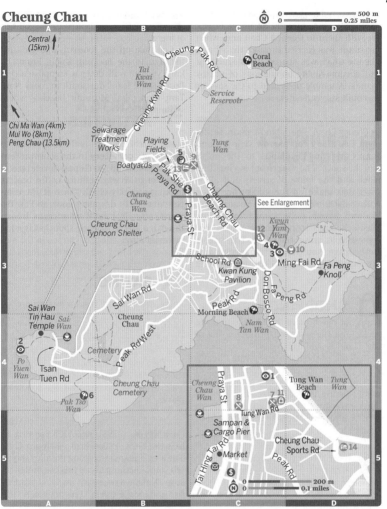

Cheung Chau

from Pak Tai Temple, this 40-year-old bakery supplies *ping on bao* (peace and prosperity buns), the round white buns with a lucky red stamp, for the Bun Festival. You can get the fresh-from-the-steamer buns, traditionally filled with sesame paste, lotus-seed paste or red-bean paste, at 2pm every day. No English sign – look for the line.

🍷 DRINKING & NIGHTLIFE

HING KEE BEACH BAR   BAR

(興記士多; ☎2981 3478; Kwun Yam Wan beach; ⊙10am-8pm; 🚢Cheung Chau) This hole-in-the-wall drinking spot at quiet Kwun Yam Wan beach is a store and bar combo, and a popular hang-out for villagers and those in the know. Auntie Hing (the owner) does good grub with her home-grown herbs.

🛍️ SHOPPING

MYARTS   ACCESSORIES, CRAFT

(☎2332 9985; 3 Tung Wan Rd; ⊙11am-7pm Wed-Mon; 🚢Cheung Chau) Of the many craft boutiques in Cheung Chau village, this hip little spot stands out for its made-in–Hong Kong

jewellery and accessories with fun local themes. Look out for earrings shaped like Hong Kong egg tarts, handmade ukuleles painted with dragons and koi by an expat artisan, and arty hand-drawn postcards.

🏃 SPORTS & ACTIVITIES

SAMPAN RIDES   BOAT TOUR

(🚢Cheung Chau) A great way to see the harbour and soak up the fishing-village atmosphere is to charter a sampan for half an hour (expect to pay HK$70 to HK$120 depending on the day, the season and the demand). Most sampans congregate around the cargo pier in Cheung Chau village, but virtually any small boat you see in the harbour can be hired as a water taxi. Just wave and two or three will come forward. Be sure to agree on the fare first.

CHEUNG CHAU WINDSURFING CENTRE   WINDSURFING

(☎2981 8316; http://ccwindc.com.hk; Kwun Yam Wan beach; ⊙10am-6pm) Windsurfing has always been a popular pastime on Cheung Chau, and Hong Kong's only Olympic gold medallist to date, Lee Lai-shan, who took

---

CHEUNG CHAU'S BUN FESTIVAL

Cheung Chau's annual **Bun Festival** (www.cheungchau.org) honours the Taoist god Pak Tai and is one of Asia's most unique celebrations. It takes place over four days in late April or early May, traditionally starting on the sixth day of the fourth moon. During the festival, the island is packed with tourists and locals cramming buns into their mouths, listening to drummers and offering incense at the temples.

The festival is best known for its bun towers: bamboo scaffolding up to 20m high covered with sacred rolls. If you visit Cheung Chau a week or so before the festival, you'll see the towers being built in front of Pak Tai Temple.

At midnight on the designated day, hundreds of people clamber up the towers to snatch the buns for good luck. The higher the bun, the greater the luck, so everyone tries to reach the top. In 1978 a tower collapsed under the weight of the climbers, injuring two dozen people. The race didn't take place again for over two decades until it was revived – with strict safety controls – in 2005.

The third day of the festival features a procession of floats, stilt walkers and people dressed as characters from Chinese legends and opera. Most interesting are the colourfully dressed 'floating children' who are carried through the streets on long poles, cleverly wired to metal supports hidden under their clothing. The supports include footrests and a padded seat.

Offerings are made to the spirits of all the fish and livestock killed and consumed over the previous year. During the four-day festival, the whole island goes vegetarian.

TUNG LUNG CHAU
....

Left alone at the eastern entrance to Victoria Harbour, uninhabited 'East Dragon Island' is Hong Kong's premier spot for rock climbing and stargazing.

Tung Lung Fort (東龍洲炮台; 🚇Tung Lung Chau), on the northeastern corner of the island, is evidence that the island was once considered strategic enough for protection. Built in the late 17th or early 18th century, it was attacked a number of times by pirate bands before being abandoned in 1810. The fort once consisted of 15 guardhouses and was armed with eight cannons, but little of it remains today except for the outline of the exterior walls. There's an **information centre** (⊙9am-4pm Wed-Mon) with pictures illustrating the history of the fort.

On the northern coast of the island is one of the earliest and largest in-situ **rock carvings** in the territory. The tortuous lines of the dragon-shaped carving (which measure 2.4m by 1.8m) are still clearly visible, and the walk down to the cliff is a leisurely one.

There are a couple of stores on the way to the fort that sell sandwiches, instant noodles and herbal tea on the weekends. You can pitch your tent in the campground below the fort or in the area near the lighthouse (access via the Holiday Store), which overlooks the stunning South China Sea. Camping facilities are primitive though.

Kaido run from Sai Wan Ho on Hong Kong Island via Joss House Bay on the Clearwater Bay Peninsula in the New Territories. There is a single sailing each way on Thursdays (round trip HK$40), with more regular services only on weekends and public holidays. A weekend and holiday service also operates from Sam Ka Tsuen near Yau Tong MTR.

the top prize in windsurfing at the 1996 Atlanta Olympics, grew up here. At the northern end of Kwun Yam Wan, Lee's uncle runs the Cheung Chau Windsurfing Centre, where you can try out the sport for yourself (day-long beginner classes HK$1100; sign up a week ahead). Windsurfers, kayaks and stand-up paddleboards are available for rental as well.

🛏 SLEEPING

Depending on the day of the week and the season, half a dozen kiosks opposite the ferry pier rent studios and apartments.

CHEUNG CHAU B&B   B&B $
(📞2986 9990; www.bbcheungchau.com.hk; 12-14 Tung Wan Rd, 2 Pak She Rd; r Sun-Thu

from HK$620, Fri/Sat from HK$750/950; 🖥; 🚇Cheung Chau) An alternative to the island's only hotel and the rooms offered by kiosks, this B&B (more like a small hotel) has two locations in the village. Some of the brightly painted rooms are quite compact, so look before you commit to make sure you don't get a tiny one.

WARWICK HOTEL   HOTEL $$
(📞2981 0081; www.warwickhotel.com.hk; Cheung Chau Sports Rd, Tung Wan beach; r/ste Mon-Fri HK$1160/2040, Sat & Sun HK$1580/2420; 🚇Cheung Chau) This 71-room concrete carbuncle on the butt of Tung Wan beach is the only game in town, but it does offer wonderful views across to Lamma and Hong Kong Island. Heavy discounts are available, so call to check.

Macau

Macau Peninsula p220

Lying 65km to the west of Hong Kong, Macau is a city of duality. Its fortresses, churches and the culinary traditions of its former Portuguese colonial masters speak to a uniquely Mediterranean style on the China coast. These are intermixed with the customs, alleys, temples and shrines of its Chinese heritage. On the other hand, the Special Administrative Region (SAR) of Macau is the 'Vegas of the East', the only place in China where gambling is legal.

The Islands: Taipa & Coloane p241

Taipa was once two islands that were slowly joined together by silt from the Pearl River. A similar physical joining has happened to Taipa and Coloane because of land reclamation from the sea. The new strip of land joining the two islands is known as Cotai (from Co-loane and Tai-pa). Taipa has rapidly urbanised and it's hard to imagine that just a few decades ago it was an island of duck farms and boat yards. The small island of Coloane was a haven for pirates until 1910. Today it retains Macau's old way of life, though luxurious villas are finding their way onto the island.

 TOP SIGHT
RUINS OF THE CHURCH OF ST PAUL

Also known as 'the Gate to Nowhere', the ruins of the Church of St Paul are the most treasured icon in Macau. Once a Jesuit church in the early 17th century, all that remains of it now are the facade and the stairway. However, with its statues, portals and engravings that effectively make up a sermon in stone, it's one of the greatest monuments to Christianity in Asia.

The church was designed by an Italian Jesuit and built in 1602 by Japanese Christian exiles and Chinese craftsmen. After the expulsion of the Jesuits, a military battalion was stationed here. In 1835 a fire erupted in the kitchen of the barracks, destroying everything, except what you see today.

The facade has five tiers. At the top is a dove, representing the Holy Spirit, surrounded by stone carvings of the sun, moon and stars. Beneath that is a statue of the infant Jesus accompanied by the implements of the Crucifixion. In the centre of the third tier stands the Virgin Mary being assumed bodily into heaven along with angels and two flowers: the peony, representing China, and the chrysanthemum, a symbol of Japan. Just below the pediment, on the right side of the facade, is a dragon surmounted by the Holy Virgin. To the right of the Virgin is a carving of the tree of life and the apocalyptic woman (Mary) slaying a seven-headed hydra; the Japanese *kanji* next to her reads: 'The holy mother tramples the heads of the dragon'.

The facade is approached by six flights of 11 stairs each, with an attractive balustrade running up each side.

The small **Museum of Sacred Art & Crypt** (天主教藝術博物館和墓室, Museu de Arte Sacra e Cripta; Map p226; Rua de São Paulo; ⊙9am-6pm; ☑8A, 17, 26, disembark at Luís de Camões Garden) **FREE** contains carved wooden statues, silver chalices and oil paintings, as well as the remains of Vietnamese and Japanese Christians martyred in the 17th century.

DON'T MISS

➡ Facade details
➡ The stairway
➡ Museum of Sacred Art
➡ Crypt & ossuary

PRACTICALITIES

➡ 大三巴牌坊, Ruinas de Igreja de São Paulo
➡ Map p226
➡ Travessa de São Paulo
➡ admission free
➡ ☑8A, 17, 26, disembark at Luís de Camões Garden

Macau Peninsula

Explore

Take bus 3 from the Macau–Hong Kong Ferry Terminal to Largo do Senado (Macau's main square) and visit the Church of St Dominic, Lou Kau Mansion and other sights around the square. Wander up to the Ruins of the Church of St Paul, then Monte Fort and the Macau Museum above it; allow two hours for these three sights. Before leaving this area, check out Nga Tcha Temple and browse for souvenirs at the shops near the steps. Wander southwest through the tiny streets towards the Inner Harbour, stopping at the Mandarin's House and St Joseph's Seminary & Church. After lunch head over to the A-Ma Temple and the Moorish Barracks for a look, before cabbing it north to the lovely St Lazarus quarter for more history and culture.

The Best...

➡ **Sight** Ruins of the Church of St Paul (p219)

➡ **Place to eat** Clube Militar de Macau (p237)

➡ **Place to drink** Macau Soul (p239)

Top Tip

All the big-name casinos have free shuttle services to and from the ferry terminals, the border gate and the airport. Anyone can use these buses – no questions asked. You'll see them outside the ferry terminals and the casinos. Ask for a timetable at the casinos.

Getting There & Away

➡ **Air** For airline details, check the website of **Macau International Airport** (☑2886 1111; www.macau-airport.com) on Taipa. **Sky Shuttle** (☑in Hong Kong 2108 9898; www.skyshuttlehk.com) runs a 15-minute helicopter shuttle between Macau and Hong Kong (HK$4100, every 30 minutes from 9am to 11pm).

➡ **Boat to China** Frequent ferries operated by the **Yuet Tung Shipping Co** (Map p226; ☑2877 4478; www.ytmacau.com/index.php) run to Wānzǎi in Zhuhai (MOP$129, 15 minutes) from 8am to 4.15pm departing Macau Inner Harbour (pier 11A), just off Rua das Lorchas. Check its website for the less frequent ferries from Taipa Ferry Terminal to Shékǒu and the airport in Shēnzhèn.

➡ **Sampans & ferries** These boats (MOP$12.50, MOP$20 departure tax, hourly 8am to 4pm) run to Wānzǎi from a small pier near where Rua das Lorchas meets Rua do Dr Lourenço Pereira Marques.

TEMPLES FOR LESSER-KNOWN DEITIES

Macau has a few interesting temples dedicated to important but less-worshipped gods.

Na Tcha Temple (哪吒廟; Map p226; 6 Calçada de Sao Paulo; ⊗8am-5pm; 🚍3, 4, 6A, 8A, 18A, 19) There's no better symbol of Macau's cultural diversity than Na Tcha Temple sitting quietly beside a major Christian monument – the Ruins of the Church of St Paul. Built around 1888, it was dedicated to the child god of war to halt the plague occurring at that time. The wall outside, often said to be a section of Macau's old city walls, in fact belonged to the former St Paul's College located at the ruins.

Nu Wa Temple (女媧廟; Map p226; cnr Rua das Estalagens & Travessa dos Algibebes; ⊗9am-5pm; 🚍3, 6, 26A) This tiny temple in a faded yellow building, also built in 1888, was consecrated to the serpent-like Nu Wa – the Chinese equivalent of Gaia, the creator goddess. Unlike most other divinities worshipped in Macau, Nu Wa does not offer services associated with the sea. Instead, she gives divine assistance to marital and fertility matters. Her likeness sits among those of other deities in the cluttered and smoky temple.

Hong Kung Temple (康公廟; Map p226; cnr Rua das Estalagens & Rua de Cinco de Outubro; ⊗8am-6pm; 🚍3, 6, 26A) This peaceful, 200-year-old temple is dedicated to Li Lie, a Han-dynasty general. The boat-shaped sculpture in the main hall is used to offer wine to the deities during religious festivities.

➡**Boat to Hong Kong** TurboJet (www. turbojet.com.hk) has the most sailings. The one-hour trip departs most from the Hong Kong–Macau Ferry Terminal and Macau Maritime Ferry Terminal; see TurboJet's website for services to Hong Kong International Airport. CotaiJet (www.cotaijet.com.mo) departs every half-hour from 7.30am to midnight, and runs between the Taipa Temporary Ferry Terminal and Hong Kong–Macau Ferry Terminal; a feeder shuttle-bus service drops off at destinations along the Cotai Strip. Check CotaiJet's website for services to Hong Kong International Airport.

Need to Know

➡**Area code** ☑853
➡**Location** 60km southwest of Hong Kong.
➡**Tourist office** (p336)

◉ SIGHTS

You'll find the lion's share of Macau's museums, churches, gardens and interesting architecture on the peninsula. In 2005 Unesco recognised this wealth by adding the Historic Centre of Macau, comprising eight squares and 22 historic buildings, to its World Heritage list. At many of the heritage sites, seniors over 60 and children under 11 are admitted free – just ask. The Macau Museums Pass (MOP$25) allows entry to a half-dozen museums over a five-day period.

◉ Central Macau Peninsula

LEAL SENADO   HISTORIC BUILDING
Map p226 (民政總署大樓; ☑2857 2233; 163 Avenida de Almeida Ribeiro; ⊙9am-9pm Tue-Sun; ☐3, 6, 26A, 18A, 33, disembark at Almeida Ribeiro) Facing Largo do Senado is Macau's most important historical building, the 18th-century 'Loyal Senate', which houses the Instituto para os Assuntos Cívicos e Municipais (IACM; Civic and Municipal Affairs Bureau). It is so-named because the body sitting here refused to recognise Spain's sovereignty during the 60 years that it occupied Portugal. In 1654, a dozen years after Portuguese sovereignty was re-established, King João IV ordered a heraldic inscription to be placed inside the entrance hall, which can still be seen today.

ⓘ BROWSING IN THE OLD CITY

Window-shopping in the old part of town, such as on Rua dos Ervanários and Rua de Nossa Senhora do Amparo near the Ruins of the Church of St Paul, can be a great experience. You'll see shops selling stamps, jade, incense and goldfish.

You can also look for antiques or replicas on and around Rua das Estalagens and Rua de São António. Rua de Madeira and Rua dos Mercadores, which lead up to Rua da Tercena have stores selling mah-jong tiles and birdcages. These are lovely streets to walk around, even if you don't buy anything.

Stores selling pork jerky, egg rolls and almond cookies are scattered all over town. Standards are pretty much the same everywhere, so just hop into the nearest one.

Inside the entrance hall is the **IACM Temporary Exhibition Gallery** (民政總署臨時展覽廳; Map p226; ☑8988 4100; 163 Avenida de Almeida Ribeiro; ⊙9am-9pm Tue-Sun; ☐3, 6, 26A, 18A, 33, disembark at Almeida Ribeiro) **FREE**. On the 1st floor is the **Senate Library** (民政總署圖書館; Map p226; ☑2857 2233; ⊙1-7pm Tue-Sat) **FREE**, which has a collection of some 18,500 books, and wonderful carved wooden furnishings and panelled walls.

RUINS OF THE CHURCH OF ST PAUL   RUIN
See p219.

MONTE FORT   FORT
Map p226 (大炮台, Fortaleza do Monte; ⊙7am-7pm; ☐7, 8, disembark at Social Welfare Bureau) Just east of the ruins, Monte Fort was built by the Jesuits between 1617 and 1626 as part of the College of the Mother of God. Barracks and storehouses were designed to allow the fort to survive a two-year siege, but the cannons were fired only once, during the aborted attempt by the Dutch to invade Macau in 1622. Now the ones on the south side are trained at the gaudy Grand Lisboa Casino like an accusing finger. On the outside of the southeastern wall, about 6m from the ground, under a cannon, is a sealed rectangular opening. This was a door used by soldiers patrolling the old city wall that was connected to the fort at a right angle.

Macau Peninsula

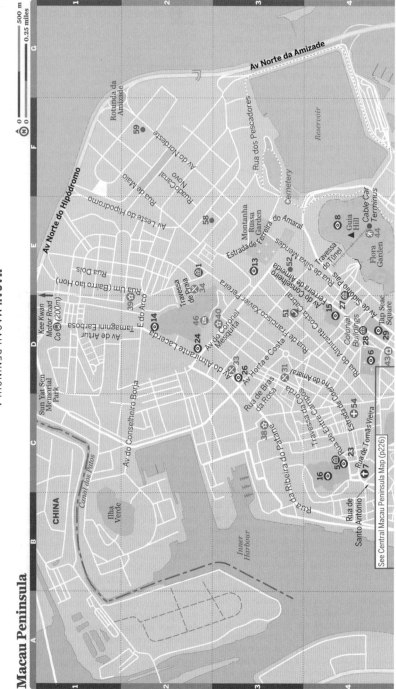

N 0
0

500 m
0.25 miles

Av Norte da Amizade

Rotunda da
Amizade

59

Av do Nordeste

RuadoCanal
Novo

Rua dos Pescadores

Reservoir

58

Av Leste do Hipódromo

Av Norte do Hipódromo

Rua de Maio

Montanha
Russa
Garden

Estrada de Ferreira do Amaral

13

52

1

Cemetery

Travessa do Túnel

8
Guia
Hill

Cable Car
Terminus

Flora
Garden

44

Av de Sidónio Pais

15
21

Kee Kwan
Motor Road
Co (200m)

Rua Um (Barrio Iao Hon)
Rua Dois

E do Arco

39

Travessa
de Praia

34

46

40

51

Av do Conselheiro Ferreira de Almeida

Rua de Francisco Xavier Pereira

Travessa de Silva Mendes

Av de Artur Tamagnini Barbosa

14

24

Av do Coronel
Mesquita

Colonial
Buildings

28

6

43

29

Tap Seac
Square

Av do Almirante Lacerda

33

26

Av Horta e Costa

31

Rua do Campo

Rua de Bras
da Rosa

Rua da Ribeira do Patane

Av do Conselheiro Borja

Sun Yat Sen
Memorial Park

Ilha
Verde

Canal dos Patos

CHINA

Inner
Harbour

38

Travessa do Corda

Rua de Pedro Coutinho

54

7

23

5

16

Rua de Tomás Vieira

Rua de
Santo António

See Central Macau Peninsula Map (p226)

G

F

E

D

C

B

A

1

2

3

4

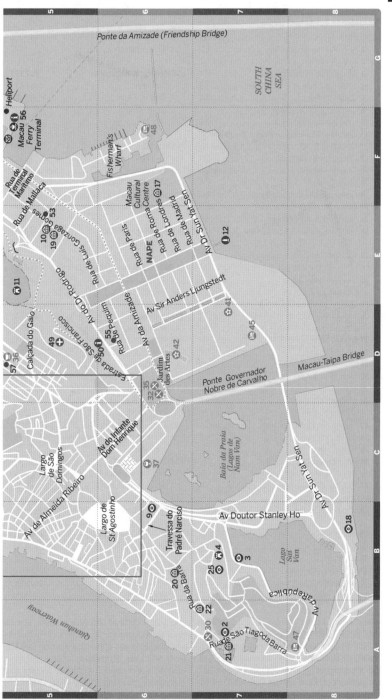

Macau Peninsula

MACAU MUSEUM   MUSEUM
Map p226 (澳門博物館, Museu de Macau;
☎2835 7911; www.macaumuseum.gov.mo; 112
Praceta do Museu de Macau; admission MOP$15,
15th of month free; ⏰10am-5.30pm Tue-Sun; ☐7,
8, disembark at Social Welfare Bureau) This interesting museum inside Monte Fort will

give you a taste of Macau's history. The 1st
floor introduces the territory's early history
and includes an elaborate section on Macau's religions. Highlights of the 2nd floor
include a recreated firecracker factory and
a recorded reading in the local dialect by
Macanese poet José dos Santos Ferreira

(1919–93). The top floor focuses on new architecture and urban-development plans.

ST JOSEPH'S SEMINARY & CHURCH CHURCH

Map p226 (聖若瑟修院及聖堂, Capela do Seminario Sao Jose; Rua do Seminario; ⊗church 10am-5pm; 🚇9, 16, 18, 28B) St Joseph's, which falls outside the tourist circuit, is one of Macau's most beautiful models of tropicalised baroque architecture. Consecrated in 1758 as part of the Jesuit seminary (not open to the public), it features a white and yellow facade, a scalloped entrance canopy (European) and the oldest dome, albeit a small one, ever built in China. The most interesting feature, however, is the roof that features Chinese materials and building styles.

LOU KAU MANSION HISTORIC BUILDING

Map p226 (盧家大屋, Casa de Lou Kau; 🖉8399 6699; 7 Travessa da Sé; ⊗10am-5.30pm Tue-Sun; 🚇3, 4, 6A, 8A, 19, 33) FREE Built around 1889, this Cantonese-style mansion with southern European elements belonged to merchant Lou Wa Sio (aka Lou Kau), who also commissioned the Lou Lim Ioc Garden (p234). Behind the grey facade, an intriguing maze of open and semi-enclosed spaces blurs the line between inside and outside. The flower-and-bird motif on the roof can also be found in the Mandarin's House and A-Ma Temple. Free guided tours in Chinese on weekends (from 10am to 7pm).

MANDARIN'S HOUSE HISTORIC BUILDING

Map p222 (鄭家大屋, Caso do Mandarim; 🖉2896 8820; www.wh.mo/mandarinhouse; 10 Travessa de Antonio da Silva; ⊗10am-5.30pm Thu-Tue; 🚇28B, 18) FREE Built around 1869, the Mandarin's House, with over 60 rooms, was the ancestral home of Zheng Guanying, an influential author-merchant whose readers had included emperors, Dr Sun Yatsen and Chairman Mao. The compound features a moon gate, tranquil courtyards, exquisite rooms and a main hall with French windows, all arranged in that labyrinthine style typical of certain Chinese period buildings.

ST LAZARUS CHURCH DISTRICT NEIGHBOURHOOD

Map p226 (瘋堂斜巷, Calcada da Igreja de Sao Lazaro; www.cipa.org.mo; 🚇7, 8) A lovely neighbourhood with colonial-style houses and cobbled streets. Designers and independents like to gather here, setting up shop and organising artsy events, such as the weekly Sun Never Left – Public Art Performance (p239), Tai Fung Tong Art House (p229), G32 (p228) and the Old Ladies' House are also here.

OLD LADIES' HOUSE HISTORIC BUILDING

Map p226 (仁慈堂婆仔屋, Albergue SCM or Albergue da Santa Casa da Misericórdia; 🖉2852 2550; www.albcreativelab.com; 8 Calcada da Igreja de Sao Lazaro; ⊗noon-7pm Wed-Mon; 🚇7, 8) The Old Ladies' House was a shelter for Portuguese refugees from Shànghǎi in WWII, and later a home for elderly women. It's now run by an art organisation, Albergue SCM, which organises cultural events here. The two yellow colonial-style buildings sit in a poetic courtyard with magnificent old camphor trees. Fashion boutique Lines Lab (p241) and Portuguese grocery shop Mercearia Portuguesa (p240) are here.

MUSEUM OF THE HOLY HOUSE OF MERCY MUSEUM

Map p226 (仁慈堂博物館, Núcleo Museológico da Santa Casa da Misericórdia; 🖉2857 3938; 2 Travessa da Misericórdia; adult/child MOP$5/ free; ⊗10am-1pm & 2.30-5.30pm Tue-Sun; 🚇3, 6, 26A) In the heart of Largo do Senado is Macau's oldest charitable institution (c 1569). The house once sheltered orphans and prostitutes in the 17th and 18th centuries. Today it's a museum with an eclectic collection that includes religious sculptures, ancient porcelain, and the skull of its founder and Macau's first bishop, Dom Belchior Carneiro.

CHURCH OF ST DOMINIC CHURCH

Map p226 (玫瑰堂, Igreja de São Domingos; Largo de São Domingos; ⊗10am-6pm; 🚇3, 6, 26A) Northeast of Largo do Senado, this baroque church with a beautiful altar and a timber roof was founded by three Spanish Dominican priests from Acapulco, Mexico, in the 16th century, though the current structure dates to the 17th century. It was here, in 1822, that the first Portuguese newspaper was published on Chinese soil. The former bell tower now houses the **Treasury of Sacred Art** (聖物寶庫, Tresouro de Arte Sacra; Map p226; ⊗10am-6pm) FREE, an Aladdin's cave of ecclesiastical art and liturgical objects exhibited on three floors.

DOM PEDRO V THEATRE HISTORIC BUILDING

Map p226 (崗頂劇院, Teatro Dom Pedro V; 🖉2893 9646; Calçada do Teatro, Largo de St

Central Macau Peninsula

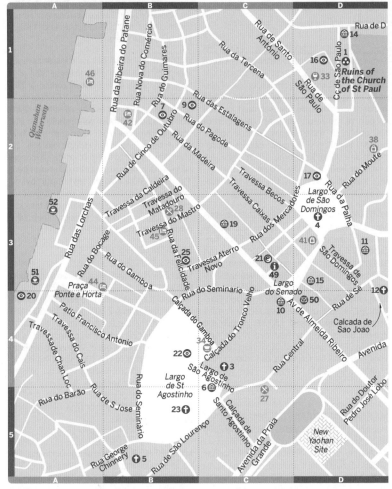

MACAU MACAU PENINSULA

Agostinho; ⊙10am-6pm Wed-Mon; 🚌3, 4, 6A, 8A, 19) Opposite the Church of St Augustine, Dom Pedro V, a colonnaded, neoclassical theatre in green and white, is the oldest (1858) Western-style theatre in China, and remains an important cultural venue for the Macanese community.

⭐ SIR ROBERT HO TUNG LIBRARY LIBRARY
Map p226 (何東圖書館; 3 Largo de St Agostinho; ⊙10am-7pm Mon-Sat, 11am-7pm Sun; 🚌9, 16, 18) This charming building founded in the 19th century was the country retreat of the late tycoon Robert Ho Tung who purchased it in 1918. The colonial edifice featuring a dome,

an arcaded facade, Ionic columns and Chinese-style gardens, was given a modern extension by architect Joy Choi Tin Tin not too long ago. The new four-storey structure in glass and steel has Piranesi-inspired bridges connecting to the old house and a glass roof straddling the transitional space.

CHURCH OF ST LAWRENCE CHURCH
Map p226 (聖老楞佐教堂, Igreja de São Lourenço; Rua de São Lourenço; ⊙10am-5pm Tue-Sun, 1-2pm Mon; 🚌9, 16, 18, 28B) One of Macau's three oldest churches, St Lawrence was originally constructed of wood in the 1560s, then rebuilt in stone in the early 19th cen-

on the first Saturday of Lent, followed by thousands of devotees.

PAWNSHOP MUSEUM HISTORIC BUILDING

Map p226 (典當業展示館, Espaço Patrimonial – Uma Casa de Penhores Tradicional; ☎2892 1811; 396 Avenida de Almeida Ribeiro; admission MOP$5; ☉10.30am-7pm, closed 1st Mon of month; ☐2, 3, 7, 26A) This museum housed inside the former Tak Seng On ('virtue and success') pawnshop offers an atmospheric glimpse into Macau's pawnshop business, which dates back to the Qing dynasty. Built in 1917, it comprises an office, a lobby and an eight-storey, fortress-like tower. On display is equipment from the original establishment, safes where goods were stored and financial records.

GOVERNMENT HEADQUARTERS BUILDING

Map p222 (澳門特別行政區政府總部, Sede do Governo; cnr Avenida da Praia Grande & Travessa do Padré Narciso; ☐3, 6A, 9, 9A, 16) South of the Church of St Lawrence is the headquarters of the Macau SAR government. This pillared, rose-coloured building with two stories and three wings was built in 1849 for a Portuguese noble. It's open to the public two days a year, usually in September or October.

SAM KAI VUI KUN TEMPLE TAOIST, TEMPLE

Map p226 (三街會館; 10 Rua Sui do Mercado de São Domingos; ☉8am-6pm; ☐3, 4, 6A, 26A) Literally 'a community hall for three streets', this temple was a meeting place for merchants and an adjudication court, before the Chinese Chamber of Commerce came into existence in 1912. It's dedicated to Kwan Yu, the god of war and justice. It gets particularly busy in May, June and July when locals celebrate three festivals in the god's honour.

CHINESE READING ROOM BUILDING

Map p226 (八角亭圖書館; Rua de Santa Clara; ☉9am-noon & 7pm-midnight; ☐2A, 6A, 7A, 8) This former drinks booth (c 1926), known as the 'Octagonal Pavilion' in Chinese, is a library with red windows and a slip of a staircase linking the two floors. It's a serene place where middle-aged and elderly men go to read newspapers for free.

STREET OF HAPPINESS STREET

Map p226 (福隆新街; Rua da Felicidade; ☐3, 6, 26A) Not far west of Largo do Senado is Rua da Felicidade (Street of Happiness). Its shuttered terraces were once Macau's

tury. The neoclassical church has a magnificent painted ceiling and one of its towers once served as an ecclesiastical prison. Enter from Rua da Imprensa Nacional.

CHURCH OF ST AUGUSTINE CHURCH

Map p226 (聖奧斯定教堂, Igreja de Santo Agostinho; No 2, Largo de St Agostinho; ☉10am-6pm; ☐3, 4, 6, 26A) The foundations of this church date from 1586 when it was established by Spanish Augustinians, but the present structure was built in 1814. The high altar has a statue of Christ bearing the cross, which is carried through the streets during the Procession of the Passion of Our Lord

Central Macau Peninsula

main red-light district. Several scenes from *Indiana Jones and the Temple of Doom* were shot here. The government has plans to repaint the famous red shutters in the original colour – green. But whether it's wise to change the distinguishing feature of so iconic a landmark remains to be seen.

LIN FUNG TEMPLE   TEMPLE

Map p222 (蓮峰廟, Lin Fung Miu; Avenida do Almirante Lacerda; ⊗7am-5pm; ➌1A, 8, 8A, 10, 28B) Dedicated to Kwun Yum, the goddess of mercy, this Temple of the Lotus was

built in 1592, but underwent several reconstructions from the 17th century. It used to host mandarins from Guǎngdōng province when they visited Macau. The most famous of these imperial visitors was Commissioner Lin Zexu who was charged with stamping out the opium trade.

G32   HISTORIC BUILDING

Map p226 (☎2834 6626; 32 Rua de Sao Miguel; ⊗free guided tours 2.30-5pm Sat & Sun; ➌7, 8) This three-storey tenement building has been restored as a middle-class Macanese home from the 1960s and '70s, with wooden floorboards, floral wallpaper and retro furniture. A narrow staircase takes you to the roof, where you'll see a unique skyline formed by Chinese buildings, Unesco-protected monuments and casino kitsch.

TAI FUNG TONG
ART HOUSE   HISTORIC BUILDING

Map p226 (大瘋堂藝舍; ☑2835 3537; 7 Calcada de Sao Lazaro; ◎2-6pm Tue-Sun; ☐7, 8) Featuring a mix of Chinese and European architectural styles, this unusual-looking mansion was built almost a century ago by a philanthropist. It's now occupied by a nonprofit that promotes the area's Chinese heritage. The house has a collection of traditional Chinese artefacts and a calligrapher is sometimes here to demonstrate ink-and-brush calligraphy.

TAP SEAC GALLERY   GALLERY

Map p222 (塔石藝文館, Galeria Tap Seac; www.macauart.net/ts; 95 Avenida Conselheiro Ferreira de Almeida; ◎10am-7pm Tue-Sun; ☐) One of a handful of 1920s houses surrounding Tap Seac Sq, this building features a European-style facade and Moorish arched doors. The gallery inside hosts excellent contemporary art exhibitions. The original patio in the middle of the house has been kept, which creates a light-filled, relaxing setting.

TAP SEAC SQUARE   SQUARE

Map p222 (塔石廣場, Praca do Tap Seac; ☐7, 8) This beautiful square surrounded by important historic buildings from the 1920s (Cultural Affairs Bureau, Tap Seac Health Centre, Central Library, Library for Macau's Historical Archives, Tap Seac Gallery) was designed by Macanese architect Carlos Marreiros. Marreiros also created the Tap Seac Health Centre, a contemporary interpretation of Macau's neoclassical buildings.

AFA (ART FOR ALL SOCIETY)   GALLERY

Map p222 (全藝社; ☑2836 6064; www.afamacau.com; 3rd fl, Edificio da Fabrica de Baterias N E National, 52 Estrada da Areia Preta; ◎noon-7pm Mon-Sat; ☐8, 8A, 18A, 7) Macau's best contemporary art can be seen at this nonprofit gallery, which has taken Macau's art worldwide and holds monthly solo exhibitions by Macau's top artists. AFA is near the Mong Há Multi-Sport Pavilion (望廈體育館). Disembark from the bus at Rua da Barca or Rua de Francisco Xavier Pereira. Alternatively, it's a 20-minute walk from Largo do Senado.

OX WAREHOUSE   ARTS CENTRE

Map p222 (牛房倉庫, Armazem de Boi; ☑2853 0026; http://oxwarehouse.blogspot.com; cnr Avenida do Coronel Mesquita & Avenida do Almirante Lacerda; ◎noon-7pm Wed-Mon; ☐4, 5, 25, 26A, 33) This atmospheric former slaughterhouse is run by a nonprofit that hosts contemporary exhibitions, workshops and performances by local and visiting artists. Much of the work is engagingly experiential. Even if nothing's on, the architecture of the old buildings here makes it worthwhile to come for a peek.

MACAU CATHEDRAL   CHURCH

Map p226 (大堂(主教座堂), A Sé Catedral; Largo da Sé; ◎8am-6pm; ☐3, 6, 26A, 18A) East of Largo do Senado is this cathedral. It's not a particularly attractive structure, consecrated in 1850 and rebuilt in 1937 in concrete. It has some notable stained-glass windows and is very active during major Christian festivals and holy days in Macau.

MACAU'S SWORD DESIGNER

One of Macau's most accomplished artists, Antonio Conceição Júnior (aka Antonio Cejunior) custom-designs blades (www.arscives.com/bladesign) inspired by his city, mythology and the modern world.

The charismatic Antonio has designed Eastern and Western swords, as well as hybrids such as one featuring a Western-style blade with a guard inspired by the Harley Davidson wheel. Antonio does not manufacture the swords himself, but he will recommend North American bladesmiths. Interested parties should email Antonio at antonio.cejunior@gmail.com. Expect about two weeks for the design and a designer's fee of US$3000.

Formerly a director of the Museum of Macau, Antonio's repertoire spans fashion, jewellery, book covers and stamps for Macau.

⊙ Southern Macau Peninsula

MACAU MUSEUM OF ART
MUSEUM

Map p222 (澳門藝術博物館, Museu de Arte de Macau; ☑8791 9814; www.mam.gov.mo; Macau Cultural Centre, Avenida Xian Xing Hai; adult/child MOP$5/2, Sun free; ⊙10am-6.30pm Tue-Sun; ☑1A, 8, 12, 23) This excellent five-storey museum has well-curated displays of art created in Macau and China, including paintings by Western artists like George Chinnery, who lived in the enclave. Other highlights are ceramics and stoneware excavated in Macau, Ming- and Qing-dynasty calligraphy from Guǎngdōng, ceramic statues from Shíwān (Guǎngdōng) and seal carvings. The museum also features 19th-century Western historical paintings from all over Asia, and contemporary Macanese art.

MACAU CULTURAL CENTRE
BUILDING

Map p222 (澳門文化中心, Centro Cultural de Macau; ☑2870 0699; www.ccm.gov.mo; Avenida Xian Xing Hai; ⊙9am-7pm Tue-Sun; ☑1A, 8, 12, 23) This US$100-million centre with an area of 45,000 sq metres is the territory's prime venue for cultural performances. It's beside the wonderful Macau Museum of Art. Creative Macau (創意空間; ☑2875 3282; www.creativemacau.org.mo; Ground fl, Macau Cultural Centre; ⊙2-7pm Mon-Sat) is an art space that runs exhibitions and poetry readings on the Cultural Centre's ground floor.

A-MA TEMPLE
TEMPLE

Map p222 (媽閣廟, Templo de A-Ma; Rua de São Tiago da Barra; ⊙7am-6pm; ☑1, 2, 5, 6B, 7) A-Ma Temple was probably already standing when the Portuguese arrived, although the present structure may date from the 16th century. It was here that fisherfolk once came to replenish supplies and pray for fair weather. A-Ma, aka Tin Hau, is the goddess

MACAU'S INNER BEAUTIES

Between the historic and the flashy, Macau has a lot to offer architecturally to those with patience and a good eye.

Lovely Libraries

By the way they relate to their surroundings, Macau's libraries show how tiny proportions can be beautiful.

Sir Robert Ho Tung Library (p226) A 19th-century villa and its glass-and-steel extension rising above a garden, with Piranesi-like bridges between the two.

Chinese Reading Room (p227) Retirees and students come to the 'Octagonal Pavilion', built in 1926, to read the news and to study.

Sr Wong Ieng Kuan Library (p234) An oasis of calm in the Luís de Camões Garden, between a boulder that juts into the interior, and a banyan tree that frames the entrance.

Coloane Library (p243) Grotesque but cute, this mini Grecian temple (c 1917) has a pediment containing the word 'library' in Chinese and Portuguese, and disproportionately fat columns.

Modernist Marvels

Macau has an important heritage of modernism, especially in the Inner Harbour area, that is little known outside the city.

Pier 8 (8號碼頭; Map p226; Rua do Dr Lourenco Pereira Marquez; ☑5, 7) A stunner in grey, 50 paces south of Macau Masters Hotel; best views from the **South Sampan Pier** (Map p226) next door.

East Asia Hotel (東亞酒店; Map p226; cnr Rua do Guimares & Rua da Madeira; ☑5, 7) Chinese art deco in mint green; a little shabby, very chic.

Penha Hill (p231) 'Bishop's Hill' is littered with the stylish villas of the wealthy.

Red Market (Almirante Lacerda; p236) This art-deco building houses a bustling wet market.

of the sea, from which the name Macau is derived. It's believed that when the Portuguese asked the name of the place, they were told 'A-Ma Gau' (A-Ma Bay). In modern Cantonese, 'Macau' (Ou Mun) means 'gateway of the bay'.

MOORISH BARRACKS HISTORIC BUILDING

Map p222 (Calçada da Barra, Barra Hill; ☐18, 28) These former barracks (c 1874) were designed by an Italian in a neoclassical style inspired by Moorish architecture, to accommodate Muslim Indian policemen from Goa. The confusion of Muslims with Moors was due to the fact that dated Cantonese refers to Indians as 'moh loh cha' and 'moh loh' is a transliteration of 'Moorish'. You can't enter the building, now occupied by the Macau Maritime Administration. Turn right as you leave A-Ma Temple; a 10-minute uphill walk will take you here.

PENHA HILL NEIGHBOURHOOD

Map p222 (西望洋山, Colina da Penha; ☐6, 9, 16) Towering above the colonial villas along Avenida da República is Penha Hill, the most tranquil and least-visited area of the peninsula. From here you'll get excellent views of the central area of Macau. Atop the hill is **Bishop's Palace** (主教府; Map p222), built in 1837 and a residence for bishops (not open to the public), and the **Chapel of Our Lady of Penha** (主教山小堂, Ermida de Nossa Senhora da Penha; Map p222; Top of Penha Hill; ⊙9am-5.30pm; ☐6B, 9, 16, 28B), once a place of pilgrimage for sailors.

MARITIME MUSEUM MUSEUM

Map p222 (海事博物館, Museu Marítimo; ☑2859 5481; www.museumaritimo.gov.mo; 1 Largo do Pagode da Barra; adult MOP\$3-10, child free; ⊙10am-5.30pm Wed-Mon; ☐1, 2, 5, 6B, 7, 10) The highlights here are the interactive displays detailing the maritime histories of Portugal and China, the artefacts from Macau's seafaring past, and the mockups of boats – including the long, narrow dragon boats used during the Dragon Boat Festival – and a Hakka fishing village.

AVENIDA DA REPÚBLICA NEIGHBOURHOOD

Map p222 (☐6, 9, 16) Avenida da República, along the northwest shore of Sai Van Lake, is Macau's oldest Portuguese quarter. There are several grand colonial villas not open to the public here. The former Bela Vista Hotel, one of the most-storied hotels in Asia, is now the residence of the Portuguese consul-

general. Nearby is the ornate **Santa Sancha Palace**, once the residence of Macau's Portuguese governors, and now used to accommodate Portuguese state guests. Not too far away are beautiful, abandoned art-deco-inspired buildings.

KUN IAM STATUE & ECUMENICAL CENTRE MONUMENT

Map p222 (觀音像及觀音蓮花苑, Estátua de Kun Iam e Centro Ecuménico Kun Iam; Avenida Dr Sun Yat Sen; ⊙ecumenical centre 10am-6pm Sat-Thu; ☐10A, 17) This 20m-tall bronze figure, emerging Virgin Mary–like from a 7m-high lotus in the outer harbour, is probably the only statue in the world of the goddess of mercy that is not facing the sea. The lotus shelters a small ecumenical centre, which distributes pamphlets on Buddhism.

GRAND PRIX MUSEUM MUSEUM

Map p222 (大賽車博物館, Museu do Grande Prémio; ☑8798 4108; Basement, CAT, 431 Rua de Luís Gonzaga Gomes; adult/child MOP\$10/free; ⊙10am-8pm Wed-Mon; ☐1A, 3, 10) Cars from the Macau Formula 3 Grand Prix, including the bright-red Triumph TR2 driven by Eduardo de Carvalho that won the first Grand Prix in 1954, are on display here, while simulators let you test your racing skills.

MACAU WINE MUSEUM MUSEUM

Map p222 (Museu do Vinho de Macau; ☑8798 4188; Basement, CAT, 431 Rua de Luís Gonzaga Gomes; wine tasting MOP\$15; ⊙10am-8pm Wed-Mon; ☐1A, 3, 10, 10B, 10X, 23, 28A) **FREE** Over 1100 types of wine are on display at the only museum in Macau where beverages are allowed. About 90% of these are of Portuguese origin, including the oldest bottle – the Porto 1815. For MOP\$15, you can have a tasting of selected bottles. There is also a rundown of Portugal's various wine regions, and a (rather bland) display of wine racks, barrels, presses and tools. It's right next to the Grand Prix Museum.

MACAU TOWER LANDMARK

Map p222 (澳門旅遊塔, Torre de Macau; ☑2893 3339; www.macautower.com.mo; Largo da Torre de Macau; adult/child observation deck MOP\$135/70; ⊙10am-9pm Mon-Fri, 9am-9pm Sat & Sun; ☐9A, 18, 23, 26, 32) At 338m, Macau Tower looms above the narrow isthmus of land southeast of Avenida da República. You can stay put on the observation decks on the 58th and 61st floors, or challenge yourself to a bungee jump or some other form of extreme sport.

MACAU MACAU PENINSULA

1. Chapel of St Francis Xavier (p242)
This 1928 chapel is home to paintings of the infant Christ with a Chinese Madonna.

2. Macau Tower (p231)
The observation deck offers sweeping views and the opportunity for extreme sports, including bungee jumping.

3. Portuguese egg tarts
Pastéis de nata (sweet and creamy Portuguese-style egg tarts) are just one example of the influence of Portuguese cuisine in Macau.

4. Casino Lisboa
Nearly 40 casinos line Macau's seafront (p240), where gamblers, mostly from mainland China, come to try their luck on the tables.

◉ Northern Macau Peninsula

GUIA FORT & GUIA CHAPEL   FORT, CHURCH

Map p222 (東望洋炮台及聖母雪地殿聖堂, Fortaleza da Guia e Capela de Guia; ⏰chapel 9am-5.30pm; 🚍2, 2A, 6A, 12, 17, 18 Flora Garden stop) As the highest point on the peninsula, Guia Fort affords panoramic views of the city and, when the air is clear, across to the islands and China. At the top is the stunning Chapel of Our Lady of Guia built in 1622 and retaining almost 100% of its original features, including some of Asia's most valuable frescoes. Next to it stands the oldest modern **lighthouse** on the China coast – an attractive 15m-tall structure that is closed to the public.

You could walk up, but it's easier to take the Guia cable car that runs from the entrance of **Flora Gardens** (Jardim da Flora; Map p222; Travessa do Túnel; ⏰7.30am-8.30pm), Macau's largest public park.

LOU LIM IEOC GARDEN   GARDENS

Map p222 (盧廉若公園, Jardim Lou Lim Ieoc; 10 Estrada de Adolfo de Loureiro; ⏰6am-9pm; 🚍2, 2A, 5, 9, 9A, 12, 16) Locals come to this lovely Suzhou-style garden to practise taichi, play Chinese music, or simply to relax among its lotus ponds and bamboo groves. The Victorian-style **Lou Lim Ieoc Garden Pavilion** (盧廉若公園, Pavilhão do Jardim de Lou Lim Ieoc; Map p222; ☎8988 4100; 10 Estrada de Adolfo Loureiro; ⏰9am-7pm Tue-Sun; 🚍2, 2A, 5, 9, 9A, 12, 16) was where the Lou family received guests, including Dr Sun Yatsen, and is now used for exhibitions. Adjacent to the garden is the **Macao Tea Culture House** (澳門茶文化館, Caultura do Chá em Macau; Map p222; ☎2882 7103; Lou Lim Ieoc Garden, Avenida do Conselheiro Ferreira de Almeida; admission free; ⏰9am-7pm Tue-Sun; 🚍2, 2A, 5, 9, 9A, 12, 16), displaying Chinese tea-drinking culture with exhibits of teapots and paintings related to the coveted drink.

KUN IAM TEMPLE   TEMPLE

Map p222 (觀音廟, Templo de Kun Iam; 2 Avenida do Coronel Mesquita; ⏰7am-5.30pm; 🚍1A, 10, 18A, stop Travessa de Venceslau de Morais) Macau's oldest temple was founded in the 13th century, but the present structures date back to 1627. Its roofs are embellished with porcelain figurines and its halls are lavishly decorated. Inside the main one stands the likeness of Kwun Yum, the goddess of

mercy; to the left of the altar is a statue of a bearded arhat rumoured to represent Marco Polo. The first Sino-American treaty was signed at a round stone table in the temple's terraced gardens in 1844.

LUÍS DE CAMÕES GARDEN & GROTTO   GARDENS

Map p222 (白鴿巢公園, Jardim e Gruta de Luís de Camões; Praça de Luís de Camões; ⏰6am-10pm; 🚍8A, 17, 26) This relaxing garden with dappled meandering paths is dedicated to the one-eyed poet Luís de Camões (1524–80), who is said to have written part of his epic *Os Lusíadas* in Macau, though there is little evidence that he ever reached the city. You'll see a bronze bust (c 1886) of the man here. The wooded garden attracts a fair number of chess players, bird owners and Chinese shuttlecock kickers. The **Sr Wong Ieng Kuan Library** (白鴿巢公園黃營均圖書館, Praça de Luís de Camões; Map p222; ☎2895 3075; ⏰8am-8pm Tue-Sun) is also here.

CASA GARDEN   HISTORIC BUILDING

Map p222 (東方基金會會址; 13 Praça de Luís de Camões; ⏰garden 9.30am-6pm daily, gallery open only during exhibitions 9.30am-6pm Mon-Fri; 🚍8A, 17, 26) Sitting quietly east of the Luís de Camões Garden is this beautiful colonial villa built in 1770. It was the headquarters of the British East India Company when it was based in Macau in the early 19th century. Today it's the headquarters of the Oriental Foundation, and includes a gallery, **Museu do Oriente** (東方基金會博物館; Map p222; 13 Praça de Luís de Camões; ⏰during exhibitions 9.30am-6pm Mon-Fri; 🚍8A, 17, 26), that mounts interesting art exhibitions.

CHURCH OF ST ANTHONY   CHURCH

Map p222 (聖安多尼教堂, Igreja de Santo António; cnr Rua de Santo António & Rua do Tarrafeiro; ⏰7.30am-5.30pm; 🚍8A, 17, 26) Next to the roundabout outside Casa Garden, St Anthony's, built from 1558 to 1608, is one of Macau's oldest churches, and the Jesuits' earliest headquarters. The local Portuguese used to hold wedding ceremonies here, hence the church's name in Cantonese: Fa Vong Tong (Church of Flowers).

OLD PROTESTANT CEMETERY   CEMETERY

Map p222 (基督教墳場, Antigo Cemitério Protestante; 15 Praça de Luís de Camões; ⏰8.30am-5.30pm; 🚍8A, 17, 26) As church law forbade the burial of non-Catholics on hallowed

SLEEPING IN THE MACAU PENINSULA

The vast majority of new hotels in Macau are aimed at the moneyed rather than budget travellers, so you have to look hard for good budget sleeping options. But for those with the cash, there are world-class choices.

San Va Hospedaria (新華大旅店; Map p226; ☑8210 0193, reservations 2857 3701; www.sanvahotel.com; 65-67 Rua da Felicidade; d $190-220, tw $320-360, tr $380; ☑3, 6, 26A) Built in 1873, San Va, with its green partitions and retro tiles, is about the cheapest and most atmospheric lodging in town – Wong Kar-wai filmed parts of *2046* here. However it's also very basic, with shared bathrooms and no air-conditioning (just fans).

Ole London Hotel (澳門英京酒店; Map p226; ☑2893 7761; 4-6 Praça de Ponte e Horta; d MOP$420-500; ☒@☎; ☑2, 7, 10A) A stone's throw from the Inner Harbour, this place has smart, clean rooms. They are small, but given its location and rates you can't really complain. Bigger discounts apply if you book via www.macau.com.

Pousada de Mong Há (澳門望廈迎賓館; Map p222; ☑2851 5222; www.ift.edu.mo; Colina de Mong Há; r MOP$700-1300, ste MOP$1300-1800; ☻☒@☎; ☑5, 22, 25) Sitting atop Mong Há Hill near the ruins of a fort built in 1849 is this Portuguese-style inn run by students at the Institute for Tourism Studies. Rooms are well appointed, with some having computers, and the service is attentive. Rates include breakfast. Discounts of 25% to 40% midweek and off season.

5Footway Inn (五步廊旅舍; Map p226; www.5footwayinn.com; 8 Rua de Constantino Brito; d & tw MOP$700, tr MOP$900; ☻☒☎; ☑1, 2, 10, 5, 7) This Singapore-owned accommodation converted from a love motel has 23 small clean rooms, vibrant paintings in communal areas and excellent English-speaking staff. Rates include a self-service breakfast. It's opposite the Sofitel Macau at Ponte 16, which means you can take the latter's free shuttle buses to and from the ferry terminal.

Hotel Sintra (澳門新麗華酒店; Map p226; ☑2871 0111; www.hotelsintra.com; Avenida de Do João IV; r MOP$1500-2000, ste from MOP$2500; ☒☎; ☑3, 11, 22) Spotless rooms and professional staff make this centrally located three-star hotel a great-value option. Our only complaints are the slow-moving lift and the massive LED screen of the Grand Emperor Hotel nearby, which is visible from some rooms. Discounts of up to 50% midweek.

Mandarin Oriental (文華東方; Map p222; ☑8805 8888; www.mandarinoriental.com/macau; Avenida Dr Sun Yat Sen, Novos Aterros do Porto Exterior; r MOP$2088-4000, ste MOP$4788-6588; ☻☒@☎☒) A great high-end option, the Mandarin has everything associated with the brand – elegance, superlative service, comfortable rooms and excellent facilities. Though relatively small, it's a refreshing contrast to the glitzy casino hotels.

Pousada de São Tiago (澳門聖地牙哥古堡酒店; Map p222; ☑2837 8111; www.saotiago.com.mo; Fortaleza de São Tiago da Barra, Avenida da República; ste MOP$3000-5400; ☻☒@☎☒; ☑6, 9, 28B) Built into the ruins of the 17th-century Barra Fort, the landmark São Tiago is the most romantic place to stay in Macau. No other hotel has such a rich history. All 12 rooms are elegantly furnished suites. Discounts of up to 35% off season. The restaurant La Paloma is here.

Sofitel Macau at Ponte 16 (澳門十六浦索菲特大酒店; Map p226; ☑8861 0016; www.sofitel.com/gb/asia/index.shtml; Rua do Visconde Paço de Arcos; r MOP$1520-2220, ste from MOP$4500; ☻☒@☎; ☑1, 2, 10, 5, 7) This reasonably priced luxury hotel offers some atmospheric views of the sleepy Inner Harbour and the Ruins of the Church of St Paul on the other side. The rooms are large, with contemporary decor and plush, inviting beds.

Rocks Hotel (萊斯酒店; Map p222; ☑2878 2782; www.rockshotel.com.mo; Macau Fisherman's Wharf; r MOP$1880-2880, ste from MOP$4080; ☻☒@☎; ☑3A, 5, 23) All rooms at this elegant Victorian-style boutique hotel have a balcony – most with a view of the bay. Unlike most hotels of this price in Macau, the Rocks doesn't have a casino attached. It's also located in a relatively quiet area.

SLEEPING IN MACAU: NEED TO KNOW

Rates

Most large hotels add a 10% service charge and 5% government tax to the bill. Rates shoot up on Friday and Saturday, while during the week you can find incredible deals at travel agencies and through the following:

Macau.com (www.macau.com)

Agoda (www.agoda.com)

Shun Tak Centre (信德中心; Map p368; 200 Connaught Rd Central, Hong Kong)

Macau Ferry Terminal Check for information in the arrivals hall.

Shuttle Buses

Most midrange and top-end hotels have shuttle buses to/from the ferry terminal and, for those on the Cotai Strip, also to/from the peninsula.

Accommodation Price Ranges

Breakfast is usually included in the rates for hotels marked $$ and $$$.

$ under MOP$700

$$ MOP$700-2000

$$$ over MOP$2000

ground, this cemetery was established in 1821 as the last resting place of (mostly Anglophone) Protestants. Among those interred here are Irish-born artist George Chinnery (1774–1852), and Robert Morrison (1782–1834), the first Protestant missionary to China and author of the first Chinese-English dictionary.

CEMETERY OF ST MICHAEL THE ARCHANGEL
CEMETERY

Map p222 (西洋墳場, Cemitério de São Miguel Arcanjo; 2a Estrada do Cemitério; ⊙8am-6pm; 🚍7, 7A, 8) This cemetery, northeast of Monte Fort, contains tombs and sepulchres that can only be described as baroque ecclesiastical works of art. Near the main entrance is the **Chapel of St Michael** (聖彌額爾小堂, Capela de São Miguel; Map p222; ⊙10am-6pm), which is a doll-sized, pea-green church with a tiny choir loft and pretty porticoes.

SUN YAT SEN MEMORIAL HOUSE
MUSEUM

Map p222 (國父紀念館, Casa Memorativa de Doutor Sun Yat Sen; ☎2857 4064; 1 Rua de Silva Mendes; ⊙10am-5pm Wed-Mon; 🚍2, 2A, 5, 9, 9A, 12) **FREE** This mock-Moorish house (c 1910) commemorates Dr Sun Yatsen's (1866–1925) brief stay in Macau where he gathered support to overthrow the Qing dynasty. You'll see documents and personal belongings of the 'Father of the Chinese Republic'. Inter-

estingly, Sun himself had never lived in the house, though it was built by his son, and his first wife Lu Muzhen lived here until she died in 1952.

RED MARKET
MARKET

Map p222 (紅街市大樓, Mercado Almirante Lacerda; cnr Avenida do Almirante Lacerda & Avenida Horta e Costa; ⊙7.30am-7.30pm; 🚍23, 32) Designed by Macanese architect Júlio Alberto Basto, this three-storey art-deco building with a clock tower houses a lively wet market. It was so-named because of the red bricks used in its construction.

✗ EATING

While Macau's Chinese cuisine is excellent, most people come here for Macanese or Portuguese food. Whatever cooking you're after, making reservations is a must in midrange and fine-dining places.

★ LUNG WAH TEA HOUSE
CANTONESE $

Map p222 (龍華茶樓; ☎2857 4456; http://lungwahteahouse.com; 3 Rua Norte do Mercado Aim-Lacerda; dim sum from MOP$14, tea MOP$10, meals MOP$50-180; ⊙7am-2pm; 🖪; 🚍23, 32) There's grace in the retro furniture and the casual way it's thrown together in this airy Cantonese teahouse (c 1963). Take a booth by the windows overlooking the Red Market where the teahouse buys its produce every day. There's no English menu; just point and take. Lung Wah sells a fine array of Chinese teas.

O PORTO
MACANESE $

Map p222 (☎2859 4643; 17 Travessa da Praia; meals MOP$160; ⊙12.30-2pm & 6.30-10.30pm Thu-Tue; 🖼; 🚌2, 10, 12) Not to be confused with O Porto Interior on Rua do Almirante Sérgio, this modest place serves decent and affordable Macanese dishes, with a few luxuries: chequered tablecloths, football paraphernalia and warm service. It's near the steps leading to Mong Há Hill.

CHAT YIN
BURMESE $

Map p222 (七賢小食店; ☎2837 6297; 1 Rua de Bras da Rosa, San Kiu; noodles MOP$16-34; ⊙7.30am-6pm; 🚌23, 32) Located in the 'three-lamp' district known for its Burmese cuisine, this joint whips up a sumptuous Burmese fish soup with noodles and the hearts of banana trees.

CHEONG KEI
CANTONESE $

Map p226 (祥記麵家; ☎2857 4310; 68 Rua da Felicidade; noodles MOP$20-55; ⊙11.30am-11.30pm; 🚌3, 6, 26A) Peak-time queues at the door even before the Michelin recommendation are a clue that this long-standing noodle joint has a loyal following. Try the noodles tossed with shrimp roe. There are just a few communal tables; be prepared to trade elbows with the locals.

★CLUBE MILITAR
DE MACAU
PORTUGUESE $$

Map p226 (澳門陸軍俱樂部; ☎2871 4000; www.clubemilitardemacau.net; 975 Avenida da Praia Grande; meals MOP$150-400; ⊙1.45-2.30pm & 7-10.30pm Mon-Fri, noon-2.30pm & 7-10pm Sat & Sun; 🚌6, 28C) Housed in a distinguished colonial building, with fans spinning lazily above, the Military Club takes you back in time to a slower and quieter Macau. The simple and delicious Portuguese fare is complemented by an excellent selection of wine and cheese from Portugal. The MOP$153 buffet is excellent value. Reservations are required for dinner and weekend lunches.

ALFONSO III
PORTUGUESE $$

Map p226 (亞豐素三世餐廳; ☎2858 6272; 11a Rua Central; meals MOP$300; ⊙11.30am-2.30pm & 6-9.30pm; 🖼; 🚌3, 6, 26A) A short

MACAU CHOW

A typical Macanese menu features an enticing stew of influences from Chinese and South Asian cuisines, and the cooking of former Portuguese colonies in Africa, India and Latin America. Coconut, tamarind, chilli, jaggery (palm sugar) and shrimp paste can all feature.

A famous Macanese speciality is *galinha africana* (African chicken), made with coconut, garlic and chillies. Other popular dishes include *casquinha* (stuffed crab), *minchi* (minced meat cooked with potatoes and onions) and *serradura* (a milk pudding).

You'll find Portuguese dishes here too, such as *arroz de pato* (rice with duck confit) and *leitão assado no forno* (roasted suckling pig).

stroll southwest of Leal Senado is this tiny, family-run restaurant that has won a well-deserved reputation among Macau's Portuguese community. Service is patchy, but no one seems to mind. Tables are often in short supply, so phone ahead.

A LORCHA
MACANESE, PORTUGUESE $$

Map p222 (船屋葡國餐廳; ☎2831 3193; 289 Rua do Almirante Sérgio; meals MOP$300-500; ⊙12.30-2.30pm & 6.30-10.30pm Wed-Mon; 🖼; 🚌1, 5, 10) 'The Sailboat' is listed in every guidebook. One reason for its popularity is that it's within walking distance of the A-Ma Temple. If you go not expecting outstanding creativity, you'll enjoy its solid Portuguese and Macanese fare. Portions are generous.

★GUINCHO A GALERA
PORTUGUESE $$$

Map p222 (葡國餐廳; ☎8803 7676; 3rd fl, Hotel Lisboa, 2-4 Avenida de Lisboa; meals MOP$550-1800; ⊙noon-2.30pm & 6.30-10.30pm; 🚌3, 10) The international branch of Portugal's

ℹ️ MEAL PRICES

This price guide is for the approximate cost of a two-course meal with drinks.

$ under MOP$200

$$ MOP$200-400

$$$ over MOP$400

MACAU MACAU PENINSULA

A BUDDING CAFE CULTURE

Good cafes and patisseries have been sprouting all over Macau in recent years, offering a professional cuppa or some serious cakeage to those craving quietude from the hurry of the city.

Terra Coffee House (Map p226; ☑2893 7943; 1 Largo de St Agostinho; ☺11am-8pm; ☎; 🚍9, 16) This tiny haven overlooking pretty St Augustine Sq will make you forget you're only a five-minute walk away from heaving Largo do Senado. Stop here for a strong and carefully crafted cuppa after visiting the nearby Sir Robert Ho Tung Library.

Single Origin (單品; Map p222; ☑6698 7475; www.singleorigincoffee.com; 19 Rua de Abreu Nunes; coffees MOP$35; ☺11.30am-8pm Mon-Sat, 2-7pm Sun; ☎; 🚍2, 4, 7, 7A, 8) This airy corner cafe, opened by coffee professional Keith Fong, makes a mean shot of espresso. You can choose your poison from a daily selection of 10 beans from various regions. If you can't decide, the well-trained barristas are more than happy to help.

Communal Table (Map p226; ☑6677 9985; 29c Rua Formosa; ☺noon-8pm; ☎; 🚍2, 7, 8, 8A, 9) This neat little-sister shop of Single Origin specialises in blends, and touts its homemade sandwiches and pastries, most of which are reasonably good.

Passione Cafe (品嚐咖啡店; Map p243; www.passione-cafe.com; 49 Rua Direita Carlos Eugenio; ☺11am-8pm; ☎; 🚍22, 28A, 26) This inviting cafe makes decent coffee and refreshing fruit tea (MOP$22 to MOP$40), as well as chunky waffle sandwiches (from MOP$50). The airy split-level space is flooded with natural light on a sunny day, which makes it hard to leave.

Kafka Sweets & Gourmandises (卡夫卡; ☑2882 0086; www.kafkasweets.com; 152 Rua de Braga, Taipa; ☺1.30-10pm; ☎; 🚍30, 34) Arguably Macau's best French-style patisserie outside of the hotels, Kafka is run by Le Cordon Bleu–trained Nicole Lei and her partner. The tastefully minimalist shop is named after Franz Kafka, because 'Braga' is Portuguese for Prague, where Kafka was born.

famous Fortaleza do Guincho, this luxuriously decorated restaurant brings Portuguese haute cuisine to Macau. The menu features well-executed classical dishes, with a couple of Macanese additions. Set meals are available at lunch (from MOP$300) and dinner (from MOP$600).

EIGHT
CANTONESE $$$

Map p226 (8餐廳; ☑8803 7788; www.grandlisboahotel.com; 2nd fl, Grand Lisboa Hotel, Avenida de Lisboa; meals MOP$350-1500; ☺11.30am-2.30pm & 6.30-10.30pm; 🚍3, 10, 28B) With water (a symbol for money) cascading down the wall, crystal-dripping chandeliers and an auspicious numeral for a name, the Eight can only belong to a casino. Granted, it's a stellar restaurant set apart from similar places by its solid dim sum, the chef's creativity and three Michelin stars. Getting a table is almost impossible without a reservation.

ROBUCHON AU DÔME
FRENCH $$$

Map p226 (☑8803 7878; www.grandlisboahotel.com/dining-Robuchon_au_Dome-en; 43rd fl, Grand Lisboa Hotel, Avenida de Lisboa; lunch/

dinner set menu from MOP$400/1588; ☺noon-2.30pm & 6.30-10.30pm; 🚍3, 10) Encased in a glass dome, this is arguably the most tastefully decorated of the casino restaurants. And as one of two Macau restaurants with three Michelin stars, it has everything you'd associate with the celebrated Robuchon name: fine decor, exquisite Gallic creations and impeccable service. The wine cellar with 8000 bottles is one of the best in Asia.

LA PALOMA
SPANISH, MEDITERRANEAN $$$

Map p222 (芭朗瑪餐廳; ☑2837 8111; www.saotiago.com.ma; 2nd fl, Pousada de São Tiago, Avenida da República; mains MOP$250-410; ☺7am-11pm; 🚍9) 'The Dove' sits on the foundations of a 17th-century fortress – one of Macau's most romantic spots and a welcome change from the casino restaurants. Hence any meal or drink here – be it a protracted Spanish feast under modern chandeliers, or a glass of *vinho do porto* (port wine) on the terrace – should be accompanied by a walk around the premises.

TIM'S KITCHEN
CHINESE $$$

Map p222 (桃花源小廚; ☑8803 3682; www.
hotelisboa.com; Shop F25, East Wing, Hotel
Lisboa, 2-4 Avenida de Lisboa, Praia Grande;
meals MOP$300-1500; ⊙noon-2.30pm & 6.30-
10.30pm; ☒3, 6, 26A) At Tim's, with one
Michelin star, fresh ingredients are meticu-
lously prepared using methods that pre-
serve or highlight their original flavours,
resulting in dishes that look simple but
taste divine – a giant 'glass' prawn shares
a plate with a sliver of Chinese ham; a crab
claw lounges on a cushion of winter melon
surrounded by broth.

🍷 DRINKING & NIGHTLIFE

★ MACAU SOUL
BAR

Map p226 (澳感廊; ☑2836 5182; www.macau
soul.com; 31a Rua de São Paulo; ⊙3-10pm Sun,
Mon & Thu, to midnight Fri & Sat; ☒8A, 17, 26) An
elegant haven in wood and stained glass,
where twice a month a jazz band plays to
a packed audience. On most nights though,
Thelonious Monk fills the air as customers
chat with the owners and dither over their
430 Portuguese wines. Opening hours vary;
phone ahead.

CINNEBAR
BAR

Map p222 (霞酒廊; ☑8986 3663; Ground fl,
Wynn Macau, Rua Cidade de Sintra, Novos Ater-
ros do Porto Exterior; ⊙3pm-1am Sun-Thu, to
2am Fri & Sat; ☎; ☒8, 10A, 23) Cinnebar has a
fantastic combination of swish and casual:
classy surroundings indoors and a relaxed
atmosphere in its outdoor seating area
around the swimming pool. Some exoti-
cally blended cocktails are served in this
lobby bar.

SINGING BEAN
COFFEE

Map p222 (音樂豆咖啡; ☑2838 9118; Macau
Tower, Largo da Torre de Macau; ⊙noon-9.30pm
Mon-Fri, 11am-9.30pm Sat & Sun; ☎; ☒9A, 18,
23, 26, 32) A pleasant and surprisingly af-
fordable coffee shop that also offers decent
Western and Macanese chow. If the weather
permits, take a table outside, and walk up
to the railing for views of the harbour and
people doing extreme sports from the tower.

SKY 21 LOUNGE
LOUNGE

Map p222 (☑2822 2122; www.sky21macau.
com; 21st fl, AIA Tower, 215a-301 Avenida Com-
ercial de Macau; ⊙6.30pm-2am Sun-Thu, to 3am
Fri & Sat, happy hour 5-9pm; ☎; ☒18, 23, 32)
Zen and cyber come together in this sleek
lounge-bar with alfresco seating and pan-
oramic views. There's a DJ and live jazz on
some days of the week, and special parties
on Saturdays.

☆ ENTERTAINMENT

★ LIVE MUSIC ASSOCIATION
LIVE MUSIC

Map p222 (現場音樂協會; www.lmamacau.com;
11b San Mei Industrial Bldg, 50 Avenida do Coronel
Mesquita; ☒3, 9, 32, 12, 25) The go-to place for
indie music in Macau, this excellent dive
inside an industrial building has hosted lo-
cal and overseas acts, including Cold Cave,
Buddhistson, Mio Myo and Pet Conspiracy.
See the website for what's on. Macau indie
bands to watch out for include WhyOceans
(www.whyoceans.com) and Turtle Giant
(www.turtlegiant.com).

SUN NEVER LEFT – PUBLIC ART PERFORMANCE
LIVE MUSIC

Map p226 (黃昏小叙-街頭藝術表演; www.
cipa.org.mo; Rua de Sao Roque; ⊙3-6pm Sat &
Sun; ☎; ☒7, 8) Every weekend artists at St
Lazarus Church District set up shop on the
picturesque Rua de Sao Roque, selling art
and handicrafts. Buy coffee from a nearby
cafe and sip it as you browse and enjoy the
live music.

RUI CUNHA FOUNDATION
CULTURAL VENUE

Map p226 (官樂怡基金會, Fundacao Rui Cunha;
☑2892 3288; http://ruicunha.org; 749 Avenida
da Praia Grande; ⊙gallery 10am-7pm; ☒2A, 6A,
7A, 8) From its airy venue in the heart of the
peninsula, this foundation promotes the

ℹ️ EVENTS & TICKETS

The website www.macau.com has
events listings and a ticket-booking
service. You can also book tickets to
most events through **Macau Ticket**
(Map p222; ☑2855 5555; www.macau
ticket.com; 71b Avenida Conselheiro Fer-
reira De Almeida) and **Cotai Ticketing**
(www.cotaiticketing.com).

The monthly events calendar for
upmarket entertainment is *Destination
Macau*, available at Macau Government
Tourist Office outlets and larger hotels.

Macau identity through a thoughtfully curated series of art exhibitions, literary readings and recitals. These are held alongside thought-provoking seminars on Macau's legal and social systems.

COMUNA DE PEDRA
DANCE

Map p222 (石頭公社; ☑6628 0064; http:// comunadepedra.blogspot.com) This edgy but elusive contemporary-dance company has performed everywhere – in parks, on rooftops, in factories, and on stage in Macau and overseas. Pinto Livros (p241) has updates.

CAO BOX
LIVE MUSIC

Map p222 (噪格; ☑6623 6091; www.caobox.net; 4th fl, Edificio Industrial Wan Kau, 35 Avenida do Almirante Lacerda; ☒1, 3, 4, 6A, 26, 26A, 33, N1A) A rehearsal studio for bands that sometimes morphs into an indie dive. It's on the 4th floor of an industrial building. See its website for updates.

🛍 SHOPPING

MERCEARIA PORTUGUESA
FOOD

Map p226 (☑2856 2708; www.merceariaportu guesa.com; 8 Calçada da Igreja de São Lazaro; ☉1-9pm Mon-Fri, noon-9pm Sat & Sun; ☒7, 8) The charming Portuguese corner shop opened by a film director and actress has a small but well-curated selection of provisions, which includes honey, chinaware, wooden toys and jewellery from Portugal, gorgeously packaged and reasonably priced.

FUTURA CLASSICA
BEAUTY

Map p226 (☑2835 8378; www.futuraclassica. com; 1A, Calcada da Rocha; ☉noon-8pm; ☒3, 6, 26 A, 18A, 33) This dizzyingly sweet-smelling shop is the Asian distributor of Claus Porto, a Portuguese brand of luxury soap and beauty products. It's a great place to shop for souvenirs. Prices range from MOP$50 to MOP$1000.

BRIGHT LIGHTS, SIN CITY

Gargantuan monuments in all forms of postmodern kitsch have taken over Macau's seafront. The change began when casino mogul Stanley Ho's monopoly ended in 2002 and Las Vegas operators set up shop in competition. There are now close to 40 casinos in Macau, their total gaming revenue surpassing all of the world's major gambling jurisdictions combined.

Table games are the staple at casinos here – mostly baccarat, then roulette and a dice game called *dai sai* ('big small'). You'll hardly hear any whooping and clunking – slot machines make up only 5% of total casino winnings (versus Vegas' 60%). Drunks are also hard to come by, as Chinese players believe that booze dulls their skill. Over 80% of gamblers and 95% of high rollers come from mainland China. The latter play inside members-only rooms where the total amount wagered on any given day can exceed a country's GDP.

For recreational players, the only thing to watch out for is harassment by tip hustlers – scam artists who hang around tables acting like your new best friend. They may steal your chips, nag you for a cut, or try to take you to a casino that'll tip them for bringing clients.

Casinos are open 24 hours. To enter, you must be 18 years or older and properly dressed.

MGM Grand Macau (澳門美高梅; Map p222; Grande Praça, Avenida Dr Sun Yat Sen, Macau Peninsula; ☒8, 3A, 12) With its younger vibe and less over-the-top decor, MGM Grand is pleasant for an air-conditioned walk-through even if you don't play the tables. It's also got more bars than the other casinos.

Grand Lisboa Casino (新葡京; Map p226; ☑2838 2828; Avenida de Lisboa, Macau Peninsula; ☒3, 10) The only Macau-born casino, the plush Grand Lisboa, with its glowing bulb exterior and flaming-torch-shaped tower, has become the landmark by which people navigate the peninsula's streets.

Wynn Macau Casino (永利娛樂場; Map p222; ☑2888 9966; Wynn Macau, Rua Cidade de Sintra, Novos Aterros do Porto Exterior, Macau Peninsula; ☒8, 10A) Vegas-style Wynn is arguably the classiest of the lot, with every game imaginable (up to MOP$2500 minimum bet) and original Matisse and Renoir paintings on the premises.

PINTO LIVROS
BOOKS

Map p226 (边度有书; http://blog.roodo.com/pintolivros; 1a Veng Heng Bldg, 31 Largo do Senado; ☺11.30am-11pm; ☐3, 6, 26A) This upstairs reading room overlooking Largo do Senado has a decent selection of art and culture titles, a few esoteric CDs and two resident cats.

LINES LAB
CLOTHING

Map p226 (www.lineslab.com; Shop A3, 8 Calçada da Igreja de São Lazaro; ☺1-8pm Tue-Sun; ☐7, 8) Two Lisbon-trained designers opened this boutique in the Old Ladies' House art space and created edgy Macau-inspired clothes and bags for it.

WORKER PLAYGROUND
CLOTHING

Map p222 (☑2875 7511; Ground fl, Edificio Cheung Seng, 83A Avenida do Conselheiro Ferreira de Almeida; ☺3-10pm; ☐) Worker Playground makes solid-quality baseball jackets, biker pants, and fashionably androgynous garments for men and women. The brand pays tribute to the old Workers' Stadium, a nostalgic landmark that was razed to make way for the Grand Lisboa Casino.

MACAO FASHION GALLERY
CLOTHING

Map p226 (澳門時尚廊; ☑2835 3341; www.macaofashiongallery.com; 47 Rua de São Roque; ☺10am-8pm Tue-Sun; ☐7, 8) A boutique on the ground floor displaying the creations of Macau designers, and a (underwhelming) gallery on the upper floors with exhibitions that change every three months and showcase fashion-related artefacts.

G17 GALLERY
CERAMICS

Map p226 (陶藝廊; ☑2834 6626; 17a Rua de Sao Miguel; ☺10am-7pm Mon-Sat, 2-6pm Sun; ☐7, 8) A small gallery that showcases and sells ceramics and pottery crafted by Macau's artists.

🏃 SPORTS & ACTIVITIES

AJ HACKETT
ADVENTURE SPORTS

Map p222 (☑8988 8656; http://macau.ajhackett.com) New Zealand–based AJ Hackett organises all kinds of adventure climbs up and around the Macau Tower.

GRAND PRIX
SPECTATOR SPORT

(☑2855 5555; www.macau.grandprix.gov.mo) The biggest sporting event of the year is the Macau Formula 3 Grand Prix, held in the third week of November. The 6.2km Guia circuit starts near the Grand Lisboa Casino and follows the shoreline along Avenida da Amizade, going around the reservoir and back through the city.

HIKING
HIKING

There are two trails on Guia Hill in central Macau Peninsula that are good for a stroll or jog. The **Walk of 33 Curves** (1.7km) circles the hill; inside this loop is the shorter **Fitness Circuit Walk**, with 20 exercise stations. You can access these by the Guia cable car.

The Islands: Taipa & Coloane

Explore

Jump on a bus to Coloane village and take an easy two-hour stroll around, soaking up the ambience and making stops at the Chapel of St Francis Xavier and Tam Kong Temple. Then take a bus to the Cotai Strip to the mega casino resorts where you can play the tables or catch a free show. Then it's on to Taipa. Wander through Taipa village to Avenida da Praia and spend an hour inside the Taipa Houses-Museum. Rua da Cunha is the place to go for a nice Macanese meal after you've checked out Taipa's assortment of Chinese temples.

The Best...

➡ **Sight** Taipa Houses-Museum (p242)
➡ **Place to eat** António (p245)
➡ **Place to drink** Macallan Whisky Bar & Lounge (p246)

Top Tip

Cycling is a great way to see Taipa and Coloane. In Taipa, 有記士多 on 11 Rua dos Negotiantes, near Pak Tai Temple, has bikes for rent. In Coloane, Dang Rang (東榮單車行) on Rua do Meio, does the same.

Getting There & Away

➜**Bus** Between the peninsula and Taipa: 11, 22, 28A, 30, 33, AP1. Between the peninsula and Coloane via Taipa: 21, 21A, 2521, 21A, 25, 26, 26A.

Need to Know

➜**Area code** ☑853

➜**Location** Taipa is 2.5km from Macau Peninsula and 39.3km away from Hong Kong; Coloane is 5.6km from Macau Peninsula and 39.3km from Hong Kong.

➜**Tourist office** There is a MGTO information counter at the Taipa Temporary Ferry Terminal.

⊙ SIGHTS

⊙ Taipa

TAIPA HOUSES-MUSEUM   MUSEUM

Map p243 (龍環葡韻住宅式博物館, Casa Museum da Taipa; ☑2882 7103; Avenida da Praia, Carmo Zone, Taipa; adult/student MOP$5/2, child & senior free, Sun free; ⊙10am-5.30pm Tue-Sun; ☐11, 15, 22, 28A, 30, 33, 34) The pastel-coloured villas (c 1921) here were once the summer residences of wealthy Macanese. House of the Regions of Portugal showcases Portuguese costumes. House of the Islands looks at the history of Taipa and Coloane, with displays on traditional industries, such as fishing and the manufacture of fireworks. Macanese House offers a snapshot of life in the early 20th century.

MUSEUM OF TAIPA & COLOANE HISTORY   MUSEUM

Map p243 (路氹歷史館, Museu da História da Taipa e Coloane; ☑2882 5361; Rua Correia da Silva, Taipa; adult/student MOP$5/2, child & senior free, Tue free; ⊙10am-5.30pm Tue-Sun; ☐11, 15, 22, 28A, 30, 33, 34) This museum has a display of excavated relics and other artefacts on the 1st floor, while the 2nd floor contains religious objects, handicrafts and architectural models.

CHURCH OF OUR LADY OF CARMEL   CHURCH

Map p243 (Igreja de Nossa Senhora de Carmo; Rue da Restauração; ☐22, 28A, 26) Built in 1885, this pretty church stands on a hill overlooking the harbour, the scenic Taipa village and the pastel-coloured Taipa Houses-Museum.

POU TAI TEMPLE   TEMPLE

(菩提禪院, Pou Tai Un; 5 Estrada Lou Lim Ieok; ⊙9am-6pm; ☐21A, 22, 25, 25X, 26A, 28A) A picturesque temple founded in the 19th century by Buddhist monks, Pou Tai has an enormous bronze statue of Lord Gautama in its main hall, and prayer pavilions and orchid greenhouses scattered around the complex. The monks also operate a vegetarian restaurant (p245).

TAIPA VILLAGE   VILLAGE

Map p243 (☐22, 26, 33) The historical part of Taipa is best preserved in this village in the south of the island. With a tidy sprawl of traditional Chinese shops and some excellent restaurants, the village is punctuated by colonial villas, churches and temples. Avenida da Praia, a tree-lined esplanade with wrought-iron benches, is perfect for a leisurely stroll.

PAK TAI TEMPLE   TEMPLE

Map p243 (Rua do Regedor; ☐22, 28A, 26) Pak Tai Temple sits quietly in a breezy square framed by old trees. It is dedicated to a martial deity – the Taoist God (Tai) of the North (Pak). This god defeated the Demon King, who was terrorising the universe. A pair of Chinese lions guards the entrance to the temple. On the third day of the third lunar month each year, Cantonese opera performances take place here.

⊙ Coloane

CHAPEL OF ST FRANCIS XAVIER   CHURCH

Map p244 (聖方濟各教堂, Capela de São Francisco Xavier; Rua do Caetano, Largo Eduardo Marques, Coloane; ⊙10am-8pm; ☐15, 21A, 25, 26A) This chapel, which was constructed in 1928, contains paintings of the infant Christ with a Chinese Madonna, and other reminders of Christianity and colonialism in Asia. This is a quirky place painted in yellow and embellished with red lanterns. In front of the chapel are a monument and fountain surrounded by four cannonballs that commemorate the successful (and final) routing of pirates in 1910.

Taipa

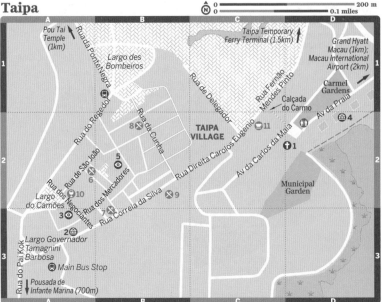

TEMPLES

TEMPLE

(☉8.30am-5.30pm; 🚌15, 21A, 25, 26A) Between Travessa de Caetano and Travessa de Pagode is a dainty **Kwun Yum Temple** (觀音廟; Map p244), a mere altar inside a walled compound. To the southeast in Largo Tin Hau Miu is **Tin Hau Temple** (天后廟; Map p244). At the south end of Avenida de Cinco de Outubro, **Tam Kong Temple** (譚公廟; Map p244; Avenida de Cinco de Outubro, Largo Tam Kong Miu; ☉8.30am-5.30pm; 🚌15, 21A, 25, 26A) is dedicated to a Taoist god of seafarers. To the right of the main altar is a long whale bone carved into a model of a dragon boat.

MACAU GIANT PANDA PAVILION

ZOO

(大熊貓館, Pavihao do Panda Gigante de Macau; ☎2833 7676; www.macaupanda.org.mo; Seac Pai Van Park, Coloane; admission MOP$10; ☉10am-1pm & 2-5pm Tue-Sun; ♿; 🚌15, 21A, 25, 26, 26A, 50) Coloane offers a convenient and inexpensive opportunity to see a panda. The cuddly one is kept inside a purpose-built pavilion inside Seac Pai Van Park (p244). There are six hour-long viewing sessions daily, from 10am to 4pm. Other animals on display include peacocks, monkeys and a toucan.

COLOANE LIBRARY

LIBRARY

Map p244 (路環圖書館; Rua de Cinco de Outubro, Coloane; ☉1-7pm Mon-Sat; 🚌21A, 25, 26A)

Taipa

☉ Sights (p242)

1 Church of Our Lady of Carmel D2
2 Museum of Taipa & Coloane
    History.. A3
3 Pak Tai Temple....................................... A3
4 Taipa Houses-Museum....................... D2
5 Taipa Village... B2

☓ Eating (p245)

6 A Petisqueira.. A2
7 António.. B3
8 O Santos... B2
9 Tai Lei Loi... B2

☉ Drinking & Nightlife (p246)

10 Old Taipa Tavern................................. A2
11 Passione Cafe...................................... C2

This mini Grecian temple, built in 1917, still functions as a public library.

HÁC SÁ BEACH

BEACH

(黑沙海灘; 🚌21A, 25, 26A) Hác Sá (Black Sand) is Macau's most popular beach. The sand is indeed a blackish colour and makes the water look somewhat dirty, but it's clean. Lifeguards are on duty from May to October. The stalls just off the beach rent out parasols

Coloane

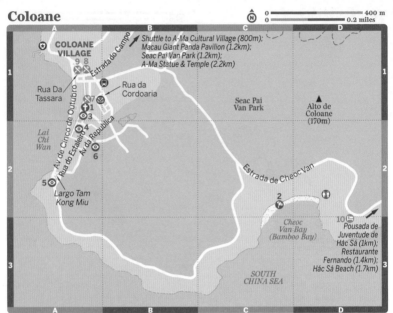

Coloane

⊙ Sights	(p242)
1 Chapel of St Francis Xavier	A1
2 Cheoc Van Beach	C2
3 Coloane Library	A1
4 Kun Iam Temple	A2
5 Tam Kong Temple	A2
6 Tin Hau Temple	A2

⊗ Eating	(p245)
7 Café Nga Tim	A1
8 Espaco Lisboa	A1
9 Lord Stowe's Bakery	A1

⊕ Sleeping	(p246)
10 Pousada de Juventude de Cheoc Van	D3

for MOP$60 a day, with a MOP$100 deposit (but you'll need to bring your parasol back).

A-MA STATUE & TEMPLE   MEMORIAL
(媽祖像及媽閣廟, Estátua da Deusa A-Ma; Estrada do Alto de Coloane; ⊙temple 8am-7.30pm) Atop Alto de Coloane (176m), this 20m-high white jade statue of the goddess who gave Macau its name was erected in 1998. It's the best part of a touristy 'cultural village' that

also features **Tian Hou Temple**. A free bus runs from the A-Ma ornamental entrance gate (媽祖文化村石牌坊) on Estrada de Seac Pai Van (bus 21A, 25, 50) half-hourly from 8am to 6pm. You can also reach both by following the Coloane Trail (Trilho de Coloane) from Seac Pai Van Park.

CHEOC VAN BEACH   BEACH
Map p244 (竹灣海灘; Estrada de Cheoc Van; ▣21A, 25, 26A) About 1.5km down Estrada de Cheoc Van, which runs east and then southeast from Coloane village, is the beach at Cheoc Van (Bamboo Bay), smaller but more idyllic than Hác Sá beach. There are changing rooms and toilets and, in season, lifeguards on duty (from 10am to 6pm Monday to Saturday, from 9am to 6pm Sunday, May to October).

SEAC PAI VAN PARK   PARK
(石排灣郊野公園; Estrada de Seac Pai Van; ⊙9am-6pm Tue-Sun, aviary 9am-5pm Tue-Sun; ▣21A, 26A, 50) **FREE** At the end of Cotai, this 20-hectare park, built in the wooded hills on the western side of the island, has somewhat unkempt gardens, the Macau Giant Panda Pavilion (p243), a lake with swans and other waterfowl, and a walk-through aviary.

✖ EATING

✖ Taipa

A PETISQUEIRA
PORTUGUESE $

Map p243 (葡國美食天地; ☑2882 5354; 15 Rua de São João, Taipa; meals MOP$150-500; ⏱12.30-2.15pm & 6.45-10pm Tue-Sun; 🚻; 🚌22, 28A) 'The Snackery' is an amicable place with myriad Portuguese choices set in an obscure alley. It serves its own *queijo fresca da casa* (homemade cheese). Try the bacalao five ways, and baked seafood with rice.

POU TAI TEMPLE RESTAURANT
CHINESE, VEGETARIAN $

(5 Estrada Lou Lim Ieok; dishes MOP$40-60; ⏱11am-8pm Mon-Sat, 9am-9pm Sun; 🚻🚻) This verandah vegetarian restaurant, set in Pou Tai Temple (p242) in northern Taipa, is a great find.

TAI LEI LOI
CHINESE $

Map p243 (大利來記; ☑2882 7150; www.taileiloi.com.mo; 35 Rua Correia da Silva, Taipa; dishes MOP$30; ⏱8am-6pm; 🚻; 🚌22, 26) South China's most famous pork-chop bun is made here – a shop founded in 1960 as a street stall by the mother of the current owner. Succulent slices of pork (or, alternatively, slivers of fish) are coupled with warm, chewy buns that emerge from the oven daily at 2pm sharp.

BANZA
PORTUGUESE $$

(百姓餐廳; ☑2882 1519; 154a & b, G & H, Block 5, Edificio Nam San Garden, Avenida de Kwong Tung, Taipa; meals MOP$200-500; ⏱noon-3pm & 6.30-11pm Tue-Sun; 🚌11, 16, 28A) This welcoming place run by a Portuguese former lawyer is known for its well-executed fish dishes and Portuguese classics. If you'd like, Banza could also recommend a bottle from his interesting selection of Portuguese wines.

O SANTOS
MACANESE $$

Map p243 (☑2882 7508; 20 Rua da Cunha, Taipa; meals MOP$200-350; ⏱lunch & dinner; 🚻; 🚌22, 26) Despite its location on the touristy Rua da Cunha, charming O Santos keeps its standards up. Patrons have been coming back for the chicken and rice in blood and friendly banter with the owner (a former naval chef) for 20 years.

★ ANTÓNIO
PORTUGUESE $$$

Map p243 (安東尼奧; ☑2899 9998; www.antoniomacau.com; 7 Rua dos Clerigos, Taipa; meals MOP$350-1200; ⏱noon-10.30pm; 🚌22, 26) The cosy mahogany-framed dining room, the meticulously thought-out menu and the entertaining chef, António Coelho, all make this the go-to place for traditional Portuguese food. If you can only try one Portuguese restaurant in Macau, make it this one.

✖ Coloane

CAFÉ NGA TIM
MACANESE $

Map p244 (雅憩花園餐廳; Rua do Caetano, Coloane; mains MOP$70-200; ⏱noon-1am; 🚻; 🚌21A, 25, 26A) We love the Chinese-Portuguese food, the small-town atmosphere, the view of the Chapel of St Francis Xavier, the prices and the owner – a guitar-and *erhu*-strumming ex-policeman named Feeling Wong.

LORD STOWE'S BAKERY
BAKERY $

Map p244 (澳門安德魯餅店; Rua do Tassara, Coloane; ⏱7am-10pm; 🚻; 🚌21A, 25, 26A) This bakery commemorating Andrew Stowe, the English baker who lived in Macau,

LOCAL KNOWLEDGE

COLOANE'S STILT HOUSES

Macau was a fishing village before gambling was legalised in the mid-19th century. Now the only vestiges of that idyllic past are found in Coloane.

Along the coastline, on Rua dos Navegantes in Coloane's old fishing village, there are a few stilt houses and shipyards. These huts of colourful corrugated metal, extending like chunky chopsticks out into the harbour, were once landing spots for house boats. A couple have been turned into dried seafood shops, such as Loja de Peixe Tong Kei (棠記魚舖) at Largo do Cais, the square just off the charming old pier of Coloane.

From the square, take the slope to the right of the Servicos de Alfangega building. After two minutes, you'll see the cavernous cadaver of a shipyard, also on stilts.

SLEEPING IN TAIPA & COLOANE

Macau Peninsula has the greatest range of accommodation that is close to the major sights. Lodging on the islands comprises big casino hotels or reasonably priced options that are a little out of the way.

Pousada de Juventude de Cheoc Van (Map p244; ☑2888 2024; www.dsej.gov.mo; Rua de António Francisco, Coloane; dm/tw/q from MOP$100/160/120; ❉❖; ☐21A, 25, 26A) This government-run, beachside hostel is excellent value, but conditions apply. You'll need to book three months in advance and own an International Youth Card, International Youth Hostel Card or similar. It's closed to tourists in July and August. More details on the website.

Pousada de Juventude de Hác Sá (☑2888 2702, 2888 2701; www.dsej.gov.mo; Rua de Hác Sá Long Chao Kok, Coloane; dm Sun-Fri MOP$50-80, Sat additional MOP$20-40; ❉❖; ☐21A, 25, 26A) Similar deal as the Cheoc Van youth hostel, but with more beds and recreation space. It's 400m uphill from the beach on Rua de Hác Sá Long Chao Kok. Showers and toilets are shared, though its website says otherwise.

Pousada de Infante Marina (皇庭海景酒店; ☑2883 8333; www.pousadamarinainfante.com; Avenida Marginal Flor de Lotus, Taipa; r MOP$865-1369, ste MOP$1918; ❂❉@❖) An old-fashioned hotel sandwiched between the Galaxy casino and a river. Service can be cavalier but the rooms are clean and relatively large. If you book online, you get wi-fi and the minibar for free. Otherwise, there's no wi-fi and you have to pay to use the minibar. Rooms facing the Galaxy have surreal views, especially at night.

Grand Hyatt Macau (☑8868 1234; http://macau.grand.hyatt.com; City of Dreams, Estrada do Istmo, Cotai; r MOP$1300-3200, ste from MOP$2300; ❂❉@❖❐; ☐35, 50) The most tasteful of the casino hotels on the Cotai Strip, the Grand Hyatt is part of the City of Dreams complex. The massive rooms come with glass-and-marble showers, bath-tubs and a full battery of technology.

continues to make his renowned *pastéis de nata* (MOP$8), a sweet and creamy Portuguese-style egg-tart pastry.

BARBECUE STALLS
NEAR HÁC SÁ BEACH   BARBECUE $

(Rua de Hác Sá Long Chao Kok, Coloane; skewers MOP$15-45; ⊗11am-3pm; ⓕ; ☐21A, 25, 26A) Just off Hác Sá beach is a row of barbecue stalls – some with tables – emitting the mouth-watering aromas of grilled meat and seafood.

RESTAURANTE FERNANDO   PORTUGUESE $$

(法蘭度餐廳; ☑2888 2264; 9 Hác Sá beach; meals MOP$150-270; ⊗noon-9.30pm; ⓕ; ☐21A, 25, 26A) Possibly Coloane's most famous restaurant, Fernando's easy-breezy atmosphere makes it perfect for a protracted seafood lunch by the sea, as its devoted customers would agree. The bar stays open till midnight.

ESPACO LISBOA   PORTUGUESE, MACANESE $$$

Map p244 (里斯本地帶餐廳; ☑2888 2226; 8 Rua das Gaivotas, Coloane; meals MOP$250-800; ⊗noon-3pm & 6.30-10pm Thu & Sun-Tue, noon-10.30pm Fri & Sat; ⓕ; ☐21A, 25, 26A) The home-style dishes here are solidly good, but what makes this two-storey restaurant in Coloane village unique is the combination of Portugal-inspired decor and a Chinese village house – in other words, the space (*'espaco'*).

🍷 DRINKING & NIGHTLIFE

★MACALLAN WHISKY BAR & LOUNGE   BAR

(☑8883 2221; www.galaxymacau.com; 203, 2nd fl, Galaxy Hotel, Cotai; ⊗5pm-1am Mon-Thu, to 2am Fri & Sat; ☐25, 25X) Macau's best whisky bar is a traditional affair featuring oak panels, Jacobean rugs and a real fireplace. The 400-plus whisky labels include representatives from Ireland, France, Sweden and India, and a 1963 Glenmorangie.

CLUB CUBIC   CLUB

(☑6638 4999; www.cubic-cod.com; 2105-02, Level 2, City of Dreams, Estrada do Istmo, Cotai;

⏰11.30pm-6am Mon-Sat; 🚌50, 35) The massive and flashy Club Cubic at the Hard Rock Hotel has themed rooms and a large disco ball. There are DJs mixing a variety of tunes, including hip hop, techno and Korean pop, pumped out of the club's top-notch sound system.

OLD TAIPA TAVERN

PUB

Map p243 (好客鄉村餐廳; 21 Rua dos Negociantes, Taipa; ☎; 🚌22, 28A, 26) A location near the Pak Tai Temple makes laid-back OTT a sublime spot to watch the comings and goings in the centre of Taipa village.

☆ ENTERTAINMENT

HOUSE OF DANCING WATER

THEATRE

(水 舞間; ☎8868 6688; http://thehouseofdancingwater.com; City of Dreams, Estrada do Istmo, Cotai; tickets MOP$580-980; 🚌50, 35) 'The House of Dancing Water', Macau's most expensively made show, is a breathtaking melange of stunts, acrobatics and theatre designed by Franco Dragone, the former director of Cirque du Soleil. The magic revolves around a cobalt pool the size of several Olympic-sized swimming pools, over, around, into and under which a cast of 80 perform hair-raising stunts dressed in glorious costumes.

🏃 SPORTS & ACTIVITIES

🏃 Taipa

CYCLING

CYCLING

Taipa has two cycling trails. **Taipa Grande Trail** (bus 21A, 26, 28A) can be accessed via a paved road off Estrada Colonel Nicolau de Mesquita, near the United Chinese Cemetery. **Taipa Pequena Trail** (bus 21A, 33, 35) is reachable by way of Estrada Lou Lim Ieok, behind the Regency Hotel. A store,

有記士多 on 11 Rua dos Negotiantes, near Pak Tai Temple and two shops up from Old Taipa Tavern, has bikes for rent at MOP$20 per hour; it's open from 9am to 7pm. Cycling across the Macau–Taipa bridges is prohibited.

HIKING

HIKING

The **Little Taipo Trail** (Trilho de Taipa Pequena) is a 2km-long circuit around a hill (111m) in northwestern Taipa, reachable via Estrada Lou Lim Ieok. The 2.2km-long **Taipo Trail** (Trilho de Taipa Grande) rings Taipa Grande, a 160m-high hill at the eastern end of the island. You can access the trail via a short paved road off Estrada Colonel Nicolau de Mesquita.

🏃 Coloane

COLOANE TRAIL

HIKING

Coloane's and Macau's longest trail, the 8100m Trilho de Coloane, begins in the mid-section of Estrada do Alto de Coloane and winds around the island. (To get there, take bus 21A and get off at stop Estrata do Campo, then enter Estrata Militar across the road; after 600m, turn right.) You can make a detour to Alto de Coloane (170m) to see the A-Ma Statue.

The shorter **Coloane Northeast Trail** (Trilho Nordeste de Coloane), near Ká Hó, runs for 3km. Other trails that offer good hiking include the 1.5km-long **Altinho de Ká Hó Trail** and the 1.5km-long **Circuito da Barragem de Hác Sá**, which both loop around the reservoir to the northwest of Hác Sá beach.

MACAU GOLF & COUNTRY CLUB

GOLF

(澳門高爾夫球鄉村俱樂部; ☎2887 1188; www.macaugolfandcountryclub.com; 1918 Estrada de Hác Sá, Coloane; 🚌15) One of three tournament courses in greater China, the scenic 18-hole, par-71 course connected to the Westin Resort has special weekday tee times for non-members. The driving range allows players to hit balls into the South China Sea.

MACAU THE ISLANDS: TAIPA & COLOANE

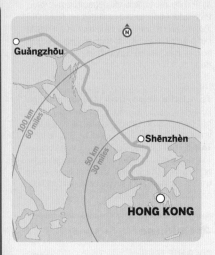

Day Trips from Hong Kong

Shēnzhèn p249

For most day visitors, Shēnzhèn is mostly about bargain shopping (followed by a cheap massage or good dim sum). Although the bargains are still Shēnzhèn's main draws, many exciting cultural spaces have emerged that are subverting the city's reputation for vacuous consumerism. Shēnzhèn hosts the Bi-City Biennale of Urbanism/Architecuture and China's major music festivals all have SZ editions. You can buy a five-day, Shēnzhèn-only visa at the Lo Wu border crossing (Americans, and sometimes British, excluded).

Guǎngzhōu p254

Known to many as Canton, Guǎngzhōu, the capital of Guǎngdōng province, is a sprawling city with 12 million people that may seem chaotic to the uninitiated. But with patience, you'll discover graceful Chinese gardens, magnificent temples, throbbing indie dives, tea houses rich with culture, and sites of uprisings that changed the history of China. And fittingly enough, in Canton, you'll find Cantonese cuisine at its best.

Shēnzhèn

Explore

On arriving at Shēnzhèn train station, take bus 101 or 204 for an hour's ride west to Window of the World in Nánshān District. Spend about two hours there, before taking the metro to the next two stops east, respectively Huáqiáochéng station and Qiáochéngdōng station, to visit art galleries and the OCT-LOFT Art Terminal. Have a snack at one of the cafes at OCT-LOFT, before heading east to Chēgōngmiào station to shop for knock-off designer furniture and a proper lunch. Then head east to the Shēnzhèn Museum near Shìmín Zhōngxīn station to get some context for your impressions. Spend an hour or so there. If you're up for more shopping, check out Luóhú Commercial Centre, and enjoy dinner in the Luóhú District, before catching the train back to Hong Kong.

The Best...

➡ **Sight** OCT-LOFT (p249)

➡ **Place to eat** Phoenix House (p252)

➡ **Place to shop** Century Furnishings Central Mall (p253)

Top Tip

At Dōngmén Market, you can have clothes, drapes or bedcovers custom-made for same-day pick-up. Place your order in the morning, do your sightseeing and pick up your goods before dinner. With clothes, stick to straightforward designs, and try to provide an image of what you want.

Getting There & Away

➡ **Train** MTR's Lo Wu–bound or Lok Ma Chau–bound trains (1st/2nd class HK$72/36 if you start from Hung Hom) are the most convenient transport to Shēnzhèn from Hong Kong. The first train to Lo Wu/Lok Ma Chau leaves Hung Hom station at 5.30/5.35am, the last at 11.07/9.35pm, and the trip takes about 44/49 minutes. Both connect with the metro in Shēnzhèn once across the border.

➡ **Bus** Frequent buses run by **China Travel Tours Transportation Services** (CTS; ☑2764 9803; http://ctsbus.hkcts.com) head to the Huánggǎng border crossing (near Lok Ma Chau) and Shēnzhèn Bay (深圳湾)

at Shékǒu from multiple departure points including Metropark Hotel in Causeway Bay, and CTS branches in Wan Chai, Sheung Wan, Mong Kok and Prince Edward. Fares range from HK$40 to HK$50 (one way). Shēnzhèn has a cheap and efficient network of buses and minibuses (tickets ¥2 to ¥7).

➡ **Boat** The **Chu Kong Passenger Transportation Company** (☑2858 3876; www.cksp.com.hk) has six jet-cat departures (economy/1st class HK$140/180, one hour) daily from the Hong Kong-Macau Ferry Terminal to Shékǒu port from 10am to 8.30pm. Fourteen ferries depart from Hong Kong airport (HK$220, 30 minutes one way) between 9am and 9.45pm.

Getting Around

➡ **Metro** Shēnzhèn has five metro lines (www.szmc.net). Fares start from ¥2 for the first 4km. Line 1 stretches from the Luóhú border crossing to the airport, passing through the Window of the World theme park. Line 4 starts at Fútián Check Point station, where passengers can interchange from Lok Ma Chau station across the border in Hong Kong. You can buy a ¥20 pass at any metro station and make unlimited trips within a 24-hour period.

➡ **Taxi** In Shēnzhèn, the first 2km cost ¥10, with each additional kilometre ¥2.40.

Need to Know

➡ **Area code** ☑86 (0)755

➡ **Tourist office** (Shēnzhèn Tourist Consultation Centre, 深圳市旅游局旅游咨询中心; ☑8232 3045; Ground fl, Shēnzhèn train station, east exit; ◷9am-6pm) Free and reasonably detailed maps available on request. There's another branch at Fútián Port that keeps the same hours.

➡ **Visa** See p314 for details.

◉ SIGHTS

OCT-LOFT   ARTS CENTRE

(华侨城创意文化园; Huáqiáochéng Chuàngyì Wénhuàyuán; ☑2691 1976; Enping Jie, Huáqiáochéng, Nánshān District; ◷10am-5.30pm; Ⓜ Qiáochéngdōng, exit A) The sprawling OCT-LOFT complex, converted from austere communist-era factories, is one of the best places to see contemporary art in Shēnzhèn, and makes for a wonderful browse-as-you-

Shēnzhèn

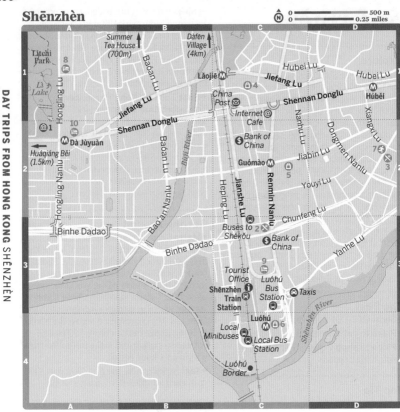

stroll experience. Large exhibition spaces and private galleries (many closed on Mondays) are complemented by chilled cafes, restaurants with exposed ventilation ducts, quirky fashion boutiques, a gem of a bookstore, and the obligatory 'lifestyle' outlets.

Turn right as you exit the metro station and follow the signs.

SHĒNZHÈN MUSEUM   MUSEUM
(深圳博物馆新馆; Shēnzhèn Bówùguǎn Xīnguǎn; ☏8201 3036; www.shenzhenmuseum.com.cn; East Gate, Block A, Citizens' Centre, Fuzhong Sanlu, Fútián District; ⊗10am-6pm Tue-Sun; Ⓜ Line 4, Shìmín Zhōngxīn, exit B) **FREE** The hulking Shēnzhèn Museum provides a solid introduction to Shēnzhèn's short yet dynamic history of social transformation, both before and after the implementation of Deng Xiaoping's policies of reform. Highlights include propaganda art popular in the 1940s and the colourful scale models in the folk culture hall.

HÉ XIĀNGNÍNG ART GALLERY GALLERY

(何 香凝美術館; Héxiāngníng Měishúguǎn; ☑2660 4540; www.hxnart.com; 9013 Shennan Lu; ⊙9.30am-4.30pm Tue-Sun; Ⓜ Huáqiáochéng, exit C) **FREE** The esoteric permanent collection here features Japanese-influenced Chinese water paintings by He Xiangning (1878–1972), the late master of modern Chinese art and well-known revolutionary. These are complemented by temporary exhibits that range from avant-garde Chinese art to Western works of an experimental nature. The gallery is one metro stop from OCT-Loft.

GUĀNLÁN ORIGINAL
PRINTMAKING BASE VILLAGE

(观澜版画原创产业基地; Guānlán Bǎnhuà Yuán-chuàng Chǎnyè Jīde; ☑2978 2510; www.guanlan-prints.com/en/; Dàshuǐtián, Niúhú, Bǎo'ān District; ☑312, M258, M285, M288, M338, M339 to Guānlán Printmaking Base stop, ☑B650, B768, B769, E4 to Guānlán jiēdàobàn zhàn (观澜街道办站)) At this 300-year-old village, rows of quaint black-and-white houses exuding a modest, functional elegance unique to Hakka architecture are occupied by the workshops and galleries of printmaking artists from China and overseas. The village, with its tree-lined paths and lotus ponds, is open all day, but the galleries keep different hours. The journey from downtown Shēnzhèn takes about 1½ hours.

OCT ART & DESIGN GALLERY GALLERY

(华·美术馆; Huá Měishùguǎn; ☑3399 3111; www.oct-and.com; 9009 Shennan Lu; adult/child ¥15/8; ⊙10am-5.30pm Tue-Sun; Ⓜ Huáqiáochéng, exit C) The bare interiors of this former warehouse are filled with the works of excellent mainland and international graphic designers. Exhibits change frequently. It's a glass-encased steel structure adjacent to Hé Xiāngníng Art Gallery.

WINDOW OF THE WORLD THEME PARK

(世界之窗, Shìjiè Zhīchuāng; ☑2660 8000; www.szwwco.com; adult/child under 12yr ¥160/80; ⊙9am-10.30pm, ☑90 or 245 from Shēnzhèn Bay Port, Ⓜ Shìjiè Zhīchuāng, exit J) Just a few minutes' walk from the OCT Art & Design Gallery is a series of dated theme parks that are always packed with snap-happy Chinese tourists. They're fun destinations for a family day out. Window of the World sports a collection of scale replicas of famous world monuments. Foreigners being misidentified as part of the exhibits is not unheard of.

DÀPÉNG FORTRESS VILLAGE

(大鹏所城; Dàpéng Suǒchéng; ☑0755-8431 5618; Dàpéng Town, Lónggǎng District; adult/student & senior ¥20/10; ⊙10am-6pm) This walled town and lively village built 600 years ago lies on Shēnzhèn's eastern edge. Stately mansions, fortress gates and ornate temples from the Ming and Qing dynasties are the main attractions. Board bus 360 at Yínhú bus station or near China Regency Hotel on Sungang Lu. The journey takes about 90 minutes. At Dàpéng bus station (Dàpéng zǒngzhàn; 大鹏总站), change to bus 966. A taxi from Luóhú costs ¥190.

OCT EAST AMUSEMENT PARK, RESORT

(东部华侨城, Dōngbù Huáqiáochéng; ☑2503 18 37; www.octeast.com; Dàméishā, Yán Tián District; admission ¥160-300; ⊙9.30am-6pm) Some 20km east of downtown Shenzhen is OCT East, an upmarket theme-park-cum-resort. Think Universal Studios plus Chinese Disneyland with a mock Swiss village, a golf complex, a scenic tea valley and luxury hotels thrown in. You can rent a car inside the park to tour around in. Sightseeing Bus 1, which leaves from Window of the World, with stops at Dìwáng Dàxià (Shennan Lu), has its last stop at the park. A taxi from Luohu train station is about Y70.

🍴 EATING

Being a city of immigrants, Shēnzhèn offers some excellent regional Chinese cooking, such as Hunanese and Sichuanese, in addition to Cantonese cuisine. The food courts in shopping malls like **The MixC** (Ⓜ Dàjùyuàn, exit C3) and **Coco Park** (Ⓜ Gòuwù Gōngyuán, exit C) have some decent options for budget travellers.

LAUREL DIM SUM, CANTONESE $

(丹 桂轩; Dānguìxuān; ☑8232 3668; Renmin Nanlu; 人民南路; dim sum ¥8-28, dishes ¥40-180; ⊙7am-11pm) An excellent modern dim sum restaurant on the 5th floor of Luóhú Commercial City. Tables are a little close together, but the environment is pleasant and service is warm.

MÁOJIĀ RESTAURANT HÚNÁN $$

(毛 家飯店, Máojiāfàndiàn; ☑8221 6569; 2033 Chunfeng Lu, 2nd fl, Yúnjǐng Háoyuán, Luohu; meals ¥50-110; ⊙10am-10pm; ☑387 from Luóhú train station) This decent Húnán restaurant honours Mao Zedong, who was a native of

Húnán. It's decked out with Mao paraphernalia, including a copper bust of the Chinese leader and a few poems he penned. Nonspicy options include sliced pumpkin with dates and 'Mao family' roast pork. Disembark at Chūnfēngwànjiā bus stop and walk for five minutes.

SUMMER TEA HOUSE   VEGETARIAN, DIM SUM $

(静颐茶馆, Jìngyí Cháguǎn; ☏2557 4555; www.jingyi2000.com/; 7th & 8th fl, Jìntáng Dàxià, 3038 Ba o'an Nanlu; dishes ¥50-80; ◉10am-1am; ✐) Tucked away in an office building near Xīhú Bīnguǎn is this vegies' favourite in Shēnzhèn, with healthy ingredients, a relaxing tea-tasting area and a smoke-free dining hall. There's no English menu, but colourful pictures illustrate the dishes. Vegetarian dim sum is available even for dinner. There are more filling options too, if you're hungry.

WEST LAKE SPRING   HANGZHOU $

(西湖春天, Xīhú Chūntiān; ☏8211 6988; 3019 Sungang Donglu, 2nd-3rd fl, Parkway Tower; dishes ¥21-260; ◉10am-11pm; 🚍18, get off at Xīhú Bīnguǎn) This Hángzhōu restaurant gets the thumbs-up from locals. Signature dishes such as *lóngjǐng xiārén* (龙井虾仁; stir-fried freshwater shrimp with longjing tea leaves; ¥88) and *sòngsǎo yúgēng* (宋嫂鱼羹; yellow croaker soup; small/large ¥48/58) are delicately flavoured like they should be. There's no English menu, but the Chinese menu has pictures.

PHOENIX HOUSE   DIM SUM, CANTONESE $$

(凤凰楼, Fènghuánglóu; ☏8207 6688, 8207 6338; 4002 Huaqiang Beilu, East Wing, Pavilion Hotel; lunch ¥60-80, dinner ¥100-350; ◉7.30am-11pm; Ⓜ Huáqiánglù, exit A) One of the best Cantonese restaurants in town, but expect noisy waits for 30 minutes or more after 11.30am. Some of the dim sum can be ordered by the piece – good when you're dining alone.

🍷 DRINKING & NIGHTLIFE

Finding a venue in Shēnzhèn for anything from a quiet drink to a raucous knees-up after a hard day of bargaining is easy. There are upmarket bars below Citic City Plaza (中信城市广场, Zhōngxìn Chéngshì Guǎngchǎng), at Coco Park in Fútián and SeaWorld (海上世界, Hǎishàng Shìjiè) in Shékǒu.

YĪDÙTÁNG   BAR

(一渡堂; ☏8610 6046; Enping Lu, Block F3, OCT-LOFT, Huáqiáochéng, Nánshān District; ◉11.30am-2am; Ⓜ Qiáochéngdōng, exit A) International and local indie bands play almost every night after 10pm at this warehouse-turned-bohemian-haunt in OCT-LOFT. It's a pleasant place with large glass panes, a soaring ceiling (from which chandeliers hang) and velvet armchairs placed next to brick walls. During the day, it's an upmarket cafe.

☆ ENTERTAINMENT

BROWN SUGAR   LIVE MUSIC

(皇冠科技园; Hóngtáng Guànzi; www.hongtanggu an.com; Tairan Jiulu, Fútián District, Ground fl, Block 2, Huángguān Kējì Yuán; tickets ¥40-120; ◉2pm-midnight Sun-Thu, to 2am Fri & Sat; Ⓜ Chēgōngmiào, exit C) Sandwiched between a garage and a hair salon near the entrance of Crown Technology Park (皇冠科技園, Huángguān Kējìyuán), this loft-like bar is where local and foreign indie bands play every weekend from 9pm. Run by young musicians, it sports eclectic furniture and paintings displayed on bare concrete walls.

At the metro exit, turn right and walk to the end of the road, then make a left. You should see the park entrance on your right after two minutes.

B10 LIVE HOUSE   LIVE MUSIC

(☏8633 7602; Shantou Jie, northern section, OCT-LOFT, Huáqiáochéng, Nánshān District; Ⓜ Qiáochéngdōng, exit A) A huge warehouse conversion that morphs into a live house when there are no exhibitions going on. It's located on the north side of the Block B10 in the northern section of OCT-LOFT.

🛍 SHOPPING

Interior designers and shrewd homeowners in Hong Kong are increasingly turning to Shēnzhèn to hunt for furniture and furnishings, including knock-off designer furniture. Unless you want a genuine Eames chair or Artemide lamp, most replicas in Hong Kong and overseas were made in Shēnzhèn anyway. Many places will pack and ship overseas, and if customers are prepared to haggle, vendors may lower the marked price by 30% to 50%.

Shoppers won't leave Shēnzhèn empty-handed, though quality can vary. Some shops

INDIE MUSIC FESTIVALS

Shēnzhèn's indie music scene is rocking, and there's irrefutable proof – China's largest indie music events, **Strawberry Music Festival** (草莓音乐节; Cǎoméi Yīnyuè Jié; www. modernsky.com; ⏲May) and **Midi Music Festival** (迷笛音乐节; Mídí Yīnyuè Jié; www.midifestival.com), have had Shēnzhèn editions since 2013–14. Both events feature the strongest bands from China, Taiwan and Hong Kong performing for three days. Midi takes place at the end of the year and Strawberry is usually in May. Check their websites for details.

have been known to be cavalier about following specs and maintaining quality for larger items such as a set of cabinets on order. So shop around, and shop hard.

DÀFĒN VILLAGE ARTS & CRAFTS

(大芬村, Dàfēncūn; ☑8473 2633; www.dafenvillageonline.com; Dafen, Buji, Lónggǎng District) A real eye-opener: 600 studios-cum-stores, churning out thousands of copies of Rembrandt, Renoir and Picasso paintings every week, and some original work. Prices start from ¥300. It's also a good place to stock up on art supplies, with prices about 50% cheaper than in downtown Shēnzhèn. Bus 306 from Shēnzhèn's Luóhú station takes you to the village in about an hour. A taxi ride costs around ¥80.

DŌNGMÉN MARKET MARKET

(东门市场, Dōngmén Shìchǎng; ⏲10am-10pm; ⓂLǎojiē, exit A) A chaotic market popular for tailored suits, skirts, curtains and bedding. Be careful of pickpockets.

HUÁQIÁNG BĚI COMMERCIAL ST ELECTRONICS

(华强北商业街, Huáqiángběi Shāngyèjiē; ⓂHuáqiánglù, exit A) For electronics, Huáqiáng Běi is a living, breathing eBay, with shops and malls for blocks on end selling the latest tech gadgets, audiovisual equipment, android tablets, Bluetooth headsets, nonbranded laptops and accessories at rock-bottom prices.

★OLD HEAVEN BOOKS BOOKS

(旧天堂书店, Jiùtiāntáng Shūdiàn; ☑8614 8090; oldheavenbooks@gmail.com; Room 120, Block A5, northern section, OCT-LOFT, Huáqiáochéng, Nánshān District; ⏲11am-10pm; ⓂQiáochéngdōng, exit A) A bookstore specialising in cultural and academic titles, that also doubles up as music store (vinyls anyone?). Gigs sometimes take place in the adjoining cafe. Located in the northern section of OCT-LOFT, it's up the street perpendicular to B10 Live House, on the left-hand side.

KINGGLORY PLAZA CLOTHING, ACCESSORIES

(金光华广场, Jīnguānghuà Guǎngchǎng; ☑8261 1100; www.kingglory.com.cn; 2028 Renmin Nanlu, Luóhú District; ⓂGuómào, exit A) Sitting atop the Guómào metro station, this modern shopping mall is where many Hong Kong day trippers hang out. It's more upscale than the much older Luóhú Commercial City one station away, featuring local and imported clothing and lifestyle brands, and a handful of decent restaurants.

LUÓHÚ COMMERCIAL CITY CLOTHING

(罗湖商业城, Luóhú Shāngyè Chéng; ☑8233 8178; www.tosz.com; Renmin Nanlu; ⏲11am-midnight) An old favourite of Hong Kong day trippers, this multistorey mall, right next to the Luóhú train station, has 1000 stalls selling handbags, household fabric, clothing, accessories, knick-knacks and DVDs, as well as massage parlours, salons for manicures and acrylic nails, and even dental clinics. Most shops are open 10.30am to 10pm.

CENTURY FURNISHINGS CENTRAL MALL HOMEWARES

(世纪中心家居广场, Shìjìzhōngxīn jiājūguǎng Chǎng; ☑8371 0111; www.sz-sjzx.com; Shennan Dadao, west of Xiāngmì Hú Water Park, Fútián District; ⏲9.30am-8pm Mon-Fri, to 8.30pm Sat & Sun; ⓂChēgōngmiào, exit A) This mall has a whopping 30,000 sq metres of retail space for homewares. There are three main zones. A and B sell mainly tiles, and bathroom and shower gadgets; C is all about lamps. A cab from Shēnzhèn's Luóhú station costs about ¥40.

GALAXY & TOP LIVING HOMEWARES

(星河第三空间, Xīnghédìsān Kōngjiān; www.topliving.cn; 3069 Caitian Lu, Galaxy Century Bldg, Fútián District; ⓂGǎngshà, exit B) A one-stop mall for mid-to-upper-range furnishings that features some imported brands such as Simmons, Markor Furnishings and Ligne Roset. If you take a cab from Luóhú station, it's about ¥50.

🏃 SPORTS & ACTIVITIES

QUEEN'S SPA & DINING   SPA
(皇室假期, Huángshì Jiàqī; ☎8225 3888; Chunfeng Lu, B1-5th fl, Golden Metropolis Bldg; ☺24hr; Ⓜ Guómào, exit B) Shenzhen offers an assortment of body-perfecting services, from massage through body scrubbing to manicure. Queen's Spa & Dining near Guómào metro pampers with aromatherapy and different types of body massage (¥138 to ¥280; a minimum tip of ¥30 is mandatory). With the pools, the fruit bar and sleeping capsules, it's easy to lose days inside.

🛏 SLEEPING

Hotels in Shēnzhèn discount deeply during the week, slicing as much as 60% off the regular rack rate, though you should ask for a discount no matter when you go.

★SHĒNZHÈN LOFT
YOUTH HOSTEL   HOSTEL $
(深圳侨城旅友国际青年旅舍, Shēnzhèn Qiáochéng Lǚyǒu Guójì Qīngnián Lǚshè; ☎8609 5773; www.yhachina.com; 7 Xiangshan Dongjie, OCT-LOFT, Huáqiáochéng, Nánshān district; 南山区，华侨城香山东街7号; dm from ¥65, d from ¥200, ste from ¥370; ☺⚹@☎; Ⓜ Qiáochéngdōng, exit A) Located in a tranquil part of OCT-LOFT, near the junction of Enping Jie and Xiangshan Dongjie, this immaculate YHA hostel has over 50 private rooms, all with showers, and dormitory-type accommodation with shared bathrooms. The staff are well-trained and helpful. There's wi-fi in the lobby only.

NEW MELBOURNE HOSTEL   HOSTEL $
(墨尔本一家, Mò'ěrběn Yījiā; ☎158 2076 6520; 1435113378@qq.com; Unit 1801, Lìjǐng Dàshà, 1008 Hongling Zhonglu; 红岭中路1008 号,荔景大厦1801室; dm from ¥70; ☺⚹@☎; Ⓜ Dàjùyuàn, exit B) Three spotless dormitory rooms (two women's, one men's) with a total of 18 bed spaces, run by John, the well-mannered English-speaking owner. Some rooms overlook a river and a park. The building is a 10-minute stroll on Hongling Zhonglu from the metro station.

SHĒNZHÈN VISION
FASHION HOTEL   BOUTIQUE HOTEL $$
(深圳视界风尚酒店; Shēnzhèn Shìjiè Fēngshàng Jiǔdiàn; ☎2558 2888; www.visionfashionhotel.com; 5018 Shennan Donglu; 深南东路5018号; d

¥486-1880; ⚹@☎; Ⓜ Dàjùyuàn, exit B) Inside a theatre complex is this boutique hotel featuring eclectic designs in its rooms. Some are chic, some bizarre. Its prime location and quiet environment make it a very good choice. Discounts of 50% to 70% available.

SHANGRI-LA   HOTEL $$$
(香格里拉大酒店, Xiānggélǐlā Dàjiǔdiàn; ☎8233 0888; www.shangri-la.com/shenzhen; 1002 Jianshe Lu; d ¥1700-2010, ste ¥3500; ☎) This classic, luxury hotel, about 150m from Luóhú train station, is one of the best places to stay in Luóhú District, and offers free wi-fi. Rooms are spacious and sparkling.

Guǎngzhōu

Explore

If you're arriving in the morning, beat the crowds to the New Guǎngdōng Museum (it closes at 5pm and is closed on Monday) in the southeastern district of Zhūjiāng New Town. Don't forget to take a peek at the fabulous Guǎngzhōu Opera House close by. That should take about two hours. Hop on the metro and head west to the Chén Clan Ancestral Hall to spend an hour, then make a beeline for the stunning Mausoleum of the Nányuè King (it closes at 5.30pm) in the Yuèxiù District. Follow this with a leisurely stroll among the famous landmarks inside Yuèxiù Park. Depending on time available and interest, you can reverse the order, or replace New Guǎngdōng Museum with a trip to Shāmiàn Island in the southwest.

The Best...
➡**Sight** Mausoleum of the Nányuè King (p255)
➡**Place to eat** Pānxī Restaurant (p260)
➡**Place to drink** Kuí Garden (p261)

Top Tip

Most taxi drivers in Guǎngzhōu are migrant workers who don't know the city well. If possible, flag down the rare yellow or red cabs, which are driven by local drivers.

Getting There & Away
➡**Train** The most hassle-free transport

to Guǎngzhōu is to take the high-speed intercity trains from Hung Hom station to Guǎngzhōu East train station (two hours). It has 12 departures between 7.25am and 8.01pm, returning from Guǎngzhōu the same number of times from 8.19am to 9.32pm. One-way tickets cost HK$230/190 in 1st/2nd class for adults and HK$115/95 for children aged five to nine.

➡**MTR** One-way and return tickets for Guǎngzhōu can be booked in advance at MTR stations in Hung Hom, Mong Kok, Kowloon Tong and Sha Tin, and at MTR Travel at Admiralty station, or with a credit card on the MTR website (www. it3.mtr.com.hk) or via the Tele-Ticketing Hotline (2947 7888).

➡**Hi-speed train** A cheaper way to get from Hong Kong to Guǎngzhōu is to board a hi-speed train once you go across the Lo Wu border to Shēnzhèn. They run frequently between Shēnzhèn and Guǎngzhōu East train station (¥80 to ¥100, 1¼ hours) from 6.20am to 11.30pm.

➡**Bus** CTS has frequent buses from Metropark Hotel in Causeway Bay and many CTS branches in Hong Kong to Guǎngzhōu (¥110). The trip takes 2½ hours.

Getting Around

➡**Metro** Guǎngzhōu metro (www.gzmtr. com) has nine metro lines in full service and covers most of the sights. Depending on the line, the metro runs from about 6.20am to 11pm. Fares start from ¥2 for the first 4km.

➡**Taxi** The flagfall is ¥10 for the first 2.5km, and ¥2.60 for every additional kilometre. A trip from the main train station to Shēnzhèn Island should cost between ¥30 and ¥40. A taxi to/from the airport will cost about ¥200.

Need to Know

➡**Area code** ☑86 (0)20

➡**Location** 185km from Hung Hom station

➡**Tourist Office** (☑020-8333 6888; 8 Qiaoguang Lu, China Travel Service, CTS, 广州中国旅行社, Zhōngguó Lǚxíngshè; ⊙8.30am-6pm Mon-Fri, 9am-5pm Sat & Sun; MHǎizhū Guǎngchǎng, exit A) Located next to Hotel Landmark Canton, it offers various tours and books tickets.

➡**Visa** Get it in advance in Hong Kong or Macau; see p314 for details.

👁 SIGHTS

MAUSOLEUM OF THE
NÁNYUÈ KING   MAUSOLEUM
(西汉南越王博物馆; Nányuèwáng Mù; ☑3618 2920; www.gznywmuseum.org/nanyuewang/index. html; 867 Jiefang Beilu; admission ¥12; ⊙9am-4.45pm; MLine 2, Yuèxiù Gōngyuán, exit E) This superb mausoleum from the 2000-year-old Nányuè kingdom is one of China's best museums. It houses the tomb of Zhao Mo, second king of Nányuè, who was sent south by the emperor in 214 BC to quell unrest and establish a sovereign state with Guǎngzhōu as its capital. Don't miss Zhao Mo's jade burial suit – the precious stone was thought to preserve the body.

YUÈXIÙ PARK   PARK
(越秀公园; Yuèxiù Gōngyuán; ☑8666 1950; 988 Jiefang Beilu; ⊙6am-9pm; MLine 2, Yuèxiù Gōngyuán) A statue of the symbol of Guǎngzhōu – the five rams (五羊) that supposedly carried the five immortals who founded the city – stands guard at this park. On a hilltop is red-walled Zhènhǎi Tower (镇海楼; Zhènhǎi Lóu), built in 1380 as a watchtower to keep out pirates. The tower is home to the excellent **Guǎngzhōu City Museum** (广州博物馆; Guǎngzhōushì Bówùguǎn; ☑8355 0627; www.guangzhoumuseum.cn/en/main.asp; admission ¥10; ⊙9am-5pm; MLine 2, Yuèxiù Gōngyuán), which traces the city's history from the neolithic period. To the east is Guǎngzhōu Art Gallery, which has embroidery, ivory carvings and displays on the city's trading history with the West.

CHÉN CLAN
ANCESTRAL HALL   HISTORIC SITE
(陈家祠; Chénjiā Cí; ☑8181 4559; 34 Enlong Li, Zhongshan Qilu; admission ¥10; ⊙8.30am-5.00pm; MLine 1, Chénjiācí, exit D) An all-in-one ancestral shrine, Confucian school and 'chamber of commerce' for the Chen clan, this compound was built in 1894 by the residents of 72 villages in Guǎngdōng, where the Chen lineage is predominant. There are 19 buildings in the traditional Lǐngnán style, all featuring exquisite carvings, statues and paintings, and decorated with ornate scrollwork throughout.

MOSQUE DEDICATED
TO THE PROPHET   MOSQUE
(怀圣寺; Huáishèng Sì; ☑8333 3593; 56 Guangta Lu; ⊙daybreak to sundown; MLine 1, Xīmén Kǒu) The original building is believed to be

Guǎngzhōu

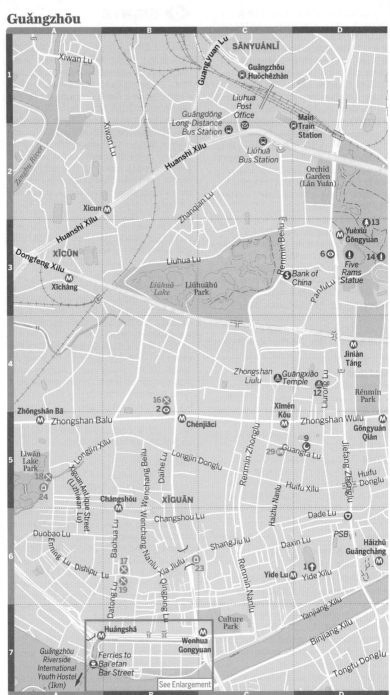

Xiwan Lu

Guāngyuán Lu

SĀNYUÁNLǏ

Guǎngzhōu
Huǒchēzhàn

Liuhua
Post
Office

Guǎngdōng
Long-Distance
Bus Station

Main
Train
Station

Xiwan Lu

Liúhuā
Bus Station

Huanshi Xilu

Orchid
Garden
(Lán Yuán)

Zengbu River

Zhanqian Lu

Xicun

Huanshi Xilu

Yuèxiù
Gōngyuán

13

Dongfeng Xilu

XĪCŪN

Renmin Beilu

6

14

Five
Rams
Statue

Xīchǎng

Liuhua Lu

Liúhuā
Lake

Liúhuāhú
Park

Bank of
China

Panfu Lu

Jìniàn
Táng

Rénmín
Park

Zhongshan
Liulu

Guāngxiào
Temple

12

Zhōngshān Bā

16

Zhongshan Balu

2

Chénjiācí

Xīmén
Kǒu

Zhongshan Wulu

Liurong lu

Gōngyuán
Qián

Liwǎn
Lake
Park

18

24

Longjin Xilu

Xiguan Antique Street
(Liuzhiwan Lu)

Chángshòu

Longjin Donglu

Renmin Zhonglu

29

Guangta Lu

9

Huifu Xilu

Haizhu Nanlu

Jiefang Zhonglu

Huifu
Donglu

Duobao Lu

Changshou Lu

XĪGUĀN

W. Wenchang Nanlu

Baohua Lu

Daihe Lu

ShangJiu lu

Dade Lu

Daxin Lu

PSB

Hǎizhū
Guǎngchǎng

Enning Lu

Dishipu Lu

17

19

Datong Lu

Xia Jiulu

Qingping Lu

23

Renmin Nanlu

Yide Lu

1

Yide Xilu

Huángshā

Ferries to
Bai'etan
Bar Street

Wenhua
Gongyuán

Culture
Park

Yanjiang Xilu

Binjiang Xilu

Tongfu Donglu

Guǎngzhōu
Riverside
International
Youth Hostel
(1km)

See Enlargement

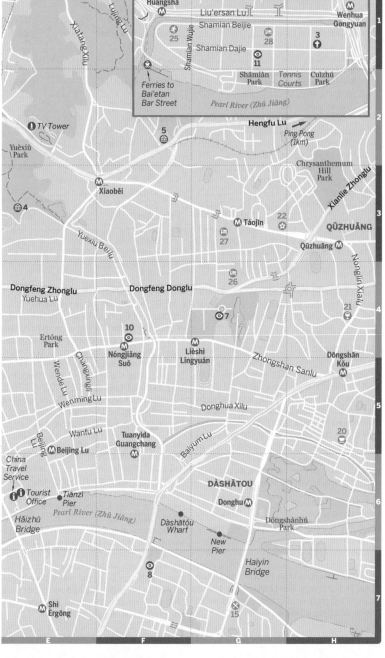

0 — 1 km
0 — 0.5 miles

Inset map:

0 — 400 m
0 — 0.25 miles

Huángshā

Liu'ersan Lu

Shamian Beijie

Shamian Wujie

Shamian Dajie

Wenhua Gongyuan

25

28

3

11

Shāmiàn Park

Tennis Courts

Cuìzhú Park

Pearl River (Zhū Jiāng)

Main map:

Lujing Lu

Xiatang Xilu

TV Tower

Yuèxiù Park

5

Hengfu Lu

Ping-Pong (1km)

Chrysanthemum Hill Park

Xíaoběi

Xianlie Zhonglu

4

Yuexiu Beilu

Táojīn

22

QŪZHUĀNG

27

Qūzhuāng

Nonglin Xialu

Dongfeng Zhonglu

Yuehua Lu

Dongfeng Donglu

26

7

21

Ertóng Park

10

Nóngjiāng Suǒ

Lièshì Língyuán

Zhongshan Sanlu

Dōngshān Kǒu

Changxing li

Wende Lu

Wenming Lu

Donghua Xilu

Wanfu Lu

Beijing Lu

Tuanyida Guangchang

Baiyum Lu

20

China Travel Service

Tourist Office

Tiānzì Pier

Beijing Lu

DÀSHĀTÓU

Donghu

Pearl River (Zhū Jiāng)

Hǎizhū Bridge

Dàshātóu Wharf

New Pier

Dōngshānhú Park

8

Haiyin Bridge

Shì Èrgōng

15

Guǎngzhōu

founded here in 627 by Abu Waqas, an uncle of the prophet Mohammed. The present mosque dates from the Qing dynasty.

TEMPLE OF THE SIX BANYAN TREES
BUDDHIST TEMPLE

(六榕寺; Liùróng Sì; ☏8339 2843; 87 Liurong Lu; admission ¥5, pagoda ¥10; ⊙8am-5pm; ☒56) This Buddhist temple was built in AD 537 to enshrine Buddhist relics that were brought over from India and placed in the octagonal **Decorated Pagoda** (Huā Tǎ). The temple was given its current name by the exiled poet Su Dongbo in 1099, who waxed lyrical over the (now gone) banyans in the courtyard. You can see the characters 'six banyans' (liùróng) that he wrote above the gates.

CATHEDRAL OF THE SACRED HEART
CHURCH

(石室圣心大教堂; Shíshì Jiàotáng; 368 Yide Lu; Ⓜ Line 2, Hǎizhū Guǎngchǎng) The French were granted permission to build this impressive twin-spired Roman Catholic cathedral after the second Opium War, between 1863 and 1888. It features a neo-Gothic style and is constructed entirely of granite, with massive towers reaching a height of 48m.

SHĀMIÀN ISLAND
HISTORIC SITE

(沙面岛; Shāmiàn Dǎo; Ⓜ Line 1, Huángshā) To the southwest of Guǎngzhōu is the dappled oasis of Shāmiàn Island. It was acquired as a foreign concession in 1859 after the two Opium Wars. Shamian Dajie, the main boulevard, is a gentle stretch of gardens dotted by old houses, cafes and galleries. The **Church of Our Lady of Lourdes** (天主教露德圣母堂; Tiānzhǔjiào Lùdé Shèngmǔ Táng; 14 Shamian Dajie; ⊙8am-6pm; Ⓜ Line 1, Huángshā), built by the French in 1892, is on the eastern end.

MEMORIAL MUSEUM OF GENERALISSIMO SUN YATSEN'S MANSION
HISTORIC SITE

(孙中山大元帅府; Sūn Zhōngshān Dàyuánshuài Fǔ; ☏8901 2366; www.dyshf.com; 18 Dongsha Jie, Fangzhi Lu; ⊙9am-4.30pm Tue-Sun; Ⓜ Line 2, Shì Èrgōng) FREE Sun Yatsen lived in this restored mansion when he established governments in Guǎngzhōu in 1917 and 1923. The beautiful complex comprises two Victorian-style buildings housing displays on the history of Guǎngzhōu in the revolutionary era, as well as Sun's living quarters. A cab from Shāmiàn Island costs about ¥40, and from Shì Èrgōng station, about ¥20.

YÚYÌN MOUNTAIN VILLA   GARDENS

(馀荫山房; Yúyīn Shānfáng; ☎3482 2187; Náncūn, Pā nyú; adult/child ¥18/9; ☺8am-6pm; Ⓜ Line 1, Dàshí, exit A) One of Guǎngdōng's four famous classical gardens, this graceful property was built in 1871 by an official of the Qing court. It incorporates the landscaping styles of Sūzhōu and Hángzhōu, and the features of Lǐngnán architecture. The result is a photogenic collection of pavilions, terraces, halls, bridges and lakes. The Waterside Pavilion commands a different vista on each of its eight sides; the Deep Willow Room features ancient art and coloured 'Manchu' windows, aka 'four-season windows', which create an illusion of changing seasons by altering the hue of the outside scenery.

Turn left when you leave the metro. There's a stop for the Route 8 feeder bus to Qīxīnggǎng Gōngyuán (七星岗公园; ¥2). Disembark at Nánshān Gōngyuán (南山公园), the 20th stop, after half an hour. Cross to the opposite and leafy side of the road. Bus 30 (¥2) from the stop there takes you to the entrance of Yúyìn Mountain Villa just one stop away.

WHAMPOA MILITARY ACADEMY   MUSEUM

(黄埔军校; Huángpǔ Jūnxiào; ☎8820 1082; ☺9am-5pm Tue-Sun; Ⓜ Line 2, Chìgǎng, exit C1) FREE This academy on Chángzhōu Island (长洲岛; Chángzhōu Dǎo) was founded in 1924 by the Kuomintang to train military elites. Many of the graduates went on to fight in important conflicts and civil wars. The present structure has a museum dedicated to the revolutionary history of modern China. After leaving the metro, board bus 262 on Xingang Zhonglu to Xīnzhōu Pier (新洲码头; Xīnzhōu Mǎtou). Ferries (¥2) to the academy depart every hour from 7.40am to 7.40pm.

Ferries leave from the pier every 20 minutes between the rush hours of 7.50am to 9.30am. Private boats will also make the 10-minute trip to the island for ¥40.

XĪNHÀI REVOLUTION MUSEUM   MUSEUM

(辛亥革命纪念馆, Xīnhàigémìng Jìniànguǎn; ☎8252 5897; Junxiao Lu, Huángpǔ Qū; ☺9am-5pm Tue-Sun; ☒383, 430, Ⓜ Dàxuéchéng Běi) FREE The 18,000-sq-metre museum has some 7,000 well-curated but propaganda-ish exhibits on the revolution, famous Cantonese revolutionaries, and the life of Sun Wan, Sun Yatsen's daughter. Take bus 383 or 430 and disembark at Chángzhōujie, or take line 4 of the metro and get off at Dàxuéchéng Běi,

then take bus 383 to Chángzhōujie and walk for five minutes.

PEASANT MOVEMENT INSTITUTE   HISTORIC SITE

(农民运动讲习所; Nóngmín Yùndòng Jiǎngxísuǒ; ☎0 20-8333 3936; 42 Zhongshan Silu; ☺9am-4.30pm Tue-Sun; Ⓜ Nóngjiǎng Suǒ) FREE The institute was established in 1924 by the Chinese Communist Party at the site of a former Confucian temple. Mao Zedong and Zhou Enlai both taught here, before the school closed in 1926. You can see Mao Zedong's re-created personal quarters and even his bed.

MEMORIAL GARDEN TO THE MARTYRS   MEMORIAL

(烈士陵园; Lièshì Língyuán; admission ¥3; ☺8am-7pm; Ⓜ Line 1, Lièshì Língyuán) East of the Institute on Zhongshan Sanlu, the garden commemorates those killed on 13 December 1927 under the orders of Chiang Kaishek. The massacre occurred when a small group of workers, led by the CCP, were gunned down by Kuomintang forces. Over 5000 lives were lost.

GUǍNGZHŌU MUSEUM OF ART   MUSEUM

(广州艺术博物院; Guǎngzhōu Yìshù Bówùyuàn; ☎8 365 9337; www.gzam.com.cn; 13 Luhu Lu; ☺9am-5pm Tue-Fri, 9.30am-4.30pm Sat & Sun; ☒10, 84, 109, 297, 808, Ⓜ Line 5, Xiǎoběi) FREE This massive museum has an extensive collection of Chinese art from ancient to contemporary. The emphasis is on calligraphic works and paintings, especially those created in the Lǐngnán area. Rare Tibetan tapestries are displayed on the top floor.

NEW GUǍNGDŌNG MUSEUM   MUSEUM

(广东省博物馆新馆; Guǎngdōngshěng Bó wùguǎn Xīnguǎn; ☎3804 6886; www.gd museum.com; 2 Zhujiang Donglu, Zhūjiāng New Town; ☺9am-4pm Tue-Sun; Ⓜ Line 3, Zhūjiāng Xīnchéng, exit B1) FREE This ultramodern museum has an extensive collection illuminating the human and natural history of Guǎngdōng, as well as Cantonese art, literature and architecture. Inspired by the Chinese lacquer box, the museum's appearance is a striking contrast against the curvilinear design of the Guǎngzhōu Opera House further to the west.

GUǍNGZHŌU OPERA HOUSE   BUILDING

(广州大剧院; Guǎngzhōu dà jù yuàn; ☎3839 2666, tour bookings 3839 9847; www.chgoh.org; 1 Zhujiang Xilu; admission ¥30, tours in English per person ¥200;

⊘9am-4.30pm, closed Mon, tours 10am, 11am, 2pm, 3pm & 4pm; Ⓜ Line 3, Zhūjiāng Xīnchéng, exit B1) Authored by architect Zaha Hadid, southern China's biggest performance venue has transformed the area with its other-worldly appearance. With futuristic glass panels knitted together to form subtle curves, it's been described as pebbles on the bed of the Pearl River. To enter, you have to join one of five 45-minute daily tours. Tours in English require booking a day in advance.

The visit will allow you to see the ethereal opera hall with its 4200 LED lights and floor planks from Russia, as well as the state-of-the-art rehearsal studios.

REDTORY
VILLAGE

(员村四横路128号, Hóngzhuān Chǎng; ☑ 8557 84 70; www.redtory.com.cn/english/redtory.php; 128 Yuancun Sihenglu; 员村四横路128號; ⊘ 6am-midnight; Ⓜ Line 3, Yúncūn, exit B) The Bauhaus structures of Guǎngdōng Canned Food Factory (c 1958) are now stuffed with the galleries, bookstores and cafes of Redtory art village. The art is underwhelming, but the dated architecture and the old factory equipment on display make a visit worthwhile. Turn right from the metro exit and make your way to the alley immediately behind the one you're on. About 200m down the alley, turn left into a dirt road.

 EATING

Guǎngzhōu is especially famous for its dim sum. In Xīguān District there are many tiny restaurants featuring locally well-known *xīguān xiǎochī* (snacks and dessert), where you can bump elbows with locals. A large expat population means there are also many restaurants serving international cuisines.

CHÉN CLAN ANCESTRAL HALL FOOD STALLS
CANTONESE $

(陈家祠大排档, Chénjiācí Dàipáidàng; Enlong Li, Zhongshan Qilu; per person ¥40-60; ⊘ from 7pm; Ⓜ Line 1, Chénjiācí, exit D) Locals munch on *kǎoshēngháo* (烤生蚝; grilled oysters), *jiāoyánxiā* (椒盐虾; pepper salt shrimp) and *chǎoxiè* (炒蟹; stir-fried crab) at the outdoor food stalls that appear every evening in an alley next to Chén Clan Ancestral Hall (p255). It's clean by food-stall standards.

NÁNXÌN
DESSERTS $

(南信; ☑ 8138 9904; 47 Dishipu Lu; desserts ¥7-15; ⊘ 10am-midnight; Ⓜ Chángshòu Lù) Popular stop for desserts, including *shuāngpínǎi* (双皮奶; steamed egg white with milk).

BǏNGSHÈNG RESTAURANT
CANTONESE $$

(炳胜海鲜酒家, Bǐngshàng Hǎixiān Jiǔjiā; ☑ 020-34 28 6910; 33 Dongxiao Lu; dishes from ¥48; ⊘ 11am-midnight; ☐ 293, 886) This exquisite Cantonese restaurant surprises us every time we visit, and the price is right! Shùndé (a town south of Guǎngzhōu) cuisine is the speciality here, where freshwater fish is prepared in many different ways. The *dòufuhuā zhēngxiègāo* (豆腐花蒸蟹羔; bean curd with crab roe) and *hǎilú cìshēn* (海鲈刺身; sea bass sashimi) are outstandingly tasty. Also try the *cuìpí chāshāo* (脆皮叉烧; crispy barbecued pork). It has a handful of branches in town but the newest one in Zhūjiāng New Town is by far the best. No English menu; grab a Chinese friend to communicate.

PĀNXĪ RESTAURANT
DIM SUM $$

(泮溪酒家, Pānxī Jiǔjiā; ☑ 8172 1328; 151 Longjin Xi lu; dishes from ¥40; ⊘ 7.30am-midnight; Ⓜ Chángshòu Lù) Housed in a majestic garden, this ginormous restaurant serves some of the best dim sum in town. It's also one of the all-time favourites for the elders in Guǎngzhōu. Wake up early. It's impossible to get a table after 8.30am.

TÁO TÁO JŪ RESTAURANT
DIM SUM $$

(陶陶居, Táotáojū Jiǔjiā; ☑ 020-8139 6111; 20 Di shipu Lu; dim sum per portion ¥7-23; ⊘ 7am-midnight) Táo Táo Jū is old name in Canton's history of yum cha, a fact unfortunately obscured by all the shine and glitter in its modern decor. The standard of its dim sum, however, is still solid. But it's a pain if you're indecisive – there are over 200 items! The 1st floor serves dim sum all day.

🍷 DRINKING & NIGHTLIFE

Guǎngzhōu has a number of international-style bars where, in addition to sinking chilled Tsingtao and imported beers, you can scoff pizza, burgers, rice or noodles.

SUN'S
LOUNGE

(☑ 8977 9056; www.sunsgz.com; B25-26 Yuejiang Xilu; ⊘ 7am-2am Sun-Thu, to 5am Fri & Sat; ☐ 779, 765 (final stop)) The best of the lot in Zhūjiāng 'Party Pier' (珠江琶醍), Sun's lets you sip cocktails on couches by the river or dance to electronic music.

⭐ **KUÍ GARDEN** CAFE

(逵园; Kuí Yuán; ☎8765 9746; 9 Xuguyuan Lu; 恤孤 院路9号; ⏰10am-midnight; Ⓜ Line 1, Dōngshānkǒu, exit F) From its location inside th e gorgeous Kuí Garden in the historic Dōngshān area, this cafe serves decent coffee and canapes during the day and morphs into a bar at night. Stylish, warm-toned seatin g areas occupy the rooms of the original residence. Built in 1922, the house is famous for its Western architectural features that include colonnaded verandahs and a portico.

Th ere's a small exhibition space on the ground floor and a light-flooded shop on the top floor that is breathtaking to look at but do esn't sell much. Both the gallery and the shop close at 10pm.

PING PONG LIVE MUSIC

(乒 乓空间, Pīngpāng Kōngjiān; ☎2829 6306; 60 Xi anlie Donghenglu, Starhouse 60; ⏰6pm-2am) Th is bohemian place is where you'll find li ve music, theatrical performances and art exhibitions. It's hard to find, though. Tell the taxi driver to drop you at the rear entrance of Xīnghǎi Conservatory (星海音乐学院后门; Xīnghǎi Yīnyuè Xuéyuàn Hòumén) and make sure they haven't taken you to Xīnghǎi Concert Hall on Èrshā Island!

WILBER'S BAR

(☎3761 1101; 62 Zhusigang Ermalu; ⏰5pm-midnight Sun-Thu, to 2am Fri & Sat; Ⓜ Qūzhuāng) Wilber's is a gem that is hidden down an alley in a historical villa. It has something for everyone: the patio is popular with ladies looking for a qu iet natter, indoors is a gay-friendly drinking den, and upstairs is a fine-dining restaurant. It serves the best martinis and margaritas in town.

☆ **ENTERTAINMENT**

T he comprehensive events-listings website **Gu angzhou Stuff** (www.gzstuff.com) is an invaluable resource for what's happening.

VELVET CLUB

(S īróngbā; ☎8732 1139; 403 Huanshi Donglu, Ground fl, International Electronic Tower; beer ¥65, co cktails ¥60; ⏰7.30pm-3am; Ⓜ Xiǎoběi) A famous club, popular with local and international DJs. With a full range of tunes to suit everybody, it's one of the best bets for a good night out. It's gay friendly too.

C UNION LIVE MUSIC

(喜窝, Xǐwō; ☎3584 0144; 115 Shuiyin Lu; ⏰7pm-2am) C Union hosts a good mix of bands playing jazz, R&B and reggae. It's behind the Chéngshìhuì (城市会) building, in the Yuèxiù District. Only accessible by taxi.

⭐ **191 SPACE** LIVE MUSIC

(1 91Space 音乐主题酒吧, 191 Space Yīnlè Zhǔtí Ji ǔba; ☎8737 9375; www.191space.com; 191 Gu angzhou Dadao Zhonglu; 广州大道中路191 号; ⏰8pm-2am; Ⓜ Line 5, Wǔyángcūn, exit A) Two steps from the metro exit, this is a throbbing dive that features live indie gigs from China and overseas every weekend.

T UNION LIVE MUSIC

(凸空间, Tū Kōng Jiān; ☎3659 7623; http:// weibo.com/uniontutu; G/F, 361-365 Guangzhou Dadaozhong; 广州大道中路361-365号; Ⓜ Yángjī, exit B) A rustic-looking cafe that hosts performances by local and overseas acts. The genre tends towards modern folk and singer-songwriter, but postrock and heavy metal have been featured too. It's next to a 7 Days Inn.

GUĂNGZHŌU OPERA HOUSE THEATRE

(广州大剧院, Guǎngzhōu Dàjùyuàn; ☎3839 2666, 3839 2888; http://gzdjy.org; 1 Zhujiang Xilu; ⏰9am-4.30pm, closed Mon; Ⓜ Line 3, Zhūjiāng Xīnchéng, ex it B1) Guǎngdōng's premier performance venue.

🛍 **SHOPPING**

Guǎngzhōu is a terrific place for cheap and ch eerful shopping. Prices are reasonably cheap, and there are gems in its haystack of goods.

FĀNGCŪN TEA MARKET TEA

(芳村茶叶市场, Fāngcūn Cháyè Shìchǎng; Fangcun Dadao; Ⓜ Fāngcūn, exit C) A sprawling market with block after block of tea shops, along wi th malls selling tea and teaware. Most ta rget wholesale traders but retail is often possible.

XĪGUĀN ANTIQUE STREET ANTIQUES

(西 关古玩城, Xīguān Gǔwánchéng; Lizhiwan Lu; Ⓜ Line 5, Zhōngshān Bālù) This street sells everything from ceramic teapots to Tibetan rugs. Even if you're not in the mood to load up your pack with ceramic vases, it's a wonderful place in which to browse. Note that most artefacts here are known to be fakes.

FĀNG SUŎ COMMUNE — BOOKS

(方所, Fāngsuŏ; ☑3868 2327; MU35, Tai Koo Hui, 383 Tianhe Lu; ⊙10am-10pm; ⓂLine 1, Shípáiqiáo) Occupying some 2000 sq m in a classy mall, this elegant bookstore also sells clothes, homewares and coffee. There are more than 90,000 titles, mostly Chinese.

XIA JIULU/SHANG JIULU — CLOTHING

Literally 'Up Down Nine Street', this pedestrianised street in one of the oldest parts of the city, where buildings retain elements of both Western and Chinese architecture, is a good place to look for discounted clothing.

🏃 SPORTS & ACTIVITIES

GUĂNGZHŌU STAR
CRUISES COMPANY — RIVER CRUISE

(☑8333 2222) The Guangzhou Star Cruises Company has evening cruises on the Pearl River (Y38 to Y148, 1½ hours) every 15 minutes between 6.40pm and 9.30pm. Boats leave from the **Tiānzǐ Pier** (Tiānzǐ Mǎtou; Beijing Lu), just east of Hǎizhū Bridge (Hǎizhū Qiáo; catch metro line 2 from Hǎizhū Guǎngchǎng station), and head down the river as far as Èrshā Island (Èrshā Dǎo) before turning back.

SHĀMIÀN TRADITIONAL
CHINESE MEDICAL CENTRE — MASSAGE

(沙面国医馆, Shāmiàn Guóyīguǎn; ☑8121 8383; www.gzshamian.com.cn; 85-87 Shamian Beijie, 沙面北街85-87号; ⊙8.30am-10pm) Shamian Traditional Chinese Medical Centre, at the western end of the island, offers body massage for ¥268 an hour. Consultation of a Chinese doctor (through an inhouse interpreter) is ¥21. Appointments are not accepted.

🛏 SLEEPING

Hotels in Guǎngzhōu are expensive. Prices rise even higher during the Canton Trade Fair in spring and autumn. But don't be put off by the posted rates – most hotels offer discounts from 30% to 60%, depending on the season. Top-end places add a 15% service charge to the quoted room rates. Most hotels have in-room broadband internet access.

7 DAYS INN — HOTEL

(7天连锁酒店, Qītiān Liánsuǒ Jiǔdiàn; fax 020-8364 4488; 32 Huale Lu; r¥199-329; ⓂTáojīn) This chain hotel is the cheapest decent option amid the five-star enclave in Yuèxiù (越秀) district. It's behind the Garden Hotel.

LAZY GAGA — HOSTEL $

(春田家家, Chūntián Jiājiā; ☑8192 3232, 8192 3199; www.gagahostel.com; 215 Haizhu Zhonglu; 海珠中路215号; dm ¥55-65, d & tw ¥168-198, tr ¥225; ⓂXiménkǒu, exit B) Only five minutes' walk from the metro, Lazy Gaga has 45 cheerful rooms and homey communal areas enlivened by colourful walls and furniture. Guests can have free use of the spotless kitchen and the pleasant staff members are up for a chat when they're not busy. In-room lockers come thoughtfully embedded with chargers for mobile devices.

GUĂNGZHŌU RIVERSIDE
INTERNATIONAL YOUTH HOSTEL — HOSTEL $

(广州江畔国际青年旅舍, Guǎngzhōu Jiāngpàn Guójì Qīngnián Lǚshè; ☑2239 2500; www.yhachina. com; 15 Changdi Jie, 长堤街15号; dm ¥60, s ¥260, d ¥280-340, tr ¥410; @🛜; ⓂLine 1, Fāngcūn, exit B1) Located in Fāngcūn next to a bar street, this YHA-affiliated hostel has spotless rooms and a welcoming vibe.

Turn right from the metro exit and go through the back lane next to the hospital to reach tree-lined Luju Lu (陆居路). Turn left and walk towards the river. Then make a right and you'll see the hostel after five minutes. Ferries depart frequently from Huángshā pier on Shāmiàn Island to Fāngcūn pier right in front of the hostel.

GUĂNGDŌNG VICTORY HOTEL — HOTEL $$$

(胜利宾馆, Shènglì Bīnguǎn; ☑8121 6688; www. vhotel.com; 53 & 54 Shamian Beijie; 沙面北街53、54号; r from ¥800, tr ¥1180, ste ¥1380-3880; ✱@🛜) There are two branches of the Victory Hotel on Shāmiàn Island: an older one at 54 Shamian Beijie (enter from 10 Shamian Sijie) and a newer wing (胜利宾馆(新楼)) at 52 Shamian Nanjie. Both offer decent value for money.

★ GARDEN HOTEL — HOTEL $$$

(花园酒店, Huāyuán Jiǔdiàn; ☑8333 8989; www. thegardenhotel.com.cn; 368 Huanshi Donglu; 环市东路368号; r/ste from ¥3200/5200; ✱@🛜; ⓂLine 5, Táojīn) One of the most popular luxury hotels in Guǎngzhōu with waterfalls and lovely gardens in the lobby and on the 4th floor. The rooms are just as classy. Bookings essential.

🛏 Sleeping

In a city where real estate is the price of gold, money makes all the difference when you're seeking accommodation. If you have cash, you'll be spoiled for choice, so wide is the range of luxurious places. The midrange options are less mind-blowing but adequate, while further down, the pickings get thinner – the defining feature here is hostels with tiny rooms.

New Trends

Since the easing of cross-border travel restrictions by China in 2003, mainland visitors have become the single largest market for Hong Kong. As most of them are middle-class and here to shop, they seek out midrange lodging in central locations. This has led to a proliferation of hotels and serviced apartments falling in the middle of the price spectrum that cater to these tourists, and an increase in prices of accommodation in general. More and more hotels, including upmarket ones, are offering long-stay deals.

It's worth noting that during peak seasons, the rates at some of the midrange hotels, especially those in Wan Chai, Yau Ma Tei and Tsim Sha Tsui, can be up to five times the low-season rates. This discrepancy is not as marked in top-end hotels or the cheapest places.

Keep in mind that whatever your budget, accommodation costs are higher in Hong Kong than in most other Asian cities, but cheaper than in Europe and the US. The rates published here are the rack rates which hotels use for reference, which are not the same as the daily or seasonal rates.

Top-End Hotels

Hong Kong's luxury hotels are locked in an arms race for the dollars of affluent travellers. Their weapons are superstar restaurants, lavish spa complexes and smooth service catering to your most footling whims. It doesn't come cheaply though. Prices for top-of-the-range hotels start from close to HK$2000 per room. A few of them offer comfort, amenities

and service that compete with or surpass that of the world's finest five-star hotels.

Midrange Hotels

While midrange hotels used to be generic establishments with little to distinguish one from another, many new places have sprung up that are uniquely cool to look at and easy on the pocket, with rates hovering between HK$1000 and HK$2000 and dipping to budget range in the low season. Rooms at these places tend to be small and come with wi-fi connection, limited cable TV and room service.

Guesthouses

Dominating the lower end of the accommodation market are guesthouses, usually a block of tiny rooms squeezed into a converted apartment or two. Often several guesthouses operate out of the same building. Your options are greater if there are two of you; find a double room in a clean guesthouse for HK$200 to HK$300 and your accommodation costs will fall sharply. Some offer dormitory accommodation for those on tight budgets.

Though rooms are small, the places listed here are clean and cheerily shabby or neat and austere, rather than grim and grimy. All have air-con and most have TVs, phones and private bathrooms. Anything under HK$900 should be considered budget.

Depending on the season, try to negotiate a better deal, as a lot of places will be eager to fill empty rooms. Most guesthouses offer

LOW-SEASON DISCOUNTS

Don't be shocked by the rack rates! Many hotels slash prices by up to 70% for nightly stays outside the peak season.

➡ Garden View (p269)
➡ Harbour View (p269)
➡ City Garden Hotel Hong Kong (p270)
➡ BP International Hotel (p276)
➡ Stanford Hillview Hotel (p276)
➡ Kowloon Hotel Hong Kong (p277)
➡ Knutsford Hotel (p276)
➡ Hotel Panorama (p277)
➡ Eaton Smart (p278)
➡ Cosmopolitan Hotel (p270)
➡ Ovolo (p268)
➡ Bauhinia (p268)
➡ Royal Garden (p277)

some sort of internet access, from a communal PC to free in-room wi-fi.

Serviced Apartments

Those staying in Hong Kong for longer than a month may be interested in serviced apartments. These range in size from studios to three-bedroomers, and usually come with a kitchen, cooking and eating utensils, maid service and laundry facilities. Plusher ones may even have DVD players, a pool and a gym.

Hostels & Campsites

The **Hong Kong Youth Hostels Association** (香港青年旅舍協會, HKYHA; ☎2788 1638; www.yha.org.hk; Shum Mong Rd, Shop 118, 1st fl, Fu Cheong Shopping Centre, Sham Shui Po; HI card under/over 18yr $70/150; ☺9am-7pm Mon-Fri, 10am-5pm Sat; Ⓜ Nam Cheong, exit A) maintains seven hostels affiliated with Hostelling International (HI). It also sells HKYHA and HI cards. If you haven't applied for membership in your own country, visit the HKYHA office or the hostels to do so. Be sure to take along a visa-sized photo and ID.

All HKYHA hostels have separate toilets and showers for men and women, and cooking facilities. They provide blankets, pillows and sheet bags. Most have lockers available.

Prices for a bed in a dormitory range from HK$50 to HK$260 a night, depending on the hostel and whether you are a junior (under 18 years of age) or senior member.

The Country & Marine Parks Authority (p186) maintains 41 basic campsites in the New Territories and Outlying Islands that are intended for walkers and hikers.

Facilities

Unless otherwise specified, all rooms listed here have private bathrooms and air-conditioning, and all but the cheapest will have cable TV in English. Almost all mid-range to top-end hotels, and most guest-houses, offer broadband and/or wi-fi access, as well as computers for guests' use. All hotels midrange and above, and some budget places have nonsmoking floors, or are non-smoking.

Accommodation Websites

Lonely Planet (hotels.lonelyplanet.com) Has listings of hostels, B&Bs and hotels, and an online booking service.

Hong Kong Hotels Association (www.hkha.org) For booking hotels that are members of the association.

Discover Hong Kong (www.discoverhongkong.com) Hotel search based on location and facilities.

Asia Travel (www.hongkonghotels.com) Has better deals than others.

Hotel.com (www.hotels.com/Hong-Kong) Specialises in cheap lodging.

Traveller Services (www.traveller.com.hk) For accommodation in Hong Kong, Macau and Shēnzhèn.

Phoenix Services Agency (www.statravel.hk) Online booking of relatively affordable accommodation.

Hong Kong Tourism Board (www.discoverhongkong.com) Lets you search some 200 licensed hotels and guesthouses in Hong Kong.

Lonely Planet's Top Choices

Peninsula Hong Kong (p276) World-class luxury and colonial elegance.

Mira Moon (p269) A Chinese fairy-tale theme and all the gadgets you can dream of.

Urban Pack (p274) Bunk beds in Tsim Sha Tsui come with a chilled vibe and pub crawls.

Upper House (p271) A Zen-like atmosphere, yoga on the lawn and warm service overlooking the hills in Admiralty.

Hyatt Regency Tsim Sha Tsui (p276) A self-assured veteran offering comfort and understated luxury.

YHA Mei Ho House Youth Hostel (p274) Airy lodgings converted from historic '50s housing in Sham Shui Po.

Best by Budget

$

YHA Mei Ho House Youth Hostel (p274) Fine views and immaculate rooms in an off-the-way historic housing estate.

Urban Pack (p274) Unbeatable dormitory-type lodging, especially if you love to party.

Helena May (p267) Affordable elegance in Admiralty.

YesInn (p269) A colourful hostel with lively communal areas.

Mariner's Club (p272) Offers great value in Tsim Sha Tsui, mostly to seafarers.

$$

Madera Hong Kong (p275) Smart rooms and warm service more than make up for lack of space.

99 Bonham (p267) Sleek, spacious rooms just a hop away from Central.

Mira Moon (p269) Exceptional decor and fancy gadgets.

T Hotel (p272) It's hard to believe the sparkling rooms here are run by hospitality students.

Salisbury (p275) A fabulous, YMCA-managed option that's (naturally) hard to book.

$$$

Peninsula Hong Kong (p276) One of the most elegant and richly storied hotels in Asia.

Upper House (p271) Where state-of-the-art (rooms) goes Zen (decor, atmosphere).

Mandarin Oriental (p267) Repeatedly voted one of the world's best hotels.

Four Seasons (p267) Wields award-winning restaurants and much more.

Hyatt Regency Tsim Sha Tsui (p276) Ticks all the boxes.

Best for Design

W Hong Kong (p277) Fanciful urban aesthetics that's almost too cool for school.

Madera Hong Kong (p275) Boldly coloured decor reminiscent of the movie sets of Pedro Almodóvar.

Mira Moon (p269) Taking a famous Chinese legend to new and creative heights.

Hotel Icon (p276) Stunning views and quietly opulent design-oriented interiors.

Landmark Oriental (p267) Subtle elegance infuses every nook and corner.

Best for Quirkiness

Boat Moksha (p272) A floating B&B with panoramic views of the sea.

Mingle Place by the Park (p270) Tiny rooms with eclectic quasi-vintage artefacts.

Cosmopolitan (p270) Stands right next to a spooky cemetery in Happy Valley.

NEED TO KNOW

Price Ranges
Nightly rates for a double room:

$	Up to HK$900
$$	HK$900–1900
$$$	Over HK$1900

Monthly rates for a one-bedroom apartment:

$	Up to HK$15,000
$$	HK$15,000–25,000
$$$	Over HK$25,000

High Season
When big trade fairs come to town, accommodation in Wan Chai, Causeway Bay and Tsim Sha Tsui is very tight and prices rocket. Check exact dates at www.discoverhongkong.com.

➡ January, March to early May (trade-fair season and Labour Day holiday)

➡ National Day holiday (first 10 days of October)

➡ Ching Ming Festival (usually in April)

➡ Chinese New Year (late January or February)

Reservations
Booking a room is not essential outside peak periods, but during the shoulder and low seasons, you can get discounts of up to 50% off daily rates if you book online, through a travel agent or with the Hong Kong Hotels Association, which has reservation centres on level 5 of the airport.

Taxes
Most midrange and top-end hotels and a small number of budget places add 10% service and 3% government tax to your bill.

SLEEPING

Where to Stay

Neighbourhood	For	Against
Hong Kong Island: Central	Close to the Star Ferry Pier, famous skyscrapers and luxury malls; within walking distance of bars and eats; good transport links.	The nearest eats, sleeps, bars and shops are pricey; gets quiet after office hours.
Hong Kong Island: The Peak & the Northwest	In the thick of the nightlife and dining action; close to the Peak and the historic sites in Sheung Wan.	Sloping topography, hence more trips uphill and downhill; districts further west are quiet and away from the action.
Hong Kong Island: Wan Chai & the Northeast	Good for Hong Kong Park, Happy Valley Racecourse and shopping; abundant eating and drinking options; great transport links.	Wan Chai and Causeway Bay are traffic-choked and crowded; districts further east are a little worn and far away.
Hong Kong Island: Aberdeen & the South	Great for Aberdeen Typhoon Shelter, Stanley Market, Horizon Plaza, swimming and hiking around Repulse Bay and Shek O.	Not central; frequent traffic jams near Aberdeen Tunnel; limited sleeps, eats, bars and shops.
Kowloon	Convenient for Hong Kong Museum of Art and Hong Kong Museum of History; best views of the harbour; great for shopping, eating, even 'slumming'; cool mix of old and new, high-brow and low-heel; great transport links.	Crowded and traffic-choked around Nathan Rd; some areas can be touristy and/or a little seedy.
New Territories	Fewer crowds, fresher air; handy for outdoor sports, nature tours, walled villages; prices generally lower.	Far from the action; fewer eats, sleeps, bars and shops; little to do at night.
Outlying Islands: Lamma, Lantau & Cheung Chau	Laid-back vibe and nice setting; good for seafood on Lamma, windsurfing on Cheung Chau, hiking the Lantau Trail and loads of beaches.	Longer time spent commuting; fewer eats, sleeps, bars and shops; activities dependent on weather.

🛏 Hong Kong Island: Central

The lion's share of Hong Kong Island's luxury hotels is in Central, catering predominantly to moneyed leisure travellers and busy, corporate types. The service and facilities you'll find here are the best in town. Whether it's child-minding service, dinner reservations or combating jetlag you need, it will be done with efficiency, and possibly a smile.

⭐ **HELENA MAY** HOTEL **$**
Map p362 (梅夫人婦女會主樓; ☑2522 6766; www.helenamay.com; 35 Garden Rd, Central; s/d HK$510/670, studios per month HK$15,520-20,230; ☑23) If you like the Peninsula's colonial setting but not its price tag, this grand dame could be your cup of tea. Founded in 1916 as a social club for single European women in the territory, the Helena May (p74) is now a private club for women of all nationalities and a hotel with 43 creaky but charming rooms.

Rooms in the main building are women-only with shared bathrooms, while the rent-by-month studios in an adjacent building are also open to men. You must be 18 or above to stay at the Helena May. The building is a stone's throw from the Peak Tram Terminus and the Zoological & Botanical Gardens.

⭐ **FOUR SEASONS** LUXURY HOTEL **$$$**
Map p362 (四季酒店; ☑3196 8888; www.fourseasons.com/hongkong; 8 Finance St, Central; r HK$4800-8100, ste HK$9800-65,000; ☯☎☒; Ⓜ Hong Kong, exit F) The Four Seasons arguably edges into top place on the island for its amazing views, pristine service and location close to the Star Ferry Pier, Hong Kong station and Sheung Wan. Also on offer are palatial rooms, a glorious pool and spa complex, and award-winning restaurants Caprice (p79) and Lung King Heen (p78).

MANDARIN ORIENTAL LUXURY HOTEL **$$$**
Map p362 (文華東方酒店; ☑2522 0111; www.mandarinoriental.com/hongkong; 5 Connaught Rd, Central; r HK$5300-7400, ste HK$8000-65,000; ☯☎☒; Ⓜ Central, exit J3) The venerable Mandarin has historically set the standard in Asia and continues to be a contender for the top spot, despite competition from the likes of the Four Seasons.

The styling, service, food and atmosphere are stellar throughout and there's a sense of gracious, old-world charm. The sleek **Landmark Oriental** (Map p362; ☑2132 0088; www.mandarinoriental.com/landmark; 15 Queen's Rd, Central; r HK$3500-6800, ste HK$9300-45,000; ☯☎☒), just across the way, offers modern luxury, but with a business vibe.

🛏 Hong Kong Island: The Peak & the Northwest

MIA CASA BOUTIQUE HOTEL **$**
(輝豪酒店; ☑3752 2988; www.miacasa.com.hk; 2 Hau Wo St, Kennedy Town; s/d from HK$600/800, ste HK$1200-1300, Fri & Sat extra HK$100; ☎; 🚋Kennedy Town terminus) Mia Casa, close to the Kennedy Town tram terminus, has 33 clean rooms just large enough to swing a cat in. A bed occupies 70% of that; the rest is split between a tiny bathroom and a luggage rack. Some suites have balconies. It's a good option if you just need a clean bed to sleep in.

⭐ **99 BONHAM** BOUTIQUE HOTEL **$$**
Map p368 (☑3940 1111; www.99bonham.com; 99 Bonham Strand, Sheung Wan; Ⓜ Sheung Wan, exit A2) This hotel has 84 unusually large rooms (for Hong Kong). These are stylishly minimalist, featuring a palette of white, black and grey. The hotel also has a small gym, a business centre and a rooftop terrace where you can go for a smoke surrounded by resplendent views. There's no F&B (food and beverage) outlet but an abundance of eateries await just out the door.

PUTMAN APARTMENT **$$**
Map p366 (☑2233 2233; www.theputman.com; 202-206 Queen's Rd, Central; studios HK$1100-1300, apt HK$2800-3200, studio/apt per month from HK$22,000/52,000; ☯☎; Ⓜ Sheung Wan, exit A or E) Behind the art-deco-inspired glass facade, this designer outfit has three cool-toned studios for shorter stays and 25 one-bedroom flats for long-term rental. Each flat occupies an entire storey and the floor-to-ceiling windows allow a lot of natural light. You also get space (the flats are 120 sq metres and the studios are 30 to 40 sq metres) and impeccable taste here. The kitchens come with designer cooking utensils, crockery, stemware and laundry facilities. Prices include membership to a gym nearby.

OVOLO
BUSINESS HOTEL **$$**

Map p366 (☑3423 3286; www.ovolohotels.com; 286 Queen's Rd Central, Sheung Wan; r HK$3800; @ 🛜; MSheung Wan, exit D1) All 60 smoke-free rooms, some with connecting doors, are clean and compact (14 to 18 sq metres), with low beds and a minimalist Japanese-influenced design. Guests are showered with freebies including breakfast, minibar, use of a small gym, self-service laundry and booze every evening in the 24-hour lounge. Ask about the in-city wi-fi service. Rates are usually between HK$200 and HK$2000.

BAUHINIA
SERVICED APARTMENT, HOTEL **$$**

Map p368 (寶軒酒店; ☑3426 3333, 2156 3000; www.apartments.com.hk; 119-121 Connaught Rd, Central; 1-bed flat per month from HK$26000, 2-bed from HK$35,000, daily r HK$2200; @ 🛜; MSheung Wan, exit A1) Bauhinia now has 42 rooms for daily rental in addition to its original serviced apartments. Rooms are small but spotless and you can't complain about the location, which is right next to the MTR station. Daily rates outside the high season hover between HK$1000 and HK$2000. Staff are friendly and service efficient. Enter from Man Wah Lane.

BUTTERFLY ON HOLLYWOOD
BOUTIQUE HOTEL **$$**

Map p368 (晉逸好萊塢精品酒店; ☑2850 8899; 263 Hollywood Rd, Sheung Wan; r HK$1200-1600, ste HK$1800-2400; @ 🛜; 🚌26) A well-located hotel with good service and small but adequate rooms, some of which feature a wacky (or tacky) tinsel-town theme. Tips: 'City View' rooms have no windows; rooms ending in '01' face buildings; the smoking floors are 6, 16 and 17. Rates are usually between HK$800 and HK$1200, but can soar to HK$5000 – ask before you book.

MERCER
BOUTIQUE HOTEL **$$**

Map p366 (尚圜; 29 Jervois St, Sheung Wan; r/ste from HK$1680/2800; @ 🛜🛝; MSheung Wan, exit A2) There are 15 rooms and 40 one-bedroom suites at this modern, conveniently located hotel. Decked out in beige with lots of mirror surfaces, they offer a host of freebies – wi-fi, minibar, local calls and breakfast, and, for the suites, coffee machines. There's a small gym and lap pool for the sporty, while smokers can puff away in the 1st-floor lounge.

HOTEL LBP
BUSINESS HOTEL **$$**

Map p368 (西關酒店; ☑2681 9388; www.hotel-lbp.com.hk; 77-91 Queen's Rd W, Sheung Wan; r HK$1220-1740, monthly package from HK$25,000; @ 🛜; MSheung Wan, exit A2) Just 600m west of Sheung Wan MTR station, this is a good-value choice – each of the 46 rooms has at least 21 sq metres, a reasonable size by Hong Kong standards. The decor won't wow you, but the rooms are clean and comfortable enough. Rooms facing south offer views of Hollywood Rd Park.

LAN KWAI FONG HOTEL
BOUTIQUE HOTEL **$$**

Map p366 (蘭桂坊酒店@九如坊; ☑3650 0000; www.lankwaifonghotel.com.hk; 3 Kau U Fong, Central; r/ste from HK$1300/3200; @ 🛜; MSheung Wan, exit E2) This well-located hotel (not to be confused with Hotel LKF) is closer to Soho than Lan Kwai Fong. The Chinese decor with a contemporary twist adds an interesting touch to the reasonably spacious digs. The service is top-notch.

IBIS
HOTEL **$$**

Map p368 (上環宜必思酒店; ☑2252 2929; www.ibishotel.com; 18-30 Des Voeux Rd W, Sheung Wan; r from HK$950; @; 🚌5B from Central) The 550-room Ibis offers a more affordable option in an expensive part of town. The rooms and facilities are decent, but do not expect luxury. The highlight here is the warm service by staff dressed perpetually in polo tees and a smile which lends the hotel a relaxing, resort-like flair. Prices are in the hundreds if you book online. Hotel Ibis is just around the corner from Western Market (p90).

COURTYARD BY MARRIOTT HONG KONG
BUSINESS HOTEL **$$$**

(香港萬怡酒店; ☑3717 8888; www.marriott.com/hotels/travel/hkgcy-courtyard-hong-kong; 167 Connaught Rd W; r HK$1300-3000, ste from HK$2600; @ 🛜; 🚌5 or 5B from Central) This hotel juggles luxury with limited space, and it works. Most rooms offer harbour views and are smartly decorated with modern furnishings. The plump beds and high-thread-count sheets guarantee you a good night's sleep. Service is impeccable. There's an Airbus stop across the street.

HOTEL LKF
HOTEL **$$$**

Map p366 (隆堡蘭桂坊酒店; ☑3518 9688; www.hotel-lkf.com.hk; 33 Wyndham St, Central; r HK$2600-6000, ste from HK$10,000; @ 🛜;

Ⓜ Central, exit D2) Located on the upper, flatter section of Wyndham St, Hotel LKF is arguably the best gateway to the Lan Kwai Fong action, but is far enough above it not to be disturbed by it. It has high-tech rooms in muted tones and they brim with all the trimmings you'll need: fluffy bathrobes, espresso machines and free bedtime milk and cookies. There's a plush spa and yoga studio in the building.

🛏 Hong Kong Island: Wan Chai & the Northeast

Admiralty, with easy access to Hong Kong Park, the Pacific Place mall and the Asia Society Hong Kong Centre, has a handful of high-end hotels. Wan Chai, favoured by trade-fair regulars and mainland tourists, has midrange lodging, with a sprinkling of cheaper guesthouses and some high-end options near the Convention & Exhibition Centre. In addition to good-value midrange options, Causeway Bay is relatively well served by inexpensive guesthouses, especially on or around Paterson St. During the low season guesthouses often struggle to fill beds and rooms; most will offer discounts to anyone staying longer than a few nights.

YESINN HOSTEL $

Map p374 (☑2213 4567; www.yesinn.com; 472 Hennessy Rd, 2nd fl, Nan Yip Bldg, Causeway Bay; dm HK$159-469, r HK$199-459; Ⓜ Causeway Bay, exit F2) This funky, vibrant hostel attracts backpackers from all over the world, as evidenced by their signatures on the building's chalkboard paint ceiling. There are both single-sex and mixed dorms, as well as private rooms, all brightly painted. The small reception area is made up for by the excellent roof deck, sometimes the site of hostel-sponsored barbecues.

The hostel entrance is at the side of the building on the corner. Private rooms are in a building across the street. The neon, shopping and late-night sushi of Causeway Bay are a two-minute walk. YesInn has sister hostels in Fortress Hill and Kowloon.

COSMO BOUTIQUE HOTEL $

(☑3552 8388; www.cosmohotel.com.hk; 375-377 Queen's Rd E, Wan Chai; r/ste from HK$650/1000; 😊 🛜; Ⓜ Causeway Bay, exit A) Aiming for boutiquey ambience, this good-value hotel on the quiet side of Wan Chai has lovely rooms done in cool whites and greys with modish pops of bright orange. The cheaper rooms have frosted-glass windows, so no view. Not to be confused with its pricier sister hotel, the Cosmopolitan (p270), just down the block.

HARBOUR VIEW HOTEL $

Map p372 (香港灣景國際; ☑2802 0111; www.theharbourview.com.hk; 4 Harbour Rd, Wan Chai; r from HK$750; @ 🛜; 🚇18, Ⓜ Wan Chai, exit A5) Close to the water in Wan Chai, this 320-room hotel is good value for the location. It offers simply furnished but adequate rooms, and exceptionally friendly staff. Some rooms overlook a dark courtyard which can be a bit creepy; pay an extra HK$200 for a room facing the street. Rates can drop nearly 50% in low season.

★ MIRA MOON BOUTIQUE HOTEL $$

(☑2643 8888; www.miramoonhotel.com; 388 Jaffe Rd, Wan Chai; r HK$1400-3000; 🛜; Ⓜ Wan Chai, exit A1) 🍃 The new kid on the block is also the coolest. Decor at this 91-room boutique hotel riffs on the Chinese fairy tale of the Moon Goddess and the Jade Rabbit – stylised rabbit wall art, oversized Chinese lanterns, graphic peony floor mosaics. For all its hipness, the hotel's staff is warm and helpful, and the architecture is ecofriendly to boot.

It's all about the details here. Freestanding bathtubs in the 'Half Moon' and 'Full Moon' rooms are to die for, while the more budget-friendly 'New Moon' rooms offer walk-in showers. All rooms come with a phone, which guests can take with them for free 3G and local and international calls. There's free soy milk and soda in the minifridge, and the room's iPad connects to the TV. Amenities include a 24-hour gym, a Spanish-Chinese fusion tapas restaurant and (naturally) a house DJ.

GARDEN VIEW HOTEL $$

Map p370 (女青年會園景軒; ☑2877 3737; http://the-garden-view-ywca.hotel-rn.com; 1 MacDonnell Rd, Central; r/ste HK$1800/2800, per month from HK$25,000; @ 🛜; 🚌green minibus 1A) Straddling the border of Central and the Mid-Levels, this YWCA-run hotel is favoured by families and professionals. Its 133 rooms overlook the Zoological & Botanical Gardens (p76) and are close to a supermarket.

Accommodation here is plain but quiet and functional, and comes with an outdoor swimming pool. No free wi-fi. Rates drop to HK$1000 in the low season.

SHAMA
SERVICED APARTMENTS $$

Map p374 (☑2202 5555; www.shama.com; 8 Russell St, 7th fl, Causeway Bay; r per day from HK$1500, apt per month from HK$28,300; @☎; MCauseway Bay, exit A) These are among the most attractive serviced apartments in town, in a block opposite Times Square shopping mall. Ranging from fairly spacious studio flats to two-bedroom apartments, they're all tastefully furnished and exceedingly comfortable. Features and extras include wi-fi, daily maid service, DVD equipment, laundry facilities and membership to gyms. Studios and one-bedrooms have no minimum stay.

CITY GARDEN HOTEL HONG KONG
HOTEL $$

(城市花園酒店; ☑2887 2888; www.citygarden. com.hk; 9 City Garden Rd, North Point; r HK$800-2850; @☎; MFortress Hill, exit A) Only five minutes' walk from Fortress Hill MTR station, this exceptionally well-turned-out business hotel also boasts large rooms (by local standards), good service, free and fast wi-fi and a generous discounting policy. Enter from the corner of Electric Rd and Power St.

MINI HOTEL CAUSEWAY BAY
BOUTIQUE HOTEL $$

Map p374 (☑3979 1111; www.minihotel.hk; 8 Sun Wui Rd, Causeway Bay; r from HK$740; MCauseway Bay, exit F1) Exactly as the name suggests, this centrally located Causeway Bay property offers teeny-weeny rooms, some as small as 100 sq ft. Cool architectural details – parquet floors, crown molding, recessed lighting – and an uber-hip, art-filled lobby help make up for what it lacks in size. Best for visitors more interested in being out on the town than relaxing in their room.

COSMOPOLITAN HOTEL
HOTEL $$

(香港麗都酒店; ☑3552 1111; www.cosmopolitanhotel.com.hk; 387-397 Queen's Rd E, Wan Chai; r/ste from HK$900/1800; @☎; MCauseway Bay, exit A) The views here are unusual – Hong Kong Cemetery to the south and the Happy Valley Racecourse to the east. If tombstones spook you out, request a room with frosted windows; that said, rooms facing the racecourse are supposed to have better feng shui. All rooms are sunny and bright and come with 11 pillow choices!

Cosmopolitan is actually closer to Queen's Rd East in Wan Chai than to Causeway Bay, but there's a shuttle service to the latter. Look for online deals for as much as 35% off. Not to be confused with the Cosmo (p269), its sister hotel down the block.

MINGLE PLACE BY THE PARK
HOTEL $$

Map p372 (☑2838 1109; www.mingleplace.com; 143 Wan Chai Rd, Wan Chai; r HK$750-2000, per month HK$1500-24,000; @☎; MWan Chai, exit A3) This five-storey hotel is housed in a restored 1960s tenement building with a small garden. Teeny rooms are 'original 1960s style' which means bare bones with some quirky vintage paraphernalia like retro alarm clocks and tea sets. Some rooms, including the cubicle-sized 'lite' rooms, have tiny balconies. No lift.

CHARTERHOUSE HOTEL
HOTEL $$

(☑2833 5566; www.charterhouse.com; 209-219 Wan Chai Rd; r/ste from HK$700/1500; ☎; ☑23) On the leafy side of Wan Chai, you're almost getting top-end accommodation for low-midrange rates. Rooms are plush, clean and perfumed (allergy sufferers, beware) if not brand-new, and staff are friendly and eager to please.

CAUSEWAY CORNER
APARTMENTS $$

Map p374 (銅鑼閣; ☑2838 3211; www.causewaycorner.com; 18 Percival St, Causeway Bay; per night HK$1100-1800, per month HK$15,500-23,000; @☎; MCauseway Bay, exit C) Ideal for longer stays, this serviced apartment block has 105 units that come with showers, microwave oven, fridge, eating utensils and twice-a-week maid service. Compact rooms are neat and pleasantly furnished, and there's a coin-operated laundry facility.

REGAL ICLUB HOTEL
BUSINESS HOTEL $$

Map p372 (☑3669 8668; www.regalhotel.com; 211 Johnston Rd, Wan Chai; r HK$900-2300; @☎; MWan Chai, exit A3) ✐ This modern 99-room hotel in the heart of Wan Chai is a good choice if functionality and location are more important to you than large rooms, clockwork service and a lavish breakfast. It bills itself as the first carbon-neutral hotel in Hong Kong, and is 100% smoke-free.

Y-LOFT YOUTH SQUARE HOSTEL
HOSTEL $$

(☑3721 8989; www.youthsquare.hk; 238 Chai Wan Rd, Chai Wan; tw/tr low season HK$700/900, high season HK$1200/1800, ste HK$3000; @🛜; Ⓜ Chai Wan, exit A) If you don't mind trading 20 extra minutes on the MTR for an excellent budget option, you'll be rewarded with large, clean and cheerful rooms atop a community youth centre in Chai Wan (not Wan Chai!). Popular with students from mainland China on semesters abroad, the vibe here is more upscale dormitory than backpacker hostel.

The beaches and bazaar of Stanley are only 15 minutes away by bus from the 16X bus stop opposite the MTR station. To reach the hostel from exit A, go straight through the youth centre to the footbridge and take the first exit on your right. Reception's on the 12th floor. Staff are very friendly.

WIFI BOUTIQUE HOTEL BUSINESS HOTEL $$
(📞2558 8939; www.wifihotel.com.hk; 366 Lockhart Rd, Wan Chai; r HK$800-2000; 🛜; Ⓜ Causeway Bay, exit C) Ignore the lightless lobby and the odd disco ambience of the mirrored elevators, and you'll be rewarded with bright, pleasant rooms done up in earth tones. A favourite with mainland shoppers.

★ UPPER HOUSE BOUTIQUE HOTEL $$$
Map p370 (📞2918 1838; www.upperhouse.com; 88 Queensway, Pacific Pl, Admiralty; r/ste from HK$4500/12,000; @🛜; Ⓜ Admiralty, exit F) Every corner of this boutique hotel spells zen-like serenity – the understated lobby, the sleek eco-minded rooms, the elegant sculptures, the warm and discreet service and the manicured lawn where guests can join free yoga classes. Other pluses include a free and 'bottomless' minibar, and easy access to the Admiralty MTR station.

Guests of the Upper House can pay to use the pool facilities of nearby hotels. This is a superb alternative to luxury options in Central and Admiralty, if you don't mind fewer luxuries.

LANSON PLACE HOTEL $$$
Map p374 (📞3477 6888; www.lansonplace.com; 133 Leighton Rd, Causeway Bay; r HK$1520-3800; @🛜; Ⓜ Causeway Bay, exit F) This plush hotel is an oasis of calm and class amid the Causeway Bay din. The spacious rooms blend classic style with modern fittings and feature lavish bathrooms. There's plenty of public lounging space and a concierge service. If you get one of the corner rooms, there are windows overlooking two different streets.

GRAND HYATT HOTEL LUXURY HOTEL $$$
Map p372 (君悦酒店; 📞2588 1234; www.hongkong.grand.hyatt.com; 1 Harbour Rd, Wan Chai; r HK$3600-6000; @🛜🏊; 🚇18, Ⓜ Wan Chai, exit A5) With a towering black-and-gold lobby, a string quartet on the mezzanine and an enormous emerald on display by the concierge, this vast convention hotel ain't subtle. Rooms are huge and sport desks bristling with technology, marble-clad bathrooms and some great views.

While you're here, be sure to sip some bubbles at the classy Champagne Bar (p124) or indulge in a facial in the hushed and opulent Plateau spa on the 11th floor.

EAST HONG KONG BUSINESS HOTEL $$$
(📞3968 3808; www.east-hongkong.com; 29 Taikoo Shing Rd, Taikoo Shing, Quarry Bay; r/ste from HK$1700/4800; @🛜🏊; Ⓜ Tai Koo, exit D1) This sleekly cool business hotel has 345 clean, bright rooms decorated with contemporary art and minimalist furniture. Corner harbour-view rooms, commanding good views, cost more than rooms on the lower floors which look on to buildings nearby. The 32nd-floor bar, Sugar (p126), is spectacular for sunset cocktails.

ISLAND SHANGRI-LA HONG KONG LUXURY HOTEL $$$
Map p370 (港島香格里拉大酒店; 📞2877 3838; www.shangri-la.com; Supreme Court Rd, Pacific Pl, Admiralty; r/ste from HK$3900/5600; @🛜🏊; Ⓜ Admiralty, exit F, via Pacific) This monolithic hotel offers plush digs with an early-'90s vibe. Comfortable (though not particularly chic) rooms are matched by a good gym, a swimming pool and excellent service. Take a quick ride up the bubble lift that links the 39th and 56th floors; you'll catch a glance of the hotel's signature 60m-high painting, a mountainous Chinese landscape that's quite impressive.

J PLUS BOUTIQUE HOTEL $$$
Map p374 (📞3196 9000; www.jplushongkong.com; 1-5 Irving St, Causeway Bay; r HK$1500-2800; @🛜; Ⓜ Causeway Bay, exit F) This stylish boutique hotel occupies a prime location in Causeway Bay within walking distance of bus, tram and MTR stations. The Philippe Starck–inspired rooms are small but clean, cool and modern. Some taxi drivers may not know it, so tell them you're going to the Regal hotel which is right across the street.

PARK LANE HONG KONG HOTEL $$$

Map p374 (柏寧酒店; ☑2293 8888; www.parklane.com.hk; 310 Gloucester Rd, Causeway Bay; r HK$1700-7000; @🛜❄; MCauseway Bay, exit E) With restful views of Victoria Park to the east and busy Causeway Bay to the west, the Park Lane is a good choice for those who want to be both in and out of the action. The higher rooms have much nicer views. Park Lane is favoured by tourists who are here to shop, so the lobby and the entrance area can get noisy and crowded. There's also a large gym.

METROPARK HOTEL HOTEL $$$

Map p374 (維景酒店; ☑2600 1000; www.metroparkhotelcausewaybay.com; 148 Tung Lo Wan Rd, Causeway Bay; r HK$1100-2800; @🛜❄; MTin Hau, exit B) This flashy tower overlooking Victoria Park makes the most of its easterly location, with 70% of its 243 rooms boasting sweeping city-harbour views through floor-to-ceiling windows. Rooms are bright but the basic ones don't have bathtubs. Check the website for discounts and packages.

🛏 Hong Kong Island: Aberdeen & the South

BOAT MOKSHA HOUSEBOAT $

Map p376 (☑6935 9091; www.airbnb.com/rooms/65117; Shum Wan Rd, Wong Chuk Hang, Aberdeen; r HK$760-1000; @🛜❄; ☐72A from Causeway Bay, 75 from Central, below Exchange Sq) Finally, there's a nonterrestrial lodging option in this archipelago of 260-plus islands. This cosy houseboat moored on the eastern side of Aberdeen is a floating B&B that offers 360-degree sea views, modern facilities and very comfy beds. The front deck room is reasonably sized so you don't need to squeeze. Upstairs, the suite room is an affordable luxury.

Owner Saral is not always around, but his friendly helper will look after you. Booking in advance is a must. To get there, take bus 72A or 75 towards Aberdeen and alight at the terminus. Water taxis (HK$7) will take you to the boat from the dock opposite the bus terminus.

JOCKEY CLUB MT DAVIS YOUTH HOSTEL HOSTEL $

(☑2817 5715; www.yha.org.hk; 123 Mount Davis Path, Pok Fu Lam; member/nonmember high season HK$210/245, low season HK$160/195) If you're not afraid of ghosts (Mt Davis, an isolated Pok Fu Lam peak, is said to be haunted) then this newly refurbished hostel may be for you. Though it's not walking distance from anything, it makes up for it with a free shuttlebus and killer views of Victoria Harbour. Must be a Hong Kong Youth Hostels Association (p325) member, or arrive with one.

★ T HOTEL HOTEL $$

(T酒店; ☑3717 7388; www.vtc.edu.hk/thotel; 145 Pokfulam Rd, VTC Pokfulam Complex, Pok Fu Lam; r from HK$900; @🛜❄; ☐7, 91 from Central, 973 from Tsim Sha Tsui) Ah, we almost don't want to tell you about this gem on the island! The 30-room T, perched high in the serene neighbourhood of Pok Fu Lam, is entirely run by students of the local hospitality training institute. The young trainees are attentive, cheerful and very eager to hone their skills. Rooms are sparkling and spacious, and offer ocean or mountain views.

The food and beverage outlets, run by the famous culinary school in the complex, provide excellent Chinese and Western meals.

🛏 Kowloon

Splendour rubs shoulders with squalor in Kowloon. There is a huge range of hotels and guesthouses, catering to all budgets, between the two extremes. Tsim Sha Tsui has a number of top-end hotels, some glamorous, some anonymous. Things start getting cheaper as you go north. Yau Ma Tei has several midrange options, plus cheap, basic hotels and a good assortment of guesthouses.

★ MARINER'S CLUB HOTEL $

Map p380 (海員之家; ☑2368 8261; www.marinersclub.org.hk; 11 Middle Rd, Tsim Sha Tsui; s/d without bathroom from HK$370/520, with bathroom from HK$550/750, ste from HK$1100; @🛜❄; MEast Tsim Sha Tsui, exit K) Anyone can book this great budget option, but they'll ask for mariner's ID or proof of shipping-company employment at check-in. However, we've had reports that they're not very strict about this and prices for shipping companies are about HK$80 more for each category. The hotel has 100 rooms – 30 new (4th and 5th floors; the only ones with wi-fi) and 70 old – austere-looking with retro furniture and black-and-red vinyl flooring.

BUDGET BLOCKS IN TSIM SHA TSUI

Chungking Mansions

Say 'budget accommodation' and 'Hong Kong' in one breath and everyone thinks of **Chungking Mansions** (重慶大廈, CKM; Map p378; 36-44 Nathan Rd, Tsim Sha Tsui; MTsim Sha Tsui, exit F). Built in 1961, CKM is a labyrinth of homes, guesthouses, Indian restaurants, souvenir stalls and foreign-exchange shops spread over five 17-storey blocks in the heart of Tsim Sha Tsui (p146). According to anthropologist Gordon Mathews, it has a resident population of about 4000 and an estimated 10,000 daily visitors. Over 120 different nationalities – predominantly South Asian and African – pass through its doors in a single year.

Though standards vary significantly, most of the guesthouses at CKM are clean and quite comfortable. It's worth bearing in mind, however, that rooms are usually the size of cupboards and you have to shower right next to the toilet. The rooms typically come with air-con and TV and, sometimes, a phone. Many guesthouses can get you a Chinese visa quickly, most have internet access and some have wi-fi and laundry service.

Bargaining for a bed or room is always possible, though you won't get very far in the high season. You can often negotiate a cheaper price if you stay more than, say, a week, but never try that on the first night – stay one night and find out how you like it before handing over more rent. Once you pay, there are usually no refunds.

Dragon Inn (龍滙賓館; Map p378; 2368 2007; dragoinn@netvigator.com; flat B5, 3rd fl, B Block; s HK$320-490, d HK$380-680, honeymoon rooms HK$600-700, tr HK$530-620, q HK$560-680; 🕾) This place is owned by the chairperson of the Incorporated Owners of CKM – a shrewd and helpful lady. It has squeaky-clean rooms with private bathrooms, drinking water and a hairdryer; there are discounts for students, seniors and repeat customers. (Yes, the email is spelt 'dragoinn'.)

Holiday Guesthouse (Map p378; 2316 7152, 9121 8072; fax 2316 7181; flat E1, 6th fl, E Block; s HK$250-600, d HK$350-700; @🕾) An upmarket Nepali-run place with 23 pleasant rooms.

Yan Yan Guest House (欣欣賓館; Map p378; 2366 8930, 9489 3891; fax 2721 0840; flat E1, 8th fl, E Block; s HK$150-240, d HK$180-240; 🕾) This is one of the last of the Chinese-owned guesthouses in the overwhelmingly subcontinental E Block. Wi-fi reception is better in the front rooms. New Yan Yan Guesthouse (新欣欣賓館; Map p378; 2723 5671; Flat E5, 12th fl, E Block; 🕾), in the same block, is managed by the same people.

Park Guesthouse (百樂賓館; Map p378; 2368 1689; fax 2367 7889; flat A1, 15th fl, A Block; s HK$250, d HK$450, without bathroom HK$200; 🕾) A basic but welcoming 45-room guesthouse that comes recommended by readers.

Mirador Mansion

It was at **Mirador Mansion** (Map p378; 54-64 Nathan Rd, Tsim Sha Tsui; MTsim Sha Tsui, exit D2) – and not Chungking Mansions – where Wong Kar-wai filmed most of *Chungking Express* (1994).

Hello HK (您好小棧; Map p378; http://helloinn.mysinablog.com; Block A7, 6th fl, Mirador Mansion; r HK$320-500) Three small and clean ensuite rooms (two doubles and one triple), three dorm-type rooms, and a corridor where you can make coffee and use the communal laptop make up Hello HK. Run by the helpful Ivan, it's secure with password door keylock and electronic lockers. Forget about knocking on the door without a reservation; they won't even open it.

Cosmic Guest House (宇宙賓館; Map p378; 2369 6669; www.cosmicguesthouse.com; flats A1-A2, Block F1, 12th fl; s HK$200, d & tw HK$300, tr HK$390-450, q HK$380-520, f from HK$500; @🕾) With some 80 beds, this is one of the largest guesthouses in town. It's clean and quiet with big and bright rooms (well, those with windows) and a very helpful owner. There's internet access in every room. Some even have rain showers...wedged into 1-metre-sq bathrooms!

The Mariner's Club, overlooking the Middle Road Children's Playground, was opened in 1967 for visiting 'China coasters'. It offers a lazy, old-world charm, as well as a first-rate swimming pool and a chapel with Catholic and Anglican services.

YHA MEI HO HOUSE YOUTH HOSTEL
HOSTEL $

(美荷樓青年旅舍; ☑3728 3500; www.meiho-house.hk; 70 Berwick St, Block 41, Shek Kip Mei Estate, Sham Shui Po; dm member HK$260, d HK$810, family HK$1620; ☎; ⊠A21, ⓂSham Shui Po, exit D2) This youth hostel, converted from public housing units, features immaculate rooms and dorm-type lodgings, as well as a **museum** (美荷樓生活館; ⊙9.30am-5pm Tue-Sun) and **cafe** (☑3728 3454; HK$30-60; ⊙7am-11pm; ☎). Lockers with inbuilt chargers are provided, but not toiletries. After leaving the MTR, go straight into Kweilin St, then turn right into Un Chau St. After a block, make a left into the underground walkway, turning left again as you exit.

Mei Ho House was among the first batch of resettlement blocks built to house the 58,000 homeless survivors of a devastating blaze, known commonly as the 'Shek Kip Mei Fire', that broke out in 1953. As such, it marks the beginning of Hong Kong's public housing policy.

★URBAN PACK
HOSTEL $

Map p378 (休閑小窩; ☑2732 2271; www.urban-pack.com; 99-101 Nathan Rd, unit 1410, 14th fl, Haiphong Mansion, Tsim Sha Tsui; dm HK$220-300; ☎; ⓂTsim Sha Tsui, exit A1) If your idea of a great hostel involves a chilled vibe, lots of interaction with fellow travellers, and bar-hopping with the owners, Urban Pack is *the* place for you. Run by two friendly Canadian-Chinese, Albert and Jensen, Urban Pack also offers solid dorm rooms (mixed and women's), sophisticated showering facilities (rain showerheads anyone?), free coffee, and even a massage chair.

YESINSPACE
SERVICED APARTMENT $

Map p383 (悅思服式公寓; ☑3427 6000; www.yesinspace.com; 10 Anchor St, 4th fl, Tai Kok Tsui; s per month HK$9500, d HK$12,500; ☎; ⓂMong Kok, exit A2) All 54 rooms and apartments here are nonsmoking and simply furnished, not unlike a college dorm room. There's a pantry and an electric stove for your culinary needs, as well as a working

desk and a closet. Your neighbours will be mainland expats and foreign university students on exchange programs.

ALOHAS HOSTEL
HOSTEL $

Map p382 (愛樂活旅舍; ☑5117 3470; www.alohas.com.hk; 231 Nathan Rd, flat A, 7th fl, Kam Ling Bldg, Jordan; s HK$300-400, d HK$600, tr HK$900; ⓂJordan, exit C1) With the exception of the single, all eight rooms here have private bathrooms. Though tiny, they're reasonably clean with white walls embellished by the whimsical art of a Taiwanese illustrator. The English-speaking staff are polite and helpful. Guests are given a card key which they can use to open their rooms and the front door.

CITY ECONO GUESTHOUSE
GUESTHOUSE $

Map p382 (京樺旅館; ☑2730 0212; www.cityecono.com; 227 Nathan Rd, 6th fl, Cumberland House, Jordan; s/d/tr/q from HK$450/550/700/800; ☎; ⓂJordan, exit C2) This old-fashioned family-run guesthouse is safe and conveniently located, but to get to the lift lobby from Nathan Rd you have to negotiate a long flight of stairs. All 16 rooms are neat and small; bathrooms are also clean, but cramped and fitted with ageing gadgets. Ask for a room with windows.

INNSIGHT
GUESTHOUSE $

Map p378 (悠悠客舍; ☑2369 1151; www.innsight.hk; 9 Lock Rd, 3rd fl, Tsim Sha Tsui; r HK$600-800; ⓐ☎; ⓂTsim Sha Tsui, exit H) Fabulous location, warmly decorated rooms and a cosy pantry are the fortes here. The owner Carmen makes an effort to please, even providing free shampoo and bath gel, which makes it easy to overlook the fact that the showers are not encased in stalls. If you want a wider bed, ask for a Comfort Double. Rates are around HK$1100 during Christmas.

HOP INN ON HANKOW
HOSTEL $

Map p378 (☑2881 7331; www.hopinn.hk; 19-21 Hankow Rd, flat A, 2nd fl, Hanyee Bldg, Tsim Sha Tsui; s HK$410-530, d & tw HK$520-790, tr HK$650-980, q HK$1020-1200; ⓐ☎; ⓂTsim Sha Tsui, exit C1) This nonsmoking hostel has a youthful vibe and nine spotless and dainty rooms, each sporting illustrations by a different Hong Kong artist. The rooms without windows are quieter than the ones that have them. The other branch, Hop Inn on

Carnarvon (p275), has newer rooms in an older building. Both branches offer free in-room wi-fi and will help to organise China visas.

HOP INN ON CARNARVON   HOSTEL $

Map p380 (☑2881 7331; www.hopinn.hk; 33-35 Carnarvon Rd, 9th fl, James S Lee Mansion, Tsim Sha Tsui; s HK$410-530, d & tw HK$520-790, tr HK$650-980, q HK$1020-1200; ☎; ⓂTsim Sha Tsui, exit A2) Similar to the original Hop Inn on Hankow (p274), this newer branch is excellently located and the small rooms feature illustrations by local artists (check out the one by Sim Chan!). Hot water supply in the showers is sometimes unsteady at this branch.

HOTEL PANDORA   HOTEL $

Map p382 (潘多拉酒店; ☑3727 4888; www.hotelpandora.hk; 321 Nathan Rd, 9th fl, Jordan; d/tr/q/ste from HK$400/550/600/850; ☎; ⓂJordan, exit C2) Pandora, with 105 rooms (the smallest shoe-box-sized), sits atop hostess clubs and massage parlours like a modern oasis. Sure, you may bump into a couple of drunk men in the slow-moving lift, but apart from that, it's safe. Some bookings come with free breakfast which is served in an airy, light-flooded cafe. Pandora is popular with mainland tourists.

CARITAS LODGE   GUESTHOUSE $

Map p383 (明愛賓館; ☑2339 3777; www.caritas-chs.org.hk; 134 Boundary St, Mong Kok; s HK$504-720, d HK$574-820; @☎; ⓂMong Kok East, exit C or D) With just 40 rooms, this place is as nice as its sister guesthouse, Caritas Bianchi Lodge (p276), but the rooms are smaller and it's further afield. Still, you couldn't get much closer to the bird market, and the New Territories is (officially) just across the road. Rates include breakfast.

NIC & TRIG'S   GUESTHOUSE $

Map p383 (☑6333 5352; rooms@nostalgic.org; 703 Shanghai St, Mong Kok; r from HK$400; ☎; ⓂPrince Edward, exit C1) Run by a friendly hipster couple, this place inside a 'walk-up' tenement building (c 1957) has atmospheric rooms inspired by retro Hong Kong. Toilet and shower areas are shared; provisions are basic. If you need anything, just ask. The owners are happy to give you restaurant and sightseeing tips. Email and they will tell you how to get there.

★ SALISBURY   HOTEL $$

Map p378 (香港基督教青年會; ☑2268 7888; www.ymcahk.org.hk; 41 Salisbury Rd, Tsim Sha Tsui; dm HK$300, s/d/ste from HK$1000/1200/2200; @☎❄; ⓂTsim Sha Tsui, exit E) If you can manage to book a room at this fabulously located place, you'll be rewarded with professional service and excellent exercise facilities. Rooms and suites are comfortable but simple, so keep your eyes on the harbour: that view would cost you five times as much at the Peninsula next door. The dormitory rooms are a bonus but restrictions apply.

The four-bed dorm rooms are meant for short-stay travellers, hence no one can stay there more than seven consecutive nights and walk-in guests aren't accepted if they've been in Hong Kong for more than seven days; check-in is at 2pm. The same restrictions do not apply to the other rooms of the Salisbury. Sports enthusiasts will love it here – the hotel has a 25m swimming pool, a fitness centre and a climbing wall. The 7th floor is the smoking floor.

★ MADERA HONG KONG   BOUTIQUE HOTEL $$

Map p382 (木的地酒店; ☑2121 9888; www.hotelmadera.com.hk; 1-9 Cheong Lok St, Yau Ma Tei; r HK$1200-4000, ste HK$4200-9000; ⓂJordan, exit B1) A spirited addition to Kowloon's midrange options, Madera is close to the Temple Street Night Market (p142) and the Jordan MTR station. The decent-sized rooms come in neutral tones accented with the bold, vibrant colours of Spanish aesthetics. Madera (meaning 'wood') also has a ladies' floor, a hypo-allergenic floor, and a tiny but adequate gym room.

PENTAHOTEL   HOTEL $$

(貝爾特酒店; ☑3112 1933; www.pentahotels.com; 19 Luk Hop St, San Po Kong; r from HK$1300; @☎; ⓂDiamond Hill, exit A2) Eclectic 'retro Hong Kong' artefacts and a fake fireplace decorate the dimly-lit communal spaces of this hotel at a slightly out-of-the-way location. The rooms, however, are more conventionally stylish, and the service is reassuring. Pentahotel is a 10-minute walk south from Diamond Hill MTR station. They also run a free shuttle service to the MTR and shopping hot spots.

The smoking floors are 5th, 6th, 18th, 29th and 30th.

SLEEPING KOWLOON

BP INTERNATIONAL HOTEL
HOTEL **$$**

Map p378 (龍堡國際酒店; ☎2376 1111; www.
bpih.com.hk; 8 Austin Rd, Tsim Sha Tsui; r/ste
from HK$1900/6500; @☎; MJordan, exit C)
This enormous hotel overlooks Kowloon
Park (p146). The rooms are of a reasonable
standard and some of the more expensive
ones have good harbour views. The fam-
ily rooms have bunk beds, which is good if
you're travelling with kids. Haggle before
you book: depending on the season and
day of the week, prices are often reduced
by 50%.

KNUTSFORD HOTEL
HOTEL **$$**

Map p380 (樂仕酒店; ☎2377 1180; www.ac-
esitehotel.com; 8 Observatory Ct, Tsim Sha Tsui;
s HK$1000, d HK$1200-1800; ☎; MTsim Sha
Tsui, exit B1) The 28 coffin-sized rooms here
feel quite airy, thanks to savvy use of glass
and whites. The service, by contrast, can be
nonchalant. The hotel is in a quiet corner
of Tsim Sha Tsui's old residential quarter,
yet close to the watering holes of Knutsford
Tce. Tall people will find the beds cramped.

STANFORD HILLVIEW HOTEL
HOTEL **$$**

Map p380 (仕德福山景酒店; ☎2722 7822;
www.stanfordhillview.com; 13-17 Observatory
Rd, Tsim Sha Tsui; r HK$1480-2680, ste from
HK$3180; ☎; MTsim Sha Tsui, exit B1) At the
eastern end of Knutsford Tce, the Stanford
is a decent choice if you prize location over
new rooms and top-notch service. Sitting
on a quiet knoll, the Stanford is just sec-
onds away from the bars on Knutsford Tce
and a downhill stroll from the old quarter
of Tsim Sha Tsui. Huge discounts are avail-
able during the low season.

MINDEN
HOTEL **$$**

Map p380 (棉登酒店; ☎2739 7777; www.
theminden.com; 7 Minden Ave, Tsim Sha Tsui; r
HK$1300-1800, ste HK$3000; @; MTsim Sha
Tsui, exit G) This 64-room hotel, tucked away
on relatively quiet Minden Ave, is well located for both Tsim Sha Tsui and East Tsim
Sha Tsui MTR stations, and very reasonable
value. The lobby is packed with an eclectic
mix of Asian and Western curios and furnishings, while the rooms are serene and
comfortable, with all the amenities you'd
expect included in the rates.

CARITAS BIANCHI LODGE
GUESTHOUSE **$$**

Map p382 (明愛白英奇賓館; ☎2388 1111; www.
caritas-chs.org.hk/eng/bianchi_lodge.asp; 4
Cliff Rd, Yau Ma Tei; s HK$1350, d & tw HK$1600,

f HK$2100; ☎; MYau Ma Tei, exit D) This 90-
room guesthouse run by a Catholic NGO
is just off Nathan Rd (and a stone's throw
from Yau Ma Tei MTR station), but the rear
rooms are quiet and some have views of
King's Park. All rooms are clean with pri-
vate bathrooms. The wait for lifts can be
long, especially at night. Breakfast is in-
cluded in the rates.

★HYATT REGENCY
TSIM SHA TSUI
LUXURY HOTEL **$$$**

Map p380 (尖沙咀凱悅酒店; ☎2311 1234; www.
hongkong.tsimshatsui.hyatt.com; 18 Hanoi Rd,
Tsim Sha Tsui; s/d/ste from HK$1200/4200/3600;
@☎; MTsim Sha Tsui, exit D2) Top marks
to this classic that exudes understated elegance and composure. Rooms are plush
and relatively spacious with those on the upper floors commanding views over the city.
Black-and-white photos of Tsim Sha Tsui
add a thoughtful touch to the decor. The
lobby gets crowded at times, but the helpful and resourceful staff will put you at ease.

★PENINSULA
HONG KONG
LUXURY HOTEL **$$$**

Map p378 (香港半島酒店; ☎2920 2888; www.
peninsula.com; Salisbury Rd, Tsim Sha Tsui; r/
ste from HK$4080/7880; @☎; MTsim Sha
Tsui, exit E) Lording it over the southern tip
of Kowloon, Hong Kong's finest hotel ex-
udes colonial elegance. Your dilemma will
be how to get here: landing on the rooftop
helipad or arriving in one of the hotel's
14-strong fleet of Rolls Royce Phantoms.
Some 300 classic European-style rooms
sport wi-fi, CD and DVD players, as well as
marble bathrooms.

Many rooms in the 20-storey annexe
also offer spectacular harbour views; in the
original building you'll have to make do
with the glorious interiors. There's a top-
notch spa and swimming pool, and Gaddi's
(p156) is one of the best French restaurants
in town.

HOTEL ICON
LUXURY HOTEL **$$$**

Map p380 (唯港薈; ☎3400 1000; www.hotel-
icon.com; 17 Science Museum Rd, Tsim Sha Tsui;
r HK$2200-4100, ste HK$3000-6500; @☎;
MEast Tsim Sha Tsui, exit P1) The rooms at this
teaching hotel of a local university are modern and spacious, and the service is warm.
Icon is a 10-minute walk from the MTR and
there's a shuttle service to the more central
parts of Tsim Sha Tsui. Not all rooms have

harbour views and children are not allowed into the terrace lounge, but overall, it's great value for money.

Hotel Icon is within walking distance of the Science Museum (p149), the Hong Kong Museum of History (p140) and the northern section of the Tsim Sha Tsui East Promenade (p141).

CHI RESIDENCES
SERVICED APARTMENTS $$$

Map p382 (☑3443 6888; www.chi-residences.com; 314 Nathan Rd, Jordan; per month HK$24,100-60,000; @☏; ⓜJordan, exit B2) All 57 rooms (410 sq ft to 900 sq ft) are spick and span which makes up for the lack of space of the smaller ones. The beds are also surprisingly comfortable and the environment is quiet, despite the apartments' central location. That said, the wi-fi and the showers could be more efficient. Enter from Nanking St.

MIRA
LUXURY HOTEL $$$

Map p378 (☑2368 1111; www.themirahotel.com; 118-130 Nathan Rd, Tsim Sha Tsui; s/d HK$3200/4500, ste from HK$5000; @☏🏊; ⓜTsim Sha Tsui, exit B1) The Mira impresses with colour-themed rooms, designer chairs and a darkened entrance so cool you'd expect to see a bouncer. The guestroom gadgets aren't too shabby either – a mobile phone for use in Hong Kong, an iPod dock, flatscreen TV...that said, the 'standard rooms' have low ceilings and thin walls (pray for a quiet neighbour!). Service is inconsistent though staff are generally helpful.

The Mira is just across Nathan Rd from Kowloon Park (p146).

KOWLOON HOTEL HONG KONG
HOTEL $$$

Map p378 (九龍酒店; ☑2929 2888; www.thekowloonhotel.com; 19-21 Nathan Rd, Tsim Sha Tsui; s from HK$2000, d HK$2100, ste from HK$3900; @☏; ⓜTsim Sha Tsui, exit E) The Kowloon Hotel has a dated feel, with its 1990s techno aesthetic and a lobby evoking an airport lounge. Nevertheless, the hotel is popular for its unflappable service, central location and decent if rather small rooms. Rates drop dramatically in the low season.

INTERCONTINENTAL HONG KONG
LUXURY HOTEL $$$

Map p380 (香港洲際酒店; ☑2721 1211; www.intercontinental.com; 18 Salisbury Rd, Tsim Sha Tsui; r HK$6000-9000, ste from HK$11,000; @☏🏊; ⓜTsim Sha Tsui, exit F) Occupying arguably the finest waterfront spot in the territory, the InterContinental tilts at modernity while bowing to colonial traditions, such as a fleet of navy-blue Rolls Royces, doormen liveried in white and incessant brass polishing. The emphasis on service ensures a lot of return customers, from rock stars to business VIPs. The lobby lounge bar (p158) has the best views in Hong Kong.

ROYAL GARDEN
LUXURY HOTEL $$$

Map p380 (帝苑酒店; ☑2721 5215; www.rghk.com.hk; 69 Mody Rd, Tsim Sha Tsui; r/ste from HK$3600/16,100; @☏🏊; 🚌5C or 8, ⓜEast Tsim Sha Tsui, exit P1) The 422-room Royal Garden is one of the best options in the eastern part of Tsim Sha Tsui. From the blonde-wood and chrome lobby to the rooftop sports complex with million-dollar views, the Royal Garden ticks all the boxes. The rooms are highly specced with huge, comfortable beds. You should be able to secure large discounts off the quoted rates.

EMPIRE KOWLOON
HOTEL $$$

Map p380 (尖沙咀皇悦酒店; ☑3692 2222; www.empirehotel.com.hk; 62 Kimberley Rd, Tsim Sha Tsui; r/ste from HK$1600/3200; @☏🏊; ⓜTsim Sha Tsui, exit B2) This hotel offers decent rooms and an excellent indoor atrium swimming pool and spa. It's in the old residential quarter of Tsim Sha Tsui. Check the website for promotions.

HOTEL PANORAMA
HOTEL $$$

Map p380 (麗景酒店; ☑3550 0388; www.hotelpanorama.com.hk; 8A Hart Ave, Tsim Sha Tsui; r/ste from HK$3000/10,000; @☏; ⓜEast Tsim Sha Tsui, exit N) You'll find panoramic views at this hotel – but only above the 17th floor. The lower rooms overlook buildings nearby, which may not be to everyone's liking. That said, all rooms are tastefully furnished, and the breezy Sky Garden on the 40th floor offers great vistas. The tourist desk helps to organise China visas. Low-season discounts are available.

W HONG KONG
LUXURY HOTEL $$$

(☑3717 2222; www.whotels.com; 1 Austin Rd W, Tsim Sha Tsui; r from HK$2500, ste HK$8000; @☏🏊; ⓜKowloon, exit C1) W is famous for its uberstylish interiors. Rooms are named 'wonderful', 'spectacular', 'fantastic', and appropriately so, in particular the ones with stunning vistas above the 35th floor. Equally breathtaking are the gym with harbour views and the 'highest pool in the city' (72nd floor). W is right on top of Kowloon Station and Elements mall (p164).

RITZ-CARLTON HONG KONG
LUXURY HOTEL $$$

(麗思卡爾頓酒店; ☑2263 2263; www.ritzcarlton.com; 1 Austin Rd W, Tsim Sha Tsui; r HK$7200-9900, ste from HK$13,000; @🛜☒; Ⓜ Kowloon, C1 or D1) Sitting on Kowloon Station, this out-of-the-way luxury hotel is the tallest hotel on earth (lobby's on the 103rd floor). And to echo the theme of excess, the decor is over-the-top with imposing furniture and a superfluity of shiny services; the service is stellar; Tin Lung Heen (p158) serves top-notch Chinese food; and the views on a clear day are mindblowing.

EATON SMART
HOTEL $$$

Map p382 (香港逸東「智」酒店; ☑2782 1818; www.hongkong.eatonhotels.com; 380 Nathan Rd, Yau Ma Tei; r HK$2350-3200, ste from HK$3250; @🛜☒; Ⓜ Jordan, exit B1) Leave the chaos of Nathan Rd behind as you step into the Eaton's grand lobby. The rooms are relatively large and most, except some of the 'superior' rooms, are well maintained. Staff are courteous and there's a rooftop pool. Booking on the internet can halve the quoted rates and there are 'linger longer for less' rates. Enter from Pak Hoi St.

CITYVIEW
HOTEL $$$

Map p382 (城景國際; ☑2771 9111; www.thecityview.com.hk; 23 Waterloo Rd, Yau Ma Tei; r HK$1880, tr HK$2280, ste from HK$3080; @🛜☒; Ⓜ Yau Ma Tei, exit A2) All 413 rooms at this YMCA-affiliated hotel are clean and smart, featuring mellow colour tones and stylish fabrics. The service is also impeccable. The hotel occupies a quiet corner between Yau Ma Tei and Mong Kok. It's a short stroll from Yau Ma Tei Theatre (p152) and the Yau Ma Tei Wholesale Fruit Market (p149).

LANGHAM PLACE HOTEL
HOTEL $$$

Map p383 (朗豪酒店; ☑3552 3388; www.hongkong.langhamplacehotels.com; 555 Shanghai St, Mong Kok; r HK$2100-3700, ste from HK$3300; @🛜☒; Ⓜ Mong Kok, exit C3) Peering out from one of the rooms of this colossal tower hotel, you'd never suspect that you were in Mong Kok. It's a triumph for the district. Special guestroom features include multifunction IP phones, DVD players, marble bathrooms and room safes that can fit (and recharge) a laptop. The rooftop pool, gym and spa command great views over Kowloon.

Understand Hong Kong

Hong Kong Today

Just a few years ago, most Hong Kong residents would say return to Chinese rule did not bring many changes, but since then, for many, things have gone downhill. Rising tensions with mainland China and the Běijīng government dominate Hong Kong politics and public sentiment these days, putting the 'One Country, Two Systems' experiment in peril. In just 15 years, Běijīng has highly politicised a city that was known for its political antipathy during 150 years of British rule.

Best on Film

The Grandmaster (2013) Wong Kar-wai's stylish martial arts drama about the life of Wing Chun grandmaster Ip Man.

Infernal Affairs (2002) A crime-thriller directed by Andrew Lau and Alan Mak that inspired Scorsese's *The Departed*.

Night and Fog (2010) Auteur Ann Hui's darkly realistic drama on domestic violence and the lives of migrant women.

Election I and **II** (2005 and 2006) A complex two-part crime noir about elections inside a Triad society.

Comrades: Almost a Love Story (1996) Two mainland migrants take a reality check in the maddening city.

Best in Print

City at the End of Time: Poems by Leung Ping-kwan (Ed Esther Cheung; 2012) Leung Ping-kwan aka Yesi was Hong Kong's unofficial poet laureate.

The Hungry Ghosts (Anne Berry; 2009) Restless spirits haunt this excellent tale.

Hong Kong: A Cultural History (Michael Ingham; 2007) The definitive title in this category.

Triad (Derek Lambert; 1991) A gripping British police superintendent vs Chinese underworld yarn.

The State of Play

Hong Kong has witnessed much political strife since the turn of the decade. Critics of the Government have focused on a long list of increasingly intractable issues, from slow democratic reform and the perceived collusion between the government and big businesses, to stifling property prices and the perceived drain on public resources by mainland migrants. The involvement of Běijīng's Hong Kong–based proxies around Leung Chun-ying's ascent to the top post in town marks a definitive dynamics shift in the local political landscape, and serves as an ominous forewarning of worsening political turbulence.

While many hope that Leung can turn his populist overtures into action, for instance, by providing more social housing, the combination of divisive party politics and the lack of a democratic mandate has caused many to condemn the Government as a weak one, and hopelessly so when faced with vested interests as strong as the largest developers.

Basic Economics

Inflation hit a 16-year high in 2011 and, while it may have slowed down since, the truth is that for many, Hong Kong has become a depressingly expensive place to live. The costs of living are racing ahead of spending power, and punters even have to pay double for the luxury to dream about winning the lottery after the price of a Mark Six ticket went up to HK$10 in 2010. Hong Kong has more billionaires than most countries, but many more struggle to meet fairly basic levels of subsistence. Despite reasonable economic growth in the past few years, Hong Kong's economy has become increasingly reliant on the financial sector and the spending power of mainland tourists.

A New Era

There's a prevailing mood in Hong Kong today that the city has passed its heyday. Once savvy and confident, many Hong Kongers are worried about what they see as Běijīng's attempt at homogenisation. To stimulate growth, the Hong Kong Government has allowed more mainland Chinese to travel to the city, which breeds even more discontent among critics as mainland tourists dominate shopping areas and tourist attractions. But despite the general mood of anxiety, all is not doom and gloom. If anything, the multiple challenges that are confronting the city are stirring a strong spirit among many people to defend their core values (namely, the rule of law and civil liberties), and to actively define who they are, rather than who they're not.

New Waves

Protest marches, often feisty and carnival-esque, take place just about every other Sunday in Hong Kong. Young people are increasingly coming to the forefront of resistance, such as when they spearheaded tens of thousands of people, including parents, to take to the streets in July 2012 to protest the introduction in schools of 'national education' classes that they fear will lead to political brainwashing.

At the same time, Hong Kong is still the only place in the whole of China where the crackdown on the Tiān'ānmén pro-democracy uprising of 4 June 1989 can be openly commemorated. In 2014 a massive crowd (180,000 according to organisers; 99,500, to police) turned out for the 25th anniversary of the 4 June candlelight vigil. As Běijīng desperately searches for a formula of soft power to project on the international stage, the answers it needs may well lie in the rebellious tendencies of its semi-autonomous territory in the south.

Part of the city's growing assertion of its own distinctive identity is an increasing drive among the young population to preserve Hong Kong's social heritage. Funky collectives have flowered in the past few years to document the social history of storied neighbourhoods caught in the tide of urban redevelopment, such as Wan Chai and Yau Ma Tei. The perennial tussle for space in the city has also seen the growth of alternative music venues and urban farms in old factory buildings. As always, there's more than meets the eye in this pulsating metropolis, which has time and again shown an extraordinary ability to rebound, adapt and excel.

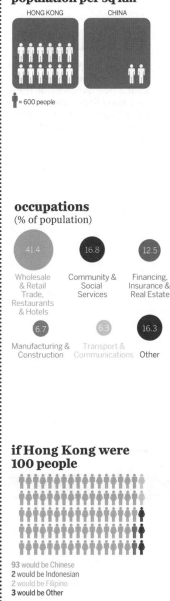

population per sq km

HONG KONG   CHINA

≈ 600 people

occupations
(% of population)

41.4 — Wholesale & Retail Trade, Restaurants & Hotels

16.8 — Community & Social Services

12.5 — Financing, Insurance & Real Estate

6.7 — Manufacturing & Construction

5.3 — Transport & Communications

16.3 — Other

if Hong Kong were 100 people

93 would be Chinese
2 would be Indonesian
2 would be Filipino
3 would be Other

History

The name Hong Kong came from the Cantonese *heung gawng* ('fragrant harbour' or 'incense harbour'), which was inspired by the scent of sandalwood incense piled at what is now Aberdeen, on the western edge of the island. In the very long scale of history, Hong Kong as we know it today has existed for a mere blink of an eye. But there was a lot going on in the region before that wintry morning in 1841 when a contingent of British marines clambered ashore and planted the Union Jack on the western part of Hong Kong Island, claiming it for the British Crown.

Early Inhabitants

Hong Kong has supported human life since at least the Middle Neolithic Period (c 4000–2500 BC). Artefacts uncovered at almost 100 archaeological sites in the territory suggest that the inhabitants of these settlements shared similar cultural characteristics to the people who lived in the Pearl River delta. The remnants of Bronze Age habitations (c 1500–220 BC) unearthed on Lamma and Lantau Islands, as well as the eight extant geometric rock carvings along Hong Kong's coastline, also indicate that these early peoples practised a folk religion involving animal worship.

Archaeologists say Hong Kong's Stone Age inhabitants enjoyed a relatively nutritious diet of iron-rich vegetables, small mammals, shellfish and fish harvested far offshore. Early Chinese historical records call the diverse maritime peoples along China's southeastern coasts the 'Hundred Yue' tribes, which potentially included some of Hong Kong's prehistoric inhabitants.

The Five Great Clans

The first of Hong Kong's mighty 'Five Clans' – Han Chinese, whose descendants hold political and economic clout to this day – began settling the area around the 11th century. The first and most powerful of the arrivals was the Tang, who initially settled around Yuen Long (the walled village of Kat Hing Wai is part of this cluster).

The Tang clan was followed by the Hau and the Pang, who spread around present-day Sheung Shui and Fanling. These three clans were followed by the Liu in the 14th century and the Man a century later.

The Cantonese-speaking newcomers called themselves *bun day* (Punti), meaning 'indigenous' or 'local' – which they clearly weren't. They looked down on the original inhabitants, the Tanka, many of whom had been shunted off the land and had moved onto the sea to live on boats.

TIMELINE	4000–1500 BC	214 BC	AD 1000–1400
	Small groups of neolithic hunter-gatherers and fisherfolk settle in coastal areas; a handful of tools, pottery and other artefacts are the only remnants left by these nomads.	Chinese emperor Qin Shi Huang conquers present-day Guǎngxī, Guǎngdōng and Fújiàn after a long period of war. Hong Kong comes under greater cultural influence from the north.	Hong Kong's Five Clans –Tang, Hau, Pang, Liu and Man – settle in what is now the New Territories and build walled villages in the fertile plains and valleys.

An Imperial Outpost

Clinging to the southern edge of the Chinese province of Canton (now Guǎngdōng), the peninsula and islands that became the territory of Hong Kong counted only as a remote pocket in a neglected corner of the Chinese empire. The Punti flourished until the struggle that saw the moribund Ming dynasty (1368–1644) overthrown. The victorious Qing (1644–1911), angered by the resistance put up by southerners loyal to the ancien régime, ordered in the 1660s a forced evacuation inland of all the inhabitants of China's southeastern coastal area, including Hong Kong.

More than four generations passed before the population was able to recover to its mid-17th-century level, boosted in part by the influx of the Hakka (Cantonese for 'guest people'), who moved here in the 18th century and up to the mid-19th century. A few vestiges of their language, songs, folklore and cooking survive, most visibly in the wide-brimmed, black-fringed bamboo hats sported by Hakka women in the New Territories.

The discovery of coins and pottery from the Eastern Han dynasty (AD 25–220) on Lantau and at several important digs, including a tomb at Lei Cheng Uk in central Kowloon, attests to the growing Han influence in Hong Kong at the start of the first millennium.

Arrival of the Outer Barbarians

For centuries the Pearl River estuary had been an important trading artery centred on the port of Canton (now Guǎngzhōu). Some of the first foreign traders (or 'outer barbarians') were Arab traders who entered – and sacked – the settlement as early as the 8th century AD. Similarly, the Ming emperors regarded their subjects to the south as an utterly un-civilised bunch. It was therefore fitting that the Cantonese should trade with the 'outer barbarians'.

Regular trade between China and Europe began in 1557 when Portuguese navigators set up a base in Macau, 65km west of Hong Kong. Dutch traders came in the wake of the Portuguese, followed by the French. British ships appeared as early as 1683 from the East India Company concessions along the coast of India, and by 1711 the company had established offices and warehouses in Guǎngzhōu to trade for tea, silk and porcelain.

In 1276 the boy emperor Duan Zong and his younger brother, Bing, were forced to flee to Hong Kong as the Mongols swept aside the remaining army of the Song dynasty (AD 960–1279). After Mongol ships defeated the tattered remnants of the imperial fleet in a battle on the Pearl River, the Song dynasty was definitively ended.

The First Opium War & British Hong Kong

China did not reciprocate Europe's voracious demand for its products, for the most part shunning foreign manufactured goods. The foreigners' ensuing trade deficit was soon reversed, however, after the British discovered a commodity that the Chinese did want: opium.

The British, with a virtually inexhaustible supply of the drug from the poppy fields of India, developed the trade aggressively. Consequently, opium addiction spread out of control in China, and the country's silver reserves became perilously drained.

1557	1644	1683	1757
Portuguese navigators set up a base in Macau, and are followed by Dutch and then French traders. Regular trade begins between China and Europe.	The Ming dynasty (1368–1644) is overthrown by the Qing dynasty, which reigns until 1911.	British East India Company ships begin to arrive, and by 1711 the company has established offices and warehouses in Guǎngzhōu, to trade for tea, silk and porcelain.	An imperial edict restricts European trade to the *cohong* (local merchants guild) in Guǎngzhōu; growing discontent with the trading system sets the stage for the First Opium War.

In late 1838 Emperor Dao Guang (r 1820–50) appointed Lin Zexu, governor of Húnán and Húběi and a Mandarin of great integrity, to stamp out the opium trade. His rather successful campaign would ultimately lead to the First Opium War (or First Anglo-Chinese War) of 1839–42.

In January 1841 a naval landing party hoisted the British flag at Possession Point (now Possession St) on Hong Kong Island. Subsequently, the Treaty of Nanking abolished the monopoly system of trade, opened five 'treaty ports' to British residents and foreign trade, exempted British nationals from all Chinese laws and ceded the strategically useful island of Hong Kong to the British 'in perpetuity'.

Hong Kong formally became a British possession on 26 June 1843, and its first governor, Sir Henry Pottinger, took charge. A primitive, chaotic and lawless settlement soon sprang up.

> Today's Triads still recite an oath of allegiance to the Ming, but their loyalty these days is to the dollar rather than the vanquished Son of Heaven.

Growing Pains

What would later be called the Second Opium War (or Second Anglo-Chinese War) broke out in October 1856. The victorious British forced the Chinese to sign the Convention of Peking in 1860, which ceded Kowloon Peninsula and Stonecutters Island to Britain. Britain was now in complete control of Victoria Harbour and its approaches.

THE TRIADS

Hong Kong's Triads, which continue to run the territory's drug, prostitution, people-smuggling, gambling and loan-sharking rackets, weren't always the gangster operations they are today.

They were founded as secret and patriotic societies that opposed the corrupt and brutal Qing (Manchu) dynasty and aided the revolution that eventually toppled it in 1911. The fact that these organisations had adopted Kwan Tai (or Kwan Yu), the god of war and upholder of righteousness, integrity and loyalty, as their patron, lent them further respectability. The Triads descended into crime and vice during the Chinese Civil War (1945–49), and came in droves to Hong Kong after the communists came to power in 1949. Today they are the Chinese equivalent of the Mafia.

The communists smashed the Triad-controlled drug racket in Shànghǎi after the 1949 revolution. Having long memories and fearing a repeat could occur with the looming 1997 handover, many Hong Kong–based hoods moved their operations to ethnic-Chinese communities in countries such as Thailand, the Philippines, Australia, Canada and the US. Since 1997, however, many Triads have moved back into Hong Kong and have even expanded their operations onto the mainland.

The definitive work on the Triads is *Triad Societies in Hong Kong* by WP Morgan (1960), a former subinspector with the Royal Hong Kong Police.

1773	1799	1841	1842
Opium smuggling to China skyrockets after the British East India Company monopolises production and export of Indian opium.	China's silver reserves drain rapidly as opium addiction sweeps through China. The Qing emperor issues an edict banning opium trade in the country.	British marines plant the Union flag on the western part of Hong Kong Island, claiming the land for the British Crown.	China cedes Hong Kong Island to Britain.

As the Qing dynasty slid into major chaos towards the end of the 19th century, the British government petitioned China to extend the colony into the New Territories. The June 1898 Convention of Peking handed Britain a larger-than-expected slice of territory that included 235 islands and ran north to the Shumchun (Shēnzhèn) River, increasing the colony's size by 90%.

A Sleepy Backwater

While Hong Kong's major trading houses, including Jardine Matheson and Swire, prospered from their trade with China, the colony hardly thrived in its first few decades. Fever, bubonic plague and typhoons threatened life and property, and at first the colony attracted a fair number of criminals and vice merchants.

Gradually Hong Kong began to shape itself into a more substantial community. Nonetheless, from the late 19th century right up to WWII, Hong Kong lived in the shadow of the treaty port of Shànghǎi, which had become Asia's premier trade and financial centre.

The colony's population continued to grow thanks to the waves of immigrants fleeing the Chinese Revolution of 1911, which ousted the decaying Qing dynasty and ushered in several decades of strife, rampaging warlords and famine. The Japanese invasion of China in 1937 sparked another major exodus to Hong Kong's shores.

Hong Kong's status as a British colony would offer the refugees only a temporary haven. The day after Japan attacked the US naval base at Pearl Harbor on 7 December 1941, its military machine swept down from Guǎngzhōu and into Hong Kong.

Conditions under Japanese rule were harsh, with indiscriminate killings of mostly Chinese civilians; Western civilians were incarcerated at Stanley Prison on Hong Kong Island. Many Hong Kong Chinese fled to Macau, administered by neutral Portugal.

> 'Albert is so amused at my having got the island of Hong Kong', wrote Queen Victoria to King Leopold of Belgium in 1841. At the time, Hong Kong was little more than a backwater of about 20 villages and hamlets.

The Road to Boomtown

After Japan's withdrawal from Hong Kong, and subsequent surrender in August 1945, the colony looked set to resume its hibernation. But events both at home and on the mainland forced the colony in a new direction.

The Chinese Civil War (1945–49) and the subsequent communist takeover of China caused a huge number of refugees – both rich and poor – to flee to Hong Kong. The refugees brought along capital and cheap labour which would prove vital to Hong Kong's economic takeoff. On a paltry, war-torn foundation, local and foreign businesses built a huge manufacturing (notably textiles and garments) and financial services

1860	1894	1895	1898
Under the Convention of Peking, China cedes Kowloon Peninsula and Stonecutters Island to Britain, giving Britain complete control of Victoria Harbour and its approaches.	Bubonic plague breaks out in Hong Kong, killing 2500 of mainly local Chinese; trade suffers badly.	Future Chinese national hero Sun Yatsen plots an insurrection in southern China from his base in Hong Kong; it fails and the British ban Sun from the territory.	China hands the New Territories to Britain in a 99-year lease, which begins on 1 July 1898 and ends at midnight on 30 June 1997.

centre that transformed Hong Kong into one of the world's great economic miracles.

Hong Kong's stability received a battering at the height of the Cultural Revolution in 1967, as local procommunist groups instigated a series of anticolonial demonstrations, strikes and riots. The violence soon mushroomed into bombings and arson attacks, and the colony's economy was paralysed for months. The riot came to an end in December 1967, when Chinese Premier Zhou Enlai ordered the procommunist groups to stop.

A Society in Transition

After the 1967 crisis the colonial government initiated a series of reforms to alleviate social discontent and to foster a sense of belonging to Hong Kong. In the next decade the government introduced more labour laws, and invested heavily in public housing, medical services, education and recreational activities for youth.

Although Hong Kong's stock market collapsed in 1973, its economy resumed its upward trend later in the decade. The 'Open Door' policy of Deng Xiaoping, who took control of China in the confusion after Mao Zedong's death in 1976, revived Hong Kong's role as the gateway to the mainland and it boomed. By the end of the 1980s Hong Kong was one of the richest places in Asia, second only to Japan in GDP per capita.

The 1997 Question

Few people gave much thought to Hong Kong's future until 1979, when the governor of Hong Kong, Murray MacLehose, raised the issue with Deng Xiaoping on his first official visit to Běijīng. Britain was legally bound to hand back only the New Territories – not Hong Kong Island and Kowloon, which had been ceded to it forever. However, the fact that nearly half of Hong Kong's population lived in the New Territories by that time made it an untenable division.

It was Deng Xiaoping who decided that the time was ripe to recover Hong Kong, forcing the British to the negotiating table. The views of Hong Kong people were not sought whatsoever. The inevitable conclusion laid to rest the political jitters and commercial concerns that had in 1983 seen the Hong Kong dollar collapse – and subsequently be pegged to the US dollar.

Despite soothing words from the Chinese, British and Hong Kong governments, over the next 13 years the population of Hong Kong were to suffer considerable anxiety at the possible political and economic consequences of the handover.

In the early years of British Hong Kong, opium dens, gambling clubs and brothels proliferated; just a year after Britain took possession, an estimated 450 prostitutes worked out of two-dozen brothels, including a fair number of foreign prostitutes clustered in Lyndhurst Tce, which today is home to a hip bar scene.

In the early 1970s, the construction of the first three 'New Towns' (Sha Tin, Tsuen Wan and Tuen Mun) commenced, marking the start of a massive and unprecedented public-housing program that would, and still does, house millions of Hong Kong people.

1911	1937	1941	1962
The colony's population expands as large groups of immigrants flee the Chinese Revolution on the mainland.	Pouncing on a country weakened by a bloody civil war, Japan invades China; as many as 750,000 mainlanders seek shelter in Hong Kong over the next three years.	British forces surrender to Japanese forces on Christmas Day; the population in Hong Kong is more than halved during almost four years of Japanese occupation.	The great famine caused by the Great Leap Forward in China drives 70,000 people to flee into Hong Kong in less than three months.

One Country, Two Systems

Under the Sino-British Joint Declaration on the Question of Hong Kong of December 1984, Hong Kong would be reborn as a Special Administrative Region (SAR) of China. This meant its capitalist system would be permitted to continue, while across the border China's version of socialism would continue. The Chinese catchphrase for this was 'One Country, Two Systems'.

The Basic Law for Hong Kong, the future SAR's constitution, preserved Hong Kong's English common-law judicial system and guaranteed the right of property and ownership, as well as other key civil liberties. The SAR would enjoy a high degree of autonomy with the exception of foreign affairs and matters of defence.

Despite these assurances, many families and individuals had little faith in a future Hong Kong under Chinese rule, and a so-called brain drain ensued when tens of thousands left the colony for the United States, Canada, Australia and New Zealand towards the end of the 1980s.

Tiān'ānmén & Its Aftermath

The concern of many Hong Kong people over their future turned to out-and-out fear on 4 June 1989, when the Chinese army killed pro-democracy demonstrators in Běijīng's Tiān'ānmén Square.

Tiān'ānmén was a watershed for Hong Kong. Sino-British relations deteriorated, the stock market fell 22% in one day and a great deal of capital left the territory for destinations overseas.

The Hong Kong government sought to rebuild confidence by announcing plans for a new airport and shipping port in what was the world's most expensive (HK$160 billion or US$20.6 billion) infrastructure project of the day.

The Tiān'ānmén protests had strengthened the resolve of those people who either could not or would not leave, giving rise to the territory's first official political parties. In a bid to restore credibility, the government introduced a Bill of Rights in 1990 and the following year gave Hong Kong citizens the right to choose 18 of the 60 members of the Legislative Council (LegCo), which until then had essentially been a rubber-stamp body chosen by the government and special-interest groups.

Democracy & the Last Governor

One of the first parties to emerge was the United Democrats of Hong Kong, led by outspoken democrats Martin Lee and Szeto Wah. The pair, initially courted by China for their anticolonial positions and appointed to the committee that drafted the Basic Law, subsequently infuriated

In the aftermath of the Tiān'ānmén Square protests of 1989, an underground smuggling operation, code-named Yellow Bird, was set up in Hong Kong to spirit many activists to safety overseas. Meanwhile Hong Kong–based Chinese officials who had criticised the killings were either yanked from their posts or sought asylum in the West.

HISTORY ONE COUNTRY, TWO SYSTEMS

1967	1971	1976	1982
Riots and bombings by procommunist groups rock Hong Kong; armed Chinese militia cross the border, killing five policemen and penetrating 3km into the New Territories before pulling back.	A former child actor called Bruce Lee lands his first adult leading role in the kung fu film *The Big Boss*; it becomes a smash around the world.	Deng Xiaoping takes control of China after Mao Zedong's death, and revives Hong Kong's role as the gateway to the mainland.	British PM Margaret Thatcher visits Běijīng to begin talks on Hong Kong's future. Two years of closed-door wrangling between the Chinese and British ensues.

Běijīng by publicly burning copies of the proto-constitution in protest over Tiān'ānmén. China denounced them as subversives.

Chris Patten, Hong Kong's 28th – and last – British governor, arrived in 1992, pledging that democracy reforms would be sped up. China reacted by levelling verbal attacks at Patten and threatening the post-1997 careers of any pro-democracy politicians or officials. When these tactics failed, China targeted Hong Kong's economy. Talks on certain business contracts and infrastructure projects straddling 1997 suddenly came to a halt, including the new airport program.

Sensing that it had alienated even its supporters in Hong Kong, China backed down and in 1994 gave its blessing to the new airport at Chek Lap Kok. It remained hostile to direct elections, however, and vowed to disband the democratically elected legislature after 1997. It eventually did what it said by installing an interim rubber-stamp body which would serve until June 1998.

As for the executive branch of power, China organised an 'election' in December 1996 to select Hong Kong's first postcolonial leader. But Tung Chee Hwa (1937–), the Shànghǎi-born shipping magnate hand-picked to be the SAR's first chief executive, won approval by retaining Patten's right-hand woman, Anson Chan, as his chief secretary and Donald Tsang as financial secretary.

CHINA'S HONG KONG INVASION PLAN

The peaceful agreement that eventually settled the status of Hong Kong was by no means a foregone conclusion in the decades leading up to it. The key negotiators have since revealed just how touchy China felt about Hong Kong and how close it came to retaking the territory by force.

Margaret Thatcher, the British prime minister who negotiated the deal, said later that Deng Xiaoping, then China's leader, told her he 'could walk in and take the whole lot this afternoon'.

She replied that China would lose everything if it did. 'There is nothing I could do to stop you,' she said, 'but the eyes of the world would now know what China is like.'

Lu Ping, the top Chinese negotiator, recently confirmed that this was no bluff on Deng's part. Deng feared that announcing the date for the 1997 handover would provoke serious unrest in Hong Kong, and China would be compelled to invade as a result.

According to Lu, China had also been hours away from invading during 1967, at the height of the chaotic Cultural Revolution, when a radical faction of the People's Liberation Army (PLA) was poised to invade the British colony during procommunist riots. The invasion was called off only by a late-night order from Premier Zhou Enlai to the local army commander, Huang Yongsheng, a radical Maoist who had been itching to invade.

1984	1989	1990	1997
Hong Kong's future is sealed in the Sino-British Joint Declaration on the Question of Hong Kong; the city's capitalist system will continue after 1997.	More than a million Hong Kong people march in support of the pro-democracy movement in Běijīng; the Chinese army kills protesting students in and around Tiān'ānmén Square.	The government introduces a Bill of Rights and in 1991 gives Hong Kong citizens the right to choose 18 of the 60 members of the Legislative Council (LegCo).	The rain falls, Chris Patten cries and Hong Kong returns to Chinese sovereignty; avian flu breaks out, leaving six dead. Tung Chee Hwa is sworn in as Hong Kong's first chief executive.

On the night of 30 June 1997, the handover celebrations held in the purpose-built extension of the Hong Kong Convention & Exhibition Centre in Wan Chai were watched by millions of people around the world. Chris Patten shed a tear while Chinese President Jiang Zemin beamed and Prince Charles was outwardly stoic (but privately scathing, describing the Chinese leaders in a diary leaked years later to the British tabloids as 'appalling old waxworks').

So the curtain fell on a century and a half of British rule, and the new Chief Executive Tung summed up Chinese feelings about the handover with the words: 'Now we are masters of our own house'.

Hong Kong Post-1997

Almost as soon as the euphoria of the 1997 handover faded, things started going badly in Hong Kong. The financial crisis that had rocked other parts of Asia began to be felt in Hong Kong at the end of 1997. A strain of deadly avian flu saw the city slaughter more than one million chickens.

The credibility of the SAR administration was severely damaged in 1999 when the government challenged a High Court ruling that upheld residency rights for China-born offspring of Hong Kong citizens, regardless of the parents' residency status at the time of the child's birth. The ruling was based on certain clauses of the Basic Law, and the government calculated that it would potentially make 1.67 million people from the mainland eligible for right of abode in the territory. The SAR administration appealed to the standing committee of the National People's Congress (NPC), China's rubber-stamp parliament, to reinterpret these clauses. The NPC complied, and ruled that at least one parent must already have acquired permanent residency status at the time of the birth.

As a result, the mainland stands accused of interfering in Hong Kong's judicial independence via intrusion into the city's legal system, and the apparent withholding of universal suffrage from Hong Kong citizens. Clearly the mainland government wields huge influence, but in the first few years after the handover (at least up until the historic 500,000-strong antigovernment protests of 1 July 2003, which changed Běijīng's stance on Hong Kong), it largely chose to tread lightly, honouring the spirit of the handover agreement to a great extent.

The Clamour for Democracy

Tung Chee Hwa's first term is remembered as much for his confusing housing policy, which many blamed for a sustained fall in property prices, as for such vacuous infrastructure proposals as a Chinese medicine port. Despite his poor standing in the polls, Tung was returned for a second five-year term in March 2002.

Hong Kong is the only place under Chinese rule that still mourns those killed in 1989. Every year on 4 June, tens of thousands of people gather at Victoria Park to attend a candlelight vigil held in commemoration of those who lost their lives.

2003	2009	2010	2010
SARS all but shuts down Hong Kong for weeks. The Closer Economic Partnership Agreement with the mainland government provides favourable business opportunities.	Hong Kong's population exceeds seven million and the unemployment rate grows to almost 5% in the face of the world's worst economic crisis since the Great Depression.	LegCo approves HK$66.9 billion for the Hong Kong portion of the Guǎngzhōu–Hong Kong high-speed rail link, following 25 hours of heated debate.	The pro-democracy camp splits over a government reform package which ensures a slightly more representative LegCo but gives no definitive date on universal suffrage in all elections.

Controversy continued to dog his time in office, however, most notably in March 2003, with the government's failure to contain the Severe Acute Respiratory Syndrome (SARS) epidemic at an early stage, provoking a torrent of blame. The outbreak killed 299 people, infected 1755 and all but closed Hong Kong down for weeks.

In July 2003 the government caused further controversy when it tried to turn Article 23 of the Basic Law into legislation; the National Security Bill raised fears that Hong Kong's press freedom and civil liberties would be undermined. In the face of massive public protests – of 500,000 people or more – the government shelved the bill indefinitely.

In March 2005 Tung announced his resignation as chief executive. His replacement was the bow-tie-wearing chief secretary Sir Donald Tsang, who had continuously served as Hong Kong's financial secretary since before the handover through 2001, when he became the city's number-two public official.

Compared to Tung, Tsang was a welcome replacement for both the Běijīng powerbrokers and the Hong Kong public. In 2007 Tsang was easily re-elected with Běijīng's blessing. However, he soon suffered an erosion of public confidence when he was seen to renege on a series of promises, including delaying a highly anticipated consultation on reforming the electoral process for the chief executive and legislature to make the 2012 polls more democratic.

The clamour for democracy reached a crescendo in 2010 as two landmark political events took place in successive months. In May five pro-democracy lawmakers were re-elected to LegCo after they collectively resigned four months earlier in the hope that the resulting by-elections would serve as a de-facto referendum on universal suffrage. The pro-Běijīng parties boycotted the contests, however, and the quintet's campaign came unstuck, even though they could claim to have been returned to the chamber by a respectable vote.

The pro-democracy parties had in fact been divided over the political strategy behind the forced by-elections, and the long-running differences among the key players imploded the following month when the biggest of them all, the Democratic Party, sided with the government in a new political reform package that would see LegCo earn a slightly increased percentage of popularly elected seats at the expense of delayed universal suffrage for the entire legislature and for the election of Hong Kong's chief executive.

The calls for democracy have continued since, most notably around the election (by a 1200-member body of predominantly pro-Běijīng notables) of the SAR's fourth chief executive in March 2012. Leung Chun-ying, a stalwart in Hong Kong politics with impeccably close links to Běijīng, defeated the long-time hopeful and former civil-service chief Henry Tang.

In the wake of the Tiān'ānmén Square killings, local Hong Kong people with money and skills made a mad dash to emigrate to any country that would take them. During the worst period more than 1000 people were leaving each week, especially for Canada and Australia.

2011	2011	2012	2012
A minimum wage of HK$28 per hour takes effect, and inflation hits a 16-year high.	Public hospitals stop accepting reservations from pregnant mainland women through year's end; immigration officials block 1930 heavily pregnant women from crossing the border.	Property surveyor Leung Chun-ying begins his term as the fourth Hong Kong SAR chief executive after beating former civil-service head Henry Tang in a scandal-plagued election.	Tens of thousands take to the streets to protest a new national education curriculum that they fear will brainwash students with communist propaganda.

In June 2014 an unofficial referendum on making the election of the city's CE more democratic garnered votes from over 787,000 Hong Kong residents – the equivalent of more than 22% of the city's 3.5 million registered voters. Following this, on 1 July 2014, an estimated 510,000 people turned out for a pro-democracy protest march on the anniversary of the handover, though the police put the figure at 98,600.

A Changed City?

Visitors returning to Hong Kong since July 1997 would see and feel little material difference walking around the city today. Perhaps the most striking thing for returning visitors from the West is the influx of a new breed of visitor: mainland Chinese, who now make up nearly 70% of the territory's visitor numbers.

In many ways Hong Kong has benefited from closer ties with the mainland. The growth in Hong Kong's tourism would have been impossible without the influx of mainland tourists, and the Closer Economic Partnership Agreement signed with the mainland government in 2003 provided favourable business opportunities to Hong Kong.

However, the seemingly headlong rush for the Chinese tourist dollar, with the attendant proliferation of luxury stores in areas such as Causeway Bay and Canton Rd in Tsim Sha Tsui, has pushed up shop rentals across the board, fuelling inflation and taking many small traders off Hong Kong's once accommodating streetscape. Similarly, the property market, flush with cash from mainland speculators, has become prohibitively expensive for ordinary folk. Of most concern to many Hong Kong people are the tens of thousands of mainland Chinese migrants and pregnant women who have poured into the city in the past decade or so (any child born in Hong Kong, even to noncitizens, has a right of abode). Worries abound that the influx is putting a strain on Hong Kong's public services, and there are fears that the cultural – and material-wealth – differences between locals and 'mainlanders' could provide more fodder for both sensationalist and sobering news headlines in the years to come.

While closer ties with the mainland have often been met with unease, might history one day identify an equal and opposite reaction going on? Hong Kong's dazzling success and core values arguably exert 'soft' power that influences thinking on the mainland. It might be hard to measure, but in the enclave that sheltered and inspired fathers of powerful mainland movements (Sun Yatsen and Zhou Enlai), it should not be dismissed.

What is certain is that, more than 15 years on from the handover, Hong Kong people are asking questions about their identity more intensely than ever as Hong Kong and mainland China, for better or worse, increasingly intertwine.

A measure of just how successful the handover had generally been came in a 2007 BBC interview with Margaret Thatcher. Marking the 10th anniversary of the handover of Hong Kong from Britain to China, Thatcher, to her own surprise, deemed China's overall performance a success.

2014	2014	2014
Archaeological finds at an MTR site in East Kowloon show that Hong Kong's history in the Sung dynasty may have been far richer than had been popularly believed.	A massive crowd (180,000 according to organisers; 99,500, to police) turn out for the 25th anniversary of the 4 June candlelight vigil that marks the Tiān'ānmén demonstration in 1989.	The chief executive states that the city may limit tourist arrivals as an influx of Chinese visitors stirs discontent.

Arts

Hong Kong's arts scene is more vibrant than its reputation suggests. There are musical ensembles of all persuasions, an assortment of theatre groups, Chinese and modern dance troupes, and numerous art organisations. The West Kowloon Cultural District is one of Asia's most ambitious cultural projects. Government funds allow organisers to bring in top international performers, and the number of international arts festivals hosted here seems to grow each year.

Top Museums for Hong Kong Art

....

Hong Kong Museum of Art (Tsim Sha Tsui)

....

Hong Kong Arts Centre (Wan Chai)

....

Asia Society Hong Kong (Admiralty)

Art

Hong Kong is one of the three most important art auction centres in the world, along with New York and London. Theoretically, it can only get stronger, given that China has already surpassed the US as the world's largest market for art and antiques. Despite some industry concern about the ability of the Chinese market to promote stable, long-term growth, Hong Kong will continue to ride the bull wave nimbly – and with gusto – for as long as the overheated market keeps its lid on.

Contemporary Hong Kong art tends not to bother too much with grandiose narratives about nationhood and religion, preferring to take an introverted view of the world and expressing visions of Chinese-ness outside of the national frame.

The best sources for information on Hong Kong and Asian art are *Asian Art News* (www.asianartnews.com), the free monthly *Art Map* (www.artmap.com.hk), the **Asia Art Archive** (☎2815 1112; www.aaa.org.hk; 233 Hollywood Rd, 11th fl, Hollywood Centre; ◷10am-6pm Mon-Sat) and the **Hong Kong International Association of Art Critics** (www.aicahk.org).

Roots

In general, Chinese painters of the past were interested in traditional forms and painting processes – not necessarily composition and colour. Brush strokes and the utensils used to produce them are of vital importance and interest. In traditional Chinese art, change for the sake of change was never the philosophy or the trend; Chinese artists would compare their work with that of the master and judge it accordingly.

The influential Lingnan School of Painting, founded by the watercolourist Chao Shao-an (1905–98) in the 1930s and relocated to Hong Kong in 1948, attempted to move away from this tradition. It combined traditional Chinese, Japanese and Western artistic methods to produce a rather decorative style, and dominated the small art market in Hong Kong for the next two decades.

The most distinct group of painters and sculptors to appear in Hong Kong were the proponents of the New Ink Painting movement who came to prominence in the late 1960s. Most had strong links to China or its cultural heritage. The movement aimed at reconciling Chinese and Western ideas by steering traditional Chinese ink painting towards abstract expressionism. Lui Shou-kwan (1919–75), who arrived in Hong Kong in 1948, was the earliest and the best known of the New Ink Painting artists. Lui worked for the Yau Ma Tei ferry as a pier inspector and taught in his spare time. Speaking no English, his only experience of the West was through pictures and books borrowed from the British Council library. Many of the artists who became associated with the movement were his students.

The only major artist to break free of the era's dominant style was Luis Chan (1905–95). Born in Panama, Chan came to Hong Kong at the age of five, where he learnt to paint from art magazines and a correspondence course. Stylistically, Chan was a loner with no apparent allegiance to any tradition. He was also a genius who, particularly in his post-60s works, transformed Hong Kong into a fantastical realm of dreams and hallucinations. His 1976 painting *Ping Chau* is a bizarre interpretation of the somnolent outlying island which is at once puzzling and endearing.

Avant-Garde

The 1980s and '90s saw the coming of age of artists born after WWII, many of whom had received their training abroad. Less burdened by the need to reconcile East and West, they devoted their efforts to defining avant-garde art, often through Western mediums. They were also politically engaged. Wong Yan-kwai, a painter educated in France, was arguably the most influential artist of that period and is still one of the most accomplished today. His powerful paintings in vibrant colours are free of any social or historical context. Wong's mural graces Club 71 in Central.

London-trained Antonio Mak (1951–94) is Hong Kong's most famous contemporary sculptor and is known for his figurative pieces in cast bronze. He focused on the human figure as well as on animals important in Chinese legend and mythology (eg horses and tigers), and was greatly influenced by Rodin.

Salisbury Gardens, leading to the entrance of the Hong Kong Museum of Art in Tsim Sha Tsui, is lined with modern sculptures by contemporary Hong Kong sculptors. Dotted among the greenery of Kowloon Park is Sculpture Walk, with 30 marble, bronze and other weather-resistant works by both local and overseas artists, including a bronze by Mak called *Torso* and one by Britain's late Sir Eduardo Paolozzi (1924–2005) called *Concept of Newton*.

Contemporary

Compared to their predecessors, Hong Kong's young artists – those born in the '70s and '80s – take a more internalised view of the world. They are overwhelmingly unfussed with orthodox Chinese culture and older generations' attempts to amalgamate East and West. Instead, they're often looking for (or perhaps, trying to retrieve) something that is uniquely Hong Kong. Nonetheless, their works show eloquence in a host of mediums, from Wilson Shieh's cheeky urban paintings using Chinese *gōngbǐ* (fine-brush) techniques to Jaffa Lam's sculpture installations.

ARTS ART

Antonio Mak's work employs much visual 'punning'. In his *Bible from Happy Valley* (1992), a racehorse is portrayed with a winglike book made of lead across its back. The word 'book' in Cantonese has the same sound as 'to lose (at gambling)'.

ART SPACES & GALLERIES

Nonprofit exhibition spaces in Hong Kong include **Para/Site Artspace** (藝術空間; ☎2517 4620; www.para-site.org.hk/pre.htm; 4 Po Yan St; ⊙noon-7pm Wed-Sun), the most consistent and promising of the local artists' cooperatives; **Fotan Art Studios** (www.fotanian.com), a labyrinth of artists' lofts in vacated factory buildings set against the rolling hills of Fo Tan; the nine-storey Jockey Club Creative Arts Centre (p153), which was converted from an industrial building and houses artists' studios; and Cattle Depot Artist Village (p153), a one-time slaughterhouse that is home to a colony of local artists. The best time to visit Fotan Art Studios and the JCCAC is during their open studios (see their websites for the dates). Admission is free to almost all commercial galleries in Hong Kong.

Cantonese opera performers

Chow Chun-fai's background across a wide spectrum of media has seen him work between different art forms, such as photographs from classical paintings, or paintings from films. Adrian Wong's playful works involve his family connections to prominent names in the local entertainment industry, and indigenous superstitions. Kacey Wong's exciting installations can usually move about and invariably involve some kind of Hong Kong theme or common household treasure recast in a jovial light. His *Sleepwalker* (2011) contraption imbues the bunk bed – an indispensable fixture in Hong Kong's tight living spaces – with life and speaks to a mass aspiration, or doomed desperation, for a more humane habitat.

Photography

Hong Kong is endowed with internationally competitive photographers, and some of their works can be seen in the Hong Kong Heritage Museum.

Working in black and white, documentary photographer Yau Leung (1941–97) captured some of the most stunning and iconic images of 1960s Hong Kong, while art photographer So Hing-keung focuses on the shadows, figurative and literal, of the city in creations known for their psychological depth. Hong Kong–born, London-based visual artist Kurt Tong explores his multilayered identity, family heritage and memories through thoughtful documentary photography. *In Case it Rains in Heaven* (2010), his best-known project, is presented like a high-end shopping catalogue of stylised portraits of paper-made objects burnt as offerings for the deceased. The combustible items honoured by Tong run the gamut of modern human desires in Chinese societies.

Street Art & Other Arts

Street graffiti was almost nonexistent or largely unrecognised in Hong Kong until the passing in 2007 of the self-proclaimed 'King of Kowloon' (aka Tsang Tsou-choi), who for decades had smothered the city with

There are only about four Tsang Tsou-choi works left on Hong Kong's streets today (with three subject to the mercy of the elements), but you won't miss the concrete pillar that bears his imperial treatise at the Star Ferry pier in Tsim Sha Tsui.

his trademark rambling, childlike calligraphy that cursed the Queen of England for 'usurping' his rightful land. His irrepressible daily reveries and inimitable visual style eventually inspired many artists and designers, and won him exhibitions both at home and abroad.

Street art has grown in Hong Kong since, perhaps with the King's benediction. This trend in part stems from a new-found confidence among a younger generation of artists to express their dissatisfaction with the social problems of the day using means that are more open and combative. After the April 2011 arrest in mainland China of the prominent artist and activist Ai Weiwei, a number of artists in Hong Kong came forth with a dose of creative surprise to raise public awareness of his case and to rally for his release. Most memorably, Ai-inspired graffiti stencils appeared on pavements, overpasses and walls for five nights straight around the city, thanks to a lone operator known only as 'Tangerine'.

Equally unorthodox in its use of public space is Street Art Movement, a new group that stages seemingly impromptu gallery shows in the most ordinary of common spaces. In March 2012 the group organised an art ride along the Tsuen Wan line on the MTR, sketching and clipping their finished drawings onto laundry lines that they strung up inside the train carriages as fresh interest poured in at every station.

Contemporary ceramics is another field in which Hong Kong artists enjoy an edge beyond the city's borders. Fiona Wong, one of the city's best-known ceramic artists, makes life-sized sculptural works of clothing, shoes and other familiar items.

The Leisure and Cultural Services Department (www.lcsd.gov.hk) regularly stages free arts and entertainment shows at its venues throughout the territory.

Music

Western Classical

Western classical music is very popular in Hong Kong. The city boasts the Hong Kong Philharmonic Orchestra, the Hong Kong Sinfonietta and the City Chamber Orchestra of Hong Kong. Opportunities to see big-name soloists and major orchestras abound, especially during the Hong Kong Arts Festival in February/March. The **Hong Kong International Piano Competition** (http://chshk.brinkster.net), with its star-studded jury, is held every three years in October/November. The **Hong Kong Academy for Performing Arts** (www.hkapa.edu) has free concerts almost daily.

Jazz

The best times to experience world-class jazz in the city are during the **Hong Kong International Jazz Festival** (www.hkijf.com), which takes place in the final quarter of the year, and the Hong Kong Arts Festival in February/March. Hong Kong also has a small but zealous circle of local musicians, including the 17-piece **Saturday Night Jazz Orchestra** (www.saturdaynight-jazz.com), which plays big-band sounds every month. Other names to watch out for include guitarist Eugene Pao, the first local jazz artist to sign with an international label, and pianist Ted Lo, who has played with Astrud Gilberto and Herbie Hancock.

Traditional Chinese

You won't hear much traditional Chinese music on Hong Kong streets, except perhaps the sound of the doleful *dī-daa* (a clarinet-like instrument played in funeral processions); the hollow-sounding *gú* (drums) and crashing *luó* (gongs) and *bat* (cymbals) at lion dances; the *èrhú* (a two-stringed fiddle), favoured by beggars for its plaintive sound; or strains of Cantonese opera wafting from the radio of a minibus driver. You can sample this kind of music in a form adapted to a symphony-orchestra model at concerts given by the **Hong Kong Chinese Orchestra** (www.hkco.org).

For more authentic fare, check out a Chinese opera or the Temple Street Night Market, where street performers deliver operatic excerpts.

Canto-Pop

Originally designed for sports events, the Hong Kong Coliseum in Hung Hom is the prime venue for Canto-pop concerts. In the past, only the superstars could perform here, but now practically anyone with a bit of fame in the local entertainment industry can come and throw a bash.

Hong Kong's home-grown popular-music scene is dominated by 'Canto-pop' – compositions that often blend Western rock, pop and R&B with Chinese melodies and lyrics. Rarely radical, the songs invariably deal with such teenage concerns as unrequited love and loneliness; to many they sound like the American pop songs of the 1950s. The music is slick and eminently singable – thus the explosion of karaoke bars throughout the territory. Attending a Canto-pop concert is to see the city at its sweetest and most over the top, with screaming, silly dancing, day-glo wigs and enough floral tributes to set up a flower market.

Canto-pop scaled new heights from the mid-1980s to mid-1990s and turned singers like Anita Mui, Leslie Cheung, Alan Tam, Priscilla Chan and Danny Chan into household names in Hong Kong and among Chinese communities around the world. The peak of this Canto-pop golden age came with the advent of the so-called Four Kings: thespian/singer Andy Lau, Mr Nice Guy Jacky Cheung, dancer-turned-crooner Aaron Kwok and teen heart-throb Leon Lai.

It never quite reached that altitude again. Subsequent arrivals such as Běijīng waif Faye Wong, Sammi Cheung, Kelly Chen and proto-hunk Nicholas Tse assumed the throne for a time. But today most stars are a packaged phenomenon. Singers from the mainland and Taiwan – singer/songwriter Jay Chou is one example – are competing with local stars and gaining new fans here, and the strongest influences on local music are now coming from Japan and Korea. There are also acts making their mark from the edge of the mainstream, such as Ellen Lo and Eman Lam, two 'urban folk' singer-songwriters, and My Little Airport, a dapper act whose irreverent multilingual lyrics are often speckled with Chinglish.

Theatre

Much theatre in Hong Kong is Western in form, if not content. Traditional Chinese theatre can still be experienced, but Western theatre has been very influential. Most productions are staged in Cantonese, and a large number are by Hong Kong writers. The fully professional **Hong Kong Repertory Theatre** (www.hkrep.com) and **Chung Ying Theatre Company** (www.chungying.com) put on Cantonese productions, often with English titles. **Theatre du Pif** (www.thtdupif.com), formed by a Scottish-Chinese couple, puts on innovative works incorporating text, movement and visuals, in English and/or Cantonese. **Hong Kong Players** (www.hongkongplayers.com), consisting of expatriate amateurs, mounts classical and modern productions in English, while **Zuni Icosahedron** (www.zuni.org.hk) creates conceptual multimedia works known for their experimental format.

The Cantonese opera Sunbeam Theatre seems to face a closure crisis every few years when its lease expires. The most recent crisis, in February 2012, was averted only when a group of private benefactors intervened at the last minute.

Among the more popular venues are the Fringe Club theatres in Central. The Hong Kong Cultural Centre, Hong Kong Academy for the Performing Arts, Hong Kong City Hall and the Hong Kong Arts Centre all host foreign productions, ranging from large-scale Western musicals to minimalist Japanese theatre.

Chinese Opera

Chinese opera *(hei kuk)*, one of the three oldest dramatic art forms in the world, is a colourful, cacophonous spectacle featuring music, singing, martial arts, acrobatics and acting. Admittedly, it can take some getting used to. Female characters, whether played by men or women, sing in falsetto. The instrumental accompaniment often takes the form of drum-ming, gonging and other nonmelodic punctuation. And the whole affair can last four to six hours. But the costumes are splendid and the plots are adapted from legends and historical tales with universal themes. If you attend a performance by a leading Cantonese opera troupe such as Chor Fung Ming, you'll experience some of the best moments of Chinese opera.

Cantonese opera *(yuet-kek)* is a regional variety of Chinese opera that flourished in Hong Kong, particularly in the 1950s when opera virtuosi fleeing China composed and performed a spate of original works in the territory. But eventually the limelight shifted to the sleek, leather-clad kid on the block – cinema – and things have been going downhill for Cantonese opera since. A shortage of performance venues is a problem. At present there are only two venues, Sunbeam Theatre in North Point and the recently restored Yau Ma Tei Theatre, dedicated to the promotion and development of Chinese opera.

The best way to experience Cantonese opera is to attend a *sun kung hei* (performance for the gods) in a temporary theatre. During major Chinese festivals such as the Lunar New Year, Mid-Autumn Festival and Tin Hau Festival, rural communities invite troupes to perform. The performances usually take place on a makeshift stage in a temple or a bamboo shed. It is a jovial, laid-back event for the whole family that lasts several days.

For a more formal experience, try the Hong Kong Arts Festival in February/March. **Ko Shan Theatre** (www.lcsd.gov.hk/CE/CulturalService /KST) also has Cantonese opera offerings. But the most reliable venue for opera performances year-round is Sunbeam Theatre, while Yau Ma Tei Theatre is expected to also develop an active show calendar on the other side of the harbour. At other times, you might stumble upon a performance at the Temple Street Night Market nearby.

You can also check out the enlightening Cantonese-opera display at the Hong Kong Heritage Museum, where the Hong Kong Tourist Board (HKTB) offers a Chinese-opera appreciation course every Saturday from 2.30pm to 3.45pm.

Other varieties of Chinese opera being performed in Hong Kong by local and/or visiting troupes include Peking opera, a highly refined form that uses almost no scenery but different kinds of traditional props; and Kun opera, the oldest form and one designated a Masterpiece of the Oral and Intangible Heritage of Humanity by Unesco.

> Liu Yichang (1918–), Hong Kong's most respected senior writer, is the author of the stream of consciousness novella *Tête-bêche* which inspired Wong Kar-wai's *In the Mood for Love*.

ART VERSUS INVISIBILITY: LEUNG PING-KWAN

Hong Kong poet Leung Ping-kwan, aka 'Ya Si', born in 1948, fills us in on the literary scene.

Why is food one of your favourite metaphors? When Hong Kong was returned to China in 1997, the West says, 'Poor you!', and China tells us, 'You should be happy!' But the reality is neither... We carry on loving and eating. So instead of heroic tragedies, I write about the wear and tear of daily life, about history, about our emotional complexities through food and romance.

What are some of the features of Hong Kong literature? A mature urban sensibility. It was exploring the individual's psychology when mainland Chinese literature focused on collective values, experimenting with modernism when the latter was writing realist narratives about the building of a nation. Today the best mainland fiction is that depicting the lives of peasants – rural problems are the concern of contemporary China; but portrayals of urban life or foreign cultures tend to be melodramatic and clichéd. By contrast, Hong Kong literature talks about both with much greater sophistication.

Why is Hong Kong literature so 'invisible'? We don't have our own literary museum; our government does not promote literature through international cultural exchange. Our society and its representative media are commercially oriented and lack cultural vision. Hong Kong literature has evolved for the most part under colonial rule.

Literature

Hong Kong has long suffered from the misconception that it does not have a literature of its own, but, in fact, the city has seen a thriving microclimate in the vast landscape of Chinese literature, where the same sun shining on other parts of China has spawned distinct smells, textures and voices.

From the 1920s to the 1940s, Hong Kong was a haven for Chinese writers on the run. These émigrés continued their writing here, their influence lasting until the 1970s when the first generation of writers born and/or raised locally came into their own. The relative creative freedom offered by the city has spawned works in a variety of genres and subjects, from prose poems to experimental novels, from swordplay romance to life as a make-up artist for the dead.

Hong Kong Collage: Contemporary Stories and Writing (ed Martha PY Cheung; 1998) is an important collection of fiction and essays by 15 contemporary local writers. *To Pierce the Material Screen: an Anthology of Twentieth Century Hong Kong Literature* (ed Eva Hung; Renditions; 2008) is a two-volume anthology featuring established figures, younger names and emerging voices, and spans 75 years. In *From the Bluest Part of the Harbour: Poems from Hong Kong* (ed Andrew Parkin; 1996), 12 modern poets reveal the emotions of Hong Kong people in the run-up to 1997. For critical articles on Hong Kong literature, check out the special Hong Kong issue (winter 2008) of the *Journal of Modern Literature in Chinese* (Lingnan University of Hong Kong).

The major literary festival in the city is the **Hong Kong Literary Festival** (www.festival.org.hk), which seems to be held in a different month every year.

The website www.renditions.org has excellent info on Chinese literature published in English. Hong Kong University Press (www.hku press.org) also publishes works by local Chinese writers.

TRANSLATED HONG KONG FICTION

The Cockroach and Other Stories (1995) by Liu Yichang Liu Yichang (1918–), Hong Kong's most respected senior writer, is believed to have written the first stream-of-consciousness novel in Chinese literature. 'The Cockroach' is a Kafkaesque exploration of psychology and philosophy. In 'Indecision', a woman is torn between staying in Hong Kong and returning to her mad husband in Shànghǎi.

Islands and Continents: Short Stories (2007) by Leung Ping-kwan Anti-heroes enter the limelight against the background of Hong Kong history. In 'Postcolonial Affairs of Food and the Heart', a man devours the culinary and erotic delights of other cultures in a bid to find his identity. Leung has also published the bilingual *Travelling with a Bitter Melon: Selected Poems (1973–1998)*.

Love in a Fallen City: And Other Stories by Eileen Chang Chang (1920–95) is considered by some to be the best modern Chinese writer. In the title story set during WWII, a divorcée pursues a liaison with a playboy from Shànghǎi to Hong Kong. Director Ann Hui made it into a film starring Chow Yun-fat. Chang also wrote *Lust, Caution*, a tale of love and espionage, which was adapted for film by Ang Lee.

My City: A Hong Kong Story (1993) by Xi Xi This novel offers a personal vision of Hong Kong in the '60s and '70s through the lives of a telephone repairman, his family, friends and, come to think of it, pineapples and stationery. *Asia Weekly* ranked it one of the top 100 works of 20th-century Chinese fiction.

Renditions Nos 47 & 48: Hong Kong Nineties (1997) Two writers to watch in this collection of 1990s Hong Kong fiction are Wong Bik-wan (1961–) and Dung Kai-cheung (1969–). Wong, a flamenco dancer, writes with a violent passion. 'Plenty and Sorrow' is a tale about Shànghǎi, with a chunk of cannibalism thrown in. Dung recreates the legend of the Father of Chinese Agriculture in 'The Young Shen Nong'.

Cinema

Once known as the 'Hollywood of the Far East', Hong Kong was for decades the third-largest motion-picture industry in the world (after Mumbai and Hollywood) and the second-largest exporter. Now it produces a few dozen films each year, down from well over 200 in the early 1990s. Yet Hong Kong film continues to play an important role on the world cinema stage as it searches for a new identity in the Greater China market.

Martial Arts

Hong Kong cinema became known to the West when a former child actor appeared as a sinewy hero in a kung fu film. But before Bruce Lee unleashed his high-pitched war cry in *The Big Boss* (1971), the kung fu genre was alive and kicking. The *Wong Fei-hung* series, featuring the adventures of a folk hero, has been named by the *Guinness Book of Records* as the longest-running cinema serial dedicated to one man, with roughly a hundred episodes made from 1949 to 1970 alone. The works of the signature directors of the period – Chang Cheh, whose macho aesthetics seduced Quentin Tarantino, and King Hu, who favoured a more refined style of combat – continue to influence films today.

Jackie Chan & Jet Li

The decade after Lee's death saw the leap to stardom of two martial artists: Jackie Chan and Jet Li. Chan's blend of slapstick and action, as seen in *Snake in the Eagle's Shadow* (1978), a collaboration with action choreographer Yuen Wo-ping (who choreographed the action on *Crouching Tiger, Hidden Dragon* and *The Matrix*), became an instant hit. He later added stunts to the formula, resulting in the hits *Police Story* and the *Rush Hour* series. Li garnered international acclaim when he teamed up with director Tsui Hark in *Once Upon a Time in China* (1991). Despite his reputation for tampering with a print just hours before its premiere, Tsui introduced sophisticated visuals and rhythmic editing into the martial-arts genre, most notably in Hong Kong's first special-effects extravaganza, *Zu: Warriors from the Magic Mountain* (1983). As a producer, he helped to create John Woo's gangster classic *A Better Tomorrow* (1986).

The One-Armed Swordsman (1967), directed by Chang Cheh, was one of the first of a new style of martial-arts films featuring male heroes and serious bloodletting.

Contemporary Martial-Arts Films

Fast forward to the 21st century, when a Bruce Lee craze briefly returned on the 35th anniversary of his death with the release of *Ip Man* (2008), a fawning semi-speculative biopic of Lee's mentor. A sequel, *Ip Man 2* (2011), was more chop socky and less solemn, though the nationalist-hero treatment still applied, with a Sinophobic British pugilist in postwar Hong Kong replacing Japanese soldiers as the enemy. Also cashing in on Lee's revived legend is *Bruce Lee, My Brother* (2010), a coming-of-age comedy based on a published recollection of childhood memories that the master's siblings shared of their famous brother.

WALTER BIBIKOW / GETTY IMAGES ©

Avenue of the Stars (p141)

Similarly nostalgic is *Gallants* (2010), a retro comedy in which various kung fu stars of yesteryear pay a feisty homage to an old genre. The low-budget film won Best Picture at the 2011 Hong Kong Film Awards. *Ashes of Time Redux* (2008) is a shorter cut of Wong Kar-wai's haunting 'non-action action movie' of the same name from 1994.

New Wave

Tsui Hark belonged to the New Wave, a group of filmmakers of the late 1970s and '80s who grew up in Hong Kong, and were trained at film schools overseas as well as in local TV. Their works had a more contemporary sensibility, unlike those of their émigré predecessors, and were more artistically adventurous.

Once Upon a Time in China (1991) is the first of Tsui Hark's five-part epic that follows folk hero Wong Fei-hung (Jet Li) as he battles government officials, gangsters and foreign entrepreneurs to protect his martial-arts school in 19th-century China.

Ann Hui, Asia's top female director, is a New Waver who has won awards both locally and overseas. *Song of the Exile* (1990), a tale about the marriage between a Japanese woman and a Chinese man just after the Sino-Japanese War, won Best Film at both the Asian Pacific Film Festival and the Rimini Film Festival in Italy.

International Acclaim

The 1990s saw Hong Kong gaining unprecedented respect on the global film-festival circuit. Besides Ann Hui, Wong Kar-wai received Best Director at the Cannes Film Festival for *Happy Together* in 1997. Auteur of the cult favourite *Chungking Express* (1994), Wong is famous almost as much for his elliptical mood pieces as for his disregard of shooting deadlines. In the same year, Fruit Chan bagged the Special Jury Prize at the Locarno International Film Festival with *Made in Hong Kong*, an edgy number shot on film stock Chan had scraped together while working on other projects.

Tough Times & New Direction

Due to changes in the market, in the 1990s the Hong Kong film industry sank into a gloom from which it has not recovered. The return to China also presented problems related to censorship or, more often, self-censorship. But there have been sunny patches, too. *Infernal Affairs* (2002), directed by Andrew Lau and Alan Mak, made such an impact on its release that it was heralded as a box-office miracle, though it suffered some loss in translation in Martin Scorsese's remake, *The Departed*. *Election* (2005) and *Election 2* (2006), by master of Hong Kong noir Johnnie To, also enjoyed immense critical and box-office success.

Echoes of the Rainbow (2010), a rather maudlin tale about the battling spirit of Hong Kong people in the turbulent 1960s, won a Crystal Bear at the Berlin Film Festival. Meanwhile, veteran thespian Deanie Ip won the Best Actress award at the Venice Film Festival for her role as a traditional housemaid in Ann Hui's *A Simple Life* (2011), an elegant drama about ageing and loneliness.

The past few years have also seen a string of big-budget Hong Kong–China collaborations, most notably the *Ip Man* series and *Bodyguards and Assassins* (2009), a story of anti-Qing intrigue set in 1905 Hong Kong. The trend of growing cooperation with the wealthy – and lucrative – Chinese market looks set to take hold as local filmmakers seek new ways to finance their celluloid (or digital) fantasies.

The Warlords (2007), directed by Peter Chan, is a period war film about sworn brothers forced to betray one another by the realities of war – showing it's possible to please both Hong Kong and mainland audiences.

Film Festivals & Awards

The Hong Kong International Film Festival (every March/April), now in its third decade, is the best in Asia and boasts a laudable if precarious balance of art-house choices and titles offering red-carpet opportunities. The Hong Kong Film Awards is also among the most respected in this part of the world. The Hong Kong Film Archive is a treasure trove of Hong Kong films and resources on them.

Hong Kong in Film

Hong Kong has been the setting of many Western-made films, including *Love is a Many-Splendored Thing* (1955), starring William Holden, and Jennifer Jones as his Eurasian doctor paramour, with great shots on and from Victoria Peak; *The World of Suzie Wong* (1960), with Holden again and Nancy Kwan as the pouting bar girl from Wan Chai; and *The Man with the Golden Gun* (1974), with Roger Moore as James Bond and filmed partly in a Tsim Sha Tsui topless bar. More recently, in *The Dark Knight* (2008), Christian Bale's Batman performed one of his trademark escapes from Two International Finance Centre (although a planned scene in which the superhero would drop from a plane into the harbour was axed after the film's producers found the water quality could pose a potential health danger). An excellent source for spotting familiar locations is the two-part freebie *Hong Kong Movie Odyssey Guide* from the Hong Kong Tourist Board (HKTB).

Days of Being Wild (1990), set in the 1960s, is a star-studded piece directed by Wong Kar-wai and steered along by the characters' accounts of seemingly mundane events. It won Best Picture at the 1991 Hong Kong Film Awards.

CINEMA TOUGH TIMES & NEW DIRECTION

Architecture

Welcome to the most dazzling skyline in the world. We defy you not to be awed as you stand for the first time at the harbour's edge in Tsim Sha Tsui and see Hong Kong Island's majestic panorama of skyscrapers march up those steep, jungle-clad hills. This spectacle has been created because in Hong Kong buildings are knocked down and replaced with taller, shinier versions almost while your back is turned. The scarcity of land, the strains of a growing population and the rapacity of developers – as well as the opportunism of the common speculator – drive this relentless cycle of destruction and construction.

Heritage Preservation

Pre-Colonial Buildings

Tsui Sing Lau Pagoda (Yuen Long)

Tang Ancestral Hall (Yuen Long)

Yu Kiu Ancestral Hall (Yuen Long)

Sam Tung Uk Museum (Tsuen Wan)

Victorian & Edwardian Buildings

Central Police Station (Soho)

Nam Koo Terrace (Wan Chai)

Kam Tong Hall (The Mid-Levels)

Western Market (Sheung Wan)

The government's disinterest in preserving architecturally important buildings went almost entirely unregretted by most until very recently. The destruction of the iconic Star Ferry Terminal in Central marked a surprising reversal in public apathy. Heartfelt protests greeted the wrecking balls in late 2006, but to no avail.

However, in the wake of the protests the government announced that the Streamline Moderne–style Wan Chai Market would be partially preserved (though a luxury apartment tower has risen over it).

Meanwhile the nearby Pawn, a flashy drinking hole converted from four old tenements and a century-old pawn shop, is a running sore with heritage activists who argue that the Urban Renewal Authority has short-changed the public by refusing to list the building's rooftop terrace as an unrestricted public space. Similarly, the former Marine Police Headquarters in Tsim Sha Tsui, now yet another hotel-cum-shopping centre, has disappointed many after the original landscape was razed.

There have been some bright spots, however, most notably when the government stopped the demolition of the magnificent King Yin Lei (1937), a private, Chinese Renaissance–style mansion on Stubbs Rd over Happy Valley. Even more significantly, the government launched in 2008 a scheme for the 'revitalisation' of historic monuments, which allows NGOs to pitch for the use of these buildings. The nascent program has already seen the restoration of the Old Tai O Police Station and the distinctive pre-WWII shophouse Lui Seng Chun.

Despite these positive examples of heritage preservation, the reality remains that the imperatives of the property market, in the name of urban redevelopment, continue to dictate the city's future and its connection with the past. The deep, protracted uncertainty over the fate of the West Wing of the former Government Secretariat in Central – a fine model of understated elegance and a vital place of contact between the former colonial administration and the people – shows that no building in Hong Kong, no matter how valued its architectural and historical heritage, is truly safe from the bulldozers.

Traditional Chinese Architecture

About the only examples of 19th-century Chinese architecture left in urban Hong Kong are the popular Tin Hau temples, including those at Tin Hau near Causeway Bay, Aberdeen, Stanley and Yau Ma Tei. Museums in Chai Wan and Tsuen Wan have preserved a few 18th-century Hakka village structures. More substantial physical reminders of the past lie in the New Territories and the Outlying Islands, where walled villages, fortresses and even a 15th-century pagoda can still be seen.

East-Meets-West Architecture

Architectural cross-play had already been in vogue long before 'soy sauce Western' appeared in colonial Hong Kong. Largely the preserve of the wealthy and the religious, local examples of fusion architecture have not earned the same level of public recognition accorded to some outright, nostalgia-jerking colonial landmarks.

The abandoned Shek Lo Mansion in Fanling (1925) resembles a Kaiping *diāolóu* (a fortified tower that blends Chinese and Western architectural elements) across the border in Guǎngdōng. The Anglican St Mary's Church, at 2a Tai Hang Rd in Causeway Bay, is a somewhat comical Orientalist exercise from 1937 while a subtle Eurasian interior graces the cathedral-like Buddhist temple at the contemporaneous Tung Lin Kok Yuen, at 15 Shan Kwong Rd in Happy Valley.

Tai Hang's Lin Fa Kung is a small Kwun Yum temple with a unique octagonal design and side entrances reminiscent of a medieval Catholic chapel.

Colonial Architecture

Most of the colonial architecture left in the city is on Hong Kong Island, especially in Central, such as the former Legislative Council building (1912) and Government House, residence of all British governors from 1855 to 1997. In Sheung Wan there is Western Market (1906), and in

Revitalised Heritage

Lui Seng Chun (Sham Shui Po)

Béthanie (Pok Fu Lam)

Explosives Magazine (Admiralty)

Old Tai O Police Station (Tai O)

Crown Wine Cellars (Aberdeen)

Mei Ho House Youth Hostel (Sham Shui Po)

ARCHITECTURE TRADITIONAL CHINESE ARCHITECTURE

PETE SEAWARD / LONELY PLANET ©

HSBC building (p72)

the Mid-Levels the Edwardian-style Old Pathological Institute, now the Hong Kong Museum of Medical Sciences (1905). The Old Stanley Police Station (1859) and nearby Murray House (1848) are important colonial structures on the southern part of Hong Kong Island.

The interesting **Hong Kong Antiquities & Monuments Office** (☑2721 2326; www.amo.gov.hk; 136 Nathan Rd; ☺9am-5pm Mon-Sat), located in a British schoolhouse that dates from 1902, has information and exhibits on current preservation efforts.

Neo-
Classical
Buildings
....
*Former Legislative
Council Building
(Central)*
....
*Hung Hing Ying
Building, Univer-
sity of Hong Kong
(The Mid-Levels)*

Contemporary Architecture

Hong Kong's verticality was born out of necessity – the scarcity of land and the sloping terrain have always put property at a premium in this densely populated place. Some buildings, such as Central Plaza and International Commercial Centre, have seized height at all costs; a privileged few, such as the Hong Kong Convention & Exhibition Centre and the windowless Hong Kong Cultural Centre, have pulled off audacious moves to go horizontal.

Internationally celebrated modern architecture in the city includes the Hong Kong & Shanghai Bank building in Central and the Hong Kong International Airport in Chep Lap Kok (opened in 1998) – both by English architect Norman Foster, in Late-Modern high-tech style – as well as IM Pei's soaring symphony of triangular geometry that is the Bank of China Tower.

For more on Hong Kong's contemporary architecture, pick up a copy of the illustrated pocket guide *Skylines Hong Kong*, by Peter Moss (2006), or the more specialist *Hong Kong: A Guide to Recent Architecture* (1998), by Andrew Yeoh and Juanita Cheung.

Distinctively Urban Vistas

For thrill-seekers, a seemingly ordinary tram ride across the northern shore of Hong Kong Island often feels more like an impossible hurtle through an endless canyon of high-rises. Indeed, similar psychogeography can be experienced in much of urban Hong Kong. While the bulk of the buildings here may be uninspired office and apartment blocks sprouting cheek-by-jowl throughout the territory, there are perverse spectacles to be found as various forms of the built environment routinely challenge conventional notions of scale and proportion to achieve their purpose.

Modernism
....
*Bank of China
Buildings
(Central)*
....
*International
Finance Centre
(Central)*
....
*Hongkong &
Shanghai Bank
Building (Central)*
....
*Hong Kong Inter-
national Airport
(Lantau)*

A classic example is the tumbledown Oceanic Mansion (1010-1030 King's Rd), a forbidding cliff of pulverised dwellings that soars above a tight, sloping bend in the shadows of a country park in Quarry Bay. Near the western end of the tramline in Kennedy Town, Hill Rd Flyover is a towering urban racetrack that lures traffic from the rarefied heights of Pok Fu Lam to the siren call of Central, *Blade Runner*–like.

The same sense of space or freedom can rarely be manufactured by the many luxury real-estate projects you will see in Hong Kong, however, even if they've been romantically christened with names like Sorrento, Leguna Verde or Cullinan. Tiny living spaces remain the norm in this city.

Those interested in the future of the city's urban landscape can visit the **Hong Kong Planning & Infrastructure Exhibition Gallery** (☑3102 1242; www.infrastructuregallery.gov.hk; 2 Murray Rd, ground fl, Murray Rd Multistorey Car Park Bldg; ☺10am-6pm Wed-Mon).

Religion & Belief

Hong Kong is arguably the only city in China where religious freedom is both provided for by law and respected in practice. Almost everyone here is brought up on certain spiritual beliefs, even though these may not always add up to the profession of a religion. And most of the time, they don't – Hong Kongers aren't a particularly religious bunch.

Early Influences

The city's early inhabitants were fishermen and farmers who worshipped a mixed bag of deities – some folk, some Taoist – notably the Kitchen God, the Earth God and the Goddess of the Sea (Tin Hau). Many sought divine protection by symbolically offering their children to deities for adoption. All villages have ancestral shrines and traditional practices are still alive in Hong Kong today, often colourfully intertwined with those of imported religions such as Buddhism and Christianity.

Confucianism

For 2000 years, the teachings of Confucius (551–479 BC) and the subsequent school of thought, called Confucianism, informed the familial system and relationships in imperial China. Yet in the revolutionary fervour of the 20th century, the philosophy that was the bedrock of Chinese civilization was blamed for a host of evils from feudal oppression and misogyny to all-round backwardness.

Two pillars of Confucian thought are respect for knowledge and filial piety. Hong Kong parents attach huge importance to academic performance; youngsters are trained to work hard as well as to treat parents and teachers with courtesy. Many adults live with their folks (though this is related to the city's exorbitant rent); almost everyone is expected to provide for their parents, though whether they do is another matter.

Confucian ideals are not carved in stone and Hong Kongers are known for their remarkable ability to adapt different traditions for their convenience. Parents and schools increasingly value independent thinking and vocalising one's opinion, though speaking to an elder like an equal is still frowned upon. Dining with the family is a must in the Lunar New Year but the meal may take place in a restaurant.

Perhaps the Confucian precept most unwittingly embraced by Hong Kongers is the right to remonstrate. Mencius (372–289 BC), a celebrated Confucian philosopher, proposed the concept of a 'divine right of rebellion'. This is enacted daily by protesters and activists in Hong Kong.

Buddhism

Buddhism is Hong Kong's dominant religion. It was first introduced here in about the 5th century, when the monk Pui To set up a hermitage in the western New Territories. The area, a stop on the ancient route linking Persia, Arabia and India to Guǎngzhōu, is regarded as the birthplace of Buddhism in the territory.

The ancestors of Hong Kong's small Parsee community migrated to the city from Mumbai in the early colonial period. Some were buried in a tiny Parsee Cemetery in Happy Valley. Despite their small number, the Parsees' influence had been great. At one time, three of the 13 board members of HSBC were Parsee. It was also a Parsee who founded the Star Ferry.

Although a tiny fraction of the population is purely and devoutly Buddhist, about a million practise some form of the religion, and use its funeral and exorcism rites. Some followers abstain from meat on certain days of the month, others for longer periods; few are strict vegetarians.

Buddhist organisations here focus on providing palliative care and spiritual services. Every year on Remembrance Day (11 November), they hold a ceremony for the souls of the victims of the two World Wars and the Japanese invasion. Buddhist funerals are dignified affairs that can be quite elaborate, with some ceremonies lasting 49 days – the time it purportedly takes an average soul to find the conditions for its rebirth. Prayers are chanted every seven days to help the soul find rebirth in a higher realm ('happy human' versus 'cockroach', for instance). On the seventh day, souls are believed to revisit their homes. Everyone in the family stays in their room to avoid crossing paths with the loved one.

In 1997 the government made a day in May or June a public holiday to mark the birthday of the Buddha, Siddhārtha Gautama, replacing the Queen's Birthday. Followers gather at temples where they douse statues of Buddha with water, an act that signifies purification of one's soul. They also eat green cookies made with the bitter Indian pluchea herb, as eating them represents passing through prickles to better pastures.

> Some 80% of funeral rites in Hong Kong are presided over by Taoist priests. These are noisy affairs with cymbals and *suona*, a Chinese reed instrument. Some have elaborate rituals featuring props from coins to flaming swords that are meant to ensure the soul lets go of its worldly relationships.

Taoism

Taoism is an indigenous Chinese religion over 2000 years old. Though never declared a national faith, its presence is ubiquitous in most aspects of Chinese life. Unlike evangelical religions, Taoism simply offers its services, whether it's treatment for illness or protection from evil spirits, to everyone within its locale.

The Hong Kong horse-racing season, and all construction and filming projects, are preceded by Taoist rituals to appease the nature deities and ensure good feng shui. During the first two weeks of the Lunar New Year, people of all creeds and faiths pay their respects at Taoist temples. Taoist priests preside over the majority of funeral rites in Hong Kong.

Due to Taoism's intimate ties with mundane life, its temples tend to be colourful. Taoism and folk religion have always been willing bedfellows as both prescribe a harmonious coexistence between humans and nature, respect for the environment, and the belief that everything has a spirit. In some instances they are so well integrated that it's hard to tell them apart. Taiping Qingzhao, celebrated in Cheung Chau as the Bun Festival, features a Taoist priest performing the main ceremony, Buddhist monks leading the worship of local gods, with a little bit of Confucianism and even a few tourism gimmicks thrown in for good measure.

> **Religious Reads**
> ....
> *Changing Church and State Relations in Hong Kong 1950–2000*, by Beatrice Leung and Chan Shun-hing (2003)
> ....
> *Imperial to International: A History of St John's Cathedral, Hong Kong*, by Stuart Wolfendale (2013)
> ....
> *Islam in Hong Kong: Muslims and Everyday Life in China's World City*, by Paul O'Connor (2012)
> ....
> *The Daoist Tradition: An Introduction*, by Louis Komjathy (2013)

Christianity

Hong Kong's Christian community has over 800,000 followers, with Protestants outnumbering Roman Catholics and having more young believers. About a third of the Catholics are Filipina domestic helpers. Most churches offer services in Cantonese and English, and some also in Tagalog.

Christianity has been in Hong Kong since the mid-19th century. In the early days, the Hong Kong Catholic Church provided support to the missionaries travelling to and from China, and served the Catholics in the British Army as well as Portuguese merchants and their families from Macau. In the ensuing decades, both Catholics and Protestants began working for the local community, founding schools, hospitals and welfare organsations. These services were, as they are now, open to followers and non-followers alike.

Macau's History & Culture

Ou Mun, Macau's Chinese name, means Gateway of the Bay. This is what the Portuguese sought when they arrived in the 16th century – a trading gateway in Asia. Trade did prosper, and Macau's colonial buildings tell of its former glory. But Portugal's decline as a colonial power and Hong Kong's rise as the dominant trading post changed the course of history for Macau.

History

Arrival of the Portuguese

The first Portuguese contingent, led by Jorge Álvares, set foot on Chinese soil in 1513 at a place they called Tamaõ, about 80km southwest of the mouth of the Pearl River. However, the exposed anchorage there forced the Portuguese traders to search for a better port.

At the time, Macau was inhabited by a small number of mostly Cantonese-speaking farmers and fisherfolk from Fújiàn. In 1557 officials at Guǎngzhōu let the Portuguese build temporary shelters on the peninsula in exchange for customs dues and rent. The Portuguese also agreed to rid the area of the pirates that were endemic at the time. Neither side expected that for the next 400-plus years, the Portuguese would dominate Macau's history.

A Trading Powerhouse

Macau grew rapidly as a trading centre. Acting as agents for the Chinese merchants, who were forbidden to leave the country by imperial decree, Portuguese traders traded for Chinese goods that they then took to other ports for trading.

During the late 16th century, the Portuguese in Macau were at the forefront of all international commerce between China and Japan. In 1586 Macau was conferred the status of a city by the Portuguese Crown: Cidade de Nome de Deus (City of the Name of God).

By the beginning of the 17th century, Macau was home to several thousand residents, including about 900 Portuguese, Christian converts from Malacca and Japan, and a large number of slaves from colonial outposts in Africa, India and the Malay Peninsula. Many Chinese moved to

---

4000 BC
Archaeological finds from Hác Sá and Ká Hó bays on Coloane island suggest that Macau was inhabited in neolithic times.

AD 500
Macau serves as a stop in the Maritime Silk Road for merchant ships travelling between Southeast Asia and Guǎngzhōu.

1277
Mongols invade China during the Southern Song dynasty; some 50,000 people seek refuge in Macau.

1513
The Portuguese, under Jorge Álvares, land in the Pearl River Delta of China.

1557
The Ming court leases Macau to Portugal for tribute paid to Běijīng; the Portuguese build the first walled village in Macau.

1560–80
Jesuits and Dominicans arrive in Macau, turning it into a Catholic missionary hub.

1601
The Dutch attack Macau. Further raids culminate in a full-scale – but ultimately unsuccessful – invasion in 1622, prompting construction of the Guia Fort.

1680
Lisbon appoints the first Portuguese governor of Macau. Macau's role as a major trading port is in decline.

Macau from across the border, working as traders, craftspeople, hawkers and labourers; by the close of the century, their numbers reached 40,000.

Besides trading, Macau had also become a centre of Christianity in Asia. Among the earliest missionaries was Francis Xavier of the Jesuit order, who was later canonised.

The Portuguese in Macau, along with their Macanese descendants, created a home away from home, with luxurious villas overlooking the Praia Grande and splendid baroque churches, paid for with the wealth generated by their monopoly on trade between China and Japan.

Portuguese Decline

In 1580 Spanish armies occupied Portugal and, for more than 60 years, three Spanish kings ruled over the country and its empire. In the early years of the 17th century, the Dutch moved unsuccessfully to seize the rich Portuguese enclaves of Macau, Nagasaki and Malacca.

The Portuguese felt that they should follow in the footsteps of the British and push China for sovereignty over Macau, a territory they had occupied for three centuries. Negotiations began in 1862, although it was not until 1887 that a treaty was signed in which China effectively recognised Portuguese sovereignty over Macau in perpetuity.

With the advent of the steamship, however, there were fewer trans-shipments from Chinese ports going through Macau. The enclave's future economy was greatly assisted by the legalisation of gambling in the 1850s, but by the close of the 19th century the ascent of the British colony and the decline of the Portuguese territory had become irreversible.

Macau in the 20th Century

By the turn of the 20th century, Macau was little more than a haven for Chinese refugees fleeing war, famine and political oppression. Among them was Sun Yatsen, founder of the Republic of China, who lived in Macau before the 1911 revolution.

In the mid-1920s large numbers of Chinese immigrants arrived, fleeing civil strife in China. Then, during WWII, people from Hong Kong and China, as well as Asian-based Europeans, took refuge in Macau, a neutral port. By 1943 the population had increased to 500,000. There was another influx of Chinese refugees in 1949 when the communists took power in China.

In 1974 the new left-wing government in Portugal began to divest Portugal of the last remnants of its empire. Lisbon tried to return Macau to China, but the word from Běijīng was that China wished Macau to remain as it was – at least for the time being.

In 1986 China and Portugal began negotiations on returning Macau to China, and an agreement was signed the following April. Under the so-called Sino-Portuguese Pact, Macau would become a Special Ad-

Colonial Portuguese architecture survives throughout Macau, infused with Chinese features and the styles of Portugal's trading partners and former colonies. In Hong Kong, by contrast, the Western model was transplanted with far fewer adaptations.

GANG VIOLENCE

The years 1996 to 1998 were a grim time for Macau and its all-important tourism industry – during this time an escalating number of gangland killings took place. Some 40 people were killed as senior Triad leaders jostled for control of lucrative gambling rackets, and one international hotel was raked with AK-47 gunfire.

As the handover approached, China put pressure on Portugal to clean up its act. The government issued a new anti-Triad law calling for a lengthy prison term for anyone found to be a senior leader. Wan Kwok Koi, a prominent Triad leader, was arrested and sentenced to 15 years; many other Triad members fled overseas. The violence was calmed, though Triad activity in Macau was by no means stamped out.

ministrative Region (SAR) of China. On 20 December 1999, 442 years of Portuguese rule officially ended. Like Hong Kong, the Macau SAR is supposed to enjoy a 'high degree of autonomy' for 50 years in all matters except defence and foreign affairs.

Macau has directly elected some of the members of its Legislative Assembly since the assembly's founding in 1976 but, unlike Hong Kong, it didn't rush last-minute proposals to widen the franchise or speed up democratisation. The existing legislature served throughout the handover, unlike in the British territory.

Macau after 1999

In 2001 casino licences were liberalised. This led to an influx of mostly American casinos, and in 2006 Macau supplanted Las Vegas as the world's gambling capital, bringing about a drastic socio-economic shift. While the casino industry has become the primary driver of economic growth, it has also increased Macau's income inequality. The ever-expanding industry has also caused a labour shortage, as its high-paying jobs requiring little or no professional skills have lured many young people into giving up their studies. The labour shortage also led to an influx of illegal migrant workers and has become a rallying cause of labour protests in Macau.

Culture

While traditional culture among the Chinese of Macau is similar to that of Hong Kong, the Macanese community – a tiny community of the descendents of intermarriages between Portuguese and Asians – has a vastly different culture that has evolved through the centuries. The Macanese have unique food, festivals and traditions, and even their own dialect called Patuá, a Creole language derived mainly from Malay, Sinhalese, Cantonese and Portuguese. José dos Santos Ferreira (1919–93), aka Adé, was a poet who wrote in Patuá.

Macau has far greater linguistic complexity than Hong Kong. Cantonese, English, Portuguese, Mandarin and Patuá are all spoken in Macau, not to mention the minorities that speak Thai, Tetun, Indonesian, Filipino and Burmese. Today, however, English is used and understood more widely than Portuguese. Some Macau residents are worried that the growing influence of English and Mandarin will dilute the character of Macau, to the detriment of its culture.

For the vast majority of Macau Chinese people, Taoism and Buddhism are the dominant religions. The Roman Catholic Church, however, is still going strong with followers making up about 6% of the population.

Architecture

Macau has a unique heritage consisting of both Portuguese and Chinese architecture. What often appears at a glance to be 'Portuguese' architecture is actually a complex fusion of Portuguese and Chinese building

---

1851
Taking advantage of China's weakness during the Opium War, Portugal occupies Taipa and later takes control of Coloane in 1864.

1865
The Portuguese turn Macau into a major point on the slave-trade circuit. *Dea del Mar* sets sail from Macau with 550 slaves from southern China; only 162 survive the journey to Tahiti.

1937–45
Macau enjoys a brief period of prosperity as a neutral port during WWII.

1949
Communists take over China and declare the Protocol of Lisbon an 'unequal treaty'.

1966
Violent riots break out in Macau. The government proposes that Portugal leaves, but, fearing the economic shock to Hong Kong, the Chinese refuse the offer.

1974
The new left-wing government in Portugal decides to relinquish all its colonies, including those in Africa and the Indonesian archipelago.

1999
Macau returns to China on 20 December as a Special Administrative Region (SAR), ending almost 450 years of Portuguese rule.

2001
The liberalisation of casino licences leads to an economic boom, but polarises Macau society.

styles, techniques and materials, with influences from other parts of Asia such as Goa, the Philippines and Malacca, and contributions from the Italian and Spanish missioners who infused it with their sensibilities and traditions. Generally the only buildings in the city that are wholly Chinese or Portuguese are temples and fortresses.

Examples of Mediterrasian architecture abound, including the Ruins of the Church of St Paul, and 'Portuguese' churches. Even Chinese residences sport a mix of influences. The Mandarin's House has Western-style arches and window panels inlaid with mother-of-pearl, a technique of ornamentation practised in India, the Philippines and other parts of Asia. Inside another residence, the Lou Kau Mansion, neoclassical balustrades and stained-glass windows embellish a Chinese maze behind a grey facade.

Macau has a strong heritage of modernism. As well as the modernist villas on Bishop Hill, the 'Red Market', Pier 8 and the East Asia Hotel are fine examples of Chinese art deco.

The 'old city' – around Rua das Estalagens, Rua de Madeira, Rua dos Mercadores, Rua da Tercena and Rua de Felicidade (Street of Happiness) – has clan-related structures comprising an alley and a communal altar, as well as humble, one- or two-storey Chinese houses from agricultural times.

Literature

The most active literary organisation in Macau is the nonprofit Association of Stories in Macao (ASM), which promotes, through publishing, the poetry and fiction of Macau-based authors in English or in translation. The founder of ASM is Christopher (Kit) Kelen, an Australian poet and critic, who has lived in Hong Kong and Macau for close to 20 years.

Kelen has been bringing together the different writers in Macau (and sometimes even Hong Kong) who write in Chinese, English and Portuguese. His efforts have given rise to 100-plus publications, including solid anthologies of Macau, Chinese and Australian poetry. Of these the two anthologies of Macau poetry are: *I Roll the Dice: Contemporary Macao Poetry* (2008) and *Portuguese Poets of Macau* (2010). The first features the works of contemporary Chinese-speaking poets in Macau, as well as poetry by Portuguese- or English-speaking residents of Macau. The second contains the works of some 40 poets, rendered into English. Contributors include contemporary poets and early writers who have left their mark on Macau, such as Portugal's national poet, Luís de Camões (1524–80), and the symbolist poet Camilo de Almeida Pessanha (1867–1926) who was buried in the Cemetery of St Michael the Archangel.

Painting

Macau can lay claim to having spawned or influenced a number of artists, some born in the territory and some from Guǎngdōng Province. Their work is on display in the Macau Museum of Art, while some of Macau's best contemporary art can be seen at AFA Macau.

The most important Western artist to have lived in Macau was George Chinnery (1774–1852). Other influential European painters who spent time in Macau include the Scottish physician Thomas Watson (1815–60), Chinnery's pupil Frenchman Auguste Borget (1808–77), and watercolourist Marciano António Baptista (1826–96), who was born in Macau.

Guan Qiaochang (1825–60), another of Chinnery's pupils, was a Chinese artist who painted in the Western style and worked under the name Lamqua.

Survival Guide

Hong Kong Transport

GETTING TO HONG KONG

Most international travellers arrive and depart via Hong Kong International Airport. Travellers to and from mainland China can use ferry, road or rail links to Guăngdōng and points beyond. Hong Kong is accessible from Macau via ferry or helicopter.

More than 100 airlines operate between Hong Kong International Airport and some 160 destinations around the world. Flights include from New York (16 hours), Los Angeles (15 hours), Sydney (9½ hours), London (12 hours) and Běijīng (3½ hours). There are regular buses connecting Hong Kong with major destinations in neighbouring Guăngdōng province. Twelve trains run daily from Hong Kong to Guăngzhōu (two hours), and trains to Běijīng (23½ hours) and Shànghăi

(18½ hours) run on alternate days. Visas are required to cross the border to the mainland.

Regularly scheduled ferries link the China Ferry Terminal in Kowloon and/ or the Macau Ferry Terminal on Hong Kong Island with a string of towns and cities on the Pearl River Delta, including Macau. Trips take two to three hours.

Flights, cars and tours can be booked online at lonelyplanet.com.

Air

There are flights between Hong Kong and around 40 cities in mainland China, including Běijīng, Chéngdū, Kūnmíng and Shànghăi. One-way fares are a bit more than half the return price.

Cathay Pacific Airways (CX; ☑2747 1888; www.cathaypacific.com) Hong Kong's

major international airline has flights to 20 cities in mainland China.

Dragonair (KA; ☑3193 3888; www.dragonair.com) Owned by Cathay Pacific, Dragonair specialises in regional flights and flies to 20-plus cities in mainland China.

Hong Kong Airlines (HX; ☑3151 1888; www.hongkongairlines.com) Cheaper airline that specialises in regional routes, including 17 cities in mainland China.

Hong Kong International Airport

Designed by British architect Sir Norman Foster, the **Hong Kong International Airport** (HKG; ☑2181 8888; www.hkairport.com) is on Chek Lap Kok, a largely reclaimed area off Lantau's northern coast. Highways, bridges (including the 2.2km-long Tsing Ma Bridge, one of the world's

---

CLIMATE CHANGE & TRAVEL

Every form of transport that relies on carbon-based fuel generates CO_2, the main cause of human-induced climate change. Modern travel is dependent on aeroplanes which might use less fuel per kilometre per person than most cars but travel much greater distances. The altitude at which aircraft emit gases (including CO_2) and particles also contributes to their climate change impact. Many websites offer 'carbon calculators' that allow people to estimate the carbon emissions generated by their journey and, for those who wish to do so, to offset the impact of the greenhouse gases emitted with contributions to portfolios of climate-friendly initiatives throughout the world. Lonely Planet offsets the carbon footprint of all staff and author travel.

longest suspension bridges) and a fast train link the airport with Kowloon and Hong Kong Island.

The two terminals have a wide range of shops, restaurants, cafes, ATMs and moneychangers.

Hong Kong Tourism Board (HKTB; ☑2508 1234; www.discoverhongkong.com) Maintains information centres in Buffer Halls A and B located after Customs in Terminal 1.

Hong Kong Hotels Association (香港酒店業協會, HKHA; ☑2769 8822, 2383 8380; www.hkha.org; ⊙7am-midnight) Counters are located inside the Buffer Halls. HKHA deals with midrange and top-end hotels only; it does not handle hostels, guesthouses or other budget accommodation.

China Travel Service (中國旅行社, CTS; ☑2261 2472; www.ctshk.com; ⊙7am-10pm) Has four counters in the terminals, including one in Arrival Hall A which issues China visas (normally takes one working day).

AIRPORT EXPRESS
The **Airport Express line** (☑2881 8888; www.mtr.com.hk) of the Mass Transit Railway (MTR) is the fastest (and most expensive, other than a taxi) way to get to and from Hong Kong International Airport.

Departures Trains depart every 10 to 12 minutes from 6am to 1am daily to Hong Kong station (HK$100) in Central, calling at Kowloon station (HK$90) in Jordan and at Tsing Yi island (HK$60) en route; the full trip takes 24 minutes.

Fares Adult return fares, valid for a month, are HK$180/160/110. Children three to 11 years pay half-fare. You can also buy an Airport Express Travel Pass, which allows three days of unlimited travel on the MTR and Light Rail and one/two trips on the Airport Express (HK$220/300).

Tickets Vending machines dispense tickets at the airport and train stations en route.

Shuttle buses Airport Express has two shuttle buses on Hong Kong Island (H1 and H2) and five in Kowloon (K1 to K5), with free transfers for passengers between Hong Kong and Kowloon stations and major hotels. The buses run every 12 to 20 minutes between 6.12am and 11.12pm. Schedules and routes are available at Airport Express and MTR stations and on the Airport Express website.

Checking bags If you are booked on a scheduled flight and taking the Airport Express to the airport, most airlines allow you to check in your bags and receive your boarding pass from 90 minutes to one day before your flight at Hong Kong or Kowloon Airport Express stations (open 5.30am to 12.30am).

BUS
There are also good bus links to/from the airport. These buses have plenty of room for luggage, and announcements are usually made in English, Cantonese and Mandarin notifying passengers of hotels at each stop. For more details on the routes, check the 'Transport' section at www.hkairport.com.

Departures Buses run every 10 to 30 minutes from about 6am to between midnight and 1am. There are also quite a few night buses (designated 'N').

Fares Major hotel and guesthouse areas on Hong Kong Island are served by the A11 (HK$40) and A12 (HK$45) buses; the A21 (HK$33) covers similar areas in Kowloon.Bus drivers in Hong Kong do not give change, but it is available at the ground transportation centre at the airport, as are Octopus cards. Normal returns are double the one-way fare. Unless otherwise stated, children aged between three and 11 years and seniors over 65 pay half-fare.

Tickets Buy your ticket at the booth near the airport bus stand.

LIMOUSINE
There are limousine service counters in the arrivals hall and at the ground transportation centre, including **Parklane Limousine Service** (☑2730 0662; www.hongkonglimo.com) and **Intercontinental Hire Cars**

TAXI FARES FROM THE AIRPORT

DESTINATION	FARE (HK$)
Central, Admiralty, Wan Chai, Causeway Bay (Hong Kong Island)	280-320
Tsim Sha Tsui, Jordan, Yau Ma Tei, Mong Kok, Hung Hom (Kowloon)	230-230
Sha Tin (New Territories)	280
Tsuen Wan (New Territories)	200
Tung Chung (Lantau)	45-55

(☑3193 9333; www.trans-island.com.hk). In a car seating up to four people, expect to pay HK$650 to HK$810 to destinations in Hong Kong Island and urban Kowloon and from HK$600 to HK$1000 to the New Territories.

Train

One-way and return tickets for Guăngzhōu, Běijīng and Shànghǎi can be booked 60 days in advance at MTR stations in Hung Hom, Mong Kok, Kowloon Tong and Sha Tin, and at MTR Travel at Admiralty station. Tickets to Guăngzhōu can also be booked with a credit card on the **MTR website** (www.it3. mtr.com.hk) or via the **Tele-Ticketing Hotline** (☑2947 7888).

Shēnzhèn

Reaching Shēnzhèn is a breeze. Just board the MTR East Rail and ride it to Lo Wu or Lok Ma Chau; the mainland is 200m away. The first

train to Lo Wu/Lok Ma Chau leaves Hung Hom station at 5.30/5.35am, the last at 11.07/9.35pm, and the trip takes about 44/49 minutes. The border crossing at Lo Wu opens at 6.30am and closes at midnight. The crossing at Lok Ma Chau is open around the clock.

Guăngzhōu

High-speed intercity trains leave Hung Hom station for Guăngzhōu East train station 12 times a day between 7.25am and 8.01pm, returning from that station the same number of times from 8.19am to 9.32pm. The trip takes approximately two hours. One-way tickets cost HK$230/190 in 1st/2nd class for adults and HK$115/95 for children aged five to nine. A cheaper but less convenient option is to take the MTR East Rail train to Lo Wu, cross through immigration into Shēnzhèn and catch a local train from there to Guăngzhōu. There are frequent high-speed trains

(¥80 to ¥100, 52 minutes to 1¼ hours) that run throughout the day.

Běijīng & Shànghǎi

There are direct rail links between Hung Hom and both Shànghǎi and Běijīng. Trains to Běijīng West train station (hard/soft/deluxe sleeper from HK$808/1125/1339) depart on alternate days at 3.15pm, arriving at 1.08pm the following day. Trains to Shànghǎi (hard/soft/deluxe sleeper from HK$874/1234/1491) also depart on alternate days at 3.15pm, arriving at 10am the following day.

Bus

Several transport companies in Hong Kong offer bus services to Guăngzhōu, Shēnzhèn airport and other destinations in the Pearl River Delta. In addition, at Hong Kong International Airport buses run by CTS and Trans-Island link Hong Kong International Airport with many points in southern China.

China Travel Tours Transportation Services (CTS; ☑2764 9803; http://ctsbus. hkcts.com; 78-83 Connaught Road, CTS House, Central)

Trans-Island Limousine Service (☑3193 9333; www. trans-island.com.hk) Mainland destinations from Hong Kong include Dōngguǎn, Fóshān, Guăngzhōu, Huìzhōu, Kāipíng, Shēnzhèn's Bǎoān airport and Zhōngshān.

CHINA VISAS

Everyone except Hong Kong Chinese residents must have a visa to enter mainland China. Visas can be arranged by **China Travel Service** (中國旅行社, CTS; ☑2261 2472 ; www.ctshk.com; ☺7am-10pm), the mainland-affiliated agency; a good many hostels and guesthouses; and most Hong Kong travel agents.

At the time of writing, holders of Canadian, Australian, New Zealand and most EU passports – but not USA ones – can get a single visa on the spot for around HK$150 at the Lo Wu border crossing, the last stop on the MTR's East Rail. This particular visa limits you to a maximum stay of five days within the confines of the Shēnzhèn Special Economic Zone (SEZ). The queues for these visas can be interminable, so it is highly recommended that you shell out the extra money and get a proper China visa before setting off, even if you're headed just for Shēnzhèn. If you have at least a week to arrange your visa yourself, you can go to the **Visa Office of the People's Republic of China** (☑3413 2424; www. fmcoprc.gov.hk; 26 Harbour Rd, 7th fl, Lower Block, China Resources Centre, Wan Chai; ☺9am-noon & 2-5pm Mon-Fri). For further details see www.fmprc.gov.cn.

Ferry

Chu Kong Passenger Transportation Company (☑2858 3876; www.cksp. com.hk) provides regularly scheduled ferries that link the **China Ferry Terminal** (中港碼頭; China Hong Kong City,

33 Canton Rd, Tsim Sha Tsui) in Kowloon and/or the **Hong Kong–Macau Ferry Terminal** (Shun Tak Centre, 200 Connaught Rd, Sheung Wan) on Hong Kong Island with a string of towns and cities on the Pearl River Delta – but not central Guǎngzhōu or Shēnzhèn.

Mainland destinations from Hong Kong include:

Shékǒu One hour

Shùndé Two hours

Zhàoqìng Four hours

Zhōngshān 1½ hours

Zhūhǎi 70 minutes

A fast ferry service called the **Skypier** (☎2215 3232) links Hong Kong airport with seven Pearl River Delta destinations: Shékǒu near Shēnzhèn, Shēnzhèn Fúyǒng, Dōngguǎn, Zhōngshān, Zhūhǎi, Nánshā and Macau. The service enables travellers to board ferries directly without clearing Hong Kong customs and immigration. Book a ticket prior to boarding from the ticketing desks located in the transfer area on Arrivals level 5 close to the immigration counters. An air-side bus then takes you to the ferry terminal.

GETTING AROUND HONG KONG

Hong Kong is small and crowded, and public transport is the only practical way to move people. The ultramodern Mass Transit Railway (MTR) is the quickest way to get to most urban destinations. The bus system is extensive and as efficient as the traffic allows, but it can be bewildering for short-term travellers. Ferries are fast and economical and throw in spectacular harbour views at no extra cost. Trams are really just for fun.

MTR

The **Mass Transit Railway** (MTR; ☎2881 8888; www.mtr.com.hk; fares HK$4-25) is the name for Hong Kong's rail system comprising underground, overland and light rail (slower tram-style) services. Universally known as the 'MTR', it is clean, fast and safe and transports some four million people daily.

Though it costs slightly more than bus travel, the MTR is the quickest way to get to most destinations in Hong Kong.

Train

There are 84 stations on nine underground and overland lines, and a Light Rail network that covers the northwest New Territories. Smoking, eating and drinking are not permitted in MTR stations or on the trains, and violators are subject to a fine of HK$5000.

Departures Trains run every two to 14 minutes from around 6am to sometime between midnight and 1am.

Fares Tickets cost HK$4 to HK$25, but trips to stations bordering mainland China (Lo Wu and Lok Ma Chau) can cost up to HK$50. Children aged between three and 11 years and seniors over 65 pay half-fare. Ticket machines accept notes and coins and dispense change.

Tickets Once you've passed through the turnstile to begin a journey you have 90 minutes to complete it before the ticket becomes invalid. If you have underpaid (by mistake or otherwise), you can make up the difference at an MTR service counter next to the turnstile.

Peak hours If possible, it's best to avoid the rush hours: 7.30am to 9.30am and 5pm to 7pm weekdays.

Toilets There are toilets in many MTR stations, though sometimes you have to ask to find them.

Exits MTR exit signs use an alphanumerical system and there can be as many as a dozen to choose from. We give the correct exit for sights and destinations wherever possible, but you may find yourself studying the exit table from time to time and scratching your head. There are always maps of the local area at each exit.

Light Rail Lines

The MTR's Light Rail system is rather like a modern, air-conditioned version of the trams in Hong Kong, but it's much faster. It runs in the northwest New Territories.

Departures The Light Rail operates from about 5.30am to between 12.15am and 1am. Trams run every four to 12 minutes, depending on the line and time of day.

Fares Fares are HK$4.10 to HK$6.50, depending on the number of zones (from one to five) travelled; children and seniors over 65 pay from HK$2 to HK$3.10.

Tickets If you don't have an Octopus card, you can buy single-journey tickets from vending machines on the platforms. There are no gates or turnstiles and customers are trusted to validate their ticket or Octopus card when they board and exit.

Travel & Tourist Passes

Octopus Card (☎2266 2222; www.octopuscards.com) The Octopus Card is a rechargeable 'smart card' valid on the MTR and most forms of public transport in Hong Kong. It also allows you to make

HONG KONG TRANSPORT GETTING AROUND HONG KONG

MTR: FUN FACTS, FAST FICTION

Hong Kong's MTR stations are colour-coded and colourfully storied.

Platform design Colour-coding adds personality to drab underground environments and enables passengers on crowded trains to quickly locate themselves. The most chromatically interesting stations are on the Kwun Tong Line. Kowloon Tong is light blue – 'Tong' means 'pool'. Wong Tai Sin takes 'wong' or 'yellow'. Diamond Hill is charcoal flecked with silver. Navy with rainbow stripes stands for Choi Hung ('rainbow'). Lai Chi Kok on the Tsuen Wan Line is orange-red because that's the colour of a ripe lychee ('lai chi'). Interchange stations, Central and Mong Kok, sport eye-catching red.

Calligraphy Platforms on the Island Line, which tend to be less spacious, show the station names in ancient Chinese script. The graceful calligraphy is supposed to have a soothing effect on waiting passengers.

Ancient superstition Traditional Chinese are apprehensive about digging activities because spirits are believed to reside underground. When the MTR was commissioning its construction in the 1970s, many local companies refused to bid. Like other high-risk industries in Hong Kong, construction has an informal code of ethics based on superstition.

Haunted? Ghost stories about the MTR abound. A woman in a red dress is said to have leapt onto the tracks in Yau Ma Tei, but no corpse could be found. There are tales of children playing in the tunnel between Lai King and Mei Foo, vanishing just when the train hits them; and a victim of an industrial accident in white overalls, dangling his legs from a swing made from a high-pressure electric cable between Choi Hung and Kowloon Bay. Staff lit incense, offered apologies, and he was never seen again.

purchases at retail outlets across the territory (such as convenience stores and supermarkets). The card costs HK$150 (HK$70 for children and seniors), which includes a HK$50 refundable deposit and HK$100 worth of travel. Octopus fares are about 5% cheaper than ordinary fares on the MTR. You can buy one and recharge at any MTR stations.

Airport Express Travel Pass (1/2 trips on Airport Express HK$220/300) Also allows three consecutive days of unlimited travel on the MTR.

MTR Tourist Day Pass (adult/child 3-11yr HK$55/25) Valid on the MTR for 24 hours after the first use.

Tourist Cross-Boundary Travel Pass (1/2 days consecutive travel HK$85/120) Allows unlimited travel on the MTR and two single journeys to/from Lo Wu or Lok Ma Chau stations.

Bus

Hong Kong's extensive bus system will take you just about anywhere in the territory. Since Kowloon and the northern side of Hong Kong Island are so well served by the MTR, most visitors use the buses primarily to explore the southern side of Hong Kong Island, the New Territories and Lantau Island.

Departures Most buses run from 5.30am or 6am until midnight or 12.30am, though there are smaller numbers of night buses that run from 12.45am to 5am or later.

Fares Bus fares cost HK$4.70 to HK$52, depending on the destination. Fares for night buses cost from HK$6 to HK$32. You will need exact change or an Octopus card.

Bus stations On Hong Kong Island the most important bus stations are the bus terminus in **Central** (Exchange Sq) and the one at **Admiralty**.

From these stations you can catch buses to Aberdeen, Repulse Bay, Stanley and other destinations on the southern side of Hong Kong Island. In Kowloon the **Star Ferry bus terminal** has buses heading up Nathan Rd and to the Hung Hom train station.

Route information Figuring out which bus you want can be difficult, but **City Bus** (2873 0818) and **First Bus** (2136 8888; www.nwstbus. com.hk), owned by the same company, and **Kowloon Motor Bus** (KMB; 2745 4466; www.kmb.hk) provide user-friendly route search on their websites. KMB also has a route app for smartphones.

Lantau Most parts of Lantau Island are served by the **New Lantao Bus** (2984 9848; www.newlantaobus.com). Major bus stations are located in Mui Wo ferry terminal and Tung Chung MTR station.

Minibus

Minibuses are vans with no more than 16 seats. They come in two varieties: red and green.

Red minibuses The red minibuses (HK$4 to HK$22) are cream-coloured with a red roof or stripe, and they pick up and discharge passengers wherever they are hailed or asked to stop along fixed routes. The destination and price are displayed on a card propped up on the windscreen, but these are often only written in Chinese. You usually hand the driver the fare when you get off, and change is given. You can use your Octopus card on certain routes.

Green minibuses Maxicabs (HK$4 to HK$24), commonly known as 'green minibuses', are also cream-coloured but with a green roof or stripe, and they make designated stops. You must put the exact fare in the cash box when you get in or you can use your Octopus card. Two popular routes are the 6 (HK$5.70) from Hankow Rd in Tsim Sha Tsui to Tsim Sha Tsui East and Hung Hom station in Kowloon, and the 1 (HK$9.20) to Victoria Peak from next to Hong Kong station.

Boat

Despite Hong Kong's comprehensive road and rail public-transport system, the territory still relies very much on ferries to get across the harbour and to reach the Outlying Islands. The cross-harbour Star Ferry services are faster and cheaper than buses and the MTR. They're also great fun and afford stunning views. While Lantau can be reached by MTR and bus, for the other Outlying Islands ferries remain the only game in town.

Star Ferry

You can't say you've 'done' Hong Kong until you've taken a ride on a **Star Ferry** (天星小輪; ☑ 2367 7065; www.star-ferry.com.hk; adult HK$2.50-3.40, child HK$1.50-2.10; Ⓜ Hong Kong, exit A2), that wonderful fleet of electric-diesel vessels with names like *Morning Star*, *Celestial Star* and *Twinkling Star*.

There are two Star Ferry routes, but by far the most popular is the one running between Central (Pier 7) and Tsim Sha Tsui (every six to 12 minutes from 6.30am to 11.30pm). Quite frankly, there's no other trip like it in the world. Try to take a trip on a clear night from Kowloon to Central. It's not half as dramatic in the opposite direction.

Star Ferry also links Wan Chai with Tsim Sha Tsui (every eight to 20 minutes from 7.20am to 11pm). The coin-operated turnstiles do not give change, but you can get change from the ticket window or use an Octopus card.

Outlying Islands Ferries

Regular ferry services link the main Outlying Islands to Hong Kong. Fares are reasonable and the ferries are comfortable and usually air-conditioned. They have toilets, and some have a basic bar that serves snacks and cold drinks. The ferries can get very crowded on Saturday afternoon and all day Sunday, especially in the warmer months.

FERRY COMPANIES

Three separate ferry companies operate services to the outlying islands from the ferry terminal in Central. Another, Tsui Wah Ferry Service, offers services to less-visited but scenic spots.

Discovery Bay Transportation Service (☑ 2987 7351; www.hkri.com) Provides fast-speed regular ferry between Central (Pier 3) and Discovery Bay on Lantau Island.

Hong Kong & Kowloon Ferry Co (HKKF; ☑ 2815 6063; www.hkkf.com.hk) Serves destinations on Lamma and Peng Chau only.

New World First Ferry (NWFF; ☑ 2131 8181; www.nwff.com.hk) NWFF boats sail to/from Cheung Chau, Peng Chau and Lantau, and connect all three via an interisland service (regular/deluxe class/fast ferry HK$12.60/19.70/24.60), every 1¾ hours from 6am to 10.50pm.

Tsui Wah Ferry Service (☑ 2527 2513, 2272 2022; www.traway.com.hk) Has slower ferries from Ma Liu Shui (15 minutes' walk from the University MTR station) to Tap Mun Chau and Sai Kung

---

HAILING A CROSS-HARBOUR TAXI

Hailing a cross-harbour taxi can be a frustrating task. There are three main ways to snag one:
➜ Look for a taxi with its lights on, but its 'Out of Service' sign up. This generally means the taxi is looking for a cross-harbour fare.
➜ Find a (rare) cross-harbour taxi stand.
➜ Hail a cab with a sort of 'walk like an Egyptian' gesture, snaking your arm as if in imitation of a wave. Taxis potentially interested in cross-harbour fares will stop to negotiate.

Peninsula (twice daily); from Ma Liu Shui to Tung Ping Chau (only on weekend and public holidays); and from Aberdeen to Po Toi Island (on Tuesday, Thursday, Saturday and Sunday).

Tram

Hong Kong's venerable old trams, operated by **Hongkong Tramways Ltd** (☑ 2548 7102; www.hktramways. com; fares HK$2.30), are tall and narrow double-decker streetcars. They are slow, but they're cheap and a great way to explore the city. Try to get a seat at the front window on the upper deck for a first-class view while rattling through the crowded streets.

For a flat fare of HK$2.30 (dropped in a box beside the driver as you disembark, or use Octopus) you can rattle along as far as you like over 16km of track, 3km of which wends its way into Happy Valley. Trams operate from 6am to midnight and arrive every couple of minutes. There are six routes but they all move on the same tracks along the northern coast of Hong Kong Island. The longest run (Kennedy Town–Shau Kei Wan, with a change at Western Market) takes about 1½ hours.

Peak Tram

The **Peak Tram** (☑2522 0922; www.thepeak.com.hk; Lower Terminus 33 Garden Rd, Central; one-way/return adult HK$28/40, seniors over 65 &

child 3-11yr HK$11/18; ⏱7am-midnight) is not really a tram but a cable-hauled funicular railway that has been scaling the 396m ascent to the highest point on Hong Kong Island since 1888. It is thus the oldest form of public transport in the territory. It's such a steep ride that the floor is angled to help standing passengers stay upright.

The Peak Tram runs every 10 to 15 minutes from 7am to midnight. The lower terminus is behind the St John's Building. The upper tram terminus is in the **Peak Tower** (128 Peak Rd) . Avoid going on Sunday and public holidays when there are usually long queues. Octopus cards can be used.

Between 10am and 11.40pm, open-deck (or air-conditioned) bus 15C (HK$4.20, every 15 to 20 minutes) takes passengers between the bus terminus near Central Ferry Pier 7 and the lower tram terminus.

Taxi

Hong Kong taxis are a bargain compared with those in other world-class cities. With more than 18,000 cruising the streets of the territory, they're easy to flag down, except during rush hour, when it rains or during the driver shift-change period (around 4pm daily).

Taxis are colour-coded:
➧ 'Urban taxis' – those in Kowloon and on Hong Kong Island – are red with silver roofs and they can go anywhere except Lantau.

➧ New Territories taxis are green with white tops.
➧ Lantau taxis are blue.

You need to take a red taxi in New Territories if your destination is in Hong Kong, Kowloon or the city centres of the new towns in New Territories.

Availability When a taxi is available, there should be a red 'For Hire' sign illuminated on the meter that's visible through the windscreen. At night the 'Taxi' sign on the roof will be lit up as well. Taxis will not stop at bus stops or in restricted zones where a yellow line is painted next to the kerb.

Language Some taxi drivers speak English well; others don't know a word of English. It's never a bad idea to have your destination written down in Chinese.

Seat belts The law requires that everyone in a vehicle wears a seat belt. Both driver and passenger(s) will be fined if stopped by the police and not wearing a seat belt, and most drivers will gently remind you to buckle up before proceeding.

Extra fees There is a luggage fee of HK$5 per bag, but (depending on the size) not all drivers insist on this payment. It costs an extra HK$4 to HK$5 to book a taxi by telephone. There are no extra late-night charges and no extra passenger charges. Passengers must pay the toll if a taxi goes through the many Hong Kong harbour or

TAXI FARES

TYPE OF TAXI	FIRST 2KM (HK$)	COST PER EVERY ADDITIONAL 200M & MINUTE OF WAITING
Urban taxi (red)	22	HK$1.60 (HK$1 if fare exceeds HK$78)
New Territories taxi (green)	18.50	HK$1.40 (HK$1 if fare exceeds HK$60.50)
Lantau taxi (blue)	17	HK$1.40 (HK$1.20 if fare exceeds HK$143)

mountain tunnels or uses the Lantau Link to Tung Chung or the airport. Though the Cross-Harbour Tunnel costs only HK$10, you'll have to pay HK$20 if, say, you take a Hong Kong taxi from Hong Kong Island to Kowloon. If you manage to find a Kowloon taxi returning 'home', you'll pay only HK$10. (It works the other way round as well, of course.)

Paying Try to carry smaller bills and coins; most drivers are hesitant to make change for anything over HK$100.

Tipping You can tip up to 10%, but most Hong Kong people just leave the little brown coins and a dollar or two.

Complaints Though most Hong Kong taxi drivers are scrupulously honest, if you feel you've been ripped off, take down the taxi or driver's licence number (usually displayed on the sun visor in front) and call the **Transport Complaints Unit hotline** (☏2889 9999) or the **Transport Department hotline** (☏2804 2600) to lodge a complaint. Be sure to have all the relevant details: when, where and how much.

Lost property If you leave something behind in a taxi, ring the **Road Co-op Lost & Found hotline** (☏187 2920); most drivers turn in lost property.

Car & Motorcycle

Hong Kong's maze of one-way streets and dizzying expressways isn't for the faint-hearted. Traffic is heavy and finding a parking space is difficult and very expensive. If you are determined to see Hong Kong under your own steam, do yourself a favour and rent a car with a driver.

Road rules Vehicles drive on the left-hand side of the road in Hong Kong, as in the UK, Australia and Macau, but *not* in mainland China. Seat belts must be worn by the driver and all passengers, in both the front and back seats. Police are strict and give out traffic tickets at the drop of a hat.

Drivers licence Hong Kong allows most foreigners over the age of 18 to drive for up to 12 months with a valid licence from home. It's still a good idea to carry an International Driving Permit (IDP) as well.

Hire

Car-hire firms accept IDPs or driving licences from your home country. Drivers must usually be at least 25 years of age.

Ace Hire Car (☏2572 7663, 2893 0541; www.acehirecar.com.hk; 49-51A Sing Woo Rd, Flat F, 1st fl, Nam Wing Building, Happy Valley; ☐1 from Des Voeux Rd Central) Hires chauffeur-driven Mercedes Benz for HK$250 per hour (minimum two to five hours, depending on location).

Avis (☏2890 6988; www.avis.com.hk; 183 Queen's Rd E, Hopewell Centre, Wan Chai; Ⓜ Wan Chai, exit B2) Hires a Corolla/Camry/BMW for a day/weekend/week for HK$930/1200/1500, nearly double on weekends. A chauffeur-driven Toyota is HK$600 per hour.

Bicycle

Cycling in urbanised Kowloon or Hong Kong Island would be suicide, but in the quiet areas of the islands (including southern Hong Kong Island) and the New Territories, a bike can be a lovely way to get around. It's more recreational than a form of transport, though – the hilly terrain will slow you down (unless you're mountain biking). Be advised that bicycle-hire shops and kiosks tend to run out of bikes early on weekends if the weather is good.

TOURS

Despite its size, Hong Kong has a profusion of organised tours. There are tours available to just about anywhere in the territory and they can make good a option if you only have a short time in Hong Kong or don't want to deal with public transport. Some tours are standard excursions covering major sights on Hong Kong Island, such as the Peak and Hollywood Rd, while other tours take you on harbour cruises, out to the islands or through the New Territories.

Some of the best tours are offered by the **Hong Kong Tourism Board** (HKTB; ☏2508 1234; www.discoverhongkong.com), and tours run by individual companies can usually be booked at any HKTB branch.

Harbour Tours

The easiest way to see the full extent of Victoria Harbour from sea level is to join a circular **Star Ferry Harbour Tour** (☏2118 6201; www.starferry.com.hk/tour), of which there are a number of different options. Most of the tours depart from the Star Ferry Pier in Tsim Sha Tsui, but there are also departures from the piers at Central and Wan Chai; see the website for details.

Single daytime round trip Departs hourly between 2.05pm and 7.05pm daily; costs HK$85/77 adult/concession (children aged three to 12 years and seniors over 65).

Night round trip departs at 6.55pm and 8.55pm and is HK$160/144 for adult/concession.

Symphony of Lights Harbour Cruise Departs at 7.15pm or 7.55pm depending on the season and takes in the nightly sound-and-light show over Victoria Harbour; it costs HK$180/162.

If you prefer fancier harbour tours, some operators offer tours with drinks, food and even buffet!

Hong Kong Ferry Group (☑2802 2886; www.cruise.com.hk; adult/child HK$330/230) Offers two harbour cruises in a large boat with buffet dinner and live band performance).

Water Tours (☑2926 3868; www.watertours.com.hk) Six different tours of the harbour, as well as dinner and cocktail cruises, are available. Tours include the Morning Harbour & Noon Day Gun Firing Cruise (adult/child 2-12 yrs HK$250/160), the Harbour Lights (adult/child HK$310/220) and the Lei Yue Mun Seafood Village Dinner Cruise (adult/child HK$510/480).

Nature Tours

Eco Travel (☑3105 0767; www.ecotravel.hk) This eco-travel company offers tours exploring Hong Kong's fishing and ocean culture, wetlands tours, a nature bike tour, and a trip to the Geopark of the northern New Territories. Some are only in Cantonese – check ahead regarding English availability.

Hong Kong Dolphinwatch (香港海豚觀察; ☑2984

1414; www.hkdolphinwatch.com; 15th fl, Middle Block, 1528A Star House, 3 Salisbury Rd, Tsim Sha Tsui; adult/child HK$420/210; ⊙cruises Wed, Fri & Sun) Hong Kong Dolphinwatch was founded in 1995 to raise awareness of Hong Kong's wonderful pink dolphins and promote responsible ecotourism. It offers 2½-hour cruises to see them in their natural habitat every Wednesday, Friday and Sunday year-round (adult/child HK$420/210). Guides assemble in the lobby of the Kowloon Hotel Hong Kong (九龍酒店; ☑2929 2888; www.thekowloonhotel.com; 19-21 Nathan Rd, Tsim Sha Tsui; Ⓜ Tsim Sha Tsui, exit E) in Tsim Sha Tsui at 9am for the bus to Tung Chung via the Tsing Ma Bridge, from where the boat departs; the tours return at 1pm. About 97% of the cruises result in the sighting of at least one dolphin; if none are spotted, passengers are offered a free trip. Between 100 and 200 misnamed Chinese white dolphins (*Sousa chinensis*) – they are actually bubble-gum pink – inhabit the coastal waters around Hong Kong, finding the brackish waters of the Pearl River estuary to be the perfect habitat. Unfortunately these glorious mammals, which are also called Indo-Pacific humpback dolphins, are being threatened by environmental pollution, and their numbers are dwindling.

Kayak and Hike (☑9300 5197; www.kayak-and-hike.com) The seven-hour Sai Kung Geopark kayak tour provides an exciting option for exploring the beauty of Sai Kung. It takes you to a kayak base at nearby Bluff Island in a junk, from where you paddle to a beach to enjoy swimming and snorkelling. Departs 8.45am at Sai Kung old pier (HK$700

per person). You need to pack your lunch.

Walk Hong Kong (☑9187 8641; www.walkhongkong.com) Offers a range of hiking tours to some of the most beautiful places in Hong Kong – for example, deserted beaches in Sai Kung (per person HK$800, 8½ hours), Dragon's Back in Shek O (per person HK$500, four hours), hexagonal volcanic column wall in Sai Kung (HK$800, 8½ hours) – as well as half-day local market tours (HK$450).

City & Culture Tours

Big Foot Tours (☑6075 2727; www.bigfoottour.com) Small group tours tailored to your interests really get behind the scenes of daily Hong Kong life. Itineraries can focus on food (wanna try snake soup?), architecture, nature, or whatever strikes your fancy, and guides are full of interesting facts. Four-hour tours are about HK$500 to HK$800 per person, depending on group size.

Big Bus Company (☑2723 2108; www.bigbustours.com; adult/child 24hr HK$425/340) A good way to get your bearings in the city is on the hop-on, hop-off, open-topped double-deckers. Three tours are available: the Kowloon Route takes in much of the Tsim Sha Tsui and Hung Hom waterfront; the Hong Kong Island Route explores Central, Admiralty, Wan Chai and Causeway Bay; and the Green Tour goes to Stanley Market and Aberdeen.

Heliservices (☑2802 0200; www.heliservices.com.hk) If you hanker to see Hong Kong from on high (and hang the expense), Heliservices has chartered Aerospatiale Squirrels for up to five passengers. A quickie harbour tour is HK$1200 per seat, while the 15-minute Hong Kong skyline flight is HK$8500.

Splendid Tours & Travel (☑2316 2151; www.splendid. hk) Runs the Sai Kung coastal tour, a six-hour cruise that explores the beautiful coastline, peaceful waters and diverse geological formations of Sai

Kung, the 'back garden of Hong Kong'. It includes a stop at the Unesco World Heritage site, Hung Shing Temple, on Kau Sai Chau. Departs at 8.20am at the Excelsior Hotel at 281 Gloucester Rd, Causeway Bay (HK$720 per person).

Sky Bird Tours (☑2736 2282; www.skybird.com.hk) A traditional lifestyle tour. Learn all about taichi, feng shui and Chinese tea with a four-hour

tour (HK$298 per person). Tours depart 7.30am from the Excelsior Hotel in Causeway Bay and 7.45am from the Salisbury YMCA at 41 Salisbury Rd, Tsim Sha Tsui on Monday, Wednesday and Friday.

Gray Line (☑2368 7111; www.grayline.com.hk; adult/child 3-11yr from HK$560/460) Has a one-day tour taking in Man Mo Temple, Victoria Peak, Aberdeen and Stanley Market.

Macau Transport

GETTING TO MACAU

Most travellers arrive in Macau by ferry from Hong Kong. If you are coming from mainland China, you can take the ferry or a bus from Guǎngdōng, or fly from select cities.

Macau International Airport is connected to a limited number of destinations in Asia. If you are coming from outside Asia and destined for Macau, your best option is to fly to Hong Kong International Airport and take a ferry to Macau without going through Hong Kong customs.

Nationals of Australia, Canada, the EU, New Zealand and most other countries (but not US citizens) can purchase their China visas at Zhūhǎi on the border, but it will ultimately save you time if you get one in advance. These are available in Hong Kong (p314) or in Macau from **China Travel Service** (中國旅行社, CTS; Map p222; ☑2870 0888; www.cts.com.mo; Nam Kwong Bldg, 207 Avenida do Dr Rodrigo Rodrigues; ☉9am-6pm), usually in one day.

Sea

Ferry and catamaran tickets can be booked in advance at the ferry terminals, through travel agencies or online. You can also buy tickets on the spot, though advance booking is recommended if you travel on weekends or public holidays as tickets are often in high demand. There is a standby queue at the pier for passengers wanting to travel before their ticketed sailing. You need to arrive at the pier at least 15 minutes before departure, but you should allow 30 minutes because of occasional long queues at immigration.

You are limited to 10kg of carry-on luggage in economy class, but oversized or overweight bags can be checked in.

To/From Hong Kong

The vast majority of travellers make their way from Hong Kong to Macau by ferry. The journey takes just an hour and there are frequent departures throughout the day, with reduced service between midnight and 7am.

Most ferries depart from the **Hong Kong–Macau Ferry Terminal** (Map p368; Shun Tak Centre, 200 Connaught Rd, Sheung Wan) on Hong Kong Island or the **China Ferry Terminal** (中港碼頭; Map p378; China Hong Kong City, 33 Canton Rd, Tsim Sha Tsui) in Kowloon, and arrive at the Macau Maritime Ferry Terminal (in the outer harbour) or the **Taipa Temporary Ferry Terminal** (☑2885 0595).

TurboJet (Map p368; ☑2859 3333; www.turbojet.

com.hk) has regular departures from the Hong Kong–Macau Ferry Terminal (every 15 minutes) and the China Ferry Terminal (every 30 minutes) to Macau from 7am to midnight, and less frequent service after midnight. Fares are HK$159/309 (economy/superclass), and it costs about 10% more on weekends and 20% more for night service (6.15pm to 6.30am).

CotaiJet (☑2885 0595; www.cotaijet.com.mo) has high-speed catamarans connecting the Hong Kong–Macau Ferry Terminal and the Taipa Temporary Ferry Terminal every half-hour between 7.30am and midnight. Fares are HK$160/213 (Cotai class/Cotai first) and it costs about 10% more on weekends and 20% more for night service (after 6pm). Free shuttles at the ferry terminal in Taipa will take you to destinations along the Cotai Strip.

To/From Mainland China

TurboJet (Map p368; ☑2859 3333; www.turbojet.com.hk) has 11 departures from the Macau Maritime Ferry Terminal daily to the port of Shékǒu in Shēnzhèn between 9.45am and 8.45pm. The journey takes one hour and costs MOP$222/351 (economy/super class). Eleven ferries return from Shékǒu between 8.15am and

7.30pm. TurboJet also has nine departures to Shēnzhèn airport (MOP$222/377, one hour) from 9.40am to 7.30pm and two departures to Nánshā in Guǎngzhōu (MOP$180/280) at 10.45am and 4.15pm.

Yuet Tung Shipping Co (Map p226; ☑2877 4478; www.ytmacau.com/index. php) has ferries connecting Macau (Taipa Temporary Ferry Terminal) with Shékǒu (MOP$222). The boat departs from Macau at 11am, 2pm, 5.30pm, 6.30pm and 8.30pm and takes 1½ hours. Ferries also leave from the Macau Maritime Ferry Terminal for Wānzǎi in Zhūhǎi (MOP$30). Departures are every half-hour between 8am and 4.15pm, returning half an hour later.

Land

Macau is an easy gateway by land into mainland China. Simply take bus 3, 5 or 9 to the **border gate** (關閘; Portas do Cerco; ☉7am to midnight) and walk across. A second – and much less busy crossing – is the **Cotai Frontier Post** (☉9am-8pm) on the causeway linking Taipa and Coloane, which allows visitors to cross the Lotus Flower Bridge by shuttle bus (MOP$4) to Héngqín in Zhūhǎi. Buses 15, 21 and 26 will drop you off at the crossing.

If you want to travel further afield in China, buses run by **Kee Kwan Motor Road Co** (歧關車路有限公司; ☑2893 3888; ☉7.15am-9pm) leave the bus station at the border gate. Buses for Guǎngzhōu (MOP$77, 2½ hours) depart every 15 minutes or so, and for Zhōngshān (MOP$40, one hour) every 20 minutes between 8am and 6.30pm. There are many buses to Guǎngzhōu (MOP$150) and Dōngguǎn (MOP$150) from Macau International Airport.

Air

There are regular flights between Macau and Běijīng, Hángzhōu, Nánjīng, Níngbō, Shànghǎi and Xiàmén and less frequent flights to Chéngdū, Chóngqìng, Fúzhōu, Héféi, Nánníng, Tàiyuán, Wǔhàn and Wúxī in China. Check www.macau-airport.com for timetable and airline information.

Macau International Airport

Located on Taipa Island, **Macau International Airport** (☑2886 1111; www. macau-airport.com) is only 20 minutes from the city centre. It has frequent services to destinations including Bangkok, Chiang Mai, Kaohsiung, Kuala Lumpur, Manila, Osaka, Seoul, Singapore, Taipei and Tokyo.

If you are flying into Macau, ask your hotel if it has a pick-up service – many midrange and all luxury hotels do. A taxi from the airport to the town centre should cost about MOP$60, plus a surcharge of MOP$5. Large bags cost an extra MOP$3.

The airport bus AP1 (MOP$4.20) leaves the airport and zips around Taipa before heading to the Macau Maritime Ferry Terminal and the border gate. The bus stops at a number of major hotels en route and departs every five to 12 minutes from 6.30am to midnight. Other services run to Praça de Ferreira do Amaral (MT1 and MT2) and Coloane (bus 26).

Helicopter

Travel to Macau by helicopter is a viable option and is becoming increasingly popular for residents and visitors alike. **Sky Shuttle** (☑in Hong Kong 2108 9898; www.skyshuttlehk.com) runs a 15-minute helicopter shuttle service between Macau and Hong Kong (HK$4100, tax included) with daily flights

leaving every half-hour between 9am and 11pm. Flights arrive and depart in Macau from the roof of the Macau Maritime Ferry Terminal. In Hong Kong, departures are from the helipad atop the ferry pier that is linked to **Shun Tak Centre** (信德中心; Map p368; 200 Connaught Rd Central, Sheung Wan, Hong Kong) in Sheung Wan.

Sky Shuttle also has a helicopter shuttle linking Macau with Shēnzhèn six times a day from 10.15am to 7.45pm (11.45am to 8.30pm from Shēnzhèn) for HK$5800. The trip takes about 15 minutes.

GETTING AROUND MACAU

Public Transport

Public buses and minibuses run by **TCM** (☑2885 0060; www.tcm.com.mo), **Transmac** (☑2827 1122; www.transmac. com.mo) and **Reolian** (☑2877 7888; www.reolian.com.mo) operate from 6am until shortly after midnight. Fares – MOP$3.20 on the peninsula, MOP$4.20 to Taipa Village, MOP$5 to Coloane Village and MOP$6.40 to Hác Sá beach – are dropped into a box upon entry (exact change needed), or you can pay with a Macau Pass, which can be purchased from various supermarkets and convenience stores. The card costs MOP$130 at first purchase, which includes a refundable deposit of MOP$30. A minimum of MOP$50 is required to add money to the card each time. Expect buses to be very crowded.

The *Macau Tourist Map* has a full list of bus company routes and it's worth picking one up from one of the Macau Government Tourist Office (MGTO) outlets. You can also check the routes online. The two most useful buses on the peninsula are buses 3 and 3A, which run between the ferry terminal and the city centre, near the post office. Both continue up to the border crossing with the mainland, as does bus 5, which can be boarded along Avenida Almeida Ribeiro. Bus 12 runs from the ferry terminal, past the Lisboa Hotel and then up to Lou Lim Ioc Garden and Kun Iam Temple. The best services to Taipa and Coloane are buses 21A, 25 and 26A. Buses to the airport are AP1, 26, MT1 and MT2.

Taxi

Flag fall is MOP$15 for the first 1.6km and MOP$1.50 for each additional 230m.

There is a MOP$5 surcharge to go to Coloane; travelling between Taipa and Coloane is MOP$2 extra. For yellow radio taxis, call ☎2851 9519 or ☎2893 9939.

Car & Motorcycle

The streets of Macau Peninsula are a gridlock of cars and mopeds that will cut you off at every turn. The following companies offer rentals as well as cars with drivers:

Avis Rent A Car (Map p222;☎2872 6571; www. avis.com.mo; Room 1022, Ground fl, Macau Maritime Ferry Terminal; ☺10am-1pm & 2-4pm) Hires out cars from

MOP$800 to MOP$1600 per day (can be 10% to 20% more expensive on weekends). Chauffeur-driven services start from MOP$360 per hour. It also has an office at the Grand Lapa Hotel car park (open 8am to 10pm).

Burgeon Rent A Car (Map p222;☎2828 3399; www. burgeonrentacar.com; Shops O, P & Q, Block 2, La Baie Du Noble, Avenida Do Nordeste) Hires Kia cars with the cheapest model starting at MOP$450 for the first nine hours. The cheapest car with chauffeur costs MOP$230 per hour with a minimum of two hours.

Hong Kong Directory A–Z

Customs Regulations

➡ The duty-free allowance for visitors arriving in Hong Kong (including those coming from Macau and mainland China) is 19 cigarettes (or one cigar or 25g of tobacco) and 1L of spirits.

➡ There are few other import taxes, and you can bring in reasonable quantities of almost anything.

Discount Cards

Hostel Card

A Hostelling International (HI) card, or the equivalent, is of relatively limited use in Hong Kong, as there are only seven HI-affiliated hostels here, and most are in remote locations in the New Territories. If you arrive without a card and want to stay in one of these hostels, you can apply for one from the **Hong Kong Youth Hostels Association** (HKYHA; ☑2788 1638; www.yha.org.hk; Sham Mong Rd, Shop 118, 1st fl, Fu Cheong Shopping Centre, Sham Shui Po, Kowloon; HI card under/over 18yr HK$70/150; ⊙9am-7pm Mon-Fri, 10am-5pm Sat; ⓂNam Cheong, exit A) or upon arrival at the hostel.

Seniors Card

Many attractions in Hong Kong offer discounts for people aged over 60 or 65. Most of Hong Kong's museums are either free or half-price for those over 60, and most forms of public transport offer a 50% discount to anyone over 65. A passport or ID with a photo should be sufficient proof of age.

Student, Youth & Teacher Cards

The International Student Identity Card (ISIC, www.wysetc.org), a plastic ID-style card with your photograph, provides discounts on some forms of transport and cheaper admission to museums and other sights. If you're aged under 26 but not a student, you can apply for an International Youth Travel Card (IYTC) issued by the Federation of International Youth Travel Organisations (FIYTO), which gives much the same discounts and benefits. Teachers can apply for the International Teacher Identity Card (ITIC).

Hong Kong Student Travel, based at **Sincerity Travel** (永安旅遊; Map p378; ☑2730 2800; 3 Salisbury Rd, rm 833-834, Star House, Tsim Sha Tsui; ⊙9.30am-8pm Mon-Sat, noon-6pm Sun), can issue you any of these cards instantly for HK$100. Make sure you bring your student ID or other credentials along with you.

HONG KONG MUSEUMS PASS

This pass allows multiple entries to seven of Hong Kong's museum. Passes valid for seven consecutive days cost HK$30. They're available from **Hong Kong Tourism Board** (HKTB; ☑2508 1234; www.discoverhongkong.com) outlets and participating museums. Note that these seven museums are all free on Wednesdays.

➡ Hong Kong Museum of Coastal Defence (Hong Kong Island)

➡ Dr Sun Yat-sen Museum (Hong Kong Island)

➡ Hong Kong Science Museum (Kowloon)

➡ Hong Kong Museum of History (Kowloon)

➡ Hong Kong Museum of Art (Kowloon)

➡ Hong Kong Space Museum, excluding Space Theatre (Kowloon)

➡ Hong Kong Heritage Museum (New Territories)

Electricity

220V/50Hz

Emergency

Police, Fire and Ambulance (☎999)

Gay & Lesbian Travellers

Those travelling to Hong Kong will find a small but vibrant and growing gay-and-lesbian scene in the Special Administrative Region (SAR). It may not compete with the likes of London or Sydney, but Hong Kong has come a long way all the same, and the annual **Pride Parade** in November now attracts rainbow flag-wavers by the thousands.

In 1991 the Crimes (Amendment) Ordinance removed criminal penalties for homosexual acts between consenting adults over the age of 18. Since then gay groups have been lobbying for legislation to address the issue of discrimination on the grounds of sexual orientation. Despite these changes, however, Hong Kong Chinese society remains fairly conservative, and it can still be

risky for gays and lesbians to come out to family members or their employers.

Contact **Pink Alliance** (www.tcjm.org) for information about LGBTQ culture and events in Hong Kong. Check out the latest events in Hong Kong's first free gay lifestyle magazine, *Dim Sum Magazine* (www.dimsum-hk.com).

Health

The occasional avian- or swine-flu outbreak notwithstanding, health conditions in the region are good. Travellers have a low risk of contracting infectious diseases compared to much of Asia. The health system is generally excellent. However, observe good personal and food hygiene and take antimosquito measures to prevent infectious diseases. If your health insurance doesn't cover you for medical expenses abroad, consider supplemental insurance.

Diseases

DENGUE FEVER

Dengue is a viral disease transmitted by mosquitoes, and there are occasional outbreaks in Hong Kong. Unlike the malaria mosquito, the *Aedes aegypti* mosquito, which transmits the dengue virus, is most active during the day, and is found mainly in urban areas, in and around human dwellings. Signs and symptoms of dengue fever include a sudden onset of high fever, headache, joint and muscle pains (hence its old name, 'breakbone fever') and nausea and vomiting. A rash of small red spots sometimes appears three to four days after the onset of fever.

You should seek medical attention as soon as possible if you think you may be infected. A blood test can exclude malaria and indicate the possibility of dengue fever. There is no specific treatment for dengue. Aspi-

rin should be avoided, as it increases the risk of haemorrhaging. The best prevention is to avoid mosquito bites at all times by covering up, and using insect repellents containing the compound DEET and mosquito nets.

GIARDIA

This is a parasite that often jumps on board when you have diarrhoea. It then causes a more prolonged illness with intermittent diarrhoea or loose stools, bloating, fatigue and some nausea. There may be a metallic taste in the mouth. Avoiding potentially contaminated foods and always washing your hands can help prevent giardia.

HEPATITIS A

Hepatitis A is a virus common in Hong Kong and Macau, and is transmitted through contaminated water and shellfish.

HEPATITIS B

While this is common in the area, it can only be transmitted by unprotected sex, sharing needles, treading on a discarded needle, or receiving contaminated blood in very remote areas of China.

INFLUENZA

Hong Kong has a bad flu season over the winter months from December to March. Symptoms include a cold (runny nose etc) with a high fever and aches and pains. You should wash your hands frequently, avoid anybody you know who has the flu and consider getting a flu shot before you travel.

Environmental Hazards

MOSQUITOES

These are prevalent in Hong Kong. You should always use insect repellent during warm and hot weather and if you're bitten, use hydrocortisone cream to reduce swelling.

CENTIPEDES

Lamma Island is home to large red centipedes, which

have a poisonous bite that causes swelling and discomfort in most cases, but can be more dangerous (and supposedly in very rare cases deadly) for young children.

WILD BOARS & DOGS
Wild boars and aggressive dogs are a minor hazard in some of the more remote parts of the New Territories. Wild boars are shy and retiring most of the time but are dangerous when they feel threatened, so give them a wide berth and avoid disturbing thick areas of undergrowth.

SNAKES
There are many snakes in Hong Kong, and some are deadly, but you are unlikely to encounter any. Still, always take care when bushwalking, particularly on Lamma and Lantau Islands. Go straight to a public hospital if bitten; private doctors do not stock antivenene.

Recommended Immunisations
There are no required vaccinations for entry into Hong Kong or Macau unless you will be travelling to the mainland or elsewhere in the region.

Water
Hong Kong tap water conforms to World Health Organization standards and is considered safe to drink, though many locals prefer bottled for reasons of flavour and prestige.

Internet Access
Getting online in Hong Kong – long since fully cabled with broadband – should be a breeze.

Free wi-fi Increasingly available in hotels and public areas, including the airport, public libraries, key cultural and recreational centres, large parks, major MTR stations (eg Central

and Causeway Bay), shopping malls and an increasing number of cafes and bars. You can also get a free 60-minute PCCW Wi-Fi pass, available at HKTB visitor centres.

PCCW account You can also purchase a PCCW account online or at convenience stores and PCCW stores and access the internet via any of PCCW's 7000-plus wi-fi hot spots in Hong Kong. Buy a 3G rechargeable SIM card from the shops of **PCCW** (www2.pccwmobile. com), **SmarTone** (www. smartone.com) and other service providers. The card price is similar and can offer phone and data for as little as HK$28 per day.

If you don't have a computer there are a few options where you can log on:

Central Library (Map p374; 3150 1234; www.hkpl. gov.hk; 66 Causeway Rd, Causeway Bay; 10am-9pm Thu-Tue, 1-9pm Wed) Free access.

Pacific Coffee Company (Map p366; 2537 1688; www. pacificcoffee.com; 43 Lyndhurst Tce, ground fl, the Workstation, Central; 7am-11pm Mon-Wed, to 1am Thu-Sat, 8am-11pm Sun) Free access with purchase; this is one of scores of branches in Hong Kong.

Left Luggage
MTR train and ferry Left-luggage lockers are in major stations, including the Hung Hom station; the West Tower of the Shun Tak Centre in Sheung Wan, from where the Macau ferry departs; and the China ferry terminal in Tsim Sha Tsui. Luggage costs between HK$20 and HK$30 for each hour (depending on the locker size).
Airport The Hong Kong Airport Express station **left-luggage office** (2261 0110; level

3, Terminal 2; per hr/day HK$12/140; 5.30am-1.30am) charges per item. Generally the machines don't use keys but spit out a numbered ticket when you have deposited your money and closed the door. You have to punch in this number when you retrieve your bag, so keep it somewhere safe or write the number down.

Accommodation Most hotels and even some guesthouses and hostels have left-luggage rooms and will let you leave your gear behind, even if you've already checked out and won't be staying on your return. There is usually a charge for this service, so be sure to enquire first.

Legal Matters
➡ Carry your passport all the time. As a visitor, you are required to show your identification if the police require it.

➡ *All* forms of narcotics are illegal in Hong Kong. Whether it's heroin, opium, 'ice', ecstasy or marijuana, the law makes no distinction. If police or customs officials find dope or even smoking equipment in your possession, you can expect to be arrested immediately.

➡ If you run into legal trouble, contact the **Legal Aid Department** (2537 7677; 24hr hotline), which provides residents and visitors with representation, subject to a means and merits test.

Maps
Most popular trails have maps at the starting point and bilingual signs along the trails. If you're heading for any of Hong Kong's four major trails, you can get a copy of the trail map produced by the Country & Marine Parks Authority, which is available

at the Map Publication Centres.

Map Publication Centre North Point (☑2231 3187; 333 Java Rd, 23rd fl, North Point Government Offices; ☺8.45am-5.30pm Mon-Fri)

Map Publication Centre Yau Ma Tei (Map p382; ☑2780 0981; 382 Nathan Rd; ☺8.45am-5.30pm Mon-Fri)

Medical Services

The standard of medical care in Hong Kong is generally excellent but expensive. Always take out travel insurance before you travel. Healthcare is divided into public and private, and there is no interaction between the two. Public and private hospitals with 24-hour accident and emergency departments are listed following.

Clinics

There are many English-speaking general practitioners, specialists and dentists in Hong Kong, who can be found through your consulate, a private hospital or the *Yellow Pages*. If money is tight, take yourself to the nearest public-hospital emergency room and be prepared to wait. The general enquiry number for hospitals is ☑2300 6555.

Hospitals & Emergency Rooms

In the case of an emergency, all ambulances (☑999) will take you to a government-run public hospital where, as a visitor, you will be required to pay a hefty fee for using emergency services. Treatment is guaranteed in any case; people who cannot pay immediately will be billed later. While the emergency care is excellent, you may wish to transfer to a private hospital once you are stable.

HONG KONG ISLAND
Ruttonjee Hospital (律敦治醫院; Map p372;☑2291 2000; 266 Queen's Rd East, Wan Chai) Public.

Queen Mary Hospital (瑪麗醫院;☑2255 3838; 102 Pok Fu Lam Rd, Pok Fu Lam) Public.

KOWLOON
Hong Kong Baptist Hospital (瑪嘉烈醫院; ☑2339 8888; 222 Waterloo Rd, Kowloon Tong) Private.

Princess Margaret Hospital (瑪嘉烈醫院;☑2990 1111; 2-10 Princess Margaret Hospital Rd, Lai Chi Kok) Public.

Queen Elizabeth Hospital (伊利沙伯醫院; Map p382; ☑2958 8888; 30 Gascoigne Rd, Yau Ma Tei) Public hospital in Kowloon.

NEW TERRITORIES
Prince of Wales Hospital (威爾斯親王醫院; Map p185;☑2632 2211; 30-32 Ngan Shing St, Sha Tin) Public.

Pharmacies

➜ Pharmacies are abundant; they bear a red-and-white cross outside and there should be a registered pharmacist available inside.

➜ In Hong Kong many medications can be bought over the counter without a prescription, but always check it is a known brand and that the expiry date is valid.

➜ Birth-control pills, pads, tampons and condoms are available over the counter in pharmacies, as well as in stores such as Watson's and Mannings.

Money

The local currency is the Hong Kong dollar (HK$), which is divided into 100 cents. Bills are issued in denominations of HK$10, HK$20, HK$50, HK$100,

HK$500 and HK$1000. There are little copper coins worth 10¢, 20¢ and 50¢, silver-coloured HK$1, HK$2 and HK$5 coins, and a nickel and bronze HK$10 coin.

Three local banks issue notes: HSBC (formerly the Hongkong & Shanghai Banking Corporation), the Standard Chartered Bank and the Bank of China (all but the HK$10 bill).

ATMs

➜ Automated Teller Machines (ATMs) can be found almost everywhere in Hong Kong and are almost always linked up to international money systems such as Cirrus, Maestro, Plus and Visa Electron.

➜ Some HSBC so-called Electronic Money machines offer cash withdrawal facilities for Visa and MasterCard holders.

➜ American Express (Amex) cardholders have access to Jetco ATMs and can withdraw local currency and travellers cheques at Express Cash ATMs in town.

Changing Money

Hong Kong has no currency controls; locals and foreigners can bring, send in or take out as much money as they like.

Banks Hong Kong banks generally offer the best rates, though two of the biggest ones (Standard Chartered Bank and Hang Seng Bank) levy a HK$50 commission for each transaction for those who don't hold accounts. Avoid HSBC, where this charge is HK$100. If you're changing the equivalent of several hundred US dollars or more, the exchange rate improves, which usually makes up for the fee.

Moneychangers Licensed moneychangers, such as Chequepoint, abound in touristed areas, including

Tsim Sha Tsui. While they are convenient (usually open on Sundays, holidays and late into the evenings) and take no commission per se, the less-than-attractive exchange rates offered are equivalent to a 5% commission. These rates are clearly posted, though if you're changing several hundred US dollars or more you might be able to bargain for a better rate. Before the actual exchange is made, the moneychanger is required by law to give you a form to sign that clearly shows the amount due to you, the exchange rate and any service charges. Try to avoid the exchange counters at the airport or in hotels, which offer some of the worst rates in Hong Kong.

Black market No foreign-currency black market exists in Hong Kong. If anyone on the street does approach you to change money, assume it's a scam.

Credit Cards

Accepted cards The most widely accepted credit cards in Hong Kong are Visa, MasterCard, Amex, Diners Club and JCB – and pretty much in that order. It may be an idea to carry two, just in case.

Surcharge Some shops in Hong Kong add a surcharge to offset the commission charged by credit companies, which can range from 2.5% to 7%. In theory, this is prohibited by the credit companies, but to get around this many shops will offer a 5% discount if you pay with cash.

Lost or stolen cards If a card is lost or stolen, you must inform both the **police** (☏2527 7177) and the issuing company as soon as possible; otherwise, you may have to pay for the purchases that have been racked up on your card. Some

24-hour numbers for cancelling cards include the following:
American Express (☏2811 6122)
Diners Club (☏2860 1888)
MasterCard (☏800 966 677)
Visa (☏800 900 782) Might be able to help you should you lose your Visa card, but in general you must deal with the issuing bank in the case of an emergency.

Tipping

Hong Kong isn't particularly conscious of tipping and there is no obligation to tip, say, taxi drivers; just round the fare up, or you can throw in a dollar or two more.

Porters It's almost mandatory to tip hotel porters HK$10 to HK$20, and for porters at the airport, HK$2 to HK$5 a suitcase is normally expected. The porters putting your bags on a push cart at Hong Kong or Kowloon Airport Express station do not expect a gratuity, though; it's all part of the service.

Hotels and restaurants Most hotels and many restaurants add a 10% service charge to the bill. Feel free to leave a few dollars extra if the service has been good. If there is no service charge, whether or not you tip depends on the type of restaurant. Tipping is not expected in local, casual restaurants like noodle shops, but 10% is the norm in upscale or Western-style restaurants.

Travellers Cheques & Cards

➡ Travellers cheques and their modern equivalent, ATM-style cards that can be credited with cash in advance, offer protection from theft but are becoming less common due to the preponderance of ATMs.
➡ Most banks will cash travellers cheques, and they all

charge a fee, often irrespective of whether you are an account holder or not.
➡ If any cheques are lost or stolen, contact the issuing office or the nearest branch of the issuing agency immediately. **American Express** (☏3002 1276) can usually arrange replacement cheques within 24 hours.

Newspapers & Magazines

➡ The main English-language newspaper in the city is the daily broadsheet *South China Morning Post* (www.scmp.com), which has always toed the government line, both before and after the handover. It has the largest circulation and is read by more Hong Kong Chinese than expatriates.
➡ The livelier and slightly punchier tabloid *Hong Kong Standard* (www.thestandard.com.hk), published Monday to Saturday (weekend edition), is harder to find.
➡ The Běijīng mouthpiece *China Daily* (www.chinadaily.com.cn) also prints a Hong Kong English-language edition of its paper.
➡ Hong Kong has its share of English-language periodicals, including a slew of homegrown (and Asian-focused) business-related magazines. *Time*, *Newsweek* and the *Economist* are all available in their current editions.

Opening Hours

The following list summarises standard opening hours:
Banks 9am to 4.30pm or 5.30pm Monday to Friday, 9am to 12.30pm Saturday
Offices 9am to 5.30pm or 6pm Monday to Friday (lunch hour 1pm to 2pm)

Museums 10am to between 5pm and 9pm; closed Monday, Tuesday or Thursday

Restaurants 11am to 3pm and 6pm to 11pm

Shops Usually 10am to 8pm

Post

Hong Kong Post ([☏]2921 2222; www.hongkongpost. com) is generally excellent; local letters are often delivered the same day they are sent and there is Saturday delivery. The staff at most post offices speak English, and the green mail boxes are clearly marked in English.

Receiving Mail

If a letter is addressed c/o Poste Restante, GPO Hong Kong, it will go to the GPO on Hong Kong Island. Pick it up at counter No 29 from 8am to 6pm Monday to Saturday only. If you want your letters to go to Kowloon, have them addressed as follows: c/o Poste Restante, Tsim Sha Tsui Post Office, 10 Middle Rd, Tsim Sha Tsui, Kowloon. Overseas mail is normally held for two months and local mail for two weeks.

Sending Mail

On Hong Kong Island, the **General Post Office** (中央郵政局; Map p362; 2 Connaught Pl, Central; ⊙8am-6pm Mon-Sat, 9am-5pm Sun) is just east of the Hong Kong station. In Kowloon, the **Tsim Sha Tsui Post Office** (尖沙咀郵政局; Map p378; ground & 1st fl, Hermes House, 10 Middle Rd, Tsim Sha Tsui; ⊙9am-6pm Mon-Sat, to 2pm Sun) is just east of the southern end of Nathan Rd. Post office branches elsewhere keep shorter hours and usually don't open on Sunday.

You should allow five days for delivery of letters, postcards and aerogrammes to the UK, Continental Europe and Australia, and five to six days to the USA. Private companies offering courier

delivery service include the following; all three have pick-up points around the territory.

COURIER SERVICES

Many MTR stations have DHL outlets, including the **MTR Central branch** (Map p362; [☏]2877 2848) next to exit H, and the **MTR Admiralty branch** (Map p370; [☏]2529 5778) next to exit E.

DHL International ([☏]2400 3388; www.dhl.com.hk/en)

Federal Express ([☏]2730 3333; www.fedex.com/ hk_english)

UPS ([☏]2735 3535; www.ups. com/content/hk/en/index.jsx)

POSTAL RATES

Local mail is HK$1.70 for up to 30g. Airmail letters and postcards for the first 20/30g are HK$2.90/5.50 to most of Asia and HK$3.70/6.50 elsewhere, and HK$150/160 respectively per kilogram. Aerogrammes are HK$2.50/3.70 to Asia/elsewhere.

SPEEDPOST

Letters and small parcels sent via Hong Kong Post's **Speedpost** ([☏]2921 2288; www.hongkongpost.com/speed-post) should reach any of 210 destinations worldwide within two days and are automatically registered. Speedpost rates vary enormously according to destination; every post office has a schedule of fees and a timetable.

Public Holidays

Western and Chinese culture combine to create an interesting mix – and number – of public holidays in Hong Kong and Macau. Determining the exact date of some of them is tricky, as there are traditionally two calendars in use: the Gregorian solar (or Western) calendar and the Chinese lunar calendar.

New Year's Day 1 January

Chinese New Year 19–21

February 2015, 8–10 February 2016

Easter 3–7 April 2015, 25–28 March 2016

Ching Ming 5 April 2015, 3 April 2016

Labour Day 1 May

Buddha's Birthday 25 May 2015, 14 May 2016

Dragon Boat (Tuen Ng) Festival 20 June 2015, 9 June 2016

Hong Kong SAR Establishment Day 1 July

Mid-Autumn Festival 27 September 2015, 15 September 2016

China National Day 1 October

Chung Yeung 21 October 2015, 10 October 2016

Christmas Day 25 December

Boxing Day 26 December

Radio

The following are Hong Kong's most popular English-language radio stations:

AM 864 Hit parade.

Metro Plus News; 1044AM.

RTHK Radio 3 Current affairs and talkback; 567AM, 1584AM, 97.9FM and 106.8FM.

RTHK Radio 4 Classical music; 97.6–98.9FM.

RTHK Radio 6 BBC World Service relays; 675AM.

The *South China Morning Post* publishes a daily schedule of radio programs.

Safe Travel

Hong Kong is generally a very safe place, but as everywhere, things can go awry.

After dark Although it is safe to walk around just about anywhere in the territory after dark, it's best to stick to well-lit areas. Tourist districts, such as Tsim Sha Tsui, are heavily patrolled by the police. In the event of an emergency, ring [☏]999.

Theft Hong Kong has its share of local pickpockets and thieves. Carry as little cash and as few valuables as possible, and if you put a bag down, keep an eye on it. This also applies to restaurants and pubs, particularly in touristy areas such as the Peak Tram. If your bag doesn't accompany you to the toilet, don't expect to find it when you return.

Reporting If you are robbed, you can obtain a loss report for insurance purposes at the police station in the area in which the crime occurred. For locations and contact details of police stations in Hong Kong, visit www.police.gov.hk and click on 'e-Report Room'.

Taxes & Refunds

There is no sales tax in Hong Kong.

Telephone

International Calls & Rates

Codes Hong Kong's 'country' code is ☑852. To call someone outside Hong Kong, dial ☑001, then the country code, the local area code (you usually drop the initial zero if there is one) and the number.

Rates Remember that phone rates in Hong Kong are cheaper from 9pm to 8am on weekdays and throughout the weekend. If the phone you're using has the facility, dial ☑0060 first and then the number; rates will be cheaper at any time.

Phonecards You can make International Direct Dial (IDD) calls to almost anywhere in the world from most public telephones in Hong Kong, but you'll need a phonecard, available from most phone service providers, such as PCCW's Hello card. You can buy phonecards at any PCCW

branch, and at 7-Eleven and Circle K convenience stores, Mannings pharmacies or Vango supermarkets.

Outlets PCCW (☑2888 2888; www.pccw.com) has retail outlets throughout the territory, where you can buy phonecards, mobile phones and accessories. The most convenient shop for travellers is the Central branch (113 Des Voeux Rd, Ground fl; ⊘10am-8.30pm Mon-Sat, 11am-8pm Sun). There's also a Causeway Bay branch (46-54 Yee Wo St, G3, Ground fl, Mc-Donald's Bldg; ⊘10am-10pm Mon-Sun).

Local Calls & Rates

Rates All calls made from private phones in Hong Kong are local calls and therefore free. As in the rest of the world, payphones are increasingly rare. Hotels charge from HK$3 to HK$5 for local calls.

Numbers All landline numbers in the territory have eight digits (except ☑800 toll-free numbers and specific hotlines).

Mobile Phones

Coverage Hong Kong locals are addicted to their mobile telephones, which work everywhere, including in the harbour tunnels and on the MTR.

Access Any GSM-compatible phone can be used here.

Purchase PCCW and other service providers sell mobile phones and accessories along with rechargeable SIM cards (HK$98). Local calls work out to cost between 6¢ and 12¢ a minute (calls to the mainland are about HK$1.80/minute).

Useful Numbers

The following are some important telephone numbers and codes. Both the telephone directory and the *Yellow Pages* can be consulted online at www.yp.com.hk.

International dialling code	☑001
International directory enquiries	☑10015
Local directory enquiries	☑1081
Collect calls/ reverse-charge	☑10010
Time and temperature	☑18501
Weather	☑187 8200

Time

➡ Hong Kong time is eight hours ahead of GMT and London; 13 hours ahead of New York; 16 hours ahead of San Francisco; the same time as Singapore, Manila and Perth; and two hours behind Sydney.

➡ Hong Kong does not have daylight-saving time.

Toilets

Compared to most global cities, Hong Kong has a vast number of public toilets. All MTR stations have toilets, but sometimes finding them requires asking. Markets, villages and parks also have facilities. Almost all public toilets have access for people with disabilities, and baby-changing shelves in both men's and women's rooms. Equip yourself with tissues, though; public toilets in Hong Kong are often out of toilet paper.

Tourist Information

Information The enterprising and energetic **Hong Kong Tourism Board** (HKTB; ☑2508 1234; www.discover hongkong.com) is one of the most helpful and useful tourist organisations in the world. Staff are welcoming and have reams of information. Most of its literature is free, though it also sells a few useful publications and books, as well as postcards, T-shirts and souvenirs.

Hotline While on the ground in Hong Kong, phone the **HKTB Visitor Hotline** (☑2508 1234; ⊙9am-6pm) if you have a query or problem, or you're lost. Staff are eager to help.

Visitor Centres HKTB Visitor Information & Service Centres can be found on Hong Kong Island, in Kowloon, at Hong Kong International Airport on Lantau Island, and in Lo Wu, which is on the border with the mainland. Outside these centres and at several other places in the territory you'll be able to find iCyberlink screens, from which you can conveniently access the HKTB website and database 24 hours a day.

Hong Kong International Airport HKTB Centres
(Map p202; Chek Lap Kok; ⊙7am-11pm) There are centres in Halls A and B on the arrivals level in Terminal 1 and the E2 transfer area.

Hong Kong Island HKTB Centre (港島旅客諮詢及服務中心; Map p374; Peak Piazza; ⊙8am-9pm)

Kowloon HKTB Centre (香港旅遊發展局; Map p378; Star Ferry Concourse, Tsim Sha Tsui; ⊙8am-8pm)

Lo Wu HKTB Centre (羅湖旅客諮詢及服務中心; 2nd fl, Arrival Hall, Lo Wu Terminal Bldg; ⊙8am-6pm)

Travel Agencies

You'll find travel agencies everywhere in Hong Kong, but the following are among the most reliable and offer the best deals on air tickets:

Concorde Travel (Map p366; ☑2526 3391; www.concorde-travel.com; 8-10

On Lan St, 1st fl, Galuxe Bldg, Central; ⊙9am-5.30pm Mon-Fri, to 1pm Sat) This is a long-established and highly dependable agency owned and operated by Aussie expats.

Natori Travel (樂途旅遊有限公司; Map p366; ☑2810 1681; www.natoritvl.com; 33 Queen's Rd, Room 2207, Melbourne Plaza, Central; ⊙9am-7pm Mon-Fri, to 4pm Sat) Readers have long used and recommended this place.

Phoenix Services Agency (峯寧旅運社; Map p380; ☑2722 7378; 22-26 Austin Ave, Room 1404, 14th fl, Austin Tower, Tsim Sha Tsui; ⊙9am-6pm Mon-Fri, to 4pm Sat) Phoenix is one of the best places in Hong Kong to buy air tickets, get China visas and seek travel advice. It is also the Hong Kong agent for the student and discount-travel company STA Travel.

Traveller Services (Map p378; ☑2375 2222; www.traveller.com.hk; 1 Wang Kwong Rd, Kowloon Bay, 18E, Tower B, Billion Centre; ⊙9am-6pm Mon-Fri, to 1pm Sat) Very reliable for good-value air tickets.

Travellers with Disabilities

People with disabilities have to cope with substantial obstacles in Hong Kong, including the stairs at many MTR stations, as well as pedestrian overpasses, narrow and crowded footpaths, and steep hills. On the other hand, some buses are accessible by wheelchair, taxis are never hard to find, most buildings have lifts (many with Braille panels) and MTR stations have Braille maps with recorded information. Wheelchairs can negotiate the lower decks of most ferries.

Easy Access Travel (香港社會服務聯會; ☑2855 9360; www.rehabsociety.org.hk; 7

Rehab Path, ground fl, HKSR Lam Tin Complex, Lam Tin, Kowloon) Offers tours and accessible transport services.

Transport Department (www.td.gov.hk) Provides guides to public transport, parking and pedestrian crossing for people with disabilities.

Visas & Passports

Passports A passport is essential for visiting Hong Kong, and it needs to be valid for at least one month after the period of your stay in Hong Kong. Carry your passport at all times as this is the only form of identification acceptable to the Hong Kong police.

Visa-free visitors The vast majority of travellers, including citizens of Australia, Canada, the EU, Israel, Japan, New Zealand and the USA, are allowed to enter the Hong Kong Special Administrative Region (SAR) without a visa and stay for 90 days. Holders of British passports can stay up to 180 days without a visa, but British Dependent Territories and British Overseas citizens not holding a visa are only allowed to remain 90 days. Holders of many African (including South African), South American and Middle Eastern passports do not require visas for visits of 30 days or less. You can check visa requirements at www.immd.gov.hk/en/services/hk-visas/visit-transit/visit-visa-entry-permit.html.

Longer stays Anyone wishing to stay longer than the visa-free period must apply for a visa before travelling to Hong Kong.

Visas If you do require a visa, you must apply beforehand at the nearest Chinese consulate or embassy; for addresses and contact information, consult the website www.fmprc.gov.cn/eng/wjb/zwjg.

Mainland China If you plan on visiting mainland China, you must have a visa; see p314.

Visa extensions You have to apply for visa extensions in person at the **Hong Kong Immigration Department** (Map p372; ☑2824 6111; www.immd.gov.hk; 7 Gloucester Rd, 2nd fl, Immigration Tower, Wan Chai; ☺8.45am-4.30pm Mon-Fri, 9-11.30am Sat) seven days from visa expiry. Check www.immd.gov. hk/en/services/hk-visas/visit-transit/visit-visa-entry-permit. html for more details.

Weights & Measures

Although the international metric system is in official use in Hong Kong, traditional Chinese weights and measures are still common. At local markets, meat, fish and produce are sold by the *léung*, equivalent to 37.8g, and the *gàn* (catty), which is equivalent to about 600g. There are 16 *léung* to the *gàn*. Gold and silver are sold by the *tael*, which is exactly the same as a *léung*.

Women Travellers

Hong Kong is a safe city for women, though common-sense caution should be observed, especially at night. Few women – visitors or residents – complain of bad treatment, intimidation or aggression. Having said that, some Chinese men regard Western women as 'easy'. If you are sexually assaulted, call the **Rape Crisis Centre Hotline** (☑2375 5322).

Macau Directory A–Z

Much of the advice given for Hong Kong (p325) also applies to Macau, in particular that regarding health and environmental hazards.

Customs

Customs formalities are few. The duty-free quota for visitors is 100 cigarettes and 1L of spirits.

Electricity

220V/50Hz

Emergency

Police, Fire and Ambulance (☑999)

24-Hour Tourists' Emergency Hotline (☑110, ☑112)

Internet Access

Free Wi-Fi

You can access free public wi-fi in select government premises, tourist hot spots and public areas daily from 8am to 1am the following day. See www.wifi.gov.mo for details.

Most cafes and hotels in Macau have free wi-fi.

Paid Wi-Fi

You can buy prepaid phonecards from CTM, ranging from MOP$50 to MOP$130, to enjoy mobile broadband; or buy a mobile broadband pass for unlimited internet access for either one day (MOP$120) or five days (MOP$220).

Left Luggage

There are electronic lockers on both the arrivals and departures levels of the Macau ferry terminal. They cost MOP$20 or MOP$25 (depending on the size of your luggage) for the first two hours, and MOP$25/30 for each additional 12-hour period.

There is also a left-luggage counter on the departures level of Macau International Airport that's open 24 hours.

It charges MOP$10 hourly and MOP$80 daily.

Legal Matters

The legal age for gambling in Macau is 18 for tourists.

Possession of any kind of illicit drugs can lead to imprisonment.

Maps

The helpful and informative Macau Government Tourist Office (MGTO) distributes the excellent (and free) *Macau Tourist Map,* with major tourist sights and streets labelled in English, Portuguese and Chinese, small insert maps of Taipa and Coloane, and bus routes marked.

Medical Services

Macau's two hospitals both have 24-hour emergency services.

Centro Hospitalar Conde Saõ Januário (山頂醫院; Map p222; ☑2831 3731; Estrada do Visconde de São Januário) Southwest of Guia Fort.

Hospital Kiang Wu (鏡湖醫院; Map p222; ☑2837 1333; Rua de Coelho do Amaral) Northeast of the ruins of the Church of St Paul.

Money

Macau's currency is the pataca (MOP$), which is divided up into 100 avos. Bills are issued in denominations of MOP$10, MOP$20, MOP$50, MOP$100, MOP$500 and MOP$1000. There are little copper coins worth 10, 20 and 50 avos, and silver-coloured MOP$1, MOP$2, MOP$5 and MOP$10 coins.

The pataca is pegged to the Hong Kong dollar at the rate of MOP$103.20 to HK$100. As a result, exchange rates for the pataca are virtually the same as for the Hong Kong dollar. Hong Kong bills and coins (except the HK$10 coins) are accepted everywhere in Macau. When you spend Hong Kong dollars in big hotels, restaurants and department stores, usually your change will be returned in that currency, but this may not apply at smaller establishments and when you're in a taxi. Try to use up all your patacas before leaving Macau.

Most ATMs allow you to choose between patacas and Hong Kong dollars, and credit cards are readily accepted at Macau's hotels, larger restaurants and casinos. You can also change cash and travellers cheques at the banks lining Avenida da Praia Grande and Avenida de Almeida Ribeiro, as well as at major hotels.

Tipping is not a must, but is expected. MOP$10 or MOP$20 will do for hotel porters, and tip around 10% of restaurant bills.

Opening Hours

Banks Open from 9am to 5pm weekdays and to 1pm on Saturday.

Government offices Usually open from 9am to 1pm and 2.30pm to 5.30pm (or 5.45pm) on weekdays.

Post

Correios de Macau, Macau's postal system, is efficient and inexpensive.

The **main post office** (郵政總局; Map p226; ☎2832 3666; 126 Avenida de Almeida Ribeiro; ◷9am-6pm Mon-Fri, 9am-1pm Sat) faces Largo do Senado; pick up poste restante from counter 1 or 2. There are other post offices in Macau Peninsula, including a **Macau ferry terminal branch** (Map p222; ☎2872 8079; Macau Ferry Terminal; ◷10am-7pm Mon-Sat).

EMS Speedpost is available at the main post office. Other companies can also arrange express forwarding:

DHL (Map p222; ☎2837 2828; Ground fl, Edificio Tong Nam Ah Campo, 100 Rua de Roma)

Federal Express (Map p222; ☎2870 3333; 54F, Edificio Hung On Centre, Avenida de Marciano Baptista)

UPS (Map p222; ☎2875 1616; 35, 43 & 49 Travessa de Venceslau de Morais, Centro Industrial de Macau)

Public Holidays

New Year's Day 1 January

Chinese New Year 19–21 February 2015, 8–10 February 2016

Easter 5–6 April 2015, 27–28 March 2016

Ching Ming 4 April

Labour Day 1 May

Buddha's Birthday 25 May 2015, 14 May 2016

Dragon Boat (Tuen Ng) Festival 20 June 2015, 9 June 2016

Mid-Autumn Festival 27 September 2015, 15 September 2016

China National Day 1 October

Chung Yeung 21 October 2015, 10 October 2016

All Souls' Day 2 November

Feast of the Immaculate Conception 8 December

Winter Solstice 22 December 2015, 21 December 2016

Macau SAR Establishment Day 20 December

Christmas Eve 24 December

Christmas Day 25 December

Safe Travel

Violent crime against visitors in Macau is rare but pickpocketing and other street crime can occur in busy areas.

Take extra caution with passports and valuables in crowded areas and when visiting casinos late at night.

Telephone

Local calls are free from private telephones; at a public payphone they cost MOP$1 for five minutes. Most hotels will charge you MOP$3.

Macau's telephone service provider is Companhia de Telecomunicações de Macau (CTM) There are several conveniently located CTM branches in Macau:

Avenida de D. Joao IV (Map p226; 12-14 Avenida de D. Joao IV; ◷10.30am-7.30pm)

Rua Pedro Coutinho (澳門電訊總店; Map p222; 25 Rua Pedro Coutinho, Pedro Coutinho Shop; ◷10.30am-8pm) Two blocks northeast of the Lou Lim Ioc Garden.

Phone Codes

The international access code for every country, except Hong Kong, is ☎00. If you want to phone Hong Kong, dial ☎01 first, then the number you want; you do not need to dial Hong Kong's country code (☎852). To call Macau from abroad – including from Hong Kong – the country code is ☎853.

Phonecards

All pay phones permit International Direct Dialling (IDD) using an Easy Call phonecard available for purchase from CTM for MOP$100. Rates are cheaper from 9pm to 8am on weekdays and all day Saturday and Sunday. Prepaid SIM cards are available from CTM for MOP$50 (for local calls) and MOP$50/100/130 (with IDD and international roaming), which allow internet access through mobile broadband.

Useful Numbers

International directory assistance ☏101

Local directory assistance ☏181

Tourist Information

The **Macau Government Tourist Office** (澳門旅遊局, MGTO; Map p226; ☏8397 1120; www.macautourism.gov. mo; Edificio Ritz, 9 Largo do Senado) is a well-organised and helpful source of information. It dispenses a large selection of free literature, including pamphlets on everything from Chinese temples and Catholic churches to fortresses, gardens and walks. The MGTO also runs a 24-hour **tourist hotline** (☏2833 3000) and a 24-hour **tourists' emergency hotline** (☏110 or 112).

MGTO has a Hong Kong branch and half a dozen outlets scattered all over Macau.

Macau Ferry Terminal (Map p222; ☏2872 6416; ◷9am-10pm)

Macau International Airport (☏2886 1418; Mezzanine level; ◷10am-10pm)

Travellers with Disabilities

Macau is not exactly friendly to travellers with disabilities. The historical part of Macau sits on a hilly landscape and pavement is often uneven, though some major sights do have provisions for disability access. The newer parts, eg around the Cotai Strip, are flat and have wider streets.

Macau law requires accessible facilities in public buildings (usually in the form of a ramp) and disabled parking bays in public parking lots. Traffic lights generally have audible signals to help the sight-impaired cross the street.

Public transport, including taxis, is not equipped to accommodate people with physical disabilities. The airport is quite accessible, but accessing the ferries from Hong Kong to Macau would require assistance from the staff.

Visas

Most travellers, including citizens of the EU, Australia, New Zealand, the USA, Canada and South Africa, can enter Macau with just their passports for between 30 and 90 days.

Travellers who do require visas can get them, valid for 30 days, on arrival in Macau. They cost MOP$100/50/200 per adult/child under 12 years/ family.

You can get a single one-month visa extension from the Macau **Immigration Department** (澳門入境處; Map p222; ☏2872 5488; Edificio Conforseg, Praceta de 1 de Outubro; ◷9am-5pm Mon-Fri).

Language

Cantonese is the most popular Chinese dialect in Hong Kong, Guǎngzhōu and the surrounding area. Cantonese speakers can read Chinese characters, but will pronounce many characters differently from a Mandarin speaker.

Several systems of Romanisation for Cantonese script exist, and no single one has emerged as an official standard. In this chapter we use Lonely Planet's pronunciation guide designed for maximum accuracy with minimum complexity.

Pronunciation

Vowels

a	as the 'u' in 'but'
ai	as in 'aisle' (short sound)
au	as the 'ou' in 'out'
ay	as in 'pay'
eu	as the 'er' in 'fern'
eui	as in French *feuille* (eu with i)
ew	as in 'blew' (short and pronounced with tightened lips)
i	as the 'ee' in 'deep'
iu	as the 'yu' in 'yuletide'
o	as in 'go'
oy	as in 'boy'
u	as in 'put'
ui	as in French *oui*

Consonants

In Cantonese, the ng sound can appear at the start of a word. Practise by saying 'sing along' slowly and then do away with the 'si'.

WANT MORE?

For in-depth language information and handy phrases, check out Lonely Planet's *China phrasebook*. You'll find it at **shop.lonelyplanet.com**, or you can buy Lonely Planet's iPhone phrasebooks at the Apple App Store.

Note that words ending with the consonant sounds p, t, and k must be clipped in Cantonese. You can hear this in English as well – say 'pit' and 'tip' and listen to how much shorter the 'p' sound is in 'tip'.

Many Cantonese speakers, particularly young people, replace an 'n' sound with an 'l' if a word begins with it – náy (you), is often heard as láy. Where relevant, this change is reflected in our pronunciation guides.

Tones

Cantonese is a language with a large number of words with the same pronunciation but a different meaning, eg g$\underline{w}$àt (dig up) and gwàt (bones). What distinguishes these homophones is their 'tonal' quality – the raising and the lowering of pitch on certain syllables. Tones in Cantonese fall on vowels (a, e, i, o, u) and on the consonant n.

To give you a taste of how these tones work, we've included them in our red pronunciation guides in this chapter – they show six tones, divided into high and low pitch groups. High-pitch tones involve tightening the vocal muscles to get a higher note, whereas low-pitch tones are made by relaxing the vocal chords to get a lower note. The tones are indicated with the following accent marks:

à	high
á	high rising
a	level
$\underline{à}$	low falling
$\underline{á}$	low rising
$\underline{a}$	low

Basics

Hello.	哈佬 。	hàa·ló
Goodbye.	再見 。	joy·gin
How are you?	你幾好啊嗎？	láy gáy hó à maa
Fine.	幾好 。	gáy hó

Excuse me. (to get attention)	對唔住 。	deui·ǹg·jew
Excuse me. (to get past)	唔該借借 。	ǹg·gòy je·je
Sorry.	對唔住 。	deui·ǹg·jew
Yes.	係 。	hai
No.	不係 。	ǹg·hai
Please ...	唔該……	ǹg·gòy ...
Thank you.	多謝 。	dàw·je
You're welcome.	唔駛客氣 。	ǹg·sái haak·hay

What's your name?
你叫乜嘢名 ？　　láy giu màt·yé méng aa

My name is ...
我叫……　　ngáw giu ...

Do you speak English?
你識唔識講
英文啊 ？　　láy sìk·ǹg·sìk gáwng
yìng·mán aa

I don't understand.
我唔明 。　　ngáw ǹg mìng

Accommodation

campsite	營地	yìng·day
guesthouse	賓館	bàn·gún
hostel	招待所	jiù·doy·sáw
hotel	酒店	jáu·dim

Do you have a ... room?	有冇…… 房 ？	yáu·mó ... fáwng
single	單人	dàan·yàn
double	雙人	sèung·yàn

How much is it per ...?	一……幾多 錢 ？	yàt ... gáy·dàw chín
night	晚	máan
person	個人	gaw yàn

air-con	空調	hùng·tiù
bathroom	沖涼房	chùng·lèung· fáwng
bed	床	chàwng
cot	BB床	bi·bì chàwng
window	窗	chèung

Directions

Where's ...?
……喺邊度?　　... hái bìn·do

What's the address?
地址係 ？　　day·jí hai

KEY PATTERNS

To get by in Cantonese, mix and match these simple patterns with words of your choice:

When's (the next tour)?
(下個旅遊團
係)幾時 ？　　(haa·gaw léui·yàu·tèwn
hai) gáy·sì

Where's (the station)?
(車站)喺邊度 ？　　(chè·jaam) hái·bìn·do

Where can I (buy a padlock)?
邊度可以
(買倒鎖) ？　　bìn·do háw·yí
(máai dó sáw)

Do you have (a map)?
有冇 (地圖) ？　　yáu·mó (day·tò)

I need (a mechanic).
我要(個整車
師傅) 。　　ngáw yiu (gaw jíng·chè
sì·fú)

I'd like (a taxi).
我想 (坐的士) 。　　ngáw séung (cháw dìk·sí)

Can I (get a stand-by ticket)?
可唔可以 (買
張後補飛) 呀 ？　　háw·ǹg·háw·yí (máai
jèung hau·bó fày) aa

Could you please (write it down)?
唔該你 (寫落嚟)?　　ǹg·gòy láy (sé lawk lài)

Do I need (to book)?
駛唔駛 (定飛
先)呀 ？　　sái·ǹg·sái (deng·fày
sìn) aa

I have (a reservation).
我 (預定)咗 。　　ngáw (yew·deng) jáw

behind	後面	hau·min
left	左邊	jáw·bìn
near ...	……附近	... fu·gan
next to ...	……旁邊	... pàwng·bìn
on the corner	十字路口	sap·ji·lo·háu
opposite	對面	deui·min
right	右邊	yau·bìn
straight ahead	前面	chìn·min
traffic lights	紅綠燈	hùng·luk·dàng

Eating & Drinking

What would you recommend?
有乜嘢好介紹 ？　　yáu màt·yé hó gaai·siu

What's in that dish?
呢道菜有啲乜嘢 ？　　lày do choy yáu dì màt·yé

That was delicious.
真好味 。　　jàn hó·may

Cheers!
乾杯 ！　　gàwn·buì

I'd like the bill, please.
唔該我要埋單 。　　ǹg·gòy ngáw yiu màai·dàan

I'd like to book a table for ...	我想訂張檯，……嘅。	ngáw séung deng jèung tóy ... ge
(eight) o'clock	(八)點鐘	(bàat) dím·jùng
(two) people	(兩)位	(léung) wái

I don't eat ...	我唔吃……	ngáw ǹg sik ...
fish	魚	yéw
nuts	果仁	gwáw·yàn
poultry	雞鴨鵝	gài ngaap ngàw
red meat	牛羊肉	ngàu yèung yuk

Key Words

appetisers	涼盤	lèung·pún
baby food	嬰兒食品	yìng·yi sik·bán
bar	酒吧	jáu·bàa
bottle	樽	jèun
bowl	碗	wún
breakfast	早餐	jó·chàan
cafe	咖啡屋	gaa·fè·ngùk
children's menu	個小童菜單	gaw siú·tung choy·dàan
(too) cold	(太)凍	(taai) dung
dinner	晚飯	máan·faan
food	食物	sik·mat
fork	叉	chàa
glass	杯	bùi
halal	清真	chìng·jàn
high chair	高凳	gò·dang
hot (warm)	熱	yit
knife	刀	dò
kosher	猶太	yàu·tàai
local specialities	地方小食	day·fàwng siú·sik
lunch	午餐	ńg·chàan
market	街市	gàai·sí
main courses	主菜	jéw·choy
menu (in English)	(英文)菜單	(yìng·màn) choy·dàan
plate	碟	díp
restaurant	酒樓	jáu·làu
(too) spicy	(太)辣	(taai) laat
spoon	羹	gàng
supermarket	超市	chiù·sí
vegetarian food	齋食品	jàai sik·bán

Meat & Fish

beef	牛肉	ngàu·yuk
chicken	雞肉	gài·yuk
duck	鴨	ngaap
fish	魚	yéw
lamb	羊肉	yèung·yuk
pork	豬肉	jèw·yuk
seafood	海鮮	hóy·sìn

Fruit & Vegetables

apple	蘋果	pìng·gwáw
banana	香蕉	hèung·jiù
cabbage	白菜	baak·choy
carrot	紅蘿蔔	hùng·làw·baak
celery	芹菜	kàn·choy
cucumber	青瓜	chèng·gwàa
fruit	水果	séui·gwáw
grapes	葡提子	pò·tài·jí
green beans	扁荳	bín·dau
lemon	檸檬	lìng·mùng
lettuce	生菜	sàang·choy
mushroom	蘑菇	màw·gù
onion(s)	洋蔥	yèung·chùng
orange	橙	cháang
peach	桃	tó
pear	梨	láy
pineapple	菠蘿	bàw·làw
plum	梅	mui
potato	薯仔	sèw·jái
spinach	菠菜	bàw·choy
tomato	番茄	fàan·ké
vegetable	蔬菜	sàw·choy

Other

bread	麵包	min·bàau
egg	蛋	dáan
herbs/spices	香料	hèung·liú
pepper	胡椒粉	wù·jiù·fán
rice	白飯	baak·faan
salt	鹽	yìm
soy sauce	豉油	si·yàu
sugar	砂糖	sàa·tàwng
vegetable oil	菜油	choy·yàu
vinegar	醋	cho

SIGNS

入口	Entrance
出口	Exit
廁所	Toilets
男	Men
女	Women

Drinks

beer	啤酒	bè·jáu
coffee	咖啡	gaa·fè
juice	果汁	gwáw·jàp
milk	牛奶	ngàu·láai
mineral water	礦泉水	kawng·chèwn·séui
red wine	紅葡萄酒	hùng·pò·tò·jáu
tea	茶	chàa
white wine	白葡萄酒	baak·pò·tò·jáu

Emergencies

Help!	救命！	gau·meng
Go away!	走開！	jáu·hòy
I'm lost.	我蕩失路 。	ngáw dawng·sàk·lo
I'm sick.	我病咗 。	ngáw beng·jáw

Call a doctor!
快啲叫醫生！ faai·dì giu yì·sàng

Call the police!
快啲叫警察！ faai·dì giu gíng·chaat

Where are the toilets?
廁所喺邊度？ chi·sáw hái bìn·do

I'm allergic to ...
我對……過敏 。 ngáw deui ... gaw·mán

Shopping & Services

I'd like to buy ...
我想買…… ngáw séung máai ...

I'm just looking.
睇下 。 tái haa

Can I look at it?
我可唔可以睇下？ ngáw háw·ǹg·háw·yí tái haa

How much is it?
幾多錢？ gáy·dàw chín

That's too expensive.
太貴啦 。 taai gwai laa

Can you lower the price?
可唔可以平啲呀？ háw·ǹg·háw·yí pèng dì aa

There's a mistake in the bill.
帳單錯咗 。 jeung·dàan chaw jáw

QUESTION WORDS

How?	點樣？	dím·yéung
What?	乜嘢？	màt·yé
When?	幾時？	gáy·sì
Where?	邊度？	bìn·do
Who?	邊個？	bìnz·gaw
Why?	點解？	dím·gáai

ATM	自動提款機	ji·dung tài·fún·gày
credit card	信用卡	seun·yung·kàat
internet cafe	網吧	máwng·bàa
post office	郵局	yàu·gúk
tourist office	旅行社	léui·hàng·sé

Time & Dates

What time is it?
而家幾點鐘？ yi·gàa gáy·dím·jùng

It's (10) o'clock.
（十）點鐘 。 (sap)·dím·jùng

Half past (10).
（十）點半 。 (sap)·dím bun

morning	朝早	jiù·jó
afternoon	下晝	haa·jau
evening	夜晚	ye·máan
yesterday	尋日	kàm·yat
today	今日	gàm·yat
tomorrow	听日	tìng·yat

Monday	星期一	sìng·kày·yàt
Tuesday	星期二	sìng·kày·yi
Wednesday	星期三	sìng·kày·sàam
Thursday	星期四	sìng·kày·say
Friday	星期五	sìng·kày·ńg
Saturday	星期六	sìng·kày·luk
Sunday	星期日	sìng·kày·yat

January	一月	yàt·yewt
February	二月	yi·yewt
March	三月	sàam·yewt
April	四月	say·yewt
May	五月	ńg·yewt
June	六月	luk·yewt
July	七月	chàt·yewt
August	八月	baat·yewt
September	九月	gáu·yewt
October	十月	sap·yewt
November	十一月	sap·yàt·yewt
December	十二月	sap·yi·yewt

Transport

Public Transport

boat	船	sèwn
bus	巴士	bàa·sí
plane	飛機	fày·gày

NUMBERS

1	一	yàt
2	二	yi
3	三	sàam
4	四	say
5	五	ńg
6	六	lụk
7	七	chàt
8	八	baat
9	九	gáu
10	十	sạp
20	二十	yị·sạp
30	三十	sàam·sạp
40	四十	say·sạp
50	五十	ńg·sạp
60	六十	lụk·sạp
70	七十	chàt·sạp
80	八十	baat·sạp
90	九十	gáu·sạp
100	一百	yàt·baak
1000	一千	yàt·chìn

taxi	的士	dìk·sí
train	火車	fáw·chè
tram	電車	dịn·chè

When's the ... (bus)?	……（巴士）幾點開？	... (bàa·sí) gáy dím hòy
first	頭班	tàu·bàan
last	尾班	máy·bàan
next	下一班	hạa·yàt·bàan

A ... ticket to (Panyu).	一張去（番禺）嘅……飛。	yàt jèung heui (pùn·yẽw) ge ... fày
1st-class	頭等	tàu·dáng
2nd-class	二等	yị·dáng
one-way	單程	dàan·chịng
return	雙程	sèung·chịng

What time does it leave?
幾點鐘出發？　　　gáy·dím jùng chèut·faa

Does it stop at ...?
會唔會喺……停呀？　wuí·ńg·wuí hái ... tịng aa

What time does it get to ...?
幾點鐘到……？　　gáy·dím jùng do ...

What's the next stop?
下個站叫乜名？　　hạa·gaw jạam giu màt méng

I'd like to get off at ...
我要喺……落車。　ngáw yiu hái ... lạwk·chè

Please tell me when we get to ...
到……嘅時候，唔該叫聲我。　do ... ge sị·hạu ńg·gòy giu sèng ngáw

Please stop here.
唔該落車。　　　　ńg·gòy lạwk·chè

aisle	路邊	lọ·bìn
cancelled	取消	chéui·siù
delayed	押後	ngaat·hạu
platform	月台	yéwt·tòy
ticket window	售票處	sạu·piu·chew
timetable	時間表	sị·gaan·bíu
train station	火車站	fó·chè·jạam
window	窗口	chèung·háu

Driving & Cycling

I'd like to hire a ...	我想租架……	ngáw séung jò gaa ...
4WD	4WD	fàw·wiù·jàai·fù
bicycle	單車	dàan·chè
car	車	chè
motorcycle	電單車	dịn·dàan·chè

baby seat	BB座	bị·bì jaw
diesel	柴油	chàai·yàu
helmet	頭盔	táu·kwài
mechanic	修車師傅	sàu·chè sì·fú
petrol	汽油	hay·yàu
service station	加油站	gàa·yàu·jàam

Is this the road to ...?
呢條路係唔係去……㗎？　lày tiụ lọ hại·ńg·hại heui ... gaa

Can I park here?
呢度泊唔泊得車㗎？　lày·dọ paak·ńg·paak·dàk chè gaa

How long can I park here?
我喺呢度可以停幾耐？　ngáw hái lày·dọ háw·yí tịng gáy·lọy

Where's the bicycle parking lot?
喺邊度停單車？　háy·bìn·dọ ting dàan·chè

The car/motorbike has broken down at ...
架車/電單車係……壞咗。　gaa chè/dịn·dàan·chè hái ... wạai jáw

I have a flat tyre.
我爆咗肽。　ngáw baau·jáw tàai

I've run out of petrol.
我冇晒油。　ngáw mọ saai yáu

I'd like my bicycle repaired.
我想修呢架車。　ngáw séung sàu lày gaa chè

GLOSSARY

arhat – Buddhist disciple freed from the cycle of birth and death

bodhisattva – Buddhist striving towards enlightenment

cha chaan tang – local tea cafe serving Western-style beverages and snacks and/or Chinese dishes

cheongsam – a fashionable, tight-fitting Chinese dress with a slit up the side (*qípáo* in Mandarin)

dai pai dong – open-air eating stall, especially popular at night, but fast disappearing in Hong Kong

dim sum – literally 'touch the heart'; a Cantonese meal of various tidbits eaten as breakfast, brunch or lunch and offered from wheeled steam carts in restaurants; see also yum cha

dragon boat – long, narrow skiff in the shape of a dragon, used in races during the Dragon Boat Festival

feng shui – Mandarin spelling for the Cantonese *fung sui* meaning 'wind water'; the Chinese art of geomancy that manipulates or judges the environment to produce good fortune

Hakka – a Chinese ethnic group who speak a different Chinese language than the Cantonese; some Hakka people still lead traditional lives as farmers in the New Territories

hell money – fake-currency money burned as an offering to the spirits of the departed

HKTB – Hong Kong Tourism Board

junk – originally Chinese fishing boats or war vessels with square sails; diesel-powered, wooden pleasure yachts, which can be seen on Victoria Harbour

kaido – small- to medium-sized ferry that makes short runs on the open sea, usually used for nonscheduled services between small islands and fishing villages; sometimes spelled kaito

kung fu – the basis of many Asian martial arts

mah-jong – popular Chinese game played among four persons using tiles engraved with Chinese characters

MTR – Mass Transit Railway

nullah – uniquely Hong Kong word referring to a gutter or drain and occasionally used in place names

Punti – the first Cantonese-speaking settlers in Hong Kong

sampan – motorised launch that can only accommodate a few people and is too small to go on the open sea; mainly used for interharbour transport

SAR – Special Administrative Region of China; both Hong Kong and Macau are now SARs

SARS – Severe Acute Respiratory Syndrome

si yau sai chaan – 'soy sauce Western'; a cuisine that emerged in the 1950s featuring Western dishes of various origins prepared in a Chinese style

taichi – slow-motion shadow-boxing and form of exercise; also spelt tai chi or t'ai chi

tai tai – any married woman but especially the leisured wife of a businessman

Tanka – Chinese ethnic group that traditionally lives on boats

Triad – Chinese secret society originally founded as patriotic associations to protect Chinese culture from the influence of usurping Manchus, but today Hong Kong's equivalent of the Mafia

wan – bay

wet market – an outdoor market selling fruit, vegetables, fish and meat

yum cha – literally 'drink tea'; common Cantonese term for dim sum

MENU DECODER

Fish & Shellfish

baau-yew	鮑魚	abalone
daai-haa	大蝦	prawn
haa	蝦	shrimp
ho	蠔	oyster
lung haa	龍蝦	rock lobster
yau-yew	魷魚	squid
yew	魚	fish
yew chi	魚翅	shark's fin
yew daan	魚蛋	fish balls, usually made from pike

Meat & Poultry

gai	雞	chicken
jew sau	豬手	pork knuckle
jew-yuk	豬肉	pork
ngaap	鴨	duck
ngau yuk	牛肉	beef
ngaw	鵝	goose
paai guat	排骨	pork spareribs
yew jew	乳豬	suckling pig

Pastries

bo lo baau	菠蘿包	pineapple bun
gai mei baau	雞尾包	cocktail bun

Rice & Noodle Dishes

baak-faan	白飯	steamed white rice
chaau-faan	炒飯	fried rice
chaau-min	炒麵	fried noodles
faan	飯	rice
fan-si	粉絲	cellophane noodles or bean threads
haw-fan	河粉	wide, white, flat rice noodles that are usually pan-fried
juk	粥	congee
min	麵	noodles
sin-haa haa wan-tan	鮮蝦餛飩	wontons made with prawns
wan-tan min	餛飩麵	wonton noodle soup

yau-jaa-gwai	油炸鬼	'devils' tails'; dough rolled and fried in hot oil

Sauces

gaai laat	芥辣	hot mustard
ho yau	蠔油	oyster sauce
laat jiu jeung	辣椒醬	chilli sauce
si yau	豉油	soy sauce

Soups

aai yuk suk mai gang	蟹肉粟米羹	crab and sweet corn soup
baak-choy tawng	白菜湯	Chinese cabbage soup
daan faa-tawng	蛋花湯	'egg flower' (or drop) soup; light stock into which a raw egg is dropped
dung-gwaa tawng	冬瓜湯	winter-melon soup
wan-tan tawng	餛飩湯	wonton soup
yew-chi tawng	魚翅湯	shark's-fin soup
yin waw gang	燕窩羹	bird's-nest soup

Vegetarian Dishes

chun gewn	春卷	vegetarian spring rolls
gai lo may	雞滷味	mock chicken, barbecued pork or roast duck
gam gu sun jim	金菇筍尖	braised bamboo shoots and black mushrooms
law hon jaai	羅漢齋	braised mixed vegetables
law hon jaai yi min	羅漢齋伊麵	fried noodles with braised vegetables

Cantonese Dishes

baak cheuk haa	白灼蝦	poached prawns served with dipping sauces
chaa siu	叉燒	roast pork
ching chaau gaai laan	清炒芥蘭	stir-fried Chinese broccoli
ching jing yew	清蒸魚	whole steamed fish served with spring onions, ginger and soy sauce
geung chung chaau haai	薑蔥炒蟹	sautéed crab with ginger and spring onions
haai yuk paa dau miu	蟹肉扒豆苗	sautéed pea shoots with crab meat
ho yau choi sam	蠔油菜心	*choisum* with oyster sauce
ho yau ngau yuk	蠔油牛肉	deep-fried spare ribs served with coarse salt and pepper
jaa ji gai	炸子雞	crispy-skin chicken
jiu yim yau·yew	椒鹽魷魚	squid, dry-fried with salt and pepper
mui choi kau yuk	霉菜扣肉	twice-cooked pork with pickled cabbage
sai laan faa daai ji	西蘭花帶子	stir-fried broccoli with scallops
siu ngaap	燒鴨	roast duck
siu yew gaap	燒乳鴿	roast pigeon
siu yew jew	燒乳豬	roast suckling pig
yìm guk gai	鹽焗雞	salt-baked chicken, Hakka-style

Dim Sum

chaa siu baau	叉燒包	steamed barbecued-pork buns
cheung fan	腸粉	steamed rice-flour rolls with shrimp, beef or pork

ching chaau si choi	清炒時菜	fried green vegetable of the day
chiu·jau fan gwaw	潮州粉果	steamed dumpling with pork, peanuts and coriander
chun gewn	春卷	fried spring rolls
fan gwaw	粉果	steamed dumplings with shrimp and bamboo shoots
fu pay gewn	腐皮卷	crispy tofu rolls
fung jaau	鳳爪	fried chicken feet
haa gaau	蝦餃	steamed shrimp dumplings
law mai gai	糯米雞	sticky rice wrapped in a lotus leaf
paai gwat	排骨	small braised spare ribs with black beans
saan juk ngau yuk	山竹牛肉	steamed minced-beef balls
siu maai	燒賣	steamed pork and shrimp dumplings

Chiu Chow Dishes

bing faa gwun yin	冰花官燕	cold, sweet bird's-nest soup served as a dessert
chiu·jau lo 0seui ngaw	潮州滷水鵝	Chiu Chow braised goose
chiu·jau yew tong	潮州魚湯	aromatic fish soup
chiu·jau yi min	潮州伊麵	pan-fried egg noodles served with chives
dung jing haai	凍蒸蟹	cold steamed crab
jin ho beng	煎蠔餅	oyster omelette
sek lau gai	石榴雞	steamed egg-white pouches filled with minced chicken
tim·sewn 0hung·siu haa/ haai kau	甜酸紅燒蝦/蟹球	prawn or crab balls with sweet, sticky dipping sauce

Northern Dishes

bak·ging tin ngaap	北京填鴨	Peking duck
chong baau yeung yuk	蔥爆羊肉	sliced lamb with onions served on sizzling platter
gaau·ji	餃子	dumplings
gon chaau ngau yuk si	乾炒牛肉絲	dried shredded beef with chilli sauce
haau yeung·yuk	烤羊肉	roast lamb
sewn laat tong	酸辣湯	hot-and-sour soup with shredded pork (and sometimes congealed pig's blood)

Shanghainese Dishes

baat bo faan	八寶飯	steamed or pan-fried glutinous rice with 'eight treasures', eaten as a dessert
chong yau beng	蔥油餅	pan-fried spring onion cakes
chung·ji wong yew	松子黃魚	sweet-and-sour yellow croaker with pine nuts
daai jaap haai	大閘蟹	hairy crab (an autumn and winter dish)
fu gwai gai/ hat yi gai	富貴雞/ 乞丐雞	'beggar's chicken'; partially deboned chicken stuffed with pork, Chinese pickled cabbage, onions, mushrooms, ginger and other seasonings, wrapped in lotus leaves, sealed in wet clay or pastry and baked for several hours in hot ash

gon jin say gwai dau	乾煎四季豆	pan-fried spicy string beans
hung·siu si·ji·tau	紅燒獅子頭	Braised 'lion's head meatballs' – over-sized pork meatballs
jeui gai	醉雞	drunken chicken
lung jeng haa jan	龍井蝦仁	shrimps with 'dragon-well' tea leaves
seung·hoi cho chaau	上海粗炒	fried Shànghǎi-style (thick) noodles with pork and cabbage
siu lung baau	小籠包	steamed minced-pork dumplings

Sichuan Dishes

ching jiu ngau yok si	青椒牛肉絲	sautéed shredded beef and green pepper
daam daam min	擔擔麵	noodles in savoury sauce
gong baau gai ding	宮爆雞丁	sautéed diced chicken and peanuts in sweet chilli sauce
jeung chaa haau ngaap	樟茶烤鴨	duck smoked in camphor wood
maa ngai seung sew	螞蟻上樹	'ants climbing trees'; cellophane noodles braised with seasoned minced pork
maa paw dau fu	麻婆豆腐	stewed tofu with minced pork and chilli
say·chewn ming haa	四川明蝦	Sichuan chilli prawns
wui gwaw yuk	回鍋肉	slices of braised pork with chillies
yew heung ke ji	魚香茄子	sautéed eggplant in a savoury, spicy sauce

Behind the Scenes

SEND US YOUR FEEDBACK

We love to hear from travellers – your comments keep us on our toes and help make our books better. Our well-travelled team reads every word on what you loved or loathed about this book. Although we cannot reply individually to your submissions, we always guarantee that your feedback goes straight to the appropriate authors, in time for the next edition. Each person who sends us information is thanked in the next edition – the most useful submissions are rewarded with a selection of digital PDF chapters.

Visit **lonelyplanet.com/contact** to submit your updates and suggestions or to ask for help. Our award-winning website also features inspirational travel stories, news and discussions.

Note: We may edit, reproduce and incorporate your comments in Lonely Planet products such as guidebooks, websites and digital products, so let us know if you don't want your comments reproduced or your name acknowledged. For a copy of our privacy policy visit lonelyplanet.com/privacy.

OUR READERS

Many thanks to the travellers who used the last edition and wrote to us with helpful hints, useful advice and interesting anecdotes:
Dagmar Kemmling, Dallas Baron, David Bonsor, Kylie Winkworth, Meaghan McGurga, Nick Williams, Norman Mok Chor Shek, Ole Haagen Nielsen, Peter Guth, Werner Bruyninx

AUTHOR THANKS

Piera Chen

Thanks to Ulysses Hwang, Yangi, Jackal Tam, and Antonio Cejunior for making research for this book an exciting journey. Gratitude also goes to Janine Cheung, Lambda Li, Zoe Lau and Yuen Ching-sum for their generous assistance; and to Tina So and Carmen Ng for their kindness and companionship. Finally I must acknowledge my husband Sze Pang-cheung and my muse Clio for their patience, understanding and wonderful support.

Emily Matchar

Thanks to the entire Lonely Planet team. Thanks to Marie Kobler and Tim Bonebrake for their excellent Lamma suggestions, and to Michael Johnson for his helpful restaurant advice. Thanks to my friends and, especially, to my husband, Jamin Asay, for being so willing to help me try out Hong Kong's many, many restaurants and bars.

ACKNOWLEDGMENTS

Cover photograph: Chinese-style pagoda, Hong Kong; Songquan Deng/Alamy.

THIS BOOK

This 16th edition of Lonely Planet's *Hong Kong* was researched and written by Piera Chen and Emily Matchar. The previous edition was written by Piera Chen and Chung Wah Chow. This guidebook was commissioned in Lonely Planet's London office, and produced by the following:

Destination Editor Megan Eaves

Coordinating Editor Monique Perrin

Product Editor Kate Mathews

Senior Cartographer Julie Sheridan

Book Designer Virginia Moreno

Senior Editor Karyn Noble

Assisting Editors Michelle Bennett, Bruce Evans, Justin Flynn, Gabrielle Stefanos

Assisting Cartographer Diana Von Holdt

Cover Researcher Naomi Parker

Thanks to Kate Chapman, Indra Kilfoyle, Katie O'Connell, Sunny Or, Martine Power, Dianne Schallmeiner, Eleanor Simpson, John Taufa, Amanda Williamson, Juan Winata

Index

See also separate subindexes for:

✗ **EATING P353**

🍺 **DRINKING & NIGHTLIFE P354**

☆ **ENTERTAINMENT P355**

🛍 **SHOPPING P356**

🏃 **SPORTS & ACTIVITIES P356**

🛏 **SLEEPING P357**

🍸 DRINKING & NIGHTLIFE

INDEX ENTERTAINMENT

INDEX ENTERTAINMENT

Hong Kong Maps

Sights
- Beach
- Bird Sanctuary
- Buddhist
- Castle/Palace
- Christian
- Confucian
- Hindu
- Islamic
- Jain
- Jewish
- Monument
- Museum/Gallery/Historic Building
- Ruin
- Sento Hot Baths/Onsen
- Shinto
- Sikh
- Taoist
- Winery/Vineyard
- Zoo/Wildlife Sanctuary
- Other Sight

Activities, Courses & Tours
- Bodysurfing
- Diving
- Canoeing/Kayaking
- Course/Tour
- Skiing
- Snorkelling
- Surfing
- Swimming/Pool
- Walking
- Windsurfing
- Other Activity

Sleeping
- Sleeping
- Camping

Eating
- Eating

Drinking & Nightlife
- Drinking & Nightlife
- Cafe

Entertainment
- Entertainment

Shopping
- Shopping

Information
- Bank
- Embassy/Consulate
- Hospital/Medical
- Internet
- Police
- Post Office
- Telephone
- Toilet
- Tourist Information
- Other Information

Geographic
- Beach
- Hut/Shelter
- Lighthouse
- Lookout
- Mountain/Volcano
- Oasis
- Park
- Pass
- Picnic Area
- Waterfall

Population
- Capital (National)
- Capital (State/Province)
- City/Large Town
- Town/Village

Transport
- Airport
- Border crossing
- Bus
- Cable car/Funicular
- Cycling
- Ferry
- MTR station
- Monorail
- Parking
- Petrol station
- Skytrain/Subway station
- Taxi
- Train station/Railway
- Tram
- Underground station
- Other Transport

Note: Not all symbols displayed above appear on the maps in this book

Routes
- Tollway
- Freeway
- Primary
- Secondary
- Tertiary
- Lane
- Unsealed road
- Road under construction
- Plaza/Mall
- Steps
- Tunnel
- Pedestrian overpass
- Walking Tour
- Walking Tour detour
- Path/Walking Trail

Boundaries
- International
- State/Province
- Disputed
- Regional/Suburb
- Marine Park
- Cliff
- Wall

Hydrography
- River, Creek
- Intermittent River
- Canal
- Water
- Dry/Salt/Intermittent Lake
- Reef

Areas
- Airport/Runway
- Beach/Desert
- Cemetery (Christian)
- Cemetery (Other)
- Glacier
- Mudflat
- Park/Forest
- Sight (Building)
- Sportsground
- Swamp/Mangrove

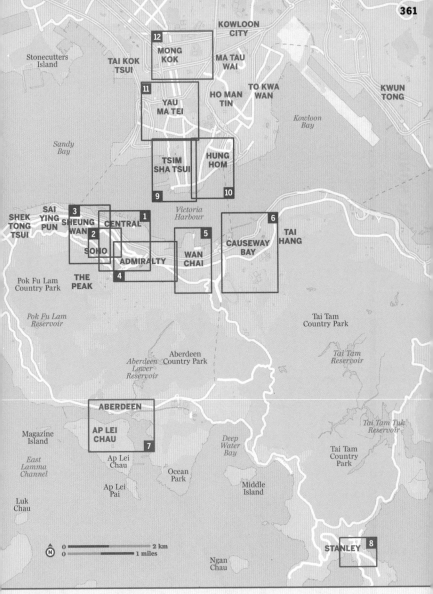

Stonecutters
Island

TAI KOK
TSUI

12 MONG
KOK

KOWLOON
CITY

MA TAU
WAI

KWUN
TONG

11 YAU
MA TEI

HO MAN
TIN

TO KWA
WAN

*Sandy
Bay*

*Kowloon
Bay*

TSIM
SHA TSUI

HUNG
HOM

9

10

*Victoria
Harbour*

SHEK
TONG
TSUI

SAI
YING
PUN

3 SHEUNG
WAN

1 CENTRAL

2
SOHO

ADMIRALTY

4

5 WAN
CHAI

6 CAUSEWAY
BAY

TAI
HANG

Pok Fu Lam
Country Park

THE
PEAK

*Pok Fu Lam
Reservoir*

Tai Tam
Country Park

*Aberdeen
Lower
Reservoir*

Aberdeen
Country Park

*Tai Tam
Reservoir*

ABERDEEN

AP LEI
CHAU

7

Magazine
Island

*East
Lamma
Channel*

Ap Lei
Chau

Ocean
Park

*Deep
Water
Bay*

*Tai Tam Tuk
Reservoir*

Tai Tam
Country
Park

Ap Lei
Pai

Middle
Island

Luk
Chau

0 ———— 2 km
0 ———— 1 miles

STANLEY 8

Ngan
Chau

CENTRAL HONG KONG

Key on p364

200 m
0.1 miles

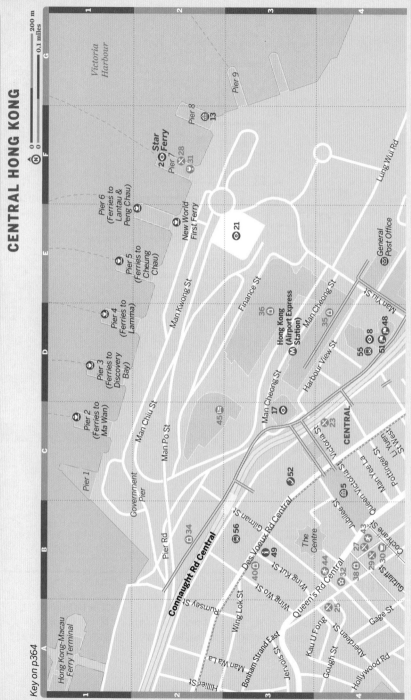

Victoria Harbour

Pier 9

Pier 8
13

Star Ferry
2 Pier 7 **28**
31

Pier 6
(Ferries to Lantau & Peng Chau)

New World First Ferry

Pier 5
(Ferries to Cheung Chau)

21

Pier 4
(Ferries to Lamma)

Lung Wui Rd

Pier 3
(Ferries to Discovery Bay)

General Post Office

Man Kwong St

Finance St

Man Cheong St

Man Yiu St

Pier 2
(Ferries to Ma Wan)

36

Hong Kong (Airport Express Station)

35

55

8

48

51

Harbour View St

Pier 1

Man Chiu St

45

Man Cheong St

17

Man Po St

23

CENTRAL

Victoria St

Government Pier

52

Queen Victoria St

Man Yee La

Li Yuen St West

Pier Rd

34

56

Gilman St

5

Jubilee St

Cochrane St

Pottinger St

Connaught Rd Central

40

49

Des Voeux Rd Central

Wing Kut St

The Centre

44

Queen's Rd Central

27

43

32

38

29

30

Gutzlaff St

Rumsey St

Wing Lok St

Wing Wo St

25

Kau U Fong

Gage St

Hillier St

Bonham Strand East

Jervois St

Man Wa La

Gough St

Aberdeen St

Hollywood Rd

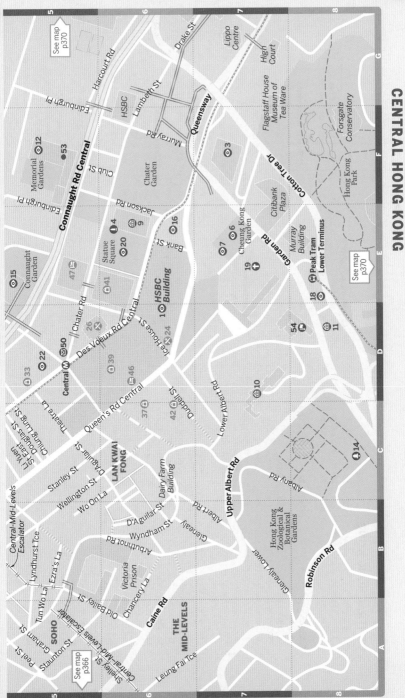

LAN KWAI FONG & SOHO *Map on p366*

Key on p365

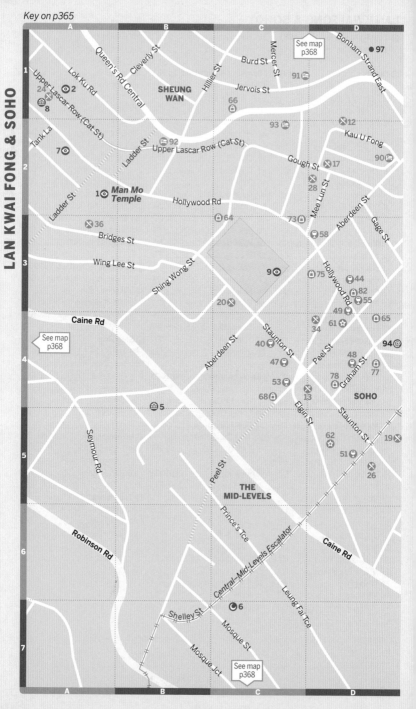

LAN KWAI FONG & SOHO

SHEUNG WAN

Queen's Rd Central

Cleverly St

Hillier St

Burd St

Mercer St

Jervois St

Bonham Strand East

● 97

91

66

93

12

Kau U Fong

Upper Lascar Row (Cat St)

Lok Ku Rd

24

2

8

Tank La

7

Ladder St

92

Upper Lascar Row (Cat St)

Gough St

17

90

28

Mee Lun St

Aberdeen St

Gage St

1 **Man Mo Temple**

Hollywood Rd

64

73

58

36

9

75

44

82

55

Bridges St

Hollywood Rd

49

65

Wing Lee St

Shing Wong St

20

34

61

94 @

Caine Rd

See map p368

Aberdeen St

40

Staunton St

Peel St

48

Graham St

78

77

47

53

68

13

SOHO

5

Elgin St

Seymour Rd

Peel St

Staunton St

62

19

THE MID-LEVELS

51

26

Prince's Tce

Robinson Rd

Central–Mid-Levels Escalator

Caine Rd

Leung Fai Tce

6

Shelley St

Mosque St

Mosque Jct

See map p368

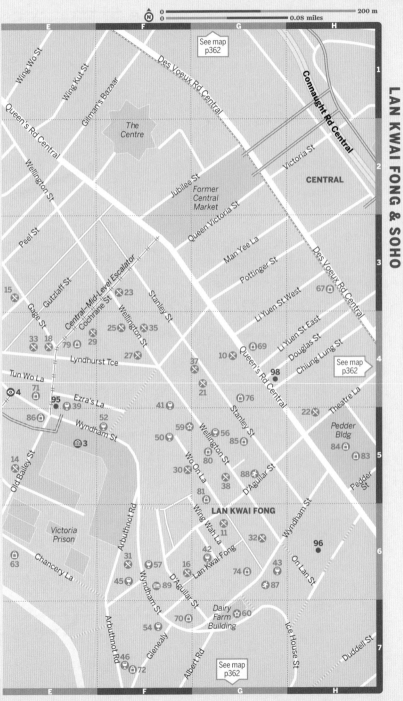

SHEUNG WAN

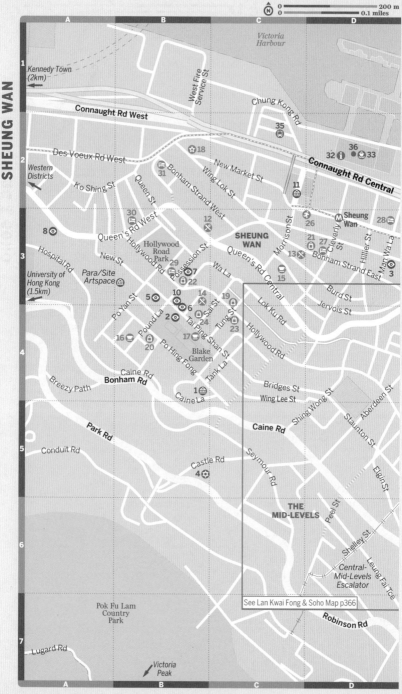

See Lan Kwai Fong & Soho Map p366

SHEUNG WAN

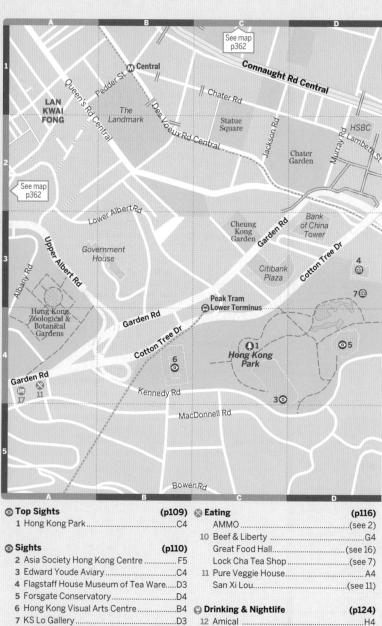

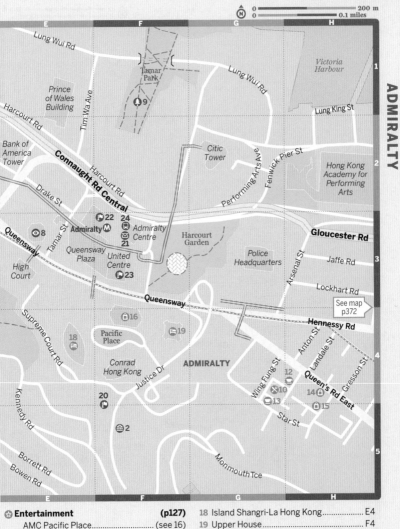

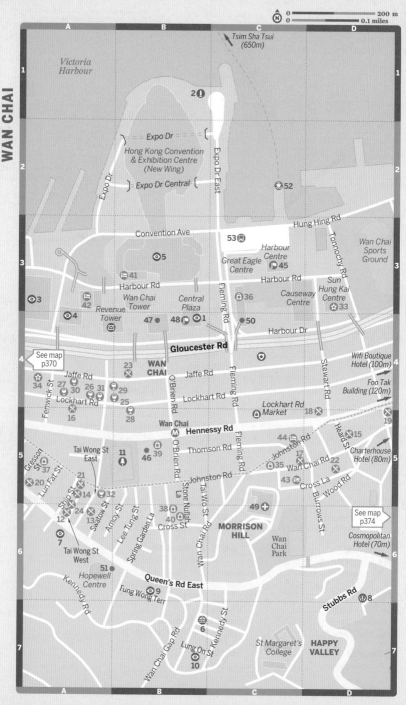

WAN CHAI

Tsim Sha Tsui (650m)

Victoria Harbour

Expo Dr

Expo Dr

Expo Dr East

Hong Kong Convention & Exhibition Centre (New Wing)

Expo Dr Central

52

Convention Ave

Hung Hing Rd

Tonnochy Rd

Wan Chai Sports Ground

5

53

Harbour Centre

Great Eagle Centre

45

41

Harbour Rd

Harbour Rd

Sun Hung Kai Centre

42

Wan Chai Tower

Central Plaza

Fleming Rd

36

Causeway Centre

33

3

Revenue Tower

4

47

48

1

50

Harbour Dr

Gloucester Rd

WAN CHAI

23

Jaffe Rd

Jaffe Rd

Fenwick St

Stewart Rd

Wifi Boutique Hotel (100m)

34

27

30

26

31

29

Lockhart Rd

Lockhart Rd

Fleming Rd

Foo Tak Building (120m)

16

25

28

Lockhart Rd Market

18

19

Wan Chai

Hennessy Rd

44

Johnston Rd

Head St

15

Tai Wong St East

11

46

39

O'Brien Rd

Thomson Rd

17

Wan Chai Rd

22

Charterhouse Hotel (80m)

Gresson St

37

21

Stone Nullah La

Johnston Rd

35

Cross La

43

Wood Rd

20

14

32

Lun Fat St

Ship St

24

13

38

40

Cross St

49

Burrows St

See map p374

12

7

Swatow St

Amoy St

Lee Tung St

Spring Garden La

MORRISON HILL

Wan Chai Park

Cosmopolitan Hotel (70m)

Tai Wong St West

51

Hopewell Centre

Kennedy Rd

Queen's Rd East

Fung Wong Terr

9

Stubbs Rd

8

Wan Chai Gap Rd

Lung On St

6

Kennedy St

St Margaret's College

HAPPY VALLEY

10

WAN CHAI

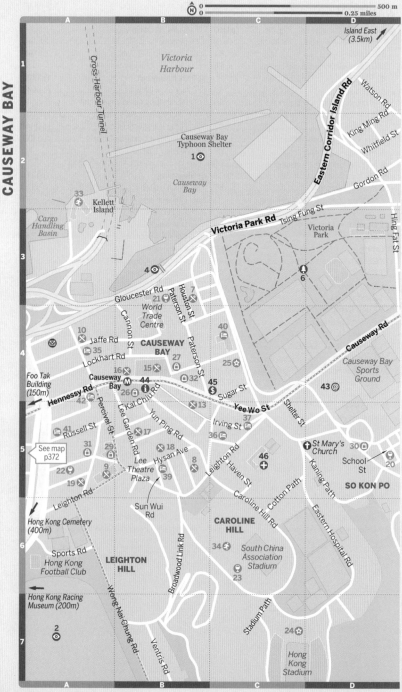

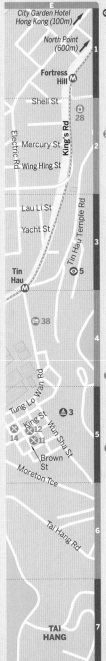

◉ Sights (p114)

1 Causeway Bay Typhoon
   Shelter.....................B2
2 Happy Valley
   Racecourse.....................A7
3 Lin Fa Temple.....................E5
4 Noonday Gun.....................B3
5 Tin Hau Temple.....................E3
6 Victoria Park.....................C3

⊗ Eating (p118)

Citysuper.....................(see 31)
7 Delicious Kitchen.....................B3
8 Farm House.....................B5
9 Fiat Caffe.....................A5
10 Forum.....................A4
11 Go Ya Yakitori.....................E5
   Ho Hung Kee.....................(see 26)
12 Hong Kee Congee
   Shop.....................E5
13 Iroha.....................B5
   Irori.....................(see 22)
14 Lab Made Ice Cream.....................E5
   School Food.....................(see 31)
15 Sogo.....................B4
16 Sushi Fuku-suke.....................B4
17 Tai Ping Koon.....................B5
18 West Villa.....................B5
19 Yu.....................A5

⊙ Drinking & Nightlife (p125)

20 Buddy Bar.....................D5
21 Dickens Bar.....................B3
22 Executive Bar.....................A5
23 Inn Side Out.....................C6

⊛ Entertainment (p127)

24 Hong Kong Stadium.....................C7
25 Windsor Cinema.....................C4

⊙ Shopping (p127)

Eslite.....................(see 26)
26 Hysan Place.....................B4
27 Island Beverley Mall.....................B4
28 Mountain Services.....................E2
29 Muji.....................A5
30 Papabubble.....................D5
   Sogo.....................(see 15)
31 Times Square.....................A5
32 Two Girls.....................B4

⊙ Sports & Activities (p129)

Happy Valley Sports
   Ground.....................(see 2)
33 Royal Hong Kong
   Yacht Club.....................A2
34 South China
   Athletic
   Association.....................C6
   Victoria Park.....................(see 6)

⊜ Sleeping (p269)

35 Causeway Corner.....................A4
36 J Plus.....................C5
37 Lanson Place.....................C5
38 Metropark Hotel.....................E4
39 Mini Hotel
   Causeway Bay.....................B5
40 Park Lane Hong
   Kong.....................C4
41 Shama.....................A5
42 YesInn.....................A4

ⓘ Information

43 Central Library.....................D4
44 Hong Kong Island
   HKTB Centre.....................B4
45 HSBC.....................C4
46 St Paul's Hospital.....................C5

ABERDEEN

Map labels:

Pok Fu Lam Village (2.3km);
Kennedy Town (5.5km)

Hong Kong Trail (1km)

Yue Kwong Rd

Aberdeen Main Rd

Old Main St
Aberdeen Main Rd
Tung Sing Rd
Chengtu St
Nam Ning St

ABERDEEN

Aberdeen Centre

Aberdeen Praya Rd
Promenade

Fish Market

Private Sampans

Aberdeen Harbour

Hung Shing St

Main St–Ap Lei Chau

Ap Lei Chau Bridge Rd

Ap Lei Chau

Ap Lei Chau Praya Rd

Lei Tung Estate Rd

Lee Wing St

Lee Nam Rd

AP LEI CHAU

Sham Wan

Welfare Rd

Shum Wan Rd

Wong Chuk Hang Rd

Heung Yip Rd

Aberdeen Tunnel (1.6km)

Ocean Park (Waterfront Section 1.3km); Cable Car (1.3km)

Ocean Park Summit Section (2km)

500 m
0.25 miles

STANLEY

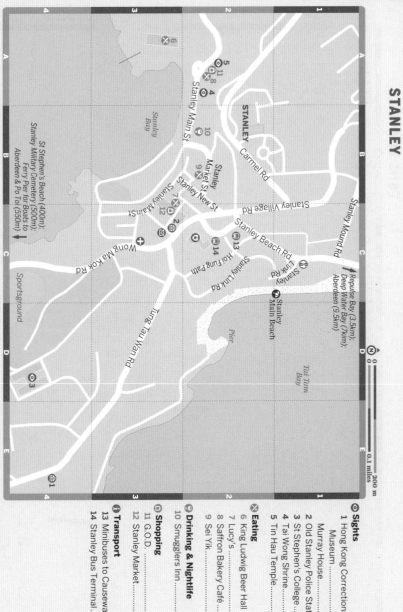

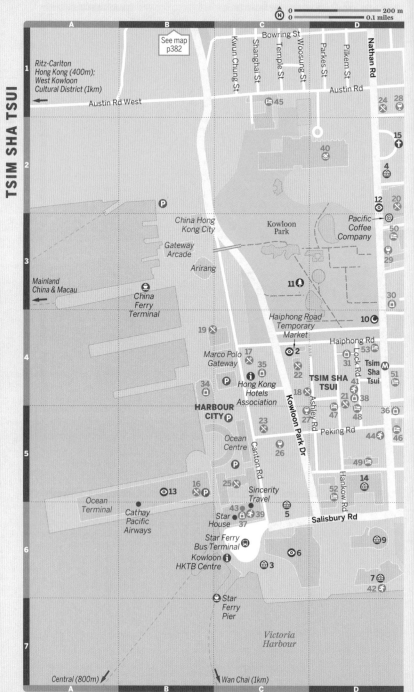

TSIM SHA TSUI

See map p382

Bowring St

Kwun Chung St

Shanghai St

Temple St

Woosung St

Parkes St

Pilkem St

Nathan Rd

Ritz-Carlton
Hong Kong (400m);
West Kowloon
Cultural District (1km)

Austin Rd

Austin Rd West

45

40

24

28

15

4

China Hong
Kong City

Kowloon Park

Pacific
Coffee
Company

12

20

@

50

29

Gateway
Arcade

Arirang

30

Mainland
China & Macau

China
Ferry
Terminal

11

Haiphong Road
Temporary
Market

Haiphong Rd

10

53

19

2

31

Lock Rd

Tsim
Sha
Tsui

M

Marco Polo
Gateway

17

35

22

TSIM SHA
TSUI

41

51

34

Hong Kong
Hotels
Association

18

Ashley Rd

21

38

36

HARBOUR
CITY

27

47

48

Peking Rd

44

46

Ocean
Centre

23

26

Canton Rd

Kowloon Park Dr

49

Ocean
Terminal

13

16

25

Sincerity
Travel

14

52

Hankow Rd

Cathay
Pacific
Airways

43

39

Star
House

37

5

Salisbury Rd

Star Ferry
Bus Terminal

Kowloon
HKTB Centre

3

6

9

7

42

Star
Ferry
Pier

Victoria
Harbour

Central (800m)

Wan Chai (1km)

TSIM SHA TSUI

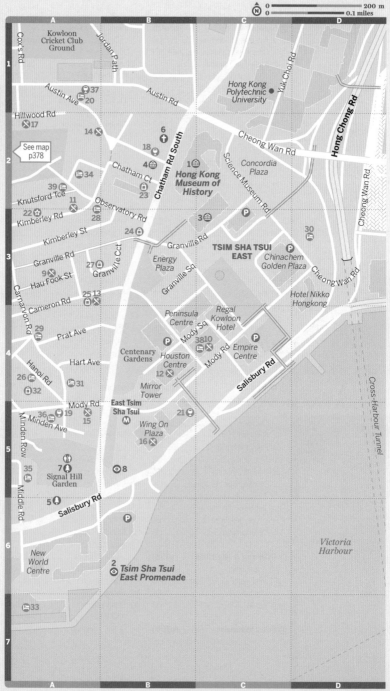

See map p378

Kowloon Cricket Club Ground

Hong Kong Polytechnic University

Hong Kong Museum of History

TSIM SHA TSUI EAST

Chinachem Golden Plaza

Hotel Nikko Hongkong

Peninsula Centre

Regal Kowloon Hotel

Empire Centre

Centenary Gardens

Houston Centre

Mirror Tower

East Tsim Sha Tsui

Wing On Plaza

Signal Hill Garden

New World Centre

Tsim Sha Tsui East Promenade

Victoria Harbour

Cross-Harbour Tunnel

Salisbury Rd

Concordia Plaza

Energy Plaza

Granville Sq

Mody Sq

Mody Rd

Science Museum Rd

Cheong Wan Rd

Hong Chong Rd

Yuk Choi Rd

Chatham Rd South

Austin Rd

Austin Ave

Hillwood Rd

Knutsford Tce

Kimberley Rd

Kimberley St

Granville Rd

Hau Fook St

Cameron Rd

Prat Ave

Hart Ave

Hanoi Rd

Mody Rd

Minden Ave

Minden Row

Middle Rd

Carnarvon Rd

Observatory Rd

Granville Cct

Jordan Path

Cox's Rd

Chatham Ct

HUNG HOM

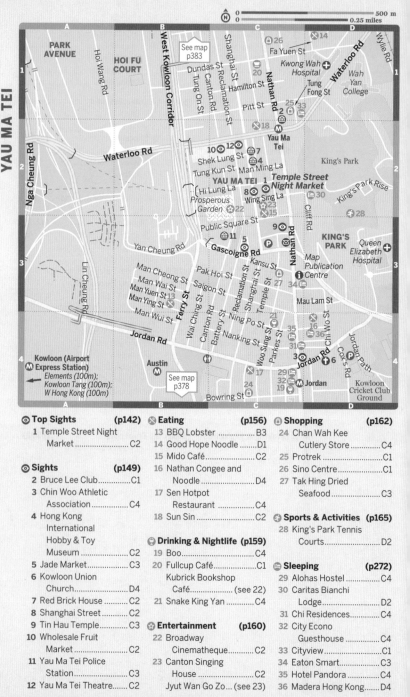

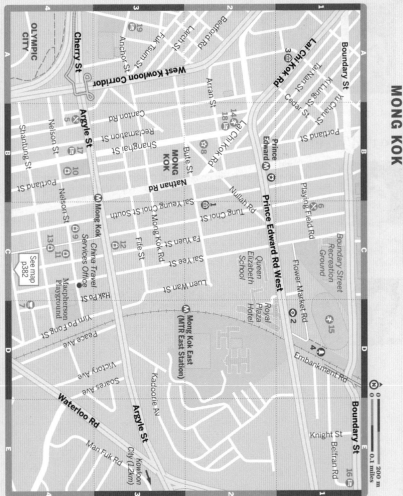

MONG KOK

383

OLYMPIC CITY

West Kowloon Corridor

MONG KOK

Prince Edward Rd West

Mong Kok East (MTR East Station)

Royal Plaza Hotel

Queen Elizabeth School

Kowloon City (1.2km)

See map p382

Our Story

A beat-up old car, a few dollars in the pocket and a sense of adventure. In 1972 that's all Tony and Maureen Wheeler needed for the trip of a lifetime – across Europe and Asia overland to Australia. It took several months, and at the end – broke but inspired – they sat at their kitchen table writing and stapling together their first travel guide, *Across Asia on the Cheap*. Within a week they'd sold 1500 copies. Lonely Planet was born.

Today, Lonely Planet has offices in Franklin, London, Melbourne, Oakland, Beijing and Delhi, with more than 600 staff and writers. We share Tony's belief that 'a great guidebook should do three things: inform, educate and amuse'.

Our Writers

Piera Chen

Coordinating author, Hong Kong Island: Central, Hong Kong Island: The Peak & the Northwest, Kowloon, Macau, Day Trips from Hong Kong Born to a Shanghainese father and a Pekingese mother in Hong Kong, Piera studied literature at Pomona College and works as a writer in her native city. She currently divides her time among Hong Kong, Běijīng, Vancouver, and various exotic holiday destinations, real and imagined. Piera's acquaintance with southern China began when she paid visits to relatives in Guǎngdōng and Macau as a child. It was during these sojourns that she learnt how to coax away a water leech and developed a taste for Portuguese cheeses. Piera has written over half a dozen titles for Lonely Planet.

Emily Matchar

Hong Kong Island: Wan Chai & the Northeast, Hong Kong Island: Aberdeen & the South, New Territories, Outlying Islands Emily Matchar has contributed to some two dozen Lonely Planet guides, and writes for newspapers and magazines all over the world. A native of North Carolina in the southern USA, she currently lives near the top of the world's longest outdoor escalator in Hong Kong.

Published by Lonely Planet Publications Pty Ltd
ABN 36 005 607 983
16th edition – Jan 2015
ISBN 978 1 74321 473 2
© Lonely Planet 2015   Photographs © as indicated 2015
10 9 8 7 6 5 4 3 2 1
Printed in China